Reordering the World

❧

Reordering the World

Essays on Liberalism and Empire

Duncan Bell

PRINCETON UNIVERSITY PRESS

Princeton and Oxford

Jacket art: Coiling the Atlantic Telegraph cable in one of the
tanks on board the *Great Eastern* (engraving). © Look and
Learn / Illustrated Papers Collection / Bridgeman Images

Library of Congress Cataloging-in-Publication Data

Bell, Duncan, 1976– author.
Reordering the world : essays on liberalism and empire / Duncan Bell.
pages cm
Includes bibliographical references and index.
9780691138787 (hardcover : alk. paper)
1. Liberalism—Great Britain—History.   2. Imperialism—
History.   3. Great Britain—Colonies—History.
JC574.2.G(Great Britain)   2015027893

British Library Cataloging-in-Publication Data is available

This book has been composed in Garamond Pro and Ideal Sans

Printed on acid-free paper. ∞

Printed in the United States of America

1 3 5 7 9 10 8 6 4 2

FOR DOROTHY, WITH LOVE AND THANKS

CONTENTS

꤯

Part III: Thinkers

ACKNOWLEDGMENTS

The essays collected in this volume were written over a period of more than a decade, and along the way I have accumulated numerous personal and intellectual debts. I'd like to thank the following for their generous support and penetrating discussions about political theory and imperial history: David Armitage, Peter Cain, Michael Freeden, Ian Hall, Zaheer Kazmi, Karuna Mantena, Jeanne Morefield, Isaac Nakhimovsky, and Richard Tuck. In Cambridge, Joel Isaac, Duncan Kelly, and Peter Mandler are ideal interlocutors. The great Istvan Hont provided intellectual encouragement and friendship over many years. I miss him greatly. Casper Sylvest has commented incisively on just about everything I've written, and for that act of supererogatory endurance, and much else besides, I'm deeply grateful to him. Moreover, I thank him for allowing me to reprint our jointly authored essay as chapter 10 of this volume. The following all commented on one or more of the chapters: Robert Adcock, Jens Bartelson, Mark Bevir, Alex Bremner, Chris Brooke, David Cannadine, Greg Claeys, Linda Colley, David Craig, Mary Dietz, Saul Dubow, Daniel Deudney, Mark Goldie, John Gunnell, Ian Hunter, Ben Jackson, Charles Jones, Stuart Jones, Peter Katzenstein, Ira Katznelson, Daniel O'Neill, Martti Koskenniemi, Ron Krebs, Chandran Kukuthas, Anthony Lang, Michael Ledger-Lomas, Joanna Lewis, Patchen Markell, Mark Mazower, Iain McDaniel, Jennifer Mitzen, Robert Nichols, Jon Parry, Nicholas Phillipson, Quentin Skinner, Katherine Smits, Tim Stanton, Gareth Stedman Jones, Anders Stephanson, Miles Taylor, Colin Tyler, Cheryl Welch, Brian Young, and Bernardo Zacka. Caroline Ashcroft and Eliza Garnsey did stellar work helping to prepare the manuscript. Kathleen Cioffi has been an exemplary production editor. Ben Tate has been a marvelously positive and sympathetic editor. Above all, Sarah Fine has been a constant source of inspiration, as have our daughters, Juliet and Alice. Thanks to one and all.

A number of institutions have provided essential practical and financial support. The Centre of International Studies, and now the Department of Politics and International Studies, both at the University of Cambridge, have been admirably collegial environments in which to pursue serious scholarly work at the intersection of political theory, history, and international relations. The same is true of Christ's College, Cambridge. The Minda de Gunzburg Center for European Studies at Harvard hosted me for a productive period of sabbatical leave. The Leverhulme Trust has been a magnificent sponsor of the humanities and social sciences in the United Kingdom, and I have benefitted greatly from their largesse, first with the award of an Early Career Fellowship, and more recently, with a Philip Leverhulme Prize. These have given me invaluable time to conduct research for some of the chapters in this book.

Finally, I am grateful to the editors and publishers for permission to reprint the following material:

Chapter 3: "What Is Liberalism?," *Political Theory*, 42/6 (2014), doi: 10.1177/0090591714535103, ptx.sagepub.com

Chapter 4: "Ideologies of Empire," in *The Oxford Handbook of Political Ideologies*, ed. Michael Freeden, Marc Stears, and Lyman Tower Sargent (2013), reproduced by permission of Oxford University Press, global.oup.com

Chapter 5: "Empire," in *Historicism in the Victorian Human Sciences*, ed. Mark Bevir (Cambridge: Cambridge University Press, forthcoming). Reprinted with permission

Chapter 6: "The Idea of a Patriot Queen? The Monarchy, the Constitution, and the Iconographic Order of Greater Britain, 1860–1900," *Journal of Imperial and Commonwealth History*, 34/1 (2006), 3–22, www.tandfonline.com

Chapter 7: "Imagined Spaces: Nation, State, and Territory in the British Colonial Empire, 1860–1914," in *The Primacy of Foreign Policy in British History*, ed. William Mulligan and Brendan Simms (Basingstoke: Palgrave, 2010), reproduced with permission of Palgrave Macmillan

Chapter 8: "The Project for a New Anglo Century: Race, Space, and Global Order," in *Anglo-America and Its Discontents: Civilizational Politics Beyond East and West*, ed. Peter Katzenstein (London: Routledge, 2012)

Chapter 9: "John Stuart Mill on Colonies," *Political Theory*, 38/1 (2010), doi: 10.1177/0090591709348186, ptx.sagepub.com

Chapter 10: "International Society and Victorian Political Thought: Herbert Spencer, T. H. Green, and Henry Sidgwick," with Casper Sylvest, *Modern Intellectual History*, 3/2 (2006) © Cambridge University Press. Reprinted with permission

Chapter 12: "Republican Imperialism: J. A. Froude and the Virtue of Empire," *History of Political Thought*, 30/1 (2009), reproduced courtesy of Imprint Academic

Chapter 13: "Alter Orbis: E. A. Freeman on Empire and Racial Destiny," in *Making History: Edward Augustus Freeman and Victorian Cultural Politics*, ed. G. A. Bremner and Jonathan Conlin (2015), reproduced by permission of Oxford University Press, global.oup.com

Chapter 14: "Democracy and Empire: Hobson, Hobhouse, and the Crisis of Liberalism," in *British International Thought from Hobbes to Namier*, ed. Ian Hall and Lisa Hill (Basingstoke: Palgrave, 2009), reproduced with permission of Palgrave Macmillan

This book is dedicated to my wonderful mother, Dorothy.

Reordering the World

CHAPTER 1

Introduction

༁

Reordering the World

[C]entral to the lives of all empires have been the ways in which they have been
constituted through language and their own self-representations: the
discourses that have arisen to describe, defend, and criticize them, and the
historical narratives that have been invoked to make sense of them.[1]

—JENNIFER PITTS

From the earliest articulations of political thinking in the European tradition to its most recent iterations, the nature, justification, and criticism of
foreign conquest and rule has been a staple theme of debate. Empires, after all,
have been among the most common and the most durable political formations
in world history. However, it was only during the long nineteenth century that
the European empire-states developed sufficient technological superiority
over the peoples of Africa, the Americas, and Asia to make occupation and
governance on a planetary scale seem both feasible and desirable, even if the
reality usually fell far short of the fantasy. As Jürgen Osterhammel reminds us,
the nineteenth century was "much more an age of empire than . . . an age of
nations and nation-states."[2] The largest of those empires was governed from
London.

Even the most abstract works of political theory, Quentin Skinner argues,
"are never above the battle; they are always part of the battle itself."[3] The ideo-

---

[1] Pitts, "Political Theory of Empire and Imperialism," *Annual Review of Political Science*, 13
(2010), 226.

[2] Osterhammel, *The Transformation of the World*, trans. Patrick Camiller (Princeton, 2014),
392. On the nineteenth-century imperial order, see also C. A. Bayly, *The Birth of the Modern
World, 1780–1914* (Oxford, 2004); Jane Burbank and Frederick Cooper, *Empires in World History* (Princeton, 2010), chs. 10–11. On some of the distinctive features of Victorian imperialism,
see Duncan Bell, "Victorian Visions of Global Order," in *Victorian Visions of Global Order*, ed. Bell
(Cambridge, 2007), 1–25.

[3] Skinner, *Hobbes and Republican Liberty* (Cambridge, 2008), xvi.

logical conflict I chart in the following pages was one fought over the bitterly contested terrain of empire. The main, though not the only, combatants I survey are British liberal political thinkers—philosophers, historians, politicians, imperial administrators, political economists, journalists, even an occasional novelist or poet. Multifaceted and constantly mutating, liberalism was chiefly a product of the revolutionary ferment of the late eighteenth century, of the complex dialectic between existing patterns of thought and the new egalitarian and democratic visions pulsating through the Euro-Atlantic world. A squabbling family of philosophical doctrines, a popular creed, a resonant moral ideal, the creature of a party machine, a comprehensive economic system, a form of life: liberalism was all of these and more. Intellectuals were central to the propagation and renewal of this expansive ideology, though they were far from the only agents involved. From Bentham to Hobson, from Macaulay to Mill, from Spencer to Sidgwick, a long parade of thinkers helped sculpt the contours of the evolving tradition, elaborating influential accounts of individual freedom, moral psychology, social justice, economic theory, and constitutional design. Liberal thinkers wrote extensively about the pathologies and potentialities of empire, developing both ingenious defenses and biting critiques of assorted imperial projects. The conjunction of a vibrant intellectual culture and a massive and expanding imperial system makes nineteenth-century Britain a vital site for exploring the connections between political thought and empire in general, and liberal visions of empire in particular. The vast expanses of the British empire provided both a practical laboratory and a space of desire for liberal attempts to reorder the world.

Reordering the World collects together a selection of essays that I have written over the last decade. Some explore the ways in which prominent thinkers tackled the legitimacy of conquest and imperial rule, while others dissect themes that pervaded imperial discourse or address theoretical and historiographical puzzles about liberalism and empire. They are united by an ambition to probe the intellectual justifications of empire during a key period in modern history. The materials I analyze are the product of elite metropolitan culture, including works of technical philosophy and recondite history, but also pamphlets, speeches, editorials, periodical articles, and personal correspondence. Such sources helped constitute the intellectual lifeblood of Victorian political discourse, feeding into the creation of a distinctive "imperial commons," a globe-spanning though heavily stratified public constituted in part through the production and circulation of books, periodicals, and newspapers.[4] The bulk of the volume focuses on the late Victorian and Edwardian eras, the years that Eric Hobsbawm once characterized as the "age of empire."[5]

---

[4] See Antoinette Burton and Isabel Hofmeyr, "The Spine of Empire?," in *Ten Books That Shaped the British Empire*, ed. Burton and Hofmeyr (Durham, NC, 2014), 1–28. Later, of course, radio, cinema, and television added new dimensions to the imperial commons.

[5] Hobsbawm, *The Age of Empire, 1875–1914* (London, 1987).

During that period the empire assumed a newfound significance in political argument, looming large over debates on a plethora of issues from social policy to geopolitical strategy and beyond. However, I also explore earlier currents of political thinking, and trace some of the echoes of nineteenth-century ideologies across the twentieth century and into the present.

Political Thought and Empire

As late as 2006 Anthony Pagden could write that the study of empire had until recently been "relegated to the wastelands of the academy."[6] It was dragged in from the cold during the 1980s as postcolonial scholarship percolated through the humanities (and more unevenly across the social sciences). Imperial history was rejuvenated, moving swiftly from the periphery to the center of historical research, where it remains ensconced to this day.[7] Political theory, like political science more broadly, has proven rather more resistant to the imperial turn. During the postwar years the field was characterized by a revealing silence about both the history of empire and the wave of decolonization then overturning many of the governing norms and institutions that had shaped the architecture of world order for five centuries.[8] Adam Smith remarked in the *Wealth of Nations* that the "discovery" of the Americas was one of the "most important events recorded in the history of mankind," and he and his contemporaries, as well as many of their nineteenth-century heirs, wrestled incessantly with its meaning and consequences.[9] Political theorists barely registered its passing.[10] Mainstream approaches to the subject, at least

[6] Pagden, "The Empire's New Clothes," *Common Knowledge*, 12/1 (2006), 36.

[7] For accounts of the revival, see Linda Colley, "What Is Imperial History Now?," in *What Is History Now?*, ed. David Cannadine (Basingstoke, 2002); John Mackenzie, "The British Empire," *Journal of Imperial and Commonwealth History*, 43/1 (2015), 99–124; Dane Kennedy, "The Imperial History Wars," *Journal of British Studies*, 54/1 (2015), 1–22.

[8] For exceptions that prove the rule, see Hannah Arendt, *The Origins of Totalitarianism* [1951] (New York, 1985), pt. 2; John Plamenatz, *On Alien Rule and Self-Government* (London, 1960); Louis Hartz, ed., *The Founding of New Societies* (New York, 1964). Yet imperial questions often intruded in unexpected places; see, for example, James Tully's analysis of the subtle imperial entailments of Isaiah Berlin's seminal essay on liberty. Tully, " 'Two Concepts of Liberty' in Context," in *Isaiah Berlin and the Politics of Freedom*, ed. Bruce Baum and Robert Nichols (Abingdon, 2013), 23–52.

[9] Smith, *An Inquiry into the Nature and Causes of the Wealth of Nations* [1776], ed. R. H. Campbell, Andrew S. Skinner, and W. B. Todd (Oxford, 1976), bk. 4, ch. 7, p. 166. The only other event of equal significance, he wrote, was the opening of "a passage to the East Indies by the Cape of Good Hope." For a brilliant account of Smith and his context, see Istvan Hont, *Jealousy of Trade* (Cambridge, MA, 2005); Hont, *The Politics of Commercial Society*, ed. Béla Kapossy and Michael Sonenscher (Cambridge, MA, 2015).

[10] The same was true of much postwar social science. For conflicting interpretations of the role of empire and decolonization in International Relations, the scholarly field dedicated to the analysis of world politics, see Nicolas Guilhot, "Imperial Realism," *International History Review*, 36/4

in the Anglo-American tradition, continue to argue about the nature of justice, democracy, and rights, while ignoring the ways in which many of the
ideas and institutions of contemporary politics have been (de)formed or inflected by centuries of Western imperialism—"this half millennium of tyranny against diverse civilisational forms of self-reliance and association"[11]—
and the deep complicity in this enterprise of the canon from which they draw
inspiration, concepts, arguments, and authority. While a persistent tattoo of
criticism has been maintained by dissident scholars, it has made little impact
on the core concerns or theoretical approaches of the field.[12]

Historians of political thought have been more willing to take empire and
its multifarious legacies seriously, tracing the ways in which European thinkers grappled with projects of imperial conquest and governance.[13] One of the
guiding themes of this scholarship—sometimes rendered explicit, sometimes
lurking in the wings—has been a concern with the relationship between liberal political thought and empire, between the dominant ideology of the contemporary Western world and some of the darkest, most consequential entanglements of its past.[14] Both the political context for this scholarly
reorientation and the stakes involved in it are clear. Against a backdrop of
numerous "humanitarian intervention" operations, blood-letting in Iraq, Afghanistan and beyond, the forever war against terror, challenges from competing theocratic fundamentalisms, the specter of neoliberal globalization,
and a burgeoning interest in questions of global poverty and inequality, the
ethico-political status of liberalism has been put in question. Is it necessarily
an imperial doctrine or a welcome antidote to imperial ambition? Perhaps liberals should face up to their imperial obligations rather than ducking them?
"Nobody likes empires," Michael Ignatieff argues, "but there are some problems for which there are only imperial solutions."[15] If so, what are they? Alternatively, is it possible to foster anti-imperial forms of politics, liberal or other-

---

(2014), 698–720; Robert Vitalis, *White World Order, Black Power Politics* (Ithaca, 2015). See also
John Hobson, *The Eurocentric Conception of World Politics* (Cambridge, 2012), chs. 8–13.

[11] James Tully, "Lineages of Informal Imperialism," in *Lineages of Empire*, ed. Duncan Kelly
(Oxford, 2009), 29.

[12] For acute criticisms of this tendency, see Charles Mills, "Decolonizing Western Political Philosophy," *New Political Science*, 37/1 (2015), 1–24. The partial exception to this claim is the literature on historical injustice.

[13] For influential examples, see Richard Tuck, *The Rights of War and Peace* (Oxford, 1999);
Anthony Pagden, *Lords of All the World* (London, 1995); David Armitage, *The Ideological Origins
of the British Empire* (Cambridge, 2000). The literature is discussed in Pitts, "Political Theory of
Empire"; David Armitage, *Foundations of Modern International Thought* (Cambridge, 2013), pt. 1.

[14] Valuable earlier accounts include Bernard Semmel, *Imperialism and Social Reform* (Cambridge, MA, 1960); Semmel, *The Rise of Free Trade Imperialism* (Cambridge, 1970); Eric Stokes,
The English Utilitarians and India (Oxford, 1959); A. P. Thonton, *The Imperial Idea and Its Enemies* (London, 1959); Donald Winch, *Classical Political Economy and Colonies* (Cambridge,
1965).

[15] Ignatieff, *Empire Lite* (London, 2003), 11.

wise, in an increasingly interdependent world? Such concerns permeate the febrile debate. In chapter 2 I discuss some of the main trends in the scholarship, as well as identifying some of its weaknesses

Throughout the book I treat liberalism chiefly as an actor's category, a term to encompass thinkers, ideas, and movements that were regarded as liberal at the time. (In chapter 3, I discuss the origins and development of liberal discourse in Britain and the United States.) Nineteenth-century British liberalism drew on multiple sources and was splintered into a kaleidoscope of ideological positions, some of which overlapped considerably, while others pulled in different directions. Indeed one of the main purposes of *Reordering the World* is to highlight the ideological complexity and internal variability of liberalism, and in doing so to call into question sweeping generalizations about it. Benthamite utilitarianism, classical political economy, the historical sociology of the Scottish Enlightenment, Comtean positivism, partially digested German, French, and Greek philosophy, an emergent socialist tradition, the expansive legacies of republicanism, assorted forms of political theology, miscellaneous evolutionary theories, the democratic ethos inherited from the revolutionary era, the comforting embrace of Burkean organicism: all (and more) fed the cacophony. They cross-fertilised to spawn various identifiable articulations of liberal thinking, several of which are discussed in the following chapters. These include liberal Whig ideology (Macaulay, for example), forms of radical liberalism (including, in their different ways, Richard Cobden, John Stuart Mill, and Herbert Spencer), and late Victorian "new liberalism" (most notably J. A. Hobson and L. T. Hobhouse).[16] This list is far from exhaustive, of course, and the period was also populated by multiple ideological hybrids, idiosyncratic figures whose ideas are hard to categorize, and less conspicuous or long-lived threads of political thinking. While they differed in many respects, including the philosophical foundations of their ideas and the public policies they endorsed, all shared a commitment to individual liberty, constitutional government, the rule of law, the ethical significance of nationality, a capitalist political economy, and belief in the possibility of moral and political progress.[17] But the ways in which they interpreted, combined, and lexically ordered these abstract ideas, as well as the range of institutions they prescribed as necessary for their realization, varied greatly. So too did their

---

[16] For different perspectives on Victorian liberalism, see Richard Bellamy, *Liberalism and Modern Society* (Cambridge, 1992); Bellamy, ed., *Victorian Liberalism* (Abingdon, 1990); John Burrow, *Whigs and Liberals* (Oxford, 1988); Stefan Collini, *Public Moralists* (Oxford, 1991); Michael Freeden, *The New Liberalism* (Oxford, 1978); Elaine Hadley, *Living Liberalism* (Chicago, 2010); Simon Gunn and James Vernon, eds., *The Peculiarities of Liberal Modernity in Imperial Britain* (Berkeley, 2011); Peter Mandler, ed., *Liberty and Authority in Victorian Britain* (Oxford, 2006); J. P. Parry, *The Politics of Patriotism* (Cambridge, 2009).

[17] Note that this is an empirical claim about the ideological commitments of Victorian liberalism, not a conceptual or normative evaluation of the necessary or sufficient elements of liberal political thinking in general. For further discussion on this methodological issue, see chapter 3.

attitudes to empire, though few rejected all its forms, and most (as I will argue) endorsed the formation of settler colonies.

British imperial expansion was never motivated by a single coherent ideology or a consistent strategic vision. This was the grain of truth in the historian J. R. Seeley's famous quip that the empire seemed to have been "acquired in a fit of absence of mind."[18] Characterized by instability, chronically uncoordinated, and plagued by tensions between and within its widely dispersed elements, it was "unfinished, untidy, a mass of contradictions, aspirations and anomalies."[19] Yet despite this, or perhaps because of it, the empire was a subject of constant deliberation, celebration, denunciation, and anxiety.[20] It was, as Jennifer Pitts notes in the epigraph, partly constituted (and contested) through language and legitimating representations. One of the main goals of imperial ideologists was to impose order on the untidy mass, to construct a coherent view of the past, present, and future that served to justify the existence of the empire, while their critics repeatedly stressed the manifest dangers of embarking on foreign conquest and rule. Imperial themes were woven through the fabric of nineteenth-century British political thinking, from the abstract proclamations of philosophers to the vernacular of parliamentary debate through to quotidian expressions of popular culture. Conceptions of liberty, nationality, gender, and race, assumptions about moral equality and political rationality, debates over the scope and value of democracy, analyses of political economy, the prospects of "civilization" itself: all were inflected to varying degrees with imperial concerns, explicit or otherwise.

While each chapter can be read as a self-contained study of a particular topic, two general themes run through the book. The first is the pivotal importance of *settler colonialism.* As I argue in greater detail in chapter 2, the welcome revival of imperial history in the 1980s produced its own lapses and silences, one of the most significant of which was the sidelining of settler colonialism—or "colonization" as it was called at the time—in accounts of the long nineteenth century. There is a considerable historical irony involved in this redistribution of attention, given that the sub-discipline of imperial history was created at the turn of the twentieth century as part of a conscious effort to proselytize the superiority of the settler empire over other imperial

[18] Seeley, *The Expansion of England* (London, 1883), 8.

[19] John Darwin, *The Empire Project* (Cambridge, 2011), xi. Darwin's work offers a powerful structural account of the empire as a fragile, fragmented system, the fate of which was ultimately dependent on wider geopolitical currents largely outside British control. For some brief reflections on his work, see Duncan Bell, "Desolation Goes before Us," *Journal of British Studies*, 54/4 (2015), 987–93.

[20] My understanding of ideology has been influenced by the work of Michael Freeden and Quentin Skinner. See, for example, Freeden, *Ideologies and Political Theory* (Oxford, 1998); Freeden, *The Political Theory of Political Thinking* (Oxford, 2013); Skinner, *Visions of Politics*, vol. 1 (Cambridge, 2002). See also the discussion in chapter 4, section 2.

spaces, above all India.[21] While (what became) Australia, Canada, New Zealand, and South Africa were far less heavily populated than India, they nevertheless played a crucial role in the liberal imperial imagination, especially during the "age of empire." In recent years the imbalance has been corrected and settler colonialism is once again a lively source of historical debate.[22] Replicating the earlier pattern of omission, however, much of the literature on nineteenth-century British imperial political thought has consistently underplayed the significance of the colonies. Among other things, this has led to a skewed understanding of liberal accounts of empire. As I hope to demonstrate, acknowledging the importance of settler colonialism in nineteenth-century political thought unsettles some of the main ways in which scholars have interpreted the nature of "imperial" and "anti-imperial" arguments since the late eighteenth century.

The second recurrent theme is the multivalent role that historical consciousness performed in shaping visions of empire. While it is certainly arguable that political economists were the most influential imperial ideologists in the first half of the century, historians assumed this mantle in the second half. From James Mill and Macaulay to Froude and Seeley, historians were among the most prominent imperial thinkers, writing and rewriting the history of empire to bolster specific political projects.[23] Their messages resonated in a culture obsessed with the past and the lessons it purportedly encoded.[24] The "English," Seeley observed in 1880, "guide ourselves in the great political questions by great historical precedents."[25] Historical-mindedness, as it was often called, structured political argument, rendering some lines of reasoning more intelligible, more perspicacious, and more plausible, than others. Precedent, tradition, organic development: all were invoked *ad infinitum*. It was this obsession with history that prompted A. V. Dicey to complain that it was better to be found guilty of "petty larceny" than to admit to skepticism about the universal validity of the historical method or to remain unconvinced by

---

[21] See, in particular, Amanda Behm, "The Bisected Roots of Imperial History," *Recherches Britanniques*, 1/1 (2011), 54–77. For the educational networks binding Greater Britain, see Tamsin Pietsch, *Empire of Scholars* (Manchester, 2013).

[22] See the references in chapter 2, section 3.

[23] On James Mill, see Javeed Majeed, *Ungoverned Imaginings* (Oxford, 1992); on Macaulay, see Catherine Hall, *Macaulay and Son* (London, 2012); on Seeley, see chapter 11. Tadhg Foley argues that from the 1830s onwards, colonization was "theorized and justified by the hired-prize fighters of empire totally in economic terms." Foley, " 'An Unknown and Feeble Body,' " in *Studies in Settler Colonialism*, ed. Fiona Bateman and Lionel Pilkington (Basingstoke, 2011), 10. However, this sweeping contention is implausible, especially when directed at the second half of the nineteenth century.

[24] For an insightful recent analysis, see Theodore Koditschek, *Liberalism, Imperialism, and the Historical Imagination* (Cambridge, 2011).

[25] Seeley, "Political Somnambulism," *Macmillan's Magazine*, 43 (1880), 32.

the patent superiority of "historical-mindedness."[26] Three of my chapters are thus dedicated to the imperial thought of renowned late Victorian historians. But the imaginative significance of history was not confined to the writings of professional scholars. Rather, a sense of the importance of historical time—of the legitimating functions of precedent and tradition, of appeals to ancient authorities and the rhetoric of longevity, of the temporal logic of decline and fall, of the uses and abuses of historical analogies and metaphors, of the political possibilities inherent in the technological "annihilation" of time and space—helped animate and condition imperial discourse.

Structure of the Book

Offered as an invitation for further reflection rather than an exhaustive account of the topic, *Reordering the World* seeks to illuminate significant aspects of imperial debate and potentially open up new lines of inquiry. The book is divided into three parts. The first, "Frames," contains three essays that probe the diverse meanings of liberalism and empire. Part II, "Themes," comprises four historical essays that examine some salient topics in Victorian imperial thought (and beyond). The six chapters in the third part, "Thinkers," dissect the imperial political thought of influential philosophers and historians, focusing in particular (though not exclusively) on their accounts of settler colonialism. Chapter 2 was written especially for this volume, while chapter 11 combines new research with some previously published materials.[27] The remaining chapters were originally published in edited volumes and academic journals spanning the fields of political theory, history, and international relations. I have made only minor changes to them, occasionally excising some of the original text to avoid undue repetition, correcting stylistic infelicities where possible, and identifying connections and disjunctions between the chapters where appropriate.

Chapter 2 opens with a discussion of the mutable vocabulary of empire and liberalism, before analyzing some of the most important recent scholarship on the subject. I argue that despite the excellence of much of this work, it exhibits two recurrent flaws. First, it tends to overlook the significance of set-

[26] Dicey, *Introduction to the Study of the Law of the Constitution*, 4th ed. (London, 1893), 14. On the ubiquity of "historical mindedness" in Victorian culture, see also Lord Acton, "Inaugural Lecture on the Study of History," in *Lectures on Modern History*, ed. J. N. Figgis and R. V. Laurence (London, 1906), 22. On the role of historical imagination in Victorian political thinking, see especially John Burrow, *Whigs and Liberals* (Oxford, 1988); Stefan Collini, Donald Winch, and John Burrow, *That Noble Science of Politics*, (Cambridge, 1983), chs. 6–7.

[27] As well as including a considerable amount of new research, chapter 11 synthesizes material from several chapters of Bell, *The Idea of Greater Britain* (Princeton, 2007); as well as Bell, "Unity and Difference," *Review of International Studies*, 31/3 (2005), 559–79.

tler colonialism in the political imagination of the Victorians and their successors. In particular, many British liberals regarded settler colonialism as a preferable model of empire to the conquest and alien rule associated with India, and they invested their hopes in assorted projects of colonial reform. The colonies, they argued, were spaces of political freedom for their (white, "civilized") inhabitants, and as such they were not burdened by the moral and political dangers associated with the despotic rule prevalent throughout the rest of the empire. This made them ideal communities for the articulation of liberal ideas and institutions. Second, I argue that much work on political theory and empire is constrained by "canonical" approaches to intellectual history. Focusing on a narrow range of "major" thinkers can be illuminating— I do so myself in several chapters—but it can also lead to oversights and omissions, especially when trying to capture broad patterns of thinking. In particular, attempts to divine a connection between the inner essence of liberalism and imperialism efface the complexity and messiness of the historical record. To investigate imperial discourse it is necessary to dig deeper into the imperial commons, incorporating an extensive archive of intellectual production.

The following two chapters explore each side of the "liberal empire" compound. Isaiah Berlin once described freedom as "a term whose meaning is so porous that there is little interpretation that it seems able to resist."[28] Something similar could be said about liberalism. Challenging conventional understandings of the liberal tradition, chapter 3 presents both a theoretical argument and a historical interpretation. Theoretically, I propose that liberalism can be characterized as the sum of the arguments that have been classified as liberal, and recognized as such by other self-proclaimed liberals, over time and space. The historical argument suggests that between 1850 and 1950 the meaning of liberalism was transformed in the Anglo-American world. For most of the nineteenth century, liberalism was commonly viewed as a product of late eighteenth-century revolutionary turmoil, but it was reimagined during the opening decades of the twentieth century, its origins pushed further back in time and its scope expanded massively, such that it came to be seen as the overarching ideology of Western modernity. This transmutation was profoundly influenced by the wars fought against "totalitarianism," both hot and cold. I illustrate this example of ideological shape-shifting by tracing how John Locke came to be conscripted as a paradigmatic liberal during that period. Demonstrating the instability of "liberalism" as a category, this analysis challenges the unreflective manner in which the term is employed in contemporary scholarly inquiry—including (but not only) in debates over liberalism and empire. The final chapter in the section anatomizes different types of argument made about empire, especially during the last couple of hundred years. I distinguish between political ideologies, theories, and imaginaries,

[28] Berlin, "Two Concepts of Liberty" [1958], in *Liberty*, ed. David Miller (Oxford, 1991), 168.

before sketching an ideal-typical account of ideologies of justification, governance, and resistance. Throughout, I emphasize the variety of arguments available to both advocates and critics of empire and colonialism, the patchwork forms they often assumed in political disputation, and some of their contemporary legacies.

Chapter 5 examines how historical time was conceptualized in imperial debate, focusing in particular on the diverse invocations of classical models of empire. Contrary to most scholarship on the subject, I argue that Victorian imperialists were often keen to escape the gravitational pull of the ancients, because the resonant lesson they drew from the Romans and the Greeks was that empires were self-dissolving, that they were fragile and temporary forms of political order rather than the basis for permanence and stability. Roman experience taught that empires eventually collapsed in ruins, Greek experience that settler colonies only thrived when formally independent of the "mother country." Neither vision appealed to those aiming to create a resilient imperial formation, and so they borrowed selectively from the hallowed past, arguing that unlike its predecessors and potential competitors the British empire was not condemned to repeat the ostensible pattern of all human history. I demarcate two popular argumentative strategies. One attempted to reconcile progress and empire by insisting that the British were unique in some important respect—usually their self-proclaimed ability to harmoniously combine "libertas et imperium" in a manner appropriate for an industrial, democratic age.[29] The other was to argue that Greater Britain—the settler colonies plus the "mother country"—constituted a radically new type of political association. According to such accounts, empire was transfigured into something else: a federation, a transcontinental state, a multinational commonwealth. It had transcended its originary form. This novel type of polity was not subject to traditional anxieties about dissolution, corruption, or overextension, but was instead a pioneering manifestation of political trends reshaping world order at the time. It heralded the future rather than embodying the past.

Chapters 6 and 7 analyze aspects of the debate over Greater Britain that I didn't cover in my earlier book on the subject.[30] The first discusses how the monarchy was figured in arguments about imperial federation. Queen Victoria was assigned two main functions. First, it was argued that the august institution of the monarchy could act as a marker of stability and constitutional fidelity in a globe-spanning imperial polity, thus reassuring skeptics that a strong thread of historical continuity ran through proposals for uniting Brit-

[29] The problematic of liberty and empire ran through modern European political thought. For the period until the end of the eighteenth century, see David Armitage, "Empire and Liberty," in *Republicanism*, vol. 2, ed. Martin van Gelderen and Quentin Skinner (Cambridge, 2002), 29–47.

[30] Bell, *The Idea of Greater Britain*.

ain and the settler colonies. The British political tradition would be reinforced, rather than undermined, by the creation of an imperial federal structure. This line of argument formed the basis for an audacious account of constitutional patriotism. Secondly, an idealized representation of Victoria served as an anchor for national identity across vast geographical distances, her popularity binding the far-flung peoples of her realm in close communion. Or so it was claimed. I also contend that the way in which she was often represented in imperial debate echoed an older civic humanist language of "patriot kingship," a fantasy vision of the monarch as the enemy of corruption, the protector of the people, and the strong but benevolent leader of a dynamic commercial people. Chapter 7, meanwhile, argues that the purported scope of the "people" and the "public" was transformed in debates over colonial unification. Both were conceptually decoupled from the state and imaginatively extended to encompass the geographically fragmented settler empire. As innovative communications technologies revolutionized understandings of time and space, so thinkers began to envision new forms of political and cultural solidarity on a global scale.[31] Greater Britain was conceptualized as a discrete political space populated by a unified "people"—coded typically as either a superior "race" or "nation"—and governed by a constitutional monarchy sensitive to the preferences of an emergent transoceanic public. This spatial extension prefigures recent debates about the possibility of creating a global public sphere.

The final chapter in the section steps back from the patterns of Victorian political argument, and seeks to locate the intellectual history of the British empire in a wider frame. It reads the debates over Greater Britain as a formative moment in what I term the "project for a new Anglo century"—the repeated attempt to create the political and social conditions necessary to secure the global domination of the "Anglo-Saxon" or "English-speaking" people. These were variations on the theme of white supremacism, a racial vision of global governance that frequently served as both a grounding assumption and a prescriptive conclusion throughout the nineteenth and much of the twentieth century. Towards the close of Victoria's reign Gilbert Murray, leading classicist and liberal political thinker, voiced a widely shared supposition.

> There is in the world a hierarchy of races. The bounds of it are not, of course, absolute and rigid . . . but on the whole, it seems that those nations which eat more, claim more, and get higher wages, will direct and rule the others, and the lower work of the world will tend in the long-

---

[31] For more on the transformation of conceptions of time and space, see Duncan Bell, "Dissolving Distance," *Journal of Modern History*, 77/3 (2005), 523–62; Bell, *The Idea of Greater Britain*, ch. 3.

run to be done by the lower breeds of men. This much we of the ruling colour will no doubt accept as obvious.[32]

While the specific theoretical frameworks and vocabularies used to justify this "hierarchy of races" mutated over time, it was nevertheless usually accepted as "obvious," the commonsense of the geopolitical imagination. After outlining the overlapping debates about Greater Britain and the possibilities of an Anglo-American (re)union, I follow these ideas through the twentieth century and into our own world. I delineate four models that drew inspiration (and sometimes personnel) from the earlier Victorian debates: Anglo-American, imperial-commonwealth, democratic unionist, and world federalist. I conclude by discussing recent accounts of Anglo-world supremacy, suggesting that they should be interpreted as the latest iterations of a long-standing racialized vision of world order.

Section III examines the political thinking of some key Victorian public intellectuals, chiefly historians and philosophers. I start with a reading of John Stuart Mill. Recent scholarship on Mill has greatly improved understanding of his arguments about the ethical defensibility of imperial rule, and in particular his account of India, but it has tended to ignore or downplay his extensive writings on colonization. Yet this was a subject that Mill returned to frequently throughout his long and illustrious career. While initially he regarded colonization as a solution to the "social problem" in Britain, he came to believe that its legitimacy resided primarily in the universal benefits—civilization, peace, and prosperity—that it generated for humanity as a whole. In the final years of his life Mill seemed to lose faith in the project. Confronted with the political intransigence and violence of the settlers, yet refusing to give up on the settler empire altogether, his colonial romance gave way to a form of melancholic resignation.

Chapter 10—which was co-authored by Casper Sylvest—discusses the content and boundaries of liberal internationalism. An ideology that imagined a world of self-determining nation-states gradually socialized into cooperative interaction through international commerce, law, and incremental democratization, it was typically predicated on a distinction between "civilized" and "uncivilized" peoples, applying one set of arguments to those within the privileged circle and another to those who fell outside it. Many (but not all) of its fundamental assumptions about the nature and direction of progress in the international system were shared by large swathes of the Victorian and Edwardian intellectual elites. It remains a potent force to this day, the domi-

---

[32] Murray, "The Exploitation of Inferior Races in Ancient and Modern Times," in *Liberalism and the Empire,* by F. W. Hirst, Gilbert Murray, and J. L. Hammond (London, 1899), 156. On Murray's theoretical account of empire and international politics, see Christopher Stray, ed., *Gilbert Murray Reassessed* (Oxford, 2007), chs. 11–12; Jeanne Morefield, *Covenants without Swords* (Princeton, 2004).

nant internationalist ideology of the modern West.[33] The chapter examines how the very different philosophical systems crafted by T. H. Green, Henry Sidgwick, and Herbert Spencer issued in similar prescriptions for the international system.[34] They diverged, though, over the legitimacy of empire, with Sidgwick adumbrating a fairly conventional liberal civilizational imperialism, Green largely silent on the issue, and Spencer a fierce critic.

Then it is the turn of the historians. In an account of Edward Freeman's lifework, J. A. Doyle observed that it was "scarcely possible" to avoid comparisons between Froude, Freeman, and Seeley. All three scaled the heights of the blossoming professional discipline in Britain. Seeley was Regius Professor of Modern History at Cambridge from 1869–1895, Freeman held the equivalent chair in Oxford from 1884–1892, whereupon he was succeeded (albeit briefly) by Froude. All three were leading public moralists, contributing to debates on a plethora of issues beyond their putative historical expertise.[35] Despite their many and varied differences, there was one "point of community" that united them. "To each of them history was something more than an inspiring and impressive drama. Each fully acknowledged the truth . . . that the things of history happened for an example; that it is only by a knowledge of history that the citizen can attain a clear understanding of the duties and responsibilities which lie about him." Yet this similarity, Doyle continued, produced divergent conclusions: "[I]t would be hard to imagine political ideas or conceptions of national life differing more widely than did those held by Freeman and those of his two contemporaries."[36] So it appeared to each of them and many of their readers.

It was a late Victorian platitude that Seeley's *The Expansion of England* (1883) and Froude's *Oceana* (1886) played a pivotal role in reorienting British attitudes to the settler colonies and stoking the fire of popular imperialism. "The work of Seeley and Froude in one sphere of literary activity, of Kipling in another, and the strong personality of Mr. Chamberlain . . . combined to draw

[33] For a recent critical analysis, see Beate Jahn, *Liberal Internationalism* (London, 2013). For a more positive account, see John Ikenberry, "Liberal Internationalism 3.0," *Perspectives on Politics*, 7/1 (2009), 71–87. See also the essays in Tim Dunne and Trine Flockhart, eds., *Liberal World Orders* (Oxford, 2013).

[34] For a more detailed analysis, covering the work of historians and lawyers as well as philosophers, see Casper Sylvest, *British Liberal Internationalism, 1880–1930* (Manchester, 2009). For a general history, see Mark Mazower, *Governing the World* (London, 2012), pt. 1.

[35] Doyle, "Freeman, Froude, Seeley," *Quarterly Review*, 182/364 (1895), 296. Doyle was a Fellow of All Souls, Oxford, best known for his multivolume history of the British colonization of North America. Doyle, *The English in America*, 5 vols. (London, 1882–1907). For the institutional and cultural context of this professionalization, see Reba Soffer, *Discipline and Power* (Stanford, 1994); Philippa Levine, *The Amateur and the Professional* (Cambridge, 1986); Peter Slee, *Learning and a Liberal Education* (Manchester, 1986). Their intellectual and social milieu is brilliantly evoked in Collini, *Public Moralists*.

[36] Doyle, "Freeman, Froude, Seeley," 296.

the outposts of the realm into a closer union," wrote one informed observer.[37] Half a century later Hannah Arendt underlined their significance in her discussion of imperialism in *The Origins of Totalitarianism*.[38] Disagreeing fundamentally over the appropriate way to study and write history—Froude harking back to the narrative mode of Macaulay, Seeley impressed by the rigorous historical positivism imported from Germany—they were nevertheless both ardent imperial federalists, keen to formally unite the scattered elements of the British colonial system. C. A. Bayly has argued that the decades prior to the outbreak of war in 1914 can be seen as an "idealist" age, with both nationalism and empire "tinctured with religion."[39] In chapter 11 I argue that Seeley's political thought, including his wildly popular account of empire, was structured by concepts—nation, history, state, civilization—that he interpreted in theological terms. I read his vision of world order as an idiosyncratic expression of "cosmopolitan nationalism," an attempt to reconcile human universality with national particularity. Moreover, I contend that although he never outlined his plans for Greater Britain in any detail, he was committed to the creation of a federal nation-state encompassing Britain and its settler colonies. Chapter 12 engages Froude's elusive political thought. I start by distinguishing two modes of justifying imperialism, a "liberal civilizational" model (as articulated by John Stuart Mill) that did so principally in terms of the benefits that it bestowed on subject populations, and a "republican" model that focused instead on a specific set of benefits—glory, honor, virtue—that accrued to the imperial state. The remainder of the chapter offers a "republican" interpretation of Froude's writings on settler colonialism, arguing that both his diagnosis of the problems besetting modern Britain and his prescribed solutions were derived in part from his reading of the fate of the Roman Republic.

Freeman pursued a relentless intellectual vendetta against Froude, frequently challenging his credentials as a serious historian.[40] Freeman and Seeley had more in common: both were fairly conventional liberals, albeit of different stripes, and both concurred on the intimate connection between history and politics. But Freeman scorned the vision of empire articulated by

---

[37] W. Alleyne Ireland, "The Victorian Era of British Expansion," *North American Review*, 172/533 (1901), 563. See also Ireland, "The Growth of the British Colonial Conception," *Atlantic Monthly*, April 1899, 488–98; J. H. Muirhead, "What Imperialism Means" [1900], in *The British Idealists*, ed. David Boucher (Cambridge, 1997), 244.

[38] Arendt, *The Origins of Totalitarianism*, 181–82. For Arendt on empire, see Richard King and Dan Stone, eds., *Hannah Arendt and the Uses of History* (Oxford, 2007), pt. 1; A. Dirk Moses, "Das römische Gespräch in a New Key," *Journal of Modern History*, 85/4 (2013), 867–913.

[39] Bayly, "Michael Mann and Modern World History," *Historical Journal*, 58/1 (2015), 334.

[40] On Freeman's campaign against Froude, see Ian Hesketh, "Diagnosing Froude's Disease," *History and Theory*, 47/3 (2008), 373–95.

Seeley and Froude. Chapter 13 unpacks the intellectual sources of his skepticism. Drawing in particular on the history of federalism—a subject on which he was the recognized authority—he argued that plans for uniting the colonies were absurd, based on a flagrant misunderstanding of both the federal idea and the true meaning of empire. Properly understood, the history of empire instilled the need for colonial independence, not unification. But it would be a mistake to exaggerate Freeman's anti-imperial credentials, or characterize him (following Doyle) as the antithesis of Seeley and Froude, because he shared with them a belief in the unity and superiority of the "English-speaking race." His preferred political vehicle for this racial vision of world order was an alliance, cemented by common citizenship, between Britain and the United States, countries that were ordained to lead and police the world.[41] Like many critics of formal empire during the period, Freeman was nevertheless committed to a hierarchical conception of global politics predicated on white racial supremacy.

The final full chapter analyzes two renowned "new liberal" thinkers, J. A. Hobson and L. T. Hobhouse, focusing in particular on how they conceived of the relationship between democracy, empire, and international politics between the late 1890s and the First World War. I start by highlighting how they positioned themselves in relation to the past and present of the mutating liberal tradition, before turning to examine their writings on settler colonialism, showing how they both supported projects for the unification of Greater Britain, albeit in a qualified manner. Posterity has been kind to Hobson, who is usually remembered as one of the major anti-imperial thinkers of the twentieth century (not least because of his influence on Lenin).[42] Yet his writings present a rather more complicated picture, for he was not opposed to empire in all its forms, only to what he saw as pathological variants of it, and he was a keen advocate of settler colonialism. Hobhouse, meanwhile, sketched an idealized account of the colonial empire. He argued that if transmuted into a federal institution it would be compatible with democracy, in a manner that traditional forms of empire were not, and as such it could serve as a privileged agent of progress, fermenting the democratization of the international system and acting as a template for a future "international state." Like many liberal thinkers, both Hobson and Hobhouse invested far more political hope in settler colonialism that in other modes of empire-building.

---

[41] For more on the late Victorian interest in cooperation (even union) with the United States, including visions of "isopolitan citizenship," see Duncan Bell, "Before the Democratic Peace," *European Journal of International Relations*, 20/3 (2014), 647–70; Bell, "Beyond the Sovereign State," *Political Studies*, 62/2 (2014), 418–34. I address the topic in a forthcoming book, *Dreamworlds of Empire*.

[42] Lenin, *Imperialism* [1917], in *Selected Works* (Moscow, 1963), 1:667–766.

In the brief coda, I revisit some of the main lines of argument developed in the preceding chapters. Reiterating the centrality of historical-mindedness and settler colonialism in nineteenth-century visions of empire, I finish with some tentative suggestions about the need to "de-colonize" liberalism, to seek ways to acknowledge and transcend the legacies of colonial occupation and rule, rather than either ignoring this tainted history or rejecting liberalism altogether.

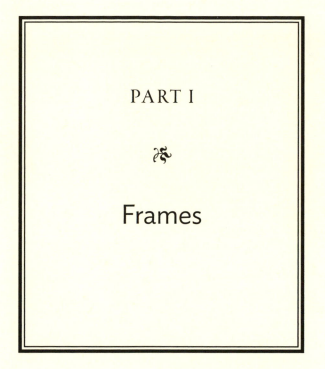

PART I

Frames

The Dream Machine

২৯

On Liberalism and Empire

In the empire, one might say, liberalism had found
the concrete place of its dreams.[1]

—UDAY SINGH MEHTA

The relationship between liberalism and empire has been a recurrent topic of debate among political theorists and intellectual historians during the last two decades. The timing is no coincidence. In the "new world order" purportedly hatched by the dissolution of Cold War certainties, liberals and their critics sought to diagnose the virtues and vices of the triumphant ideology.[2] Evaluating the present triggered an urgent turn to history, as the record of liberal engagement with empire was scoured for lessons, precedents, and forecasts. As old arguments have been reanimated and mobilized, so political thought has been articulated in the register of historical investigation. In this chapter I survey the scholarly field, concentrating in particular on work that emphasizes the centrality of British imperial ideology in the long nineteenth century, from the turmoil of the American and French Revolutions to the onset of the First World War.[3] During that extraordinary period Britain was both the crucible of liberal political thinking and the most extensive imperial formation in history.

Liberalism was a protean phenomenon, a shape-shifting amalgam of philosophical arguments and political-economic practices encompassing diverse views on the self, society, economy, and government. Its ideological reach and complexity grew steadily as the century unfolded. By 1860 liberals of different

---

[1] Mehta, *Liberalism and Empire* (Chicago, 1999), 37.

[2] For a challenge to such certainties, see Duncan Bell and Joel Isaac, eds., *Uncertain Empire* (Oxford, 2012).

[3] For global accounts of the period, see Chris Bayly, *The Birth of the Modern World, 1780–1914* (Oxford, 2004); Barry Buzan and George Lawson, *The Global Transformation* (Cambridge, 2015); Jürgen Osterhammel, *The Transformation of the World* (Princeton, 2014).

stripes were beginning to converge on a relatively stable "internationalist" doctrine that championed the benefits of conjoining international commerce and international law, but such arguments applied only (or primarily) to relations between purportedly "civilized" states.[4] Then, as now, liberals remained divided over the question of empire. Most supported it, but then so too did most non-liberals, and liberal imperialists differed over the forms of empire they defended, the intensity of support they offered, and perhaps most significantly, the justificatory arguments that they articulated. There were also assorted liberal critics of empire, though they were always in a minority. Reductive generalizations about "liberalism and empire," whether directed at the heyday of the British empire or the contemporary world, are usually more misleading than illuminating.

Two main weaknesses run through scholarly commentary on liberalism and empire: a tendency to overlook the significance of *settler colonialism* and an over-reliance on *canonical* interpretations of liberalism. I address both in this chapter. Settler colonialism played a crucial role in nineteenth-century imperial thought, and liberalism in particular, yet it has largely been ignored in the burst of writing about the intellectual foundations of the Victorian empire. Utilizing canonical interpretations of liberalism, meanwhile, has generated some skewed claims about the historical connections between liberal political thought and empire.

Languages of Empire

The study of liberal attitudes to empire is beset with conceptual, historical, and semantic difficulties. To say something perspicacious about the relationship between X and Y, it is vital to have a clear sense of their meaning, but "liberalism" and "empire" both rank among the most polysemous concepts in the modern political lexicon, and as a result debates about their relationship are often characterized by confusion. Since there is no settled agreement on their meaning, the selection of definitions—and thus the determination of conclusions—is the product of an opaque combination of scholarly sensibility, disciplinary socialization, and political commitments. The bulk of the literature produced by political theorists employs a plausible but relatively narrow understanding of empire—chiefly what John Plamenatz termed "alien rule," the conquest and governance of distant populations and territories.[5]

---

[4] For a detailed exposition, see Casper Sylvest, *British Liberal Internationalism, 1880–1930* (Manchester, 2009). See also the discussion in chapter 10. For further comments on the nature of liberalism, and for bibliographical references on the topic, see chapters 1 and 3.

[5] Plamenatz, *On Alien Rule and Self-Government* (London, 1960). This was one of only a handful of books written by a political theorist during the Cold War that addressed the question of empire. For an attempt to resuscitate it, see Brian Barry, "On Self-Government," in *The Nature of*

This definitional preference conditions a particular range of questions and answers.

Scholarship on liberal political theory and empire is divided by three main issues. First, there is profound disagreement over whether the relationship is *rejectionist, necessary,* or *contingent.* The *rejection thesis* posits that liberalism and imperialism are mutually exclusive, that authentic liberals cannot be imperialists. In contrast, the *necessity thesis* asserts that imperialism is an integral feature of liberal political thought—that to be a proper liberal is to be committed to the legitimacy of (liberal) empire. Those espousing the *contingency thesis* argue that liberal normative commitments do not necessarily entail support for empire. Instead, the imperialism of liberal writers, past and present, can be explained either through reference to superseded historical conditions or by disaggregating discrete strands of liberalism, some of which are more susceptible to imperial temptation than others. The political and theoretical repercussions of this disagreement are palpable, not least because it raises the question of whether forms of non-imperial liberalism are even possible.

The second line of divergence concerns the extent to which the history of liberalism contaminates its contemporary expressions. While overlapping with the first point, this is nevertheless a distinct issue. Even if one denies the necessity thesis, it might still be argued that liberal assumptions, categories, and institutions cannot escape their original imperial entanglements—that the history of Western conquest is so deeply implicated in shaping the present order that it permeates liberal political thinking and practice, as well as the ways in which it is perceived in places with long experience of European intervention. Such an argument is normatively indeterminate. One version embraces the continuities, viewing the history of empire as a fertile resource for contemporary projects of imperial world ordering.[6] Another, less celebratory, response acknowledges the deep historical roots of contemporary liberal political ideas, but suggests that this historical lineage does not in itself invalidate them. Their "genealogy," Anthony Pagden argues, should not be "counted as grounds for dismissing them."[7] To do so, proponents of this line charge, would be to commit the genetic fallacy, the mistake of evaluating something solely in terms of its origins. But the most common line of argument maintains that liberals can and should escape the burdens of imperial history; that the liberalism of today is (or can be) radically different from that which went

---

Political Theory, ed. David Miller and Larry Siedentop (London, 1983), 121–54. For a recent defense of "alien rule" (understood in broader terms), see Michael Hechter, *Alien Rule* (Cambridge, 2013).

[6] For a prominent example, see Niall Ferguson, *Empire* (London, 2003).

[7] Anthony Pagden, *The Burdens of Empire* (Cambridge, 2015), 37. For a more detailed account, see Pagden, "Human Rights, Natural Rights, and Europe's Imperial Legacy," *Political Theory,* 31 (2003), 171–99. This essay is reprinted in *Burdens,* on pages 243–63.

before. The third main source of disagreement concerns the historical trajectory of liberalism. This dispute is often tied up with the long-standing historical debate about the origins of liberalism, with some tracing the ideology to
early modern Europe, and in particular the seventeenth century, while other
scholars (myself included) claim that it is best seen as a product of the late
eighteenth century. One line of argument posits that the history of liberal political thought has always been thoroughly imperial (whether through conceptual necessity or otherwise), another that it is marked by significant ideological variability and ruptures. The most common line, which I return to
later in this chapter, suggests that the late eighteenth century witnessed a
major transition in liberal visions of empire, an ideological break that allows
us to draw a firm line between the epochs. Others, though, propose different
historical chronologies, identify alternative discursive shifts, or place greater
emphasis on long-run continuities in liberal thinking.

While pure examples of the rejection and necessity theses are (and always
have been) rare, liberals have developed a range of argumentative strategies
that articulate weak forms of the rejectionist line. In the late nineteenth century, for example, it was common to distinguish between *imperialism* (an un-
justified form of aggressive expansionism) and *empire* (a potentially legitimate
form of political order). This distinction was central to Gladstone's fierce critique of Disraeli's romantic defense of imperialism.[8] "Liberalism and Imperialism," the historian J. L Hammond wrote at the turn of the twentieth century, "differ in their morals, their manners and their ideals." Whereas the
former (represented by Cobden, Bright, and Spencer) was pacific in intent,
the latter was militaristic, and whereas liberals affirmed the value of nationality, imperialists rejoiced in the "funerals of other nationalities."[9] Yet empire
was legitimate if it was motivated by broadly liberal ambitions and functioned
according to broadly liberal norms. Thus Hammond could argue that even as
they firmly rejected imperialism, true liberals recognized that the possession
of empire imposed a "special obligation to act with self-control and
moderation."[10] Dismissive of imperialism, he praised the value of settler colonialism. L. T. Hobhouse adopted a similar argument, insisting that the "central principle" of liberalism was self-government, whereas imperialists hymned
the "subordination of self-government to Empire," and that as such they were
antithetical ideological positions. Like Hammond, though, he nevertheless
suggested that if understood properly—in his case as "a great aggregation of

---

[8] Peter Cain, "Radicalism, Gladstone, and the Liberal Critique of Disraelian 'Imperialism,'" in
Victorian Visions of Global Order, ed. Duncan Bell (Cambridge, 2007), 215–39. For the liberal critique of "imperialism," see also Miles Taylor, "Imperium et Libertas?," *Journal of Imperial and Commonwealth History*, 19 (1991), 1–23.

[9] Hammond, "Colonial and Foreign Policy," in *Liberalism and the Empire*, by Hammond,
Hirst, and Murray (London, 1899), 196.

[10] Ibid., 171.

territories enjoying internal independence while united by some common bond"—the pursuit of empire was compatible with liberalism.[11]

Echoing this distinction, liberal internationalists today often scramble to differentiate "hegemony" from "empire," with the former typically construed as normatively desirable and the latter as both obsolete and objectionable. Thus John Ikenberry celebrates American global leadership in the post-1945 era as a victory of liberal hegemony, while castigating the imperial depredations of the George W. Bush administration. This argument presupposes a restrictive definition. "If empire has any meaning," he maintains, "it refers to political control by a dominant state of the domestic and foreign policy of weaker countries."[12] Hegemony is different. In an empire, "the lead state operates unilaterally and outside the order, whereas in a hegemonic order, the lead establishes multilateral rules and institutions that it itself operates within." As with the late Victorian attempt to separate empire from imperialism, the line between empire and hegemony is often hard to sustain. Ikenberry, for example, anoints Victorian Britain and the postwar United States as the two "great historical cases of liberal hegemony," but since Britain was an empire-state the historical (as opposed to ideological) value of the distinction he draws is unclear.[13] Not everyone is convinced by such acts of semantic jujitsu. Niall Ferguson, a proud liberal imperialist, is right to observe that "hegemony" is "really just a way to avoid talking about empire," and that it is only convincing if one assumes an implausibly narrow definition of the latter.[14] Indeed it can be seen as a rhetorical move within imperial ideology rather than a disinterested description of an alternative political formation. The history of imperial ideology is in part a story of contestation over the vocabulary of domination.

Another mode of argument maintains that the spread of capitalism will ultimately render imperialism obsolete. The most influential twentieth-century version was developed by Joseph Schumpeter, who equated liberalism with *laissez-faire* capitalism and declared that in its purest form it was hostile to imperialism. "[W]here free trade prevails," he predicted, "no class has an interest in forcible expansion as such."[15] Imperialism was an atavistic throw-

[11] Hobhouse, *Democracy and Reaction* [1904], ed. Peter Clarke (Brighton, 1972), 48, 154; Hobhouse once defined imperialism as "the doctrine of racial ascendency and territorial aggression." Hobhouse, "The Growth of Imperialism," *Speaker* (January 25, 1902), 474. I examine his views in chapter 14.

[12] Ikenberry, "Liberalism and Empire," *Review of International Studies*, 30 (2004), 619. If, on the other hand, "empire is defined more loosely as a hierarchical system of political relationships in which the most powerful state exercises decisive influence, the postwar American system indeed qualifies" (619).

[13] Ikenberry, "Liberalism and Empire," 615, 616. For more on liberal hegemony, see Ikenberry, *Liberal Order and Imperial Ambition* (London, 2006).

[14] Ferguson, "Hegemony or Empire?," *Foreign Affairs*, 82/5 (2003), 160.

[15] Schumpeter, *Imperialism and Social Classes* (New York, 1955), 75. See also Bernard Semmel, *The Liberal Ideal and the Demons of Empire* (Baltimore, 1993), 167–76.

back to a feudal age. Such arguments temporalize liberal anti-imperialism, implying that at some (indefinite) point in the future an authentic post-imperial liberal political order will emerge. Schumpeter inherited a long-standing line of reasoning about the emergent conditions and likely consequences of commercial society. Benjamin Constant's assault on the "spirit of conquest," Herbert Spencer's historical sociology of industrial society, Richard Cobden's relentless promotion of free trade, Hobson's critique of the financial "taproot" of imperialism, Norman Angell's account of the irrationality of war in an economically interdependent world: all posited that the development of capitalism would lead eventually to the supersession of the will-to-empire.[16] Yet none of them rejected empire in all its forms, and nor did they think that capitalism was always and everywhere opposed to imperialism. Indeed specific instantiations of capitalism were key to their respective explanations for the persistence of imperialism in the industrial age. Only in the long run would the perfection of the liberal capitalist order consign imperialism to the proverbial dustbin of history. Lineal descendants of this argument can be found in Panglossian cheerleading for neoliberal globalization.

James Tully's work illustrates the political and theoretical stakes involved in defining empire. Rejecting a narrow conception of empire-as-alien-rule, and of imperialism as the policy dedicated to the creation of such an empire, he adopts a much broader interpretation in order to critique the manifold continuities between the past and present. He contends that Western political thought has long articulated the right (even duty) of purportedly "advanced" states to remake the world in their own image, a self-defined mission that has been undertaken in the name of various related ideals: "to improve, to civilise, develop, modernise, constitutionalise, democratise, and bring good governance and freedom."[17] From this perspective, virtually all extant liberal political thought has been corrupted by its entanglement with empire. Tully also delineates various modalities of imperial rule. The subtlest is *informal imperialism*, under which there is no need to govern populations and territories through formal-legal means because the most powerful states "induce local rulers to keep their resources, labour, and markets open to free trade dominated by western corporations and global markets, thereby combining 'empire and liberty.'"[18] This account dissolves the distinction between hegemony and empire. In the nineteenth century, "free trade imperialism" was one of the

[16] Constant, "The Spirit of Conquest" [1814], in *Political Writings*, ed. Biancamaria Fontana (Cambridge, 1988), 51–81; Angell, *The Great Illusion* (London, 1910). See also Peter Cain, "Capitalism, Aristocracy and Empire," *Journal of Imperial and Commonwealth History*, 35/1 (2007), 25–47.

[17] Tully, "Lineages of Contemporary Imperialism," in *Lineages of Empire*, ed. Duncan Kelly (Oxford, 2009), 11. On Tully's vision, see Duncan Bell, "To Act Otherwise," in *On Global Citizenship*, ed. David Owen (London, 2014), 181–207.

[18] Tully, "Lineages of Contemporary Imperialism," 13. Here he draws on a seminal article,

main instruments through which Britain integrated much of Latin America into the global capitalist system. During the twentieth century, and especially after the defeat of Nazi and Soviet alternatives, it emerged as the preferred mode of domination by the leading powers, chiefly the United States. On this account, modernization, development, and globalization are best characterized as "the continuation of Western imperialism by informal means and through institutions of global governance."[19] The domain of empire, then, extends far beyond alien rule. Yet although Tully presents one of the most sweeping accounts of the imperial legacy of Western thought, he stops short of endorsing the necessity thesis. In Wittgensteinian terms, he argues that imperialism is only a contingent feature of dominant theoretical languages and practices, and that as such it does not exhaust them. The imperial dimensions of liberalism can thus be transcended or eliminated, at least in principle. A similar line is adopted by Charles Mills, who argues that despite its deep historical complicity in racism and imperialism, liberalism—albeit of a radically transformed kind—can be salvaged.[20] Both argue that liberal political thinking is capable of redemption.

Writing against the grain, some liberals acknowledge an intrinsic connection, with Ignatieff and Ferguson perhaps the best-known examples.[21] According to Alan Ryan, liberal imperialism is the doctrine that "a state with the capacity to force liberal political institutions and social aspirations upon nonliberal states and societies is justified in so doing," and in light of this he argues both that "liberalism *is* intrinsically imperialist" and that we should "understand the attractions of liberal imperialism and not flinch," before immediately warning against "succumbing to that attraction," chiefly on the pragmatic grounds that imperialism usually doesn't work in practice. The implication, of course, is that if it did work liberal imperialism would be legitimate in a wide range of cases.[22] While the vast majority of contemporary liberals would reject Ryan's framing of the issue, insisting that there is a fundamental difference between humanitarian intervention and imperialism, that difference is rarely spelt out, and when it is the reasoning is usually based on a very narrow conception of empire and imperialism. Once again, it is the

Ronald Robinson and John Gallagher, "The Imperialism of Free Trade," *Economic History Review*, 6 (1953), 1–15.

[19] Tully, *Public Philosophy in a New Key* (Cambridge, 2008), 2:7.

[20] Tully, *Strange Multiplicity* (Cambridge, 1995); Mills, "Occupy Liberalism!," *Radical Philosophy Review*, 15/2 (2012), 305–23.

[21] For a powerful critique of their uses of history, and much else besides, see Jeanne Morefield, *Empires without Imperialism* (Oxford, 2014).

[22] Ryan, "Liberal Imperialism" [2004], in *The Making of Modern Liberalism* (Princeton, 2012), 107, 122. For a sophisticated liberal account of the practical difficulties of humanitarian intervention, and the normative implications to be drawn from this, see Michael Doyle, *The Question of Intervention* (New Haven, 2015). Doyle, though, exaggerates the differences between past modes of imperialism and current ideas and practices.

choice of definitions (and the interpretation of polyvalent political terms) that shapes the parameters of the theoretical debate, as well as its political complexion.

The bulk of the recent literature on liberalism and empire employs variations on the theme of historical contingency. Scholars differ chiefly over where they place the emphases and on how much continuity and change they discern in the historical development of liberal ideology. In the following section, I outline some of the key contributions to this debate.

Intertextual Empire: Writing Liberal Imperialism

Uday Singh Mehta's *Liberalism and Empire,* published in 1999, set the terms for much of the recent scholarship.[23] His sophisticated analysis is as much epistemological as ethical. Drawing principally on John Locke and John Stuart Mill, he contends that liberalism encodes a particular vision of historical development and a preordained response to it. Incapable of respecting the "unfamiliar," defined in terms of radical difference, liberal thought is marked by a "singularly impoverished understanding of experience."[24] When liberals confronted alterity they (almost) invariably judged it through reference to an antecedently fixed standard of evaluation, rooted in Eurocentric conceptions of what it means to be fully human and/or a legitimate society. While liberalism claimed the mantle of universalism—the "cosmopolitanism of reason"—it was deeply parochial, seeking "relentlessly" to "align or educate the regnant forms of the unfamiliar with its own expectations."[25] Indians were thus portrayed as backward due to their failure to conform to purported universal norms of rational conduct. On this account, the liberal dream of disembodied reason is a cognitive technology for imaginatively assimilating the unfamiliar to a pre-given local structure of rationality. Liberal empire is the product of a

---

[23] Mehta's timing was exemplary. In April that year, British Prime Minister Tony Blair gave a speech in Chicago presenting the case for "humanitarian" intervention in Kosovo, invoking the "doctrine of the international community." It synthesised many of the liberal arguments that had been percolating around Western politics elites and academic discourse during the preceding few years. Subsequently, this line of thinking was formalised into the doctrine of "Responsibility to Protect." For supportive accounts, see Alex Bellamy, *Responsibility to Protect* (Oxford, 2014); Luke Glanville, *Sovereignty and the Responsibility to Protect* (Chicago, 2014). For a critique, see Philip Cunliffe, ed., *Critical Perspectives on the Responsibility to Protect* (London, 2011).

[24] Mehta, *Liberalism and Empire*, 11, 23. Mehta is clear he is not concerned here with authorial intent, but with "foundational commitments" (47, 1n).

[25] Ibid., 18. Intriguingly, this argument was itself employed by liberal defenders of empire. Hammond, for example, admonished "imperialists" for "that intolerance which regards every diversity of religion, of polity, as an eyesore, which sees a moribund civilization in every civilization not immediately intelligible or sympathetic to our own . . . and takes pride in its rigid Procrustean measurements of every nation by our own standard" ("Colonial and Foreign Policy," 199).

loaded encounter between abstract universalism and the concrete lifeworlds of other peoples.

According to Mehta, the nineteenth century witnessed the climacteric of the liberal "urge" to empire, as liberals grafted a heavily over-determined vision of civilization and historical progress onto a Lockean account of rationality. The result was a developmental picture that bifurcated the world into those (coded as "adults") who possessed reason and were thus capable of self-government and those (coded as "children") who required tutelage to bring them up to the required standard. Liberals, in other words, were committed to what Dipesh Chakrabarty famously termed the "waiting room" view of history, a view that "came to non-European peoples in the nineteenth century as somebody's way of saying 'not yet' to somebody else."[26] The "standard of civilization" stratified human reason as well as geographical space, identifying a differential capacity for "improvement" among assorted human groups. Underpinning Mehta's theoretical argument is a sweeping historical claim: liberalism has been an imperial ideology from its inception in seventeenth-century Europe. Its two leading figures—Locke and Mill—provide the intellectual scaffolding for enduring liberal justifications of empire.

While Mehta's argument is theoretically powerful, its scope and thus its ultimate force are obscure. He oscillates between a weak and a strong thesis. The anthropomorphic language of "urge" and "impulse"—as if liberalism was a self-realizing ideological formation—might be read as endorsing the necessity thesis. Thus he insists that the imperial urge is "integral" to the "political vision" of liberalism.[27] This is how his argument has often been interpreted. But elsewhere Mehta qualifies the contention. "Urges can of course be resisted, and liberals offer ample evidence of this ability, which is why I do not claim that liberalism *must be* imperialistic, only that the urge is *internal* to it."[28] This is equivocal. If by "urge" Mehta means that liberal thought contains theoretical resources that can be employed to justify empire, then few would dissent, but if he means either that authentic liberals must always support empire or alternatively that a special act of will or theoretical circumspection is required to stop liberals becoming imperialists—as the main thrust of the book seems to suggest—then this position is hard to sustain, not least because the concept of "urge" is too vague and indeterminate to do the explanatory work required. After all, liberalism contains plenty of other "urges," some of which can underpin the critique of empire, including a concern with the dangers of state coercion, individual freedom, toleration, collective self-government, and universal moral equality. Hence Frederick Cooper's riposte that the "urge" to

[26] Chakrabarty, *Provincializing Europe* (Princeton, 2000), 8.

[27] Mehta, *Liberalism and Empire*, 9. Italics added. "Given liberalism's universalism," he writes elsewhere, "this is definitionally the case" (48).

[28] Ibid., 20. Italics in original.

anti-imperialism is also "internal to it."[29] What matters is the lexical ordering or conceptual configuration of such "urges" in any given context, and Mehta fails to establish that the urge to empire is uniformly prioritized either across the history of liberalism or within the catholic expanses of Victorian liberal thought. Finally, it isn't clear where Mehta draws the discursive boundaries of liberalism. He suggests, for example, that anti-imperial forms of liberalism co-existed with the civilizing vision, and to make this case he counterposes the "cosmopolitanism of sentiment" articulated by Hume and especially Burke to the "cosmopolitanism of reason," defining it as part of an "other liberal tradition," though to muddy the waters further he also labels Burke a conservative.[30] If we acknowledge this other tradition, however, the ostensible "urge" to empire is not internal to liberalism, but rather to specific articulations of it. On either the weak or the strong reading, though, Mehta suggests that only through misunderstanding or suppressing some of their own basic theoretical commitments can (most) liberals avoid becoming imperialists.

Three prominent analyses—by Sankar Muthu, Jennifer Pitts, and Karuna Mantena—offer alternative accounts of the connections between universalism and the project of empire.[31] In *Enlightenment against Empire* Muthu targets the pervasive claim that late eighteenth-century intellectual life in Europe was shaped by a monolithic "Enlightenment project" complicit in imperial expansion. Despite their manifest differences, he argues that Kant, Diderot, and Herder shared philosophical commitments that underpinned a thoroughgoing critique of European conquest. The condition of possibility for anti-imperialism was a radical transformation in understanding what it meant to be human, a shift that facilitated three other philosophical claims. First, and most fundamentally, it grounded an account of basic moral equality, the view that all humans "deserve some modicum of moral and political respect" in virtue of their shared humanity. This was combined with an argument that

---

[29] Cooper, *Colonialism in Question* (Berkeley, 2005), 235.

[30] Mehta, *Liberalism and Empire*, 43, 50. Michael Bentley suggests that Mehta should simply acknowledge that the "other tradition" he identifies is an antiliberal conservative one, fully capable of "recognising other cultures in and for their authenticity and selfhood." Bentley, review, *Victorian Studies*, 43/4 (2001), 620.

[31] While I here focus on these texts, chiefly because of their influence and the scope of their historical claims, numerous other scholars have explored aspects of the topic. For some of the most interesting accounts of British imperial liberalism, see Peter Cain, "Empire and the Languages of Character and Virtue in Later Victorian and Edwardian Britain," *Modern Intellectual History*, 4/2 (2007), 1–25; Cain, "Character, 'Ordered Liberty,' and the Mission to Civilise," *Journal of Imperial and Commonwealth History*, 40/4 (2012), 557–78; Gregory Claeys, *Imperial Sceptics* (Cambridge, 2010); Daniel Gorman, *Imperial Citizenship* (Manchester, 2006); Jeanne Morefield, *Covenants without Swords*; Morefield, *Empires without Imperialism*; Nicholas Owen, *The British Left and India* (Oxford, 2007); Andrew Sartori, *Liberalism in Empire* (Berkeley, 2014); Casper Sylvest, *British Liberal Internationalism, 1880–1930*. For the European context, see Matthew Fitzpatrick, ed., *Liberal Imperialism in Europe* (Basingstoke, 2012).

humans were "fundamentally cultural beings," immersed in a complex web of attachments, the spatio-temporal variation of which produces difference. Finally, Muthu contends that Enlightenment anti-imperialism was premised on a robust account of "moral incommensurability and relativity," meaning that individuals and communities could not be judged according to a single scale of value.[32] In a retort to Mehta's starkly drawn contrast between the (abstract) universal and the (concrete) particular, Muthu suggests that when tempered by recognition of cultural agency universalism offers a potent resource for anti-imperialism. "[A]n increasingly acute awareness of the *irreducible plurality* and *partial incommensurability* of social forms, moral values, and political institutions engendered a historically uncommon, inclusive moral *universalism*."[33] His acute philosophical analysis is tethered to a historical argument. Contra Mehta, Burke was no "lone voice in the wilderness" but rather one among a constellation of brilliant thinkers who assailed the injustices of European conquest during the second half of the eighteenth century. This moment, though, was an "historical anomaly," for European thought had previously been dominated by fantasies of the "noble savage," which denied basic moral equality, while the period that followed it was defined by the victory of aggressive imperial ideologies. "By the mid-nineteenth century, anti-imperialist political thinking was virtually absent from Western European intellectual debates, surfacing only rarely by way of *philosophically obscure and politically marginal figures*."[34] I return to this bold historical claim later in the chapter.

Jennifer Pitts pushes the analysis deep into the nineteenth century. She offers a convincing corrective to Mehta, suggesting that liberalism is best understood as a "complex ideology whose exemplars share family resemblances rather than any strict doctrine."[35] It contains resources to both combat and justify empire. She too identifies a resplendent period of enlightenment anti-imperialism followed by a pronounced "turn to empire," though unlike Muthu she explicitly narrates this as part of the history of liberalism, refiguring it as an ideology born in a dazzling moment of imperial critique. Rather than its besetting original sin, exemplified by Locke's complicity in the colonization of the Carolinas, empire is posited as a tragic betrayal of its early promise. She casts Burke, Bentham, and Adam Smith in the anti-imperial role and tracks the emergence of "imperial liberalism" through James Mill's writings, before pinpointing its full realization in the work of Alexis de Tocqueville and John Stuart Mill. Pitts presents her argument as (among other things) a rejoinder to Mehta's overly reductive account of liberalism, although given Mehta's ambiguity it can also be read as a subtle fleshing out of the underdeveloped "weak

---

[32] Muthu, *Enlightenment against Empire* (Princeton, 2003), 268–69.

[33] Ibid., 282. Italics in original.

[34] Ibid., 4, 5 (and 258). Italics added.

[35] Pitts, "Political Theory of Empire and Imperialism," *Annual Review of Political Science,* 13 (2010): 218.

thesis" hinted at in *Liberalism and Empire*: the recognition of an alternative liberal tradition containing a battery of arguments to level against empire. With admirable dialectical skill, Pitts demonstrates how her catalog of anti-imperial liberals rejected European expansion and displayed considerable respect for societies at different stages of socioeconomic development. Thus while Smith deployed a stadial theory to explain the emergence of commercial society, he accounted for differential patterns of growth in terms of serendipitous historical circumstances rather than the intrinsic faults of other peoples. A "theory of progress," Pitts argues, "need not imply a pejorative assessment of less 'advanced' peoples or support for European colonial expansion."[36] However, she continues, the empathetic subtlety that characterized late eighteenth-century political thought was supplanted during the course of the nineteenth century by a crude binary division of the world into civilized/barbarian. In this narrative John Stuart Mill is presented as the apotheosis of imperial liberalism. Her historical timeline matches that of Muthu. By the mid-nineteenth century, "we find *no prominent political thinkers in Europe* questioning the justice of European empires."[37]

Karuna Mantena argues for an alternative chronology, maintaining that liberal "ethical" visions flared only for a brief moment, before being superseded with a different form of imperial justification during the second half of the nineteenth century. "Late imperial ideologies and discourses of justification were grounded in a common, conservative *opposition to the liberal project*."[38] On this account, liberal confidence in imperial progress—predicated on "the language of a civilizing rule and the goal of self-government"—was corroded by the Sepoy Rebellion of 1857 and subsequent episodes of resistance.[39] Under the influence of Henry Maine, an eminent scholar of comparative jurisprudence, imperial ideologists adopted a "culturalist" narrative, which emphasized the Sisyphean difficulty of transforming colonized spaces in the image of liberal modernity.[40] Thus from the 1860s onwards we see a "decisive turning away" from liberal arguments to a view that emphasized the protection of (newly conceptualized) "native communities."[41] Social theory rather than political philosophy provided a novel intellectual founda-

[36] Pitts, *A Turn to Empire* (Princeton, 2005), 26. For the intriguing late-Victorian afterlife of Smith's ideas, see Marc-William Palen, "Adam Smith as Advocate of Empire," *Historical Journal*, 57/1 (2014), 179–98.

[37] Pitts, *A Turn to Empire*, 2. Italics added. Pitts argues that French liberalism followed a similar trajectory in the nineteenth century, split between an anti-imperial tradition represented by Constant and Amédée Desjobert and a republican-inflected imperial liberalism articulated in de Tocqueville's writings on Algeria.

[38] Mantena, *Alibis of Empire* (Princeton, 2010), 45. Italics added.

[39] Ibid., 48.

[40] On Maine's life and thought, see also Alan Diamond, ed., *The Victorian Achievement of Sir Henry Maine* (Cambridge, 2006); Raymond Cocks, *Sir Henry Maine* (Cambridge, 1988).

[41] Mantena, *Alibis of Empire*, 1, 48. For empirical confirmation of this policy trend outside of

tion for imperial ideology.[42] Maine and his followers argued for the prolongation of empire on the grounds that intervention had so weakened traditional
communities that retreat would herald disaster. "Native society here functioned both as a pretext and solution, as an *alibi* for the fait accompli of
empire."[43] Mantena reimagines the lineage between Burke and Mill, viewing
them less as antipodes than as avatars of a tradition of "ethical" imperialism.
Mill is presented as a "crucial transitional figure," a bridge between the exuberant optimism of the 1830s and 1840s and the later period of disenchantment,
rather than the assured culmination of liberal imperial ideology.[44] The shift to
alibis had important practical effects, shaping the policy of "indirect rule" that
was enacted by British imperial administrators, including Lugard in Africa
and Cromer in Egypt. Furthermore, it established the intellectual groundwork for the League of Nations mandate system (itself a model for UN practices in the 1990s and beyond).[45]

Even as Mehta's account comes closest to the necessity thesis, he ultimately
pulls back from endorsing it, and in so doing weakens the general thrust of his
argument, leaving its theoretical and political implications unclear. Muthu
and Pitts advocate variations on the theme of contingency, with both postu-
lating a late eighteenth-century moment of anti-imperialism supplanted by an
overwhelming turn to empire. The contemporary lesson is clear: while liberalism is not intrinsically imperial, liberals must avoid replicating the corrupted
position adopted by their nineteenth-century predecessors. Mantena, meanwhile, complicates this narrative arc by stepping outside the canon and rerout-
ing the historical trajectory, suggesting that liberal imperial optimism was neither inscribed in the ideology from its very inception, as with Mehta, nor was
it as pervasive in the nineteenth century as Muthu and Pitts imply. It was instead a brief, anomalous episode tied to specific developments in the empire
in India. Diverging over the three issues I outlined earlier in the chapter—
conceptual architecture, contemporary legacy, and historical narrative—these
bold lines of argument have helped to set the coordinates for debate over liberal visions of empire during the long nineteenth century.

India, see Coel Kirkby, "The Politics and Practice of 'Native' Enfranchisement in Canada and the
Cape Colony, c.1880–1900," (PhD thesis, University of Cambridge, 2013).

[42] Mantena also develops a brilliant analysis of the recurrent instability of imperial ideology,
which she convincingly applies to the recent conflict in Iraq and its aftermath (*Alibis of Empire*,
179–81).

[43] Ibid., 11. Italics in original.

[44] Ibid., 22–39. On this account, his universalism was heavily qualified by assorted empirical
factors, leading to a more contextualized approach to imperial affairs.

[45] This reinforces other recent accounts of the imperial origins of the League and the United
Nations, including Mark Mazower, *No Enchanted Palace* (Princeton, 2009). On trusteeship, see
also William Bain, *Between Anarchy and Society* (Oxford, 2003). For a magisterial analysis of the
Mandate system, see Susan Pedersen, *The Guardians* (Oxford, 2015).

On Settler Colonialism

During the 1980s and 1990s the field of imperial history was revivified by an infusion of new theoretical approaches, the most influential of which was postcolonialism.[46] This intervention served both to illuminate and obscure. One significant consequence was a narrowing of geographical focus, with India looming so large that it sometimes performed a metonymic function, standing for empire as a whole and nearly exhausting the space of argument and interpretation.[47] As a sympathetic observer noted in 1998, "[p]ostcolonial commentary in the nineties has been remarkable in the degree of its engrossment with India."[48] The settler empire was relegated to the margins of debate, despite its historical importance. Scholars of nineteenth-century political thought have tended to follow this general trend.

The distorting effects of this gaze assume different forms. Witness, for example, the attention lavished on Edmund Burke. While Pitts offers a qualified view of his enlightened credentials, Mehta, Muthu, and Frederick Whelan celebrate him as a coruscating scourge of European imperialism.[49] Yet Burke's newfound status as a progressive hero is a product of selection bias, based on emphasizing his commentary on India while downplaying his views on other imperial spaces. India was the exception not the rule in Burke's sympathies—and even then the extent of his "anti-imperialism" is open to serious question.[50] A very different picture emerges if we turn to his writings on North America and the Caribbean. Committed to a civilizing vision of history, he promoted a reformed slave trade and denied what Muthu would call "cultural agency" to "savage" populations. Until the eve of the American Revolution he "heartily endorsed British imperial aggrandizement and colonialism, and defended at length the subjugation of Native Americans and Africans alike to that end."[51]

[46] For recent assessments, see Andrew Thompson, ed., *Writing Imperial Histories* (Manchester, 2014); John Mackenzie, "The British Empire," *Journal of Imperial and Commonwealth History*, 43/1 (2015), 99–124; Dane Kennedy, "The Imperial History Wars," *Journal of British Studies*, 54/1 (2015), 1–22.

[47] This is no longer the case. See, for example, James Belich, *Replenishing the Earth* (Oxford, 2009); John Darwin, *The Empire Project* (Cambridge, 2011); Marilyn Lake and Henry Reynolds, *Drawing the Global Colour Line* (Cambridge, 2008); Gary Magee and Andrew Thompson, *Empire and Globalization* (Cambridge, 2010). Cf. Duncan Bell, "Desolation Goes before Us," *Journal of British Studies* 54 (2015), 987–93.

[48] Balachandra Rajan, "Excess of India," *Modern Philology*, 95/4 (1998), 490.

[49] Mehta, *Liberalism and Empire*, ch. 5; Pitts, *A Turn to Empire*, ch. 3; Whelan, *Enlightenment Political Thought and Non-Western Societies* (London, 2009), ch. 4; Whelan, *Edmund Burke and India* (Pittsburgh, 1996); Muthu, *Enlightenment against Empire*, 4–5.

[50] Daniel O'Neill, "Rethinking Burke and India," *History of Political Thought*, 30/3 (2009), 492–523; Sartori, *Liberalism in Empire*, 26. For an insightful account of Burke's imperialism, see Daniel O'Neill, *Edmund Burke and the Conservative Logic of Empire* (Berkeley, 2016).

[51] Margaret Kohn and Daniel O'Neill, "A Tale of Two Indias," *Political Theory*, 34 (2006), 202.

Burke argued that British domination helped civilize those benighted souls, chiefly through prolonged exposure to commerce and Christianity.

However, the main lacuna created by focusing relentlessly on India is the downplaying (even absence) of settler colonialism in accounts of liberalism and empire. During the nineteenth and twentieth centuries the settler empire played a fundamental role in British imperial ideology, and it was central to liberal visions of world order. Indeed British liberals often privileged the settler colonies over the imperial territories in Africa, Asia, and the Caribbean, viewing them as both more legitimate and more durable. To ignore this is to miss much of what constituted the relationship between liberal political thought and empire in the nineteenth century (and beyond). It was in the settler colonies, not India, that many liberals found the concrete place of their dreams.

One possible rejoinder to this line of argument is that even if the nineteenth century has been overlooked, settler colonialism has played a formative role in elucidating the connections between liberalism and empire due to the prominence of John Locke in recent scholarship.[52] Forty years ago John Dunn observed that Locke had "worn many faces": "only begetter of the Enlightenment, self-conscious and dedicated ideologist of the rising bourgeoisie, greatest of the exponents of English liberal constitutionalism . . . majoritarian populist, most shifty and esoteric of the treasonous clerks."[53] Now add to that another face: progenitor of liberal empire. Since Locke was involved in the project to legitimate colonization in North America, and since he is now regarded as one of the founding fathers of liberalism, the inference is clear: "[T]he liberal involvement with the British empire," Mehta declares, was "largely coeval with liberalism itself."[54] On this account, liberalism was born imperial, the complicity of Locke setting a pattern that was to be repeated down the centuries and into the present. However, I am not persuaded that we can learn much about liberal accounts of empire (in general) by studying Locke. As I show in chapter 3, Locke was not widely regarded as a liberal until the twentieth century; his conscription to the canon occurred a century after liberalism emerged as an explicit body of political thinking. We would do well to remember Quentin Skinner's warning about the dangers of the "mythology

---

[52] For accounts of Locke and colonialism, see Barbara Arneil, *John Locke and America* (Oxford, 1996); Arneil, "Citizens, Wives, Latent Citizens and Non-Citizens in the *Two Treatises*," *Eighteenth-Century Thought*, 3 (2007), 209–22; James Farr, "Locke, Natural Law, and New World Slavery," *Political Theory*, 36 (2008), 495–522; Duncan Ivison, "Locke, Liberalism and Empire," in *The Philosophy of John Locke*, ed. Peter R. Anstey (London, 2003), 86–105; Jimmy Casas Klausen, "Room Enough," *Journal of Politics*, 69/3 (2007), 760–69; Herman Lebovics, *Imperialism and the Corruption of Democracies* (Durham, NC, 2006), ch. 5; James Tully, *An Approach to Political Philosophy* (Cambridge, 1993), 137–76; Jack Turner, "John Locke, Christian Mission, and Colonial America," *Modern Intellectual History*, 8 (2011), 267–97. For qualified skepticism about Locke's imperialism, see David Armitage, *Foundations of Modern International Thought*, chs. 6–7.

[53] Dunn, *The Political Thought of John Locke* (Cambridge, 1969), 5.

[54] Mehta, *Liberalism and Empire*, 4.

of prolepsis," a mythology in which the attribution of retrospective significance to an event, thinker, or text clouds understanding of their meaning to
historical actors. Indeed Skinner identifies Locke's supposed paternity of liberalism as a paradigmatic example, noting that while it might be plausible to
describe Locke as a founding figure of liberal political thought, insofar as that
is how he came to be seen, it would be a mistake to call Locke himself a liberal.[55] Moreover, the study of Locke sheds little light on imperial ideology during the nineteenth century, for he was rarely invoked by Victorian imperialists
or their successors, and their justificatory claims seldom drew on Lockean
theoretical machinery.[56] Moreover, Lockean arguments could just as easily be
employed for anti-imperial ends, as when they were utilized to defend the
rights of native property ownership in Bengal.[57] Locke's relative insignificance
at the time should induce skepticism about the general salience of his views
on empire (important as they are to understanding the character of his own
political thinking). Liberal attitudes to empire are illuminated more clearly by
turning attention to the nineteenth century, the era of liberal ascendency and
the apogee of Western imperial ambition.

Other chapters in this book explore the justificatory arguments offered in
support of the settler colonies. Here it is simply worth noting that they were
many and varied, spanning economic, geopolitical, social, and racial claims. It
is possible, though, to trace a general shift in the representation of the settler
empire, from a time when it barely registered in metropolitan consciousness
to its elevation to the very heart of political debate. During the 1830s and
1840s a group of "colonial reformers" set out to overturn the economic orthodoxy that colonies were drains on the "mother country" and colonists disrep-
utable emigrants—or worse, criminals banished beyond the horizon—worthy of little attention and even less support. The discourse of political economy
was central to the revolt, as thinkers grappled with the urgent "social question." In the late eighteenth and early nineteenth centuries, colonies had often
been thought of, if at all, as dumping grounds for excess population. As
Charles Buller explained, emigration policy was seen as "little more than
shoveling out your paupers to where they might die, without shocking their

[55] Skinner, "Meaning and Understanding in the History of Ideas," in *Visions of Politics*, 1:73–
74. While agreeing with the general thrust of this argument, and the methodological commitments that underpin it, in chapter 3 I suggest that Locke *became* a liberal in the twentieth century
through his retrospective incorporation into the (new) liberal tradition, but that this was part of a
process of conceptual and ideological expansion that rendered liberalism such an amorphous category that it is usually unhelpful as a guide to theoretical or historical interpretation.

[56] For the striking absence of Lockean accounts of property in elite metropolitan discourse, see
Andrew Fitzmaurice, *Sovereignty, Property, and Empire, 1500–2000* (Cambridge, 2014), chs. 7–9.
On the inapplicability of the category "liberalism" to early modern empires, see Fitzmaurice, "Nei-
ther Neo-Roman nor Liberal Empire," *Renaissance Studies*, 26/4 (2012), 479–91.

[57] Andrew Sartori, *Liberalism in Empire*.

betters with the sight and sound of their last agony."[58] The colonial reformers, though, sought a more far-reaching reappraisal of British political economy. Challenging Ricardian orthodoxy, they diagnosed the stagnation of the British economy as a product of excess domestic capital and labor supply, which depressed wages and profits. Their prescribed solution was "systematic colonization," which would allow for the productive export of capital and labor.[59] Looking back on the early years of the reform movement from the vantage point of 1864, the political economist J. E. Cairnes praised this collection of "visionaries" for elaborating "[f]or the first time something like a sound and complete theory of colonization." It posited that colonization "confers a double benefit: it relieves the old country from the pressure of its superabundant population, and gives a field for its unemployed capital; while, at the same time, by opening up new lands and placing their resources at her disposal, it widens indefinitely the limits which restrain her future growth."[60]

While Nassau Senior, Robert Torrens, and Herman Merivale all played important roles in proselytizing the colonial reform vision, the most significant figure was the mercurial E. G. Wakefield, who developed an ambitious scheme predicated on the role of government in regulating the distribution of colonial land. He argued that if land prices were set artificially high, profits could be utilized for supporting further emigration, towns would grow as centers of civilization, and British class hierarchies could be replicated.[61] Moreover, he insisted that contrary to existing practice, colonists should be selected for their suitability as pioneers. Above all, he and the other reformers stressed the importance of granting the new colonies a significant degree of self-

---

[58] Buller used the phrase "shoveling out paupers" to describe Robert Wilmot Horton's emigration scheme. See the discussion in H.J.M. Johnson, *British Emigration Policy, 1815–1830* (Oxford, 1972), 168. A friend of John Stuart Mill, Buller was a liberal politician and active member of the colonial reform movement. On the "somersault in British attitudes to emigration," see Belich, *Replenishing the Earth*, 145–52.

[59] The economic debate is discussed in Winch, *Classical Political Economy*.

[60] Cairnes, "Colonization and Colonial Government," *Political Essays* (London, 1873), 30, 33. He added: "The theory has now little more than an historic value" (30).

[61] The most developed version of his argument can be found in Wakefield, *A View of the Art of Colonization* (London, 1849). For other contributions to the debate, see Nassau Senior, *Remarks on Emigration* (London, 1831); Nassau Senior, *An Outline of a Science of Political Economy* (London, 1836); Robert Torrens, *Colonisation of South Australia* (London, 1835); Torrens, *Self-Supporting Colonization* (London, 1847); Merivale, *Lectures on Colonisation and Colonies*, 2 vols. (London, 1841). For analysis, see Winch, *Classical Political Economy*; Peter Burroughs, *Colonial Reformers and Canada, 1830–1849* (London, 1969); Tony Ballantyne, "Remaking the Empire from Newgate," in *Ten Books That Shaped the British Empire*, ed. Antoinette Burton and Isabel Hofmeyr (Durham, NC, 2014), 29–50. One issue on which there was considerable disagreement was the idea of a "sufficient price" for land. For differing perspectives, see Wakefield, *A View of the Art of Colonization*, 338–69; Merivale, *Lectures on Colonisation and Colonies*, lectures 14–16; John Stuart Mill, *Principles of Political Economy* [1848], in *The Collected Works of John Stuart Mill*, ed. John Robson (Toronto, 1963–91), (hereafter *Collected Works*), vol. 3, bk. 1, ch. 8.

government.[62] Under the degraded, haphazard old system, "colonies and colonists are in fact, as well as in the estimation of the British gentry, inferior, low, unworthy of much respect, properly disliked and despised by people of honour here, who happen to be acquainted with the state of society in the colonies."[63] He believed that applying the lessons of political economy would transform the image and the reality of colonization, at once remaking them as economically productive and socially respectable. This argument exerted an abiding influence on John Stuart Mill, among many others, and it is little wonder that Marx's critique of colonialism in *Capital* focused almost exclusively on Wakefield's work.[64]

The reform movement, then, reimagined the colonies as productive spaces for economic growth, outlets for helping to defuse combustible domestic social conditions, fecund territories for the reproduction of civilized societies, and as nodes in a globe-spanning imperial security apparatus. From then on, and especially following the midcentury grant of significant constitutional autonomy to the colonies in Canada and Australia, the settler empire assumed a privileged role in the political visions of many British thinkers, including—and perhaps especially—liberals. The transformation of the colonial empire threatened its ultimate dissolution. Granting self-government to the colonies, under the rubric of "responsible government," led to a widespread sense that they were inevitably bound for independence. This line was articulated most forcefully by Goldwin Smith.[65] In a similar vein, Cairnes argued that the colonial empire had "reached its natural goal." But all was not lost, and like Smith he argued that what remained would fulfill the admirable role of the ancient Greek colonies. "Instead of a great political, we shall be a great moral, unity; bound together no longer indeed by Imperial ligaments supplied from the Colonial Office, but by the stronger bonds of blood, language, and religion—by the common inheritance of laws fitted for free men, and of a literature rich in all that can keep alive the associations of our common glory in the past."[66] It was this sense of inevitability that John Stuart Mill challenged in the *Considerations on Representative Government*, arguing that although the colonies were free to seek independence it was in both their

---

[62] For a good account of the argument, see Cairnes, "Colonization and Colonial Government," 30–35.

[63] Wakefield, *A View of the Art of Colonization*, 148. See also Arthur Mills, *Systematic Colonization* (London, 1847), 33–34.

[64] Marx, *Capital*, vol. 1, in *Collected Works,* by Marx and Engels (London, 1975), ch. 33. Indeed Marx regarded him as the most significant bourgeois political economist since Ricardo. For Victorian accounts of the importance of the colonial reformers, see Alfred Caldecott, *English Colonization and Empire* (London, 1891), 131–33, who labeled them "Benthamites"; and Egerton, *A Short History of British Colonial Policy,* (London, 1897), who, despite praising Wakefield and the movement, noted their "un-English" propensity for theorizing systematically about empire (4).

[65] Smith, *The Empire* (London, 1863).

[66] Cairnes, "Colonization and Colonial Government," 58.

interest and that of the "mother country" to remain united. Anxiety about the political status of the settler colonies catalyzed a major debate over the future of the empire in the closing decades of the century.[67]

Between 1870 and the outbreak of the First World War, the settler empire assumed an unprecedented role in British political discourse. It was widely acknowledged that the colonies were vitally important elements of the imperial system, and that unless something was done, and done soon, the logic of self-government identified by Smith and Cairnes, as well as the embryonic development of settler nationalisms, would eventually lead to independence. Advocates of "imperial federation" sought to establish permanent bonds between Britain and its settler colonies, creating a vast racial polity—even a global federal state—spanning oceans and continents. Many of the leading ideologues of the movement were liberals, including Seeley, its most influential cheerleader, and numerous liberal politicians were only too happy to lend their support, including W. E. Forster and Lord Rosebery.[68] I have explored this topic at length in *The Idea of Greater Britain*, and I address it in several chapters in this book. Those opposed to such grandiose institutional plans, such as Freeman and Goldwin Smith, still tended to emphasize the importance of settler colonies, whether they remained politically bound to the "mother country" or secured independence. All thought it a topic of great significance. The historian W.E.H. Lecky was far from alone in his belief that it was "unspeakably important" to the "future of the world that the English race, through the ages that are to come, should cling as closely as possible together."[69] Indeed it was a commonplace. The colonial unification discourse blurred into another set of arguments, popular during the 1890s in particular, that demanded the "reunion" of Britain and the United States, the two great "Anglo-Saxon" powers ordained to reorder the world. As with imperial federation, plans for transatlantic reunion stretched from the moderate to the radical, from closer friendship to full federal union, and once again liberals were among the most vociferous exponents. Andrew Carnegie, James Bryce, A. V. Dicey, and W. T. Stead all advocated transatlantic (racial) union of one kind or another.[70] In chapter 8, I track some of the descendants of these arguments across the arc of the twentieth century.

[67] Mill, *Considerations on Representative Government* [1861], ch. 18. For more on his argument for retaining the colonies on a voluntary basis, see chapter 9. In 1864 Mill and Cairnes corresponded over the issue, with Mill rejecting Cairnes's arguments and reiterating the position elaborated in *Considerations*. See, for example, Mill to Cairnes, November 8, 1864, *Collected Works*, 15:965. See also the discussion in Georgios Varouxakis, *Liberty Abroad* (Cambridge, 2013), 132–34.

[68] See H.C.G Matthew, *The Liberal Imperialists* (Oxford, 1973), on liberal parliamentary support for empire and imperialism. Both served as presidents of the Imperial Federation League.

[69] Lecky, *The Empire* (London, 1893), 15.

[70] Carnegie, *The Reunion of Britain and America* (Edinburgh, 1893), 24; see also Carnegie, "Distant Possessions," *North American Review*, 167/501 (1898), 239–48. For analysis of this idea,

According to the conventional Victorian understanding of the term, "colonies" were territories claimed by emigrants from the "mother country" with the intention of founding permanent communities that replicated key aspects of the original society. This was an act—or at least a fantasy—of mimetic transfer. The aim of colonization, Gladstone proclaimed in 1858, "was to reproduce the likeness of England, as they were doing in Australia, New Zealand, North America, and the Cape, thereby contributing to the general happiness of mankind."[71] This kind of argument was predicated on an imagined isomorphism between mother country and colony. The colonies were populated, as one scholar put it, by people "predominantly blood of our blood, bone of our bone, with our language, our laws (in the main), and our manners."[72] This meant, chiefly, what we might call the *second settler empire*: the colonies in Canada, Australia, New Zealand, and (more ambiguously) South Africa. From the mid-nineteenth century onwards, the normative and legal distinction between settler colonies and the rest of the empire was inscribed evermore deeply into the elite British political imagination. Presented as radically different from—and often superior to—other imperial spaces, they were the subject of different ideologies of justification and governance.[73] For Seeley, "[t]he colonies and India are in opposite extremes. Whatever political maxims are most applicable to one, are most inapplicable to the other."[74] The liberal historian G. P. Gooch likewise emphasized the "vital distinction" between empire and colony. "In passing from Colonies to dependencies we enter a different world, to which different principles must be applied."

> Indeed the very circumstances that call forth the enthusiasm in the one case compel us, in some degree, to withhold it in the other. Where our flag flies over willing subjects and the institutions of self-government our rule may count on great reserves of moral and material strength; where it does not, our material strength may be great, but the moral basis is either weak or totally lacking.[75]

On this account, the empire was imaginatively bifurcated, with the self-governing colonies assigned to a completely separate category of rule and ethico-political judgment.

---

see Duncan Bell, "Beyond the Sovereign State," *Political Studies*, 62/2 (2014), 418–34; Bell, "Before the Democratic Peace," *European Journal of International Relations*, 20/3 (2014), 647–70.

[71] Quoted in John Darwin, *The Empire Project*, 146.

[72] Caldecott, *English Colonization and Empire*, 11. Caldecott was Dean of St. John's College, Cambridge; the book was designed for use on university courses.

[73] The distinction was a constant theme across the Victorian era and beyond. George Cornewall Lewis, *An Essay on the Government of Dependencies* (London, 1841), 169–79; Arthur Mills, *Colonial Constitutions* (London, 1856); John Stuart Mill, *Considerations on Representative Government*, ch. 18; Alpheus Todd, *Parliamentary Government in the British Colonies* (London, 1880); Henry Jenkyns, *British Rule and Jurisdiction beyond the Seas* (Oxford, 1902), 1–9.

[74] Seeley, *The Expansion of England*, 244.

[75] Gooch, "Imperialism," in *The Heart of Empire*, ed. C.F.G Masterman (London, 1901), 310.

Two key thematics underpinned the demarcation between the settler empire and other kinds of foreign rule: *racial identity* and *self-government*. Colonists were figured as always already civilized, and as carrying with them a bundle of rights and obligations that marked them indelibly as both facsimiles (or not-quite-facsimiles) of those inhabiting the mother country and radically different from (and superior to) other peoples they encountered—and especially those they invaded and dispossessed. This set of assumptions underwrote the argument for self-government. As another liberal historian, C. P. Lucas, once put it, "[t]he ground of self-government is, that those who are in the colony are on the same level in physique and intelligence with those who are in the mother country, and that, being on the spot, they are best able to take care of themselves."[76] The original inhabitants were in turn pictured as incapable, as immature, lacking in both rationality and competence, and thus as unworthy of political or social equality. The logic of settler colonialism, then, was a powerful mix of intraracial egalitarianism and interracial exclusion. The British settler empire enacted a version of what Charles Mills terms the *racial contract*: a vision of the just polity predicated on the ascription of political equality to whites and its concurrent denial to nonwhites. It thus expressed a form of *Herrenvolk* ethics, a normative system intended to structure settler societies as racially exclusive communities.[77] Indigenous peoples continue to suffer its pernicious effects.

Settler colonialism is a distinct modality of imperial governance, and one that until recently was too often conflated with, or subsumed under, more general models of domination.[78] It is a process comprising a four-dimensional interaction between the metropole from which the settlers departed, the settler colonial community, the indigenous populations whose lands and lifeworlds were transformed or occupied by the settlers, and those non-indigenous non-settlers living within or moving through the settler colonial space.[79] The intricate and shifting relations between these various elements

[76] Lucas, "Introduction," in *An Essay on the Government of Dependencies*, by George Cornewall Lewis, ed. C. P. Lucas (Oxford, 1891), xxxiii.

[77] Mills, *The Racial Contract* (Ithaca, 1997); Mills, "White Right," in *Blackness Visible* (Ithaca, 1998). For a different account of the "settler contract," see Carole Pateman and Charles Mills, *Contract and Domination* (Cambridge, 2007), ch. 2 (by Pateman). Note that Mills and Pateman employ "contract" in different senses.

[78] Lorenzo Veracini locates the origins of the concept (not the practice) in the period of decolonization in the 1950s and 1960s. "Settler Colonialism," *Journal of Imperial and Commonwealth History*, 41/2 (2013), 313–33. Settler colonialism has been central to the work of J.G.A. Pocock, though he has written little about the nineteenth century, which is why I don't engage him at greater length in this chapter. See Pocock, *The Discovery of Islands* (Cambridge, 2005); Richard Bourke, "Pocock and the Presuppositions of the New British History," *Historical Journal*, 53/3 (2010), 747–70.

[79] For theoretical accounts of the practice, see Jürgen Osterhammel, *Colonialism*, 2nd ed. (Princeton, 2005); Lorenzo Veracini, *Settler Colonialism* (Basingstoke, 2010); Patrick Wolfe, *Settler Colonialism and the Transformation of Anthropology* (London, 1999); Caroline Elkins and Susan Pedersen, "Settler Colonialism," in *Settler Colonialism in the Twentieth Century*, ed. Elkins

shape the history—and the present—of the settler colonial condition. It was typically manifested in the instantiation of a highly ambivalent form of sovereignty, a claim that settlers exerted over the indigenous populations inhabiting the land they invaded, which served as a source of friction and constant negotiation with the government of the metropolitan center.[80]

Modern settler colonialism, British or otherwise, almost invariably relies on violence against indigenous peoples and everyday forms of humiliation, exclusion, and racial segregation, some informal, some sanctioned by law. As Patrick Wolfe argues, it is an "inclusive, land-centred project that coordinates a comprehensive range of agencies, from the metropolitan centre to the frontier encampment, with a view to *eliminating* Indigenous societies."[81] Colonial eliminativism encompasses assorted practices, including assimilation, displacement, legal domination, intimidation, and the use of lethal violence, even genocide.[82] The purpose is to secure territory while destroying the sense of peoplehood of those supplanted by the settler community. This is not to suggest that all settlers, politicians, colonial advocates, and London-based officials necessarily thought of it in those terms, or that practices of colonialism were everywhere and always the same—far from it.[83] But that was what it usually entailed.[84] Even the most purportedly "benign" forms of erasure resulted

---

and Pedersen (London, 2005), 1–20; Mahmood Mamdani, "Settler Colonialism," *Critical Inquiry*, 41 (2015), 1–19. For a useful summary of the distinctive, even antithetical, character of colonialism and settler colonialism, see Veracini, "Introducing Settler Colonial Studies," *Settler Colonial Studies*, 1/1 (2011), 1–12.

[80] On settler sovereignty, see, for example, Lauren Benton, *A Search for Sovereignty* (Cambridge, 2010); Lisa Ford, *Settler Sovereignty* (Cambridge, MA, 2010). See also Ann Stoler, "On Degrees of Imperial Sovereignty," *Public Culture*, 18/1 (2006). On practices and ideologies of settler colonialism, see also Fiona Bateman and Lionel Pilkington, eds., *Studies in Settler Colonialism: Politics, Identity and Culture* (New York: Palgrave, 2011); Shaunnagh Dorsett and Ian Hunter, eds., *Law and Politics in British Colonial Thought* (Basingstoke, 2010); Lynette Russell, ed., *Colonial Frontiers* (Manchester, 2001); Annie Coombes, ed., *Rethinking Settler Colonialism* (Manchester, 2006); Alyosha Goldstein and Alex Lubin, eds., "Settler Colonialism," *South Atlantic Quarterly*, 107/4 (2008).

[81] Wolfe, "Settler Colonialism and the Elimination of the Native," *Journal of Genocide Research*, 8/4 (2006), 393. Italics added. On settler violence, see Dirk Moses, ed., *Genocide and Settler Society* (New York, 2004); Ann Curthoys, "Genocide in Tasmania," in *Empire, Colony, Genocide*, ed. Dirk Moses (New York, 2008), 229–53; Wolfe, "Settler Colonialism." On racial exclusion from the franchise in the British settler empire, see Julie Evans et al., *Unequal Rights* (Manchester, 2003); Kirkby, "The Politics and Practice of 'Native' Enfranchisement."

[82] Wolfe, "Settler Colonialism." See also Wolfe, "Recuperating Binarism," *Settler Colonial Studies*, 3/4 (2013), 257–79.

[83] On humanitarian governmentality, see Alan Lester and Fae Dussart, *Colonization and the Origins of Humanitarian Governance* (Cambridge, 2014).

[84] In the zone of greatest destruction, the population of Aboriginal Australians fell from over 750,000 to less than 50,000 during the colonial period. In the penal colony of Tasmania (once Van Diemen's Land), the local population was almost exterminated between 1803 and 1850 in a prolonged nightmare of rape, torture, disease, and murder. See Benjamin Madley, "From Terror to

in destruction. "Here, in essence, is assimilation's Faustian bargain—have our settler world, but lose your Indigenous soul. Beyond any doubt, this is a kind of death."[85] Moreover, settlement is not an autochthonous founding moment superseded by postcolonial state formation, but rather a process of domination with effects that continue to shape the lifeworlds of indigenous populations long after the formal age of empire. Invasion is a "structure not an event."[86] Indeed settler colonialism has generated some of the most challenging problems in the contemporary world, from the desperate plight of the Palestinian people to pressing questions about the rights of indigenous peoples within purportedly liberal democratic polities.[87] Political theory has barely begun to confront its implications.

The settler project incited much debate. Some celebrated the cleansing violence of its professed "civilizing" mission, while others damned it. The violence of founding was often naturalized, imagined as an inevitable fate for "savages" who came into contact with superior peoples—a sad but necessary feature of historical progress.[88] Aboriginal protection societies sprang up, and colonial officials tried to rein in the worst excesses, though such campaigns rarely managed to stop the attempted extirpation of existing communities. "[I]n spite of their human likeness," the Tasmanians, H. G. Wells wrote in *The War of the Worlds* (1898), "were entirely swept out of existence in a war of extermination waged by European immigrants in the space of fifty years."[89] Over half a century earlier, the political economist Herman Merivale was equally clear about the consequences of settler colonialism. "Desolation goes before us," he lamented, "and civilisation lags slowly and lamely behind." South Africa, Van Diemen's land, Newfoundland, the interior of the United States, New Zealand: all were marked by the "ferocity and treachery" of "civilised" men and governments.[90] In an intriguing twist on normative arguments about the rectification of historical injustice, the recognition of colonial ultra-

---

Genocide: Britain's Tasmanian Penal Colony and Australia's History Wars," *Journal of British Studies*, 47 (2008), 77.

[85] Wolfe, "Settler Colonialism," 397. For a related discussion, see Jonathan Lear, *Radical Hope* (Cambridge, MA, 2006). See also the comments in Duncan Bell, "Making and Taking Worlds," in *Global Intellectual History*, ed. Samuel Moyn and Andrew Sartori (New York, 2013), 254–82.

[86] Wolfe, "Settler Colonialism," 388. For a useful comparative perspective, see Benjamin Madley, "Tactics of Nineteenth Century Colonial Massacre," in *Theatres of Violence*, ed. Philips Dwyer and Lyndall Ryan (New York, 2012), 110–25.

[87] Duncan Ivison, Paul Patton, and Will Sanders, eds., *Political Theory and the Rights of Indigenous Peoples* (Cambridge, 2001); Mamdani, "Settler Colonialism"; Tully, *Strange Multiplicity*.

[88] Patrick Brantlinger, *Dark Vanishings* (Ithaca, 2003).

[89] Wells, *The War of the Worlds* (London, 1898), prologue.

[90] Merivale, *Lectures on Colonies and Colonisation*, 2:152. After a spell as Professor of Political Economy at Oxford, during which time he delivered his famed lectures on colonies, Merivale held a series of senior imperial administrative posts, which culminated in his appointment as Permanent Under-Secretary for India in 1860.

violence could even be invoked to legitimate empire. The Cambridge theologian and philosopher Alfred Caldecott argued that as a consequence of their despicable treatment of the Australian "nature people," the British had a moral obligation to continue the educative mission of empire: in India, "we may redeem the past."[91] Gilbert Murray outlined a similar argument. "If ever in the lifetime of the world a duty has been laid upon a nation," he wrote, "a great and manifest obligation lies on us towards our subject peoples, the duty of endeavoring by strenuous and honest sympathy, justice, and even magnanimity, to obliterate our cruel conquests, and justify our world-wide usurpation."[92] Only future empire could erase the moral stains of past empire. Merivale was optimistic that the "ferocity and treachery" in the colonies could be ameliorated. "Our errors are not of conception so much as of execution."[93] By locating (or deflecting) responsibility in this manner, such arguments denied the systemic character of the violence, reducing it to the excessive, localized behavior of a few rogue settlers.

Most accounts of settler colonialism were marked by an ideological aporia. Colonial identities are shaped by settler *mythscapes*, evocative narratives that embody claims about the origins, the legitimacy, and the destiny of the enterprise.[94] The founding moment is typically figured as heroic, the epic fabrication of new "civilized" communities in the wilderness. Legitimacy is usually grounded in a dual claim: of the civilizational superiority of the settler over the indigenous and of the productive recuperation of under-utilized or vacant land. Plotting colonial destiny was more contested, oscillating (in the British case at least) between dreams of future political independence and of assuming a vanguard role within an expansive imperial formation, a better (global) Britain. Settler mythscapes were invariably marked by a constitutive forgetting of the claims of indigenous populations.

The play of similarity and difference was central to British representations of both the colonies and India. Early in the nineteenth century, British impe-

---

[91] Caldecott, *English Colonization and Empire*, 234. On the inevitability of extinction-through-contact, he wrote the following extraordinary passage: "The past is irrevocable, and in the future men must move on. Some of these peoples are plainly passing away: they are unable to live when called upon to make a sudden and almost spasmodic effort to live in a higher stage of culture. But even for them it is not difficult to determine what should be our attitude. What is our conduct to the sick and dying among ourselves? All the alleviations and comforts we can think of are placed cheerfully at their disposal. Let it be so for these sick and dying tribes. Let us work gently as in the sick-chamber, and be ministers to their closing years in comfort, patience, and tenderness" (235).

[92] Murray, "The Exploitation of Inferior Races in Ancient and Modern Times," in *Liberalism and the Empire*, ed. Hirst, Murray, and Hammond, 157.

[93] Merivale, *Lectures on Colonies and Colonisation*, 2:152.

[94] On the notion of mythscape, see Duncan Bell, "Mythscapes," *British Journal of Sociology*, 54/1 (2003), 63–81; Bell, "Agonistic Democracy and the Politics of Memory," *Constellations*, 15/1 (2008), 148–66. On settler narratives, see also Veracini, *Settler Colonialism*, ch. 4.

rial ideologues often sought out points of similitude between the conquered and the conquerors in India, though as the century wore on the call of radical difference came to predominate.[95] But expressions of similarity can assume contrasting forms. In the Indian case, what was (occasionally) imagined was similarity despite apparent difference, a basic uniformity grounded either in professed essential human characteristics or (more frequently) a shared "Aryan" heritage, traceable to an ancient ur-race.[96] Similarity was thus embedded in a deep history of human evolutionary development that both explained its uneven progress over the preceding centuries and legitimated the hierarchical ordering of the contemporary world. It could only be rendered intelligible by ignoring surface phenomena and physical appearance. Settler colonialism was predicated on a different logic of identity. Colonists were seen as reproductions of the basic metropolitan archetype, as passing the minimum threshold of civilized life even as they often failed to live up to its very highest standards. The variation was reflected in subtly contrasting metaphors of maturity. While Chakrabarty and Mehta correctly highlight the authoritative role played by the trope of childhood in legitimating British rule in India, the rhetorical strategy was ubiquitous and assumed different forms across the space of empire.[97] Liberals routinely applied it to the settler colonies, but they did so in a way that goes to the heart of the contrasting ideological justifications of colonialism and imperialism. Whereas in India (for example) the language of childhood was applied to the individual subjects of empire, connoting a deficit of rationality and a lack of capacity for individual autonomy and collective self-government, it was applied to the colonies as a whole, not to the individual settlers. It was the political institutions and socioeconomic systems of the nascent communities that were coded as immature and in need of (some) guidance. While settlers were frequently the butt of metropolitan condescension, they were accepted as fully rational autonomous agents and granted civilizational standing. Instead, the individuated language of childhood was often displaced onto indigenous populations.

Despite general agreement on the distinctiveness of settler colonialism, there were some conceptual disputes over its exact meaning. In an influential text published in 1841, the liberal politician and writer George Cornewall Lewis defined a colony as "a body of persons belonging to one country and political community, who, having abandoned that country and community, form a new and separate society, independent or dependent, in some district which is wholly or nearly uninhabited, or from which they expel the ancient

---

[95] Metcalf, *Ideologies of the Raj* (Cambridge, 1995).

[96] On Aryanism, see Tony Ballantyne, *Orientalism and Race* (Basingstoke, 2002), and the discussion in chapter 13.

[97] Mehta, *Liberalism and Empire*, 31–33; Chakrabarty, *Provincializing Europe*. See also Ashis Nandy, "Reconstructing Childhood," in *Traditions, Tyranny, and Utopia* (Delhi, 1987), 56–76.

inhabitants."[98] "Of colonization," wrote Wakefield, "the principal elements are emigration and the permanent settlement of the emigrants on unoccupied land."[99] He then distinguished between two classes of colony, the *dependent*, which was still subject to a political connection, and the *independent*, which was not. The status of colony, then, was derived from the initial practice of colonizing rather than from any enduring formal political relationship between the founding and the founded communities. Writing half a century later, the historian Hugh Egerton instead accentuated the necessity of a *continuing* political tie. A colony, he maintained, was "a community, politically dependent in some shape or form, the majority, or dominant portion, of whose members belong by birth or origin to the Mother country, such persons having no intention to return to the Mother country, or to seek a permanent home elsewhere than in the colony."[100] These accounts differ over the kind of connection thought necessary to classify a political community as a colony. This disagreement had some substantive implications. For example, it generated divergent classifications of states that had once been formal colonies but were now independent, a question relevant for thinking about both the ontological status of the United States and the future unity of the British settler empire. On the former account, for instance, the United States was still a colony of Britain, albeit an autonomous one. "To my view," Wakefield argued, "the United States of America, formed by emigration from this country, and still receiving a large increase of people by emigration from this country, are still colonies of England."[101] On the latter account, it ceased to be a colony the moment it gained political independence. This was the most common position. Seeley evaded this thorny conceptual issue altogether in *The Expansion of England* by stipulating that the United States "are to us almost as good as a colony," since "our people can emigrate there without sacrificing their language or chief institutions or habits."[102] On this more ambiguous account, the United States was once a *de jure* colony but was now best understood as a (quasi) *de facto* one.

[98] Cornewall Lewis, *Essay*, 170. This definition was adopted by Cairnes, in "Colonization and Colonial Government," 4–5. For Cornewall Lewis's account of colonial sovereignty, see Shaunnagh Dorsett, "Sovereignty as Governance in the Early New Zealand Crown Colony Period," in *Law and Politics in British Colonial Thought*, ed. Dorsett and Hunter, 209–28.

[99] Wakefield, *A View on the Art of Colonization*, 16-17. "A colony therefore is a country wholly or partially unoccupied, which receives emigrants from a distance; and it is a colony of the country from which the emigrants proceed, which is therefore called the mother country" (16).

[100] Egerton, *A Short History of Colonial Policy*, 8–9.

[101] Wakefield, *A View on the Art of Colonization*, 17. Canada was an example of the former, Massachusetts of the latter. E. A. Freeman also referred to the United States as "independent colonies." Freeman, *Some Impressions of the United States* (London, 1883), 23. See also my discussion in chapter 13.

[102] Seeley, *The Expansion of England*, 58.

Once we expand the interpretive aperture to encompass settler colonialism, the "anti-imperialism" of the Enlightenment begins to look rather less clear-cut. As Muthu concedes, Diderot affirmed the value of colonies, while Burke was a zealous proponent of settler colonialism in North America.[103] Nor was Bentham immune. At the turn of the century he commended the socioeconomic benefits of settler colonization, and towards the end of his life he produced an unpublished plan for a new colony in South Australia.[104] Moreover, some of the most acerbic nineteenth-century "anti-imperialists" endorsed settler colonialism. In *Imperialism*, J. A. Hobson distinguished between "genuine colonialism" and "Imperialism." Whereas colonialism represented the progressive spread of civilization through settlement, imperialism meant the "expansion of autocracy." As I discuss in chapter 14, he also argued that one of the problems with the "new imperialism" of the 1880s and 1890s was that it undermined the chances of securing the unification of the British state and its settler colonies.[105] Like that of many self-professed anti-imperialists, his target was a particular species of empire, not all forms of Western control or expansion. Paying attention to settler colonialism, then, reconfigures the way in which we understand "imperialist" and "anti-imperial" arguments since the late eighteenth century.

Mehta briefly acknowledges the discrepancy between nineteenth-century justifications of empire and settler colonialism, but he draws the line in a misleading fashion. He regards the former as "crucially predicated" on notions of tutelage and kinship, while the latter involved the peopling of distant territories where there "was often an ideology and practice of exterminating aboriginal populations." Since liberals did not countenance extermination, he concludes that the topic can be left aside.[106] There are three problems with this brief account. First, as we shall see, liberal justifications of empire were not exhausted by tutelary arguments. Second, arguments for settler colonialism, liberal or otherwise, usually did not explicitly invoke extermination (though they often entailed elimination). Finally, and conversely, some liberals (including Spencer) did discuss the eventual extinction of indigenous populations, albeit as an inevitable function of historical progress rather than a policy to be actively pursued.[107]

---

[103] Muthu, *Enlightenment against Empire*, 75.

[104] E. G. Wakefield, *England and America* (London, 1833), 2:252n; Richard Mills, *The Colonization of Australia (1829–42)* [1915] (London, 1968), 152–53; Philip Schofield, *Utility and Democracy* (Oxford, 2006), 199–220.

[105] Hobson, *Imperialism* (London, 1902), 36, 27, 328–55. Hobson, though, did recognize the exterminatory dangers of settler colonization (e.g., 266–67). He later changed his mind about imperial federation. See Duncan Bell, "On J. A. Hobson's 'The Ethics of Internationalism,'" *Ethics*, 125 (2014), 220–22; and chapter 14.

[106] Mehta, *Liberalism and Empire*, 2–3n1.

[107] Patrick Brantlinger, *Dark Vanishings*.

Arguing that colonialism was compatible with (or an expression of) basic liberal normative commitments, liberal thinkers often claimed the settler world as their own progeny. It was liberals, they boasted, who brought self-government to the colonies, thus rescuing the empire from potential dissolution and laying the foundation for future British greatness. According to Hammond, "[a]ll that has made this Commonwealth great and strong is the work of Liberalism."[108] Hobhouse agreed: "The Colonial Empire as it stands today is in substance the creation of the older Liberalism."[109] This was not simply a claim about intellectual patrimony, for it was conjoined with an argument that the settler colonies were both more important and more legitimate than the dependent empire. Their high degree of internal self-government placed them on sound moral and political foundations. "Where is it that, after all, the great strength of the Empire resides," asked one liberal imperialist. "Not in the great military dependencies of India, Egypt and the Far East. No! It is in the free communities which have sprung from these shores and which have carried to the ends of the earth the name and fame of Britain and the strength of British character." This was "true Imperialism."[110] John Morley, esteemed historian and prominent liberal politician, adopted a similar line.

> By Imperialism the better men of the school understood a free and informal union with the Colonies, combined with a conscientious and tolerant government of tropical dependencies. This was in essence the conception of the Empire bequeathed by the older generation of Liberals, and precisely the antithesis of present-day Imperialism, the operative principle of which is the forcible establishment and maintenance of racial ascendency.[111]

Morley thus espoused a variation of the common distinction drawn between empire and imperialism, contrasting *old* (reputable, liberal) against *new* (degraded, aggressive) forms of imperialism.

Alterity, then, acted as a repellent not a magnet. An empire encompassing radically different institutions and populations was both fundamentally unstable and incapable of serving as a platform for further political integration. While few liberals advocated immediate withdrawal from India, or denied that Britain had a "duty" to help improve its subjects, they recognized that it

---

[108] Hammond, "Colonial and Foreign Policy," 207. See also Gooch, "Imperialism." This emphasis wasn't accepted by all liberals. Charles Dilke, for example, argued that "India ought always to be first in our minds." Dilke, *The British Empire* (London, 1899), 17.

[109] Hobhouse, *Liberalism* [1911], ed. James Meadowcroft (Cambridge, 1994), 115.

[110] A. C. Forster Boulton, "Liberalism and the Empire," *Westminster Review*, 151 (1899), 490. Forster Boulton was a successful barrister and writer.

[111] Morley, "Democracy and Reaction" [1904], *Critical Miscellanies* (London, 1908), 4:282–83. He later served as Secretary of State for India (1905–10).

was, and would always remain, alien, exotic, different—even if it was "civilized" to the point where it was ready for self-government. It was precisely because of its alien character that it was impossible to regard as a site for realizing the true destiny of the English people. After stressing the importance of permanent unity between the settler colonies and the metropole, the novelist and liberal social reformer Walter Besant observed that India, despite its undoubted value, "cannot be integrated" and that "our occupation . . . must remain, as it is, a strong, just hand, restraining and leading, but the hand of a foreigner." The future greatness of Britain resided instead in the "Anglo-Saxon" settler colonies.[112] This was one of the central claims of Seeley's influential analysis in *The Expansion of England.* "When we inquire into the Greater Britain of the future," he announced, "we ought to think much more about our colonial than our Indian empire."[113] Racial or cultural or national similarity—the three interwoven in Victorian political consciousness—exerted the greatest imaginative pull on liberal thinkers. The extended racial Self was accorded normative primacy over the alien Other.

Due to their considerable political autonomy, some liberals argued that the settler colonies were not, strictly speaking, "imperial" spaces, and that as such they no longer formed part of the British empire. As Goldwin Smith put it in 1890: "Over the colonies England has resigned all real power: they are substantially so many independent nations. The only empire, properly so called, which she now has is India."[114] Empire, the authors of *Liberalism and the Empire* wrote, was the rule of one nation over another, and the term was thus applicable to India but not to "free" Canada and Australia, which were "grander evidences of England's greatness and solider elements in her strength than all those tropical provinces which she has won as a conqueror and holds as a foreign despot."[115] Seeley argued that the British settler empire constituted a "world-state" rather than an empire, and that the latter designation was only appropriate for India. Empire, he counseled, "seems too military and despotic to suit the relation of mother-country to colonies."[116] Hammond reiterated the point: "The name 'Empire' is charged with associations for which Liberals have little liking, and they would prefer to apply the term 'Commonwealth' to the confederacy of states which make up the dominions of the Crown."[117] From this perspective, settler colonialism represented a different,

---

[112] Besant, *The Future of the Empire* (London, 1897), 124.

[113] Seeley, *Expansion of England*, 11.

[114] Smith, "The Hatred of England," *North American Review*, 150/402 (1890), 558.

[115] Hirst, Murray, and Hammond, *Liberalism and the Empire*, xv.

[116] Seeley, *The Expansion of England*, 37. On what he meant by this, see Bell, "The Victorian Idea of a Global State," in *Victorian Visions*, ed. Bell, 159–86; and chapter 11.

[117] Hammond, "Colonial and Foreign Policy," 207. The Earl of Rosebery is often credited with coining the term "commonwealth" to refer to the British empire, though it only became popular when adopted by the Round Table twenty-five years later. See Rosebery's speech in Adelaide, Janu-

perhaps nobler, kind of civilizing mission, defined by the construction of exemplary new political communities embodying the virtues of British freedom and law. Rather than civilizing backward native populations through direct tutelage, it instead helped to civilize humanity as a whole by simultaneously exporting the institutions and values of Britain to "fresh" territories, thus providing a shining model of how best to organize sociopolitical life. Combining "imperium" with "libertas" this type of empire had the potential to escape the historical fate of all previous instances, the inevitability of decline and fall (a topic I address in chapter 5). It would long outlast the transient occupation of India, Egypt, and even the Caribbean. Indeed some liberals regarded it as an embryonic form of cosmopolitical order, the herald of a future form of world government. Hence Hobhouse saw the colonial empire as a "natural outgrowth of a common sentiment," and as "one of the steps towards a wider unity which involves no backstroke against the ideal of self-government." Scanning the horizon, he offered it as a "model" of the coming "International State."[118]

A comprehensive understanding of liberal attitudes to empire, then, must pay more attention to settler colonialism than is usually the case. Settler colonies offered liberals a way of celebrating expansion and rule cleansed of traditional anxieties about foreign conquest—the perennial corrupting dynamics of empire. Instead, they were premised on a comforting fantasy about the occupation of new lands, free of established institutions and settled communities. The result was both the founding of dynamic communities and a legacy of expropriation and horrific violence. This is a bequest that "liberal democracies" face (or refuse to face) to this day.

The Tyranny of the Canon

In chapter 3 I discuss various "interpretive protocols" that scholars employ to demarcate liberalism (and other politico-intellectual traditions). The most common protocol, the *canonical*, constructs liberalism through analyzing one or more exemplary figures who are taken, whether implicitly or explicitly, to stand in for the whole. John Locke and John Stuart Mill often perform this role in the literature on liberal empire.[119] While canonical approaches have their uses, they are incapable of generating satisfactory accounts of multifac-

---

ary 18, 1884, reprinted in *The Concept of Empire*, 2nd ed., ed. George Bennett, (London, 1962), 283.

[118] Hobhouse, *Democracy and Empire*, 116. I explore Hobhouse's views in chapter 14. As I discuss in chapter 8, this vanguard notion was repeated in a variety of forms across the twentieth century.

[119] Bhikhu Parekh, "Liberalism and Colonialism," in *The Decolonization of Imagination*, ed. J. N. Pieterse and Parekh, (London, 1995), 81–98; Mehta, *Liberalism and Empire*.

eted political ideologies. Relying on an overly narrow evidentiary base, they cannot support felicitous generalizations about continuities and change in patterns of political thinking.

Mehta, Muthu, and Pitts all make bold historical claims based chiefly on interpretations of canonical thinkers. Whereas Mehta argues for a strong line of ideological continuity from Locke onwards, Muthu and Pitts identify a radical break at the end of the eighteenth century. However, the historical arcs that they carve through the long nineteenth century are in part artifacts of the canon of European political theory, a canon largely constructed during the twentieth century.[120] If we expand the range of sources analyzed, a rather different picture emerges. In contrast to the narratives of the nineteenth century presented in their work, I would argue that the liberalism of the time was just as diverse, and contained just as much critical energy, as the intellectual world of the late eighteenth century. Leading politicians and thinkers expressed disdain for territorial expansion. Auguste Comte, for one, railed against the injustice of empire, focusing his attention on the French occupation of Algeria and the British in India.[121] Cobden, to give an especially prominent British example, was both one of the most significant liberal politicians and ideologues of the age and a fierce (albeit somewhat inconsistent) critic of imperialism.[122] He believed that the spread of free trade would corrode patriotism, eradicate the feudal scourge of war, and undermine the rationale for empire. In 1850 he wrote to John Bright that the world had "never yet beheld such a compound of jobbing, swindling, hypocrisy, and slaughter, as goes to make up the gigantic scheme of villainy called the 'British rule in India.'"[123] Three years later he warned of "our insatiable love of territorial aggrandizement," and lamented the "deeds of violence and injustice which have marked every step of our progress in India."[124] Lauded as one of the greatest philosophers alive, and certainly one of the most influential, Herbert Spencer was a vitriolic critic of empire from the 1840s until his death in 1902. In an emblematic British radical idiom he decried imperialism as the

[120] In chapter 3, I develop a similar argument about how liberalism is now conventionally understood.

[121] Comte, *System of Positive Polity* [1854], ed. and trans. Richard Congreve (London, 1877 [1854]), 4:430–31. He called, for example, for the "noble restoration" of Algeria to the Arabs (364).

[122] P. J. Cain, "Capitalism, War, and Internationalism in the Thought of Richard Cobden," *British Journal of International Studies*, 5/3 (1979), 229–47; Anthony Howe and Simon Morgan, eds., *Rethinking Nineteenth-Century Liberalism* (London, 2006); Claeys, *Imperial Sceptics*, 27–36. For the context of free trade arguments against empire, see Anthony Howe, "Free Trade and Global Order," in *Victorian Visions of Global Order*, ed. Bell, 26–46.

[123] Cited in Donald Read, *Cobden and Bright* (London, 1967), 205–6. He warned: "I have a presentiment . . . that God's chastisement upon us as a nation will come from Hindoostan."

[124] Cobden, "How Wars Are Got Up in India," in *Writings of Richard Cobden* (London, 1886), 455, 458.

preserve of the governing elite, the aristocrats, military, clergy, and politicians.[125] Recoding the common trope of "civilisation versus barbarism," he
argued that the pursuit of empire threatened the "re-barbarization" of Britain.[126] But as with the Enlightenment anti-imperialists there were limits to
his critique, for he endorsed a "natural system" of settler colonization
through which people emigrated to create new communities, as long as this
was the result of private initiative not state action.[127] Libertarian settler colonialism was legitimate. Imperial ideology was marked more by continuity
than rupture across the late eighteenth and nineteenth centuries. While the
critique of alien rule was a recurrent (albeit minority) phenomenon from the
Enlightenment to the era of decolonization, it was often conjoined with support for settler colonization.

Critical of British belligerence and worried about aristocratic privilege and
the threat to domestic liberty, Cobden and Spencer epitomize an important
strand in nineteenth-century liberal international thought. But the staunchest
anti-imperialists in Victorian Britain were the Comtean positivists, prophets
of the "religion of humanity," many of whom were proud liberals.[128] Assailing
British occupation in India, Ireland, and Egypt, positivists including Edward
Beesly, Richard Congreve, and Frederic Harrison argued that the pursuit of
empire unjustly prevented national cultures from flourishing as part of a wider
universal humanity. A radical liberal and leading intellectual, Harrison offered a sustained critique of the British empire, which he once described as a
"huge crime against mankind" and the result of a "career of evil."[129] He gave a
distinctive Comtean twist to the conventional radical critique. "In the religion of Humanity," he asserted, "there are no distinctions of skin, or race, of
sect or creed; all are our brothers and fellow-citizens of the world—children
of the same great kith and kin."[130] Attacking the "military and commercial
aristocracy" for morally degrading the country through their egotistical quest
for domination, he maintained that an "empire of subjects trains up the impe-

---

[125] Spencer, "The Proper Sphere of Government" [1843], in *The Man versus the State* (Indianapolis, 1982), 220.

[126] Spencer, "Imperialism and Slavery," in *Facts and Comments* (London, 1902), 113.

[127] Spencer, "The Proper Sphere of Government," 224.

[128] For a key positivist intervention, see Richard Congreve et al., *International Policy* (London,
1866). On the positivists, see T. R. Wright, *The Religion of Humanity* (London, 1986). For their
views on empire, see Claeys, *Imperial Sceptics*, 47–122. However, as the example of Seeley shows
(see chapter 11), positivism was compatible with different positions on empire.

[129] Harrison, "Empire and Humanity," *Fortnightly Review*, 27/158 (1880), 298, 299. For his
views on empire, see also H. S. Jones, "The Victorian Lexicon of Evil," in *Evil, Barbarism and Empire*, ed. Tom Cook, Rebecca Gill, and Bertrand Taithe (Basingstoke, 2011), 126–43; Claeys, *Imperial Sceptics*, 47–122.

[130] Harrison, "Empire and Humanity," 294. For his account of the nature of moral obligations
within and beyond the state, see "The Modern Machiavelli," *Nineteenth Century*, 42/247 (1897),
462–71.

rial race to every injustice and deadens them to any form of selfishness."[131]
While many critics of empire focused almost exclusively on the baneful consequences for the imperial power, Harrison also attended to those denied the
possibility of self-determination. Taking a swipe at fellow liberals, he observed
that "[w]e do not pick and choose our oppressed nationalities to be favoured
with the blessings of self-government," and he insisted that the positivists were
"against all oppression of conquered by their conquerors; we look for the dissolution of these empires of conquest; we desire decentralisation of vast political communities, and not a never-ending system of annexations; and, above
all, we protest against military government in every form."[132] Harrison never
demanded immediate withdrawal from India, reasoning that it would be di-
sastrous for the Indians, and he concluded that until self-government was viable, it "must be governed in the sole interest of the countless millions who
compose it; and not only in their interest, but in their spirit, until the time
shall arrive when, part by part, it may be developed into normal and national
life of its own." But this concession should not blind us to the important difference between Harrison's Comtist liberalism and the Millian vision. They
diverged fundamentally on the question of imperial legitimacy and Britain's
role in the world. "We can accept neither the selfish plea of national glory, nor
the specious plea of a civilising mission."[133]

Not only did the Victorians produce a considerable body of writing deeply
critical of empire—or at least a body as critical as that found in the previous
century—they also justified empire with a wider variety of arguments than is
often acknowledged. In chapter 4 I demarcate five ideal-typical justificatory
strategies: realist-geopolitical; commercial-exploitative; civilizing; republican; and martialist. The first four studded nineteenth-century liberal accounts
of empire.[134] In public intellectual discourse liberal-civilizational arguments
predominated, while republican themes often coexisted with them, occasionally moving to the foreground. The civilizational model can be understood as

---

[131] Harrison, "Empire and Humanity," 295, 297.

[132] Ibid., 290.

[133] Ibid., 299. Andrew Fitzmaurice argues that international law, rather than a simple vehicle of
imperialism, as it has often been characterized in recent scholarship, was also a site of deep contestation over the legitimacy of empire, riven by clashes over the meaning of sovereignty and freedom:
"[I]nternational law was . . . one of the domains in which opposition to empire was most strongly
articulated." Fitzmaurice, *Sovereignty, Property and Empire*, 300. For another pluralist interpretation, see Jennifer Pitts, "Boundaries of Victorian International Law," in *Victorian Visions*, ed. Bell,
67–89. For an argument that stresses the complicity of international law in empire, see Martti Ko-
skeniemmi, *The Gentle Civilizer of Nations* (Cambridge, 2001).

[134] I find less evidence of martialist attitudes glorifying violence for its redemptive capacities
among liberal thinkers, though no doubt they were occasionally expressed. Karma Nabulsi, who
first formulated the category, argues that Seeley can be seen as an exemplary martialist. Nabulsi,
Traditions of War (Oxford, 1999), ch. 4. For a challenge to this attribution, see Duncan Bell,
"Unity and Difference," *Review of International Studies*, 31/3 (2005), 562–66.

benevolent empire

a species of the doctrine that liberal states can justifiably employ force to realize liberal ends. Its exponents assert that empire is legitimate if (and only if) it
is primarily intended to benefit the populations subjected to it. Premised on a
hierarchal conception of global politics, only some polities are regarded as displaying sufficient competence for self-government. It comes in weak and
strong forms.[135] The former diagnoses incompetent or malign *government* as
the main cause of incapacity. The remedy is the amputation of the government, by force if necessary, emancipating the subjugated people and putting
them in a position to achieve self-rule . Justified under the rubric of "humanitarian intervention," this is the most common contemporary iteration of the
idea. The strong version regards the people as the problem, imagining them as
incapable of creating or maintaining a stable and progressive political order.
The prescribed solution is cognitive, affective, and behavioral transformation
through expert liberal tutelage. During the nineteenth century this was most
commonly articulated in terms of the propensity for civilization—itself a
vague and elusive category.[136] In both cases, sovereignty is regarded as a privilege not a right: only those governments and/or peoples that have displayed
the appropriate political qualities are candidates for self-government and
equal recognition. While liberals often claimed that the ultimate goal of tutelage was the inculcation of a capacity for national self-determination, I would
argue that this is not a *necessary* feature of liberal civilizing rule.[137] Rather,
such rule is constituted by two central claims: that imperial tutelage can only
be justified in terms of the benefits it brings to the governed and that civilizing rule involves the transformation of existing societies into liberal ones
(broadly-defined). It thus encompasses the rule of law, the upholding of contracts, the development of representative institutions, the grant of a range of
civil and political liberties, and the introduction of a capitalist political economy. This menu of liberal reform does not automatically entail national self-
determination—at least in the foreseeable future—though liberals often gestured vaguely in that direction.

Such "altruistic" justificatory arguments were usually bolstered by a claim
that what liberal imperialists were advocating was radically new, something
that both distinguished them from and elevated them above all previous empires. Joseph Chamberlain, leading radical politician and arch-imperialist, argued that a palpable change could be discerned in justifications of empire, writing in 1897 that "[w]e feel now that our rule over their territories can only be

[135] This distinction is drawn in Jedediah Purdy, "Liberal Empire," *Ethics & International Affairs*, 17/2 (2003), 35–47.

[136] On the history of the idea, see Brett Bowden, *The Empire of Civilization* (Chicago, 2009);
Michael Sonenscher, "Barbarism and Civilisation" in Richard Whatmore and Brian Young (eds.),
A Companion to Intellectual History (Oxford, 2016), 288–302.

[137] See, for example, Morefield's discussion of Gilbert Murray's liberalism in *Covenants without
Swords*.

justified if we can show that it adds to the happiness and prospects of the people."[138] The American historian and political theorist William Dunning neatly summarized and dissected this line of reasoning. Supporters of the "new imperialism" that dominated the closing years of the nineteenth century liked to claim that the "modern movement is essentially altruistic—that it is founded upon duty to others rather than satisfaction of our own desires." Underlying the daunting complexity of imperial policy lay a single overarching principle, a "philosophic theory," namely that "the nation . . . must break the bonds of ethnic and geographic homogeneity and project its beneficent influence into the world at large." The modern democratic empire must, that is, act as a beacon for civilization and order in a turbulent age. Yet the professed principles and the grubby reality were very different, and Dunning argued that imperial expansion was driven principally by the insatiable desire for new markets. He looked on in horror, complaining that there was no longer "one first-class nation whose conscious aim is internal perfection rather than external dominion—not one that does not see in dependencies the indispensable proof of political competence. Constitutionalism and Nationalism have been superseded as controlling dogmas in the world's politics."[139] Moreover, there was little new under the sun, for such self-aggrandizing claims had permeated the imperial ideologies of Greece, Rome, and many others since. The new imperialism, he concluded wryly, "can hardly be said to have manifested thus far any characteristics that distinguish it from the movements in which throughout all history the powerful governments of the earth have extended their sway over the weak and incapable."[140] Its proponents were deluded in thinking otherwise.

This is correct as far as it goes. Advocates of empire have almost always boasted that they were spreading civilization to those subjected to their rule. This was an animating feature of Roman imperial ideology. Writing a thousand years after the fall of the Western Roman Empire, near the dawn of the European conquest of the earth, Francisco de Vitoria claimed that while the subjection of "barbarians" was justified, it was nevertheless subject to a "limitation": that "everything be done for the benefit and good of the barbarians, and not merely for the profit of the Spaniards."[141] Three centuries later, James Mill too was keen to stress the altruism of empire, this time of the British in India. "If we wish for the prolongation of an English government in India, which we

<hr>

[138] Chamberlain, "The True Conception of Empire" (1897), in *Mr Chamberlain's Speeches*, ed. C. Boyd, (London, 1914), 2:3.

[139] Dunning, "A Century of Politics," *North American Review*, 179/577 (1904), 812–13. Dunning was at the time a Professor of History at Columbia University. For more on his writing, see the discussion in chapter 3.

[140] Dunning, "A Century of Politics," 814–15.

[141] Vitoria, "On the American Indians (De Indis)," in *Franciso de Vitoria: Political Writings*, ed. Anthony Pagden and Jeremy Lawrence (Cambridge, 1991 [1539]), Question 1, Conclusion, sec. 23, 250–51.

do most sincerely, it is for the sake of the natives, not of England. India has never been anything but a burden; and anything but a burden, we are afraid, it cannot be rendered. But this English government in India, with all its vices, is a blessing of unspeakable magnitude to the population of Hindostan."[142] Here, though, we see a subtle shift, and one unique to the nineteenth century—the idea that not only was empire intended to benefit those subjected to it, but that this was its primary, overarching justification. What had changed over time, then, was not the basic *form* of the justificatory argument but rather the professed *content* of civilization and the *priority* accorded to it. The export of civilization had been elevated from one among several goals (or consequences) of imperial expansion to the overriding one, and at the same time it had been reimagined such that civilization now encompassed a wide variety of values compatible with liberalism, though not exclusive to it.

Republican justifications, in contrast, are primarily motivated by a concern with the character of the imperial power, legitimating empire in terms of a particular class of benefits that it generates for the state. Its proponents seek to foster individual and collective virtue in their compatriots, while encouraging the pursuit of national honor and glory. This kind of argument also has deep roots in Western political thought, traceable to Rome. Machiavelli presented one of its most powerful modern statements, combining an account of liberty at home with imperial expansion abroad.[143] Its echoes can be discerned in assorted nineteenth-century arguments. As Pitts makes clear, for example, Tocqueville advocated empire principally in terms of the reanimating effects of colonialism on French society.[144] Republican justifications were woven through nineteenth-century British defenses of empire. In chapter 12 I explore how the historian J. A. Froude offered one of the clearest expressions of it.

It is important to remember, though, that these categories are analytical abstractions, and they neither fully capture the idiosyncrasies of flesh-and-blood thinkers nor exhaust the range of imperial justifications circulating at the time. James Fitzjames Stephen presents an interesting case in point. A judge and jurisprudence scholar who served as Legal Member of the Viceroy's Council in India (1868–72), Stephen defended a hard-edged utilitarian liberalism that would govern with a "liberal imperial spirit."[145] He plays an important but contested function in scholarship on the intellectual foundations of the Victorian empire. Stephen stands at the center of the narrative in Eric Stokes's classic *The English Utilitarians and India*.[146] Mehta contends that Ste-

---

[142] James Mill, "Review of Voyage aux Indes Orientales," by Le P. Paulin De S. Barthélemy, *Edinburgh Review*, 15 (1810), 371.

[143] Mikael Hörnqvist, *Machiavelli and Empire* (Cambridge, 2004); Hörnqvist, "Machiavelli's Three Desires," in *Empire in Modern Political Thought*, ed. Muthu, 7–30.

[144] Pitts, *A Turn to Empire*, chs. 6–7.

[145] Stephen, "Liberalism," *Cornhill Magazine*, 5/25 (1862), 82.

[146] It is arguable, though, that Stokes exaggerates the importance of Stephen. See here Freder-

phen's defense of empire was illiberal, but rather than inferring from this that liberals could justify empire in a variety of ways, he resolves the interpretive conundrum by denying that Stephen was an authentic liberal. He had absorbed too much Hobbes and not enough Locke, "the true progenitor and enduring mentor of liberalism." Pitts reads him as offering a "moral" justification of empire despite his anti-democratic posturing, whereas Mantena reads Stephen's "imperial authoritarianism" as exemplifying a "distinct break" from liberal "ethical" justifications.[147]

Rather than seeing Stephen's authoritarian construal of imperial legitimacy as the culmination of an internal tendency in utilitarian thinking, indicative of a fracture in late imperial ideology, or as a quixotic antiliberal justificatory strategy, I suggest that it is better to view his work as indexing one possible liberal utilitarian pathway among many.[148] While numerous utilitarians supported the empire, there was no necessary connection between the philosophy and the political project. After all, both Bentham and Spencer were fierce critics of the empire in India. Nor did utilitarian defenses of empire follow a clear unilinear historical chronology. Writing *after* Stephen's main interventions, Henry Sidgwick, the most sophisticated nineteenth-century utilitarian, proselytized a fairly conventional liberal civilizing view, counseling that the "business" of civilized nations was to "educate and absorb" savage peoples, and he expressed admiration for the "justifiable pride" that the "cultivated members of a civilized community feel in the beneficent exercise of dominion, and in the performance by their nation of the noble task of spreading the highest kind of civilisation."[149] The "gruffian," as Stephen was known, was right to protest that his views ran counter to the dominant intellectual trends of the time.

For Stephen, liberalism was an expression of a patriotic sense of English preeminence, while the empire was an integral element of the moral and political grandeur of the country. Since the conquest and rule of India was the "greatest achievement of the race," threats to imperial supremacy presented an existential challenge.[150] This anxiety of loss underpinned both his support for

---

ick Rosen, "Eric Stokes, British Utilitarianism, and India," in *J. S. Mill's Encounter with India*, ed. Moir, Peers, and Zastoupil (Toronto, 1999), 18–33. On the variability of utilitarian responses, see also Bart Schultz and Georgios Varouxakis, eds., *Utilitarianism and Empire* (Lanham, MD, 2005).

[147] Mehta, *Liberalism and Empire*, 29–30, 198; Pitts, *A Turn to Empire*, 223; Mantena, *Alibis of Empire*, 38.

[148] His unconventional liberalism is discussed in James Colaiaco, *James Fitzjames Stephen and the Crisis of Victorian Thought* (London, 1983); K.J.M. Smith, *James Fitzjames Stephen* (Cambridge, 1988); Collini, *Public Moralists*, 280–87. For a convincing account of his political thinking, see Julia Stapleton, "James Fitzjames Stephen," *Victorian Studies*, 41/2 (1998), 243–46.

[149] Sidgwick, *Lectures on the Ethics of T. H. Green, Mr. Herbert Spencer and J. Martineau* (London, 1902), 236; Sidgwick, *The Elements of Politics* [1891], 3rd ed. (London, 1907), 256. See also the discussion in chapter 10.

[150] Leslie Stephen, *The Life of Sir James Fitzjames Stephen* (London, 1895), 398.

revenge against the Sepoy rebels of 1857 and his hatred of the "Manchester School" of political economists.[151] As he argued in *Liberty, Equality, Fraternity*, a patriotic citizenry should bask in the glory of military victories in India.[152] Rejecting Bright's argument that the British had an obligation to the Indians to make amends for the original crime of conquest, he demanded that the empire be venerated. "I deny that ambition and conquest are crimes; I say that ambition is the great incentive to every manly virtue, and conquest is the process by which every great state in the world . . . has been built up." Empire elevated the moral and material condition of its subjects, serving as a "vast bridge" from a moribund violent past to a stable and orderly future. This task, if accomplished, would constitute "the greatest feat of strength, skill and courage in the whole history of the world."[153] Here his argument came close to the republican line endorsed by his friend Froude.[154]

Yet Stephen was also committed to a version of the civilizing mission. British dominion offered an unparalleled opportunity to enact a "true liberalism" by fulfilling an obligation to rule justly.[155] The "great and characteristic task" of the British in India was to spread European civilization. They were embarked on "one of the most extensive and far-reaching revolutions recorded in history," involving the "radical change" of the institutions and ideas of countless people.[156] The "essential parts" of that civilization included peace, order, the supremacy of law, the prevention of crime, the redress of wrong, the enforcement of contracts, and the use of taxation revenue for the public good. It was thus necessary to base the law and institutions of the country "on European secular morality, on European views of political economy, and on the principle that men ought to be enabled by law, irrespective of religion, race, caste, and similar considerations, to enjoy securely whatever property they have, to get rich if they can by legal means, and to be protected in doing as they please, so long as they do not hurt others."[157] Here he sounded like Mill. This was, he concluded, the near unanimous view of the Europeans who governed India. Insofar as Stephen diverged from them, it was chiefly over the *telos* of empire. Critical of the "Divine Right of Representative Institutions,"

[151] Stephen, "Deus Ultionum," *Saturday Review*, October 15, 1867; Stephen, *Life*, 225, 310, 394.

[152] Stephen, *Liberty, Equality, Fraternity* [1873], ed. R. J. White (Chicago, 1990), 113. See also his attempt to justify the conquest, and celebrate Warren Hastings, in *The Story of Nuncomar and the Impeachment of Sir Elijah Impey* (London, 1885).

[153] Stephen, "Manchester on India," *Times*, January 4, 1878, 3.

[154] On his friendship and "intellectual sympathies" with Froude, see Stephen, *Life*, 585, 700; Ciaran Brady, *James Anthony Froude* (Oxford, 2013), 3, 16.

[155] Stephen, "Liberalism," *Cornhill Magazine*, 5/25 (1862), 82.

[156] Stephen, "Foundations of the Government of India," *Nineteenth Century*, 14/80 (1883), 559, 554, 566.

[157] Ibid., 554, 556.

the view that the "exercise of absolute power can never be justified except as a temporary expedient used for the purpose of superseding itself," Stephen advised that representative institutions were not always and everywhere appropriate (chiefly because they came into conflict with more fundamental liberal utilitarian commitments).[158] India was an unsuitable candidate. But this says as much about his hostility to democracy as a form of government as it does about his conception of India. Deeply critical of democratic institutions in British life, he grudgingly accepted that there was no point in fighting against them since they were an achieved fact. India, though, could still be saved from the blight. While he was more explicit than most other liberals about the coercive foundations of empire, and while he was skeptical about the goal of Indian self-government, he nevertheless argued that British rule was only legitimate insofar as it brought civilizational benefits to the governed. His justificatory argument, then, was an awkward fusion of liberal civilizing and republican themes, with a distinctive authoritarian flavor. Stephens's heterodox political thought highlights the internal variety of Victorian liberal ideology.

The historical narrative embedded in Mantena's powerful account of liberal supersession is also open to challenge. Recall her argument about the impact of 1857: liberal justifications "were dramatically eclipsed" and the period witnessed "a more general waning of ethical arguments and moral justifications of empire."[159] The evidence she adduces for this *general transformation* of metropolitan British liberalism is chiefly drawn from her superb interpretation of Maine's personal intellectual trajectory combined with the shift in policy enforced by the British administration in India.[160] Mantena thus sets up an equivalence, implying that British liberal ideology and Indian imperial policy developed together, from ethics to alibis of empire. Maine, Seeley, and Stephen are read as representative of a ubiquitous disillusionment with democracy that reshaped imperial ideology. Hence her claim that "a growing illiberal or antiliberal consensus" was "fuelled by domestic fears about the growth of mass democracy."[161] However, this is an overly homogenous view of British elite political culture. While there was a fairly widespread sense that the onset of democracy posed a threat to Britain and its empire, it was far from universal. It was not the only—indeed not the dominant—strand of liberal thinking.[162] Intellectual currents in Britain and India were not closely

---

[158] Ibid., 551 (and 561–63).

[159] Mantena, *Alibis of Empire*, 11, 6.

[160] The argument about Indian policy draws on Metcalf, *Ideologies of the Raj*.

[161] Mantena, *Alibis of Empire*, 43.

[162] I stress the role in disillusionment with democracy on settler colonial ideology in Bell, *The Idea of Greater Britain*, ch. 2. On liberals and democracy, see also Christopher Harvie, *The Lights of Liberalism* (London, 1976).

aligned. As Jon Wilson puts it, "British political thought and administrative practice marched to a different beat in the colonial context."[163]

The closing three decades of the century witnessed a remarkable burst of innovation in British political thinking. While the Liberal Party split over Home Rule, and even as some older liberals (including Maine) lamented the direction of popular government, other thinkers and movements were emerging or gaining ground. New conceptions of the state, of the individual, and of community flourished. More important than the pained ripostes to democracy was the emergence of collectivist forms of liberalism, challenging both older *laissez-faire* articulations and conservative critics. At a fundamental philosophical level, Sidgwick revived a tired utilitarianism in *The Methods of Ethics*, while the final third of the century witnessed an efflorescence of idealist philosophy, drawing on both ancient Greek and modern German influences. T. H. Green, Bernard Bosanquet, and J. H. Muirhead, among others, all sought to craft idealist liberal political theories.[164] In the 1890s and beyond a group of "new liberal" thinkers began to self-consciously develop a more egalitarian form of liberalism.[165] Drawing on the German historian Otto von Gierke, pluralists, including Maitland, Neville Figgis, and G.D.H. Cole, challenged the normative and ontological centrality of the sovereign state, seeking answers to political challenges in a plethora of civil society associations and overlapping sources of political authority.[166] The idealists and new liberals helped to lay the intellectual foundations for the nascent welfare state.[167] Horrified at this development, Spencer and his followers restated the case for a libertarian vision. In short, this was a period of great intellectual ferment. Liberalism was reworked for an emerging democratic age.

Moreover, and just as importantly, the liberal civilizing mission remained a central feature of imperial ideology deep into the twentieth century. Stephen's complaint about his contemporaries had been correct. In one of the most sig-

---

[163] Wilson, "Taking Europe for Granted," *History Workshop Journal*, 52 (2001), 292.

[164] Sidgwick, *The Methods of Ethics* (Cambridge, 1874). See also J. B. Schneewind, *Sidgwick's Ethics and Victorian Moral Philosophy* (Oxford, 1977); Bart Schultz, *Henry Sidgwick* (Cambridge, 2004). On idealism, see David Boucher and Andrew Vincent, *British Idealism and Political Theory* (Edinburgh, 2001); W. J. Mander, *British Idealism* (Oxford, 2011), ch. 7; Peter Nicholson, *The Political Philosophy of the British Idealists* (Cambridge, 1990); Sandra den Otter, *British Idealism and Social Explanation* (Oxford, 1996); Colin Tyler, *Idealist Political Philosophy* (London, 2006).

[165] Stefan Collini, *Liberalism and Sociology* (Cambridge, 1983); Michael Freeden, *The New Liberalism* (Oxford, 1978); Avital Simhony and David Weinstein, eds., *The New Liberalism* (Cambridge, 2001).

[166] David Runciman, *Pluralism and the Personality of the State* (Cambridge, 1997); Cécile Laborde, *Pluralist Thought and the State in Britain and France, 1900–1925* (Basingstoke, 2000); Marc Stears, *Progressive, Pluralists, and the Problems of the State* (Oxford, 2002).

[167] Michael Freeden, "The Coming of the Welfare State," in *The Cambridge History of Twentieth-Century Political Thought*, ed. Terence Ball and Richard Bellamy (Cambridge, 2006), 7–45; Jose Harris, "Political Thought and the Welfare State, 1870–1914," *Past & Present*, 135 (1992), 116–41.

nificant early twentieth-century accounts of liberalism, Herbert Samuel asserted that the "foundation of Liberalism is the moral law that the State has the duty of advancing the welfare both of its own members and of all whom it can influence." But the form of this duty varied according to the level of sociopolitical development found in communities around the world. For those in which people were both free and civilized, liberal states should adopt a stance of noninterference, interacting with them harmoniously and seeking influence, if at all, through diplomatic engagement. If a people was "civilized" but living under the iron rule of a foreign despot, liberals had a duty to offer moral, and sometimes material, support. Finally, if they were "savage or semicivilized," liberalism directed that the state "may itself undertake their government and help their progress by the gift of good laws and good administration."[168] Empire was thus a moral agent, a "civilizing and pacifying force, helpful to the progress of mankind."[169] In Millian vein, he stressed the enduring relevance of the civilizing mission.

> Independence, however valuable to a people, is not their highest good. Liberals hold that the ultimate purpose of politics is nothing narrower than to help men to advance towards the best type. No people can reach the goal, indeed, unless they have liberty; but there may be stages in the march when unrestrained liberty is rather a hindrance to them than a help. A barbarian race may prosper best if for a period, even for a long period, it surrenders the right of self-government in exchange for the teachings of civilization.

He concluded that "England is honestly seeking to teach her native subjects to be self-dependent, and in place of the barbaric license of which they are deprived, to give them in the fullness of time, and under the aegis of her own flag, a new and a better freedom."[170] This was a paradigmatic expression of the ethical justification of imperial intervention. That the empire was a virtuous engine of civilization remained a metropolitan platitude deep into the twentieth century—and beyond.

Others went further still in their encomiums for a moralized vision of imperial rule. In his textbook on the subject, Caldecott even claimed that India, under British guidance, had partially realized "Plato's conception of the GOOD STATE," shorn of its "extremes": a wise governing cadre, a courageous intermediary administrative class, a temperate mass of people, all working to-

---

[168] Herbert Samuel, *Liberalism* (London, 1902), 348. One Indian civil servant and British liberal MP went so far as to argue that the civilizing mission had *already* been successful, with British imperial education having prepared the Indians for immediate (though limited) self-government within an overarching imperial structure. Henry Cotton, "The Political Future of India," *North American Review*, 181/584 (1905), 110–16.

[169] Samuel, *Liberalism*, 325.

[170] Ibid., 330, 332.

gether in harmony. But whereas Plato thought that such a state would inevitably foster debilitating corruption, the "virtues of the Indian state are preparing for consolidation and progress."[171] Another textbook, written after the war in South Africa, hymned the empire as an "agent making for the advance of civilisation." Invoking the spirit of Tennyson, the author decreed that it was the primary instrument of global progress, and thus essential for the future development of humanity.

> Working for the gradual elimination of discord and war and for the foundation of a system of universal freedom and justice leading up to that perfectibility of which poets dream, a federation of mankind speaking a common language and governed by a common law, the British Empire could scarcely be supplanted by any other aggregation of kindred peoples. Thus the extinction of the empire would mean a distinct, and so far as one can see, an irreparable, check to the progress of the world.[172]

Edwin Arnold, a leading poet and journalist, likewise evoked the world-historical mission of the British, contrasting a Hobbesian global state of nature with the reforming cosmopolitical ambitions of the empire.

> The loss of India to England would mean the breaking up and decay of our ancient empire; the eventual spread of Slavonic and Mongolian hordes all over the vacant places and open markets of the world; the world's peace gone; again, as in the days of Belisarius, the march of sciences, arts, religions, arrested as when Omar burned the Alexandrian library; and history once more put back to the beginning of a new effort, under novel and gloomy auspices, to effect that which is the perpetual object of its course and its combinations—the final amalgamation of all the people of the globe under one law and one common faith and culture.[173]

Moreover, criticizing the coercive imposition of uniform standards of British "civilization" on India did not lead invariably to the kind of "conservatism" advocated by Maine. Ramsay MacDonald, one of the founders of the Labour

---

[171] Caldecott, *English Colonization and Empire*, 84–85. For further examples of advocacy of civilization progress, see chapter 5.

[172] J. Stanley Little, *Progress of British Empire in the Century* (London, 1903), xv. Drawn from "Lockesley Hall" (1842), Tennyson's phrase the "federation of Mankind" was routinely employed in imperial discourse. For further discussion, see Duncan Bell, *Dreamworlds of Empire* (forthcoming).

[173] Arnold, "The Duty and Destiny of England in India," *North American Review*, 154/423 (1892), 170. "But—and here comes the point—the question of questions is whether the democracy of great Britain, our household-suffrage men, who have of late come to supreme power in the realm, comprehend their Indian Empire and care to maintain it" (187).

Party and later Prime Minister, commenced his analysis of British imperialism from a position similar to Maine—indeed he went further in stressing the need to protect Indian communities from the corrosive power of imperial capitalism. "Our fundamental mistake in native policy is that we regard the native as a Briton in the making," he warned, and "the less we interfere with native administration the better."[174] The answer, though, was a democratized civilizing vision. The imperialism of a future Labour government, he stated, "does not believe in the subjugation of other nationalists; it takes no pride in the 'government' of other peoples. To its subject races it desires to occupy the position of a friend; to its self-governing imperial States it seeks to be an equal; to the world it asks to be regarded as a neighbour."[175] The aim of empire in India was ultimately the creation of a self-governing nation-state. In short, while Mantena does an admirable job of anatomizing an important and novel form of imperial ideology, she exaggerates both the homogeneity of British liberal thought at the time and the decline of liberal civilizing accounts of imperial rule.

European and American political thinking in the nineteenth century was typically predicated on a vision of the world as a space divided between competing civilizations, each at a different level of socioeconomic, political, and moral development, each populated by members of distinct races, each subject to contrasting forms of evaluation and judgment. Assumed or endorsed by British liberals and their critics, and by imperialists and those who rejected empire, few completely escaped the ideological shadow of this imagined geography. Its legacy continues to shape visions of world order.

[174] MacDonald, *Labour and the Empire* (London, 1907), 102–3.
[175] Ibid., 108–9.

CHAPTER 3

What Is Liberalism?

꙲

Like the history of anything else, history of philosophy is written by the victors.
Victors get to choose their ancestors, in the sense that they decide which
among their all too various ancestors to mention, write biographies of, and
commend to their descendants.[1]

—RICHARD RORTY

Before we can begin to analyze any specific form of liberalism we must surely
state as clearly as possible what the word means. For in the course of so many
years of ideological conflict it seems to have lost its identity completely.
Overuse and overextension have rendered it so amorphous that it can now
serve as an all-purpose word, whether of abuse or praise.[2]

—JUDITH SHKLAR

Liberalism is a specter that haunts Western political thought and practice.
For some it is a site of the modern, an object of desire, even the *telos* of history. For others it represents an unfolding nightmare, signifying either the vicious logic of capitalism or a squalid descent into moral relativism. For others
still, perhaps the majority, it is a mark of ambivalence, the ideological prereq-
uisite for living a reasonably comfortable life in affluent democratic states—
the least-worst option.

But what is liberalism? Across and within scholarly discourses, it is construed in manifold and contradictory ways: as an embattled vanguard project
and constitutive of modernity itself, a fine-grained normative political philosophy and a hegemonic mode of governmentality, the justificatory ideology
of unrestrained capitalism and the richest ideological resource for its limitation. Self-declared liberals have supported extensive welfare states and their
abolition; the imperial civilizing mission and its passionate denunciation; the

---

[1] Richard Rorty, "The Historiography of Philosophy," in *Philosophy in History*, ed. Richard
Rorty, Jerome Schneewind, and Quentin Skinner (Cambridge, 1984), 70.
[2] Judith N. Shklar, "The Liberalism of Fear" [1989], in *Political Thought and Political Thinkers*
(Chicago, 1998), 3.

necessity of social justice and its outright rejection; the perpetuation of the sovereign state and its transcendence; massive global redistribution of wealth and the radical inequalities of the existing order. Shklar's complaint that it is an "all-purpose word" is thus unsurprising, for liberalism has become the metacategory of Western political discourse.

There are several responses to "overextension." One is simply to ignore it, deploying the term as if its meaning was self-evident. Ubiquitous across the humanities and social sciences, this unreflective impulse generates much confusion. Another is to engage in "boundary work"—to demarcate and police the discourse.[3] Some influential attempts to do so have figured liberalism as a capacious tradition of traditions, with Guido De Ruggiero and Friedrich Hayek, for example, bifurcating it into British and Continental forms. The most common variation on this theme is to distinguish "classical" and "social" liberalisms.[4] Another popular response is to narrate liberal history as a story of rise or decline, triumph or tragedy. A familiar rendition bemoans the lost purity of the original. Thus Leo Strauss mourned the transition from virtuous "ancient" liberalism (reaching its apogee in Athens) to debased forms of "modern" liberalism (commencing with Machiavelli), while Sheldon Wolin averred that twentieth-century liberalism had disastrously forgotten its early skeptical enunciation.[5] Some neoconservatives have claimed the mantle, seeking, with Irving Kristol, "a return to the original sources of liberal vision and liberal energy so as to correct the warped version."[6] Declension has also been a recurrent libertarian complaint. When he came to pen his defense of "classical" liberalism in 1927, Ludwig von Mises grumbled that from Mill onwards the ideology had degenerated into socialism, a warning that Herbert Spencer had flagged half a century earlier.[7] But the development of liberalism can also be cast as progressive. Both L. T. Hobhouse and John Dewey, for example, celebrated the transfiguration of liberalism from an ideology of *laissez-faire* to one that justified the use of systematic government intervention to reduce harmful disadvantages.[8] The argument continues today with many libertari-

?
.

---

[3] On the practice of boundary-work, see Thomas Gieryn, "Boundary-Work and the Demarcation of Science from Non-Science," *American Sociological Review*, 48 (1983), 785–95.

[4] De Ruggiero, *The History of European Liberalism* [1927], trans. R. G. Collingwood (Boston, 1959); Hayek, "Liberalism" [1973], in *New Studies in Philosophy, Politics, Economics and the History of Ideas* (London, 1978), 113. Alan Ryan complicates matters by distinguishing between modern, classical, social, and libertarian variants. *The Making of Modern Liberalism* (Princeton, 2012), 23–28.

[5] Strauss, *Liberalism Ancient and Modern* (Chicago, 1968); Wolin, *Politics and Vision* (Princeton, 2004), 263.

[6] Irving Kristol, *Reflections of a Neoconservative* (New York, 1983), 75.

[7] Mises, *Liberalism* (Indianapolis, 2005), 153–54; Spencer, *The Man versus the State* [1884] (Indianapolis, 1969).

[8] Hobhouse, *Liberalism* [1911], ed. James Meadowcroft (Cambridge, 1994); Dewey, *Liberalism and Social Action* (New York, 1935), 21.

ans condemning "social" liberalism as a form of socialism and many social liberals rejecting the liberal credentials of libertarianism. All sides claim to be
heirs of the one true liberalism.

A related policing strategy is to concede the intellectual diversity of liberalism while extracting its constitutive element(s)—its ineliminable core. This
too is contested terrain. Adopting the most common line, Shklar sought to
create a "modest amount of order" by characterizing liberalism as a "political
doctrine" with "only one overriding aim: to secure the political conditions
that are necessary for the exercise of personal freedom."[9] Yet Jeremy Waldron
is right that positing a commitment to freedom as the foundation of liberalism "is to say something too vague and abstract to be helpful." Instead, he
proposes that it is best defined by a "requirement that all aspects of the social
should either be made acceptable or be capable of being made acceptable to
every last individual."[10] Ronald Dworkin, meanwhile, asserts that "a certain
conception of equality . . . is the nerve of liberalism."[11] Others insist on a cluster of commitments. The historian Gary Gerstle, for example, suggests that
liberals have always endorsed three "foundational principles," rationality,
emancipation, and progress, while John Dunn once lamented the "dismaying
number of categories" that have been claimed as central to liberal ideology,
including political rationalism, hostility to autocracy, cultural distaste for
conservatism and tradition, tolerance, and individualism.[12] Even its supposed
core has proven elusive.

In what follows I neither attempt to adjudicate between these competing
interpretations nor present a new substantive liberal theory. Instead, I seek to
reframe the way in which the liberal tradition is understood. I open with a
critique of some existing interpretive protocols used to delimit political traditions, before introducing (in section 2) a new way of conceptualizing liberalism, suggesting that it can be seen as the sum of the arguments that have been
classified as liberal, and recognized as such by other self-proclaimed liberals,
across time and space. In the second half of the chapter, I analyze the emergence and subsequent transformation of the category of liberalism in Anglo-
American political thought between 1850 and 1950. This serves as an illustrative case study of some of the methodological arguments I outline in the first
two sections. While section 3 traces the evolution of the language of liberal-

---

[9] Shklar, "Liberalism," 3. On liberty as "normatively basic," see Gerald Gaus and Shane Courtland, "Liberalism," *The Stanford Encyclopaedia of Philosophy*, ed. Edward Zalta, http://plato.stan
ford.edu/entries/liberalism/.

[10] Waldron, "Theoretical Foundations of Liberalism," *Philosophical Quarterly*, 37 (1987), 131,
127, 140.

[11] Dworkin, "Liberalism," in *A Matter of Principle* (Oxford, 1985), 183.

[12] Gerstle, "The Protean Character of American Liberalism," *American Historical Review*, 99
(1994), 1046; Dunn, *Western Political Theory in the Face of the Future* [1979] (Cambridge, 1991),
33.

ism in nineteenth-century Britain, section 4 explores how the scope of the liberal tradition was massively expanded during the middle decades of the century, chiefly in the United States, such that it came to be seen by many as the constitutive ideology of the West. Above all, I contend that this broad understanding of liberalism was produced by a conjunction of the ideological wars fought against "totalitarianism" and assorted developments in the social sciences. Today we both inherit and inhabit it.

Constructing Liberalism: Scholarly Purposes and Interpretive Protocols

There are at least three *types* of answer that can be given to the question in the title, each of which serves a different scholarly purpose. *Prescriptive* responses specify norms of correct or best usage. They delineate a particular conception of liberalism, branding it as more authentic—more truly liberal—than other claimants to the title. Such accounts vary in the core features recognized as constitutive, the interpretive methodologies utilized to identify them, and the normative stance assumed towards them. This is the most familiar type of answer. *Comprehensive* responses attempt to chart the plethora of liberal languages. Rather than prescribing a favored conception they seek to identify the *actual* range of usage, mapping the variegated topography of liberal ideology. These accounts differ in the interpretive methodologies employed and the temporal and spatial scope of inquiry. *Explanatory* responses account for the development of liberalism(s), whether understood in prescriptive or comprehensive terms. They too vary in methodology and scope. Although each kind of response is legitimate in certain circumstances, problems arise when they are misapplied or conflated. In particular, prescriptive accounts are very poor guides to understanding the internal complexity and historical development of ideologies.

Scholars also adopt different methodological strategies—*interpretive protocols*—to answer the question. To argue about a political tradition—to compare and contrast it; to chart its decline, crisis, or ascension; to pinpoint its flaws or celebrate its strengths—it is first necessary to construct it as an object of analysis. Political theorists typically employ two main protocols, either individually or in combination: *stipulative* and *canonical*. *Contextualism* offers an alternative.[13]

---

[13] Less common in political theory, *expressive* protocols are widely utilized across the humanities and social sciences. They distil the meaning of liberalism through a form of reverse engineering, working backwards from observations on (aspects of) a society to the ideas purportedly underlying it. First, certain entities—for example, public policies—are classified as "liberal," a classification usually based on the self-identification of the relevant agents or the alleged correspondence between the entity and a putative external ("liberal") standard. Second, the entities are

Stipulative accounts identify necessary (though rarely sufficient) conditions for a position to count as a legitimate exemplar of a tradition. "Liberalism" is typically constructed from interpretations of the meaning and interrelation of core concepts, such as liberty, authority, autonomy, and equality. Such accounts employ definitional fiat to demarcate the legitimate boundaries of liberalism: only those adhering to a particular cluster of assumptions and arguments count as properly liberal. We have already encountered the contrasting formulations offered by Dworkin, Gerstle, Shklar, and Waldron. History is sometimes invoked in such accounts, but it is usually what Rawls aptly termed the "philosopher's schematic version of speculative history," and while these arguments often cite historical figures—above all Locke, Kant, Mill, and now Rawls himself—their core normative arguments can be justified independently of any past expression.[14]

Traditions are usually constructed around a canon of renowned thinkers, which serves simultaneously as a reservoir of arguments, an index of historical continuity, and a powerful source of intellectual authority. *Canonical* approaches thus distil "liberal" theoretical structures from exemplary writings. The most frequent targets for this protocol are (again) Locke, Kant, Mill, and Rawls, though a host of other figures are sometimes marshaled to fit the occasion. Leo Strauss and his epigones have divined sweeping interpretations of liberal modernity from a handful of "great books." Pierre Manent, for instance, charts the unfolding of liberalism through a procession of figures stretching back to Machiavelli and Hobbes.[15] Far from being an exclusive Straussian strategy, however, this is arguably the most common protocol for constructing liberalism. As I discussed in chapter 2, for example, canonical formulations have structured arguments about the relationship between liberalism and empire. While Uday Singh Mehta grounds his influential argument that liberalism has an "urge" to empire on readings of Locke and Mill, most rejoinders—including those by Jennifer Pitts and Sankar Muthu—have likewise focused on canonical figures.

Both of these methodological strategies are valuable, even essential, for achieving particular scholarly aims. Stipulative protocols can be fruitfully employed in the elaboration of normative political philosophies and the construction of ideal types for conducting social analysis. Canonical scholarship, meanwhile, can generate insightful readings of individual thinkers. Yet nei-

---

taken to embody or express underlying ideas or values, which are then characterized as liberal. Thus: State A is classified as liberal; "liberal state" A enacts policy B. Policy B is therefore "liberal." B embodies or expresses liberal value or idea C. An expressive protocol is arguably employed in Dworkin's "theory of what liberalism is" (Dworkin, "Liberalism"). This protocol has various problems, not least debilitating circularity.

[14] Rawls, *Lectures on the History of Political Philosophy*, ed. Samuel Freeman (Cambridge, 2007), 11.

[15] Manent, *An Intellectual History of Liberalism*, trans. R. Balinski (Princeton, 1996).

ther are capable of underwriting plausible comprehensive or explanatory accounts because they cannot shed much light on the universe of liberal languages, the plethora of competing and often contradictory claims that travel under its name. Articulated in the register of philosophical abstraction, the stipulative genre is estranged from the vicissitudes of history and political practice. It is caught on the horns of a dilemma. Unless the stipulated commitments are conceptualized at a very high level of generality—for example, that liberalism prioritizes individual freedom, or that liberals are committed to toleration, liberty, and constitutional government—they will invariably fail to encompass the deep divisions between professed variants of liberalism, yet when pitched at that level they provide little guidance for pursuing the detailed reconstruction necessary for satisfactory description or explanation. Waldron's argument illustrates this mismatch. Maintaining that only those adopting his contracturalist view of justification count as properly liberal, he anoints Locke, Rousseau, and Kant as genuine liberals, while suggesting that John Stuart Mill and numerous other nineteenth-century figures (especially utilitarians) stand in an "ambiguous relation" to the tradition. On this account, then, liberalism simultaneously preexists its own self-conscious formulation and was misunderstood by many of those who played a fundamental role in its propagation. At least he admits that "many liberals may not recognise" the picture he paints.[16]

The problem with canonical protocols is that they can rarely support the generalizations they are invoked to underpin. As Mehta's argument shows, work in this vein often seems to assume that the ideas of canonical figures can stand in for, or be seen as sufficiently representative of, the tradition as a whole. This provides a defective foundation on which to build an analysis of a multifaceted political ideology. Given the internal diversity of liberalism, its national and regional variation, and its polyphonic evolution, it is exceptionally difficult to ground felicitous generalizations on the work of a handful of authors. A further problem is that this protocol often takes as given the very thing that should be investigated—the construction of the canon. The idea of a canon of great thinkers standing at the heart of a preconstituted tradition is, in part, an artifact of the professional development of academic political theory during the twentieth century.[17] It is the product of a particular moment in time, shaped by largely forgotten value-commitments and selection criteria, and arguments centered on claims distilled from the canon are thus conducted

---

[16] Waldron, "Theoretical Foundations," 128, 143–44. For another prominent example of historical gymnastics, see Stephen Holmes, "The Permanent Structure of Anti-Liberal Thought," in *Liberalism and the Moral Life,* ed. Nancy Rosenblum (Cambridge, 1989), 236–37. Holmes characterizes Spinoza, Locke, and Hume (among others) as straightforward liberals, but denies a place in the pantheon to Michael Sandel and Charles Taylor.

[17] John Gunnell, *The Descent of Political Theory* (Chicago, 1993). On the politics of canon formation in literature, see John Guillory, *Cultural Capital* (Chicago, 1993).

within a discursive echo chamber. Indeed studying the processes through which the canon crystallized can reveal as much (or more) about the dynamics of political thinking as the forensic analysis of purportedly exemplary texts.

Contextualist approaches need little introduction.[18] The bulk of such work has focused on illuminating the patterns of early modern political thinking, and at present there are no general contextual histories of liberalism—indeed its methodological precepts render such a project quixotic. Contextualists have nevertheless made an important contribution to the analysis of liberalism by challenging the assumption that it can be traced to the seventeenth century. Versions of this argument have been tendered by John Dunn, Mark Goldie, J.G.A. Pocock, Quentin Skinner, and James Tully. Pocock, for example, maintains that "liberalism" was "not used in the eighteenth century, where the adjective 'liberal' did not bear its modern meaning, and though elements were present which would in due course be assembled by means of this formula, there was no system of doctrine corresponding to its later use."[19] He concludes that no significant inferences about liberalism can be drawn from the earlier period. In particular, this strand of scholarship has repeatedly questioned Locke's elevated status as a (or the) foundational liberal.[20] It is important to recognize that this is not principally a semantic argument about the absence of the word "liberalism" in the early modern period, but rather a claim about the range of concepts and arguments available to historical actors.[21] It is about extant thought-worlds, not recoverable terminology. Yet while this body of scholarship has questioned conventional accounts of liberal history, it has rarely probed how and why that very convention emerged.

Michael Freeden has developed the most systematic contextualist account of Anglo-American liberalism. It is, he argues,

> . . . that semantic field in which the political understandings of people who regard themselves as liberals, or who others regard as liberals, may be investigated. It is a plastic, changing thing, shaped and reshaped by the thought-practices of individuals and groups; and though it needs to have a roughly identifiable pattern for us to call it consistently by the same name, "liberalism," it also presents myriad variations that reflect the questions posed, and the positions adopted, by various liberals.[22]

---

[18] For a seminal statement, see Quentin Skinner, *Visions of Politics*, vol. 1 (Cambridge, 2002).

[19] J.G.A. Pocock, *The Machiavellian Moment*, rev. ed. (Princeton, 2003), 579.

[20] Mark Goldie, "Introduction," in *The Reception of Locke's Politics*, vol. 1, ed. Goldie (London, 1999), xvii-lxxiii. For a recent powerful argument, see Tim Stanton, "John Locke and the Fable of Liberalism," *Historical Journal* (forthcoming).

[21] Ryan, *Modern Liberalism*, 9, reads it as a straightforward semantic claim.

[22] Freeden, *Liberal Languages* (Princeton, 2005), 20. See also Michael Freeden and Marc Stears, "Liberalism," in *The Oxford Handbook of Political Ideologies*, ed. Michael Freeden, Lyman Tower Sargent, and Marc Stears (Oxford, 2013), 329–48.

However, even Freeden tends to blur prescriptive, comprehensive, and explanatory arguments. Identifying Millian liberalism as the most genuine manifestation of the ideology, he finds several alternative strands wanting, including contemporary libertarianism and "American philosophical liberalism" (social liberalism following Rawls). With its focus on state neutrality, neo-Kantian conceptions of autonomy, and the possibility of specifying fixed principles of justice, as well as its abstraction from practical political activity, the latter represents a "decisive departure" from prevailing modes of liberal thought, while the former lacks "many of the attributes which bestow on the liberal profile its distinctive contours," and it is thus disqualified as "a serious contender for the current mantle of liberalism."[23] On this account, while liberalism contains no ineliminable transhistorical essence, a specific thread nevertheless expresses its most mature "established" form. Freeden's explicit anti-essentialism is thus qualified by prescriptive boundary-working methodological commitments. His general approach nevertheless points to a fruitful interpretive strategy. A comprehensive contextualist analysis of liberalism should provide a framework for grasping the diverse ways in which liberal languages emerge, evolve, and come into conflict with one another, rather than trying to distil an ahistorical set of liberal commitments from conceptual or canonical investigation.

A Summative Conception

Thomas Nagel is surely right to proclaim that "[i]t is a significant fact about our age that most political argument in the Western world now goes on between different branches of [the liberal] tradition."[24] This ideological victory is acknowledged by both self-proclaimed liberals and their critics. At the turn of the new millennium, Perry Anderson protested that "for the first time since the Reformation there are no longer any significant oppositions—that is, systematic rival outlooks—within the thought-world of the West: and scarcely any on a world scale." Writing more in sorrow than celebration, Raymond Geuss concurs: "We know of no other approach to human society that is at the same time as theoretically rich and comprehensive as liberalism and also even as remotely acceptable to wide sections of the population in Western societies."[25] Most inhabitants of the West are now *conscripts of liberalism*: the scope of the tradition has expanded to encompass the vast majority of politi-

---

[23] Freeden, *Ideologies and Political Theory* (Oxford, 1996), 227ff., 276, 278.

[24] Nagel, "Rawls and Liberalism," in *The Cambridge Companion to Rawls*, ed. Samuel Freeman (Cambridge, 2003), 62.

[25] Anderson, "Renewals," *New Left Review*, 1 (2000), 13; Geuss, "Liberalism and Its Discontents," *Political Theory*, 30 (2002), 320.

cal positions regarded as legitimate.[26] Today there is little that stands outside
the discursive embrace of liberalism in mainstream Anglo-American political
debate (and perhaps especially in academic political theory), and most who
identify themselves as socialists, conservatives, social democrats, republicans,
greens, feminists, and anarchists have been ideologically incorporated,
whether they like it or not. Useful as they are for other tasks, stipulative and
canonical protocols offer little help in interpreting this phenomenon. We thus
need a comprehensive account that can accommodate the plurality of actually
existing liberalisms, past and present, without smuggling in boundary-working
prescriptive commitments. A plausible explanation, meanwhile, must unpack
the dynamics of ideological conscription. This section introduces a comprehensive heuristic, while the remainder of the essay begins the task of explain-
ing how the meaning of Anglo-American liberalism was transformed between
1850 and 1950.

I propose the following definition (for comprehensive purposes): the liberal tradition is constituted by the sum of the arguments that have been classified as liberal, and recognized as such by other self-proclaimed liberals, across
time and space. Let us call this the *summative conception*. Adopting it offers
several benefits: it can help make sense of the discursive "overextension" and
elastic usage of the term, while avoiding unhelpful claims about pure essence
or authentic form. Moreover, it forces us to examine traditions as evolving
and contested historical phenomena, conjured into existence by the work of
many hands, shaped by scholarly knowledge-production and pedagogical regimes, and often fashioned and remade with specific politico-intellectual purposes in mind. It allows us to grasp, that is, the intricate dialectic of inten-
tional human action and unintended consequences that structure any rich
political tradition.[27]

Freeden, as we have seen, points us towards "that semantic field in which
the political understandings of people who regard themselves as liberals, or
who others regard as liberals, may be investigated." However, it is necessary to
qualify the claim about those "who others regard as liberals."[28] The problem
here is that the term is commonly used to tar opponents or to create linkages
between liberalism and political positions that liberals invariably reject. Witness the current fashion for American ultra-conservatives to conflate liberalism with both fascism and Marxism.[29] If we adopt an unqualified summative
position—defining liberalism as the totality of positions termed liberal—
then the tradition would now traverse the spectrum from fascism to commu-

---

[26] For a parallel usage to which I am indebted, see David Scott, *Conscripts of Modernity* (Durham, NC, 2004).

[27] Note that a comprehensive account is not suitable for constructing a coherent normative
political theory.

[28] Freeden, *Liberal Languages*, 20.

[29] For an example of the absurd genre, see Jonah Goldberg, *Liberal Fascism* (London, 2007).

nism. This is an implausibly expansive view. Hence the epistemic limit: only those positions *affirmed* at some point in time by groups of *self-proclaimed* liberals should be included. This allows us to map the universe of liberalism(s), though it raises another question: how widely held must a particular interpretation be for inclusion? Can any usage (by a self-proclaimed liberal) expand the boundaries of liberalism? There is no simple answer to this threshold question—scholars will adopt different inclusion criteria depending on their purposes and methodological inclinations. My own view is that to stake a claim for inclusion there must be sustained usage by numerous prominent ideological entrepreneurs over at least two generations. Otherwise, the bar for inclusion is set too low. That H. G. Wells declared himself a "liberal fascist" is nowhere near enough to warrant incorporating fascism into the liberal tradition, for barely anyone else followed him along that idiosyncratic path.[30] But contra Freeden and others, "libertarianism" clearly meets the entry criteria. So too do the social democratic arguments scorned by libertarians.

The temporal point is also important: I am not suggesting that only arguments labeled (and recognized) as liberal at Time T1 count as liberal. An argument is not expelled from the liberal tradition because it is later ascribed a different label or because liberals now happen to reject it. The tradition is constituted by the accumulation of arguments *over time*. Explicit justifications of imperialism, arguments seeking to limit suffrage on grounds of gender and racial difference, and eugenicist attempts to "perfect" the species all form part of the liberal tradition.[31] As do rejections of these positions. Rather than attempting to sanitize or inoculate liberalism by ignoring aspects no longer considered palatable, or, more subtly, relegating those aspects to superseded historical circumstances while extracting a pristine transhistorical core, we should recognize that liberalism has become a hyper-inflated, multifaceted body of thought—a deep reservoir of ideological contradictions.

In thinking about traditions, it is productive to distinguish between the identities of agents and the arguments they invoke—between being an X (liberal, socialist, fascist) and employing forms of argument that are best characterized as X. The former is a claim about self-fashioning and the construction of personae, the latter about doctrine. Although this chapter has focused on academic debates, the argument also applies to practical politics. It may well

[30] P. Coupland, "H. G. Wells' 'Liberal Fascism,'" *Journal of Contemporary History*, 35 (2000), 541–58. Goldberg uses this example to reach the opposite conclusion. Wells was suggesting that it was necessary to use methods learned from fascism to realize liberal ends.

[31] One objection to this argument is that some liberal ideas/values/commitments (e.g., the normative priority of liberty) are more central to the tradition than others. I agree with this as an empirical claim. But on my view it is neither a conceptual nor a normative necessity that all possible legitimate liberalisms will contain those ideas/values/commitments. We can imagine future iterations with a different core. Thus the centrality of, e.g., liberty is a historically contingent feature of liberalism.

being a liberal w/o acknowledging it 72

be part of the self-understanding of an American Tea Party devotee that they are fundamentally opposed to liberalism, but this identity-claim does not entail that they reject arguments central to the liberal tradition (as construed by the summative conception). In other words, despite espousing virulent strains of antiliberalism they are nevertheless committed to paradigmatic liberal positions insofar as they defend (say) neoclassical economics, libertarian social policy, and the superiority of "liberal democratic" institutions. Within political theory, the same can be said for many self-proclaimed critics of liberalism, whether post-structural, critical-theoretical, republican, communitarian, or conservative.

Another consequence of adopting the summative conception is that it dissolves a familiar but misleading picture of traditions, which are still often conceived of as self-contained bodies of thought with relatively clear and stable boundaries.[32] On this view, the interstitial spaces between established traditions are populated by hybrids—liberal-socialists, liberal-conservatives, Christian-realists. However, this fails to grasp the ideological miasma of modern politics, in which most individuals simultaneously adopt positions that are claimed by assorted traditions. The most hardened Tory or Republican, contemptuous of moderate "liberal-conservatives," is likely to propound ideas that have long been affirmed by mainstream liberals. When looking at an agent who has been classified in two or more ways—say as a liberal and a conservative—this could mean several different things. It might imply that one of the classifications is mistaken, or that they adopt a hybrid position, or alternatively that decomposing the argument will yield some elements that are genuinely "liberal" and others that are genuinely "conservative." The main problem with these options, however, is that today it is impossible to convincingly classify values (such as liberty or equality) or public policies (such as free trade or democracy promotion) as *exclusively* liberal *or* conservative (or something else). They are—they have become—both at once.[33]

The scholarly implications of tradition-construction can be significant, as the work of Domenico Losurdo demonstrates. His remarkable "counterhistory" of liberalism places considerable emphasis on the social practices characteristic of British, Dutch, and American societies.[34] He contends that the British slave trade peaked in the eighteenth century, well after liberalism was consolidated by the settlement of 1688, and that in North America chattel slavery reached its apogee in the early nineteenth century, following the victory of liberalism in the War of Independence. John Locke figures heavily in

---

[32] For prominent examples, see Sherri Berman, *The Primacy of Politics* (Cambridge, 2006); Rogers Smith, *Civic Ideals* (London, 2007).

[33] It follows that those values/policies are also now part of the conservative tradition (and hypothetically others too).

[34] Losurdo, *Liberalism*, trans. Gregory Elliott (London, 2011). Losurdo mixes canonical and expressive protocols.

both narratives. If we adopt the current conventional understanding of liberalism, as Losurdo does, this throws up a disturbing puzzle about liberal attitudes to domination, hierarchy, and exploitation, and it underpins his sweeping critique. The normative conclusions that Losurdo draws about contemporary liberalism are derived from, and are only intelligible in relation to, his interpretation of the tradition. But the puzzle dissolves if we adopt (for example) a Pocockian interpretation, because on that account neither Britain nor the United States was liberal in any meaningful sense before the nineteenth century.[35] Interpretations of tradition often shape contemporary understanding as well as historical investigation.

Liberalism before Locke

At the turn of the twentieth century, the dominant prescriptive narrative about liberalism in the English-speaking world identified it as a product of the late eighteenth and early nineteenth centuries, part of a cluster of ideological innovations that also included socialism. At the turn of the twenty-first century, the dominant narrative views it as a product of the mid-seventeenth century or earlier. In the former, the French and American Revolutions and the global spread of capitalism play a starring role; in the latter, the Glorious Revolution of 1688 and the religious wars in Europe. In the former, utility, democracy, and political economy are the guiding topics; in the later, natural rights, the social contract, and constitutionalism. In the former, radicals like Jeremy Bentham take center stage; in the latter it is almost invariably John Locke. Indeed Locke's foundational role in liberalism is today a leitmotif of political thought, promulgated by critics and adherents alike. "To the extent that modern liberalism can be said to be inspired by any one writer," Wolin counseled in *Politics and Vision*, "Locke is undoubtedly the leading candidate." Stephen Holmes agrees: "The best place to begin, if we wish to cut to the core of liberalism, is with Locke."[36] The transition from one conception to the other tells us much about the trajectory of modern politics, the sociology of knowledge, and the historicity of theoretical categories.

In his compelling account of American political thought, John Gunnell argues that liberalism only became a widely recognized category of general political discourse after the First World War, and only assumed an important role in academic political theory in the wake of the Second World War. More-

---

[35] On the problems with characterizing the nineteenth-century United States as liberal, see Daniel Rodgers, "The Traditions of Liberalism," in *Questions of Tradition*, ed. Mark Salber Phillips and Gordon Schochet (Toronto, 2004), 203–33.

[36] Wolin, *Politics and Vision*, 263; Holmes, *Passions and Constraint* (Chicago, 1995), 15. Rawls's "speculative" history traces liberalism to the Reformation and the sixteenth-century religious wars (*Lectures*, 11).

over, he contends that "it was not until after 1950 that there was even any extended discussion of Locke as a liberal."[37] Adding a British dimension to the
story complicates this picture. Both the conception of liberalism as a tradition
rooted in early modern political thought, and the identification of Locke as a
foundational liberal, emerged slightly earlier in Britain than in the United
States, and for different reasons. Yet despite this initial variation, British and
American narratives converged during the ideological battles of the middle
decades of the twentieth century, creating the expansive vision of liberalism
that dominates scholarly discourse today.

While the term "liberal" had long been used in English to denote assorted
aristocratic dispositions, mores, and pursuits, it only assumed a specifically
political meaning in the early nineteenth century. Borrowed from the Spanish
Liberales of the 1812 Constitution, the term was first employed in a deroga-
tory manner by Tories to malign their Whig opponents. During the 1820s it
was reclaimed by some radical Whigs, in a classical example of rhetorical rede-
scription, to characterize individuals and policies dedicated to nonrevolution-
ary reform, although it also became associated with the small but vocal group
of "philosophic radicals," including the young John Stuart Mill. "Liberal" was
increasingly utilized to describe the politico-economic demands of the emergent middle classes.[38] Yet it was still an obscure and marginal category: during
the 1820s and 1830s " 'liberals' were not a firmly defined group and 'liberalism' did not securely mark out a single intellectual phenomenon."[39] It was
only during the second half of the century that usage proliferated, though it
remained closely tied to the creed of the recently named Liberal Party.[40]

Despite its increasing visibility, there was little sophisticated or thorough
discussion of liberalism as an intellectual tradition until the early twentieth
century, and even then it was rare. It is barely visible in surveys of political
thought written between the 1850s and the 1930s.[41] The main political the-

---

[37] Gunnell, "The Archaeology of American Liberalism," *Journal of Political Ideologies*, 6 (2001),
131; Gunnell, *Imagining the American Polity* (Philadelphia, 2004), 183–219.

[38] Jörn Leonhard, "From European Liberalism to the Languages of Liberalisms," *Redescriptions*,
8 (2004), 17–51.

[39] D. M. Craig, "The Origins of 'Liberalism' in Britain," *Historical Research*, 85 (2012), 482. Cf.
Daisy Hay, "Liberals, *Liberales* and *The Liberal*," *European Romantic Review*, 19 (2008), 307–20.
For the European context, see Maurizio Isabella, *Risorgimento in Exile* (Oxford, 2009).

[40] The Liberal Party was created from a fissile coalition of Whigs, free-trading Tories, and Radicals. The name was first used officially in 1868, but it had been a common designation since the
1850s.

[41] See, for example, Frederick Pollock, *An Introduction to the History of the Science of Politics*
(London, 1890); William Graham, *English Political Philosophy from Hobbes to Maine* (London,
1899); Ernest Barker, *Political Thought in England from Herbert Spencer to the Present Day* (London, 1915); W. L. Davidson, *Political Thought in England from Bentham to J. S. Mill* (London,
1915); Ivor Brown, *English Political Theory* (London, 1920); Robert Murray, *The History of Political Science from Plato to the Present* (Cambridge, 1926); Lewis Rockow, *Contemporary Political
Thought in England* (London, 1925); C. E. Vaughan, *Studies in the History of Political Philosophy*, 2

ory textbook employed in Cambridge and Oxford in the late nineteenth century, Bluntschli's *The Theory of the State*, didn't use liberalism as an organizing category, and nor did Sidgwick's *Development of European Polity*, which replaced it in Cambridge. The effort to construct an authoritative liberal tradition only gained ground during the perceived "crisis of liberalism" in the Edwardian era. Fighting acrimonious battles over the future of the British state, and challenged by an emergent politically conscious labor movement, some liberals elaborated edifying genealogies to underwrite the ideological legitimacy of their cause. The most common renditions of the tradition identified the transition from the eighteenth to the nineteenth century as the formative moment. W. Lyon Blease's *Short History of English Liberalism*, published in 1913, was typical. A polemical defense of advanced liberalism written by a legal scholar, it argues that liberalism was the product of three revolutions: the industrial (starting in the 1760s), American, and French.[42]

Accounts that emphasized the Revolutionary-era origins of liberalism, defined it prescriptively as expressing a commitment to both liberty and social equality (sometimes even democracy). This move excluded earlier Whig political thought. It was a constellation of ideas that could only have emerged after the tumult of the late eighteenth century and the rise of a powerful middle class demanding political representation. In 1862, in one of the earliest analytical accounts of liberalism, James Fitzjames Stephen pinpointed the connection:

> As generally used . . . "liberal" and "liberalism" . . . denote in politics, and to some extent in literature and philosophy, the party which wishes to alter existing institutions with the view of increasing popular power. In short, they are not greatly remote in meaning from the words "democracy" and "democratic."[43]

Forty years later, William Dunning, a prominent American historian and political theorist, argued that "fundamentally, nineteenth-century Liberalism meant democracy."[44] In an essay seeking to illuminate the "Historic Bases of Liberalism," another writer distinguished liberals from Whigs by pointing to the aristocratic character and consequences of 1688. "In none of the great documents of the time," he announced, "do you find the suggestion that the people should share in the work of government," for such a conception only emerged in the wake of the French Revolution. It followed that liberalism

---

vols. (Manchester, 1925). Harold Laski was an exception, identifying liberalism as an economic ideology produced by the Industrial Revolution, though with philosophical roots in the seventeenth century. *Political Thought in England from Locke to Bentham* (London, 1920), ch. 7.

[42] Blease, *Short History of English Liberalism* (London, 1913). Blease taught law at the University of Liverpool.

[43] Stephen, "Liberalism," *Cornhill Magazine*, 5 (1862), 72–73. See also Leonard Hobhouse, *Democracy and Reaction* (London, 1904), 166.

[44] Dunning, "A Century of Politics," *North American Review*, 179/577 (1904), 803.

could only be a product of the late eighteenth century.[45] This view only began to lose popularity in the interwar years, though it did not disappear completely. In a textbook published in 1920, for example, the author declared that the "essence of Whiggism has always been the belief in individual liberty combined with the denial of social equality" and that as such "this conception is rejected by Liberals who have a far wider experience on which to frame their social judgments."[46] Other variants of the prescriptive protocol can also be discerned, including one that reduced liberalism to a species of utilitarian radicalism. Thus, A. V. Dicey wrote in 1905 of "Benthamite individualism, which, in accordance with popular phraseology, may often be called conveniently liberalism."[47]

It is both striking and symptomatic that in Britain, so often seen as the incubator of liberalism, Locke was not widely regarded as a liberal—let alone a paradigmatic one—until nearly a century after liberalism emerged as an explicit political doctrine. Several generations of self-identified liberals somehow failed to recognize him as one of their own. While Locke's nineteenth-century biographers celebrated him as one of the greatest of philosophers, their verdicts on his political writings were far less positive. Acknowledging him as a leading Whig ideologue who exerted a major influence over eighteenth-century political thinking, they almost invariably rejected his theoretical arguments as defective and obsolete.[48] In so doing they painted a microcosmic picture of his general reputation during the Victorian age: "Locke meant the *Essay*," not the *Treatises*.[49]

Most accounts of the historical development of modern political thought contended that there had been a radical break—both intellectual and politi-

---

[45] P. J. Macdonell, "Historic Bases of Liberalism," in *Essays in Liberalism* (London, 1897), 220. Hillaire Belloc also discussed the liberal tradition entirely in nineteenth-century terms ("The Liberal Tradition," 1–30).

[46] Brown, *English Political Theory*, 66. "Locke had striven hard and striven successfully for more freedom, but he had never striven hard for more equality" (66). On continuities between Whigs and Victorian liberals, see John Burrow, *Whigs and Liberals* (Oxford, 1988).

[47] Dicey, *Lectures on the Relation between Law and Public Opinion in England during the Nineteenth Century* [1914], 2nd ed., ed. Richard VandeWetering (Indianapolis, 2008), 67. The radical Whig Charles James Fox was occasionally identified as a founding father of liberalism. See A. C. Forster Boulton, "Liberalism and Empire," *Westminster Review* (1899), 486–91; N. W. Sibley, "Edmund Burke," *Westminster Review* (1897), 509; Macdonell, "Historic Bases," 226–27. Thanks to Emily Jones for discussion on this point. Jones argues that conservatism was likewise crafted as a distinctive, coherent political philosophy (with Burke at the core) during the late Victorian and Edwardian years: Jones, "Conservatism, Edmund Burke, and the Invention of a Political Tradition, c. 1885–1914," *Historical Journal*, 58 (2015), 1115–39.

[48] Lord King, *The Life of John Locke* (London, 1830); H. R. Fox-Bourne, *The Life of John Locke*, vol. 2 (London, 1876), 524–40; Thomas Fowler, *Locke* (London, 1880); A. Campbell Fraser, *Locke* (Edinburgh, 1890); Samuel Alexander, *Locke* (London, 1908).

[49] Hans Aarsleff, "Locke's Influence," in *The Cambridge Companion to Locke*, ed. Vere Chappell (Cambridge, 1997), 278. His writings on toleration were also well-known though they rarely fed into accounts.

cal—at the end of the eighteenth century. A new world had dawned, and there was little space in it for Lockean political theory. Liberalism was figured as the progeny of this gestalt switch. The historicist sensibility that permeated nineteenth-century social and political thought was antithetical to the rationalist deductions of Locke, and accounts of natural rights, natural law, and above all the social contract were widely denigrated as primitive. The eminent legal scholar Frederick Pollock was reiterating a popular line of argument when he claimed that Hume had shown decisively that "even as analysis the mere doctrine is useless." He concluded that Burke had been right to ridicule the contract as "absurd."[50] Henry Craik, a writer who later served as MP for the Combined Scottish Universities, used a more colorful insult, scorning it as "the veriest figment of pedantic theorizing that any mystified scholastic ever dreamed."[51] Another common response was to historically relativize Locke's work, viewing him as a man of (and trapped in) his time. Thus the idealist philosopher W. R. Sorley loftily declared that despite the palpable weakness of Locke's political theory, "it served its purpose as a justification of the revolution settlement in accordance with the ideas of the time."[52] Many also questioned Locke's originality, suggesting that his main political ideas were derived from others, above all Hooker. As G. P. Gooch wrote in his influential account of seventeenth-century democratic thought, "there is little in Locke that he did not find in the thinkers of the Interregnum."[53] These lines of criticism were synthesized in the first monograph on Locke's political philosophy (originally a doctoral dissertation at Columbia supervised by John Dewey): "His moral and political philosophy may well be viewed as the summation of the best thought of the seventeenth century. Though he added few ideas of his own and developed the old ideas he took from others, he is rather the ripe fulfilment of the past than the herald of the future." The author concluded that "Locke's theory of political society is decidedly weak" and offered little to contemporary political theory.[54] Locke spoke from and about a lost world.

[50] Pollock, "The Social Contract in Hobbes and Locke," *Journal of the Society of Comparative Legislation* (1907), reprinted in Pollock, *Essays in the Law* (London, 1922), 109. See also his "Locke's Theory of the State" (1904), 80–102. Pollock was unusual in suggesting that Locke envisaged the contract as hypothetical. For an example of the conventional criticism—that the contract was an (absurd) empirical claim about human history—see Edwin Wallace, "John Locke," *Westminster Review*, 107 (1877), 193.

[51] Henry Craik, "John Locke," *Quarterly Review*, 169 (1889), 490.

[52] Sorley, "John Locke," in *The Cambridge History of English Literature*, ed. Adolphus William Ward and Alfred Rayney Waller (Cambridge, 1912), 8:390. Sorely succeeded Sidgwick as the Knightbridge Professor of Philosophy at Cambridge, a post he held until 1933.

[53] Gooch, *The History of English Democratic Ideas in the Seventeenth Century* (Cambridge, 1898), 358. Gooch did not connect Locke with liberalism, though he suggested that Locke's account of self-ownership provided the theoretical basis for socialism (358).

[54] Sterling Lamprecht, *The Moral and Political Philosophy of John Locke* (New York, 1918), 6, 150–51. Representative of Locke's changing designation, Lamprecht characterized him as a "Whig and a liberal."

Nineteenth-century philosophers rarely saw Locke as a liberal or written positively about his political theory. John Stuart Mill's assessment is indicative. In the *System of Logic* he praised Locke as "that truly original genius" and a hugely talented "metaphysician," yet in the vast corpus of Mill's work there are only a handful of references to Locke's political writings.[55] His only sustained discussion is in a book review, wherein Mill follows custom in disparaging social contract theories and inalienable rights, while conceding that their proponents rightly identified the importance of limitations on government. "This is the truth," Mill notes, "which was dimly shadowed forth, in howsoever rude and unskilful a manner, in the theories of the social compact and the rights of man."[56] *On Liberty* contains one passing reference to Locke, while James Fitzjames Stephen's powerful riposte, *Liberty, Equality, Fraternity*, didn't mention him at all.[57] Elsewhere, Stephen belittled Locke as confused and outmoded. The *Second Treatise*, he argued,

> ... was in its day extremely popular, and its practical effects were no doubt great, as it furnished people with the best and most accessible popular justification for the Revolution of 1688. It would be difficult, however, to find a better illustration of the fact that we have travelled a very long road since Locke's time, and have carried the metaphysical principles of which he perceived certain aspects, to consequences which have made his political speculations appear altogether superannuated and bygone.

His conclusion was equally damning: it was worth studying once popular books "to consider the reasons why they now fall so flatly among us."[58]

Herbert Spencer was probably the most widely read English-language philosopher of the age. Across his voluminous output, Locke made only a handful of appearances, and in what he considered his finest work, *The Principles of Ethics*, Locke's theory of property was casually dismissed as "unsatisfactory."[59] T. H. Green, the leading philosophical light of the final quarter of the century, shared Mill's deep skepticism about the foundations of early modern political thought, and while he expended considerable energy grappling with Locke's epistemological writings—"at once so plausible and so hollow"—he

---

[55] Mill, *System of Logic* (1843), *Collected Works*, vol. 7, ed. John Robson (Toronto, 1974), 29, 305.

[56] Mill, "Use and Abuse of Political Terms," *Collected Works*, 18:11. In the book under discussion, George Cornewall Lewis's *Remarks on the Use and Abuse of Some Political Terms* (1832), "liberalism" is absent and Locke's views are ridiculed.

[57] Mill, *On Liberty* [1859], *Collected Works*, vol. 18; Stephen, *Liberty, Equality, Fraternity*.

[58] Stephen, "Locke on Government" (1867), *Horae Sabbaticae*, vol. 2 (London, 1892), 142.

[59] Spencer, *The Principles of Ethics*, vol. 2, [1897] (Indianapolis, 1978), 111–12. Locke warrants a few brief mentions in Spencer's earlier *Social Statics* (London, 1851). In the earlier published version of this chapter, I overlooked these earlier mentions, though they do not change the general point.

barely mentioned his political views. Dismissive of the state of nature, pre-political rights, and contractualism, Green ultimately rejected Locke's arguments as incoherent and he never viewed him as a fellow (or proto) liberal.[60] Nor did Henry Sidgwick, who characterized Locke as a philosophically misguided Whig ideologue.[61] In the Edwardian era, Graham Wallas added a post-Darwinian twist to the story by arguing that Locke's "plea for a government which should consciously realize the purposes of God" was one of many philosophical utopias rendered irrelevant by modern science.[62]

The same pattern of omission, disavowal, and scorn emerges if we turn from political theory to historical scholarship. In Leslie Stephen's important *History of English Thought in the Eighteenth Century* Locke's ideas were relegated to an archaic past. In relativizing mode, he termed Locke's arguments a "formal apology of Whiggism" and grudgingly admitted that they "did well enough for the quiet time of the eighteenth century." They were then comprehensively superseded: "That authority vanished when the French Revolution brought deeper questions for solution, and new methods became necessary in politics as in all other speculation."[63] Published during the same decade, J. R. Green's hugely popular history of England classified Locke as a Whig philosopher of 1688 before noting that the social contract had long since been regarded as obsolete.[64] Venerated throughout Europe for his prodigious erudition, Lord Acton acknowledged that Locke had been a significant historical actor while assailing the quality of his political theory: "always reasonable and sensible, but diluted and pedestrian and poor."[65] While Acton clearly regarded Locke as a notable member of the "Party of Liberty," he didn't think of him as a member of the party of liberalism. In the seminal multi-volume *Cambridge Modern History*, planned by Acton before his untimely death, Locke was again credited as an influential Whig apologist, albeit one whose political

---

[60] Green, "Introduction to Hume's Treatise of Human Nature" [1874], in *Collected Works of T. H. Green* (Bristol, 1997), 1:13; Green, *Lectures on the Principles of Political Obligation* [1886] (Bristol, 1997), 375. D. G. Ritchie was a partial exception. In the *Principles of State Interference* (London, 1891), he linked English empiricism with liberalism, and praised the continuing political relevance of Locke's writings, though he derided their philosophical value (138, 128), while in his *Natural Rights* (London, 1895), Locke was characterized as both an ideologue of 1688 and an early liberal (6, 239, 175, 186).

[61] Sidgwick, *The Development of European Polity* (London, 1903), 364–67, 417–18. Locke is largely absent from Sidgwick's *Methods of Ethics* (1874), *Principles of Political Economy* (1873), or *The Elements of Politics* (1891).

[62] Wallas, *Human Nature in Politics*, 3rd ed. (London, 1909), 178.

[63] Stephen, *History of English Thought in the Eighteenth Century*, vol. 2 (London, 1876), 150, 135. However, he later acknowledged that Locke had unwittingly laid the foundations for Bentham's radicalism: "Locke, John (1632–1704)," in *The Dictionary of National Biography* (London, 1893), 34:32.

[64] Green, *A Short History of the English People* [1874] (London, 1878), 601–2.

[65] Acton, *Lectures on Modern History*, ed. John Figgis and Reginald Laurence (London, 1906), 217.

ideas "had already been better expressed by Sidney."[66] The great F. W. Maitland likewise held a low opinion of Locke, cataloguing the many "grave faults"
of his arguments, above all a literal belief in the historical reality of the social
contract.[67] Across the Atlantic, Locke's reputation was barely higher. The standard history of political thought textbook, for example, presented a damning
account of his "illogical, incoherent system of political philosophy."[68]

Widespread skepticism about the quality and relevance of Lockean political thought was fortified by the historicist "comparative method," which did
so much to shape scholarship during the late nineteenth century.[69] Its proponents, the most influential of whom was Henry Maine, challenged deductive
models of politics and sought to root the origins and development of cus-
toms, language, social structures, and legal forms, in long-term historical-
evolutionary processes. Antipathetic to early modern natural law and utilitarianism alike, it provided yet another weapon to attack the political thinking of
the seventeenth and eighteenth centuries. It exercised a profound influence
on historical scholarship and the emerging social sciences—perhaps especially
political science—on both sides of the Atlantic.[70] In the *locus classicus* of comparativism, Maine's *Ancient Law*, Locke made a fleeting appearance as one of
the many thinkers whose ideas about the state of nature and the origins of law
were fundamentally mistaken.[71] For J. R. Seeley, the leading ideologue of the
late-Victorian empire, Locke's political thinking was simply too ahistorical to
be of value, while he didn't even warrant a mention in E. A. Freeman's *Comparative Politics*, the first book to apply the method to the development of
political institutions across time and space.[72]

Teaching in the elite English universities reflected both Locke's prominence as a "metaphysician" and his meager reputation as a political thinker. At
Oxford in the 1870s the *Essay*, though not the *Treatises* or *Letter*, was a com-

---

[66] Arthur Lionel Smith, "English Political Philosophy in the Seventeenth and Eighteenth Centuries," in *The Cambridge Modern History*, ed. Adolphus Ward, George Prothero, and Stanley
Leathes (Cambridge, 1909), 6:805, 787.

[67] Maitland, *A Historical Sketch of Liberty and Equality* (Indianapolis, 2000), 42, 52. Written
in 1875, it was only published in 1911. In his *Constitutional History of England* (Cambridge,
1908), Locke appeared very briefly as "that excellent Whig" (290).

[68] Dunning, *A History of Political Theories from Luther to Montesquieu* (London, 1905), 368.

[69] On the comparative method, see Collini, Winch, and Burrow, *That Noble Science of Politics*,
ch. 7; Sandra den Otter, "The Origins of a Historical Political Science in Late Victorian and Edwardian Britain," in *Modern Political Science*, ed. Robert Adcock, Mark Bevir, and Shannon Stimson (Princeton, 2007), 37–66.

[70] Robert Adcock, *Liberalism and the Emergence of American Political Science* (Oxford, 2014),
ch. 5; James Farr, "The Historical Science(s) of Politics," in *Modern Political Science*, ed. Adcock,
Bevir, and Stimson, 66–96; and chapter 13 in this volume.

[71] Maine, *Ancient Law* [1861] (London, 1908), 101.

[72] Seeley, *Introduction to Political Science* [1891], ed. Henry Sidgwick (London, 1919), 28;
Freeman, *Comparative Politics* (London, 1873).

pulsory text in moral and political philosophy.[73] In Ritchie's appraisal of the political science curriculum in 1891, the key authors are listed as Aristotle, Hobbes, Bluntschli, Maine, and Mill.[74] At Cambridge, William Paley's *Principles of Moral and Political Philosophy* (1785) was the standard text during the first half of the nineteenth century. While Paley briefly paid lip service to Locke's historical importance, he ignored his arguments and rejected the social contract on utilitarian grounds. Locke's fortunes didn't improve during the closing decades of the century. When Henry Sidgwick surveyed the subject in the mid-1870s, Locke failed to make the list of set authors in political philosophy, though students were expected to be familiar with Plato, Aristotle, Cicero, Hobbes, Clarke, Shaftesbury, Butler, Smith, Hume, Kant, Paley, Bentham, Whewell, Mill, and Grote.[75] The History Tripos paper in "Political Philosophy and General Jurisprudence" followed a familiar pattern. In 1875, for example, Aristotle, Guizot, Tocqueville, Mill, Gibbon, Blackstone, Austin, and Maine, but not Locke, were listed.[76]

Given Locke's tarnished reputation at the time, what are we to make of his current status as the ur-liberal? One possible answer is that it is based on a mistake—that Locke simply wasn't a liberal.[77] Another response is to insist that we have now corrected the error of earlier thinkers who failed to recognize Locke's liberalism. In other words, he had either always been a liberal or he was never one. Both positions are defensible: it is possible to extract conflicting meanings from Locke's work. But I suggest an alternative answer: Locke *became* a liberal during the twentieth century. As part of a process of *retrojection* his body of work—or at least some stylized arguments stripped from it—was posthumously conscripted to an expansive new conception of the liberal tradition.

Wars of Position: Consolidating Liberalism

The Lockean narrative was consolidated in Britain and the United States between the 1930s and the 1950s, as liberalism was reconfigured as the ideological other of "totalitarian" ideologies, left and right.[78] This was achieved

ideological other

---

[73] Mark Pattison, "Philosophy at Oxford," *Mind*, 1 (1876), 91.

[74] Ritchie, "The Teaching of Political Science at Oxford," *Annals of the American Academy of Political and Social Science*, 2 (1891), 88.

[75] Sidgwick, "Philosophy at Cambridge," *Mind*, 1 (1876), 235–46.

[76] Jean McLachlan, "The Origin and Early Development of the Cambridge Historical Tripos," *American Historical Review*, 9 (1947), 99.

[77] J.G.A. Pocock, "The Myth of John Locke and the Obsession with Liberalism," in *John Locke*, ed. Richard Ashcraft and J.G.A. Pocock (Los Angeles, 1980); Goldie, "Introduction."

[78] There is a huge literature on totalitarianism. For the most comprehensive survey of the term, see Abbott Gleason, *Totalitarianism* (Oxford, 1997).

through two key discursive moves and across two main chronological phases. The first move deepened the retrojective extension of the liberal tradition that had already begun in both Britain and the United States. The early modern account moved from being a minority report to the dominant narrative. The second development was, if anything, even more significant: the emergence and proliferation of the idea of "liberal democracy." As representative forms of political order came under sustained fire, intellectuals propagated an all-encompassing narrative that simultaneously pushed the historical origins of liberalism back in time while vastly expanding its spatial reach. For the first time, it was widely presented as either the most authentic ideological tradition of the West (a pre-1945 storyline) or its constitutive ideology (a view popular after 1945). This story began to coalesce during the 1930s, in a context of radical anxiety about the fate of liberalism. This was an era where, as Mussolini proclaimed, "all the political experiments of our day are anti-liberal."[79] Liberals and their critics fought an ideological war of position, attempting to delineate the true, prescriptive meaning of liberalism. The narrative was cemented in the more complacent postwar intellectual milieu as scholars from across the political spectrum, and from assorted academic disciplines, converged on this new all-encompassing narrative, even as they proffered radically different explanations and normative evaluations of it. Strauss, Laski, Macpherson, Hartz, and Wolin, among others, helped to fabricate the new ideological structure. Though rarely acknowledged or analyzed, the transformation of liberalism did not go completely unnoticed. In a lecture delivered in 1960, Eric Voegelin observed that "in the course of the last 30 years the image of what liberalism is has changed completely."[80] Wittingly or not, we are the heirs of this ideological labor.

The main conceptual shift that underpinned the emergence and popularization of the Lockean narrative in Britain was the conscription of Whig constitutionalism into a newly expansive vision of liberalism. This move was captured by de Ruggiero in 1933: "The ambitious designs of the radicals, curbed by the tenacious forces of tradition, fused with the older Whiggism to form a composite liberalism in which the old and the new were gradually integrated and harmonized."[81] Contra Ruggiero, however, this discursive "fusion" was largely a product of the twentieth century. Consequently, liberalism came to be viewed through a wide-angle lens, as a politico-intellectual tradition centered on individual freedom in the context of constitutional government. This expansion in ideological scope was also facilitated by shifts in the philosophical current. The eclipse of idealism in the early twentieth century, as well

[79] Mussolini, *Fascism* (1935), cited in Ira Katznelson, *Desolation and Enlightenment* (New York, 2003), 23.

[80] Voegelin, "Liberalism and Its History," *Review of Politics*, 36 (1974), 504–5.

[81] De Ruggiero, "Liberalism," in *Encyclopedia of the Social Sciences*, ed. E. R. Seligman (London, 1933), 11:438.

as powerful challenges to utilitarianism, helped to create an intellectual environment more conducive to natural rights arguments and contracturalism.
Locke, the arch-Whig, was recast—by default as much as design—as a seminal liberal thinker and a source of inspiration for an individualist account of
political life.

This retrojective process began in earnest during the Edwardian years.
Hobhouse's *Liberalism*, arguably the most popular and sophisticated discussion of liberal political theory published during the first half of the century,
played an important role in establishing the lineaments of the (new) Lockean
tradition.[82] He posited the emergence of liberalism as coeval with the development of the early modern English state. In its original Whig iteration—a
theory of the "Natural Order" centered on inalienable prepolitical rights and
the restraint of government—it embodied a "negative" form of constitutionalism that sought to eliminate obstacles to human progress. "It finds humanity oppressed, and would set it free." But, Hobhouse continued, the underlying theoretical architecture was fundamentally flawed, and only during the
nineteenth century was a positive dimension added, first by utilitarians and
more recently by "new liberals."[83] Thus Hobhouse presented the Whigs as pioneer liberals, albeit now superseded. In addition to providing fellow liberal
reformers with a powerful constitutionalist genealogy, he had another motive
for stretching the discursive boundaries of liberalism, as he was engaged in the
attempt to craft a liberal socialist politics to replace the desiccated "old liberalism" of the "Manchester School" and the Benthamites.[84] Yet this Lockean narrative, a precursor of things to come, remained marginal until the 1930s, and
scholarly and popular discussions of liberalism were most commonly tied to
the quotidian concerns of the often-embattled Liberal Party.[85] When R. G.
Collingwood wrote the translator's preface for Ruggiero's *History of European
Liberalism* in 1927, he still felt it necessary to inform his audience that the
book addressed liberalism in the "continental" not the "British" sense, as a
"name for <u>principles of constitutional liberty and representative government</u>,"
rather than a party ideology.[86]

[82] As late as 1963, C. Wright Mills claimed that *Liberalism* was the best account of the subject.
The Marxists (Harmondsworth, 1963), 25n.

[83] Hobhouse, *Liberalism*, 24–25, 8. For another clear usage, see A. W. Benn, *The History of
English Rationalism in the Nineteenth Century*, vol. 1 (London, 1906), 111. Compare Herbert
Samuel, *Liberalism* (London, 1902), which does not mention Locke and makes little effort to trace
a genealogy.

[84] Michael Freeden, *The New Liberalism* (Oxford, 1978); Stefan Collini, *Liberalism and Sociology* (Cambridge, 1983).

[85] Freeden, *Liberalism Divided* (Oxford, 1986).

[86] Collingwood, "Translator's Preface," vii. See also the comments on the difference between
the narrow (British) and expansive (Continental) uses of the term in John Morley, *Recollections*
(London, 1917), 1:21. Morley adopts the latter in his discussion.

The First World War and its aftermath also saw early attempts to self-consciously define an American liberal tradition with its origins in the seventeenth century. Progressive scholars and publicists took the lead.[87] The critic Harold Stearn was one of the first. He drew heavily on Hobhouse's account of the true meaning of liberalism, but his historical narrative had a different emphasis, focusing in particular on religious toleration and the catalytic role of Roger Williams, the seventeenth-century Protestant theologian and colonist.[88] Despite dedicating a chapter to "what liberalism is" and another to the "English heritage" of American liberalism, Locke was absent from his analysis. Interpreting liberalism as an ideology centered on religious toleration become a popular theme in American scholarship, exemplified by Vernon Parrington's hugely influential *Main Currents in American Thought*, published in the late 1920s though composed largely in the 1910s.[89] Parrington argued that liberalism was articulated originally in the natural law theories of the early Puritan settlers, who had fled from a European environment inhospitable to their radical claims to a welcoming new world in America, where liberalism could truly flourish. Though Parrington stressed the importance of Williams— "England gave us her best"[90]—he also assigned Locke a prominent role. Connecting liberalism and toleration in this manner helped to place Locke at the center of the newly formatted tradition. Whereas parliamentary constitutionalism was central to the British appropriation of Locke (via the retrojection of the Whigs), it was religious toleration (via the retrojection of key elements of Puritanism) that did much of the ideological labor in the United States.

Although some of the key building blocks were in place by 1918, the ultimate hegemony of the Lockean narrative was still far from secure. The discursive consolidation of the new account of liberalism was a product of the complex interweaving of geopolitical dynamics and disciplinary imperatives within the human sciences, especially political science and history. Indeed the academic disciplines that profess to instruct us about the nature of liberalism played a fundamental role in its transfiguration. The shift unfolded in the context of a transfer of scholarly authority from Britain to the United States.

[87] On the transition from progressivism to liberalism, see Gerstle, "Protean Character." On the transatlantic dialogue between British and American thinkers, see James Kloppenberg, *Uncertain Victory* (Oxford, 1986); Marc Stears, *Progressive, Pluralists, and the Problems of the State* (Oxford, 2002).

[88] Stearns, *Liberalism in America* (New York, 1919), 11, 16–17, 33–34. Charles Merriam dismissed it as a shallow exercise in partisan propaganda. *American Political Science Review*, 14/3 (1920), 511–12.

[89] Parrington, *Main Currents in American Thought*, 3 vols. (New York, 1927–30). Gunnell argues that Parrington's trilogy marked the "threshold of the adoption of liberalism as an American political identity—both in politics and political theory." Gunnell, "Archaeology," 132. Thanks to Robert Adcock for discussion of this topic.

[90] Parrington, *Main Currents*, 1:74.

Whereas British commentators had shaped the contours of interpretation in the late nineteenth and early twentieth centuries, exerting a profound influence (alongside German scholarship) on the development of American political science and history, by 1945 a decisive shift across the Atlantic was apparent. The new liberal narrative was thus largely a product of the American human sciences, though it was mirrored in Britain. The change in meaning is captured in the evolution of George Sabine's influential conspectus of Western political thought, which was the standard textbook in the United States during the middle decades of the twentieth century. It was one of the first major scholarly texts to discuss liberalism in any detail. Published in 1937, the first edition located the tradition squarely in nineteenth-century Britain, figuring it as a distinct position between socialism and conservatism. (Locke was not classified as a liberal.) Moreover, like so many of his contemporaries, Sabine worried that it "was a diminishing force in modern society."[91] In the revised edition of 1951, however, his account of liberalism was both more capacious and more confident, and he asserted that it now had two main senses. The first, which he associated with Fascist and Marxist critics, saw it as the "social philosophy of the industrial middle class" and thus coterminous with *laissez-faire* capitalism. Rejecting this critique, he endorsed a far broader account of liberalism as both the "culmination" of Western history and largely synonymous with democracy.[92] Here he followed political theorist Frederick Watkins who had recently celebrated liberalism as the "secular form of Western civilization" and the "modern embodiment of all the characteristic traditions of Western politics."[93] Sabine concurred: "[P]olitical liberalism has been deeply implicated in the whole development of Western culture."[94] (The ultimately unsuccessful attempt to retroject liberalism back into the ancient Greek world, thus making it coterminous with Western civilization, was one of the signature ideological moves of the era.)[95] An irony appears lost on Sabine. Whereas linking democracy and liberalism had, in the nineteenth cen-

[mao]

[91] Sabine, *A History of Political Theory* (London, 1937), 679. In 1941 he observed that "[to] give a practical definition of liberalism is virtually impossible." Sabine, "The Historical Position of Liberalism," *American Scholar*, 10 (1940–41), 490.

[92] Sabine, *A History of Political Theory* (New York, 1951), 620. In a review, Macpherson noted the shift in meaning and concluded that the "ideological atmosphere in America" made an understanding of both liberalism and Marxism "increasingly difficult." *Western Political Quarterly*, 4 (1951), 145.

[93] Watkins, *The Political Tradition of the West* (Cambridge, 1948), ix. Watkins made liberalism coextensive with freedom under the law. For an influential conservative political-theological account that adopted the same timeline but reversed the normative conclusion, see John Hallowell, *The Decline of Liberalism as an Ideology* (Berkeley, 1943); Hallowell, *Main Currents in Modern Political Thought* (New York, 1950).

[94] Sabine, review of Watkins, *Political Science Quarterly*, 64 (1949), 147–49.

[95] The phenomenon was noted in Francis Coker, "Some Present-Day Critics of Liberalism," *American Political Science Review*, 47 (1953), 1–2.

tury, served to delimit its chronological scope, it was now employed to buttress the claim that liberalism was the spiritual inheritance of the West itself.

Confusion reigned. As liberalism's boundaries were conceptually stretched,
so whatever fragile coherence it once had was lost. In the mid-1930s Dewey
moaned that "liberalism has meant in practice things so different as to be opposed to one another."[96] It only got worse. A decade later, a noted philosopher could insouciantly observe that "we, too, have our 'ideology,' inherited
from the past as the liberal tradition, the American creed, the Judeo-Christian
heritage of Western civilization or the like."[97] For many, these ideas had become interchangeable. The tendency to construct legitimating genealogies for
crude ideological ends provoked the ire of a young C. B. Macpherson, who
complained that too many scholars charting the history of Western philosophy substituted serious analysis with assertions of political faith, "using their
history to show how long and honorable an ancestry that faith has."[98] This
was an accurate diagnosis. A new piece of conceptual technology was added
when the term "neoliberalism" was coined in the late 1930s. Since the 1970s
it has served as shorthand for the valorization of the minimal state and de-
regulated market, but (to add to the confusion) it originally identified a *via
media* between unrestrained capitalism and progressive statism.[99] Commentators grumbled endlessly about the theoretical muddle. One frustrated scholar
marveled in 1948 that "[o]ne finds the term employed to defend everything
from classical economics to the Soviet interpretation of communism."[100] In
1955, Reinhold Niebuhr addressed the "confusion," arguing that liberalism
had come to denominate both a phase of human history, "the rise of a modern
technical society availing itself of democratic political forms and of capitalis-
tic economic institutions," and a specific set of partisan political commitments. It also signified two "contradictory" claims, namely, that liberty necessitated both the unleashing of capitalism and its radical restraint.[101]

A similar pattern can be discerned in Britain. The translation of de Ruggiero's *History of European Liberalism* and the publication of Laski's *The Rise*

---

[96] Dewey, *Liberalism*, 3.

[97] Arthur Murphy, "Ideals and Ideologies, 1917–1947," *Philosophical Review*, 56 (1947), 386.

[98] Macpherson, "The History of Political Ideas," *Canadian Journal of Economics and Political
Science*, 7 (1941), 564–65.

[99] On neo-liberalism, see Ben Jackson, "At the Origins of Neo-Liberalism," *Historical Journal*,
53 (2010), 129–51; Angus Burgin, *The Great Persuasion* (Cambridge, 2012). For a contemporary
attempt to distinguish Ordo-liberalism and the work of the Mont Pelerin Society, see Carl Friedrich, "The Political Thought of Neo-Liberalism," *American Political Science Review*, 49 (1955),
509–25.

[100] Boyd Martin, "Liberalism," *Western Political Quarterly*, 1 (1948), 295.

[101] Niebuhr, "Liberalism," *New Republic* (1955). He endorsed the "Lockean type of
liberalism."

of European Liberalism bolstered the early modern liberal narrative.[102] It became the norm during the 1930s and 1940s.[103] Skeptical of claims about seamless continuity, Isaiah Berlin summed up the nature and ideological appeal of what had become a popular position by 1950: "European liberalism wears the appearance of a single coherent movement, little altered during almost three centuries, founded upon relatively simple foundations, laid by Locke or Grotius or even Spinoza; stretching back to Erasmus and Montaigne, the Italian Renaissance, Seneca and the Greeks."[104] By the early 1960s Kenneth Minogue, a young theorist at the London School of Economics (LSE), could confidently assert that liberalism was a "single and continuing entity . . . so extensive that it involves most of the guiding beliefs of modern western opinion" and that John Locke was its "founding father."[105] This bold proclamation would have surprised the Fabians who had founded the LSE just over half a century before.

The new historical narrative was adopted by both critics and celebrants of liberalism. Converging on description, they diverged in both explanation and normative evaluation. From the left, for example, Laski depicted liberalism as an ideology with foundations bored deep into the bedrock of Western history: "[L]iberalism has been, in the last four centuries, the outstanding doctrine of Western civilization." It supplied the ideological scaffolding of modern capitalism. Locke was elevated to the "most representative prophet" of the new age.[106] This line of critique reappeared in the work of Laski's student Macpherson and is still popular today.[107] On the political right, meanwhile, Strauss, Voegelin, and others, also pressed variations on the early modern theme. Self-proclaimed liberals were only too happy to vaunt the robust durability and deep historical roots of their creed, bolstering its ideological armature in the face of hostile competition. Narrative convergence helped produce discursive hegemony. It was against this imposing—but quite new—ideologi-

---

[102] Laski, *The Rise of European Liberalism* (London, 1936), 9, 115. For a similar analysis, see Richard Crossman, *Government and the Governed* (London, 1939), 69–80. Laski's analysis was not unchallenged: "There is plenty of truth in this as a historical account, though it is a one-sided truth. But to speak of it as Liberalism shows a bad confusion of thought." G. C. Field, *Mind*, 45 (1936), 527.

[103] See, for example, George Catlin, *The Anglo-Saxon Tradition* (London, 1939); Catlin, *The Story of the Political Philosophers* (New York, 1939); Michael Oakeshott, ed., *The Social and Political Doctrines of Contemporary Europe* (Cambridge, 1939), xi-xviii; Thomas Cook, *History of Political Philosophy from Plato to Burke* (New York, 1936), 710–11; J. P. Mayer, *Political Thought* (London, 1939).

[104] Berlin, "Political Ideas in the Twentieth Century," *Foreign Affairs*, 28 (1950), 357.

[105] Minogue, *The Liberal Mind* (London, 1962), 2.

[106] Laski, *Rise of European Liberalism*, 9, 115.

[107] Macpherson, *The Political Theory of Possessive Individualism* (Oxford, 1962); Losurdo, *Liberalism*.

cal edifice that the contextualist scholars of the 1960s fought their rear-guard action.

Arguably, the most significant conceptual move of the interwar era was the emergence of the idea of "liberal democracy." Barely visible before 1930, in the ensuing decade it began to supplant existing appellations for Euro-Atlantic states.[108] During the 1940s and 1950s it became a commonplace.[109] As a global conflict over the proper meaning of democracy raged, the modifier "liberal" simultaneously encompassed diverse representative parliamentary systems while differentiating them from others claiming the democratic title, above all Italy, Germany, and the Soviet Union. The year after Hitler assumed power, Ernest Barker observed that the "issue of our time is hardly a simple issue of democracy versus dictatorship. Dictatorship itself claims the quality of democracy; indeed it claims the quality of a higher, a more immediate, spontaneous democracy." This was, then, a clash between "two types of democracy—the parliamentary type . . . and the dictatorial type."[110] *Liberal democracy* was the name increasingly adopted to cover the former in its conflicts against the latter. Social scientists soon began to utilize the concept, usage that was refined and normalized after 1945. By 1954 Quincy Wright could assert confidently that the concept of "liberal democracy" originated in sixteenth-century Europe, especially in England, and was powerfully articulated in Locke's political philosophy.[111] The Lockean narrative was frequently generalized into a broader claim about the Lockean-liberal character of Anglo-American (sometimes Western) societies, an interpretive strategy popularized by Louis Hartz and that was to have a profound effect on the nascent subfield of comparative politics.[112] Conjoining "liberal" to democracy automatically (and vastly) expanded the scope of those purportedly encompassed by liberalism, as supporters of "liberal democracy" were conscripted, however reluctantly, to the liberal tradition. Liberalism was thus transfigured from a

[108] See, for example, M. Parmlees, "Liberal Democracy, Fascism, and Bolshevism," *Annals of the American Academy of Political and Social Science*, 180 (1935), 47–54; J. A. Leighton, *Social Philosophies in Conflict* (New York, 1937); Alfred Zimmern, ed., *Modern Political Doctrines* (Oxford, 1939), xiv-xix; Crossman, *Government*, 286–87, 294–96; J. A. Hobson, "Thoughts on Our Present Discontents," *Political Quarterly*, 9 (1938), 47–57; E. H. Carr, *The Twenty Years' Crisis, 1919–1939* (London, 1939), 37. See Oakeshott, *Doctrines*, xvi-xix, for skeptical acknowledgement of the linguistic shift.

[109] A Google Ngram graph shows this post-1930 spike in usage: http://books.google.com/ngrams/graph?content=liberal+democracy&year_start=1800&year_end=2000&corpus=0&smoothing=3. Google Scholar also offers illustrative evidence. Scrubbed of false positives, the term "liberal democracy" is employed with the following frequency: 1900–1910: 6; 1911–1920: 33; 1921–1930: 24; 1931–1940: 143; 1941–1950: 216; 1951–1960: 374.

[110] Barker, "Democracy since the War and Its Prospects for the Future," *International Affairs*, 13 (1934), 757. On the threat, see Katznelson, *Fear Itself*.

[111] Wright, "International Law and Ideologies," *American Journal of International Law*, 48 (1954), 619.

[112] Hartz, *The Liberal Tradition in America* (New York, 1955).

term identifying a limited and contested position within political discourse to either the most authentic expression of the Western tradition or a constitutive feature of the West itself. Again, this conceptual shift was rarely acknowledged, though it didn't pass completely unremarked. Strauss noted the peculiarity, and the "serious difficulty" for interpretation, that resulted from the "fact that here and now liberalism and conservatism have a common basis; for both are based here and now on liberal democracy, and therefore both are antagonistic to Communism."[113]

The political instrumentalization of intellectual history was widespread across the Euro-Atlantic world, reaching its *reductio ad absurdum* in Bertrand Russell's declaration that "at the present time Hitler is an outcome of Rousseau; Roosevelt and Churchill, of Locke."[114] It is thus unsurprising that history provided another disciplinary space for propagating the new vision of liberalism. The "history of ideas," an emergent field combining history and philosophy that "rose like a new sign in the zodiac over large areas of American culture and education," was, like political theory, transformed by émigré scholars, including Hans Baron, Ernst Cassirer, Felix Gilbert, Raymond Klibansky, Paul Kristeller, Hajo Holborn, and Erwin Panofsky.[115] Its zealous proponents helped to define and defend a holistic "Western" civilization based on "liberal" values, and as such it was of "strategic" value in fighting totalitarianism.[116] As the classroom became a powerful vector for the transmission of the new liberal-civilizational creed, so the *Journal of the History of Ideas*, founded in 1940, served as the principal venue for its scholarly elaboration. It is no coincidence that it was the only academic journal to receive a secret subsidy from the CIA-sponsored Congress on Cultural Freedom.[117] University curricula, then, provided institutional authority for the transvaluation of liberalism. "Western civilization" courses, which flourished from the end of the First World War until the 1960s, popularized "an interpretation of history that gives the United States a common development with England and Western Europe and identifies this 'civilization' with the advance of liberty and culture." Helping to construct a mythopoeic narrative of the West as simultaneously ancient and modern, free and strong, they were the most widely taught history courses after the Second World War.[118] While claims about the intellectual coherence, historical continuity, and ethico-political superiority

---

[113] Strauss, *Liberalism*, vii. He also wrote, "The conservatism of our age is identical with what originally was liberalism" (ix). Cf. Voegelin, "Liberalism," 507; Hayek, "Liberalism," 113.

[114] Russell, *History of Western Philosophy* (London, 1945/1948), 711.

[115] Anthony Grafton, "The History of Ideas," *Journal of the History of Ideas*, 67 (2006), 1.

[116] Jotham Parsons, "Defining the History of Ideas," *Journal of the History of Ideas*, 68 (2007), 682–89.

[117] Francis Stonor Saunders, *Who Paid the Piper?* (London, 1999), 338.

[118] Gilbert Allardyce, "The Rise and Fall of the Western Civilization Course," *American Historical Review*, 87 (1982), 706; Peter Novik, *That Noble Dream* (Cambridge, 1988), 312.

of "the West" stretched back at least as far as the eighteenth century, it was only in the mid-twentieth century that this potent civilizational narrative came to be routinely classified as *liberal*. The victorious spread of liberalism and the rise of the West came to be seen as one and the same thing.

Conclusion: Conscripts of Liberalism

The nature of liberalism has been a core concern in political theory since its emergence as an academic specialism in the early twentieth century. I have criticized some prominent approaches to interpreting liberalism, introduced some methodological tools for thinking about the proliferation of liberal languages, and sketched an explanatory account of shifts in the meaning of liberalism in the Anglo-American world. The analysis has implications for both political theorists and historians. Above all, it suggests the need to be alert to the historical contingency and variability of our theoretical vocabularies and the power relations of tradition-construction. It also calls into question the general utility of "liberalism" as a category of political analysis. Current debates about the nature of liberalism—in and beyond political theory—are often distorted because of the ahistorical understanding of liberal ideology that they invoke. Conducted in a discursive echo chamber, they are often marked by a symptomatic form of collective amnesia, a problematic erasure of the political and intellectual dynamics that generated much of what is now articulated as scholarly common sense.

This chapter is intended as a modest contribution to the work of historical recovery. As Stephen wrote in 1862, "the words 'liberal' and 'liberalism,' like all other such phrases, derive a great part of their significance from the time they were invented."[119] The history of liberalism, though, is a history of constant reinvention. The most sweeping of these occurred in the middle of the twentieth century, when liberalism was increasingly figured as the dominant ideology of the West—its origins retrojected back into the early modern era, it came to denote virtually all nontotalitarian forms of politics as well as a partisan political perspective within societies. This was partly a consequence of the delegitimation of political extremes, partly a result of the vicissitudes of domestic political strife, and partly a result of political and conceptual labor performed in the developing human sciences. Karl Popper once referred to *The Open Society and Its Enemies* as his "war effort," a contribution to the fight against totalitarianism. The consolidation of Lockean liberalism was a grander, more all-encompassing variation on the same theme.

[119] Stephen, "Liberalism," 70.

CHAPTER 4

Ideologies of Empire

❦

The world in which we live is largely the product of the rise, competition, and fall of empires. To attempt a survey of the role of ideology in this vast historical panorama would be hubristic—that archetypical imperial vice. Consequently, in this chapter I limit my focus both geographically and temporally, concentrating attention on European, and principally British, imperialism during the last two hundred years. Moreover I confine it to a subset of the topics that it would be possible to discuss under the heading of ideology and empire. Even with these limitations in mind, my discussion will be synoptic and selective, drawing out some key issues while leaving many others unmentioned, or mentioned only in passing.

The terms empire and imperialism have no settled definition—indeed the attempt to control and delimit their meaning has often formed a significant dimension of ideological disputation. Contemporary scholarly definitions come in narrow and broad varieties. On a narrow view, empire connotes the direct and comprehensive political control of one polity over another. It is, Michael Doyle writes, "a relationship . . . in which one state controls the effective political sovereignty of another political society."[1] Broad definitions, meanwhile, characterize an empire as a polity that exerts decisive or overwhelming power in a system of unequal political relations, thus encompassing very diverse forms of control and influence.[2] The same variation holds for the concept of imperialism. On a narrow account, imperialism is a strategy or policy that aims to consolidate or expand a territorial empire. According to broader definitions it a strategy or policy—or even an attitude or disposition—that seeks to create, maintain, or intensify relations of inequality between political communities. A cross-cutting issue concerns the connection between formal and informal imperialism. Some restrict the term to direct intervention in, or control over, a given territory; others invoke imperialism to cover a wide range of formal and informal (nonterritorial) modes of influence.[3] This can lead to substantial variation in the application of the terms.

---

[1] Doyle, *Empires* (Ithaca, 1986), 45. See also David Abernethy, *The Dynamics of Global Dominance* (New Haven, 2000), 19.

[2] Michael Ignatieff, *Empire Lite* (London, 2003), 109; Niall Ferguson, *Colossus* (London, 2004).

[3] For discussions of different conceptions of (largely European) empire, see Anthony Pagden,

For example, utilizing a narrow definition it is possible to deny that the contemporary United States is an empire while acknowledging that it exhibits
occasional imperialist aspirations, but adopting a broader definition supports
the argument that it is and nearly always has been an empire.[4] Empire and
imperialism, then, are essentially contested concepts. Sidestepping these
thorny conceptual debates, this chapter discusses positions from across the
spectrum, not least because imperial advocates and critics have often mixed
the different accounts together. Conceptual precision is vital for the scholarly
analysis of empires, but impassioned ideological contestation rarely adheres to
strict academic conventions.

The study of empire straddles the humanities and social sciences. The last
three decades have witnessed a renaissance of interest in imperial history, a
development that has recently catalyzed the increasingly popular field of
"global history."[5] Following the work of Edward Said, Homi Bhabha, and
Gayatri Spivak, among others, scholars of comparative literature have focused
attention on the representation and legitimation of empire in diverse forms of
cultural production, from the quotidian to the avant-garde.[6] Such studies
have illuminated the pivotal role of empire in the life-worlds of the modern
"West"—indeed in their very construction. Anthropology, a field once deeply
implicated in the justification of imperial activity, now offers one of the most
incisive scholarly sites for its investigation and critique. A similar case can be
made about geography.[7] Scholarship in all of these areas has been heavily influenced, though certainly not exhausted, by a range of "postcolonial" challenges to the "Eurocentrism" of Western scholarly and popular discourse.[8]
Rather ironically, international relations (IR), a field putatively dedicated to

Lords of All the World (London, 1995); Patrick Wolfe, "History and Imperialism," *American Historical Review*, 102 (1997), 388–420; David Armitage, ed., *Theories of Empire, 1450–1800* (Aldershot, 1998); and James Muldoon, *Empire and Order* (Basingstoke, 1999).

[4] Compare, for example, John Ikenberry, *Liberal Order and Imperial Ambition* (Cambridge,
2006) and Niall Ferguson, *Empire* (London, 2003).

[5] Dominic Lieven, *Empire* (New Haven, 2002); Christopher Bayly, *The Birth of the Modern
World* (Oxford, 2004); John Darwin, *After Tamerlane* (London, 2007); James Belich, *Replenishing
the Earth* (Oxford, 2009); Jane Burbank and Frederick Cooper, *Empires in World History*
(Princeton, 2010).

[6] Said, *Orientalism* (London, 1978); Said, *Culture and Imperialism* (London, 1993); Bhabha,
The Location of Culture (London, 1994); Spivak, "Can the Subaltern Speak?," in *Marxism and the
Interpretation of Culture,* ed. Cary Nelson and Laurence Grossberg (Urbana, 1988), 271–313.

[7] For anthropology, see, from a long list, Eric Wolf, *Europe and the People without History*
(Berkeley, 1982); Marshall Sahlins, *How "Natives" Think* (Chicago, 1995); Bernard Cohn, *Colonialism and Its Forms of Knowledge* (Princeton, 1996); Ann Laura Stoler, *Along the Archival Grain*
(Princeton, 2010). For geography: Felix Driver, *Geography Militant* (Oxford, 2001); Derek Gregory, *The Colonial Present* (Oxford, 2004); Gerry Kearns, *Geopolitics and Empire* (Oxford, 2009).

[8] Partha Chatterjee, *Nationalist Thought and the Colonial World* (London, 1986); Dipesh
Chakrabarty, *Provincializing Europe* (Princeton, 2000); John Hobson, *The Eurocentric Conception
of World Politics* (Cambridge, 2012); cf. David Scott, *Conscripts of Modernity*.

the analysis of world politics, has yet to engage adequately with the practices and the legacies of imperialism. Like many of the other social sciences, the origins and early disciplinary development of IR were bound up with imperial projects, but the dominant approaches continue to conceptualize global order, past and present, in terms of the relations between autonomous states acting under conditions of "anarchy."[9] However, as I discuss in chapter 2, scholars of politics have not ignored the imperial turn entirely. Spurred on by shifts in the wider world, historians and political theorists have begun to demonstrate the assorted ways in which the history of Western political thinking is profoundly entangled with imperial encounters.

Practices of imperialism are not, of course, simply the product of a set of explicit theoretical arguments, and ideologies of empire cannot be analyzed solely through deciphering written texts. Studying ideology is an interdisciplinary endeavor, exploring social, economic, political, cultural, and intellectual phenomena. It encompasses the interpretation of texts, the study of social practices, and the analysis of visual and material culture, soundscapes, the built environment, and much more besides. For heuristic purposes it is worth drawing an ideal-typical distinction between theory, ideology, and imaginary. (In reality, the three blur together.) *Theories* are systematic articulated bodies of argumentation—the kind of accounts of empire produced by Hannah Arendt, Frantz Fanon, V. I. Lenin, John Locke, and John Stuart Mill. It is writing of this kind that has drawn the attention of historians of political thought in recent years. Following Michael Freeden, we can define *ideologies* as "clusters of ideas, beliefs, opinions, values and attitudes usually held by identifiable groups, that provide directives, even plans, of action for public policy-making in an endeavour to uphold, justify, change or criticize the social and political arrangements of a state or other political community."[10] Such ideologies include liberalism, socialism, republicanism, conservatism, and fascism. Imperial ideologies, as I use the term in this chapter, are those elements of more general patterns of thought that relate to empire. Sophisticated theories often play a crucial role in such ideologies, but they do not exhaust them. The bulk of the chapters in this volume examine material falling in either or both of these categories. Finally, ideologies are nested within, and given shape by, *so-*

---

[9] David Long and Brian Schmidt, eds., *Imperialism and Internationalism in the Discipline of International Relations* (Albany, 2005); Robert Vitalis, "The Noble American Science of Imperial Relations and Its Laws of Race Development," *Comparative Studies in Society and History*, 52 (2010), 909–38; Tarak Barkawi, "Empire and Order in International Relations and Security Studies," in *The International Studies Encyclopaedia*, ed. Robert Denmark (Oxford, 2010), 3:1360–79; Naeem Inayatullah and David Blaney, *International Relations and the Problem of Difference* (New York, 2004). Notable exceptions include, Doyle, *Empires*; Alexander Motyl, *Imperial Ends* (New York, 2001); Alexander Cooley, *Logics of Hierarchy* (Ithaca, 2005); Daniel Nexon, *The Struggle for Power in Early Modern Europe* (Princeton, 2009).

[10] Freeden, *Ideologies and Political Theory* (Oxford, 1996), 6.

cial imaginaries. Charles Taylor defines a social imaginary as "the ways people imagine their social existence, how they fit together with others, how things go on between them and their fellows, the expectations that are normally met, and the deeper normative notions and images that underlie these expectations." Among other things, imaginaries constitute "that common understanding that makes possible common practices and a widely shared sense of legitimacy."[11] Imaginaries are more basic than ideologies insofar as they establish the background cultural and cognitive conventions that structure and animate them. Just as ideologies contain multiple and often competing theories, so imaginaries are compatible with varied ideologies. One of the central contentions of this chapter is that rival ideologies of empire often share key assumptions about the nature of the social world and that this can be explained through reference to underlying imperial imaginaries.

In the next section I explore aspects of the modern imperial imaginary. In the subsequent sections I distinguish three ideal-typical aspects of imperial ideology: justification, governance, and resistance. Ideologies of justification are those patterns of thought that provide reasons, explicit or implicit, for supporting or upholding imperial activity. They seek to legitimate the creation, reproduction, or expansion of empire. Ideologies of governance articulate the modalities of imperial rule in specific contexts. Particular ideologies of justification may be compatible with diverse and conflicting ideologies of governance, while precluding others. Finally, ideologies of resistance deny the legitimacy of imperial control. They too cover a broad spectrum, ranging from moderate positions that reject only some aspects of imperial rule and seek accommodation with the existing order, through to defenses of violent rebellion and the revolutionary transcendence of the system.

Imperial Imaginaries

Social imaginaries constitute "the macromappings of social and political space through which we perceive, judge, and act in the world."[12] Throughout history they have animated imperial ideologies, underwriting relevant conceptions of time and space, philosophical anthropologies, ethical assumptions, cosmologies, and metaphysical belief systems—the "deeper normative notions and images" that Taylor suggests mold expectations about human collective

---

[11] Taylor, *Modern Social Imaginaries* (Durham, NC, 2004), 23. Taylor distinguishes imaginaries from theories, the latter explicit bodies of doctrine, the former often-unstructured background features of social existence (24–25). In line with Manfred Steger, *The Rise of the Global Imaginary* (Oxford, 2008), I suggest that ideologies occupy a middle position, nested within social imaginaries, but themselves (often) containing a variety of more or less distinguishable theories. Note that the categories are not mutually exclusive.

[12] Steger, *The Rise of the Global Imaginary*, 6.

life.[13] In ancient China, for example, imperial authority was construed as mediating between heaven and earth, with the Han Emperor serving as the "son of Heaven."[14] Early modern European imperialism had to be legitimated in Christian terms. Modern imperial ideologies, too, are rooted in a widely shared set of assumptions and beliefs about the character of the social world.

Charles Taylor and Manfred Steger have both probed the relationship between modern ideologies and social imaginaries. Steger argues that "ideologies translate and articulate the largely pre-reflexive social imaginary in compressed form as explicit political doctrine" and he contends that the key transition in the modern world is from a national imaginary to a global one, a process that was accelerated by the Second World War and is still unfolding today.[15] The modern social imaginary, on this view, is constituted by various interlocking elements, including conceptions of linear time and progress, secularization, individualism, and forms of rationality and scientific knowledge. The spatial configuration of modern politics—a system of territorial states— is the institutional expression of this imaginary. Globalization signifies the ongoing and uneven transition to an emergent "globalist" system characterized by a growing consciousness of the world as an interconnected whole. For Taylor, meanwhile, the modern social imaginary is formulated in "Lockean" terms as a society of mutual respect among free autonomous agents, and it is institutionalized in the rise of civil society, popular sovereignty, and the capitalist system of market exchange.

My primary concern here is with what I will call the imperial imaginary: those aspects of social imaginaries that pertain to the justification or governance of empire. It is not clear how empire fits into Taylor's account, a lacuna that follows from his focus on the internal constitution of discrete societies— what we might call his *methodological communitarianism*. For Taylor the modern moral order, in contrast to its medieval predecessor, "gives no ontological status to hierarchy or any particular structure of differentiation. "In other words," he writes, "the basic point of the new normative order is the mutual respect and mutual service of the individuals who make up society."[16] This fails to grasp the sociopolitical dynamics of modern imperialism, which is predicated on the hierarchical classification of peoples—the sorting and categorizing of the world in ways that denied (either temporarily or permanently) equality and autonomy to large swathes of it. Moreover, imperial practices helped fashion the internal ordering of Western societies: empire cannot be bracketed off as something that happened elsewhere. As practitioners of the "new imperial history" rightly insist, imperial metropoles and peripheries

---

[13] Taylor, *Modern Social Imaginaries*, 23.

[14] Alejandro Colás, *Empire* (Cambridge, 2007), 2.

[15] Steger, "The Changing Face of Political Ideologies in the Global Age," *New Political Science*, 31 (2009), 426.

[16] Taylor, *Modern Social Imaginaries*, 12.

need to be viewed as part of a "single analytic field"—as dynamically connected and interpenetrating.[17] Above all, the modern social imaginary, in its imperial dimensions, encodes "civilizational" (or racial) difference. This imaginary has framed European encounters with other peoples at least since the "discovery" of the Americas in the fifteenth century.[18] In the remainder of this section, I discuss three elements of the modern Euro-American imperial imaginary: civilizational difference, conceptions of time and space, and what I will call "the comparative gaze."

Perhaps the most consequential element of the modern imperial imaginary is the way in which the world is envisioned as a space of inequality and radical difference.[19] Peoples and societies are arrayed in a hierarchical manner. "Civilization," the meta-concept of the modern imperial imaginary, is the term most frequently employed to characterize this stratification. It entered European political discourse in the mid-eighteenth century, first in France and then in England.[20] But the underlying idea is not unique to modernity or to the West; the distinction was also common in Japan, China, and the Islamic states. The Chinese historiographical tradition, for example, "invariably assumed that, by virtue of its superior civilization, China stood at the centre and apex of the universe, and that its emperor enjoyed a mandate from heaven not only to rule the empire, but also to exact deference and tribute from all other peoples known and unknown to the Chinese."[21] Employing the language of "civilization" invokes a standard of assessment and a regime of difference—it demands the drawing of normatively significant boundaries between "advanced" and "backward" societies, the latter to be viewed as inferior to (and hence open to rule by) the former.

Conceptions of civilization have varied considerably in modern imperial discourse. The appellation can mark either a process or a *telos*. It can be theorized in constructivist or essentialist terms: as the product of time, chance, luck, and skill, or alternatively as the result of ingrained (usually biological) difference. Conceptions of civilization come in both dynamic and static

---

[17] Frederick Cooper and Ann Laura Stoler, "Between Metropole and Colony," in *Tensions of Empire*, ed. Cooper and Stoler (Berkeley, 1997), 4. Among historians of modern Britain there is a heated dispute about the extent to which society was (and is) shaped by empire: John Mackenzie, ed., *Imperialism and Popular Culture* (Manchester, 1986); Catherine Hall, *Civilising Subjects* (Cambridge, 2002); Bernard Porter, *The Absent-Minded Imperialists* (Oxford, 2004); Andrew Thompson, *The Empire Strikes Back* (London, 2005).

[18] On the dynamics of encounter, see Tzvetan Todorov, *The Conquest of America*, trans. R. Howard (New York, 1992).

[19] The following discussion draws on material from Duncan Bell, "Empire and International Relations in Victorian Political Thought," *Historical Journal*, 49 (2006), 281–98.

[20] J.G.A. Pocock, *Barbarism and Religion: Vol. 4* (Cambridge, 2005); Brett Bowden, *The Empire of Civilization* (Chicago, 2009).

[21] Patrick O'Brien, "Historiographical Traditions and Modern Imperatives for the Restoration of Global History," *Journal of Global History*, 1 (2006), 18.

forms. The dynamic account, which from the late eighteenth century drew in particular on the historical sociology of the Scottish Enlightenment and later on universalistic theories of progress, holds that the differential levels of ethical and material development found in societies across the world are neither inevitable nor natural. This notion permeates assorted modern ideologies, including liberalism and socialism. Proponents of static accounts, which deny the implicit moral universality of dynamic perspectives, concentrate on the purportedly immutable markers of a people or "race," arguing that progress amongst at least some groups (with Aboriginal Australians and sub-Saharan Africans regularly coded as paradigmatic) is virtually impossible. An extreme manifestation of this view, found in both scholarly and literary discourses throughout the nineteenth and early twentieth centuries, viewed the most "uncivilized" peoples as unable to socially reproduce in a world dominated by advanced white civilizations, and consequently as doomed to extinction. They were seen, in other words, as self-annihilating. As Patrick Brantlinger observes, this discourse was "a specific branch of the dual ideologies of imperialism and racism."[22] Most accounts of race and civilization in nineteenth- and twentieth-century imperial discourse blended together "cultural" and "biological" arguments to create a potent set of claims about the stratified character of world order. As such, they were figured as pervasive yet opaque *biocultural assemblages*.[23]

Assumptions about European civilizational superiority were typically shared by enthusiastic imperialists and critics of empire alike, although they interpreted them in different ways. (This is one reason why the labels "pro-imperial" and "anti-imperial," whilst perhaps unavoidable in some instances, are usually too crude for satisfactory historical and theoretical discrimination.) The justificatory argument from civilization was fairly straightforward: the civilized peoples of the world had a right, or even a duty, to spread civilization to the backward. Progress—human "improvement"—demanded it. Military and economic dominance proved to many Europeans the inherent superiority of their political and moral orders, justifying attempts to export their institutions and ideas across the globe. J. A. Hobson pinpointed the connection commonly drawn between material superiority and ethical orientation in dismissing the view that "the power to do anything constitutes a right and even a duty to do it" as "the most 'natural' of temperamental fallacies."[24] But it is important to recognize that civilization was also a key category for those critical of expansion. This position assumed several forms. First, a case could be made that the attempt to export civilization would invariably fail given the

---

[22] Brantlinger, *Dark Vanishings*, 1.

[23] For further discussion of this idea, see Duncan Bell, "Beyond the Sovereign State," *Political Studies*, 62/2 (2014), 418–21.

[24] Hobson, *Imperialism* (London, 1902), 157.

intrinsic difficulty of the task, and in particular the perceived recalcitrance of the target communities. This argument was increasingly popular towards the end of the nineteenth century, as anthropological and sociological accounts of the structure of "native" communities moved to the center of imperial debate.[25] Alternatively, even if the spread of civilization was both feasible and universally beneficial there were more efficient or humane modes of transmission available—a case made by many liberal internationalists, for whom the primary engine of transformation was international commerce. Finally, and most commonly, it could be argued that regardless of whether imperialism was an effective vehicle of civilization, it inevitably damaged the imperial metropole. The "spirit of conquest," as Benjamin Constant famously labeled it, threatened the fragile achievements of civilization itself.[26] This was the lesson that many post-Renaissance Europeans drew from the fall of Rome, and it formed a key element of the critiques of empire formulated by Bentham, Constant, Cobden, Spencer, and a long line of nineteenth-century radical political thinkers. It could also be argued, in an explicitly racist variation on this theme, that the pursuit of empire threatened the (racial) contamination of the civilized.

Conceptions of time and space structure the way in which ideologies and theories articulate political projects. Throughout history they have established the imaginative limits of the zones that empires set out to conquer and rule. In Victorian Britain, for example, novel communications technologies altered the way in which individuals perceived the physical world and the political possibilities it contained. Political forms previously regarded as utopian came to be seen as realizable. This was the period in which ideas about the "annihilation of time and space" began to be applied routinely to global politics.[27] Once again, this aspect of the imaginary was pervasive but politically indeterminate. Many saw technological developments as facilitating, even necessitating, the construction of imperial institutions that in the past would have seemed the stuff of dreams, but to others they intensified the dangers of interpolity competition. As I explore in other chapters, this cognitive revolution acted as a condition of possibility for the emergence of ideas about a globe-spanning polity, a "Greater Britain" uniting Britain and its settler colonies in the South Pacific, North America, and southern Africa. It was claimed that instantaneous global communication could, for the first time in human history, sustain the bonds of identity between the members of a community—the "Anglo-Saxon race"—scattered across oceanic distances.[28] Ideas

[25] Mantena, *Alibis of Empire*.

[26] Constant, "The Spirit of Conquest and Usurpation and Their Relation to European Civilization" [1814], in *Constant: Political Writings*, ed. B. Fontana (Cambridge, 1988), 51–165.

[27] Stephen Kern, *The Culture of Time and Space, 1880–1914* (Cambridge, MA, 1983).

[28] Seeley, *The Expansion of England*. See also the discussion in Duncan Bell, *The Idea of Greater Britain*.

about the potential scope of "the people" and the nature of "the public" were reconfigured, in a racialized precursor to contemporary debates about the emergence of a global public sphere.[29]

Finally, the constitution of specific historical sensibilities has played a vital role in the imperial imaginary. The manner in which individuals and groups emplot historical trajectories, and the process through which these representations mold narrative constructions of the present and future, help to configure the scope and content of political discourse. They generate a repertoire of analogies, metaphors, "lessons," and precedents that give shape to the field of action and determine assorted ethical imperatives about how and why to act. Cyclical conceptions of historical time have structured much Western imperial discourse. The trope of "decline and fall" infused accounts of empire from the ancient world until deep into the twentieth century—a topic that I discuss in greater detail in chapter 5. Empires, on this account, are impermanent structures, subject to the vagaries of time, and as such they are either to be rejected (as bound to end in failure) or designed in such a way as to maximize their potential longevity (to defer failure for as long as possible). Modernity saw the emergence of a novel conception of historical time tied to open-ended notions of progress, and this in turn reshaped the ways in which the temporality of empires was conceived. While modern progressivist accounts have often been haunted by nightmares of eventual dissolution, they have not been burdened with the same sense of historical inevitability. History, on this account, need not repeat itself.

Modern imperial thought has also been shaped by a *habit of comparison*, the imperial gaze stretching across the world and back through time. Other empires, past and present, have provided templates for ways of ruling, as well as cautionary tales about what to avoid. Historiography has been an authoritative mode of political thinking. European imperialists turned to the ancient world for validation, and Rome, above all, "consistently provided the inspiration, the imagery and the vocabulary for all the European Empires from early modern Spain to nineteenth century Britain."[30] Civic humanism offered ideological support for justifying global exploration, conquest, and occupation in early modern Europe, while the language of neo-Roman republicanism permeated eighteenth-century defenses of the British empire, especially in the North American colonies.[31] The most obvious manifestation of this historicized sensibility, though, resided in the frequent reiteration of the classical debate over the corrupting relationship between empire and liberty.[32] Yet comparisons between the ancients and the moderns were always selective and

---

[29] I develop this argument in chapter 7.

[30] Anthony Pagden, *Peoples and Empires* (London, 2001), 28.

[31] Andrew Fitzmaurice, *Humanism and America* (Cambridge, 2003); Mikael Hörnqvist, *Machiavelli and Empire* (Cambridge, 2004).

[32] David Armitage, *The Ideological Origins of the British Empire* (Cambridge, 2000); Pagden,

the imaginative resources extracted from Rome and Greece fed a variety of conflicting desires and demands.

Comparison could also be employed as a strategy to "deflect moral anxiety" about the governing practices of empire.[33] The brutality of conquest and imperial rule could be relativized, and thus downplayed, either by comparing it favorably to the gross atrocities of past empires (usually the Spanish) or by arguing (as was widespread in British, French, and American debates) that the subject populations were better off governed by the most beneficent imperial power, whatever its defects, than by another more rapacious state. In a related move, it could be argued that Western imperial domination was invariably better than non-European alternatives. As James Mill once wrote about India, "[e]ven the utmost abuse of European power, is better, we are persuaded, than the most temperate exercise of Oriental despotism."[34] Counter-factual reasoning was routinely put at the service of imperialism.

These elements of the imperial imaginary continue to shape our world: Western political discourse is still shadowed by the specter of the civilizing mission. Although usage of the term "civilization" declined precipitously through the twentieth century, it is at least arguable that the underlying ideas never disappeared—they were rearticulated in the form of "modernization" theory during the 1960s and 1970s and are now rendered in the more palatable language of "development" and "democratization."[35] Purportedly novel conceptions of time and space lie at the very heart of debates over globalization. During the twentieth century, the apparent "shrinking" of the world through advanced communications and transport technologies underpinned an array of proposals for trans-planetary political institutions—regional unions, democratic alliances, even federal world-states.[36] Finally, the fascination with the ancients and the power of the comparative gaze continues undiminished. In the post-9/11 world, for example, both critics and admirers of the United States have routinely compared it with the nineteenth-century British empire and with Rome, seeking to identify patterns of similarity and difference that shed light on the contemporary condition.[37] Defenders of liberal imperialism, meanwhile, still resort to cost-benefit calculations and coun-

---

Lords of All the World; David Armitage, "Empire and Liberty," in *Republicanism*, ed. Martin van Gelderen and Quentin Skinner (Cambridge, 2002), 2:29–47.

[33] Cheryl Welch, "Colonial Violence and the Rhetoric of Evasion," *Political Theory*, 31 (2003), 235–64.

[34] Mill, "Review of Voyage aux Indes Orientales," by Le P. Paulin De S. Barthélemy, *Edinburgh Review*, 15 (1810), 371.

[35] Nils Gilman, *Mandarins of the Future* (Baltimore, 2004).

[36] Wesley T. Wooley, *Alternatives to Anarchy* (Bloomington, 1988); Jo-Ann Pemberton, *Global Metaphors* (London, 2001). I discuss this topic in more detail in chapter 8.

[37] For the British comparison, see Ferguson, *Colossus*; Porter, *Empire and Superempire* (London, 2006); for Rome, see Charles Maier, *Among Empires* (Cambridge, MA, 2006); Margaret Malamud, *Ancient Rome and Modern America* (Oxford, 2008).

terfactual reasoning to argue that it was better than the available alternatives.[38]
Plus ça change?

Ideologies of Justification

Justifications of empire are often blended together in practice to form a powerful if inconsistent ideological amalgam. However, for the purposes of analytical clarity it is worth delineating some of the ideal-typical forms of argument that have been employed to justify conquest and rule in the modern era.[39]
I will briefly outline five: commercial-exploitative, realist-geopolitical, liberal-
civilizational, republican, and martialist. They embody distinct logics, although they overlap in assorted ways. It is also worth noting that each kind of
justification has found sophisticated expression in social scientific or historical
explanatory theories during the last one hundred and fifty years. Ideological
affirmation has transmuted into canons of systematic scholarship. For example, the everyday arguments of imperial strategists and military planners find
their contemporary academic analog in "realist" explanations of imperial expansion offered by IR scholars and diplomatic historians. Meanwhile, arguments once adduced on behalf of the financial benefits of empire are now the
raw material of economic historians of Western expansion. This highlights the
complex entanglement of imperial politics and the evolution of the modern
human sciences.

Realist-geopolitical arguments focus attention on power politics. According to such views, imperial consolidation or expansion is often regarded as
necessary to balance or trump the power of competing imperial states. The
world is envisaged as a chessboard, with imperial strategy a vital ingredient of
ultimate success. Imperialism is rarely seen as an end in itself but rather as a
means to secure geopolitical advantage. This was the kind of argument proffered by Bismarck in Germany and Lord Salisbury in Britain. An underlying
assumption is that scale translates into status; that the governance of large territorial spaces is a precondition for assuming the role of a "great power."
Realist-geopolitical arguments play a starring role in much IR and historical
scholarship. For example, they were central to Robinson and Gallagher's seminal work on the "official mind" of British imperialism in the nineteenth century.[40] In a recent iteration of the argument, Brendan Simms contends that
the fulcrum of British foreign policy throughout the seventeenth and eighteenth centuries was to be found in Europe, not the empire, and insofar as

---

[38] Most notably, Ferguson, *Empire*.

[39] Inconsistency is no bar to the political efficacy of an ideology; indeed there are ideological
benefits to vagueness. Freeden, "What Should the 'Political' in Political Philosophy Explore?,"
Journal of Political Philosophy, 13 (2005), 113–34.

[40] Robinson and Gallagher, with Alice Denny, *Africa and the Victorians* (London, 1961).

Britain engaged in imperial activity in North America and Asia it was primarily to maintain the balance of power within Europe.[41] One feature of this type of scholarship is that while it takes calculations of power and interest seriously, it pays little attention to wider ideological currents, focusing its attention on the views of small groups of elite policy-makers.

Commercial-exploitative arguments justify empire principally in terms of the economic benefits that it generates for the metropole (or specific interests therein). Throughout history, empires have acted as engines of wealth extraction and redistribution, moving raw materials, manufactured products, and countless people—whether administrators, domestic workers, family dependents, soldiers, or slaves—through complex circuits of production and exchange. It is unsurprising, then, that economic concerns have stood at the heart of many imperial ideologies. But the particular form of justificatory argument employed has evolved over time, especially as the state of economic "knowledge" developed. There have been, in other words, performative consequences to the evolution of the discourse of political economy, from its origins in early modern Europe to the current dominance of its neoclassical variants. Commercial-exploitative arguments tend to focus on either the extraction of raw materials from an occupied territory or on opening new markets for trade. The shift in emphasis from the former to the latter represents one of the major ideological shifts in the modern history of empire.[42] Whereas deep into the early modern era imperial conquest was often legitimated through mercantilist arguments—with the Spanish Empire in the Americas serving as an exemplar[43]—during the eighteenth century, political economists began to insist that free trade was the best strategy to secure national economic development. Adam Smith's critique of the "old colonial system" in the *Wealth of Nations* was the most sophisticated elaboration of this argument. This shifted the burden of justification: imperial territories were increasingly regarded as either economic liabilities to be discarded or (more commonly) their role in the imperial order was reimagined. They were cast as nodes in a vast global trading system—as reservoirs of cheap labor and goods, or as profitable zones for market exchange.

The relationship between capitalism and empire, then, stands at the core of debates over economic justifications of imperial rule. Marx was ambivalent about imperialism. While critical of the violence and cupidity of European expansion, he nevertheless approved of its power to transform societies stifled by moribund ("oriental") traditions.[44] The task of developing a systematic

[41] Simms, *Three Victories and a Defeat* (London, 2007).

[42] Burbank and Cooper, *Empires in World History*, 219–51; Pagden, *Peoples and Empires*, 103–77.

[43] J. H. Elliott, *Empires of the Atlantic World* (London, 2006); Pagden, *Lords of All the World*.

[44] Gareth Stedman Jones, "Radicalism and the Extra-European World," in *Victorian Visions of Global Order*, ed. Duncan Bell (Cambridge, 2007), 186–225.

theory of capitalist imperialism was taken up by many of his acolytes, among whom the most influential were Rudolf Hilferding, Rosa Luxemburg, Karl Kautsky, Nikolai Bukarin, and Vladimir Illich Lenin, who famously argued that imperialism was the "highest stage" of capitalism.[45] With the partial exception of Luxemburg, all of them focused on the dire consequences for European politics, largely ignoring the impact of empire on those subjected to it. Marxist theorizing was later reworked by scholars in colonial and postcolonial states. Most influential of all were the *dependencia* theories that emerged in the 1960s and 1970s, though as with earlier Marxist accounts, their advocates downplayed the role of ideology in seeking to explain the dynamics of imperialism.[46] (Indeed the lack of attention paid to ideology was one of the main criticisms leveled at Marxist analyses by scholars working in a postcolonial idiom.) Arguments linking capitalism to imperialism are not, of course, the preserve of Marxists. Lenin himself drew on the writings of the British radical liberal J. A. Hobson, who dedicated his seminal *Imperialism: A Study* to exposing the dynamics of the "new imperialism" of the late nineteenth century. Joining a long line of radical critics of empire, all of whom stressed the economic imperatives driving imperialism, Hobson had concluded that capitalism itself was not at fault, only a distorted financial variant of it.[47] Other important analyses of the socioeconomic conditions generating European imperialism were penned by Hannah Arendt, Karl Polanyi, and Joseph Schumpeter. Most work linking capitalism and imperialism is critical of either one or both of them, but there are exceptions. Neo-imperialists like Niall Ferguson, for example, have been quick to praise the conjoined transformative energies of capitalism and liberal empire.

It would be foolish to deny the role of capitalism in motivating modern imperial activity, but it is nevertheless worth noting that, at least in the last two hundred years or so, few prominent thinkers have justified empire solely, or even primarily, in economic terms. Even Joseph Chamberlain, a British politician famous for his arguments about the economic benefits of empire, emphasized the absolute centrality of national honor and moral character in legitimating imperialism.[48] What, then, is the relationship between imperial discourse and practice? One possibility is that the profession of noneconomic justifications is a self-serving distortion of reality—ideology in the pejorative Marxist sense. Another possibility is that most imperial thinkers were moti-

---

[45] Anthony Brewer, *Marxist Theories of Imperialism*, 2nd ed. (London, 1990); Wolfe, "History and Imperialism."

[46] Lenin, *Imperialism* [1917] (London, 1996). On dependency theory, see Brewer, *Marxist Theories of Imperialism*, 136–98.

[47] On Hobson's political economy of empire, see especially Peter Cain, *Hobson and Imperialism* (Oxford, 2002); Gregory Claeys, *Imperial Sceptics* (Cambridge, 2010).

[48] Cain, "Empire and the Languages of Character and Virtue in Later Victorian and Edwardian Britain," *Modern Intellectual History*, 4 (2007), 249–73.

vated primarily by noneconomic factors. (This option is compatible with the claim that governments and capitalist enterprises were driven by economic imperatives.) Perhaps most plausible is the idea that reflective imperialists typically had mixed motives, interweaving views on the economic gains generated by empire with a variety of other arguments, including those emphasizing its ability to protect important national (or "racial") security interests and the world-transformative power of civilization. But not all advocates of empire were quite so Panglossian. Recognizing that trade-offs were necessary, John Stuart Mill, to give one prominent example, argued that the British should retain their settler colonies if possible, but that doing so would invariably amplify their military vulnerability.[49] Costs had to be weighed against benefits. Difficult choices had to be made.

The relationship between liberalism and empire has generated a substantial body of scholarship—including many of the chapters in this volume. Arguments range from the claim that liberalism is inherently imperial to the Schumpeterian position that the two are antithetical. Both poles of the spectrum are implausible, not least because liberalism is such an inchoate ideological tradition that generalizations about its content are usually misleading. It contains resources both to justify and to critique imperialism. Despite this qualification, it is undoubtedly the case that during the last two centuries a particular strand of "liberal civilizing imperialism" has thrived. Maintaining that liberal states have a right (even a duty) to spread "civilization" to the purportedly non-civilized peoples of the world, its advocates insist that empire is only legitimate if it is primarily intended to benefit the populations subjected to it. Any other benefits that it generates are derivative and incidental. As Mill argued in *On Liberty*, "[d]espotism is a legitimate mode of government in dealing with barbarians, provided the end be their improvement, and the means justified by actually effecting that end." Giuseppe Mazzini, writing in the early 1870s, likewise endorsed the "moral mission" of civilizing imperialism, suggesting that the Europeans were destined to transform Asia and that Italy "should not lose out on this wonderful new movement."[50] At the turn of the twentieth century, Chamberlain recorded the shift towards this "altruistic" vision of empire: "[T]he sense of possession has given place to a different sentiment—the sense of obligation. We feel now that our rule over their territories can only be justified if we can show that it adds to the happiness and prospects of the people."[51] Most articulations of this argument link civilization to nationality and sovereignty. Civilization is seen as a necessary though

[49] Mill, *Considerations on Representative Government* [1861], in *Collected Works*, ed. J. Robson (Toronto, 1977), vol. 18, ch. 18.

[50] Mill, *On Liberty* [1859], *Collected Works* (Toronto, 1977), 18:224; Mazzini, "Principles of International Politics" [1871], in *Cosmopolitanism and Nations*, ed. Stefano Recchia and Nadia Urbinati (Princeton, 2009), 238.

[51] Chamberlain, "The True Conception of the Empire," 2:3.

not sufficient condition for the emergence of national self-consciousness, which in turn is regarded as essential to trigger liberal claims to the right of political self-determination. Once a society had developed to the point where it could be classified as civilized, and once it exhibited authentic national self-consciousness, it could justifiably claim independence, and the job of the liberal imperial power was complete. But the temporal coordinates were very rarely specified; freedom was deferred to some indefinite point in the future. In the meantime, attention was focused on refining the modes and modulations of imperial rule—on ideologies of governance.

Liberal civilizing imperialism coexisted with another kind of justificatory argument which we might characterize as "republican." Republican imperialism is primarily motivated by a concern with the character of the imperial power, justifying empire in terms of a particular class of benefits that it generates for the state. Its proponents seek to foster individual and collective virtue in their compatriots, while upholding national honor and glory. Any other benefits that empire generates—including economic gain and "civilization"—are derivative and incidental. This kind of argument has deep roots in Western political thought, traceable to Rome. During the nineteenth century Alexis de Tocqueville, and a range of British commentators, including the historians J. R. Seeley and J. A. Froude, articulated republican defenses of empire. Though they employed the language of civilization to classify and order the world—as we would expect, given its central role in the imperial imaginary—they tended not to justify imperialism principally in terms of its civilizing agency. For example, although Froude often boasted about the greatness of the British empire, he placed little emphasis on "civilizing" occupied territories, focusing instead on the virtues that such power fostered in the British population.[52] Republican justifications predate liberalism by centuries, and they offer a different kind of argument about the character and purpose of empire, as well as its potential fate.

Finally, we can isolate a martialist justification of empire. Martialism is the view that "war is both the supreme instrument and the ultimate realization of all human endeavour."[53] It stresses the transcendent role of violence in shaping individual and collective character. The field of battle is seen as a space for enacting a form of warrior masculinity—and for inculcating virility in a population. Although it found its most ardent supporters in *fin de siècle* Germany—including Helmut von Moltke and Heinrich von Treitschke—a "martialist *Zeitgeist*," Karma Nabulsi contends, infused the thought and practice of many British soldiers, imperial administrators, and civil servants in the nineteenth century. It was expressed, though rarely in an explicit and straightforward sense, in the utterances of writers such as Thomas Carlyle and J. A.

[52] For more on Froude's imperial thought, see chapter 12.
[53] Karma Nabulsi, *Traditions of War*, 126.

Cramb,[54] and it can also be located in the works of some of the more jingoistic British poets of the age, such as W. E. Henley, who once proclaimed that "War, the Red Angel" was the lifeblood of the nation.[55] Empire, on this view, is a space for forging character through exercising the will-to-power in rituals of destruction.

Ideologies of Governance

Governance includes the discrete institutions of government but it also encompasses the assorted practices and structures—educational systems, market orders, civil society actors, cultural agencies—though which populations are administered and regulated. It focuses, then, on the multiple vectors for creating, maintaining, and contesting political legitimacy. The modalities of governance employed to rule empires, and to construct pliant imperial subjectivities, have varied greatly across time and space. For much of human history the ability of governments to rule territory was severely constrained by practical concerns, above all the difficulties of creating effective administrative systems. Only in the last couple of hundred years—and in particular during the last century—have states gained the capacity to systematically observe, measure, and regulate large populations, thus providing the necessary conditions for the comprehensive exercise of sovereign power.[56] Governance of this kind has ascribed a central role to the construction and deployment of knowledge and expertise. In the British empire, for example, administrators and scholars were set to work classifying different castes in India, tribes in Africa, languages, legal systems, sexualities, geographies, even dreams.[57] Such exercises created the "colonial knowledge" thought necessary to police and rule space, though it was rarely as effective as its advocates proclaimed.[58] Mapping the "human terrain" as it has come to be called in the post-9/11 era, was a vital element of imperial governance.

---

[54] Ibid., 110–19.

[55] Henley, "Epilogue" [1897], in *Poems* (London, 1926), 241.

[56] James Scott, *Seeing like a State* (London, 1998); Scott, *The Art of Not Being Governed* (New Haven, 2009). The work of Michel Foucault has proven especially insightful in delineating the various modulations of power and "governmentality" involved in imperial subjugation. See, for prominent examples, Timothy Mitchell, *Colonising Egypt* (Berkeley, 1991); Mitchell, *Rule of Experts* (Berkeley, 2002); and Ann Laura Stoler, *Race and the Education of Desire* (Durham, NC, 1995).

[57] On imperial dreaming, see Erik Linstrum, "The Politics of Psychology in the British Empire, 1898–1960," *Past & Present*, 215 (2012), 214–33.

[58] Bernard Cohn, *Colonialism and Its Forms of Knowledge*; Susan Bayly, *Caste, Society and Politics in India from the Eighteenth Century to the Modern Age* (Cambridge, 1999); Nicholas Dirks, *Castes of Mind* (Princeton, 2001).

The question of whether formal or informal rule is the most effectual runs through modern imperial discourse. The scholarly debate on the topic was initiated by Robinson and Gallagher's famous argument about the "imperialism of free trade" in the nineteenth century. Where possible, they argued, the British preferred to subordinate other societies through economic instruments rather than formal occupation—"trade with informal control if possible; trade with rule when necessary."[59] Exercising *de jure* sovereignty over a political community was not indispensable to wielding profound and pervasive control over it. The mid-nineteenth century, then, was marked less by a retreat from empire, as was once commonly assumed, than a turn to novel nonterritorial forms of imperial governance. This kind of argument highlights how economic regimes—specific configurations of state, market, and knowledge—can shape modes of rule. Mike Davis, for example, argues that Britain's commitment to classical liberal economics facilitated the famines that ravaged the population of British India in the closing decades of the nineteenth century, killing uncounted millions.[60] Linking imperialism directly to liberal economic ideology opens a space for arguing that the postcolonial world remains structured by imperialism. On this account, even if formal empires have retreated to the wings, imperialism remains embedded in the structures and ideology of the current global economic order. Neoliberalism can be seen as the latest manifestation of capitalist imperialism.[61]

A key issue in imperial governance concerns the degree to which an imperial power tries to (re)construct the subjected society in its own image—the extent to which empire becomes a totalizing project. This was a contested issue in the nineteenth-century debates over how and why the British should rule India. A new generation of liberal civilizing imperialists attacked what they saw as an outdated policy in which European intervention in local Indian affairs was minimized (whether this was a realistic picture is a separate question). They were adamant that the primary aim of empire was to civilize a barbarian land and not simply to extract revenue or provide an outlet for British geopolitical ambition. These contrasting ends implied very different governing means. In particular, the civilizational model demanded a much more intrusive governance regime. The character of public education assumed a fundamental role, spawning a famous ideological dispute between "Orientalists" and "Anglicizers." Professing respect for Indian cultural achievements, the Orientalists favored allocating money to teaching Sanskrit

[59] Robinson and Gallagher, "The Imperialism of Free Trade," *Economic History Review*, 6 (1953), 13.

[60] Davis, *Late Victorian Holocausts* (London, 2003).

[61] David Harvey, *The New Imperialism* (Oxford, 2003); Harvey, *A Brief History of Neoliberalism* (Oxford, 2005); Alex Callinicos, *Imperialism and the Global Political Economy* (Cambridge, 2009).

and Arabic, while the Anglicizers insisted on making English the primary language.[62] This was the occasion for T. B. Macaulay's notorious "Minute on Indian Education," wherein he proclaimed that "a single shelf of a good European library was worth the whole native literature of India and Arabia."[63] English should be supported because it conveyed the teachings of a superior civilization—language was a vehicle for progress. At stake here was a question about both the purpose and the most appropriate governing technologies of empire.

An important transition occurred in the governing ideology of the British empire in the closing decades of the nineteenth century. Karuna Mantena has characterized this as the shift from "ethical" modes of imperialism (exemplified by John Stuart Mill) to informal "alibis" of empire (exemplified by Henry Maine). On this account, the British pulled back from the attempt to create imperial subjects in their own image, thus preparing the ground for liberal self-government, and instead turned increasingly to modes of rule that they claimed protected fragile native communities from destruction. "Rather than eradicated or aggressively modernized, native social and political forms would now be patronized as they became inserted into the institutional dynamics of imperial power."[64] Although this argument understates the extent to which "ethical" justifications continued to circulate—a theme I discussed in chapter 2—the gradual emergence of more indirect styles of governance was nevertheless highly significant. The major practical impact of this ideological shift was the transition towards government by indirect rule in Britain's African colonies and the later development of notions of trusteeship under the League of Nations.

Settler colonialism, as I dissect in various chapters in this volume, produced (and was produced by) a range of distinctive justificatory and governing strategies.[65] In a standard conceptual move, Mill distinguished two classes of British "dependencies": those composed of people of a "similar civilization" that were "capable of, and ripe for, representative government" and those, defined in hierarchical opposition, that remained "a great distance from that state."[66] The former group included Australia, Canada, New Zealand—and had once included the United States—while the latter encompassed India and British territories in the Caribbean and Africa. Since the settler colonies

---

[62] Lynn Zastoupil and Martin Moir, eds., *The Great Indian Education Debate* (London, 1999).

[63] Macaulay, "Minute of 2 February 1835 on Indian Education" [1835], in *Macaulay, Prose and Poetry*, ed. G. M. Young (Cambridge, MA, 1957), 721.

[64] Mantena, *Alibis of Empire*, 2. The shift in India is traced in Thomas Metcalf, *Ideologies of the Raj*. Again highlighting the interpenetration between the modern social sciences and empire, Mantena shows how the origins of modern social theory were inflected with imperial concerns, not least through the development of the category of "traditional society."

[65] Lorenzo Veracini, *Settler Colonialism* (Basingstoke, 2010).

[66] Mill, *Considerations on Representative Government, Collected Works*, 19:562.

were seen as already populated by civilized subjects, they were justified and governed in different ways from the rest of the empire. In India the primary target of imperial governance, and the postulated locus of the problem it sought to rectify, was the mind of the "barbarian." Discussion of the settler empire was likewise saturated with the imagery of childhood, except here the referent was different. The target was not the people, who were after all descendants or relations of the inhabitants of Britain, but rather the polities in which they lived. The collective not the individual, the whole not the part, required supervision. It was Australia, Canada, and New Zealand that were "young" and "immature." They were governed in a different manner from the rest of the British empire: from the middle of the nineteenth century, for example, they were granted increasing domestic political autonomy ("responsible government").[67] Furthermore, from the 1850s onwards most advocates of settler colonialism argued that the formal connection between "mother country" and colonies was only legitimate if subject to reciprocal assent. This stands in stark contrast to attitudes to the rest of the empire, where subjects were not regarded as sufficiently developed—politically, cognitively, or morally—to enter into such voluntaristic relations.

Violence, and the threat of violence, is a necessary element of imperial governance. Empires are typically administered through a complex pattern of central rule and local collaboration, but violence is an ever-present possibility, employed both to enforce the existing order and to challenge it. During the nineteenth century, the utility of violence triggered disagreement between otherwise putatively "liberal" defenders of empire. For Tocqueville, an ardent proponent of French rule in Algeria, empire sometimes required brutal extra-judicial measures. "In order for us to colonize to any extent," he asserted, "we must necessarily use not only violent measures, but visibly iniquitous ones," and as such it was sometimes acceptable to "burn harvests, . . . empty silos, and finally . . . seize unarmed men, women, and children."[68] This kind of position horrified John Stuart Mill and many of his followers.[69] For Mill, upholding the rule of law and treating subjects with due consideration was an indispensable element of enlightened despotism, differentiating it from illegitimate imperialism. This belief underpinned support for the campaign, in which Mill played a prominent role, to bring Governor Eyre to justice for his abuse of

---

[67] James Belich, *Replenishing the Earth*, argues that the early nineteenth century saw a "Settler Revolution" that led to the explosive settlement of two related geo-economic regions, the "American West" and the "British West" (Canada, Australia, New Zealand, and South Africa). This revolution cemented the rise of the "Anglo-world," which continues to exert great power today. For a theoretical analysis of the racial-political formation, see Srdjan Vucetic, *The Anglosphere* (Stanford, 2011).

[68] Tocqueville, "Essay on Algeria (October 1841)," in *Writings on Empire and Slavery*, ed. J. Pitts (Baltimore, 2001), 83, 70.

[69] Pitts, *A Turn to Empire*.

power in Jamaica in the 1860s.[70] However, liberal imperialists were almost invariably blind to the lived experience of imperial rule, failing to recognize that routinized violence was inescapable in governing conquered spaces. While Mill became increasingly perturbed by the prevalence of colonial violence towards the end of his life, he nevertheless continued to preach the benefits of civilizing imperialism.[71]

In recent years, the legacy of imperial governance has shaped various aspects of world order. Imperial administrative practices forged in the early twentieth century have found a new lease of life as trusteeships and protectorates have been retooled by the United Nations in the former Yugoslavia and elsewhere.[72] Methods of colonial policing, meanwhile, have been widely employed in Iraq and Afghanistan, as "counter-insurgency" activities have been launched against resistance movements of various kinds. Western militaries are far more open about the colonial origins of such strategies—forged in the battle spaces of Malaya, Algeria, and Vietnam, among others—than the governments who sent them there. Indeed learning the lessons of previous colonial wars has been a central feature of the post-9/11 national security apparatus. A further legacy of imperial governmentality can be seen in the deployment of social scientists—and above all, anthropologists—to the global south to provide the "cultural knowledge" necessary to combat insurgencies.[73]

Ideologies of Resistance

There are as many ideologies of resistance as there are of justification and governance. Excavating them would involve working at multiple levels of analysis, and in a variety of scholarly registers, spanning what James Scott labels "everyday forms of peasant resistance," through the ideas animating revolutionary movements, to the sophisticated theoretical critiques developed by philosophers.[74] For the sake of convenience, we can divide such ideologies into two broad families. The first set emanates from the imperial metropole; they constitute a form of internal opposition to the practices of imperialism. The second set is produced by subjects of imperial rule. Historically the most prominent strands of metropolitan opposition focused largely (though not exclusively) on the damage that imperialism wreaks on the imperial power itself, paying scant attention to those subjected to the violence and the routine

[70] Rande Kostal, *A Jurisprudence of Power* (Oxford, 2005).

[71] I trace Mill's shift in attitude in chapter 9.

[72] William Bain, *Between Anarchy and Society* (Oxford, 2003); James Mayall and Ricardo Soares de Oliveira, eds., *The New Protectorates* (London, 2011).

[73] John Kelly, ed., *Anthropology and Global Counterinsurgency* (Chicago, 2010).

[74] Scott, *Weapons of the Weak* (New Haven, 1985); Scott, *Domination and the Arts of Resistance* (New Haven, 1990).

humiliation of empire. The second form of imperial resistance argument focuses largely (though not exclusively) on that violence and humiliation.

The term "anti-imperialism" is often misleading when applied to ideologies of resistance. Many of the arguments lumped under the umbrella do not reject imperialism in principle—instead they focus on certain expressions of it. An important body of scholarship has sought to anatomize the tradition of "liberal" imperial critique in Western Europe, demonstrating that an array of important thinkers, including Diderot, Herder, Smith, Bentham, and Kant opposed imperial conquest.[75] Edmund Burke has also been reinterpreted as an important source of anti-imperial theorizing, albeit less convincingly.[76] Despite this opposition, however, it is worth bearing in mind that much "Enlightenment" thought was nevertheless shaped by the imperial imaginary. It is sometimes suggested that anti-imperial arguments were marginalized by the middle of the nineteenth century, supplanted by the unabashed liberal imperialism exemplified by John Stuart Mill. This is misleading, however, for the nineteenth century saw stinging attacks on empire—as passionate and comprehensive as any launched by Smith, Bentham, or Kant—from esteemed liberal philosophers (such as Herbert Spencer), politicians (such as Richard Cobden), and political economists (such as J. A. Hobson). Like the late eighteenth-century critics, though, they were rarely opposed to *all* forms of empire; the "anti-imperial" critique only cut so deep. For example, many of them opposed the violent usurpation and rule of European powers in Asia, Africa, and Latin America while simultaneously endorsing the seizure of "unoccupied" lands by European settlers—the kind of settler colonialism that led to the dispossession and death (sometimes through genocide) of innumerable people in Australasia and North America, among other places.[77] Given the ubiquity of the imperial imaginary, it is unsurprising that arguments explicitly critical of empire were nevertheless typically underpinned by racial and civilizational assumptions.

Liberalism was not an ideology confined to the metropole—it was both a product and an agent of globalization. During the course of the nineteenth century it was spread throughout the world by European imperial powers, but it was then often indigenized, adapted to local circumstances and traditions to provide a repertoire of arguments that could be utilized as part of an anti-imperial struggle. As C. A. Bayly notes, the leaders of anti-imperial protests "in places as far distant as Santiago, Cape Town and Canton invoked the notion of their 'rights' as individuals and as representatives of nations."[78] An

[75] Sankar Muthu, *Enlightenment against Empire* (Princeton, 2003); Pitts, *A Turn to Empire*.

[76] See chapter 2 for further discussion of this line of interpretation. It is convincingly challenged in Daniel O'Neill, *Edmund Burke and the Conservative Logic of Empire* (Berkeley, 2016).

[77] Dirk A. Moses, ed., *Genocide and Settler Society* (New York, 2004); Moses, *Empire, Colony, Genocide* (New York, 2008).

[78] Bayly, "European Political Thought and the Wider World during the Nineteenth Century,"

emergent Indian liberal tradition provided a powerful ideological resource to oppose empire.[79] Modern Western empires often carried the ideological virus that eventually helped to kill them.

Like liberalism, republicanism is capable of being utilized for both imperial and anti-imperial ends. Whereas republican imperialism contends that the pursuit of empire is important (or even necessary) for maintaining a virtuous political community, republican anti-imperialism asserts that the very existence of the republic is endangered by imperial activity: republican virtues are corroded by the "spirit of conquest." According to republicans, Quentin Skinner argues, "[y]ou can hope to retain your individual freedom from dependence on the will of others if and only if you live as an active citizen of a state that is fully self-governing, and is consequently neither dominating nor dominated." Offering a contemporary gloss on this venerable theme, Philip Pettit suggests that "the free individual is protected against the domination of others by the undominating and undominated state."[80] Republican anti-imperial arguments have been popular during the last couple of centuries, most notably in the United States, where the founding has been mythologized as an archetypal anti-imperial moment.[81] Today they are deployed to challenge American hegemony. Chalmers Johnson, for example, laments that the American republic is being destroyed by militarism and the pursuit of global empire—it faces nemesis, the product of hubris.[82]

The Marxist arguments I mentioned in the third section of this chapter can be seen both as attempts to explain the dynamics of imperialism and as contributions to ideologies of resistance. Marxism provided much of the intellectual impetus for anti-imperial praxis throughout the twentieth century, and variants of Marxism remain central to both anti-imperial social movements and to the politico-intellectual attack on the neoliberal order. In one of the most widely discussed recent interventions, Michael Hardt and Antonio Negri argue that we are witnessing the emergence of a new form of network "Empire."[83] On this interpretation, Empire is "a *decentred* and *deterritorialis-*

---

in *The Cambridge History of Nineteenth-Century Political Thought*, ed. Gregory Claeys and Gareth Stedman Jones (Cambridge, 2011), 835; Christian Reus-Smit, "Struggles for Individual Rights and the Expansion of the International System," *International Organization*, 65 (2011), 207–42.

[79] C. A. Bayly, *Recovering Liberties* (Cambridge, 2012).

[80] Skinner, "On the Slogans of Republican Political Theory," *European Journal of Political Theory*, 9 (2010), 100; Pettit, "A Republican Law of Peoples," *European Journal of Political Theory*, 9 (2010), 77.

[81] David Mayers, *Dissenting Voices in America's Rise to Power* (Cambridge, 2007). It was also present in Victorian Britain. See, for example, Stuart Jones's account of Frederic Harrison's republicanism, in "The Victorian Lexicon of Evil," in *Evil, Barbarism and Empire*, ed. Tom Cook, Rebecca Gill, and Bertrand Taithe (Basingstoke, 2011), 126–43. On Harrison, see chapter 2.

[82] Johnson, *Nemesis* (New York, 2007).

[83] Hardt and Negri, *Empire* (Cambridge, 2000); *Multitude* (Cambridge, 2004).

ing apparatus of rule that progressively incorporates the entire global realm within its open, expanding frontiers." Empire, they continue, can "only be conceived as a universal republic, a network of powers and counterpowers structured in a boundless and inclusive architecture."[84] (Their argument is notable among other things for underplaying the continued salience of the United States.) Traditional styles of resistance, based on nationalist forms of belonging, are as obsolete as the territorial modes of imperialism they originally challenged. Instead, Empire spawns its own agent of resistance—the "Multitude," the "productive creative subjectivities of globalization."[85] An amorphous, heterogeneous assemblage of workers, the dispossessed and the oppressed, the multitude is (somehow) supposed to offer an alternative way of being.[86] Empire dialectically generates the specific mode of resistance that will dissolve or transcend it. Other Marxist theorists have recoiled from Hardt and Negri's grandiose metaphysics of resistance, and focused instead on unraveling the social dynamics of contemporary forms of neoliberal imperialism and its alternatives.[87]

A plethora of anticolonial movements and ideologies sprang up in the world's occupied zones during the twentieth century. While impossible to do them justice in such a short space, it is worth highlighting two influential but contrasting models: the Gandhian and Fanonian. Perhaps more than any other anti-imperialist, Gandhi combined theory and practice as part of a seamless whole.[88] In *Hind Swaraj* he sketched both a stringent critique of Western civilization and elaborated an alternative nonviolent form of nationalist politics rooted in the celebration of Indian cultural practices. For Gandhi, Western civilization was poisoned by its materialism, its moral myopia, and its destructive individualism—it was hypocritical to the core. Adopting a strategy of "reversal," he denigrated the claims to normative superiority used by the British to legitimate their empire while affirming many of the "traditional" practices that they had belittled, finding in Indian civilization a productive source of ethical guidance and spiritual development.[89] True (Indian) civilization embodied the virtues—self-abnegation, duty, good conduct, self-

[84] Hardt and Negri, *Empire*, xii, 166.

[85] Ibid., 60.

[86] Hardt and Negri, *Multitude*.

[87] Harvey, *The New Imperialism*; Alexander Anievas, ed., *Marxism and World Politics* (London, 2010).

[88] Bhikhu Parekh, *Gandhi's Political Philosophy* (London, 1989); Steger, *Gandhi's Dilemma* (Basingstoke, 2000); Karuna Mantena, "Another Realism," *American Political Science Review*, 106/2 (2012), 455–70; Anthony Parel, *Gandhi's Philosophy and the Quest for Harmony* (Cambridge, 2006).

[89] On anticolonial strategies of reversal, see Margaret Kohn and Keally McBride, *Political Theories of Decolonization* (Oxford, 2011). "Reversal describes attempts to undermine power relations by valorizing the cultural markers that the colonial system had denigrated as inferior."

control—that Western culture was incapable of sustaining.[90] Mixing romantic nostalgia, hard-headed political criticism and an iconoclastic account of nationalism, *Hind Swaraj* served as a seminal (though selectively appropriated) text for the Indian Nationalist Movement and a source of inspiration for later anticolonial thinkers.

Frantz Fanon, an Algerian psychiatrist and journalist, defended a radically different kind of resistance. Drawing on Marxism and psychoanalysis, his work illuminated the complex intersections of race and economic exploitation undergirding European empires.[91] In his analyses of the social and racial dynamics of imperialism—most famously *The Wretched of the Earth*—he emphasized its extreme violence and the damaging psychic consequences for the oppressed. Like Gandhi he dissected the hypocrisy of Western universalism, deriding its claims to superiority: "[W]hen the native hears a speech about Western culture he pulls out his knife."[92] Yet he diverged from Gandhi in at least two important respects. First, he was highly ambivalent about nationalism. Recognizing it as a necessary stage of anticolonial politics, he ultimately sought to transcend it, for rather than offering a vehicle to escape colonial rule, nationalism promised to reinscribe its hierarchical structures in novel forms. Fostering national consciousness served as a symbolic way for the new postcolonial elites to mask the mimetic dynamics of exploitation. The problem of oppression was not resolved by granting formal freedom, because capitalism was necessarily exploitative and freedom-constraining. This line of argument marked a powerful move, for much early anticolonial thought and practice was framed within the terms of a national imaginary. Indeed the nationalist impulse of much anticolonial activism provided one of the main targets for a later generation of postcolonial scholars.[93] The second, and most controversial, way in which Fanon diverged from Gandhi was in his defense of the utility of violence in colonial contexts. Violence was an essential part of the anti-imperial struggle, necessary both to overcome the crushing power of the colonial state and to provide a form of catharsis for its victims. Liberation—both political and psychological—was only possible through a brutal clash of wills. It is in part through the exercise of such violence that colonial subjects can regain their agency. "At the level of individuals, violence is a cleansing force. It frees the native from his inferiority complex and from his despair and inaction; it makes him fearless and restores his self-respect."[94] Fanon's arguments resonated widely in a world caught in the throes of antico-

[90] Gandhi, *Hind Swaraj and Other Writings* [1909], ed. Anthony Parel (Cambridge, 1997), 67–68.

[91] Nigel Gibson, *Fanon* (Cambridge, 2003).

[92] Fanon, *The Wretched of the Earth* (London, 2001), 43.

[93] Chatterjee, *Nationalist Thought and the Colonial World*.

[94] Fanon, *The Wretched of the Earth*, 74.

lonial struggle, while generating sharp criticism from those who rejected his advocacy of violence, including Hannah Arendt and Michael Walzer.[95]

We are left with a question about what forms of resistance are appropriate in the contemporary world. Modern history offers a range of answers, each of which finds its contemporary exponents. Liberal and republican thinkers and activists have offered forceful criticisms of imperial action, while Marxism continues to inspire social movements throughout the world, its arguments and strategies adapted to new forms of oppression. Gandhian nonviolence still finds enthusiasts.[96] What of violent resistance? This is a topic that is rarely explored in contemporary political theory, yet if the current global order is a site of vast injustice, as many theorists suggest, should violence be ruled out? After all, to deny victims the right to resist their oppressors seems to conspire in their subjugation.[97] The ghost of Fanon has not yet been exorcised.

Conclusions

One of the most famous passages written about imperialism is found in Joseph Conrad's *Heart of Darkness*:

> The conquest of the earth, which mostly means the taking it away from those who have a different complexion or slightly flatter noses than ourselves, is not a pretty thing when you look into it too much. What redeems it is the idea only. An idea at the back of it, not a sentimental pretence but an idea: and an unselfish belief in the idea—something you can set up, and bow down before, and offer a sacrifice to.[98]

Conrad here penetrates to the core of the issues that I have discussed in this chapter. Empire is never a "pretty thing," and while no idea redeems it—despite the claims of Conrad's narrator and the protestations of contemporary neo-imperialists—modern imperialism cannot be understood adequately without grasping the ideas that have motivated its advocates, legitimated its practices, and animated resistance to it. We live in a world shaped by the histories, memories, and myths of past empires, and in which imperial power still determines the life chances of countless millions of people. It should remain a central topic of concern for students of political thought.

[95] Arendt, *On Violence* (New York, 1970); Walzer, *Just and Unjust Wars* (London, 1978), 204–6.

[96] See, for example, James Tully, *Public Philosophy in a New Key*, 2 vols. (Cambridge, 2008).

[97] For further discussion, see Duncan Bell, "To Act Otherwise," in *On Global Citizenship*, ed. David Owen (Bloomsbury, 2014), 181–207.

[98] Conrad, *Heart of Darkness*, ed. Ross Murfin, 2nd ed. (London, 1996), 21.

PART II

Themes

CHAPTER 5

Escape Velocity

꒱

Ancient History and the Empire of Time

For a long time the greatness of the ancient world lay with an
oppressive weight like an incubus upon the moderns.[1]

—J. R. SEELEY

[T]here exists, no doubt, a prevalent feeling, that, in a certain sense,
the doom of Athens is already ours.[2]

—HERMAN MERIVALE

Obsessed with decoding historical experience, the Victorians endlessly
scoured the past for lessons about how best to comprehend and navigate
their world. In his inaugural lecture at Cambridge in 1895, Lord Acton observed that the nineteenth century was saturated with "historic ways of
thought," which had come to be given the "depressing names" of "historicism
or historical-mindedness." Such was the power exerted by the injunction to
seek knowledge and guidance from the annals of history that the constitutional theorist A. V. Dicey once complained that it "was far better, as things
now stand, to be charged with heresy, than to fall under the suspicion of lacking historical-mindedness, or of questioning the universal validity of the historical method."[3] The imaginative construal of empire was no exception to this
ubiquitous cultural practice. Debates over imperial order were inflected by
two conflicting narratives of historical time, one cyclical, the other progres-

---

[1] J. R. Seeley, *Introduction to Political Science*, ed. Henry Sidgwick (London, 1896), 161.

[2] Herman Merivale, "The Colonial Question in 1870," *Fortnightly Review*, 7 (1870), 153.

[3] Acton, "Inaugural Lecture on the Study of History," *Lectures on Modern History*, ed. J. N. Figgis and R. V. Laurence (London, 1906), 22; Dicey, *Introduction to the Study of the Law of the Constitution*, 4th ed. (London, 1893), 14. For a powerful questioning of that method, see Henry Sidgwick, "The Historical Method," *Mind*, 11/42 (1886), 203–19; Sidgwick, *The Elements of Politics*,
2nd ed. (London, 1897), ch. 1. Sidgwick, like Dicey, was cognizant that he was arguing against the
grain.

sive.[4] According to the former, empires followed a predetermined trajectory: they rose, they declined, and ultimately they fell. Counseling vigilance, Goldwin Smith, one time Regius Professor of History at Oxford, warned in the late 1870s that the "decay of Empires is the theme of history."[5] According to the other conception, the nineteenth century was an age of progress, of constant human improvement, with the British imperial state in the vanguard. The "movement of humanity is not, as the ancients fancied, in cycles," declared the omnicompetent scholar-statesman James Bryce, "but shows a sustained, though often interrupted, progress."[6] Imperial discourse was shaped by an unremitting negotiation between the two positions, each of which can be seen as different modulations of historicism. Although they diverged over how the past informed the present, both posited historical experience as central to understanding contemporary politics. This was a clash of historical epistemologies, of what kind of knowledge could be ascertained from historical reflection. The progressivist view of empire was broadly Whiggish, divining in the evolution of ideas and institutions the teleological unfolding of cherished principles (most often liberty).[7] The cyclical view encoded a model of eternal return, of repetition and recurrence, in which the destiny of the empire could be discerned by grasping the shape of the past.

While belief in progress suffused Victorian political consciousness, the trope of proleptic decline supplied critics of empire with powerful ammunition. It implied that imperial orders always contained the seeds of their own destruction. Hence Smith's argument that in light of historical experience the British "policy of aggrandizement" was necessarily ruinous.[8] However, it is important to distinguish between two different conceptions of imperial cyclicality, one universal, the other more institutionally specific. The universal variant, which could draw on Polybian archetypes or Christian providentialism, viewed all human institutions—indeed all life—as subject to the same temporal dynamics. Synecdochic exemplars, empires were an instance of a general historical pattern. While unusual in Victorian Britain, this position found eloquent defenders among liberal Anglican historians, including Thomas Arnold, though it was also articulated in other idioms, such as the modified classical republicanism of the historian J. A. Froude. The history of all living things, including commonwealths, Froude proclaimed in the late 1870s, was defined by "recurring stages of growth and transformation and

---

[4] This chapter updates and extends the analysis of imperial temporality in Duncan Bell, *The Idea of Greater Britain*, ch. 8.

[5] Smith, "The Policy of Aggrandizement," *Fortnightly Review*, 22 (1877), 307.

[6] Bryce, "An Age of Discontent," *Contemporary Review*, 59 (1891), 29.

[7] It thus fits with what Mark Bevir calls "developmental historicism." Bevir, "Political Studies as Narrative and Science, 1880–2000," *Political Studies*, 54 (2006), 583–606.

[8] Smith, "The Policy of Aggrandizement." For a similar critique of American empire, see Goldwin Smith, *Commonwealth or Empire?* (New York, 1902).

decay," and as such it was imperative to recognize the ephemeral quality of imperial governance.[9] Despite its historical determinism, the universalist account allowed scope for human agency: impossible to defeat, historical fate could at least be deferred. "The life of a nation, like the life of a man, may be prolonged in honour into the fullness of its time, or it may perish prematurely, for want of guidance, by violence or internal disorders."[10] Knowledge of history could guide the wise statesman in battling time. The more popular cyclical vision regarded empire as atypical, a pathological form of political association fated to collapse due to its inherent weaknesses. Unlike the universal account, this view was compatible with the widespread Victorian belief in the sustained progressive development of humanity. It was deployed to characterize empire as an *untimely* aberration, flagrantly rejecting the spirit of the age.

Most imperialists maintained that the British empire was somehow exempt from historical precedent. Forestalling the cycle of imperial temporality, progress guaranteed an *escape velocity*, the ability to break free from the gravitational pull of imperial declension. In what follows I explore two broad variations that were articulated across the human sciences and in public debate, focusing in particular on the writings of historians. In the first, the modern British empire was figured as uniquely progressive, as capable—either in actuality or *in potentia*—of avoiding the social, economic, and political dynamics that had annihilated all previous specimens. This argument was most frequently employed in relation to India. The other strategy was to insist that the empire (or a part of it) was not really an empire at all, but rather a new form of political order that could circumvent the entropic degeneration of traditional imperial forms. To think otherwise was to make a category mistake. This argument was often applied to Britain and its settler colonies from the 1870s onwards. "Greater Britain," as the settler colonial assemblage was often termed, could attain permanence, a kind of historical grace.

The Time of Empire: Narratives of Decline and Fall

The "English," J. R. Seeley observed in 1880, "guide ourselves in the great political questions by great historical precedents."[11] Understandings of the past played a formative role in the construction, elaboration, and defense of political argument in Victorian Britain, and it was widely assumed that a proper appreciation of the vicissitudes of history could impart wisdom and sound

[9] Froude, *Caesar* (London, 1879), 2. On this dimension of Froude's imperial thought, see chapter 12.

[10] Ibid., 3–4.

[11] Seeley, "Political Somnambulism," *Macmillan's Magazine*, 43 (1880), 32. On the role of historical imagination in political thinking, see especially John Burrow, *Whigs and Liberals* (Oxford, 1988); Collini, Winch, and Burrow, *That Noble Science of Politics*, chs. 6–7.

judgment. "History ought surely in some degree . . . anticipate the lessons of time," Seeley declared in *The Expansion of England*, one of the key textbooks of the Victorian empire, and it was necessary to study it so that "we may be wise before the event."[12] Some epochs of history were far more important than others. The stories of Greece and Rome provided a common frame of reference, a claim of authority, and a productive repertoire of images and arguments for a classically educated elite to interpret contemporary culture and politics, and they played a privileged role in thinking about the nature of imperial rule.[13] Yet the Victorians disagreed profoundly over which particular lessons to draw from which particular pasts, and the meaning of history was a topic of intense ideological contestation.

They inherited—and sought to recalibrate or transvalue—one of the most venerable Western accounts of historical temporality. The *Imperium romanum*, Anthony Pagden reminds us, "has always had a unique place in the political imagination of western Europe," infusing visions of self, society, state, and empire, and it supplied the "ideologies of the colonial systems of Spain, Britain, and France with the language and political models they required."[14] The Romans had bequeathed modern Europeans an evocative metanarrative of self-dissolution: the drive for expansion corrupted the polity and inevitably led to disaster. The *topos* of decline and fall had for centuries shaped understandings of empire and the principles underlying historical development. Drawing on the history of Rome, as mediated by Sallust and Polybius, Machiavelli had argued in his *Discourses on Livy* that states would inexorably seek to expand, but that in so doing would forfeit their liberty before collapsing under the moral and constitutional strain of the quest for *grandezza*.[15] Subsequent critics of imperialism, including Montesquieu, Hume, Kant, Robertson, and Constant, likewise pointed to the moral and physical collapse of Rome to warn of a comparable fate for those who pursued rapacious military

[12] Seeley, *The Expansion of England*, 169.

[13] There is a huge literature on Victorian appropriations of the classics. See, for example, Simon Goldhill, *Victorian Culture and Classical Antiquity* (Princeton, 2012); Frank Turner, *The Greek Heritage in Victorian Britain* (London, 1984); Richard Jenkyns, *The Victorians and Ancient Greece* (Oxford, 1980); Norman Vance, *The Victorians and Ancient Rome* (Oxford, 1997); Christopher Stray, *Classics Transformed* (Oxford, 1998). For the imperial uses of the classics, see, inter alia, Mark Bradley, ed., *Classics and Imperialism in the British Empire* (Oxford, 2010); Sarah Butler, *Britain and Its Empire in the Shadow of Rome* (London, 2012); Christopher Hagerman, *Britain's Imperial Muse* (Basingstoke, 2013); Phiroze Vasunia, *The Classics and Colonial India* (Oxford, 2013).

[14] Anthony Pagden, *Lords of All the World* (London, 1998), 11. See also Pagden, *The Burdens of Empire* (Cambridge, 2015), 2–3.

[15] Machiavelli, *Discourses on Livy*, ed. Julia Conaway Bondanella and Peter Bondanella (Oxford, 1997), bk. 2. See also David Armitage, "Empire and Liberty," in *Republicanism*, ed. Martin van Gelderen and Quentin Skinner (Cambridge, 2002), 2:29–46; J.G.A. Pocock, *Barbarism and Religion, Vol. 3* (Cambridge, 2003), esp. pts. 3-5.

policies. As Hume once wrote, "[t]here seems to be a Natural Course of Things, which brings on the Destruction of great Empires."[16] Edward Gibbon's *History of the Decline and Fall of the Roman Empire* imprinted the narrative deeply into British historical consciousness: the disintegration of Rome "was the natural and inevitable effect of immoderate greatness."[17] In such accounts, the imperial dynamic was naturalized, and thus posited as unchanging, indelible, eternal. The critique of empire propagated by the "country party" Whigs during the eighteenth century warned about the corruption that destroyed Rome and threatened Britain as it carved out an empire in South Asia and the Caribbean.[18] Alive to this classical precedent, British imperial ideologists of the seventeenth and eighteenth centuries had routinely sought to avoid the fate of Rome by emphasizing the exceptional character—commercial, maritime, and free—of their new empire in North America.[19] The narrative likewise exercised the imagination of both scholars and the political elite during the Victorian age. According to Seeley, the most significant imperial thinker of the period,

> Every historical student knows that it was the incubus of the Empire which destroyed liberty at Rome. Those old civic institutions, which had nursed Roman greatness and to which Rome owed all the civilisation which she had to transmit to the countries of the West, had to be given up as a condition of transmitting it. She had to adopt an organisation of, comparatively, a low type. Her civilisation, when she transmitted it, was already in decay.[20]

The narrative of decline and fall, Julia Hell argues, is "always already part of all acts of imperial mimesis, of their imaginaries and specific articulations of space and time."[21] An inescapable bequest, and an epistemic burden, it helped to set the coordinates linking past, present, and possible futures. The premo-

[16] Hume, "Hume's Early Memoranda, 1729–1740," *Journal of the History of Ideas*, ed. E. C. Mossner, 9 (1948), 517. Hume attributed Roman decline to constitutional failures rather than moral debilitation.

[17] Gibbon, *The History of the Decline and Fall of the Roman Empire*, ed. J. B. Bury (London, 1905), 4:161. Gibbon, though, made little of the connection between the British and Roman Empire. John Robertson argues that he was more interested in the fate of universal monarchy. Robertson, "Gibbon's Roman Empire as a Universal Monarchy," in *Edward Gibbon and Empire*, ed. Rosamond McKitterick and Roland Quinault (Cambridge, 1997), 247–71. On the popularity of the trope, see Vance, *The Victorians and Ancient Rome*, 234–35; Richard Hingley, *Roman Officers and English Gentlemen* (London, 2000), ch. 3; Jenkyns, *The Victorians and Ancient Greece*, 73–77.

[18] On the Whig narrative, see Burrow, *Whigs and Liberals*. On the transmission of the critique into nineteenth-century imperial debate, see Miles Taylor, "Imperium et Libertas?," *Journal of Imperial and Commonwealth History*, 19 (1991), 1–19.

[19] David Armitage, *The Ideological Origins of the British Empire* (Cambridge, 1997).

[20] Seeley, *The Expansion of England*, 246.

[21] Hell, "The Twin Towers of Anselm Kiefer and the Trope of Imperial Decline," *Germanic Review*, 84/1 (2009), 86.

nition of the fall, of earthly annihilation, was etched into the iconographic order of empire, the reservoir of images and symbols that animated Victorian debate on the subject.[22] It was captured by Kipling in his melancholy prayer-poem "Recessional," published to mark Queen Victoria's Diamond Jubilee in 1897.

> Far called, our navies melt away;
> On dune and headland sinks the fire
> Lo, all our pomp of yesterday
> Is one with Nineveh and Tyre

Kipling's plaintive call to his compatriots was stark, even desperate: "Lest we forget—lest we forget!"[23] He later wrote that he had been "scared" by the national optimism accompanying the royal celebrations, and that he composed the poem as a "*nuzzur-wattu*," "an averter of the evil eye."[24] But perhaps the most famous representation of declension was concocted by Macaulay in his depiction of the "New Zealander." In a review of Ranke's *The Ecclesiastical and Political History of the Popes of Rome*, he had marveled at the longevity of the Catholic Church, its centuries of uninterrupted existence. In comparison, other institutions seemed fragile, ephemeral, transient. "She [the Church] may still exist in undimmed vigor when some traveler from New Zealand shall, in the midst of the vast solitude, take his stand on a broken arch of London Bridge to sketch the ruin of St. Pauls."[25] Macaulay was utilizing a familiar rhetorical device, imagining the future ruins of the metropolis in order to place the contemporary within a historical frame defined by the rise and fall of civilizations. His own rendition identified early Victorian Britain with both the magnificence of Rome and its eventual fate.[26] Thirty years later the monitory image was given haunting pictorial form in an engraving by Gustave Dore, with the "tourist New Zealander upon the broken parapets, contemplating something matching—the glory that was Greece—the grandeur that was Rome."[27] The New Zealander was the most famous Victorian example of a "scopic scenario," an image that "depicts the imperial subject contemplating the ruins of empire" while simultaneously rendering the "trope of decline and

---

[22] For further discussion of the iconographic order, see chapter 7.

[23] Kipling, "Recessional," *Times*, July 17, 1897.

[24] Ibid., *Something of Myself for My Friends Known and Unknown* (London, 1937), ch. 6.

[25] Macaulay, "History of the Popes" [1840], in *Critical and Historical Essays*, ed. A. J. Grieve (London, 1907), 2:39.

[26] On the trope, see David Skilton, "Tourists at the Ruins of London," *Cercles*, 17 (2007), 93–119. For the romantic background, see Lawrence Goldstein, *Ruins and Empire* (Pittsburgh, 1977).

[27] Gustave Doré and Blanchard Jerrold, *London* (London, 1872), 188 (the words are by Jerrold). See also Robert Dingley, "The Ruins of the Future," in *Histories of the Future*, ed. Dingley and Alan Sandison (Basingstoke, 2000), 15–33. On the general theme of ruination, see Julia Hell and Andreas Schonle, eds., *Ruins of Modernity* (Durham, NC, 2010); and for a meditation on artistic representations, Brian Dillon, *Ruin Lust* (London, 2014).

fall visible."[28] By the mid-1890s the positivist Frederic Harrison could record that it had "become a proverb, and is repeated daily by men who never heard of Macaulay, much less of von Ranke."[29]

The sepulchral voyager was put to very different ideological uses. In his unpublished *The New Zealander*, penned as a social critique in 1855–56, Anthony Trollope admitted that the British empire would eventually decline and fall but nevertheless asserted that it was possible to "postpone the coming of the New Zealander" through a combination of moderate reform and a return to traditional values.[30] Dissolution could be deferred by elevating political complacency to a principle. After inspecting the admirable sanitation facilities in New Zealand, Froude proffered a quotidian rejoinder to Macaulay's flamboyant imperial metaphysics, admitting that "I have come to believe in that New Zealander since I have seen the country."[31] Hostile to sociopolitical developments in Britain, he saw the future (or at least better toilet facilities) being constructed on the colonial periphery. Goldwin Smith invoked the time-traveler to reach a different conclusion. He drew a clear distinction between Britain and its empire, the former a site of productive energy, the latter destined to follow the pattern of all history. "There is no reason why British virtue, energy, and industry should not continue as they are, or increase with the lapse of time; and therefore, there is no reason why the New Zealander should ever moralize over the ruins of the British nation; but the man of the future, whoever he may be, is pretty sure one day to moralize over the ruins of the British Empire." The lesson was clear: "In England the strength of England lies."[32] Joseph Chamberlain, the radical Secretary of State for the Colonies, dismissed the pessimism evoked by the image, vowing that the British empire was confidently embarked on a progressive trajectory. "I do not ask you to anticipate with Lord Macaulay the time when the New Zealander will come here to gaze upon the ruins of a great dead city. There are in our present condition no visible signs of decrepitude and decay."[33] In an equally bombastic vein Arthur Conan Doyle, fabulator of Sherlock Homes and passionate imperialist, observed in his justificatory account of the South African War that Macaulay, "in his wildest dream of the future of the much-quoted New Zealander," never envisaged soldiers from that distant land coming to the relief of British forces in a conflict across the ocean.[34] The New Zealander, then, did

---

[28] Hell, "*Katechon*," *Germanic Review*, 84 (2009), 284.

[29] Harrison, *Studies in Early Victorian Literature* (London, 1895), 74. As I explored in chapter 2, positivists, including Harrison, provided some of the most stinging attacks on empire during the century. See especially Gregory Claeys, *Imperial Sceptics* (Cambridge, 2012).

[30] Trollope, *The New Zealander*, ed. N. J. Hall (Oxford, 1972), 211.

[31] Froude, *Oceana, or England and Her Colonies*, new ed. (London, 1888), 236–37.

[32] Smith, "The Policy of Aggrandizement," 308.

[33] Chamberlain, "The True Conception of Empire," 2:5.

[34] Conan Doyle, *The Great Boer War* (London, 1900), 306–7.

not travel the world to sketch the ruin of empire, but rather to help defend it against the very forces of dissolution that the image encoded. Macaulay's icon, became a fulcrum for contesting visions of the future.

The combination of narrative simplicity and analytical ambiguity helps explain the powerful resonance of the Roman plotline. At least three distinct (though often overlapping) interpretations of decline and fall percolated through Victorian political culture. First, it was frequently argued that Rome had collapsed principally as a result of the corrupting power of luxury, with moral debilitation issuing in political cataclysm. Luxury, it was thought, degraded both the political morality of the governing class and eroded the manly virtues of the populace. This account dominated both scholarly interpretation and vernacular renditions for much of the century.[35] Froude offered a suggestive rendition of the story. "Virtue and truth produced strength, strength dominion, dominion riches, riches luxury, and luxury weakness and collapse—a fatal sequence repeated so often."[36] It was favored by radical critics of empire who stressed the potential dangers of aristocratic nabobs, habituated to wielding despotic power, returning from colonial service and threatening British political virtue. "Is it not just possible," asked Richard Cobden in 1860, "that we may become corrupted at home by the reaction of arbitrary political maxims in the East upon our domestic politics, just as Greece and Rome were demoralized by their contact with Asia?"[37] Goldwin Smith worried about the political influence that wealthy Anglo-Indians might wield on their return to Britain. The danger to British national identity was clear: "No political character could be stronger or more confirmed than that of the Roman, yet by Empire it was radically changed."[38] Marshaling the authority of Gibbon (while ignoring his conclusions), Herbert Spencer claimed that "in a conspicuous manner Rome shows how ... a society which enslaves other societies enslaves itself." Extirpating the freedom of conquered peoples invariably corroded the freedom of the conquerors. "And now what is the lesson?" he demanded. "Is it that in our own case Imperialism and Slavery, everywhere else and at all times united, are not to be united?" Unfortunately, he complained, "Most will say Yes."[39] In his seminal *Imperialism: A Study*, published as war in South Africa raged, the heterodox political economist J. A. Hobson answered Cobden's question by insisting that such corruption was "inevitable." It is, he averred, "a nemesis of Imperialism that the arts and crafts of tyr-

---

[35] Linda Dowling, "Roman Decadence and Victorian Historiography," *Victorian Studies*, 28 (1985), 579–608.

[36] Froude, "Calvinism" [1871], in *Short Studies on Great Subjects* (London, 1907), 2:26.

[37] Letter to Richard Hargreaves, August 4, 1860, in John Morley, *The Life of Richard Cobden*, 2 vols. (London, 1881), 2:361.

[38] Smith, "Policy of Aggrandizement," 308.

[39] Spencer, "Imperialism and Slavery," in *Facts and Comments* (New York, 1902), 162, 165. He traces the consequences in "Re-Barbarization" (172–88).

anny, acquired and exercised in our unfree Empire, should be turned against our liberties at home."[40] But the trope could also be deployed by advocates of imperialism, as both warning and call to action. In 1885 Montagu Burrows, Professor of History at Oxford, counseled that the "danger of our not perceiving our real position is exactly the same as was experienced by the old Roman Empire. The decay of the center gradually makes its way to the extremities; and these drop off, one by one, till the seat of the Empire itself, unprotected and forlorn, goes down in the general crash."[41] It could likewise serve as a salutary admonition that the problem was not empire itself but "imperialism"—a militant, territorially-rapacious creed.[42] With Disraeli in mind, Gladstone feared that like Rome, "England, which has grown so great, may easily become little; through the effeminate selfishness of luxurious living; through neglecting realities at home to amuse herself everywhere else in stalking phantoms."[43] Available to both critics of empire and its supporters, the trope was politically indeterminate.

A second account blamed excessive imperial ambition. In the late 1870s Robert Lowe, a leading British liberal politician, suggested that the Roman precedent, and in particular the transition from the Republic to the Empire, taught important lessons. "This signal and prerogative instance, to which it would be easy to add many others, seems to show that when a nation has attained a certain amount of freedom and self-government, no step can be more fatal than a career of successful conquests."[44] "I am amused at the people who call themselves Imperialists," wrote William Harcourt, another eminent liberal politician, for "I always remember the first pages in Gibbon on the 'moderation of Augustus,' in which he shows how for the first two centuries of the greatest and wisest Empire that ever existed the cardinal principle was the non-extension of Empire, and whenever it was departed from they came to grief."[45] Although acknowledging that "moral decay" engendered by luxury had played a role in the collapse of Rome, Seeley argued that the main problem was the lack of military manpower caused by over-ambitious expansion, a

[40] Hobson, *Imperialism* (London, 1902), 158, 160. Hobson also stressed the profound difference between ancient and modern empires, seeing in the former a "genuine element of internationalism" absent from modern variants (6).

[41] Burrows, "Imperial Federation," *National Review*, 4 (1884–85), 369. An undistinguished historian, Burrows was Chichele Professor of Modern History at Oxford from 1862–1900.

[42] On the late Victorian distinction between "empire" and "imperialism," see the discussion in chapter 2.

[43] Gladstone, "England's Mission," *Nineteenth Century*, 4 (1878), 584.

[44] Lowe, "Imperialism," *Fortnightly Review*, 24 (1878), reprinted in *Empire and Imperialism*, ed. P. J. Cain (Bristol, 1999), 265. See also the warning in Frederic Seebohm, "Imperialism and Socialism," *Nineteenth Century* (1880), in *Empire*, ed. Cain, 309.

[45] Harcourt, letter to Rosebery, September 27, 1892, in A. G. Gardiner, *Life of Sir William Harcourt* (London: Constable, 1923), 2:197. Widely distrusted by imperialists, Harcourt was Chancellor of the Exchequer in 1886 and again in 1892–95.

point reiterated by Herbert Samuel, "new liberal" thinker and later senior politician. Admitting that history demonstrated every previous empire had "decayed and was dissolved," Samuel drew the lesson that imperial consolidation was preferable to further territorial conquest. "Expansion that is too rapid and too wide may open the door to all three of the causes which, singly or in combination, have brought the downfall of the empires that have preceded—attack from without, revolt from within, disunion and weakness at the centre." Benjamin Franklin, he continued,

> . . . in one of the darkest times of our history, offered to furnish Gibbon with materials for a new work, on the "Decline and Fall of the British Empire." Four generations have passed since then, and events have not given room for a book on that subject. But if in a later day some historian is called upon to take up this melancholy task, it may well be that he would have to write down an excess of ambition as the chief cause of decay, and to point out that the most fatal danger which had faced the British Empire had been an over-fervent imperialism among the British people.[46]

Finally, it was argued that the over-centralization of Roman institutions, and the concentration of power in the hands of the few, led to eventual collapse. This had been a major theme in Montesquieu's pioneering *Considerations on the Causes of the Greatness of the Romans and Their Decline* (1734). The liberal historian and politician John Morley picked up the thread, arguing that the idea of imperial federation, popular in the 1880s and 1890s, presupposed the centralization that had destroyed the Roman Empire, and that as a consequence it represented a grave threat to British political liberty.[47] Hobson too ascribed the fall of Rome to over-centralization, asserting that it conveyed "in brief the real essence of Imperialism," its inescapable dynamic.[48] Economic "parasitism" by the political elite led to ever-increasing centralization of the "instruments of government," immiserating the populace and breeding the seeds of dissent and rebellion. In *Imperium et Libertas* (1901) Bernard Holland developed another variation on the theme. "The Roman Empire perished not from over-greatness but from over-centralization, and the destruction of the provinces in favour of the metropolis." Yet he drew a different conclusion from Hobson: the "failure of the Roman experiment does not

---

[46] Seeley, "Roman Imperialism, II," *Macmillan's Magazine*, 20 (1869), 54, 47–48; Samuel, *Liberalism* (London, 1902), 342–43. Note that Seeley was inconsistent on this point (cf. Seeley, *Natural Religion* (London, 1882), 237).

[47] Morley, "The Expansion of England," *Macmillan's Magazine*, 49 (1884), 241–58.

[48] Hobson, *Imperialism*, 388. Here he drew heavily on the American scholar Brooks Adams's, *The Law of Civilization and Decay* (London, 1895).

prove that an empire which avoided this peril might not beneficially endure for a much longer period."[49] Imperial nemesis could be evaded.

The Greek model of colonization presented an alternative conception of political termination. "The ancient Greek city," explained Holland, "when its population became too large for its rocky island or edge of mainland shore, sent out a colony as a beehive sends out a swarm. The colonists took possession of a new territory and there built a city, maintaining a pious regard, except when interests clashed, for the Mother City, but not a true political connection." This system, noted Seeley, "gives complete independence to the colony, but binds it in perpetual alliance."[50] It allowed for successful expansion without the internally corrosive dynamics of empire. This prospect appealed to many early Victorians, and in particular those associated with the "colonial reform" movement, prominent from the 1820s until the 1840s. Indeed in a survey written in 1856 Arthur Mills observed that the "model of Colonial policy most frequently and prominently exhibited for the emulation of modern States is that of Greece."[51] The Roman alternative was, James Mill had argued in 1823, "so very defective," for in it the "Few" dominated the "Many" to such an extent that expansion was pursued only in the interests of the aristocratic class. Mill and assorted radical "reformers" thus argued that the Greek style of colonization, premised on peopling distant lands and establishing self-governing communities with strong affective ties to the "mother country," offered a more suitable model to emulate—although in a significant departure from the ancient precedent they were generally loathe to demand immediate independence for the colonies.[52] In the 1840s John Stuart Mill eulogized the Greek colonies for "flourishing so rapidly and so wonderfully" and for guaranteeing freedom, order, and progress, and he argued that they served as a template for British colonization.[53] The philosophic radical MP J. A. Roe-

[49] Holland, *Imperium et Libertas* (London, 1901), 13–14 (though see also his extended comparison of Rome and Britain, 265–69). Holland was a barrister. The book was reviewed positively in the *Political Science Quarterly* by the classicist John Finley and in the *American Historical Review* by the historian A. L. Lowell.

[50] Holland, *Imperium et Libertas*, 15; Seeley, *Expansion of England*, 69.

[51] Mills, *Colonial Constitutions* (London, 1856), xix-xx.

[52] Mill, "Colony," *Essays from the Supplement to the Encyclopedia Britannica, Collected Works* (London, 1995), 4, 5–9. See also the discussion of the differences between the Roman and Greek models in George Cornewall Lewis's influential, *Essay on the Government of Dependencies* (London, 1841), 115–17, where he notes the similarity between British colonization in North America and the Greek experience. He also argued that governing a dependent empire damaged the "political morality" of the imperial power (251).

[53] Mill, "Wakefield's 'The New British Province of South Australia,'" in the *Examiner*, July 20, 1843, reprinted in *Collected Works*, 23:739. For his admiration of the "Greek empire," see "Grote's *History of Greece*," vol. 2, [1853], *Collected Works*, 11:321–24. Edward Wakefield, key ideologue of early Victorian colonization and a major influence on Mill, also stressed the suitability of the Greek model: *A View on the Art of Colonization* (London, 1849), 16–17.

buck sang a similar tune. "Their colonies were very unlike those of the Roman," and had far more in common with modern British experience. In particular, the Greeks were bound by a "gentle, kindly tie" between the "mother city" and her colonial offspring, of the type "we also wish to exist, and we endeavour to create."[54] The reformers drew inspiration from the classics even as they made arguments structured by post-Smithian political economy and Benthamite utilitarianism.

The popularity of the Greek model of colonial independence waned from the 1870s onwards as advocates of Greater Britain sought to forge a *permanent* political union between Britain and the settler colonies. For the pugnacious historian E. A. Freeman—the subject of chapter 13—this unionist vision clashed disastrously with a proper understanding of colonization. He argued that although the British colonies had much in common with their esteemed Greek predecessors, there was one crucial difference: they were not *ab initio* independent. Under the Greek system, the "metropolis claimed at most a certain filial respect, a kind of religious reverence, which was for the most part freely given," whereas the British settler colonies, despite their high degree of internal self-government, were nevertheless ultimately subject to the sovereignty of the Crown. Thus arguments propounding an indissoluble Greater Britain were at once conceptually flawed and historically naïve. "Let us at least remember that what is proposed is unlike anything that ever happened in the world before."[55] This was a damning verdict from a man so sensitive to the moral and practical value of precedent, and it is little surprise that he promoted independence for the settler colonies. In an obituary note about his friend, Bryce observed that "the analogy of the Greek colonies" helped motivate Freeman's scathing criticisms of the imperial unionists, for "[h]e appeared to think that the precedent of those settlements showed the true and proper relation between a 'metropolis' and her colonies to be not one of political interdependence, but of cordial friendship and a disposition to render help, nothing more."[56] History could not be ignored.

By the turn of the twentieth century, classical accounts of imperial corruption had been reinforced by anxieties about national and racial degeneration underpinned by a range of new scientific discourses.[57] In 1908 the former

[54] Roebuck, *The Colonies of England* (London, 1849), 138. Utilitarian views of Greece were shaped heavily by George Grote's seminal *History of Greece* (1846–56). See also, Grote, "Institutions of Ancient Greece," *Westminster Review*, 5 (1826), 269–331.

[55] Freeman, "Imperial Federation," *Macmillan's Magazine*, 51 (1885), 436 and 437–38. See also Freeman, *History of Federal Government* (London, 1863), 5–26; and chapter 13.

[56] Bryce, "Edward Augustus Freeman," *English Historical Review*, 7 (1892), 502. Influenced by Thomas Arnold, Freeman was himself committed to a cyclical view of history: "Historical Cycles" in *Historical Essays*, 4th series (London, 1892), 249–58, though he tended to locate patterns of repetition *within* a political community.

[57] Daniel Pick, *Faces of Degeneration* (Cambridge, 1989).

Prime Minister, Arthur Balfour, argued that many political communities, including Rome, were corrupted by mysterious bouts of decadence, but that through a combination of science and industry the British empire could probably escape this fate.[58] He thus sought to neutralize more pessimistic renderings of the future. Perhaps the most (in)famous had been elaborated by the Australian historian and radical politician C. H. Pearson in his best-selling *National Life and Character* (1894). Although it discussed the demise of Rome in some detail, the text focused principally on the contemporary exhaustion of political space, when little territory was left for the "higher races" to colonize.[59] Only the year before, Frederick Jackson Turner had warned that the closing of the American frontier would dissipate the creative energies of American democracy.[60] Pearson predicted a similar process writ global, as the Western empires, Britain foremost among them, would be undermined by a lethal combination of their own success in conquering territory and the pernicious domestic consequences of the emerging "stationary" socialist state. After gifting civilization to the rest of the world, the imperial powers would be thrown back onto their own continent by ungrateful subjects. Torpor, luxury, and decline would follow. This account both drew on and subverted progessivist justifications of empire. While Pearson viewed empire as an agent of improvement, the combination of imperial blowback and the exhaustion of planetary space meant that the future looked grim. Implicit in this argument were two claims. First, that other, perhaps less enlightened, forms of empire might be capable of reaching escape velocity, and second, that if only new spaces were discovered the restless dynamism of empire could be effectively channeled in their direction. It was this kind of thought, perhaps, that found expression in Cecil Rhodes's wistful proclamation that he would annex the planets if he could.[61]

The Victorians, then, absorbed two contrasting lessons from their incessant meditations on the history of empire, ancient and modern. Inherited from centuries of European political thought, the first insisted that history demonstrated the inevitability of imperial decline and fall. Foretelling a future of retreat and weakness, it implied that sooner or later the British empire

[58] Balfour, *Decadence* (Cambridge, 1908).

[59] Pearson, *National Life and Character* (London, 1894). The book caused a sensation. Prior to his political career, Pearson was Professor of Modern History at King's College, London (1855–65).

[60] Turner, "The Significance of the Frontier in American History," in *Rereading Frederick Jackson Turner*, ed. J. M. Faragher (London, 1998). Jackson's frontier thesis is cited in Lord Curzon of Kedleston, *Frontiers* (Oxford, 1907), 56.

[61] Rhodes, *The Last Will and Testament of Cecil J. Rhodes*, ed. W. T. Stead (London, 1902), 190. For an intriguing, and ultimately ambivalent, narrative of the future Anglo-Saxon colonization of outer space, set in the year 2236, see Robert Cole, *The Struggle for Empire*, ed. Richard Bleiler (London, 2013). Written in 1900, Cole's novel is now regarded as the first "space opera" in science fiction. I discuss this text in Bell, *Dreamworlds of Empire* (forthcoming).

would dissolve, and with it the claims of the British to world-historical significance. The other lesson, more popular and widely disseminated, allowed for the possibility of imperial redemption. Decline was *conceivable* but not *inevitable*; the future was left open. Human choice—political decision—was thus accorded a central role, one that imperialists never tired of emphasizing. Though haunted by the image of failure, they were rarely fatalists.

Harnessing the Time Spirit: On Imperial Progress

Reflecting on his long life, Morley remarked that the nineteenth century had seen belief in progress emerge as the "basis of social thought," supplanting religion as the "inspiring, guiding, and testing power over social action." Progress, he mused, could be seen as the "Time Spirit" of the modern world.[62] Soon after he penned those words the first English-language history of the idea appeared. Its author, J. B. Bury, a prodigiously gifted historian and classicist, declared that progress was the "animating and controlling idea of western civilization." He defined it in appropriately capacious terms as the view that "civilization has moved, is moving, and will move, in a desirable direction," where the desire was identified with increased human happiness. Like Morley he argued that it had displaced religion as a source of meaning: "The fate of an ultimate happy state on this planet, to be enjoyed for future generations, has replaced, as a social power, the hope of felicity in another world."[63] On this account, the death of God was a precondition for the emergence of the idea of progress, since an active, world-shaping sense of human agency needed to escape the sociopolitical fatalism inculcated by religion.

While Bury suggested that the idea of progress was predicated on the renunciation of "active" providentialism, it came in many flavors—theological, agnostic, and secular—during the Victorian age. Ubiquitous and multivalent, belief in progress structured social and political thought in assorted ways. It was typically assumed to encompass material, institutional, and moral dimensions. Materially, it was indexed by extraordinary advances in science and technology, which transformed the conditions of both social existence and political association. "[I]n every science which deserves the name," Macaulay marveled, "immense improvement may be expected." In institutional terms it was linked primarily to the development of individual freedom and representative government. Thus Macaulay could declaim that the history of England "is emphatically the history of progress. It is the history of a constant move-

---

[62] Morley, *Recollections* (London, 1917), 2:27, 30.

[63] Bury, *The Idea of Progress* (London, 1920), vii, 2. "[I]t was not till men felt independent of Providence that they could organise a theory of Progress" (73). For more recent reflection on the notion of progress, see Reinhart Koselleck, *Futures Past*, trans. Keith Tribe (Cambridge, MA, 1985).

ment of the public mind, of a constant change in the institutions of a great society."[64] And finally, it encoded the idea that these new developments were altering the manners and *moeurs*—"character," in Victorian nomenclature—of the people.[65] Confidence in the unilinear improvement of society reached its peak in the mid-Victorian era, when the various elements of progress were often read as mutually reinforcing. Many late Victorians were rather less sanguine, believing that they did not necessarily cohere or even that they conflicted. It was a common apprehension, for example, that the relentless development of science and technology was eroding public morality, advances in one domain leading to regress in another. The impact of Darwinism, disillusionment with political reform, the dizzying tempo of social life, an increasingly tense geopolitical environment, fear of urban degeneration: all contributed to the emergence of a more melancholy attitude. Most late Victorian thinkers, however, continued to believe in the possibility of progress, of constant human improvement, even as they expressed skepticism about its inevitability.

Throughout this shift in temper the empire remained a space for the projection of fantasies about progressive development. This followed from the way in which progress was figured as the advance of civilization. The great French historian Francois Guizot had remarked in his influential *General History of Civilization in Europe* that the "first idea comprised in the word *civilization* . . . is the notion of progress, of development. It calls up within us the notion of a people advancing, of a people in a course of improvement and melioration."[66] The Victorians tended to concur. Imperialists divided the world into those civilized spaces capable of self-sustaining progress (with Britain in the vanguard) and those in which progress had stalled (such as India) or had never even begun (including most of Africa). The empire was typically figured as an engine of civilization, a means to bring enlightenment to the backward spaces of the earth. Even if progress was slowing or even under threat in the "mother country," there was still work to be done—a duty to be fulfilled—civilizing the rest of the world. Such was the conceit of many British imperialists. The most common proposition for escaping the cycle of rise and decline, then, was to insist that the British imperial model was itself uniquely progressive, a global agent of human advance. Past experience meant

[64] Macaulay, "Sir James Mackintosh" [1835], in *Critical and Historical Essays* (London, 1848), 2:219, 226.

[65] On ideals of character, see Stefan Collini, *Public Moralists* (Oxford, 1993), and, on its collective expression, Peter Mandler, *The English National Character* (London, 2006).

[66] Guizot, *General History of Civilization in Europe* [1828], ed. G. Knight (New York, 1896), 11. On John Stuart Mill and civilization, meanwhile, see Duncan Kelly, *The Propriety of Liberty* (Princeton, 2011), ch. 4. See also Duncan Bell, "Empire and Imperialism," in *The Cambridge History of Nineteenth-Century Political Thought*, ed. Gregory Claeys and Gareth Stedman Jones (Cambridge, 2012), 864–91.

nothing, except perhaps as a hortatory reminder about what not to do. Liberal empire was simultaneously a cause and a consequence of civilizational progress.

Arguing that confidence in imperial progress was undercut by the Sepoy Rebellion of 1857 and successive moments of resistance, Karuna Mantena has recently questioned the durability of this civilizational justification of imperial rule. On this account, crisis and progress were figured as irreconcilable, and a markedly different "culturalist" narrative emerged, chiefly under the influence of the eminent comparativist Henry Maine. Emphasizing the fragility of local communities and the sheer difficulty of transforming colonized spaces in the image of liberal modernity, it provided Maine and his followers with an "alibi" for the prolongation of empire on the grounds that Western intervention had so weakened traditional forms of life that withdrawal would herald disaster.[67] Valuable as it is in delineating Maine's position, this argument underestimates the continuities in British imperial discourse.[68] As I argued in chapter 2, the civilizing vision of empire remained a staple of British imperial ideology, even its core feature, throughout the 1890s and deep into the twentieth century. In an address to the Imperial Institute in 1892, the historian W.E.H. Lecky sketched a characteristically Whiggish paean to the glories of imperial progress.

> Remember what India had been for countless ages before the establishment of British rule. Think of its endless wars of race and creed, its savage oppressions, its fierce anarchies, its barbarous customs, and then consider what it is to have established for some many years over the vast space from the Himalayas to Cape Comorin a reign of perfect peace; to have conferred upon more than 250 millions of the human race perfect religious freedom, perfect security of life, liberty and property; to have planted in the midst of these teeming multitudes a strong central government, enlightened by the best knowledge of Western Europe, and steadily occupied in preventing famine, alleviating disease, extirpating savage customs, multiplying the agencies of civilization and progress.[69]

W. T. Stead used his editorial platform at the *Review of Reviews* to broadcast a vision of "responsible" imperialism—or what he also liked to call "[i]mperial-

---

[67] Mantena, *Alibis of Empire*; Mantena, "The Crisis of Liberal Imperialism," in *Victorian Visions of Global Order*, ed. Duncan Bell (Cambridge, 2007), 113–36.

[68] See also, P. J. Cain, "Character, 'Ordered Liberty,' and the Mission to Civilise," *Journal of Imperial and Commonwealth History*, 40/4 (2012), 557–78; Peter Mandler, "Looking around the World," in *Time Travelers*, ed. Adelene Buckland and Sadiah Qureshi (Chicago, forthcoming).

[69] Lecky, *The Empire* (London, 1893), 44–45. One of the most influential historians of the age, Lecky never held a formal academic post, though he was offered (and declined) the Regius Professorship of History at Oxford after Freeman's death in 1892. For an earlier version of the refrain, see James Fitzjames Stephen, "Liberalism," *Cornhill Magazine*, 5 (1862), 32.

ism within limits defined by common sense and the Ten Commandments"—aimed at improving the "semi-civilised or wholly savage races."[70] Indeed he called on the United States to assume its own responsibilities in civilizing Latin and South America. This call to assume the "White Man's burden" echoed widely during the decade as British imperialists sought to share the role of civilizing the world. Samuel too was spouting a cliché when in 1902 he lavished praise on the transformative potential of the British empire. "A barbarian race may prosper best if for a period, even for a long period, it surrenders the right of self-government in exchange for the teachings of civilization."[71] It took the industrial slaughter of the First World War to create a significant transnational intellectual revolt that challenged the civilizing mission, chiefly by questioning the link between technological development and moral progress, though even that wasn't enough to fully derail the imperial desire to reorder the world.[72]

A recurrent theme in imperial discourse was that the British empire was unique in its propagation of constitutional liberty. (The subjects of imperial coercion no doubt saw it rather differently.) The happy conjunction of altruistic civilizing ambitions (in South Asia and Africa) and a high-degree of colonial self-government (in the settler empire) was routinely praised as a matchless achievement. Combining *imperium et libertas*, as Disraeli once boasted, they had managed to achieve stable rule, ordered freedom, and beneficent civilization in a single progressive ensemble.[73] In so doing the British, with their self-proclaimed "genius" for governing, had cracked the temporal code. This "civilized" and "civilizing" imperial formation could, if managed carefully, escape the fate of all previous empires. Or so it was claimed. Writing at the turn of the twentieth century, as controversy over the war in South Africa raged, Charles Beresford, Tory MP and Admiral in the Royal Navy, celebrated freedom as the unique gift of the British. In standard Polybian vein, he catalogued the traditional causes of decline.

---

[70] Stead, "To All English-Speaking Folks," *Review of Reviews*, 1/1 (1890), 17. On Stead, see Lauren Brake et al., eds., *W. T. Stead* (Chicago, 2012).

[71] Samuel, *Liberalism*, 330.

[72] Michael Adas, "Contested Hegemony," *Journal of World History*, 15/1 (2004), 31–63.

[73] Disraeli coined the (ungrammatical) phrase in 1851. Jenkyns, *The Victorians and Ancient Greece*, 333. He claimed Roman pedigree when he reused it in 1879. Moneypenny and Buckle, *The Life of Benjamin Disraeli*, 6 vols. (London, 1910–20), 6:495. As Norman Vance notes, however, his attribution was mistaken. Cicero once wrote of *imperio ac liberte*, though he meant the power to uphold and enforce law, not territorial empire. Disraeli probably had Tacitus in mind, since he had famously been misquoted by Francis Bacon in *The Advancement of Learning* (1605), where *principatum ac libertatem* was rendered as *imperium et libertatem*, before being translated by Bolingbroke in *The Idea of a Patriot King* (1738) as "Empire and Liberty." Vance, "Anxieties of Empire and the Moral Tradition," *International Journal of the Classical Tradition*, 18/2 (2011), 251. Disraeli's phrase was widely employed in British imperial debate. See, for example, Freeman, "Imperial Federation," 444; Herbert Spencer, "Imperialism and Slavery," 117; Holland, *Imperium et Libertas*.

The great weakness of the nationalities which have been engulfed by the irresistible march of time has been the despotism which underlay their governments, the corruption which sapped their liberties, the luxury and indolence which ate into their vitality, and the remarkable fact that they became worn out and vicious, while the countries they had conquered, and the dependencies they had absorbed, at last broke away, imbued deeply with the vices and but few of the original virtues of the sovereign state.

But the "irresistible march" could be halted. Through accident or design, the British had forged an empire that could avoid the fate that befell all others. "The Anglo-Saxon has so far, chiefly owing to the mixture of blood in his veins, kept alive side by side both the military and the commercial spirit; and it is this unique combination of talents which offers the best hopes for the survival of the Anglo-Saxon as the fittest of humanity to defy the decaying process of time."[74] Bathed in philosophical idealism, the conservative historian and classicist J. A. Cramb glorified war, praised violence as a purifying force, and conceived of empire as a grand metaphysical principle, the vehicle for reason in history. It was, above all, "the highest expression of the soul of the State; it is the complete, the final consummation of the life of the State." The British empire was insulated from troubling precedents, for while the "Roman ideal moulds every form of Imperialism in Europe, and even to a certain degree in the East, down to the eighteenth century," the British offered the world a new model, "not Roman, not Hellenic." The emphasis on freedom and justice was unprecedented. "From this thraldom to the past, to the ideal of Rome, Imperial Britain, first amongst modern empires, completely breaks."[75] It was attuned to the time spirit.

As Cramb was penning his encomium to imperial power, J. M. Robertson, a prominent radical liberal, scornfully dismissed imperialist attempts to escape the shadow of Rome.

One of the most unpromising symptoms of our case is the uncomprehending way in which the British imperialist always scans the story of ancient Rome. Noting the decadence which is the upshot of the whole, he seems to suppose that somehow Christianity will avail to save later empires from the same fate, though Rome was Christianized during the decline; or that haply the elimination of chattel slavery will avert decay,

[74] Beresford, "The Future of the Anglo-Saxon Race," *North American Review*, 171/529 (1900), 803, 806.

[75] Cramb, *Reflections on the Origins and Destiny of Imperial Britain* (London, 1900), 216, 18, 23. Cramb was Professor of History at Queen's College, London. In Karma Nabulsi's terms, he can be seen as a "martialist," one of the "high priests of the temple of Janus," a species quite common in German intellectual circles at the time, though rarer in Britain. Nabulsi, *Traditions of War*, ch. 4. See also my discussion of the category in Chapter 4.

though Christian Spain was free from chattel slavery at home, or that industrialism will avail, though the Moors and the Florentines were tolerably industrial. Any theory will serve to burke the truth that the special cause of decay is just empire.[76]

Unmoved by special pleading on behalf of the British, Robertson insisted that empires always and everywhere ended in annihilation. Products of avarice and arrogance, they were devoured by their own internal pathologies. "For persistent empire in the end infallibly brings the imperator, be the process slow or speedy; and with the imperator comes in due time the decadence of empire, the humiliation and paralysis of the spirit that had aspired to humiliate its kind."[77] He repeated the message in a scathing attack on the idealist philosopher D. G. Ritchie's justification of liberal civilizing imperialism. "It seems the more necessary to point out that the *pax Romana* was of old a plea for the kind of policy defended by our imperialists to-day; and that the pursuit of that policy meant the final conquest of Rome by its own brutality and moral barbarism as surely as the conquest of the surrounding world."[78] Contra the reassuring fantasies of Cramb and Ritchie, this was the true destiny of imperial Britain.

Troubled by intimations of mortality, advocates of imperial progress often saw the empire as fragile, beset on all sides by challengers and skeptics. As Peter Cain has demonstrated, normative justifications of empire during the late nineteenth and early twentieth century depended on a complex dialectical dance of "character." It was frequently argued that British imperial greatness was largely the product of the superior character of its people, individually and collectively, and that this greatness underwrote both the capacity (military and economic strength) and the moral obligation (to spread the benefits of this character to others) motivating the pursuit of empire.[79] Moreover, the practice of imperial governance fostered the very greatness on which empire depended. "The creed of the ultra-imperialists could be simply expressed. "Character," . . . had given Britain its empire and, without that empire, character would atrophy and die and Britain's moment of greatness would quickly pass."[80] Imperial dissolution would not protect Britain but instead heralded its ruination. John Ruskin's inaugural lecture as Slade Professor of the History of Art at Oxford in 1870 included a stirring call for further imperial conquest, as the only alternative was to "perish." "She must found

---

[76] Robertson, *Patriotism and Empire*, 3rd ed. (London, 1900), 151.

[77] Ibid., 157.

[78] Robertson, "The Moral Problems of War," *International Journal of Ethics*, 11/3 (1901), 283. Cf. Ritchie, "War and Peace," *International Journal of Ethics*, 11/2 (1901), 137–58.

[79] For relevant philosophical discussion of the civilizational obligations incurred by liberal empires, see J. H. Muirhead, "What Imperialism Means," *Fortnightly Review*, 68 (1900), 177–87; Ritchie, "War and Peace."

[80] Cain, "Empire," 269.

colonies as fast and as far as she is able."[81] Expansion was the only way to avoid declension. "If the empire should dissolve," Holland warned, "England would doubtless decay and decline, exhausted by the effort of creating so many new states."[82] A process of *imperial involution* beckoned, the dismantling of the periphery leading inexorably to the degeneration of the metropole.

The universities were central to propagating the civilizational endeavor. Their importance was underscored in 1907 when Curzon, in his Romanes Lecture at Oxford, hailed the spirit of imperial patriotism and demanded that the elite arrayed before him hold the line against the forces menacing Western civilization.

> To our ancient universities, revivified and re-inspired, I look to play their part in this national service. Still from the cloistered alleys and hallowed groves of Oxford ... let there come forth the invincible spirit and the unexhausted moral fibre of our race. Let the advance guard of Empire march forth, strong in the faith of their ancestors, imbued with sober virtue, and above all, on fire with a definite purpose.[83]

Empire, then, was a bulwark against degeneration, that insidious fear stalking *fin de siècle* Victorian culture, while the elite universities were construed as institutions that could foster the imperial virtues necessary to neutralize the threat. The human sciences were assigned a crucial role, with history and classics at the forefront. Oxford was the principal site of imperial pedagogy. From the 1850s Benjamin Jowett, classicist and Master of Balliol, had been instrumental in directing graduates to the Indian Civil Service (ICS), the entrance examination for which placed great emphasis on knowledge of the classics.[84] The results were palpable. Between 1874 and 1914, 27.1 percent of Balliol graduates went to work in the ICS, while between 1888 and 1905 three successive viceroys of India were products of the College. Sidgwick and Seeley, among others, tried to replicate this intimate imperial connection in Cambridge, though with only moderate success.[85] The bequest of Cecil Rhodes, himself a proud Oxford product obsessed with the ancient world, only deepened the links between the university and the empire.[86] George Parkin, a fer-

[81] Ruskin, "Inaugural Lecture," in *The Works of John Ruskin*, ed. E. T. Cook and A. Wedderburn, 39 vols. (London, 1903–12), 20:41. See also his *Stones of Venice* (1851) on how moral decline leads to imperial collapse (*Works*, 9:17).

[82] Holland, *Imperium et Libertas*, 265.

[83] Curzon, *Frontiers*, 57–58. Curzon was serving as Chancellor of the University at the time.

[84] Richard Symonds, *Oxford and Empire* (Oxford, 1991); Vasunia, *The Classics and Colonial India*, ch. 5. Oxford graduates dominated the system (though Trinity, Dublin, also produced a disproportionate number of entrants): Symonds, *Oxford and Empire*, 180–91. Jowett's project was continued by his successor at Balliol, J. L. Strachan Davidson.

[85] Collini, Winch, and Burrow, *That Noble Science of Politics*, 354–55.

[86] Philip Ziegler, *Legacy* (London, 2008). Unable to read the original languages, Rhodes employed a team of classicists to translate all of the references found in Gibbon's *Decline and Fall*, as

vent Canadian imperialist and Secretary of the Rhodes Trust, purred that "the relation of Oxford to the Empire is exceptional."[87] Milner's "Kindergarden," that group of thrusting young imperialists who played such an important role in both the Round Table movement and the formation of the South African state, were virtually all Oxford educated.[88] The close links between Oxford and the imperial elite persisted until the era of decolonization.[89]

Even as the universities produced a steady stream of recruits for the empire, they were also generating knowledge that ultimately, though often unintentionally, helped to undermine some traditional narratives of imperial legitimation. The closing decades of the nineteenth century witnessed a tectonic shift in the scholarship on Rome. For much of the Victorian era, the popular mythopoeic narrative of decline and fall—and above all the account of corruption and decay—had been bolstered by scholarly authority. So too was the idea that the Roman world taught pertinent lessons for the present. Niebuhr's *Römische Geschichte* in particular exerted a huge influence in the early Victorian era, helping to (re)establish for the nineteenth century the "plot of Roman history as the recurrent story of the world."[90] Indeed Niebuhr himself stressed the similarities between the British and Roman empires. A series of liberal Anglican writers, including Thomas Arnold and Charles Merivale, followed Niebuhr's example in seeking to collapse the temporal distance between the ancient and modern worlds, deriving lessons for the latter from the vicissitudes of the former. Their narratives of ancient Rome were infused with a moralized vision of the cycles through which all polities moved.[91] But the credibility of this approach was challenged by the great German scholar Theodor Mommsen, whose influence increased steadily throughout the second half of the century. Providentialism was gradually superseded by a model of historical positivism, whose proponents celebrated its purported objectivity and scientific superiority over earlier, primitive accounts. In Britain, this ambition was realized above all in the writings of Bury, Acton's successor at Cambridge. In addressing the purported connection between Rome and Britain,

---

well as numerous other classical texts, an exercise in historical recovery that filled over two hundred volumes in his personal library. See Victoria Tietze Larson, "Classics and the Acquisition and Validation of Power in Britain's 'Imperial Century' (1815–1914)," *International Journal of the Classical Tradition*, 6/2 (1999), 211.

[87] Parkin, *The Rhodes Scholarship* (London, 1912), 211.

[88] On the Kindergarten, see Symonds, *Oxford and Empire*; John Kendle, *The Round Table Movement and Imperial Union* (Toronto, 1975).

[89] These connections have recently become the focus of student activism aiming to force the university to acknowledge its historical role in imperialism. The campaign, drawing on developments in South Africa, is conducted under the name "Rhodes Must Fall." André Rhoden-Paul, "Oxford Uni Must Decolonise Its Campus and Curriculum, Say Students," *Guardian*, June 18, 2015.

[90] Dowling, "Roman Decadence and Victorian Historiography," 595.

[91] Duncan Forbes, *The Liberal Anglican Idea of History* (Cambridge, 1952).

Bury argued that "luxury and immorality do not constitute, and need not be symptoms of, a disease that is fatal to the life of States," and he condemned "all reasoning founded on historical analogy" as "futile."[92]

The thesis of British exceptionalism was reinforced by a burst of prominent writings comparing the Roman and British empires that appeared after 1900. The main examples were Bryce's long essay on "The Ancient Roman Empire and the British Empire in India"; *Ancient and Modern Imperialism*, a short tract written by Evelyn Baring, the Earl of Cromer, one-time British consul-general in Egypt, then serving as President of the Classical Association; and C. P. Lucas's *Greater Rome and Greater Britain*, the product of an imperial administrator turned Oxford don.[93] To varying degrees, all drew on the shift in scholarship, and while they would have demurred from Bury's strident denial of the value of historical analogies, they were nevertheless adamant that the Roman and British empires were divided by far more than they shared. This act of disavowal served an important ideological function, allowing them to celebrate the unique virtues and continuing vitality of the British empire. All suggested that the British escaped the worst aspects of the Roman precedent—its despotism, its political centralization, its crude militarism and absence of economic creativity. Lucas, for example, asserted that "loss of freedom" cemented the unity of the Roman Empire, whereas the diffuse British empire became increasingly decentralized "as freedom has grown."[94] Writing in a symposium on his book, Cromer stressed the radical difference between the ancients and the moderns. "The records of the ancient world may be searched in vain for any guidance to show whether modern democracy . . . is capable of sustaining the burthens of Empire at all."[95] They acclaimed an empire committed to freedom and justice, driven by largely humanitarian impulses and ruling in a civilizing manner, and this allowed them to boast of British superiority over even the most magnificent of their predecessors. The only area where the Romans were more successful was their ability to "assimilate" different conquered races.[96] Yet here too the point was framed to signal the ultimate superiority of the British, for Roman success was relativized as

---

[92] Bury, "The British Empire and the Roman Empire," *Saturday Review*, June 27, 1896, 645. Bury later discarded his early positivism, emphasizing contingency and rejecting the possibility of discerning general patterns of cause and effect. *Selected Essays of J. B. Bury*, ed. Howard Temperley (Cambridge, 1930), chs. 1–5. This shift is traced in R. G. Collingwood's review (*English Historical Review*, 43/186 (1931), 461–65).

[93] Bryce, "The Roman Empire and the British Empire in India," in Bryce, *Studies in History and Jurisprudence* (Oxford, 1901), 1–71; Baring, *Ancient and Modern Imperialism* (London, 1910); Lucas, *Greater Rome and Greater Britain* (Oxford, 1912). For context, see Vasunia, *The Classics and Colonial India*.

[94] Lucas, *Greater Rome*, 141.

[95] Cromer, "History and Politics," *Classical Review*, 24 (1910), 116.

[96] Lucas, *Greater Rome*, 91–112; see also Bryce, "The Roman Empire," 54–63; Baring, *Ancient and Modern*, 72–95.

the product of a smaller, less complex polity. The British faced profound difficulties because their ambition and reach were so much grander. The texts conveyed the message that uniquely among empires the British had escaped the gravitational pull of history. All three authors were also clear about the appropriate object of analysis, insisting that only India was suitable for comparison with Rome. Governed by radically contrasting principles, the British settler colonies "differ wholly in kind."[97] Ontologically distinctive, they presented yet another way in which advocates of settler colonialism sought to circumvent the fate of empire.

The Transfiguration of Empire

Casting a skeptical eye over the British empire in 1892, the American scholar and journalist Albert Shaw found little to celebrate. "If having an 'empire' means the acquiring of control over the territory and government of people of the races who happen for one reason or another to be weak, I can see nothing in that to be ardent about." Britain assumed its place in the long inglorious history of oppressive imperial powers, and as such it stood "before the world in the garb of a perpetual candidate for dissolution." Yet hope remained, if only the British could fundamentally reform their empire by establishing it on progressive foundations, a noble task that could be achieved by creating a true imperial federation modeled on the United States. "It would be an empire consisting of self-governing Britishers, in which each individual one of 'God's Englishmen' would have rights as extensive as any of his fellows and in the central ordering of which each autonomous group would be as influential, in the proportion of its numbers, as any other."[98] Although few went as far as Shaw, many British thinkers argued that the settler empire, "Greater Britain," constituted (or could constitute) a novel form of *post-imperial* political association. As such, it could avoid the pattern of decline and fall.

The discourse of Greater Britain contained two distinct claims about novelty. The first recognized that the settler colonial system formed an integral part of the wider empire, but that it was nevertheless a new kind of imperial polity. The other denied that Greater Britain was an empire at all. While it had originated as part of an imperial order, it was now assuming a completely novel form, transfigured from empire to state (or commonwealth). On either account, Greater Britain was an unprecedented phenomenon that could be

---

[97] Lucas, *Greater Rome*, 142; see also Bryce, "The Roman Empire," 4–6; Baring, *Ancient and Modern*, 17–18.

[98] Shaw, "An American View of Home Rule and Federation," *Contemporary Review*, 62 (1892), 311–12. An Anglophile, Shaw was the editor of the *American Review of Reviews*, and thus a close associate of W. T. Stead. For his role in the foundation of American political science, see Robert Adcock, *Liberalism and the Emergence of American Political Science* (Oxford, 2014), ch. 5.

inserted into a progressive narrative of historical development. The novelty, it was commonly proclaimed, resided in the degree of self-government accorded to its constituent members and the civil and political freedoms already enjoyed by its (white) inhabitants.

At midcentury, Arthur Mills had observed that all of recorded history showed the pattern of imperial "dismemberment and decay" resulting in eventual "dissolution." "Is there any known principle of political life," he inquired, "which history permits us to hope will be exceptional and peculiar to that cluster of communities which now own the rule of England?" He answered in the affirmative. Political decentralization, and above all the granting of self-government to the settler colonies, allowed the process of decay to be circumvented.[99] Later imperial unionists sought to harness this freedom in an overarching political structure. Half a century after Mills had praised the potential of self-government, Holland argued that the British could escape the fate of Rome because they had avoided destructive over-centralization. Sacrificing "imperium" in favor of more extensive "libertas," they had saved the empire from the clutches of time. "In the British empire, apart from India, we have learned . . . to concede to the Colonies the fullest liberty consistent with the maintenance of a common tie."[100] "The British Empire of to-day, it cannot be too often repeated," intoned Hugh Egerton, another prominent historian of empire, "is without precedent in the past," chiefly because the colonies had been granted "responsible government." In light of this splendid achievement, Egerton cautioned his readers against drawing false inferences from the past: "It is at once the glory and the responsibility of nations that in their case, no ceaseless law of change is operating, to make dissolution and decay inevitable. To each generation, in its turn, is given the privilege and power to shape its own destinies."[101]

For Seeley, the former Professor of Latin and editor of Livy, the ancient world presented no important lessons for the "boundless expanses" of the settler colonies. In particular, viewing Britain as an heir to Rome was a serious error.[102] In *The Expansion of England* he argued that "[o]ur colonies do not resemble the colonies which classical students meet with in Greek and Roman history, and our Empire is not an Empire at all in the ordinary sense of the

---

[99] Mills, *Colonial Constitutions*, xxxix-xl.

[100] Holland, *Imperium et Libertas*, 14.

[101] Egerton, *A Short History of Colonial Policy* (London, 1897), 455, 478. At the time of publication, Egerton worked in the Emigrants' Information Office. On the back of its considerable success, he was elected (in 1905) the first Beit Professor of Colonial History at Oxford. He retired in 1920.

[102] Seeley, "Introduction" to *Her Majesty's Colonies* (London, 1886), xviii. For the misleading argument that Seeley saw the British as heirs to Rome, see Reba Soffer, "History and Religion," in *Religion and Irreligion in Victorian Society*, ed. R. W. Davis and R. J. Helmstadter (London, 1992), 142–43; Hingley, *Roman Officers*, 24–25.

word." He cited various reasons to account for this difference, including the "ethnological unity" of the Greater British population and the development of new communications technologies that "annihilated" time and space, facilitating the creation of a common identity and enabling effective governance across planetary distances.[103] This did not mean, however, that the classical world failed to offer Seeley any insights into the patterns of contemporary international politics, for the Roman archetype, he argued, bore some resemblance to the British mode of rule in India. While the analogy was far from exact, they did share the status of "superior races" intent on "civilizing" those under their control. As the Roman Empire in the West was "the empire of civilisation over barbarism," so the British empire in India was "the empire of the modern world over the medieval." Such comparisons, though, had nothing to do with the settlement colonies.

> The colonies and India are in opposite extremes. Whatever political maxims are most applicable to one, are most inapplicable to the other. In the colonies everything is brand-new. There you have the most progressive race put in the circumstances most favourable to progress. There you have no past and an unbounded future. Government and institutions are all ultra-English. All is liberty, industry, invention, innovation, and as yet tranquillity.

India, by contrast, "is all past and, I may almost say, has no future."[104] For Seeley, the British governed spaces defined by two contrasting temporal regimes. One was characterized by novelty, creativity, movement, and flux, and its boundless energies were perfectly suited for progressive historical development. The other was stagnant, immobile, rigid, and thus incapable of progress without exogenous shock. It was as if past and future coexisted in the same historical moment.

Two decades later William Peterson, émigré classical scholar and Principal of McGill University, was likewise emphatic that the British empire represented a departure from the patterns of history, and above all its only other competitor for historical splendor:

> It is by no means to its disadvantage or discredit that the British Empire is not altogether as other Empires have been. It was by the sword that old Rome, for instance, held what she had won by the sword. To her modern successor and representative has been left the glory of reconciling the two elements, which many of Rome's subjects found incompatible—"Empire" and "liberty." A Constitution which secures equal rights for all under the ample folds of the British flag has given a new meaning

---

[103] Seeley, *The Expansion of England*, 51.
[104] Ibid., 51, 244, 176.

to the old motto, "*Imperium et Libertas*." Never before in history has the unique spectacle been presented to the world of sovereignty wielded by the parent State on the slender basis of mutual consent.

Indeed the settler colonial world, he maintained, might be described as "a system of democratic republics under the gentle sovereignty of the Motherland."[105] Many advocates of Greater Britain deliberately eschewed centuries of imperial political thought and the historicizing trends of the time by actively dismissing the relevance of ancient empires for thinking about the future. They often sought authority in the image of America—a country that had, through the creation of a continental federal system, managed to solve many of the political problems facing the British.[106] Above all, the Americans taught that it was possible to sustain individual freedom in a vast polity, reconciling liberty and empire as Thomas Jefferson had once promised.[107] William Greswell, formerly a Professor of Classics in South Africa, accentuated the fundamental differences between the ancient empires and the modern British, and he emphasized, echoing an argument made famous by Constant, the superiority of modern freedom. "The Britannica *civitas* is a far wider, and we may be allowed to believe a far more honoured, privilege. It is a *civitas* built upon freedom not despotism, upon tolerance rather than upon force, upon voluntary effort and individual enterprise rather than upon bureaucratic orders and state diplomacy." Greswell demanded a "confederacy of the British race," but added the qualifier that it was foolhardy to "refer for guidance to ancient or modern confederacies." Rather, it was instructive to look to the edifying example set by United States.[108] In a historical irony that Macaulay might well have enjoyed, London Bridge, the shattered perch of his ubiquitous New Zealander, today sits intact in the blasted heat of Arizona, an unwitting symbol of the *translatio imperii* dreamt by many Victorian imperialists.

The purportedly federal (or quasi-federal) character of Greater Britain meant that it was something wholly new. This was yet another expression of British imperial exceptionalism. In the *Considerations on Representative Government*, Mill had referred to the colonial empire as an "unequal federation," while four decades later Leonard Hobhouse talked of the "loose, informal, quasi-Federalism of the British Colonial Empire," which he contrasted with

[105] Peterson, "The Future of Canada," in *The Empire and the Century*, ed. C. S. Goldman (London, 1905), 363–64.

[106] See Bell, *The Idea of Greater Britain*, ch. 9, for more detail. Contra Mark Bradley, I do not deny that ancient precedents informed various aspects of British imperial discourse, only that advocates of Greater Britain tended to eschew them as models to emulate. Bradley, "Introduction," in *Classics and Imperialism in the British Empire*, ed. Bradley, 16–17.

[107] On this motif in American history, see Richard H. Immerman, *Empire for Liberty* (Princeton, 2010).

[108] Greswell, "Imperial Federation," in *England and Her Colonies* (London, 1887), 7.

the "strict" American variant.[109] Some went as far as proclaiming that it already comprised a state—or, alternatively, that it should be transformed into one. Considered "as a state," argued Seeley, "England has left Europe altogether behind it and become a world-state," and he called for the consolidation of this nascent polity into a vast permanent transoceanic polity.[110] The transmutation of empire into state implied by schemes for imperial federation was acknowledged by A. V. Dicey, the leading constitutional theorist in the empire, who complained that they were demanding a "new federated state."[111] In the Edwardian years it was increasingly accepted that burgeoning colonial demands for autonomy meant that new forms of political order had to be devised. But the idea of a global Anglo-state did not disappear. In 1905 W. F. Monypenny, a leading journalist with the *Times*, conceived of the empire as a "world state," a polity defined by cultural homogeneity and unity of interests. It was, he claimed, the embodiment of a "new political conception," which "transcends nationality" while simultaneously allowing the flourishing of separate nationalities within it.[112] Leo Amery, meanwhile, wrote of the colonial empire as a "single united whole, a great world-State, composed of equal and independent yet indissolubly united States." This was, he marveled, a "new ideal," a "great federation" that corresponded to the "wider outlook and broader humanity of advancing civilization."[113] The idea of an Anglo-Saxon commonwealth was also central to the Round Table movement during the Edwardian era and beyond.[114] I pick up its echoes in chapter 8.

Other arguments stressed the priority of the periphery to the metropole. According to this picture, Britain may well be subject to the relentless logic of decline, but the settler colonies, creative offspring of an old and vulnerable world, could reach escape velocity. While Lecky believed in the progressive nature of British imperialism, he still acknowledged the power of historical precedent: "Nations, as history but too plainly shows, have their periods of decay as well as their periods of growth." But even if Britain succumbed, the

---

[109] Mill, *Considerations on Representative Government*, 565; Hobhouse, *Democracy and Reaction* [1904], ed. Peter Clarke (Brighton, 1972), 154. See also J. R. Seeley, "Georgian and Victorian Expansion," *Fortnightly Review*, 48 (1887), 136.

[110] Seeley, *The Expansion of England*, 293, 169, 75. See also Seeley, "Georgian and Victorian Expansion," 133.

[111] Dicey, *Introduction to the Study of the Law of the Constitution*, 8th ed. (London, 1915), lxxxiv. Dicey presented his own vision of an Anglo-Saxon future, focusing on an Anglo-American "isopolity" (a space of common citizenship). Duncan Bell, "Beyond the Sovereign State," *Political Studies*, 62/2 (2013), 418–34. On how federation was seen by many eighteenth-century thinkers, including the authors of *The Federalist*, as a way to reconcile liberty and empire, see Armitage, "Empire and Liberty," 45–46.

[112] Monypenny, "The Imperial Ideal," in *The Empire and the Century*, ed. Goldman, 23 and 27.

[113] Amery, "Imperial Defence and National Policy," in *Empire*, ed. Goldman, 181–82.

[114] See, for example, Lionel Curtis, *The Problem of Commonwealth* (London, 1916), 68.

future of the British "race" was guaranteed as it had spread beyond the confines of the homeland to occupy vibrant, prosperous colonies throughout the world. "[W]hatever fate may be in store for these Islands, we may at least confidently predict that no revolution in human affairs can now destroy the future ascendency of the English language and of the Imperial race."[115] The (colonial) empire assured the permanence of the British people, their ability to transcend the vagaries of political institutions. This echoed arguments that figured the colonies—above all New Zealand—as a utopian space, a "better Britain."[116]

Once again, the universities came to play a vital role in legitimating empire. Even as the new wave of Roman scholarship was starting to undermine traditional narratives of luxury, decadence, and decline, so a new field of knowledge was beginning to emerge and others were being revitalized. In Oxford, the prodigious classicist Alfred Zimmern developed a modernizing interpretation of ancient Athens that inspired the "commonwealth" vision of the British empire articulated by Lionel Curtis and other members of the Round Table.[117] The Greek model entered a period of renaissance. Meanwhile Seeley's project to inject the study of the empire into the core of the emerging professional discipline began to bear fruit. During the early years of the twentieth-century imperial history, a new academic subfield financially underwritten by imperial interests was created to proselytize a specific ideological vision: to delineate Greater Britain as a singular political unit and to insist on its central importance for the future of Britain and the world. It was the hymn sung from the newly endowed chairs of imperial history in Oxford, Cambridge, and the University of London, and its intellectual inheritance persisted long into the twentieth century.[118]

Throughout the Victorian age, then, commentators on empire wrestled with the meaning of history. This resulted in a clash between a vision predicated on either the possibility or inevitability of political progress, and a cyclical vision in which empires followed predetermined trajectories. Negotiating these temporal narratives required considerable intellectual dexterity. Most advocates of empire acknowledged the previous cycles of imperial history, but suggested that there was something radically different about the age in which

---

[115] Lecky, *Empire*, 47.

[116] Lyman Tower Sargent, "Utopianism and the Creation of New Zealand National Identity," *Utopian Studies*, 12/1 (2001), 1–18.

[117] Zimmern, *The Greek Commonwealth* (Oxford, 1911). He was later appointed to the first chair of International Relations (IR) in the world, at the University of Wales, Aberystwyth, before returning to an IR chair at Oxford. See Jeanne Morefield, "'An Education to Greece,'" *History of Political Thought*, 28 (2007), 328–61; Morefield, *Empires without Imperialism* (Oxford, 2014), ch. 1; Tomohito Baji, "Commonwealth: Alfred Zimmern and World Citizenship," PhD thesis, University of Cambridge (forthcoming).

[118] Amanda Behm, "The Bisected Roots of Imperial History," *Recherches Britanniques*, 1/1 (2011), 54–77. On the "British world" scholarly network, see Tamsin Pietsche, *Empire of Scholars* (Manchester, 2013).

they lived and the kind of empire they defended. Avatars of progress, the British had managed to birth a new form of empire, one that was not only compatible with a progressive understanding of human development, but which played a pivotal role in it. Critics demurred from this Panglossian view, suggesting that the British empire was bound to follow the course of all others, and that in doing so it threatened the very things—liberty above all—which made Britain great in the first place. The muse of history whispered to the Victorians in different voices.

CHAPTER 6

The Idea of a Patriot Queen?

✺

The Monarchy, the Constitution, and the Iconographic Order of Greater Britain, 1860–1900

> The voice of Britain, or a sinking land,
> Some third-rate isle half-lost among her seas?
> *There* rang her voice, when the full city peal'd
> Thee and thy Prince! The loyal to their crown
> Are loyal to their own far sons, who love
> Our ocean-empire with her boundless homes
> For ever-broadening England, and her throne
> In our vast Orient, and one isle, one isle,
> That knows not her own greatness[1]
>
> —ALFRED TENNYSON

Tennyson, perhaps more than any other poet, expressed the profound symbolic connection between the institution of the monarchy, the heavily mediated persona of Queen Victoria, and the vast and "ever-broadening" expanses of the British empire. Victoria's long reign saw this connection grow in power and potency, as she assumed the role of an imaginative fulcrum at the center of an unprecedented global imperial system. In a later poem—one of his most anthologized and parodied works—Tennyson anointed her the "Patriot Architect," and this chapter explores some of the ways in which this vision was articulated in the political theory of Greater Britain—the political theory proclaiming the unity of the Anglo-Saxon settler colonies and the ostensible "mother country"—during the closing decades of the nineteenth century.[2]

---

[1] Tennyson, "To the Queen" [1859], in *Poetical Works* (Oxford, 1953), 441. Italics in original.

[2] Tennyson, "On the Jubilee of Queen Victoria" [1887], *Poetical Works*, 784. On Tennyson and the empire, see especially Matthew Reynolds, *The Realms of Verse, 1830–1870* (Oxford, 2001), pt.

In his pioneering *Short History of British Colonial Policy* (1897), H. G. Egerton argued that "The Period of Greater Britain" commenced in 1886.[3] This was to place the starting point at least fifteen years too late, however, for debate over the future of the settler empire began in earnest in the early 1870s, drawing its terminological inspiration from Charles Dilke's popular travelogue *Greater Britain* (1868).[4] Faced with what appeared to be a momentous shift in the patterns of European and global politics, combined with the insidious fear of mass democracy following in the wake of parliamentary reform—the latter an issue often marginalized or ignored by historians of imperial thought—a considerable number of British political thinkers sought ways to consolidate or reinforce the apparently weakening position of the country; to secure the greatness of Britain. The most vociferous, as well as the most fractious, manifestation of this desire was the movement calling for imperial federation, a movement that at one time or another attracted luminaries as diverse as J. R. Seeley, Joseph Chamberlain, Cecil Rhodes, James Bryce, J. A. Froude, W. E. Forster, W. H. Smith, Lord Rosebery, W. T. Stead, and J. A. Hobson. The proponents of Greater Britain, and in particular the imperial federalists, represented one of a large number of competing and intersecting movements aiming to challenge and transform the way in which the British empire (and state) was understood. Drawing the support and opprobrium of some of the most prominent thinkers and politicians of the day, they expounded their views in the most high-profile outlets in British public culture, generating a large volume of articles, books, and pamphlets. Ultimately, however, they never gained substantial support outside sections of the metropolitan elite, nor did they convince enough of the leading politicians of the day, including Disraeli, Gladstone, and Salisbury, of the viability and necessity of their proposals. The campaigning drive for federation faltered and then collapsed in ignominy during the 1890s, although ideas about federal unity were to remain a staple of imperial debate until the eve of decolonization. The proponents of Greater Britain, whether they identified with the federalists or not, argued that it was essential to reconfigure relations between the "mother country" and the settler colonies, so as to form an enduring and closely integrated global polity, a worthy challenger to the reinvigorated United States, the purportedly rapacious Russians, and the nascent German state. Through a policy of massive and systematic emigration, moreover, they hoped simulta-

---

3; Tricia Lootens, "Victorian Poetry and Patriotism," in *The Cambridge Companion to Victorian Poetry*, ed. Joseph Bristow (Cambridge, 2000), 255–80.

[3] Egerton, *A Short History of British Colonial Policy* (London, 1897).

[4] Dilke, *Greater Britain*, 2 vols. (London, 1868). Other early texts include: John Robinson, "The Future of the British Empire," *Westminster Review*, 38 (1870), 47–74; John Edward Jenkins, "Imperial Federalism," *Contemporary Review*, 16 (1871), 165–88; J. A. Froude, "England and Her Colonies," *Fraser's Magazine*, 1 (1870), 1–16; Andrew Robert Macfie, "On the Crisis of the Empire," *Proceedings of the Royal Colonial Institute*, 3 (1871–72), 2–12.

neously to strengthen the colonies and diffuse the conjoined dangers of over-population and "socialism" in the United Kingdom—in the process transfiguring the emigrants into loyal imperial subjects.

A variety of different models were proposed. For some, including both Dilke and Goldwin Smith, the key was to animate the idea of a planet-spanning British national-racial community and they stopped short of suggesting significant constitutional restructuring, believing it to be counterproductive.[5] Instead, they relied on the moral power of kinship and sentiment. This vision ran parallel to an important strand in the federalist literature, which demanded the recognition and fortification of the (supposedly) strong emotional and cultural bonds between the people of the United Kingdom and the colonies. For others, however, the development of a powerful Greater Britain necessitated the creation of non-legislating Advisory Councils, or expanding the scope of the Privy Council, so as to give voice (but not substantive power) to the colonists.[6] The more ambitious federalists demanded the construction of novel institutional structures, the establishment of a system of equal representation for the colonies, and, in its most radical form, the creation of a global federal state.[7] As Seeley commented—most probably drawing on Robert Browning's poignant imagery—the result would be a "world-Venice, with the sea for the streets."[8]

The monarchy played two important functions in the political theory of Greater Britain. Although analytically separable, both of these lines of reasoning were woven together through the fabric of imperial discourse. First, the institution, stretching back over centuries, could act as a temporal stabilizer, an anchor of permanence and constitutional fidelity in a reconstituted Greater Britain. Critics of such designs would be reassured that their fears of fundamental transformation were groundless—that a thread of historical continuity ran through the proposals. The delicate balance between change and stability was an essential topic to confront in a Whiggish political culture that venerated the past, disdained revolutionary institutional upheavals, and drew constant inspiration from the evolutionary gradualism elaborated most famously by Edmund Burke.[9] Secondly, Queen Victoria—or at least an idealized representation of her—served as the linchpin for a sense of global na-

[5] See Dilke, *Problems of Greater Britain* (London, 1890), vol. 2. For Smith's comments on "Greater Britain" as a moral community, see his letter to Professor Tyndall, October 6, 1882, in *A Selection from Goldwin Smith's Correspondence*, ed. Arnold Haultain (London, 1910), 137.

[6] See, for example, Earl Grey, "How Shall We Retain the Colonies?," *Nineteenth Century,* 5 (1879), 935–54; John Sutherland, *Imperial Federation* (London, 1885).

[7] The most explicit account of global statehood is in Seeley, *The Expansion of England*, pt. 1. For the details of his analysis, see chapter 11.

[8] Seeley, *The Expansion of England*, 288. See also Robert Browning, "A Toccata of Galuppi's" [1855], in *Browning: Poetical Works, 1833–64*, ed. Ian Jack (Oxford, 1970), 579.

[9] On the centrality of history and tradition in Victorian public culture, see, in general, Stefan Collini, *Public Moralists* (Oxford, 1991); Burrow, *Whigs and Liberals* (Oxford, 1988).

tional identity. It was thought that the renown and respect that she (and the institution of monarchy itself) generated knit the distant peoples of her dominions in close communion. This sense of an imagined community was a necessary though not sufficient condition for the creation of a coherent global polity, and it was something that many of the advocates of Greater Britain, of nearly all political stripes, stressed repeatedly. Moreover, a specific (and largely inaccurate) image of Victoria figured in a distinctly "civic humanist" (or what might be labeled "civic imperial") strand of imperial political thought. Above the fray of party political intrigue, and acting as a beneficent and revered ruler—indeed as a modified expression of the Bolingbrokian humanist ideal of the Patriot King—she was seen as embodying the communal values essential for linking together the colonial populations and the "mother country."

The British empire was a complex mosaic of political regimes, social institutions, and juridical forms. The proponents of Greater Britain were determined to carve out from this intricate multiracial assemblage a unified and homogeneous political-economic space. This was no easy task, and the conception of Greater Britain relied as much on the sentimental pull of the name and its associations as it did on any systematic theoretical explication. Its advocates often relied on the emotive force of what might be termed the *iconographic order* of Greater Britain, the imaginative system of resonant symbols, stirring rituals, and vague poetic imagery that, in their writings and pronouncements, provided a coherent picture of a shared past, a troubled present, and a glorious destiny. This order comprised a constellation of semi-articulated markers of identity that sought to provide an authoritative conception of a (possible if not actual) harmonious, productive, and progressive global nation—the Union Jack, Britannia ruling the waves, the ancient constitution, hardy and loyal colonists, the sacred freedoms of the English. Seeley, with typical condescension, argued that the people were "necessarily guided by a few large, plain simple ideas."[10] One of the most powerful of these ideas was that of the patriot monarch, standing watchful guard over her magnificent realms, and signifying permanence, unity, and strength.

In subsuming the scattered Anglo-Saxon colonies under a single, emotively charged name linked indelibly to the self-understanding of the British, the promoters of Greater Britain attempted to draw distant lands within the orbit, indeed to the very heart, of the metropolitan political imagination. The name itself implied two dimensions, one spatial, one moral. Spatially it referred to the vast scope of the British nation, stretching across the planet. This was an important issue in an age obsessed with the increasing size of political units. As one federalist warned, the "present growth of the United States and Russia threatens to dwarf the old states of Europe, and wisdom counsels union

---

[10] Seeley, *The Expansion of England*, 190.

to the English nation."[11] Froude concurred: "These are not the days for small states: the natural boundaries are broken down which once divided kingdom from kingdom; and with the interests of nations so much intertwined as they are now becoming, every one feels the benefit of belonging to a first-rate Power."[12] Morally it referred to the superiority of both the people and the political system—each interacting with and shaping the other in a complex dance of political progress—of this great agglomeration of territory; Greater Britain was fully deserving of a providentially ordained position of global leadership. "The fruits of political union will . . . be found," argued one excited federalist in 1885, "in the progress of an intelligent and prosperous people, marching in the van of civilisation, for the benefit not only of themselves, but of mankind, bound together in one nationality, though widely scattered over the broad surface of the globe." He concluded: "To this position the world's history offers no parallels; beside it Rome's range of influence sinks into comparative insignificance."[13] But this vision was deeply unrealistic, not least because its devotees failed to comprehend either the skepticism of colonial elites or its lack of political feasibility in Westminster. The dissonance between fantasy and reality was typical of much of the imperial thought of the age.

Constitutional Patriotism and the Monarchy

The use of the Queen, in a dignified capacity, is incalculable. Without her in England, the present English government would fail and pass away.[14]

—WALTER BAGEHOT

The popularity of the monarchy has waxed and waned over time. The nineteenth century saw considerable fluctuations in its fortunes, as the British political system underwent profound transformation: the compromise settlement of 1688 and the constitutional lineaments of the *ancien régime* were uprooted and transfigured as a (quasi-)democratic polity slowly emerged. The monarchy demonstrated remarkable resilience and flexibility, adapting to the rapidly changing society, adopting new public faces and political roles. The Hanoverian monarchy had been associated with old age, infirmity, corruption, and greed, and the young queen Victoria, ascending to the throne in 1837, consequently appeared as a breath of fresh air, revitalizing the image of a moribund institution. Apart from a brief but vocal efflorescence of anti-

---

[11] Samuel Wilson, "Imperial Federation," *National Review*, 4 (1884), 386.

[12] Froude, "England and Her Colonies," 15. See also Froude, "England's War" [1871], reprinted in *Short Studies on Great Subjects*, 5 vols. (London, 1907), 3:276.

[13] Young, *An Address on Imperial Federation* (London, 1885), 23. On the role played by Rome and Greece in late Victorian imperial thought, see chapter 5.

[14] Bagehot, *The English Constitution* [1867], ed. Paul Smith (Cambridge, 2001), 34.

monarchical sentiment in the late 1860s, Victoria was to remain a popular and venerated Queen.[15] The reasons for this popularity are multiple and varied, and would include, at a minimum, the ideological functions of elaborate royal ceremony, the respect that her demeanor and apparent disdain for aristocratic mores generated, the vital role of the burgeoning mass media in projecting her into the imaginative lives of the public, and the close association of the monarchy with philanthropic endeavor.[16] Historians continue to debate the balance between these factors, but for our present purposes what matters most is simply that "Victoria was central to the ideological and cultural signifying systems of her age," and that this was likewise true of the iconographic order of Greater Britain.[17]

Drawing on the ideas of the French syndicalist Georges Sorel, J.D.B. Miller once claimed that imperial federation was a "utopian" project.[18] As such, in Sorel's terminology, it was an "intellectual product," a fragile construct too weak to engender a powerful attachment to its cause. The "effects of utopias," Sorel argued dismissively, have "always been to direct men's minds towards reforms which can be brought about by patching up the system." As such, they were poor at galvanizing excitement and in generating affective bonds. This is a revealing way of comprehending the historical predicament of the proponents of a Greater British polity. However, it is not a self-portrait that they would have recognized. For many, the idea acted more as a Sorellian *myth*, the antithesis of utopia. For Sorel, the myth acted as an ideal, a picture of the future, behind which people would coalesce and which served consequently to unify and motivate transformative action. Myths, he argued,

> . . . must be judged as a means of acting on the present; all discussion of the method of applying them as future history is devoid of sense. *It is the myth in its entirety which is alone important*: its parts are only of interest in so far as they bring out the main idea.

[15] On the status and popularity of anti-monarchical republicanism, see Richard Williams, *The Contentious Crown* (Aldershot, 1997); David Nash and Anthony Taylor, eds., *Republicanism in Victorian Society* (Stroud, 2003); Anthony Taylor, *"Down with the Crown"* (London, 1999); Frank Prochaska, *The Republic of Britain, 1760–2000* (London, 2000). The majority of commentators now agree that there was little mainstream support for (anti-monarchical) republicanism. Craig, "The Crowned Republic?," *Historical Journal*, 46 (2003), 167–85.

[16] David Cannadine, "The Context, Performance, and Meaning of Ritual," in *The Invention of Tradition*, ed. Eric Hobsbawm and Terence Ranger (Cambridge, 1993), 101–64; William Kuhn, *Democratic Royalism* (London, 1997); Walter Arnstein, *Queen Victoria*, (Basingstoke, 2003), ch. 4; Dorothy Thompson, *Queen Victoria*; John Plunkett, *Queen Victoria* (Oxford, 2003); Frank Prochaska, *Royal Bounty* (London, 1995).

[17] The quotation is from Homans and Munich, "Introduction," 2. For the historiographical debate, see Craig, "The Crowned Republic?"; Arnstein, *Queen Victoria*. On the importance of the monarchy for empire, see G. R. Searle, *A New England?* (Oxford, 2004), 119; Thompson, *Imperial Britain* (London, 2000), 7.

[18] Miller, "The Utopia of Imperial Federation," *Political Studies*, 4 (1956), 195–97.

Unlike utopias, myths could not be refuted; they existed as an image in the mind, and acted as a guide to action in the present.[19] They embodied the intuitive, emotional, and symbolic aspects of political action. Greater Britain was seen by many of its advocates in this sense, hence their common reluctance to propound any specific plans and their reliance on vague rhetoric about unity, glory, and destiny. Moreover, their ideas fell prey to the same problems that beset Sorel's thought. The main dilemma appeared in attempting to translate the myth of global unity, of a providential Greater Britain, into a plausible scheme in an intellectual and political environment both skeptical of their general ambitions and lacking in the revolutionary impetus that a Sorellian myth would require to function adequately (if at all).

For many of the promoters of Greater Britain, then, vagueness was a virtue. Rather than explicating systematic theoretical plans for the future, a course of action that many considered counterproductive, they often relied on passionate appeals to emotion, to shared values, and to the moral edification of their loosely sketched ideas. (This began to change in the late 1880s and through the 1890s, when the number of concrete proposals increased, with the result that, as the skeptics had warned, the plans were frequently dismissed as unworkable contributions to "practical politics.") One of the perennial problems of political theory concerns the complex relationship between ideas (and ideals) and the resources necessary to motivate action in their name. Far too often political theorists propound visions of society, and of the world more generally, that appear to most observers to be detached from the vicissitudes of everyday life. British imperial theorists were acutely aware of this problem. Not only were they keen to stress that their ideas fell within the domain of "practical politics," they also placed great emphasis on the role of sentiment in political life. "Patriotism," proclaimed Froude, "may be sentimentalism, but it is sentimentalism nevertheless which lies at the root of every powerful nationality, and has been the principle of its coherence and growth."[20] Such sentiments were generated and reproduced over time by the motivational power of a rich tapestry of symbolism, ritual, and myth. An idealized image of the constitution performed such a function in the iconographic order.[21] "All nations have their idols, the creatures of their own hands, which having manufactured, they bow down before as gods . . . The Englishman adores the British Constitution."[22] It was, after all, the constitution, signifying strength and sta-

---

[19] Sorel, *Reflections on Violence* [1908], ed. Jeremy Jennings (Cambridge, 1999), 28–29, 116–17. Italics added. Miller intimates but does not develop this point.

[20] Froude, "England and Her Colonies," 6. See, for other examples, Forster, "Imperial Federation," *Nineteenth Century*, 17 (1885), 205; Anon., "The Federation of the British Empire," *Westminster Review*, 128 (1887), 492.

[21] On the importance of the constitution, and the way in which it was contested, see the essays in James Vernon, ed., *Re-Reading the Constitution* (Cambridge, 1996); J. P. Parry, *The Politics of Patriotism* (Cambridge, 2006).

[22] Froude, "England's War," 136.

bility, which had kept at bay the revolutionary fervor that had washed over Europe, both in the 1790s and in the mid-nineteenth century.[23] And it was the constitution, so it was thought, that guaranteed the conditions necessary for protecting freedom and encouraging prosperity, thus underpinning the fragile sense of progress, both moral and material, so vital in Victorian consciousness.

The monarchy was inescapably embedded in this Panglossian constitutional patriotism. Indeed, it was fundamental to the self-understanding of the vast majority of Victorians. It was a common imperialist claim that the monarchy generated, as Walter Bagehot had asserted, a "mystic reverence" and a "religious allegiance" amongst the people. A broadly Bagehotian understanding of the "dignified" elements of the constitution pervaded the discourse of Greater Britain. Bagehot wrote in the *English Constitution* (1867) that the importance of the Queen lay in the fact that "the mass of our people would obey no one else, that the reverence she excites is the potential energy—as science now speaks—out of which all minor forces are made, and from which lesser functions take their efficiency."[24] Loyalty to, and affection for, the dignified elements of the constitution were far greater than that catalyzed by the "efficient" facets. Froude noted that the loyalty of British subjects worldwide was principally to the Queen.[25] Egerton argued that there "is in the Colonies . . . an abundant loyalty to the Queen and to the British flag, but there is little loyalty to the Imperial Parliament."[26] Edward Salmon, a keen federalist, after stressing the "innate loyalty of true Britons," likewise proclaimed that "the great majority of Englishmen are enthusiastic supporters of the Throne." It is, he continued, "an emblem of Imperial unity—a golden incarnation of the brotherhood of Australia, Canada, the Cape, Great Britain, and other centres over which the Union Jack floats." "What the disappearance of the monarchy would mean is pretty clear. With it would come the break-up of the Empire." The lesson of all of this was straightforward: "[T]he Crown and the Colonies are rapidly becoming interdependent."[27] Although this was perhaps more aspiration than astute political analysis, such beliefs led many of the pro-

---

[23] Leslie Mitchell, "Britain's Reaction to the Revolutions," in *The Revolutions in Europe, 1848–1849*, ed. R.J.W. Evans and Hartmut Pogge von Strandmann (Oxford, 2000), 83–99.

[24] Bagehot, *The English Constitution*, 4, 167. Cf. Michael Bentley, *Lord Salisbury's World* (Cambridge, 2007), ch. 6. Note that Bagehot himself was skeptical of the claim often made by the advocates of Greater Britain that a shared race (defined in cultural terms) resulted in shared interests: "It is begging the question to assume that the ties of common race and language make nations better inclined to enter into active political alliance or better suited for harmonic acting." Bagehot, "An Anglo-Saxon Alliance" [1875], in *The Collected Works of Walter Bagehot*, ed. Norman St John-Stevas (London, 1965–86), 8:356–57.

[25] Froude, *Oceana* (London, 1886), 221–22.

[26] Egerton, *Short History*, 459.

[27] Salmon, "The Crown and the Colonies," *National Review*, 14 (1889–90), 200 and 202. For his views on federation, see Salmon, "Imperial Federation," *Fortnightly Review*, 58 (1900), 1009–19.

ponents of Greater Britain to stress the importance of the monarchy in their plans for a global polity.

The relationship between crown and colonies would also be reciprocally beneficial. Imperial federation, and a strong association with the aims of Greater British unity, would aid the monarchy in times ahead. The royal family could and should play an active role in advocating, and in governing, the new polity. The future status of the colonial empire was uncertain, argued Salmon, and the chances of success for the federalist movement were slim without royal support: it was up to "the action of the Crown" whether or not Greater Britain had a future. And at a time of increasing criticism of the royal family, and in particular the more feckless offspring of Victoria, this would be a wise course of action. De Labillière suggested that the sons and brothers of the sovereign might act as colonial governors, thus entrenching the connections between the different parts of the colonial system. "Its head, the Sovereign, and Royal Family, would be felt to belong, as much to Australia, Canada, South Africa, as to the people of the British Isles—just as much as the Federal Parliament in which they would all be directly represented." And again: "The sphere of its occupations, and of its usefulness might be greatly extended, by its members being brought into constant, advantageous and agreeable contact with the people in all our dominions."[28]

Nevertheless, despite the desire of many of the federalists and the understanding amongst the leadership of the Imperial Federation League (IFL) that royal patronage was essential if they were to succeed, royal attitudes to federation were mixed. Victoria was far more taken by the orientalist splendor of the imperial dependencies, India in particular, than she was with the settlement colonies. Her interest in the latter was "intermittent at best."[29] It would seem that the Queen's heart lay always, like that of her beloved Disraeli, in the East—it was, after all, with the help of her loyal prime minister that she became Empress of India in 1876. Despite this, a number of other members of the royal family were active supporters of imperial federation. One of Victoria's daughters encouraged her to read *The Expansion of England*: "It is wonderful and so statesmanlike, so farsighted, clear, and fair." The Prince of Wales likewise expressed his admiration for Seeley's vision of Greater Britain.[30] The most outspoken support came from Victoria's son-in-law, the Marquis of Lorne. A somewhat dilettantish man of letters, Liberal Unionist MP, and fi-

[28] de Labillière, *Federal Britain* (London, 1894), 248–49.

[29] Arnstein, *Queen Victoria*, 180. On Victoria's longstanding love of and involvement with India, and the lack of connection between this and her public persona, see Miles Taylor, "Queen Victoria and India, 1837–61," *Victorian Studies*, 46 (2004), 264–74.

[30] Letter by the Crown Princess of Germany to Victoria, May 25, 1884, in *The Letters of Queen Victoria, 1879–1885*, ed. George Buckle (London, 1926), 3:506; Sir Francis Knollys, letter on behalf of the Prince of Wales, to J. R. Seeley, May 13, 1887, Seeley Papers, University of London Library, MS903/1B/19. He was also President of the Royal Colonial Institute.

nally Governor-General of Canada, he argued in *Imperial Federation* (1885) for relatively limited imperial reform, expressing his disquiet at more ambitious federalist plans advocating an overhaul of parliamentary institutions. Instead, he recommended the creation of an "Advisory Council" incorporated within a reconstructed Privy Council. Rather unsurprisingly, he emphasized the role of the Queen as a focus of global national identity, capable of generating loyalty and a sense of unity amongst her scattered subjects. During her reign, he maintained, the tie between the "mother country" and the colonies in particular was regarded,

> ... with reverence and affection, and it is that which enables all citizens of this Empire to call themselves the subjects of the Queen. Her name has acquired a magic force, the strength of which can only be realized by those who have heard the national anthem sung by men, women, and children in regions many thousands of miles distant from England. It matters not whence it be heard, for in whatever part of the world her standard flies, that strain of music, and the thoughts which come with it, make the voices ring with the true loyalty that reverences women and loves the glorious sovereignty of freedom. The fervour to be heard in such notes should count for something in the calculation men are making as to the chance of keeping shoulder to shoulder wherever British hearts are beating.[31]

Victoria was thus a central element in the iconographic order of Greater Britain, her name alone exerting a "magic force," her image linked by musical and visual rituals of national identification to the idea of freedom itself. And, Lorne stressed, the power of such emotions was an important element in fashioning and sustaining global British unity, alongside more traditional concerns with shared security interests and cold economic calculation.

An especially clear evocation of the perceived role of the Crown was provided by Francis De Labillière, originally an Australian colonist, barrister of the Middle Temple, and a driving force behind the foundation of the IFL, of which he served subsequently as honorary secretary.[32] De Labillière was a prolific booster of what he termed the "great Constitutional Empire of Greater Britain," and the monarchy played an important role in his plans.

> For our Empire ... Monarchy, even were it not the existing form of government, will have the greatest advantages. It will impart to it greater dignity, in many ways. It would be preferable, were it only to save us

---

[31] Lorne, *Imperial Federation* (London, 1885). In a letter to Sir Frederick Young, Lorne wrote that he had "little faith" in the idea of a new imperial parliament. Lorne to Young, April 10, 1884, Young Papers, Cambridge University Library, RCMS 54/2/3.

[32] On his pivotal role, see the letter from W. E. Forster, the president of the IFL, to de Labillière, May 24, 1885, in the IFL Minute Book, British Library Add Ms, 62778, 74.

from a periodical scramble for the chieftainship of the nation, between rival candidates, with months of noise, abuse, exaggeration, and party trickery.[33]

In this passage we witness, alongside the Bagehotian phraseology, an example of the widespread anxiety about the importation of American "machine politics" into British life, a fear that was especially pronounced during the 1880s.[34] There was apprehension that public life would be degraded by incessant party squabbling, the unfortunate but inevitable consequence of democratic politics. In a Greater Britain, governed by a revered constitutional monarch, such a problem would be far less marked.

Furthermore, focusing on the centrality of the monarchy allowed proponents of a federal Greater Britain to confront another challenge. One of the main criticisms leveled at federation, as a general mode of political organization, was that it ran counter to the notion of unitary sovereignty.[35] It lacked, that is, a single determinate locus of political authority. For the federalists, Victoria, as sovereign, could provide a focal point, a substitute vision for that of the unitary sovereign state. In *Imperium et Libertas* (1901) Bernard Holland argued that the Crown played a key role in the relations between the "mother country" and the colonies, providing a pivot for the "confederate" empire. However, as a new era was beginning to dawn, so too was there a "rise in importance of the Throne." In a politically decentralized federal empire, the "spiritual sovereignty" of the Crown would be of ever-increasing significance. "It is not merely the symbol but the real bond of unity" and to this "central point all lines converge from all the ends of the earth."[36] As political power was devolved, so symbolic power was reaffirmed. A monarchical federation therefore offered the most effective way to avoid issues that had long plagued more conventional notions of federation. This partly explains why some federalists were keen to argue that the American constitution, which they so often held up as a model to emulate, was simply a derivation of the late eighteenth-century British constitution. J. N. Dalton, for example, presented the American brand as a subtle reworking of existing British political forms, and even claimed that the United States was governed by the "Imperial Houses of Parliament in Congress."[37] The President, in this vision, was a tem-

---

[33] de Labillière, *Federal Britain*, 248–49.

[34] See, for example, Paolo Pombeni, "Starting in Reason, Ending in Passion," *Historical Journal*, 37 (1994), 319–41; and Murney Gerlach, *British Liberalism and the United States* (Basingstoke, 2001).

[35] Amongst the most prominent advocates of unitary sovereignty were John Austin, *The Province of Jurisprudence Determined* (London, 1832), a book that became popular only posthumously; and A. V. Dicey, *Lectures Introductory to the Study of the Law of the Constitution* (London, 1885).

[36] Holland, *Imperium et Libertas* (London, 1901), 316–17, 318.

[37] Dalton, "The Federal States of the World," *Nineteenth Century*, 16 (1884), 109. This was

porary elected monarch. American institutions were thus assimilable to the conventions of British political thought; their apparently anomalous, even antithetical, structures were merely an evolutionary development of long extant British ideas. Federation was not so alien after all. The federalists were selective in their cultural and political appropriation: in reading America through British eyes, they sought to square the circle of federation and centralized sovereign authority.

The liberal statesman W. E. Forster, a key imperial ideologue and the first president of the IFL, stressed the linkage between historical continuity, patriotism, and the Crown. In discussing the conditions necessary for the continuance of Greater Britain, he argued that "allegiance to one monarch" was at the top of the list, and that the "very essence of such continuance is a common patriotism;—the feeling throughout all the different communities that, notwithstanding the seas that roll between them, they are yet one nation; and that all their inhabitants are fellow-countrymen." He maintained that the English-speaking peoples of the world shared a common culture, for they "look at life and its problems, especially the problems of Government, with much the same eyes everywhere." This included the Americans, and he claimed that the British monarchy had more in common with the United States republic than it did with any other state. Indeed, he argued that Britain had carried the torch of republicanism further than the Americans had done:

> Many millions of our race prefer a Republic to a Monarchy. Yes, but remember these facts: first, that we so treated their fathers that we almost forced them to become Republicans; Secondly, that many of them now acknowledge that at least it is a moot question whether, as regards the real meaning of the word, and its true significance, our Limited Monarchy is not a more complete Republic than their own.

Moreover, the loyalty of the colonists was specifically to the Crown. Why was this so?

> Not merely because they honour and respect our Queen; not merely because of their personal feeling towards the Royal Lady under whose rule they have grown from childhood to lusty youth; but because they are as proud as we are of the traditions of our history, and as convinced as we are of the actual advantages of a hereditary executive.[38]

"Republicanism," the monarchy, and the empire were indissolubly yoked together.

---

certainly not a universally recognized federalist strategy. For a denial of such connections, see Seeley, *Introduction to Political Science* [1896], ed. Henry Sidgwick (London, 1923), 210.

[38] Forster, *Our Colonial Empire* (Edinburgh, 1875), 25, 22, 23.

Civic Republicanism and the Colonial Order

It might seem that there is a certain irony attendant on linking the political theory of Greater Britain to the monarchy. After all, the phrase was coined originally by the radical liberal politician Charles Dilke, who was also one of the most reviled republicans of the age, a figure ostracized by Queen Victoria and her loyal followers.[39] Miles Taylor has claimed, however, that Dilke was concerned more with the issues that had troubled the classical republicans and their post-Renaissance successors than with the existence of the monarchy itself.[40] In other words, he was interested more in the nature of political authority—in challenging the scope of and constitutional limitations on popular representation—and the character of civic life than with any drastic antimonarchical scheme. Attention to the protection of political stability, maintaining limits on the power of government, and encouraging an active and patriotic citizenry permeated *Greater Britain* (1868). It is this version of civic republicanism on which the ensuing discussion focuses. It comprised an important but neglected strand of imperial political thought, infusing much of the debate over the future of the settler empire, and in particular the envisioning of a Greater British polity. I return to the topic in chapter 12.

For Stefan Collini, Victorian political thought was marked by "survivals and mutations" of the earlier language of civic humanism, and as John Burrow, Eugenio Biagini, and Frank Prochaska have all stressed, Victorian liberalism, amorphous and multidimensional as it was, frequently served as a vehicle for time-honored civic humanist ideas, which it incorporated and transformed in various ways.[41] Translated via the transmission belts of Whiggism from the early modern debates into the late nineteenth century, republicanism played a significant, though by no means dominant, role in shaping political thinking. It was common at the time to identify Britain as a republic: Tennyson called the United Kingdom a "crown'd republic," the positivist leader Frederic Harrison claimed that "England" was "an aristocratic republic," whilst Bagehot argued that "a Republic has insinuated itself beneath the folds of a Monarchy."[42] None of these were pure republican ideals, all were partial, compromised, and mixed various political sensibilities and vocabularies—as had their eighteenth-century predecessors.[43]

---

[39] On Dilke, see especially David Nicholls, *The Lost Prime Minister* (London, 1995).

[40] Taylor, "Republics versus Empires," in *Republicanism in Victorian Society*, ed. Nash and Taylor, 25–34. Cf. Prochaska, *The Republic of Britain*, 115–24.

[41] Collini, *Public Moralists*, 108–10; Burrow, *Whigs and Liberals*; Biagini, "Neo-Roman Liberalism," *History of European Ideas*, 29 (2003), 55–72; Prochaska, *The Republic of Britain*, chs. 4–5. In the historiography of European political thought, the terms "civic humanism" and "civic republican" are often used interchangeably.

[42] Tennyson, "To the Queen," 464; Harrison, "Our Venetian Constitution," *Fortnightly Review*, 7 (1867), 278; Bagehot, *The English Constitution*, 44.

[43] On the mixed idioms of eighteenth-century republicanism, see J.G.A. Pocock, "Between

Civic imperialism—humanist language and themes applied to the expanses of the empire—permeated the discourse of Greater Britain, centered as it (often) was on equalizing political relations between the "mother country" and the colonies, protecting the constitutional freedoms of its inhabitants, challenging the crass materialism and excess luxury of the modern age, and fostering a global nation of virtuous, vigorous, imperial patriots. Found in writers as diverse as Seeley, Dilke, and even Bryce, it was displayed most prominently in Froude's *Oceana* (1886), a book written explicitly as an updated version of James Harrington's utopian fantasy *The Commonwealth of Oceana* (1656). Froude's musings were pervaded by a sense of longing for the forgotten glories of the English past, of hardy yeomen, agrarian splendor, and the "genius of English freedom"—republican nostalgia writ large, and drawn upon in the name of shaping the present and the future. A "sound nation," he wrote,

> . . . is a nation composed of sound human beings, healthy in body, strong of limb, true of word and deed—brave, sober, temperate, chaste, to whom morals are more important than wealth or knowledge—where duty is first and the rights of man are second—where, in short, men grow up and live and work, having in them what our ancestors called the "fear of God."[44]

Such was Froude's dream for the British body politic—simultaneously stretching back in time, and projected forwards. It was a dream common to many of the Greater British advocates, though most of their proposals were not quite as austere.

Victoria was sometimes (though certainly not always) represented in the political theory of Greater Britain as the embodiment of a longstanding fantasy in British political consciousness: a nineteenth-century incarnation of the model found in Bolingbroke's late humanist tract, *The Idea of a Patriot King* (1738).[45] This was not an explicit comparison, a direct and self-conscious reference to a long-dead thinker, but key features and themes of earlier interpretations of patriot kingship were invoked frequently by imperial theorists. For Bolingbroke, the ideal monarch would stand above party strife, defending the constitution at home and promoting and protecting trade abroad. They would display three proud faces to the world: the enemy of corruption, the

---

Gog and Magog," *Journal of the History of Ideas*, 48 (1987), 325–46; Gregory Claeys, "The Origins of the Rights of Labor," *Journal of Modern History*, 66 (1994), 249–90.

[44] Froude, *Oceana*, 1:154. See also Harrington, *The Commonwealth of Oceana* (London, 1656). Froude wanted to see a "commonwealth of Oceana," united "as closely as the American states are united" (91). He was, however, very critical of plans for a formal set of federal institutions, although he thought they may one day develop (395).

[45] Bolingbroke, *The Idea of a Patriot King* [1738], in *Bolingbroke's Political Writings*, ed. Bernard Cottret (London, 1997), 329–421.

father of the people, and the strong but beneficent leader of a vibrant commercial people. Moreover, the patriot king was to stand firm against dangerous entanglement on the European mainland, secure in the belief in Britain's global maritime destiny. As David Armitage has demonstrated, this idea had multiple afterlives, and it was drawn upon by radicals, revolutionaries, and later by Tories in the impassioned ideological milieu of late eighteenth- and early nineteenth-century Britain. Due to its lack of specificity, the image was "perennially applicable." Following the death of William IV, the last monarch to whom the direct appellation of "Patriot King" was applied—more as desire than accurate representation—explicit references to the humanist dimensions of the Bolingbrokian idea seem to have disappeared. Indeed, from the 1830s onwards, and in particular in the hands of Disraeli and the Young England movement, Bolingbroke was retrospectively incorporated into the Tory ideological field.[46] This was not the end of the story: the ideas that he had propagated, and that had acted as common political currency for generations, remained in circulation and can be seen resurfacing, albeit in a translated form, in late Victorian imperial thought. To many of the proponents of Greater Britain, Victoria exemplified all the moral and leadership qualities that the patriot king was supposed to possess. This was the key to her symbolic power. She also faced similar dangers. Whereas the Bolingbrokian target was oligarchic corruption and the decay of virtue, so the proponents of Greater Britain were keen to confront the corrosiveness of materialism, the greed and purported lack of patriotism displayed by capitalist businessmen, the ideas of the utilitarian political economists, and the moral decline of Britain in general. Political action in the name of public duty and the common good, not private interest, was the guarantee of the continued greatness of Britain.

Sir Frederick Young provided perhaps the most explicit articulation of this vision. An ardent liberal, Young had been a close associate of E. G. Wakefield in the colonization of New Zealand, and was a longstanding and tireless proponent of imperial federation. Instrumental in establishing the Royal Colonial Institute, of which he served as honorary secretary, he was also a prominent voice in the IFL, and later the British Empire League.[47] In his contribution to an 1876 collection of letters on federation published originally in *The Colonist*, Young stressed the necessity of binding the "whole Empire into a homogeneous and indissoluble whole," and he demanded a "radical reconstruction of the Imperial representative body."[48] Indeed, he thought that the whole

---

[46] Armitage, "A Patriot for Whom?," *Journal of British Studies*, 36 (1997), 417; Richard Faber, *Beaconsfield and Bolingbroke* (London, 1961).

[47] See the brief biographical comments in Young, *A Pioneer of Imperial Federation in Canada* (London, 1902), 215. For the extent of his advocacy, see his prolific correspondence with newspapers on federation, Young Papers, RCMS 54/III/21.

[48] Young, Letter 1, in *Imperial Federation of Great Britain and Her Colonies* (London, 1876).

scheme was best conceptualized as a planetary "national federation."[49] This was a dream to which he remained faithful until his death over thirty years later.[50] The monarchy was central to Young's scheme. His most revealing comments on the topic are found in *Exit Party* (1900), a book charting (with stunning inaccuracy) what he saw as the decline of party politics in Britain. He wrote in an ode to Victoria:

> Her Most Gracious Majesty has, thank God, been preserved to us to the present hour, if it could be imagined possible, winning more and more veneration, the admiration, and the love of many millions of her people at home and beyond the seas by her supreme tact as a ruler, no less than her charming and beautiful womanly sympathy prompting her constant and wonderful personal activity in her unceasing desire for the promotion of the welfare of her subjects, throughout the length and breadth of her world-wide dominions.[51]

Like many other commentators, Young employed a heavily gendered conception of the Queen, as a mother figure displaying not only the traditional stereotypical "masculine" qualities of leadership—strength, fortitude, strategic calculation—but adding to them such "feminine" qualities as grace, tact, and sympathy; an iron fist in a velvet glove. Just as Britain was the mother country to the colonists, so Victoria was the figurative mother to all the peoples of the global nation. This was not, however, an entirely new addition to the multifaceted reception of the idea of the patriot king. Bolingbroke had, after all, looked backwards to Elizabeth as the embodiment of the values that he cherished and desired to see replicated in future leaders. It is not a coincidence that Victoria herself was often linked in the public imagination with Elizabeth.[52] Indeed, the Elizabethan age played an important role in the iconographic order of Greater Britain. Froude celebrated the "forgotten worthies" of the time, the old sea dogs who had helped make Britain great.[53] Seeley located the origins of the "national" policy—expansion at its core—in the years of Elizabeth's rule.[54] In particular, Young admired Victoria for standing above the fray of political intrigue, guiding the ship of state without being distracted by wearisome party machinations. In this, he argued—implausibly—she dif-

[49] Young, Letter, *Morning Post*, September 2, 1897, Young Papers, 54/III/21.

[50] See, for example, Young, *Imperial Federation of Great Britain and Her Colonies*, xix–xx; Young, *On the Political Relations of Mother Countries and Colonies* (London, 1885); Young, *Exit Party* (London, 1900), 66; Young, *A Pioneer of Imperial Federation*, ch. 8.

[51] Young, *Exit Party*, 56.

[52] Nicola Watson, "Gloriana Victoriana," in *Remaking Queen Victoria*, ed. Homans and Munich, 79–105; Burrow, *A Liberal Descent* (Cambridge, 1981), 249.

[53] Froude, "England's Forgotten Worthies," *Westminster Review*, 2 (1852), 42–67.

[54] Seeley, *The Growth of British Policy* (Cambridge, 1895). He argued that this policy did not fully triumph over its "dynastic" competitor until the eighteenth century.

fered from many of her predecessors. "With regards to her Parliament . . . her relations have been of the utmost and most uninterrupted harmony from the first moment she ascended the throne."[55] Writing at the end of her long reign, Young hoped that her legacy would endure. Above all, it was essential to have a constitutional monarch standing at the head of a global imperial state. Citing James Douglas, a Canadian resident in the United States, he believed that such a monarch,

> . . . would represent in his person the traditions of the past, and embody the historical continuity of the race. Powerless to interfere arbitrarily, but not therefore bereft of influence, the creature of his subjects, though nominally the controller of their fate, his right to avert injustice and enforce fair play would exert a restraining power. Such a nominal head, called by whatever name the republican principle of the Federation would allow to be applied, would be a less dangerous and more picturesque chief than an elected president.[56]

Victoria was, De Labillière likewise contended, the "most perfect constitutional Sovereign that ever presided over a free people."[57]

The gap between vision and reality was sizeable, even by the standards of imperial political thought. Not only was Victoria more enamored with India than with the colonies, the representation of her as a disinterested leader, above and beyond party, was wholly incorrect. The political power of the monarch had been in steady decline over the course of the century, but it was still considerable, and far exceeded the limited rights ascribed to it by Bagehot.[58] Victoria meddled incessantly in the day-to-day affairs of her ministers, and she perceived her role—especially the prerogative of forming ministries—as central to the constitutional machinery of the state.[59] But the notion of her as an impartial leader was a powerful illusion. Victoria's "civic publicness" had, as John Plunkett remarks, been fostered most especially in the early years of her reign, when she was seen to represent a radical departure from her staid Hanoverian predecessors and the residues of Old Corruption, and during the second half of the century a newly vigorous and pliant media helped to sustain a potent image of her role. This image lingered throughout the rest of her reign, despite shifts in the intensity of adoration.[60] Victoria was certainly patriotic, but she was no patriot queen.

[55] Young, *Exit Party*, 56–57.

[56] Young, *A Pioneer of Imperial Federation in Canada* (London, 1902), 221–22. The quotation is taken from Douglas, *Canadian Independence* (New York, 1894), 19–20. Young says of these words that "they express so forcibly and cogently my own general sentiments on the subject" (222).

[57] de Labillière, *Federal Britain*, 251–52.

[58] Bagehot, *The English Constitution*, esp. chs. 2, 3.

[59] G.H.L. Le May, *The Victorian Constitution* (London, 1979), ch. 3; Arnstein, *Queen Victoria*, ch. 8.

[60] Plunkett, *Queen Victoria*, ch. 1.

Conclusions

In 1837 there was much talk of dissolution;
in 1897 there is thought only of unity.[61]

—EDWARD SALMON

The monarchy, the monarch, and the empire were threaded together in the iconographic order of Greater Britain. Fantasies for politically unifying Britain and its colonies were grounded in a palpable sense of anxiety; fear for the future drove the construction of an image of the world rewritten according to a British script. Imperial unity became a prominent topic during the second half of Victoria's reign because it was viewed as a necessary response to domestic political pressures and foreign competition in an age of increasing globalization. For many, it was the only way of keeping Britain great.

The monarchy was essential to this dream. This chapter has sketched the outlines of that vision—a more detailed examination would also explore the important role played by the ideal of the patriot queen in post-Repeal Act, pre-Fenian nationalist Ireland during the 1850–60s, the debate over Canadian federation (1867), and the attempt to "unite" South Africa in 1879–80. In all, Victoria stood as a symbolic marker of national and imperial sentiment, a focal point for loyalty. As an imperial figurehead, the matriarch of the British nation, she played a critical function in the matrix of British global identity and power. It was in this role that she could be seen as picking up the mantle of the patriot queen. The royal family might be criticized for waste, profligacy, inefficiency, or any number of other failings, but its existence in the British constitutional order was rarely questioned, even if the degree of its power was a subject of constant debate. The proponents of Greater Britain, on the whole, tended to reflect this common understanding of the importance of a constitutional monarchy. By emphasizing the centrality of the monarchy in their conceptions of the future, they hoped to ameliorate fears about the radical nature of many of the plans being adumbrated, and to root them in the soil of British historical tradition. A planet-spanning imperial polity—even a global state—was to be their gift to Britain, the world, and posterity itself. A timeless embodiment of the glory of the nation, ensconced safely and soundly at the center of a stable constitutional order, the monarch was at the core of this vision.

[61] Salmon, "The Colonial Empire of 1837," *Fortnightly Review*, 61 (1897), 870.

CHAPTER 7

Imagined Spaces

Nation, State, and Territory in the British Colonial Empire, 1860–1914

The old colonial system is gone. But in its place no clear and reasoned system has been adopted. The wrong theory is given up, but what is the right theory? There is only one alternative. If the colonies are not, in the old phrase, possessions of England, then they must be part of England; and we must adopt this view in earnest.[1]

—J. R. SEELEY

During the late Victorian age, and deep into the twentieth century, a fierce debate raged among members of the British political and intellectual elite over the future of the empire. Could it be adapted to new economic, social, and political circumstances? What form should it take? Fear about the future was generated by concern over both the domestic consequences of democratic reform and about the precarious geopolitical position. Britain's status as a global power was at stake. Democratic reforms, first in 1867 and then more deeply in 1884, reshaped the political landscape. Large numbers of the (male) population were enfranchised, while socialism became an evermore popular and vocal force. Many advocates of empire saw these developments as a threat, worrying that the new mass public would harbor anti-imperial sentiments. The problem was reinforced by various geopolitical trends, and above all the rise of three main competitor states. First, post-unification Germany was well on the way to becoming the dominant power on the continent, and it appeared keen to flex its muscles on the global stage. Second, Russia was seen as a menace to the empire in India, and thus to British power globally. Finally, the post-Civil War dynamism of the United States challenged British economic dominance, and as it enthusiastically embarked on foreign imperial

[1] Seeley, *The Expansion of England*, 158.

adventures in the 1890s it was figured as a formidable geopolitical competitor. To make matters worse, during the closing decades of the century Britain suffered a prolonged and severe economic depression.[2] The country seemed to be weakening at the very moment when its hegemonic position was being challenged. The dynamics between "domestic" and "foreign" were mutually reinforcing; they signaled a vicious circle, a precipitate decline.

What could be done? One of the main answers proposed to address the crisis of imperial confidence was to unite Britain with its scattered settler colonies. Australia, Canada, New Zealand, and parts of South Africa could be fused together into a vast political-economic unit, straddling the planet. The movement advocating Greater Britain, as this behemoth was often called, appealed to people across the political spectrum. Its supporters ranged from Tory peers, through liberal "public moralists" to assorted socialist leaders, including H. M. Hyndman and Keir Hardie.[3] All of them believed that it was essential, for Britain and the wider world, that the colonial empire prosper in an international system defined increasingly by huge omnicompetent political units. Yet they diverged over the ends this unity was supposed to produce, as well as over the means through which to bring about those ends. For radical liberals, always in the minority, colonial unity would help simultaneously to democratize Britain and the international system as a whole. It would constitute part of a progressive multilateral institutional order.[4] In the early years of the twentieth century, following the war in South Africa, and against the backdrop of Chamberlain's tariff reform campaign, radical support for this vision dissipated, leaving the field dominated (although not exhausted) by conservative intellectuals and politicians.[5] The dominant view, however, was that Greater Britain provided a way of securing British power while dampening the threat posed by democratic reform and any possible socialist challenge. Through a process of systematic emigration, the disruptive, corrosive potential of democracy would be neutralized as "excess" population was channeled from Britain (and in particular from its overcrowded and festering cities) into the huge open spaces of the colonies.[6] This movement, it was argued, would

[2] For useful general accounts of British society and politics at the time, see Theodore Hoppen, *The Mid-Victorian Generation, 1846–1886* (Oxford, 1998) and Geoffrey Russell Searle, *A New England?* (Oxford, 2005).

[3] On socialist support for imperial federation, see especially Gregory Claeys, *Imperial Sceptics*, ch. 3. Hyndman was leader of the Social Democratic Federation and a booster of Marx, while Hardie was a founder of the Labour Party. See also the discussion of Hobson and Hobhouse in chapter 14.

[4] See chapter 10 of this volume, and Casper Sylvest, *British Liberal Internationalism, 1880–1930* (Manchester, 2009).

[5] Daniel Gorman, *Imperial Citizenship* (Manchester, 2006); Peter J. Cain "The Economic Philosophy of Constructive Imperialism," in *British Politics and the Spirit of the Age*, ed. Cornelia Navari (Keele, 1996), 41–65.

[6] On the general fear of degeneration, see Daniel Pick, *Faces of Degeneration* (Cambridge,

simultaneously defuse the dangers of urban radicalism while populating the colonies with individuals who, as a result of a transformation in their natural and cultural environments, would be transmuted into rugged imperial patriots, citizen-subjects of the most powerful polity on earth.[7]

In this chapter I explore how *fin de siécle* imperialist intellectuals challenged some of the existing spatial categories used to map world politics, and in particular how they sought to erode the distinction between the "domestic" and the "foreign." I focus on two related issues: the imagined *globalization of domestic politics* and the emergence of ideas about a nascent *planetary public*. In the minds of many imperialists, the boundaries between the domestic and the foreign were fluid and changeable, and they developed an account of the "domestic"—or *Innenpolitik*—as a space that stretched across the face of the earth, encompassing the vast settler colonies. This was often characterized in terms of a global British nation-state—a political-cultural whole, bound by a strong sense of identity and belonging—and it implied a novel conception of a "translocal" public sphere. Julius Vogel, a prominent New Zealand politician, objected to the view that the colonies were "foreign" territories; they were instead "part of a mighty nation."[8] The advocates of Greater Britain sought to reimagine the ontological and ethical status of home and abroad, while simultaneously emphasizing the important differences between the settler colonies and the rest of the empire. I am not suggesting that this novel line of argument led to any straightforward changes in government priorities or legislation. Rather, I focus on how and why a group of well-placed individuals located at the heart of the imperial metropole attempted to shift attitudes, to transform political consciousness, in order to redirect public policy. They were what contemporary theorists of international politics call "norm-entrepreneurs."[9] Through argument and political mobilization, they were seeking to alter the terms of the debate and to institute a new vision of global political order.

Salvaging Empire

While British society and politics were partially constituted through the imperial encounter, most advocates of empire thought that foreign and imperial

1989); John Burrow, *The Crisis of Reason* (London, 2000). On republican imperialism, see also chapters 2 and 12 of this volume.

[7] For further discussion, see Bell, *The Idea of Greater Britain*, ch. 2.

[8] Julius Vogel, "Greater or Lesser Britain," *Nineteenth Century*, 1 (1877), 813; Vogel, "The British Empire," *Nineteenth Century*, 3 (1878), 617.

[9] Martha Finnemore and Kathryn Sikkink, "International Norm Dynamics and Political Change," *International Organization*, 52 (1998), 887–917; see also the discussion of "innovating ideologists," in Quentin Skinner, *Visions of Politics* (Cambridge, 2002), vol. 1, esp. chs. 7, 8, 10.

affairs failed to register sufficiently in elite consciousness, let alone among the wider public. It was a commonplace lament during the period that domestic affairs, however trivial, took priority in all but the most momentous times in national history. Wars, such as the South African War, could occasionally stir the populace from its myopic slumber, at least if they were intoxicating or exotic enough, but little else did. Whether this picture was accurate or not, it was routinely argued that both the public and the political elite downplayed or ignored the importance of international affairs in general, and imperial affairs in particular.[10] There was little new in this sense of alienation. In a speech in Westminster in 1833, Thomas Babington Macaulay complained that:

> A broken head in Cold Bath Fields produces a greater sensation among us than three pitched battles in India. A few weeks ago we had to decide on a claim brought by an individual against the revenues of India. If it had been an English question the walls would scarcely have held the members who would have flocked to the division. It was an Indian question; and we could scarcely, by dint of supplication, make a House.[11]

His sense of frustration is striking, and it was widely shared. Imperialists argued that their compatriots typically failed to grasp the precarious nature of British global power, or the roles and responsibilities associated with the possession of empire. Their writings and speeches were peppered with complaints about the failure of imperial interests and ambitions to register sufficiently with either the government or the people. John Stuart Mill was expressing a common grievance when in 1859 he bemoaned the "indifference to foreign affairs" displayed by the public, and when a decade later he castigated the "indifference of official people in England about retaining the colonies."[12] Another variation on the theme of indifference concerned the lack of vision displayed by British politicians. In a discussion of George Cornewall Lewis's ideas about the Suez Canal, for example, Walter Bagehot contended that, "[t]hose who wish that the foreign affairs of England should be managed according to a far-seeing and elaborate policy will not like such voluntary short-sightedness; but the English people themselves rather have to have the na-

---

[10] There is considerable debate over the extent to which empire did register among the public and elites (and of what might follow from this). See, for example, Michael Bentley, *Politics without Democracy*, 2nd ed. (Oxford, 1999), xviii, 182; Peter Durrans, "The House of Commons and the British Empire, 1868–1880," *Canadian Journal of History*, 9 (1974), 19–45; Bernard Porter, *The Absent-Minded Imperialists* (Oxford, 2004); Catherine Hall, *Civilizing Subjects* (Cambridge, 2002).

[11] Macaulay, "Speech on the Renewal of the East India Company Charter" [July 10, 1833], reprinted in Macaulay, *The Complete Works* (London, 1898–1906), 11:558. Cold Bath Fields was a notorious prison in London.

[12] Mill, "A Few Words on Non-Intervention" [1859], in *Collected Works* (Toronto, 1963–91), 21:17; Mill, letter to Henry Samuel Chapman, January 14, 1870, *Collected Works,* 18:1685.

tional course fixed by evident, palpable, and temporary circumstances."[13] The governing class, he implied, exhibited a distinct lack of leadership and foresight in foreign and imperial affairs, this absence mirroring the apathy of the people.

While the charge of indifference was thought to apply to nearly all aspects of imperial and foreign affairs, it was often argued that the colonial empire suffered the most of all. In an essay published in 1870, the historian J. A. Froude set out the familiar indictment, grumbling that the public was "alienated" from the settler colonies.[14] Indifference, it was argued, was leavened with ignorance, a lack of awareness about the nature and value of the empire. Speaking at the inaugural meeting of the Royal Colonial Society in 1869 the Marquis of Normanby, an eminent colonial governor, argued that "[n]o person who takes an interest in colonial matters can help being struck with the extra-ordinary ignorance that exists in this country in regard to colonial matters." At the same meeting, Baillie Cochrane, a Tory MP and one of the original leaders of the Young England movement, lamented the "indifference" prevalent among the members of the public and the political class.[15] Writing in the *Quarterly Review* in 1870, John Martineau crystallized the frustration of many imperialists when he lambasted the "carelessness and indifference with which the English Parliament, reflecting truly the apathy of the public, has treated the magnificent inheritance of our Colonial Empire."[16]

Imperial advocates tended to construct the situation as a *crisis*. They deployed the language of emergency to demonstrate the urgency of the problem, to insist on its immediacy and magnitude.[17] Theirs was an imagined cartography of fear and foreboding. This emotive idiom made possible the claim that sweeping political change was imperative, that without it the empire, and British power itself, would dissolve. Imperialists had always been haunted by a sense of potential failure, of the fragility of dominance.[18] The specter of Rome loomed over their warnings; as I argued in chapter 5, the trope of imperial

---

[13] Walter Bagehot, "Sir George Cornewall Lewis" [1863], in *Biographical Studies*, ed. Richard Holt, 2nd ed. (London, 1889), 212–13.

[14] Froude, "England and Her Colonies," *Fraser's Magazine*, 1 (1870), 4–5; L. J. Trotter, "British India under the Crown," *Contemporary Review*, 15 (1870), 113–32.

[15] Both men were responding to Lord Bury's "Inaugural Speech" [March 15, 1869], reprinted in the *Proceedings of the Royal Colonial Institute*, vol. 1 (1869–70), 51–62. George Phipps, Marquis of Normanby, had served as Governor of Nova Scotia in the 1840s; during the 1870s and 1880s he was Governor of Queensland, New Zealand, and Victoria.

[16] John Martineau, "New Zealand and Our Colonial Empire," *Quarterly Review* (1870), 128, 135.

[17] See, for example, Andrew Macfie, "On the Crisis of the Empire," *Proceedings of the Royal Colonial Institute*, 3 (1871–72), 2–12.

[18] Piers Brendon, *The Decline and Fall of the British Empire: 1781–1997*, (London, 2007); John Darwin, "The Fear of Falling," *Transactions of the Royal Historical Society*, 5th series, 36 (1986), 27–45; and the discussion of time in chapter 5.

decline and fall was etched into Victorian political consciousness. During the second half of the century, this apprehension of crisis intensified. The Sepoy Rebellion (1857) unsettled many Britons, who were simultaneously astonished at the lack of gratitude displayed by their imperial subjects and transfixed by the brutality of the revenge exacted, the "war of no pity" waged against the rebels.[19] Focusing on the violent repression of an uprising in Jamaica in 1865, the Governor Eyre controversy generated a similar set of responses.[20] Beset by unrest, populated by millions of potential insurgents, yet essential to British greatness, the empire came to be imagined as an arena of perpetual conflict and confrontation. Indeed from the late 1850s onwards the British empire was routinely figured as a space of permanent crisis. In his brilliant analysis of the conceptual history of crisis, Reinhart Koselleck writes that,

> Applied to history, "crisis," since 1780, has become an expression of a new sense of time which both indicated and intensified the end of an epoch. Perceptions of such epochal change can be measured by the increased use of crisis. But the concept remains as multi-layered and ambiguous as the emotions attached to it. Conceptualized as chronic, "crisis" can also indicate a state of greater or lesser permanence, as in a longer or shorter transition towards something better or worse or towards something altogether different. "Crisis" can announce a recurring event, as in economics, or become an existential term of analysis, as in psychology and theology. All these possible uses can be applied to history itself.[21]

And all of these possible "uses" can be found in British imperial discourse. The British *colonial* empire was both part of the problem and one possible solution to it. The modality of crisis varied between the different forms of imperial connection: for the colonial empire the main fear was not about violence or insurgency, moral corruption or strategic overstretch, but rather about secession, the dissolution of the political bond. Yet if the government acted swiftly and surely to unify the empire, to treat the colonists as full citizen-subjects of a single polity, the colonies would be integrated into a permanent structure of British dominance impervious to the crises afflicting the rest of the empire. Or so it was claimed.

There were various ways to address the crisis, to overcome the indifference. The most practical was to mobilize on behalf of an alternative vision of the empire, and during this period numerous pressure groups and campaigning

---

[19] Christopher Herbert, *War of No Pity* (Princeton, 2007).

[20] Rande Kostal, *A Jurisprudence of Power* (Oxford, 2006); Karuna Mantena, "The Crisis of Liberal Imperialism," in *Victorian Visions of Global Order*, ed. Bell (Cambridge, 2007), 89–113.

[21] Koselleck, "Crisis," *Journal of the History of Ideas*, 67 (2006), 357.

organizations, including the Imperial Federation League (IFL), were established.[22] They lobbied hard for the importance of the colonial empire. The politics of knowledge assumed a starring role: indifference to empire, it was often argued, was generated and perpetuated by a lack of relevant information. Schools and universities were failing to equip their students, all future imperial subjects, with an adequate appreciation of the past and present glories of the British empire. This was one of the main complaints leveled at the British educational system in Seeley's best-selling book *The Expansion of England*.[23] It is not a coincidence that the IFL, and cognate organizations, exerted considerable energy in supporting speaker tours, public lectures, and the production and dissemination of educational materials. It was vital, they thought, to shape the public mind. The Marquis of Lorne—liberal politician, Queen Victoria's son-in-law, and future Governor-General of Canada—argued in a speech to the Royal Geographical Society in 1886 that "knowledge and sympathy are essential to the consolidation of the empire."[24] The fact that this was thought necessary bears witness to the sense of indifference perceived by the proponents of empire. W. T. Stead, one of the pioneers of the "new journalism," went so far as to propose that Seeley be placed in charge of a college dedicated to teaching the glories of the British nation.[25] In short, the production of colonial knowledge was an integral element of the project to create a Greater British century.

The advocates of Greater Britain claimed some success in reshaping public views of the character and importance of the colonial empire, if not in fully redirecting British policy. But the feeling of indifference lingered. The historian C. P. Lucas, for example, commented in 1890 that while there had been a "change in tone and feeling towards the colonies and dependencies" over the course of the previous decade, a "spirit of indifference" was still pervasive.[26] Moreover, the expanding scope of the demos brought forth a new set of worries. Leonard Hobhouse, a leading "new liberal" and qualified supporter of imperial federation, picked out one of the main concerns, borne of a sense of frustration with the rise of the mass media. The public, he worried, remained poorly informed, with the press acting as a bar to widespread interest in or knowledge about public affairs. Fed an impoverished intellectual diet, they

[22] Andrew Thompson, *Imperial Britain* (London, 2002).

[23] On the institutional ecology of imperial campaigning, see Seeley, *The Expansion of England*. In an obituary, H.A.L. Fisher commented: "I question whether any historical work has exercised so great an influence over the general political thinking of a nation." H.A.L. Fisher, "Sir John Seeley," *Fortnightly Review*, 60 (1896), 193. For Seeley's imperial political theology, see chapter 11.

[24] Lorne, "The Annual Address on the Progress of Geography, 1885–1886," *Proceedings of the Royal Geographical Society*, 8 (1886), 420; Felix Driver, *Geography Militant* (Oxford, 1999).

[25] Stead, in *The Life of W. T. Stead*, ed. Frederick Whyte (London, 1925), 2:209–10.

[26] C. P. Lucas, "Introduction" to George Cornewall Lewis, *An Essay on the Government of Dependencies* (Oxford, 1891), xxxviii, lviii.

were interested only in reading about battles and sport. "In truth, there is not, and cannot at present be, any such thing as an effective popular control of foreign policy. The average man gives little time and much less thought to politics."[27] This message resonated across the political spectrum.

Remaking the People

One of the most intriguing elements of the debate over the future of the British empire was the way in which the imaginative scope of both "the people" and "the public" was reconfigured.[28] I am using the idea of "the people" to refer to the set of individuals within a particular polity who are conceived of as bound together by—and thus in some sense as unified through—a range of common characteristics (most frequently "race" or "nationality" or some combination of the two). As such, "the people" is not coextensive with the totality of individuals falling under the jurisdiction of a particular system of governance, for many of those individuals, including resident aliens, fall outside of the recognized boundaries of community. (Indians, for example, were not regarded as a constitutive element of the British people.) But neither is the people coextensive with "the public"; the latter is a subset of the former. The public, as I am employing the term, refers to the set of the people accorded political significance within a particular polity. They are construed as belonging to a distinct and privileged group with at least a notional role in the governance of the state. This conception is closely linked to the set of the enfranchised, but it is not necessarily reducible to it. During the Victorian era both the size of the public, and the importance accorded to it, expanded considerably. During the twentieth century, with the extension of the franchise to include (nearly) all adult men and women, this gap narrowed further, though the two categories are still far from identical.[29]

One of the most prominent ways in which imperialists in the late nineteenth century attempted to address the "crisis" was by arguing that the very terms in which the trope of indifference was articulated were flawed. The future of the colonial empire was not, they argued, chiefly a problem of foreign

[27] Hobhouse, *Democracy and Reaction* [1904], ed. P. F. Clarke (Brighton, 1973), 144–45. For more on Hobhouse, see chapter 14.

[28] I do not follow nineteenth-century usage, where there was no settled meaning for either the "people" or "public." Boyd Hilton argues that the idea of a public, as we would understand it, did not really exist before 1850. *A Mad, Bad, and Dangerous People?* (Oxford, 2006), 310–11. I use the concepts as analytical categories to help make some sense of a confused debate. For a useful theoretical discussion, see Margaret Canovan, *The People* (Cambridge, 2005).

[29] On the philosophical issues involved, see Arash Abizadeh, "Citizenship, Immigration, and Boundaries," in *Ethics and World Politics*, ed. Duncan Bell (Oxford, 2010), 358–77, and, more recently, Sarah Fine, "Democracy, Citizenship, and the Bits in Between," *Critical Review of International Social and Political Philosophy*, 14/5 (2011), 623–40.

or imperial policy; it was instead a problem of *domestic* British politics. This argument required a significant cognitive shift, the willingness to recognize that the distant and scattered colonies (and colonists) were an integral part of the British polity. As Seeley argued, once this work of imagination was complete, "Canada and Australia would be to us as Kent and Cornwall."[30] Even the most common appellation for the unity of the United Kingdom with its settler colonies—Greater Britain—served to signal the seamless continuity between the "mother country" and the colonial diaspora. This represented, then, an argument for the globalization of domestic politics: the Anglo-Saxon population(s) of the British settler colonies constituted one unified "people," spread across several noncontiguous geographical spaces.

This argument was premised on a reorientation in the perception of time and space.[31] The links between political identity, territory, and the nation were, it was claimed, challenged fundamentally by new technologies. In particular, the development of transoceanic steam ships and (above all) the construction of a network of telegraph cables had a profound effect on the political imagination.[32] The cables, boasted Rudyard Kipling, "killed their father Time." [33] This death precipitated an imaginative rescaling of planetary space and a concerted effort to rethink imperial possibilities. Imperial discourse was soon saturated by a powerful form of techno-utopianism. Routinely exaggerating the capabilities of the new technology, imperial commentators celebrated the "annihilation" of time and space, arguing that this meant that the physical limits to political association had been transcended. Repudiating a long-standing argument about the impossibility of creating strong and enduring political institutions and identities across oceanic distances, advocates of colonial unity argued that a new era had dawned, an era in which nature, previously viewed as immutable, was capable of being reshaped by the powers of human technical ingenuity. Frederick Young, one of the most prolific imperial unionists, wrote that the "marvellous and mysterious help of telegraphy" had "worked a veritable revolution in the affairs of the world."[34] W. E. Forster, an influential liberal politician and one-time president of the IFL, argued in a speech in Edinburgh in 1875 that "science has brought together the ends of

[30] Seeley, *The Expansion of England*, 63. Leo Amery, "Imperial Defence and National Policy," in *The Empire and the Century*, ed. C. S. Goldman (London, 1905), 182.

[31] For the widespread transformation in perceptions of time and space in European culture, see Stephen Kern, *The Culture of Time and Space, 1880–1918* (Cambridge, MA, 2003); Nicholas Daly, *Literature, Technology, and Modernity, 1860–2000* (Cambridge, 2004); Wolfgang Schivelbusch, *The Railway Journey* (Oxford, 1986).

[32] The Atlantic was straddled in 1866 (after an abortive attempt in 1858). Cables reached Australia in 1872, New Zealand in 1876, and South Africa in 1879.

[33] Kipling, "Deep-Sea Cables" [1896], in *Rudyard Kipling's Verse, 1885–1932* (London, 1932), 173.

[34] Young, *Proceedings of the Royal Colonial Institute*, 8 (1876–77), 118–19.

the earth, and made it possible for a nation to have oceans roll between its provinces."[35] He later stated that

> The inventions of science have overcome the great difficulties of time and space which were thought to make separation almost a necessity, and we now feel that we can look forward, not to the isolated independence of England's children, but to their being united to one another with the mother-country, in a permanent family union.[36]

This radical shift in the plasticity of nature translated into a moment of political opportunity. The unification of the colonial empire was now both possible and necessary. According to F. P. De Labilliére, an ardent proponent of the federal vision, "[t]he prospect of a Federal Empire, which five-and-twenty years ago appeared very remote, and which 50 years since seemed almost a chimera, now assumes a pressing and tangible shape."[37] "It may be said," wrote the radical Australian barrister John Edward Jenkins, that at "no very distant date steam communication with Australia will be so frequent, regular, and rapid, and the telegraph system so enlarged and cheap, that no practical difficulty would impede the working of a representative federal government."[38] The shift in perceptions of time and space was a necessary though not sufficient condition for contending that it was now feasible to create a globe-spanning political institution underpinned by a powerful sense of cultural identity.

The debate was divided over the character of this identity, however. The vision of the globe-spanning British "people" assumed two main forms. One insisted that the key binding principle—the social ontological foundation—of the people was *race*. They were, above all, Anglo-Saxon members of the "English race." As was typical in nineteenth-century Britain, usage of the term race was highly imprecise, but the definition usually focused on a combination of cultural markers—historical memories, language, shared values, habitus—circumscribed by "whiteness."[39] This view was compatible with (but did not entail) an argument that the populations of the individual colonies were themselves being transformed into new nationalities. The other account ac-

---

[35] Forster, "Our Colonial Empire," *Times*, November 6, 1875, 9; Francis de Labilliére, "British Federalism," *Proceedings of the Royal Colonial Institute*, 24 (1893), 110.

[36] Forster, *Imperial Federation* (London, 1884), 27.

[37] de Labilliére, *Federal Britain, or, Unity and Federation of the Empire* (London, 1894), 12.

[38] Jenkins, "An Imperial Confederation," *Contemporary Review*, 17 (1871), 78.

[39] Peter Mandler, "'Race' and 'Nation' in Mid-Victorian Thought," in *History, Religion, and Culture*, ed. Stefan Collini, Richard Whatmore, and Brian Young (Cambridge, 2000), 224–45; Stuart Jones, "The Idea of the Nation in Victorian Political Thought," *European Journal of Political Theory*, 5 (2006), 12–21. Since this chapter was first published, I have further developed this argument about race as "biocultural assemblage." Bell, "Beyond the Sovereign State," *Political Studies*, 62/2 (2014), 418–34.

cepted the centrality of race, but emphasized the idea of a singular nationality: the (relevant) population of Greater Britain was the British nation writ
global. Both conceptions sanctioned extensive exclusion. The indigenous
populations of the settler colonies, and the vast majority of the people that
Britain ruled over in the Caribbean, Africa, and Asia, fell outside the scope of
either account of the people. (Class and gender exclusion was more pronounced in accounts of the public.) But none of these boundaries was fixed
permanently: political contestation over the scope of both the public and the
people constituted two of the main axes of British and imperial politics in the
nineteenth and twentieth centuries.

For some imperial thinkers, the colonies were in the process of forming
new nations, or had even done so already. This process of differentiation from
the originary British nation was regarded as a consequence of the radically different physical environments, social structures, economic systems, and nascent cultural traditions in which the colonists were enmeshed. Recognition
of the increasing power of colonial nationality could lead in several directions.
It could bolster the view that the colonies should be allowed to separate, even
that this was now inevitable, and that the future of Greater Britain lay (at
most) in a moral community of the Anglo-Saxon race. This was the view of
Goldwin Smith, a prominent radical historian who was regarded as a dangerous enemy by many imperialists.[40] And as I explore in chapter 13, it was also
the position advocated by the historian E. A. Freeman, who focused in particular on the "Teutonic" racial community binding Britain and its ex-colonies
in North America. The radical liberal politician Charles Dilke, who had popularized the term "Greater Britain," defended another variation on the theme.
He sketched an environmental conception of national character, where physical and social conditions, in dynamic combination, shaped the personality of
individuals and collectives alike: Canadians and Americans, despite their (as
he saw it) common racial origins, were very different in "type." But they were
anchored in the same foundations, in a "Saxondom" that incorporated both
the United States and Greater Britain: "That which raises us above the pro-
vincialism of citizenship of little England is our citizenship of the greater 'Saxondom' which includes all that is best and wisest in the world."[41] But the belief in the growing strength of colonial "nationalism" was more commonly
used to motivate urgent calls to confront this dangerous process. Crisis
loomed if no action was taken.

The most popular view among late Victorian imperial thinkers was that the
population of Greater Britain comprised a single nationality. Seeley argued
for the "general proposition" that "Greater Britain is homogenous in nation-

---

[40] Smith, *The Empire* (London, 1863); Smith, "The Empire," in *Essays on Questions of the Day*
[1893], 2nd ed. (New York, 1894), 141–95. On Smith, see Bell, *The Idea of Greater Britain*, ch. 7.
[41] Dilke, *Greater Britain* (London, 1868), 2:150, 156.

ality."[42] De Labilliére, hoping for "the permanent political unity of our race," asserted that the "spirit of national unity has been one of the most beneficent influences in the enlightened progress of modern times. It has made Italy; it has made Germany ... National magnetism, with the power of a loadstone [sic] is drawing together Great and Greater Britain in closer Indissoluble union."[43] The historian Hugh Egerton talked of the "common nationhood" binding together the peoples of Greater Britain, while a pamphlet produced for the IFL argued that federation was "a means of securing the continued Union of our nation throughout the world."[44] The nation, in this sense, acted as a form of social cement connecting the scattered elements of the empire, and allowing it to be represented both as a natural outgrowth of England and as a cohesive whole.

In the Edwardian era, a multinational commonwealth vision began to eclipse the Seeleyan global nation-state, in recognition of the burgeoning colonial demands for national autonomy. In other words, while the notion of a global polity never disappeared, it was increasingly decoupled from the idea of a singular global nation.[45] This theme had not been absent from earlier debates, although neither was it especially prominent. For example, Lord Rosebery argued in a speech delivered in Adelaide in January 1884 that Australia could no longer be seen as a colony, but was "a nation not in aspiration or in the future, but in performance and fact." The empire, he maintained, should be regarded as "a commonwealth of nations."[46] It was this account that became increasingly popular over time, not least because it mirrored the views of the political elites in the colonies. In 1905 the eminent journalist W. E. Monypenny suggested that the empire constituted a "world state" that "transcends nationality" while simultaneously allowing the flourishing of separate nationalities within it. By escaping the clutches of both a petty-minded "national exclusiveness" and a grim centralized "Caesarian despotism," it pointed the way to a new form of political order, a truly "cosmopolitan ideal."[47] The idea of an Anglo-Saxon commonwealth was, meanwhile, central to the Round Table movement, because, as Lionel Curtis wrote in 1916, "Canadians, Aus-

[42] Seeley, *The Expansion of England*, 49; Seeley, "Introduction" to *Her Majesty Colonies* (London, 1886), xxiv–xxv.

[43] de Labilliére, *Federal Britain*, 35–171; S. Wilson, "A Scheme for Imperial Federation," *Nineteenth Century*, 17 (1885), 590; Young, *An Address on Imperial Federation* (London, 1885), 23.

[44] Egerton, *A Short History of British Colonial Policy*, 477; "What Is Imperial Federation?" [1890], *Minute Book of the General Committee of the Executive Committee of the I.F.L.*, BL, Add MS, 62779, 256.

[45] See also the discussion in Gorman, *Imperial Citizenship*.

[46] Speech in Adelaide, January 18, 1884, George Bennett, *The Concept of Empire*, 2nd ed. (London, 1962), 283; Forster, "Imperial Federation," *Nineteenth Century*, 17 (1885), 201; Douglas Cole, "The Problem of 'Nationalism' and 'Imperialism' in British Settlement Colonies," *Journal of British Studies*, 10 (1971), 160–82.

[47] Monypenny, "The Imperial Ideal," in *The Empire and the Century*, ed. Goldman, 23, 27.

tralians, and South Africans each think of themselves as nations distinct from the people of the British Isles, just as the British think of themselves as a nation distinct from the citizens of the United States." They had acquired, that is, a "national consciousness of their own."[48] Both the nation-centric and the race-centric accounts, however, embodied an argument about the global singularity of "the people."

Translocalism: Expanding the Public

The extension of the scope of the people went hand in hand with an expansion of the compass of the public, of those individuals regarded collectively as politically significant. During the nineteenth-century the size and shape of the public shifted along two dimensions: *horizontal* and *vertical*. The vertical dimension refers to the degree of formal political inclusion of a given public. This has been the focus of a very large body of scholarship; it is, indeed, the story of the development of democracy in the United Kingdom (and also of the parallel but uneven development of democracy in the individual colonies). Horizontal extension, on the other hand, refers to the spatial extent of a given public—the degree to which it is linked to particular configurations of territory. This topic has received far less scholarly attention. Yet the arguments promulgating the unification of the British colonial empire embodied a claim—sometimes made explicit, often not—about the existence (or potentiality) of an ocean-transcending public. This was a significant moment in the history of modern global consciousness, an early step on the road to the idea of a global public sphere.

At the peak of the globalization boom in the 1990s the anthropologist Arjun Appadurai argued that the contemporary nation-state—conceived of as "a compact and isomorphic organisation of territory, ethnos, and governmental apparatus"—was undergoing a profound crisis; it was in "serious trouble."[49] In particular, political loyalties and territorial sovereignty were being wrenched apart as individuals increasingly came to identify with—and feel a sense of belonging to—communities and groups that transcended, indeed challenged, the nation-state. While states remained territorial entities, political identities were often unconstrained by formal boundaries, escaping the relentless topological imperatives of modern politics. "Translocal" affiliations—affiliations, that is, to imagined communities that burst the territorially circumscribed foundations of political identity—assumed a pivotal role. "The most important feature of these emergent cartographies is that they do

---

[48] Curtis, *The Problem of Commonwealth* (London, 1916), 68; John Kendle, *The Round Table Movement and Imperial Union* (Toronto, 1975).

[49] Appadurai, "Sovereignty without Territoriality," in *The Geography of Identity*, ed. P. Yaeger (Ann Arbor, 1996), 40–59; Appadurai, *Modernity at Large* (Minneapolis, MN, 1996); Peter Mandeville, "Territory and Translocality," *Millennium*, 28 (1999), 653–67.

not appear to require horizontally arranged, contiguous, and mutually exclusive claims to territory."[50] While Appadurai maintained that translocalism could take many forms, he drew a sharp distinction between two main categories. In the first, the imagined spaces are separate from, and come into conflict with, existing state configurations. An example would be the Sikh idea of Khalistan or the Islamic ummah.[51] In the second, the idea is to rework existing configurations by extending the reach and power of one community over others. Appadurai's example is the German neo-fascist view that the Aryan peoples should be united into a single political community, thus expanding the scope of the German state.

Appadurai leaves open the question about whether such dynamics existed in the past. Here we can offer a response which gives some historical flesh to his theoretical account, while employing that account to help shed light on the dynamics of late Victorian intellectual life. First, translocal dynamics have formed a central part of the history of modernity, not least through the globalizing agencies of empire.[52] Yet, second, we also witness a significant shift within the politics of modernity, a shift that signals an important moment in the history of global consciousness. This shift was catalyzed by the transformation in the perception of time and space discussed above. As the world appeared to shrink (and as time appeared to contract) so it became possible to argue—however unrealistically—that a strong sense of affiliation and belonging could be felt with individuals scattered throughout the world. Adam Smith once referred to British colonists living in North America as "strangers."[53] In the last three decades of the nineteenth century this common (and commonsensical) understanding was overturned: distance no longer entailed alienation. Communal identification need not be rooted in or constrained by geography. This was not a novelty of the post-1989 world; it is not unique to contemporary forms of globalization. It was instead a product of the nineteenth-century communications revolution, and it spawned a major rethinking of the nature of political association, territory, and space. It was as a result of these developments that proponents of colonial unity in late Victorian and Edwardian Britain can be seen as imagining a form of globe-spanning translocal politics. However, whereas many of the examples explored by Appadurai are "counterhegemonic"—seeking to challenge the established power structures and sources of authority[54]—the attempted reworking of British

---

[50] Appadurai, "Sovereignty without Territoriality," 51.

[51] Ibid., 55.

[52] A. G. Hopkins, ed., *Globalization in World History* (London, 2002) and Tarak Barkawi, *Globalization and War* (Lanham, MD, 2006); John Gerard Ruggie, "Territoriality and Beyond," *International Organization*, 47 (1993), 139–74; Friedrich Kratochwil, "Of Systems, Boundaries and Territoriality," *World Politics*, 39 (1986), 27–52.

[53] Smith, *An Inquiry into the Nature and Causes of the Wealth of Nations*, ed. W. B. Todd (Oxford, 1976), 622.

[54] Appadurai cites (51n) Paul Gilroy, *The Black Atlantic* (Cambridge, MA, 1993).

racial-national consciousness in the Victorian age was a hegemonic project, an effort to establish and prolong the dominance of an empire through novel articulations of political identity.

Yet that project does not fit neatly into either of the two categories identified by Appadurai. The imperial unionists were neither seeking to create a space outside of or in opposition to the existing state, and nor were they chiefly focused on extending the scope of British nationality by conquering other established states. Instead, they sought to extend the scope of the British polity to encompass, on equal terms, colonial spaces that had previously been regarded as subordinate communities. It was for this reason that many of the supporters of colonial union did not regard the colonies as part of the empire—a term that connoted hierarchy and difference—but instead as integral elements of a transcontinental British state.[55] This imaginative projection involved a double process of deterritorialization and reterritorialization.[56] The British polity was no longer to be conceived of as a small group of islands lying off the northwest coast of continental Europe (deterritorialization). Instead it was to be seen as encompassing a vast range of territories in North America, the Pacific, and Southern Africa (reterritorialization). This new space was a nascent form of global state.

In envisioning a translocal cartography, the idea of the public itself was refashioned. This was a direct challenge to conventional understandings of the scope of the public sphere, which had seen it as falling within, and indeed constrained by, the territorial boundaries of the British Isles. The conventional view was compatible with the claim that the colonies had their own emergent publics, but these were nevertheless regarded as separate from, and inferior and subordinate to, that of Britain. This was the standard position adopted until the last three decades of the nineteenth century. John Stuart Mill, a defender of the value of the colonial empire, articulated it clearly in the *Considerations on Representative Government* (1861), arguing that one of the key reasons why a federation of the colonies would fail to satisfy the "rational principles of government" was that the colonists were "not part of the same public" as the British people.[57] A basic harmony of both interests and sympathies was absent. The alternative vision—the vision that found expression in the debates over Greater Britain—was of a single, translocal public sphere, encompassing the publics of the United Kingdom and the settler communities. This allowed the most ambitious imperial unionists to outline plans for the creation of representative institutions, a federal constitution, even a new imperial senate, that would bind the various publics together in a new politi-

---

[55] Bell, "The Victorian Idea of a Global State," in *Victorian Visions of Global Order*, ed. Bell, 159–86.

[56] See Appadurai, "Sovereignty without Territoriality," 54.

[57] Mill, *Considerations on Representative Government, Collected Works*, 19, 564. See also the discussion in chapter 9.

cal order. This polity was to be the home of an innovative form of imperial citizenship.[58] The public sphere, circumscribed by race, had been stretched over the face of the earth.

Conclusions

During the late Victorian and Edwardian years numerous imperial commentators sought to reimagine the British state, nation, and empire. In seeking to challenge the purported indifference of their compatriots, in attempting to respond to the perceived threats posed by both domestic and geopolitical developments, and in light of the cognitive transformations wrought by new communications technologies, many of them argued for novel understandings of territory, borders, and political identity. This prominent group sought to globalize domestic politics by arguing that a vast polity, grounded in a single people and containing a single (albeit differentiated) public sphere, could already be discerned, but that it was in danger of being lost if urgent political action was not taken to secure and strengthen it. Such a failure, they warned, would hasten the decline and fall of the British empire. Their arguments implied a refashioning of the boundaries between local and global, domestic and foreign, nation and empire.

The views that they professed—hubristic, conceited, and deeply naïve—echoed powerfully down the years, and can be seen again today in the growing interest in the so-called "Anglosphere," the globe-spanning body of the heirs of the British colonial diaspora. The main difference now, of course, is that the internal balance of power has shifted firmly across the Atlantic, with Washington assuming the mantle of imperial metropolis.[59] The echo can be heard too, albeit more indirectly, in the arguments propagating a league or concert of democracies. As Tony Smith observes, these visions often embody "a claim to cultural superiority and an encouragement to belligerent behaviour" that represent "an update of race theory."[60] They are the latest incarnation of a long-standing set of arguments about the duties of purportedly advanced states to spread, by force if necessary, the enlightened benefits of civilization to the benighted, "barbaric" corners of the earth. We would do well to ignore their dangerous clarion call.

[58] Gorman, *Imperial Citizenship*; J. Lee Thompson, *A Wider Patriotism* (London, 2007).

[59] James C. Bennett, *The Anglosphere Challenge* (New York, 2004); Bennett, *The Third Anglosphere Century* (Washington, 2007); Robert Conquest and Andrew Roberts, among others, have been pushing a similar idea in recent years. Conquest, *Reflections on a Ravaged Century* (London, 2000), 267–81; Roberts, *A History of the English-Speaking Peoples since 1900* (London, 2006). For analysis of the idea, see Srdjan Vucetic, *The Anglosphere* (Stanford, 2011).

[60] Tony Smith, *A Pact with the Devil* (London, 2007), 108.

CHAPTER 8

The Project for a New Anglo Century

❧

Race, Space, and Global Order

I believe that the twentieth century is par excellence
"The Anglo-Saxon Century," in which the English-speaking
peoples may lead and predominate the world.[1]

—JOHN RANDOLPH DOS PASSOS

Prophets have long dreamed of schemes to govern a violent and unpredict-able world. This chapter sketches a synoptic intellectual history of a prom-inent variation on the theme: the attempt to unify the constituent elements of the "Anglo-world" into a single globe-spanning community, and to harness its purported world-historical potential as an agent of order and justice.[2] Since the late nineteenth century numerous commentators have preached the ben-efits of unity, though they have often disagreed on the institutional form it should assume. These are projects for the creation of a new Anglo century.

The opening two sections of the chapter explore overlapping elements of the *fin de siècle* Anglo-world discourse. Synthesizing some of the arguments made in previous chapters in this volume, I first analyze the relationship be-tween Britain and its colonial empire, before turning to a range of intersecting arguments over the future relationship between the empire and the United States. The third section traces the echoes of these debates through the twen-tieth century, discussing the interlacing articulation of imperial-commonwealth, Anglo-American, democratic unionist, and world federalist projects. Despite important differences between them, most versions of these grand supranational schemes were heirs of the earlier debates. In the final sec-tion I discuss contemporary accounts of Anglo-world supremacy. While none

---

[1] Dos Passos, *The Anglo-Saxon Century and the Unification of the English-Speaking People*, 2nd ed. (New York, 1903), vii. Dos Passos, a prominent Republican lawyer and author, was the father of the famous novelist.

[2] For the term "Anglo-world," see James Belich, *Replenishing the Earth* (New York, 2009).

of the most radical plans came to fruition, the evolving debate over the nature of the Anglo-world formed a central element in the cultural construction of the "West," and illustrates the extravagant hopes that have been invested in the "Anglo-Saxons" over the course of a brutal century. This constitutes, then, an important strand in the history of modern political thought.

Empire, Nation, State: On Greater Britain

To govern, Foucault argues, is "to structure the possible field of action of others."[3] The second half of the nineteenth century saw a profound transformation in both the scale of the field of action and the ways in which it could be structured. It witnessed the emergence of a novel governance *episteme*—an imaginative regime wherein established conventions and presuppositions about political order were overturned.

Daniel Deudney aptly labels this the "global industrial period." The spread of the industrial revolution was a "primal development" for global politics, as new technologies intensified interactions across the planet, reshaping the material and imaginative contexts in which debates over the future took place. "As the scale and tempo of human affairs changed, a major and tumultuous reordering of large-scale political relationships and institutions seemed imminent and inevitable."[4] The thinkers of the time—the "industrial globalists"— proselytized a wide array of schemes for transcending the anarchic international system, including pan-regional imperial structures, European union, the federation of the British empire, and even the future development of a world state. The debates about the Anglo-world were an integral element of this more general discourse.

This period also saw the rearticulation of the global politics of race. In 1900, at the meeting of the Pan-African Congress in London, W.E.B. DuBois predicted that the "problem of the twentieth century" would be "the problem of the color line."[5] Fears about racial contamination were rife. A civilizational dividing line was constructed between "white" peoples and others, resulting in the initiation of numerous exclusionary practices, including racist immigration controls. This was a paradoxical process: "The imagined community of white men was transnational in its reach, but nationalist in its outcomes, bolstering regimes of border protection and national sovereignty."[6] Those debating the future of the Anglo-world insisted on carving out a space within the general identity of whiteness, establishing a stratified geo-racial imaginary.

[3] Foucault, "The Subject and Power," in *Michel Foucault*, ed. Hubert Dreyfus and Paul Rabinow, 2nd ed. (Chicago, 1983), 221.

[4] Deudney, *Bounding Power* (Princeton, 2007), 215, 219.

[5] See, in particular, the argument in DuBois, *The Soul of Black Folk* (New York, 1903).

[6] Marilyn Lake and Henry Reynolds, *Drawing the Global Colour Line* (Cambridge, 2008), 4.

Usage of the term "race" was highly imprecise, but it typically designated a combination of cultural markers—historical mythscapes, habitus, shared language, cultural values, and political ideals—circumscribed by "whiteness." It was simultaneously cultural and biological. The French, the Germans, the Russians, and the Hispanics were all considered inferior to the Anglo-Saxons. They in turn ranked higher on the scale of civilization than other nonwhite racial constellations populating the world outside the Euro-Atlantic zone and its diasporic outposts. In this conception of world politics, the basic ontological unit was race, and political institutions, including the state, were only of derivative importance.

The sweeping debate over the future of the British colonial empire was conducted under the sign of "imperial federation," while the assemblage of communities under discussion was frequently labeled "Greater Britain."[7] The debate formed a key building block in the ideological construction of the twentieth-century Anglo-world. As I argue in *The Idea of Greater Britain*, and elsewhere in this volume, it was driven by two intersecting imperatives. Fear that British relative power was threatened by the rise of formidable states—notably Germany, Russia, and the United States—led many commentators to argue for the construction of a globe-spanning political association, encompassing Britain and its settler colonies in Australia, Canada, New Zealand, and (more ambivalently) South Africa, either to balance the new threats or to deter them from attempting to compete. These geopolitical concerns were reinforced by anxieties about the onset of democracy, with many imperial observers worrying that an expanding electorate would fail to recognize the importance of the empire, concentrating its energies and ambitions on domestic reform. It was feared—prematurely as it turned out—that a democratic polity would invariably be anti-imperial. Creating a federal Greater Britain, and populating it in part through an accelerated program of "systematic" emigration from the "mother country," was thought to be one way of neutralizing these threats. Yet even some radical advocates of democracy, including J. A. Hobson, H. M. Hyndman, and Keir Hardie, saw benefits in imperial federation. For them, Greater Britain could simultaneously hasten the peaceful development of the international system and help to democratize Britain itself through the importation of progressive practices from the more egalitarian colonies.[8]

According to Hobson, great federal political communities would dominate the future, and it was thus essential to erect a "Pan-Saxon" one. As he proclaimed in *Imperialism*, "Christendom thus laid out in a few great civiliza-

---

[7] I expand on the argument in this section in Bell, *The Idea of Greater Britain*.

[8] On Hobson and Hobhouse, see chapter 14. The idea of importing reform from the colonial periphery was prevalent in wider social reform debates: Daniel Rodgers, *Atlantic Crossings* (Cambridge, MA, 2000).

tional empires, each with a retinue of uncivilized dependencies, seems to me the most legitimate development of present tendencies and one which would offer the best hope of permanent peace on an assured basis of inter-Imperialism."[9] Hobhouse, meanwhile, argued that imperial federation "is a model, and that on no mean scale, of the International State."[10] These arguments illustrate the two broad temporal logics that underpinned debates over Anglo-union deep into the twentieth century. In one of them, union represented the terminal point of future political development: the polity would take its place among other competing pan-racial or regional units. In the other, Anglo-union was figured as a transitional institutional formation, one that could serve as a template, catalyst, and leader of a future global political association.

Time was of the essence. Haunted by memories of the American Revolution, many feared that the rapidly expanding colonies would secede, either establishing independent countries or fusing with another state—most likely the United States—thus further weakening Britain. The imperial advocates were determined to refute Alexis de Tocqueville's prediction, made in the closing lines of *Democracy in America*, that Russia and America would dominate the future.[11] Greater Britain was their answer.

A significant number of British unionists fantasized about the incorporation of the United States within an imperial federation, though most of them recognized that this was unrealistic (at least in the short term). Nevertheless, America played a crucial role in imperial discourse. First, it was regarded as a potential challenger to British supremacy, thus motivating the call for action. This was especially apparent in the wake of the McKinley Tariff of 1890, which incited the demand throughout Britain and its colonies for the creation of a system of imperial preference.[12] Second, the turbulent history of American-British relations, and in particular the War of Independence, preoccupied British imperial unionists, teaching them that the demands of colonial subjects had to be treated seriously. This meant granting them greater political autonomy. And finally, the United States demonstrated the power of federalism as a political technology by proving that individual liberty was compatible with vast geographical extent. This was welcome in an age in which it was commonly believed that the future belonged to huge omnicom-

---

[9] Hobson, *Imperialism* [1902], ed. Philip Siegelman (Ann Arbor, 1997), 332.

[10] Hobhouse, *Liberalism*, ed. J. Meadowcroft (Cambridge, 1994), 116. Note that Hobson later abandoned his support for imperial federation. P. J. Cain, *Hobson on Imperialism* (New York, 2002).

[11] Tocqueville, *Democracy in America* [1835–40], trans. Henry Reeve, 2 vols. (London, 1862), 2:456–57.

[12] Marc-William Palen, "Protection, Federation and Union," *Journal of Imperial and Commonwealth History*, 38 (2010), 395–418; P. J. Cain and A. G. Hopkins, *British Imperialism, 1688–2000* (London, 2002), ch. 7.

petent political units. The radical politician Charles Dilke, author of the influential *Greater Britain*, cautioned that "[i]t is small powers, not great ones,
that have become impossible."[13] Three decades later Joseph Chamberlain,
arch-federalist and Secretary of State for the Colonies, concurred: "The days
are for great Empires and not for little States."[14] Size mattered.

The debates over Greater Britain generated hundreds of proposals, differing in ambition, detail, and rationale. Three general institutional models were
discussed.[15] The least ambitious was "extra-parliamentary" federation, wherein
a group of distinguished individuals—organized as an imperial Advisory
Council—would offer the British Parliament nonbinding advice on imperial
affairs. A more constitutionally far-reaching model was "parliamentary federalism," in which the colonies were to send elected representatives to sit in
Westminster. This had been a common exhortation since the late eighteenth
century, though it was much less popular in the closing decades of the Victorian age. Finally, "supra-parliamentary federalism" connoted the formation of
a sovereign federal chamber supervening on the individual political assemblies of the empire. This model followed the example, above all, of the United
States.[16]

The leading constitutional scholar A. V. Dicey observed that many imperial federalist proposals implied the creation of a "new federated state."[17] According to prevailing conceptions of statehood, all supra-parliamentary
schemes—and indeed most parliamentary ones—could be viewed as demanding the construction of a globe-spanning Anglo-state, a polity composed of people belonging to the same nation and/or race, governed by a system of representative institutions subordinate to a supreme federal legislative
chamber. The local legislatures would have a high degree of autonomy over
specified domains of policy, though supreme authority would reside in either
a newly created imperial chamber (sometimes labeled a "senate") or a reconfigured Parliament in Westminster. This body would determine questions of
war and peace, trade, and any other general issues that concerned the whole
polity. The case of the extra-parliamentary advocates is less straightforward,
for they were simply trying to reanimate the existing structure and were far
less willing to promote significant constitutional engineering. Many of them
did, however, predict radical developments in the future.

---

[13] Dilke, *Greater Britain* (London, 1868) 1:274, 48.
[14] Chamberlain, *The Life of Joseph Chamberlain* [1902], ed. J. L. Garvin and J. Amery (London,
1968), 177.
[15] This schema is derived from Ged Martin, "Empire, Federalism and Imperial Parliamentary
Union, 1820–70," *Historical Journal*, 16 (1973), 65–92.
[16] For an example of the former model, see Marquis of Lorne, *Imperial Federation* (London,
1885); for an example of the latter, see Francis de Labilliére, *Federal Britain* (London, 1894).
[17] Dicey, *Introduction to the Study of the Law of the Constitution*, 8th ed. (London, 1915),
lxxxiv. On contemporary ideas about statehood, see Duncan Bell, "The Victorian Idea of the
Global State," in *Victorian Visions of Global Order*, ed. Bell (Cambridge, 2007), 159–86.

Yet not all advocates of Greater Britain proposed the development of a vast federal polity. For many of them the key to the future lay in the shared identity of the British people spread across the world, and they argued that further institutionalization was unnecessary—it either fell outside the scope of "practical politics" or it was counterproductive. Instead, they maintained that it was essential to nourish the existing connections. This was the course that the British government ultimately followed. Dilke and Goldwin Smith, both leading public intellectuals and critics of imperial federal schemes, extolled the superiority of the British "race" and promoted a vision in which the Anglo-Saxons, acting as a collective of independent states, would shape the future. They supported the independence of the British settler colonies, but as a means to the end of Anglo-unity, not its termination. For Dilke, the "strongest of arguments in favour of separation is the somewhat paradoxical one that it would bring us a step nearer to the virtual confederation of the English race."[18] Both of them also included the United States in their vision. The cultural-racial conception of "virtual confederation" proved the most enduring; it remains an important factor in world politics to this day.

Arguments about both Greater Britain and Anglo-American union were premised on a cognitive revolution, a fundamental transformation in the perception of time and space. It was this, above all, that shaped the new governance *episteme*. In his *Considerations on Representative Government*, John Stuart Mill argued, in an idiom common throughout the eighteenth and much of the nineteenth centuries, that physical distance thwarted the union of Britain and its settler colonies. It contradicted the principles of "rational government" and precluded the necessary degree of communal homogeneity.[19] From the 1860s onwards, new communications technologies radically altered the way in which individuals perceived the physical world and the sociopolitical possibilities it contained, spawning fantasies about the elimination of geographical distance that prefigure late twentieth-century narratives of globalization. H. G. Wells declared that "modern mechanism" had created "an absolute release from the fixed conditions about which human affairs circled." For J. R. Seeley, the leading intellectual of the imperial federalist movement, the "unprecedented facility of communication which our age enjoys seems to be creating new types of state."[20] A Greater British state was now realizable. Techno-utopianism underpinned arguments about the existence of a trans-planetary British political community. "When we have accustomed ourselves to contemplate the whole [colonial] Empire together and call it England," Seeley proclaimed, "we shall see that here too is a United States. Here too is a homo-

[18] Dilke, *Greater Britain*, 2:157.

[19] Mill, *Considerations on Representative Government* (1861), in *Collected Works*, vol. 19, ch. 18. See also the discussion in chapter 9 of this volume.

[20] Wells, *Anticipations* [1902] (Mineola, NY, 1999), 38, 44; Seeley, *The Expansion of England*, 62.

geneous people, one in blood, language, religion, and laws, but dispersed over a boundless space."[21] Previously viewed as immutable, nature was now open to manipulation, even transcendence.

All of these projects depended on claims about the common identity of the dispersed Anglo people(s).[22] As I discussed in the last chapter, the argument assumed two main forms. One insisted that the social ontological foundation of the people was *race*. They were, above all, Anglo-Saxon or members of the "English race." This view was compatible with (but did not entail) an argument that the populations of the individual colonies were coalescing into new nationalities, and that the United States already comprised a distinct nation. The other account accepted the centrality of race, but emphasized the idea of a singular *nationality*: the (relevant) population of Greater Britain was the British (or "English") nation writ global. Both conceptions sanctioned extensive discrimination. The indigenous populations of the settler colonies, and the vast majority of the people that Britain ruled over in the Caribbean, Africa, the Middle East, and Asia—and that the USA came to rule over in Hawaii and the Philippines—fell outside the scope of either account of the singular people.

The "nationality" view prevailed among late Victorian imperial thinkers. Seeley was only the most prominent to claim that "Greater Britain is homogenous in nationality."[23] During the Edwardian years, a multinational commonwealth vision began to eclipse the Seeleyean global nation-state. This alternative option was not without precedent, for Lord Rosebery, the future British prime minister, had argued in 1884 that the empire should be regarded as "a commonwealth of nations."[24] This position became increasingly popular over time, not least because it mirrored the views of the political elites in the colonies. Greater Britain morphed into a post-national (or multinational) political association. Both the nation-centric and the race-centric accounts, however, centered on an argument about the singularity of "the people."

The imaginative extension of the scope of the people was conjoined with an expansion of the compass of the public—of the set of individuals within the totality of the people regarded as politically significant. Arguments promulgating the unification of the British colonial empire (and also Anglo-America) embodied a claim about the existence or potentiality of an ocean-spanning public. As I discuss in chapter 7, this was a racially delimited precursor to the idea of a global public sphere. Indeed one of the most conceptually innovative features of the discourse, prominent especially in the early twentieth century, was the effort to inaugurate a system of Greater Brit-

---

[21] Seeley, *The Expansion of England*, 158–59.
[22] For further details, see chapter 7.
[23] Seeley, *The Expansion of England*, 49.
[24] Bruce Bennett, *New Zealand's Moral Foreign Policy 1935–39* (Wellington, 1962), 283.

ish imperial citizenship.[25] It is possible to view the Anglo-racial imaginary as an example of what Arjun Appadurai terms "translocal" affiliation—of an emergent cartography that escaped the topological imperatives of the modern territorially bounded nation-state.[26] As time and space were reordered, so it was increasingly argued that a strong sense of identity and belonging bound Britain and its colonial populations. However, whereas many of the examples explored by Appadurai are "counterhegemonic"—seeking to challenge extant power structures and sources of authority—the attempted reworking of "Anglo-Saxon" racial-national consciousness in the Victorian age was a hegemonic project involving a double process of deterritorialization and reterritorialization.[27] The British polity was no longer to be conceived of as a small group of islands lying off the northwest coast of continental Europe (deterritorialization), but rather as incorporating a vast range of territories in North America, the Pacific, and Southern Africa (reterritorialization). A similar geo-racial logic also helped underpin arguments about Anglo-American unity.

The Reunion of the Race: On Anglo-America

The unity of the Anglo-world was not preordained. For much of the nineteenth century, relations between the British empire and the United States were antagonistic. Resentment about the colonial past, incessant disputes over the Canadian border, the bitter divide over the Civil War and its aftermath, pervasive cultural condescension from the British, and widespread Anglophobia in American public life: all fanned the flames of antipathy. Mutual suspicion was the norm. It was only during the last two decades of the century, and in particular during the late 1890s, that the animosity thawed. This "rapprochement"—and the subsequent creation of an Anglo-American security community—has long been the subject of intense scrutiny by diplomatic historians and IR specialists. Yet insufficient attention has been paid to the political thought of the episode.

It was during the 1890s that the debate over Anglo-American union moved to the center of political debate. The Venezuelan boundary dispute (1895–96) led to acrimonious exchanges between Washington and London, but it also prompted anguished commentators on both sides of the Atlantic to recoil from the prospect of war. Numerous proposals for Anglo-American union appeared. The clamor for racial unity was partly a result of the new assertiveness of the United States, for although it had been engaged in imperial

[25] Daniel Gorman, *Imperial Citizenship* (Manchester, 2006).

[26] Appadurai, "Sovereignty without Territoriality," in *The Geography of Identity*, ed. Patricia Yaeger (Ann Arbor, 1996).

[27] Ibid., 54.

conquest since its founding, the annexation of Hawaii and the Spanish-American War (1898) signaled its first sustained burst of extra-continental imperialism. This was seen as marking a new phase in American history: either a moment when the country assumed its predestined role as a great power, or when it betrayed the founding principles of the republic. Many observers on both sides of the Atlantic insisted that the British and Americans should be united, not divided, under conditions of global imperial competition. Arguments ranged from a minimalist position that simply encouraged deeper political and economic cooperation between the two "kindred" powers, through intermediate proposals seeking a formal defensive alliance, to maximalist plans for uniting the two countries in a novel transatlantic political community.

Plans for a formal alliance blended "realist" concerns over shared security interests with assertions about underlying cultural affinities. The British imperial commentator Arthur Silva White declared that schemes for a comprehensive political union were "at present impossible," but that there "remains but one expedient—an alliance, or accord, which would pave the way to concerted action in the future."[28] Yet many commentators were skeptical about such an alliance, either because they opposed closer connections in the first place, or because they thought it would instrumentalize (and potentially distort) a more fundamental form of unity.[29] The esteemed American naval strategist Alfred T. Mahan argued that it was vital to "avoid all premature striving for alliance, an artificial and possibly even an irritating method of reaching the desired end." Instead, he continued, "I would dwell continually upon those undeniable points of resemblance in natural characteristics, and in surrounding conditions, which testify to common origin and predict a common destiny."[30] A British military writer concurred, warning against the "artificial and temporary arrangements miscalled 'alliances,' which provide occupation for European chancelleries."[31] The "organic" bonds of "kinship" were sufficient. Fearful that talk about the Anglo-Saxons was dangerously triumphalist, Benjamin Harrison, the former US president, insisted that friendship was quite enough. "Are not the continuous good and close relations of the two

[28] White, "An Anglo-American Alliance," North American Review, 158 (1894), 492–93; see also Walter Besant, "The Future of the Anglo-Saxon Race," North American Review, 163 (1896), 129–43.

[29] On the former, see in particular Henry Cabot Lodge, "England, Venezuela, and the Monroe Doctrine," North American Review, 160 (1895), 651–58. Indeed Lodge, a Massachusetts senator, regarded the British empire as a dangerous geopolitical competitor.

[30] Mahan, and Charles Beresford, "Possibilities of an Anglo-American Reunion," North American Review, 159 (1894), 554.

[31] G. S. Clarke, "Imperial Responsibilities a National Gain," North American Review, 168 (1899), 141.

great English-speaking nations—for which I pray—rather imperilled than promoted by this foolish talk of gratitude and of an alliance, which is often made to take on the appearance of a threat, or at least a prophecy, of an Anglo-Saxon 'paramountcy?'"[32] This was a prescient warning.

At the core of the Anglo-American vision lay a novel set of arguments that ruptured the isomorphic relation between state, citizen, and political belonging. Advocates of racial unity frequently decoupled the state from both citizenship and patriotism. Citizenship was reimagined as a political institution grounded ultimately in racial identity, not state membership. Dicey offered the most sophisticated elaboration of the idea of common citizenship, or *isopolity*, arguing in 1897 for "the extension of common civil and political rights throughout the whole of the English-speaking people." Rejecting the idea of a transatlantic (or imperial) federation, he insisted that "reciprocal" citizenship would be enough to secure permanent unity. The idea was, he averred, simply a return to a prior condition, for such a connection had existed before the Anglo-Saxon peoples were ripped apart by the War of Independence.[33] Patriotism, meanwhile, was also reconfigured as a form of allegiance owed, in the first instance, to the race. Arguments about "race patriotism"—a term usually associated with Arthur Balfour, a future prime minister—circulated widely.[34] They implied that people were enmeshed in a concentric circle of belonging and affect, the outer (and most important) ring of which was the race. Alfred Milner, a leading imperial thinker and official, summed it up neatly: "My patriotism knows no geographical, but only racial limits . . . It is not the soil of England, dear as it is to me, but the speech, the tradition, the spiritual heritage, the principles, the aspirations of the British race."[35] Quoting Balfour, Charles Beresford, a British Tory politician and senior naval officer, observed that

> [I]n addition to our domestic patriotism and our Imperial or American patriotism, we also have an Anglo-Saxon patriotism, which embraces within its ample folds the whole of that great race which has done so much in every branch of human effort, and in that branch of human effort which has produced free institutions and free communities.[36]

[32] Harrison, "Musings upon Current Topics II," *North American Review*, 172 (1901), 354. On the history of the concept of the "English-speaking peoples," usage of which originated in the 1870s and peaked during the early decades of the twentieth century, see Peter Clarke, "The English-Speaking Peoples before Churchill," *British Scholar*, 4 (2011), 199–231.

[33] Dicey, "A Common Citizenship for the English Race," *Contemporary Review*, 71 (1897), 458.

[34] On Balfour's "race patriotism," see Jason Tomes, *Balfour and Foreign Policy* (Cambridge, 1997), chs. 2–4. On Milner, see J. Lee Thompson, *A Wider Patriotism* (London, 2007).

[35] Milner, "Credo," *Times*, July 25, 1925.

[36] Beresford, "The Future of the Anglo-Saxon Race," *North American Review*, 171 (1900), 809.

Traditional notions of state citizenship and patriotism were thus seen as acceptable only insofar as they were compatible with attachment to the wider racial encompassing group.

Andrew Carnegie, the Scottish-born industrialist, argued repeatedly for racial fusion and the "reunion" of Britain and America. Though usually lauded or reviled as an anti-imperialist, Carnegie, like Hobson, highlights how opposition to certain kinds of imperial activity—in his case, British occupation of India and Africa and the American assault on the Philippines—was consistent with ardent support for projects of racial unity or superiority. Carnegie dismissed the idea of an Anglo-American alliance as failing to grasp the far more important issues at stake. "Alliances of fighting power form and dissolve with the questions which arise from time to time. The patriotism of race lies deeper and is not disturbed by waves upon the surface." "[M]y belief," he declared, is that "the future is certain to see a reunion of the separated parts and once again a common citizenship." This federated "British-American Union" would constitute a "reunited state." Yet this vision was irreconcilable with imperial federation: the British had first to grant independence to their settler colonies, which would then be welcome to join the union as equal members.[37] Although perturbed by the South African War, and by the exuberant imperialism of the American administration, he kept faith in the transformative potential of the Anglo-Saxon race.

Skeptics were quick to point to the empirical inadequacies of unionist plans. One of their main complaints focused on the pertinence of arguments about racial unity. America, they complained, was simply not a lineal "Anglo-Saxon" descendent of Britain. "There is," one critic observed, "no fundamental reason rooted in human nature by virtue of a community of blood and religion why Americans as a nation should regard England with instinctive sympathy and friendship."[38] Another stressed the multi-ethnic composition of the American population. "What about the descendants of French men, of Germans, of Slavs, and of Scandinavians, who do not admit Anglo Saxon superiority?" And what about the Irish or African-Americans?[39] But such demographic arguments failed to register with the proponents of unity, not least because their conception of race was fluid. As one unionist observed,

> It is quite true that, if the census of descent were taken as the test, the sons or descendants of Englishmen by no means make up the majority of American citizens. But there is descent other than that of birth and a

[37] Carnegie, "Americanism versus Imperialism," *North American Review*, 162 (1899), 5–6; Carnegie, *The Reunion of Britain and America* (Edinburgh, 1893), 9; Carnegie, "The Venezuelan Question," *North American Review*, 162 (1896), 132.

[38] Mayo Hazeltine, "The United States and Great Britain," *North American Review*, 162 (1896), 597.

[39] John Fleming, "Are We Anglo-Saxons?," *North American Review*, 153 (1891), 254.

lineage beside that of blood. The unity of language, literature, and law between England and America is a threefold cord that cannot be broken. To have our English Bible, our English Shakespeare, our English Blackstone all absolutely American in reverence and influence outweighs, outvotes and overwhelms all questions of racial compositeness.[40]

In general, then, what identified the United States as an Anglo-Saxon country was its dominant political culture—its White Anglo-Saxon Protestant institutions, values, and ideals. Pointing to his own Portuguese origins, Dos Passos celebrated the American polity as a machine for turning (white) immigrants into Americans, and thus into adherents to an Anglo-Saxon creed. The "foreign element," he argued, "disappears, almost like magic, in the bosom of American nationality."[41] Carnegie, meanwhile, suggested that immigration had barely altered the racial composition of America: "[I]n race—and there is a great deal in race—the American remains three-fourths purely British . . . The amount of blood other than Anglo-Saxon or Germanic which has entered into the American is almost too trifling to deserve notice, and has been absorbed without changing him in any fundamental trait."[42] Moreover, skepticism about racial commonality did not preclude support for political union. The eminent Anglo-American archaeologist Charles Waldstein argued that the notion of "Anglo-Saxon" racial identity was both misleading and dangerous: "[I]t opens the door to that most baneful and pernicious of modern national diseases, namely, Ethnological Chauvinism." Yet he was adamant that Britain and the United States shared enough features in common to constitute "one nationality," and he toasted the future creation of "a great English-speaking Brotherhood."[43]

Cecil Rhodes was another formidable proponent of Anglo-American unity. At the heart of his vision lay an account of the fractured nature of history: its progressive course had been diverted by the catastrophic estrangement of the United States and Great Britain. This could only be put right if the two great institutional expressions of the race were reunited permanently. As a self-proclaimed "race patriot," Rhodes was largely agnostic about whether Britain or the United States should lead the Anglo-Saxons in fulfilling their destiny, suggesting that a "federal parliament" could rotate between Washington and London.[44] One of Rhodes's most practical contributions to realizing the dream of global racial dominance was the establishment of the Rhodes Trust, endowed following his death in 1902 with the intention of strengthen-

[40] William Crosswell Doane, "Patriotism," *North American Review*, 166 (1898), 318.

[41] Dos Passos, *The Anglo-Saxon Century*, 101, 104.

[42] Carnegie, *Reunion*, 9.

[43] Waldstein, "The English-Speaking Brotherhood," *North American Review*, 167 (1898), 225, 230, 238.

[44] Rhodes, *The Last Will and Testament of Cecil J. Rhodes*, ed. W. T. Stead (London, 1902), 73.

ing bonds between the elites of the Anglo-world, as well (initially) as Germany, that other Teutonic power. The radical journalist W. T. Stead agreed with his friend Rhodes that the "English-speaking race is one of the chief of God's chosen agents for executing coming improvement in the lot of mankind," and he utilized his position as a prominent author and editor to preach the gospel of Anglo-unity, seeking to "constitute as one vast federated unity the English-speaking United States of the World."[45] Like many of his contemporaries, Stead sensed a gradual intra-racial shift in the balance of power. In *The Americanization of the World*, he argued that the Americans had overtaken the British in most aspects of social and economic life, observed that Britain itself was slowly Americanizing, and determined that those ruling in London now faced a stark choice: ally with the United States in a grand project of earthly redemption, or become increasingly irrelevant as the empire slowly weakened and the settler colonies sought independence and looked to Washington for leadership. This was a cause for celebration: "[T]here is no reason to resent the part the Americans are playing in fashioning the world in their image, which, after all, is substantially the image of ourselves."[46] American success was an expression of British power, institutions, and values. This was a common trope in British accounts of Anglo-America, with Dilke, for example, boasting that "[t]hrough America, England is speaking to the world."[47]

H. G. Wells also dreamt of an Anglo enunciation of modernity. In *Anticipations*, published in 1902, he prophesized the emergence of a world state ruled over by a new techno-managerial class of "efficients"—the "kinetic men" of the future.[48] This was a theme he was to pursue, in one way or another, until his death in 1946. In this early vision, the unification of the "English-speaking" peoples assumed a central role: they were to serve as pioneers of the world-state-to-come. By the year 2000 the English-speaking people would constitute a federal state, united by "practically homogenous citizenship," with its headquarters in the United States. They would govern all the "non-white states of the present British empire, and in addition much of the South and Middle Pacific, the East and West Indies, the rest of America, and the larger part of black Africa."[49] His vision was vanguardist in a double sense. Not only were the English-speaking peoples to lead the way to a further global "synthesis," but this drive was itself led by a select group of individuals, men of energy, determination, and drive, who would help to dissolve—either through social revolution or in the wake of war—the remaining barriers to its realization found in "deliquescing" modern societies. The New Republicans would act as

---

[45] Stead, *The Americanization of the World* (New York, 1901), 100, 397.
[46] Ibid., 2.
[47] Dilke, *Greater Britain*, 318.
[48] Wells, *Anticipations*, ch. 8. On Wells, see also Deudney, *Bounding Power*, pt. 3.
[49] Wells, *Anticipations*, 146.

a largely uncoordinated "Secret Society" to help inaugurate a fresh dawn in human history. This notion of a clerisy acting behind the scenes to secure race unity was echoed by Rhodes and Stead.

Wells was not the only fiction writer to propagate Anglo-unity. Arthur Conan Doyle was another enthusiast, dedicating his historical novel *The White Company* to "the Hope of the Future, the Reunion of the English-Speaking races." He even enlisted Sherlock Holmes, who declaimed that history should not prevent "our children from being someday citizens of the same world-wide country whose flag should be a quartering of the Union Jack with the Stars and Stripes."[50] Writing to his brother William, Henry James observed in 1888 that "I can't look at the English-American world, or feel about them, anymore save as a big Anglo-Saxon total, destined to such an amount of melting together that an insistence on their difference becomes more and more idle and pedantic."[51]

While many of the proposals for unity were motivated by pragmatic security concerns, an equally large number made drastic claims about the world-transforming potential of racial unity. We can thus interpret aspects of the pre-1914 Anglo-race discourse as expressions of utopian desire.[52] A political project can be considered utopian, I submit, if and only if it invokes or prescribes the transcendence or elimination of at least one of the pervasive practices or ordering principles that shape human collective life. These include poverty, inequality, war, the state, the biochemical composition of the environment, or the ontological constitution of human beings, including death itself. Utopianism is not best employed as a synonym for any ambitious project of political change or seen as a general feature of the human condition, a universal striving for a better life. Rather, it identifies a particular species of transformative social and political thought.

The utopianism of this racial vision resided in the belief that if the United States and Greater Britain were properly aligned, the "Anglo-Saxon" race would help to bring peace, order, and justice to the earth. Carnegie argued that the "new nation would dominate the world and banish from the earth its greatest stain—the murder of men by men." Lyman Abbott, a prominent American Congregationalist theologian, dreamed of an Anglo century—even millennium. "[T]hese two nations, embodying the energy, the enterprise, and the conscience of the Anglo-Saxon race, would by the mere fact of their cooperation produce a result in human history which would surpass all that pres-

---

[50] Doyle, *The White Company* (London, 1891); Doyle, "The Adventures of the Noble Bachelor," in *The Adventures of Sherlock Holmes* (London, 1892).

[51] Letter to William James, October 29, 1888, *The Letters of Henry James*, ed. Percy Lubbock (New York, 1920), 1:141.

[52] For more on this argument, see Bell, "Dreaming the Future," in *The American Experiment and the Idea of Democracy in British Culture, 1776–1914*, ed. Ella Dzelzainis and Ruth Livesey (Aldershot, 2013), 197–210.

ent imagination can conceive or present hope anticipate."[53] For Albion Tourgée, American soldier, diplomat, and judge, the Anglo-Saxons were, quite simply, the "peacemakers of the twentieth century." Rhodes once wrote: "What an awful thought it is that if we had not lost America, or even if now we could arrange with the present members of the United States Assembly and our House of Commons, the peace of the world is secured for all eternity!" In 1891, he predicted that union with the United States would mean "universal peace" within one hundred years. Stead agreed, envisaging that "war would by degree die out from the face of the earth."[54] This, then, was the promise of an Anglo-racial utopia.

Afterlives of Empire: Anglo-America and Global Governance

During the twentieth century, proposals for supranational political unions were divided among (at least) five models. One of them emphasized regional federation, and centered above all on combining the states of continental Europe. It was this vision that ultimately had the most practical effect, though only after the cataclysm of a genocidal war. The other four—which I will label imperial-commonwealth, Anglo-American, democratic unionist, and world federalist—placed the transatlantic British-American connection at the core of global order. All were descended, in part or wholly, from the earlier Anglo-world projects. Some offered only minor modifications to earlier imperial schemes, while others pushed out in new directions. Perhaps most importantly, though, the majority of the interwar and midcentury projects regarded the "Anglo" powers as a nucleus or vanguard. And even those schemes that expanded beyond the institutional limits of the Anglo-world were almost invariably liberal democratic and capitalist in form, and as such they exemplified, even embodied, the values and institutions on which the Anglo-world was based, and over which its advocates claimed paternity.

The imperial-commonwealth model focused on the continuing role of the British empire. During the Edwardian years and beyond, the Round Table and other British imperial advocacy groups continued to campaign on behalf of Greater British unity. The imperial federalist project reached its zenith during the First World War with the creation of an Imperial War Cabinet in 1917, which incorporated the prime ministers of the dominions. This was the nearest the dream of a politically unified Greater Britain came to fruition. Yet

[53] Carnegie, *Reunion*, 12–13; Abbott, "The Basis of an Anglo-American Understanding," *North American Review*, 166 (1898), 521.

[54] Tourgée, "The Twentieth Century Peacemakers," *Contemporary Review*, 75 (1899), 886–908; Rhodes, *Last Will and Testament*, 73, 66; Stead, *The Americanization of the World*, 435. I develop this line of argument in Bell, "Before the Democratic Peace," *European Journal of International Relations*, 20/3 (2014), 647–70.

the war also accelerated calls for further independence in the colonies. While the efforts of the imperial federalists did not go completely unheralded in the United States, they found, perhaps ironically, a more receptive audience in continental Europe, with a number of them—notably Philip Kerr (Lord Lothian)—playing an important role in shaping the ideological foundations of European union.[55]

During the 1920s the balance of power continued to shift within the British empire, and as the colonies were granted further autonomy they frequently came into conflict with London.[56] In the interwar period it became increasingly popular to reimagine the empire as the "British Commonwealth"—the two terms were often used interchangeably—and to see it either as a self-contained system capable of balancing other great political orders, or as the embryonic form of a future universal political system. Britain and its settler colonies remained at the center of the model, although India and other elements of the empire were sometimes allotted subordinate roles. In the second half of the twentieth century, following decolonization, the imperial-commonwealth vision morphed into a postcolonial international organization.[57] Today it lingers on, a pale shadow of the hopes once invested in it.

The Anglo-American model centered on the Anglo-Saxon—or "English-speaking"—peoples, and in particular on a British-American axis. Relations between London and Washington continued to strengthen in the wake of the late Victorian "rapprochement," and the alliance was cemented during the First World War when the United States joined the Franco-British cause in Western Europe. It remained close for the rest of the twentieth century, though not quite as close as many of its cheerleaders, then as now, like to boast. The First World War had a catalytic effect on American foreign policy discourse, spawning the development of a powerful, though often fractious, East Coast policy elite oriented towards greater American involvement in world politics, in cooperation (even alliance) with Britain.[58] During the interwar era, a variety of institutions and informal networks were created to foster closer links between the United States and Greater Britain. They constituted an emergent epistemic community dedicated to emphasizing the importance of Anglo-world global leadership. The Council on Foreign Relations in New

[55] For the American reception, see, for example, William Roy Smith, "British Imperial Federation," *Political Science Quarterly*, 36 (1921), 274–97; George Burton-Adams, *The British Empire and a League of Peace* (New York, 1919). On the impact on European debates, see John Kendle, *Federal Britain* (London, 1997), ch. 6; Andrea Bosco, "Lothian, Curtis, Kimber and the Federal Union Movement (1938–1940)," *Journal of Contemporary History*, 23 (1988), 465–502; Michael Burgess, *The British Tradition of Federalism* (London, 1995), pt. 3; John Turner, ed., *The Larger Idea* (London, 1988).

[56] Margaret MacMillan, "Isosceles Triangle," in *Twentieth-Century Anglo-American Relations*, ed. Jonathan Hollowell (Basingstoke, 2001), 1–25.

[57] Timothy Shaw, *The Commonwealth* (London, 2008).

[58] Priscilla Roberts, "The Anglo-American Theme," *Diplomatic History*, 21/3 (1997), 333–64.

York and the International Institute of International Affairs (Chatham House) in London served as institutional hubs of Anglo-world thinking, in both its Anglo-American and British imperial-commonwealth articulations.[59]

While the 1920s saw constructive cooperation between Britain and the United States, relations during the 1930s were strained; it was only with the outbreak of war, and especially between 1940 and 1942, that the two powers were forced into a tight embrace.[60] This peaked with the signing of the Atlantic Charter in August 1941, dedicated to the promotion of "certain common principles in the national policies of their respective countries on which they base their hope for the common world," though tension continued between London and Washington over the future of the British empire. As American power increased, and it became clear that Britain would be a junior partner in any future relationship, so once again the dream of an Anglo-American order faded. Perhaps its last gasp can be found in Churchill's "iron curtain" speech in March 1946, in which he popularized the term "special relationship" and insisted that peace was impossible without "the fraternal association of the English-speaking peoples."[61] Like the contemporary Commonwealth, the "special relationship" in the postwar years was a weak imitation of the ideal that had inspired many British, and even a few American, commentators over the previous decades.

Another model envisioned the creation of a league (or concert) of democracies. Before 1945 this essentially meant a transatlantic union of the United States, Great Britain, and assorted western European countries. As such, it moved beyond the "racial" limits of the Anglo-world. In the 1950s this idea sometimes mutated into an Atlanticist vision centered on the NATO countries. The most influential interwar democratic unionist vision was propounded by Clarence Streit, a journalist with the *New York Times*. In *Union Now*, he proposed a federation, on the model of the constitution of 1787, of the fifteen democracies of the Atlantic world. The union would serve three main purposes:

(a) to provide effective common government in our democratic world in those fields where such common government will clearly serve man's

---

[59] Nicholas Cull, "Selling Peace," *Diplomacy and Statecraft*, 7 (1996), 1–28; Priscilla Roberts, "The Transatlantic American Foreign Policy Elite," *Journal of Transatlantic Studies*, 7 (2009), 163–83; Inderjeet Parmar, "Anglo-American Elites in the Interwar Years," *International Relations*, 16 (2002), 53–75; Paul Williams, "A Commonwealth of Knowledge," *International Relations*, 17 (2003), 35–58.

[60] David Reynolds, *The Creation of the Anglo-American Alliance, 1937–41* (London, 1981); Reynolds, "Roosevelt, Churchill, and the Wartime Anglo-American Alliance, 1939–45," in *The Special Relationship*, ed. William Roger Louis and Hedley Bull (Oxford, 1986), 17–41.

[61] Robert Rhodes James, ed., *Winston S. Churchill* (New York, 1974), 289. Churchill advocated a common citizenship between Britain and the USA. See Henry Butterfield Ryan, *The Vision of Anglo-America* (Cambridge, 1987), ch. 3; Richard Toye, *Churchill's Empire* (London, 2010), 240.

freedom better than separate governments, (b) to maintain independent national governments in all other fields where such government will best serve man's freedom, and (c) to create by its constitution a nucleus world government capable of growing into universal world government peacefully and as rapidly as such growth will best serve man's freedom.[62]

He followed this up with *Union Now with Britain*, in which he argued that the creation of an Anglo-American union would guarantee the defeat of the Axis.[63] Streit's later work highlights the way in which the Cold War constrained the imagination of democratic unionists. The West, figured as an "Atlantic community"—a term first used by Walter Lippmann[64]—took center stage. In 1961 Streit published *Freedom's Frontier*, suggesting that the fifteen countries of NATO already constituted the nucleus of an immanent Atlantic federal state: "Atlantica."[65] This fed into a popular Atlanticist current of thought. Expressing a common view, Livingston Hartley, a former State Department official, demanded "the political integration of the Atlantic community, the citadel and the powerhouse of freedom."[66] For many, European union and Atlantic union went hand in hand, the development of the former helping to strengthen the viability of the latter.[67] For others, though, the creation of a European union threatened the more desirable goal of Atlantic union. For Streit, avatar of Atlanticism, America needed to take the lead in creating a new order, "preferably teamed closely with Canada," while European integration threatened transatlantic division.[68]

The veteran British peace campaigner Norman Angell followed a similar trajectory to Streit. An early advocate of democratic federal union as a precursor to world federation, during the Second World War he too emphasized the vital leadership role of the Anglo-states (and the British empire) in this future global order. Like so many other post-state visionaries, he insisted that a "nucleus of authority" was required to catalyze and then direct the transition to world federation, and that this nucleus "must be the English-speaking world," by which he meant the United States and the "British peoples."[69] Rather than

---

[62] Streit, *Union Now* (New York, 1938), 2.

[63] Streit, *Union Now with Britain* (New York, 1941).

[64] Lippmann, *US Foreign Policy* (Boston, 1943), 83.

[65] Streit, *Freedom's Frontier* (New York, 1961).

[66] Hartley, *Atlantic Challenge* (New York, 1965), 92.

[67] Robert Strauz-Hupe, James Dougherty, and William Kintner, *Building the Atlantic World* (New York, 1963).

[68] Streit, "Atlantic Union," *Annals of the American Academy of Political and Social Science*, 288 (1953), 8. While Streit routinely talked of uniting "all democracies," he also stressed "Atlantic Union," thus leaving unclear the role of the non-Atlantic parts of Greater Britain.

[69] See the argumentative shift between Angell, *The Political Conditions of Allied Success* (New York, 1918), and Angell, "The English-Speaking World and the Next Peace," *World Affairs*, 105 (1942), 10.

the latest manifestation of Anglo-Saxon imperialism, he was adamant that this Anglo core could act as the embryo of a true universalism. The empire should, then, be transformed into a "nucleus of integration" rather than dissolved into independent sovereign states.[70] By the late 1950s, in Streitian vein, he was arguing that "the West" as a whole should act as the advance guard in any future transformation. "A world government would have to work on the basis of 80 or 100 nationalisms, emphasizing widely differing cultures and ways of life." The common social basis for political unity did not (yet) exist. As such, he concluded, the adoption of the "federal principle" was necessary to unify the West in the face of Soviet totalitarianism, and as an essential step on the road to a more wide-ranging union.[71] The unionist axis had shifted from the British empire, through Anglo-America, to the West as a whole, but the Anglo-world remained at the heart of the project.

The major difference between "Anglo" and "Democratic unionist" models concerns the identity claim on which they are based. The Anglo model is confined to a finite set of British diasporic communities; its potential spatial extent is delimited by a specific historical trajectory. A league of democracies is in principle more expansive, designating a community that shares a minimal set of political values and institutions, all of them hypothetically exportable. Yet in practice, at the heart of this picture, were (and are) the Anglo-states. Moreover, the values and institutions associated with such a community—the architecture of liberal-democratic capitalism—were either implicitly or explicitly ascribed by contemporaries to the British and American intellectual traditions. Once again, social science offered authoritative epistemic support. The empirical analysis, and the normative affirmation, of the Anglo-world were high on the agenda of early postwar behavioral political science. Most notably, the hugely influential idea of a "security community" was forged in the crucible of Atlanticist politics. Pioneering political scientist Karl Deutsch argued, for example, that the North Atlantic security community was anchored in the most highly integrated states, namely the United States, Canada, and the United Kingdom.[72]

The final model was a universal world polity. Ideas about world government have percolated through the history of political thought, ebbing and flowing in popularity.[73] The 1940s witnessed an efflorescence of utopian political thinking, catalyzed by the old Kantian premonition that the route to perpetual peace would most likely wind its way through the valley of death—

---

[70] Angell, "The British Commonwealth in the Next World Order," *Annals of the American Academy of Political and Social Science*, 228 (1943), 65–70.

[71] Angell, "Angell Sums Up at 85," *Freedom & Union* (December 1958), 7–11.

[72] Deutsch et al., *Political Community and the North Atlantic Area* (Princeton, 1957); see also Bruce Russett, *Community and Contention* (Cambridge, MA, 1963).

[73] For analyses of such ideas, see Derek Heater, *World Citizenship and Government* (Basingstoke, 1996); Jens Bartelson, *Visions of World Community* (Cambridge, 2009).

that a brutal war might, once and for all, force people throughout the world to recognize the necessity of federation. Advocates of a global polity typically conceived of it as a long-term ideal rather than something within immediate grasp.[74] Nevertheless, many of them called for a federal institutional structure with an Anglo nucleus, while numerous advocates of democratic or Anglo-racial union saw their own more limited goals as temporary steps on the road to—and often agents in the creation of—a universal federation.

Perhaps the most famous world federalist was Wells, who proselytized on behalf of a post-sovereign cosmopolitan order in a seemingly endless stream of publications. After the First World War he turned his attention to the creation of a functionalist world state, suggesting in vague terms that a future world polity would result from the coagulation of regional and racial groupings.[75] Like most of his contemporaries, his account of a cosmopolitan world state never escaped the ethnocentric assumptions that had marked his earlier writings. Evolving through various iterations, his vision of a future global order was rooted in the purported superiority of the Western powers, and in particular the Anglo-Americans. He longed for the (re)union of the English-speaking peoples. In 1935, for example, he argued that "the commonsense of the world demands that the English-speaking community should get together upon the issue of World Peace, and that means a common foreign policy." It also meant economic unification, for "the world revival" would not materialize "unless we homologize the financial control and monetary organization of our world-wide group of people."[76] Wells exemplified the technocratic aspect of the world federalist project, even flirting with fascist methods during the 1920s and 1930s in order to help bring about a new global order.

World federalist thinking flourished in Britain and the United States in the 1940s and early l950s, drawing in a wide array of intellectuals and politicians, from Albert Einstein and Aldous Huxley to Henry L. Stimson and John Foster Dulles. Campaigning organizations—notably the United World Federalists (1947)—were formed, politicians lobbied, newsletters and pamphlets circulated. Wendell Willkie's *One World* sold over two million copies.[77] Henry Usborne, a British Labour MP, created a Parliamentary Group for World Government and signed up over 200 MPs.[78] Under the leadership of its president, Robert M. Hutchins, the University of Chicago created a Committee to Frame a World Constitution.[79] House Concurrent Resolution 64, in 1949,

[74] Jo-Ann Pemberton, *Global Metaphors* (London, 2001); Wesley Wooley, *Alternatives to Anarchy* (Bloomington, 1988).

[75] Wells, *The Outline of History* (London, 1925), 708.

[76] Wells, *The New America* (London, 1935), 24.

[77] Dulles, *War, Peace, and Change* (New York, 1939); Willkie, *One World* (New York, 1943).

[78] For further detail, see Joseph Preston Baratta, *The Politics of World Federation*, 2 vols. (Westport, 2004), 162–64.

[79] Hutchins et al., *Preliminary Draft of a World Constitution* (Chicago, 1948); See also G. A. Borgese, *Foundations of a World Republic* (Chicago, 1953).

was proposed as a "fundamental objective of the foreign policy of the United States to support and strengthen the United Nations and to seek its development into a world federation." It secured 111 votes, including those of John F. Kennedy, Gerald Ford, Mike Mansfield, Henry Cabot Lodge, and Henry Jackson. The movement peaked in early 1950, with 150,000 members worldwide.[80]

In the shadow of the bomb, political realists had their own one world moment. John Herz and Hans Morgenthau, among others, argued that human survival demanded the creation of a world state, though both were skeptical of its plausibility.[81] The world federalist movement was stifled by the onset of the Cold War.[82] The dream of unity struggled on, finding a variety of intellectual outlets, including the World Orders Model Project most closely associated with Richard Falk.[83] But it was an early victim of bipolar ideological confrontation. Once a topic of mainstream concern for scholars, public intellectuals, journalists, and politicians, Thomas Weiss argues that today ideas about a global federal state are "commonly thought to be the preserve of lunatics."[84] Yet there are signs of a revival of interest in the idea, at least among scholars.[85] In IR, for example, Alexander Wendt and Daniel Deudney have offered theoretically sophisticated accounts of the plausibility, even inevitability, of a world state.[86]

The proponents of democratic leagues and world federation often drew inspiration from—and shared personnel with—the imperial federal movement. Lionel Curtis is a prominent example. An enthusiastic advocate of imperial and then world federalism over the course of five decades, his political thought was riddled with the tensions between universalism, Atlanticism, and imperi-

[80] Thomas Weiss, "What Happened to the Idea of World Government?," *International Studies Quarterly*, 53 (2009), 258; John Preston Baratta, "The International Federalist Movement," *Peace & Change*, 24 (1999), 342.

[81] Craig Campbell, *Glimmer of a New Leviathan* (New York, 2003); Deudney, *Bounding Power*, ch. 8.

[82] Baratta, *The Politics of World Federation*. This transition was mirrored in the mutation of an "astrofuturist" discourse that focused on the possibilities of the exploration and conquest of outer space. This discourse emerged in the interwar years in the USA, Germany, Britain, and Russia, and flowered in the second half of the century, chiefly in the USA. It reached its apotheosis with the moon landing in 1969. During the interwar period it had been largely internationalist in orientation—albeit infused with the justificatory strategies of imperialism—whereas its post-1945 fortunes saw it tied increasingly to the priorities of the national security state. DeWitt Clinton Kilgore, *Astrofuturism* (Philadelphia, 2003).

[83] Falk, *A Study of Future Worlds* (New York, 1975). Falk drew on Louis Sohn and Grenville Clark, *World Peace through World Law* (Cambridge, MA, 1958).

[84] Weiss, "World Government?," 258.

[85] For discussion, see Luis Cabrera, "World Government," *European Journal of International Relations*, 16 (2010), 511–30.

[86] Wendt, "Why a World State Is Inevitable," *European Journal of International Relations*, 9 (2003), 491–542; Deudney, *Bounding Power*.

alism.[87] Curtis's magnum opus, the sprawling politico-theological treatise *Civitas Dei*, posited that a federated British empire could serve as a kernel and a model for a future universal commonwealth of nations, because of all extant political communities it offered the most appropriate space for human personality to find its fullest expression.[88] The most difficult stage in creating a world federal state was the first one; the "most experienced commonwealths" needed to show leadership. He identified the core of the global order in the union of Great Britain, New Zealand, and Australia.[89] The Second World War only reinforced his belief in the necessity of political transformation. In the early 1950s Curtis angrily denounced intellectuals for upholding the myth of sovereign statehood; they were, he charged, "responsible for the bloodshed of this century" and "answerable for the suffering, poverty, and death that millions are now facing." Federation, with an Anglo core, was the only way to escape the killing machine. An arch Anglo-supremacist who died in 1956, Curtis was frequently hailed as one of the pioneers of the world federalist movement.[90]

A notable aspect of the debates over global order, in both the nineteenth and the twentieth centuries, was that the United States often served as a template for the future. Both American political experience and political philosophy were routinely cited as inspirational, even formative. Streit modeled his plan for an Atlantic union of democracies on the US Constitution. Indeed, he went so far as to call for a Federal Convention, similar to its namesake in Philadelphia in 1787, to deliberate over the desirability and potential form of a transatlantic union. This proposal gained the support of the Canadian Senate and dozens of US senators.[91] Twentieth-century British imperial federalists, meanwhile, regularly invoked the genius of the American founders, often interpreted through the prism of F. S. Oliver's *Alexander Hamilton*. Curtis, for example, was explicit about his debt to the *Federalist Papers;* they taught him, he recorded, about both the problem of political order and the best solution to it, fundamentally influencing his views over half a century of federalist agitation.[92] America was both model and motive. Indeed, many world federalist plans can be read as demanding the Americanization of the planet.

[87] On his life and religious views, see Gerald Studdert-Kennedy, "Christianity, Statecraft and Chatham House," *Diplomacy & Statecraft*, 6 (1995), 470–89; Deborah Lavin, *From Empire to International Commonwealth* (Oxford, 1995).

[88] Curtis, *Civitas Dei*, 3 vols. (London, 1937).

[89] Curtis, "World Order," *International Affairs*, 18 (1939), 309; cf. Curtis, *Civitas Dei*, vol. 3. Curtis also expressed admiration for Streit's alternative Atlanticist plan. Curtis, "World Order," 310; Curtis, "The Fifties as Seen Fifty Years Hence," *International Affairs*, 27 (1951), 273–84.

[90] Curtis, "The Fifties," 284. On his role as a pioneer, see Streit, "Lionel Curtis," *Freedom & Union*, 10 (1956), 10.

[91] Streit, "Atlantic Union"; Curtis, "The Fifties," 275–76.

[92] Oliver, *Alexander Hamilton* (London, 1906); Curtis, "World Order," 302–7. Deudney's

Millennial Dreams, or, Back to the Future

While today there are few advocates of a global federal state outside of universities and think tanks, the vision of a "concert" or "league" of democracies has resurfaced in public life. "Democracy" has supplanted "civilization" as the defining feature in discourses of global governance. Democratic unionist arguments have been given a powerful boost by the popularity of theories of the "democratic peace," once again highlighting the complex entanglement of twentieth-century social science with projects for global order. This line of reasoning is directly descended from the mid-twentieth-century discourse. Michael Doyle, for example, identifies Streit as the first modern commentator to point to "the empirical tendency of democracies to maintain peace among themselves."[93] Uniting liberal internationalists with neoconservatives, the idea of a league of democracies has wide ideological appeal among members of the American political elite, even if it has resonated far less in Europe. Advisors to both Barack Obama and John McCain promoted the idea during the 2008 election campaign, and McCain endorsed it.[94] It has found its most systematic articulation in the Princeton Project on National Security, coordinated by Anne-Marie Slaughter and John Ikenberry, which proposes the creation of a global "Concert of Democracies" to "institutionalize and ratify the 'democratic peace.'"[95]

Recent years have also witnessed a brief flurry of arguments focusing on the Anglo dimension of world politics—the imperial dream that never expires. They are variations on the earlier themes of imperial federation and Anglo-American unity. In addition to the old rubric of the "English-speaking peoples," a new term (coined in a science fiction novel) has entered the lexicon: the "Anglosphere."[96] Advocacy of Anglo superiority has assumed different forms. One popular version, outlined in a bestselling book and a popular television series, is Niall Ferguson's paean to British imperial power, and the

---

fascinating discussion of republican security in *Bounding Power* is also modeled on American experience.

[93] Doyle, "Liberalism and World Politics," *American Political Science Review*, 80 (1986), 1162n2; cf. Ikenberry, *After Victory* (Princeton, 2001), 178–79. For further discussion, see Duncan Bell, "Before the Democratic Peace," *European Journal of International Relations*, 20/3 (2014), 647–70.

[94] McCain, "An Enduring Peace Built on Freedom," *Foreign Affairs*, 86 (November/December 2007), 19–34. See also Ivo Daalder and James Lindsay, "Democracies of the World, Unite," *American Interest*, 2 (2007), 5–15; Francis Fukuyama, *America at the Crossroads* (London, 2006); James Huntley, *Pax Democratica* (London, 1998).

[95] Ikenberry and Slaughter, *Forging a World of Liberty Under Law* (2006), Princeton Project on National Security, 2006), accessed July 22, 2011, http://www.princeton.edu/~ppns/report/Final Report.pdf, 7.

[96] For an insightful analysis, see Srdjan Vucetic, "Anglobal Governance?," *Cambridge Review of International Affairs*, 23 (2011), 455–74; Vucetic, *The Anglosphere* (Stanford, 2011).

necessity of the American empire assuming the responsibility—the old "White Man's burden"—of hegemonic stabilizer and civilizing agent.[97] Other widely discussed proposals have emanated from the American businessman James Bennett and the British historian Andrew Roberts.

Echoing earlier discussions about the world-historical function of the telegraph, Bennett contends that the Internet can serve as a medium through which the geographically scattered but culturally and politically aligned members of the "Anglosphere" can come into closer communion, and act together for the planetary greater good.[98] He sees this as both desirable and necessary, given the likely development of other competing network "spheres"— Sino, Luso, Hispano, and Franco. He concludes that the inherited political and economic traditions of the Anglosphere mean that it is uniquely equipped to thrive in the coming century. Roberts, meanwhile, seeks to pick up where Churchill finished his own bombastic history of the English-speaking peoples.[99] Rather than advocating formal union, he outlines a vision, grounded in a hubristic reading of twentieth-century history, in which the English-speaking peoples are united by "common purposes" and in defeating waves of totalitarianism, today exemplified by Islamic fanaticism. Superior political institutions mean that when they act in unison, the whole world benefits. Roberts's vision of the English-speaking peoples is limited to the United States, the United Kingdom "and her dependencies," New Zealand, Canada, and Australia, as well as the British West Indies and Ireland—though of the latter two, the first is largely ignored while the second is routinely assailed for failing to live up to the standards set by the others. Reproducing earlier arguments about race patriotism, Roberts decenters the state: the ontological foundation of his argument is a singular people, while the political units of this singularity play a secondary function. "Just as we do not today differentiate between the Roman Republic and the imperial period of the Julio-Claudians when we think of the Roman Empire, so in the future no one will bother to make a distinction between the British Empire-led and the American Republic-led periods of English-speaking dominance."[100] The book secured him an invitation to George W. Bush's White House.[101]

None of these authors proposes a formal political union, instead hymning the powers of shared culture, traditions, and interests. But the vision of an institutionalized Anglo-union has not disappeared completely. Robert Con-

---

[97] Ferguson, *Empire* (London, 2004).

[98] Bennett, *The Anglosphere Challenge* (Lanham, MD, 2007).

[99] Roberts, *A History of the English-Speaking Peoples*. Cf. Churchill, *A History of the English-Speaking Peoples*, 4 vols. (London, 1956–58). On the term "English-speaking peoples," see Clarke, "The English-Speaking Peoples."

[100] Roberts, *A History of the English-Speaking Peoples*, 381.

[101] Jacob Weisberg, "George Bush's Favourite Historian," *Slate*, March 28, 2007, accessed July 26, 2011, http://www.slate.com/id/2162837/.

quest, eminent poet and historian, has called for the "English-speaking" countries of the world to join a "flexibly conceived Association," something "weaker than a federation, but stronger than an alliance." A "natural rather than artificial" association, this "Anglo-Oceanic" polity would act as a progressive hyperpower.[102] Like Roberts, Conquest is driven in part by a sense of anger at the duplicity of British politicians signing up to European integration, and thus betraying their true kin in the dominions and across the Atlantic.

There are notable continuities between the contemporary projects for an Anglo century and their predecessors. All have been framed by war or imperial action. While Cuba, the Philippines, and South Africa set the context for the first outburst of writing on Anglo-America, and the rise of Hitler, the Second World War, and then the onset of the Cold War helped initiate the second, today it is Iraq, Afghanistan, and the "War on Terror" that provide the general ideological milieu. All of them depend on a form of "othering," an imaginative geography of fear and loathing. Over time, the Anglo-Saxons have been arrayed against Japan, France, Russia, Germany, the Soviet Union, and now an amorphous "radical Islam." Each phase has also been predicated on hyperbolic claims about the power of new communications technologies to transform the nature and scope of political association. Since the late nineteenth century, radical visions of formal political union have been accompanied by more modest proposals for strengthening existing connections and fostering close cooperation. Yet all of these varied projects, however ambitious, have been based on claims about translocal identity and belonging. They have insisted that the members of the Anglo-world share much in common—a language, a history, a set of values, political and economic institutions, and a destiny.

But there are also some notable differences. The *fin de siècle* and mid-twentieth-century debates about supranational political unions were much wider ranging and more prominent; they drew in many of the leading public intellectuals, journalists, and politicians of the day. While the current debate over the league of democracies has a high profile, the ambitions of its proponents are far more limited than those urged by their mid-twentieth-century precursors. They do not seek to replace the state system, only to carve out a powerful coalition within it.

The contemporary Anglospheric discourse, meanwhile, is a pale imitation of previous iterations. This is partly because of its ideological coloring. Whereas the older debate crossed political lines, the contemporary discourse is almost exclusively confined to the political right, and in particular to neoconservatives. Another significant difference is that the utopian dimension of the earlier projects is largely absent. In the reheated version, the Anglosphere is figured as a force for good in the world, securing and helping to spread

---

[102] Robert Conquest, *Reflections on a Ravaged Century* (London, 2000).

freedom, democracy, and liberal capitalism—it upholds the new civilizing mission. This is a form of imperial idealism, but it is not equivalent to the earlier claims that the unity of the Anglo-Saxon race would eliminate war, or that it would inaugurate a universal world state. The messianic impulse has dissolved.

The last one hundred and fifty years, then, have seen the elaboration of numerous projects to unify or coordinate the scattered polities of the Anglo-world. Initially they centered on British imperial federation, before the focus switched to the Anglo-American relationship. Proposals for a league of democracy, Atlantic union, even world federalism were heirs of this Anglo discourse, not discrete and incompatible models of global order. They emerged from the earlier imperial-racial debates, and many of the proposals for transcending the existing system were similar in form and ambition to the projects for Anglo-world imperium. To chart the "growth of nations," Tocqueville once wrote, it is an imperative to remember that they carry with them "some of the marks of their origin."[103] The same is true of projects of global governance. We have yet to escape the will to empire and the seductive call of the civilizing mission.

[103] Tocqueville, *Democracy in America*, 13.

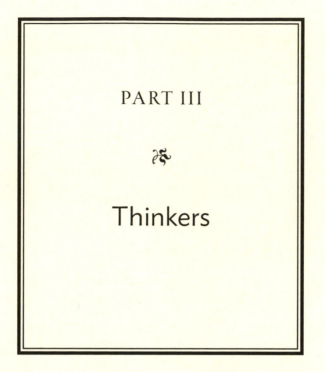

PART III

Thinkers

CHAPTER 9

John Stuart Mill on Colonies

ે૨

The question of government intervention in the work of Colonization involves
the future and permanent interests of civilization itself.[1]

—JOHN STUART MILL

During the last three decades, the study of imperialism has moved from the periphery to the center of work in the humanities and social sciences. The importance of viewing metropolitan and imperial spaces within a "single analytic field"—as dynamically connected, interpenetrating, even mutually constitutive—has been a key theme in this flourishing scholarship.[2] This productive insight points historians of political thought in two main directions. First, to the value of comparative political theory, encompassing the study of non-Western traditions and the attempt to trace the manifold ways in which political ideas circulate across and around different geo-cultural zones. And second, in drawing attention to how past thinkers conceptualized the world, how they constructed and deployed categories including the domestic, the foreign, the imperial, and the colonial.

In this chapter I explore some important yet neglected aspects of John Stuart Mill's vision of global order. Mill has played a pivotal role in the recent wave of scholarship dedicated to unraveling the entanglement of Western political thought and imperialism.[3] The reasons for this are obvious: he occupies a talismanic position in the liberal canon, and his career and writings provide fertile ground for analysis and critique. At the age of seventeen he began work at the East India Company, where he rose to high rank and left only after the company lost its charter in 1858. He continued to defend the British occupation until his death in 1873. While this scholarship has illuminated various aspects of Mill's imperial thought, especially his views on India, it has passed over other areas in near silence, and has often failed to account for the

---

[1] J. S. Mill, *Principles of Political Economy* [1848], in *Collected Works,* 3:963.

[2] Ann Laura Stoler and Frederick Cooper, "Between Metropole and Colony," in *Tensions of Empire,* ed. Cooper and Stoler (Berkeley, 1997), 4.

[3] See, for example, Uday Singh Mehta, *Liberalism and Empire* (Chicago, 1999); Jennifer Pitts, *A Turn to Empire* (Princeton, 2005); Martin Moir, Douglas Peers, and Lynn Zastoupil, eds., *J. S. Mill's Encounter with India* (Toronto, 1999); Lynn Zastoupil, *John Stuart Mill and India* (Stanford, CA, 1994).

divergent ways in which he imagined and justified different modes of imperial rule. In particular, scholars have tended to ignore or downplay his extensive writings on (settler) colonization—the establishment, as Mill saw it, of new "civilized" communities in North America and the South Pacific.[4] (Throughout the essay, I use the term colonization to denote *settler colonization*, not as a synonym for imperialism.) Historians of economic thought, meanwhile, have probed Mill's account of the political economy of colonization, but they have largely refrained from linking these arguments to other aspects of his social and political theory.[5]

In Victorian Britain it was common to delineate different types of imperial territory.[6] Mill identified two classes of British "dependencies": those composed of people of a "similar civilization" that were "capable of, and ripe for, representative government," and those, defined in hierarchical opposition, that remained "a great distance from that state."[7] The distinction between settler colonies and other imperial spaces encodes a problem, for it erases some of the key similarities between them. All forms of imperialism involved the violent dispossession of and rule over indigenous peoples. All had roots deep in the political and intellectual history of Europe. And all generated diverse forms of opposition, at home and abroad.[8] Unreflexively reproducing the categories reinscribes the presumption underlying much nineteenth-century political thought, namely that the territories settled by Europeans were "unoccupied," devoid of sovereign communities or rational autonomous agents.[9] Marx was simply following convention when he referred to "virgin

---

[4] Valuable exceptions include: Margaret Kohn and Daniel O'Neill, "A Tale of Two Indias," *Political Theory*, 34 (2006), 192–228; Katherine Smits, "John Stuart Mill on the Antipodes," *Australian Journal of Politics and History*, 51 (2008), 1–15. Both Nicholas Capaldi, *John Stuart Mill* (Cambridge, 2004), and Richard Reeves, *John Stuart Mill* (London, 2007) underemphasize colonization.

[5] Bernard Semmel, *The Rise of Free Trade Imperialism* (Cambridge, 1970); Winch, *Classical Political Economy*; R. N. Ghosh, "John Stuart Mill on Colonies and Colonization," in *John Stuart Mill*, ed. John Cunningham Wood (London, 1987), 4:354–67; Samuel Hollander, *The Economics of John Stuart Mill*, 2 vols. (Oxford, 1985), 2:753–58.

[6] George Cornewall Lewis, *An Essay on the Government of Dependencies* (London, 1841); Arthur Mills, *Colonial Constitutions* (London, 1856); Henry Jenkyns, *British Rule and Jurisdiction beyond the Seas* (Oxford, 1902), 1–9.

[7] Mill, *Considerations on Representative Government, Collected Works*, 19:562. He defines a dependency as: "outlying territories of some size and population . . . which are subject, more or less, to acts of sovereign power on the part of the paramount country" (562). See also Mill, "The East India Company's Charter" [1852], *Collected Works*, 30:49–50.

[8] See also Robert Hind, " 'We Have No Colonies,' " *Comparative Studies in Society and History*, 26 (1984), 3–35. Cf. Bruce Buchan, *Empire of Political Thought* (London, 2008).

[9] This type of argument is today often characterized in terms of *terra nullius*—the occupation of "empty land." This idea is ancient (as are the practices of conquest that can follow from it), but the terminology is a product of the late nineteenth century. Andrew Fitzmaurice, "The Genealogy of *Terra Nullius*," *Australian Historical Studies*, 129 (2007), 1–15.

soils, colonised by free immigrants."[10] Nevertheless, the distinction is important for without understanding the uses to which it was put by historical
agents, it is impossible to map the imaginative geography of empire. Despite
the similarities between the forms of conquest, there were also key differences.
Two are especially salient for interpreting Mill: the role of mass emigration
and the desire to create *permanent* "civilized" societies on distant continents.

This chapter explores Mill's defense of colonization. In his mind, Britain
and its colonies (chiefly in Canada, Australia, and New Zealand) formed part
of a single analytical field: they could not be viewed as discrete, autochthonous units. The singularity was itself predetermined by the theoretical machinery of utilitarianism and post-Ricardian political economy. He saw the
world as a space of movement and exchange, the colonies and Britain as inex-
tricably bound by flows of capital, labor, and information. This was reinforced
by his belief that progressive colonies could play a catalytic role in the global
"improvement" of humanity. Mill's arguments on the subject require reconstruction, drawing together material from books, journalism, official reports,
and personal correspondence. In what follows, I analyze three key thematics
in Mill's colonial writings: (1) his evolving account of the political economy
of colonization; (2) his views on "responsible government" and character formation; and (3) finally, his elaboration of the role played by conceptions of
physical space, and of the constitutional structure of the imperial system.

I also pursue two subsidiary lines of argument. First, I identify how Mill's
justificatory account of colonization shifted over time. We witness a movement from the particular to the universal, from arguments justifying colonization primarily in terms of the benefits that it generated for the British state
(and especially the working classes) to arguments that stressed the value of
colonization (and especially British colonization) for the world as a whole.
This signaled a subtle but significant change in emphasis, a change that sheds
light on his understanding of the trajectory of modern politics. It is explained
chiefly by his mutating perception of prevailing conditions. His account of
colonial order—like his political thought as a whole—was structured by the
dynamic interplay of general principles and interpretations of the exigencies
of social, economic, and political life. While circumstances did not radically
transform his core philosophical commitments, they did qualify them or
identify some political options (or institutional configurations) as preferable
to others.

The other line of argument focuses on how Mill framed his narrative.
David Scott has drawn attention to the literary modes of emplotment shaping
anticolonial nationalist writings and much postcolonial criticism. Both construct history, he contends, as a romantic narrative of heroic overcoming and

[10] Marx, *Capital*, vol. 1, in Karl Marx and Friedrich Engels, *Collected Works* (London, 1975),
35:751n.

redemption.[11] Jennifer Pitts, meanwhile, has emphasized the significance of "rhetorical practices" in structuring moral discourse about empire, arguing that there was a strong correlation between anti-imperialism and the authorial use of irony and humor. In Mill's "imperial liberalism" she identifies a distinct "earnestness" that distinguished him from Burke and even Bentham.[12] In the colonial context we see a transition in Mill's writings from a broadly romantic narrative to a position I label *melancholic colonialism*. Mill's colonial romance charted a story of unfolding enlightenment, in which a vanguard of far-sighted "philosophical legislators" transcended a reactionary past, opening up new vistas of human possibility. It was an optimistic story, untroubled by misgivings or doubt. Melancholic colonialism, in contrast, was marked by anxiety, even despondency, about the direction of (colonial) history, but it ultimately refused to reject the ideal, suggesting that the worst excesses could be mitigated, if not eradicated entirely. The transition occurred in the last decade of Mill's life, and was engendered above all by his increased awareness of the pathologies of colonialism, and especially the prevalence of settler violence. It signals an important shift in the way in which he conceived of the ethico-political potential of colonization.

While Mill regarded Britain and the colonies as part of a single analytic field, there were cognitive and theoretical limits to his vision. He always saw the colonies as embryonic nations, bound ultimately for independence, their sheer physical distance from Britain rendering them indissolubly separate. They did not constitute part of a *single political field*—a field in which the colonies and Britain were envisioned not simply as bound together by economic flows, shared interests, and webs of communication, but as comprising a durable political community grounded in a thick common identity. Mill never thought that Britain and its colonies formed (or could form) a single integrated polity. Around the time of his death this alternative vision, which underpinned a normative defense of the permanence of the colonial connection, came to dominate imperial discourse, pushing his position to the sidelines.

On Systematic Colonization: From Domestic to Global

Early nineteenth-century Britain was characterized by "a constant sensation of fear—fear of revolution, of the masses, of crime, famine, and poverty, of disorder and instability, and for many people even fear of pleasure."[13] Profound

---

[11] Scott, *Conscripts of Modernity*.

[12] Pitts, *A Turn to Empire*, 6. On Tocqueville's rhetorical moves, see Cheryl Welch, "Colonial Violence and the Rhetoric of Evasion," *Political Theory*, 31 (2003), 235–64.

[13] Boyd Hilton, *A Mad, Bad, and Dangerous People?* (Oxford, 2006), 31.

apprehension shadowed, and helped to motivate, political thought. Mill's political economy of colonization was shaped by two intersecting debates. The first concerned the material benefits and burdens of colonization; the second concentrated on how best to respond to the social and political turmoil that gripped Britain following the defeat of Napoleon in 1815. Focused inwards on the apparently perilous state of Britain, these concerns drove Mill's earliest forays into colonial advocacy.

Political economists had long disagreed over the value of colonies. Adam Smith had derided them as a sink for capital and labor, as had Bentham and James Mill.[14] Yet during the 1820s and 1830s, an increasing number of thinkers, including Nassau Senior, Robert Torrens, and Herman Merivale, came to view colonies in a more positive light—as potential sites of economic productivity, social amelioration, and civilizational potential.[15] At the heart of this reorientation stood Edward Gibbon Wakefield, a rogue political economist who exerted a profound influence over mid-nineteenth-century colonial discourse.[16] Marx's analysis of "The Modern Theory of Colonisation" in *Das Kapital* focused almost solely on Wakefield's arguments, while Mill regarded him as "one of the most vigorous and effective writers of our time."[17] He was to play a key role in the development of Mill's colonial vision.

Writing from a London prison—where he was interned for abducting a young heiress—Wakefield published his *Letter from Sydney* in 1829.[18] On his release, he founded the National Colonization Society (1830) to promote his views. The elderly Jeremy Bentham, a friend of Wakefield's father, was an early convert, as was the young John Stuart.[19] In 1830 Mill, then a precocious

[14] Adam Smith, *An Inquiry into the Nature and Causes of the Wealth of Nations*, ed. R. H. Campbell and A. S. Skinner (Oxford, 1976 [1776]), 4:556–641; James Mill, "Colony" [1818], in *Essays from the Supplement to the Encyclopedia Britannica, Collected Works* [1823] (London, 1995), 3–33. J. C. Wood, *British Economists and the Empire* (London, 1983), ch. 1.

[15] William Nassau Senior, *Remarks on Emigration* (London, 1831); Senior, *An Outline of a Science of Political Economy* (London, 1836); Robert Torrens, *Colonisation of South Australia* (London, 1835); Torrens, *Self-Supporting Colonization* (London, 1847); Merivale, *Lectures on Colonisation and Colonies*.

[16] On Wakefield, see W. Metcalf, ed., *Edward Gibbon Wakefield and the Colonial Dream* (Wellington, 1997).

[17] Marx, *Capital*, vol. 1, ch. 33; Mill, "Wakefield's Popular Politics," *Examiner*, January 29, 1837, *Collected Works*, 24:788. Mill still professed adherence to Wakefield's views decades later. Mill, "The Westminster Election of 1865," [1], July 3, 1865, *Collected Works*, 28:16; letter to A. M. Francis, May 8, 1869, *Collected Works*, 27:1599.

[18] It was published initially (and anonymously) in the *Morning Chronicle*; it appeared as a book, edited by Robert Gouger, and entitled *A Letter from Sydney, the Principal Town in Australasia, Together with the Outline of a System of Colonization* (London, 1830).

[19] For Bentham on colonies, see Philip Schofield, *Utility and Democracy* (Oxford, 2006), ch. 8; Pitts, *A Turn to Empire*, ch. 4. On his conversion, see Richard Mills, *The Colonization of Australia (1829–1842)* [1915] (London, 1968), 152–53; Edward Gibbon Wakefield, *England and America*, 2 vols. (London, 1833), 2:252n.

twenty-four, described emigration as a "momentous subject," constituting the "only feasible mode of removing the immediate pressure of pauperism," and throughout the following decade he proselytized on behalf of state-sponsored systematic colonization.[20] Above all, he argued, colonization could alleviate suffering among the British working classes. In 1834 he joined the recently founded South Australian Association, which included among its members a number of the other leading philosophic radicals, notably George Grote, whose work was soon to refigure the place of democracy in British political consciousness, and Sir William Molesworth, the editor of Hobbes.[21] It campaigned vociferously for the creation of a new colony in South Australia, "as like as possible to a country which is perfectly civilized, but not over-peopled."[22] While he thought that many aspects of this project were novel, the result of innovative theoretical advances in moral philosophy and political economy, Mill also suggested that in some respects it resembled the noble experiments of the ancient Greeks.

> Like the Grecian colonies, which flourished so rapidly and so wonderfully as soon to eclipse the mother cities, this settlement will be formed by transplanting an intire society, and not a mere fragment of one. English colonies have almost always remained in a half-savage state for many years from their establishment. This colony will be a civilized country from the very commencement.[23]

The "colonial reformers," as they came to be known, were the heroes of Mill's colonial romance, battling against tradition and the political establishment. And Mill himself was ready to practice what he preached: during the 1830s he considered emigrating to Australia.[24]

Jonathan Riley distinguishes between Mill's "Ricardian science" and his "liberal utilitarian art." The science "consists of abstract 'laws' or theorems which presuppose that any person is motivated primarily by a desire for wealth," while recognizing that this motive is sometimes constrained by other

[20] Mill, "The Labouring Agriculturalists," *Examiner*, December 19, 1830, *Collected Works*, 22:218.

[21] On the aims of the group, see Edward Gibbon Wakefield, *The New British Province of South Australia* (London, 1838). The "philosophic radicals" were divided over Wakefield's ideas, with Bowring, Perronet Thompson, and the *Westminster Review*, critical of them; the more influential, including Grote, Molesworth, Roebuck, Buller, both Mills, and the *London Review*, supported the plan.

[22] Mill, "Wakefield's *The New British Province of South Australia*," *Examiner*, July 20, 1834, *Collected Works*, 23:739, 742.

[23] Mill, 739. On his admiration for the "Greek empire," see also Mill, "Grote's History of Greece," vol. 2 [1853], *Collected Works*, vol. 11, esp. 321–24. On the role of Greek models in imagining British colonialism, see chapter 5 of this volume.

[24] Capaldi, *John Stuart Mill*, 107. He later bought land in New Zealand, although he never visited the country: letter to Henry Chapman, November 12, 1845, *Collected Works*, 18:687.

nonmaterial desires (such as the pursuit of leisure). The art, which was shaped by but not reducible to the science, takes the "laws" and "converts and rearranges them into a system of practical rules, and then applies the rules in concrete circumstances to promote the general welfare."[25] The distinction is important for understanding Mill's conception of colonization (although so too is recognition of Mill's deviations from Ricardian orthodoxy).[26] The science specified the reasons for the economic and social turmoil, while the art identified colonization in general—and systematic colonization in particular—as a viable solution available to enlightened political leaders, if they were willing to grasp its potential. Mill came to regard this willingness as a marker of political imagination and maturity.[27]

According to Wakefield and Mill, the social crisis in Britain was caused by a shortage of land and an excess of capital and labor. This produced low levels of growth, a stagnant labor market, and increasing unrest. Emigration to the underpopulated colonies offered the most effective answer.[28] It rendered "the vast productive resources of our colonies available for the employment and comfortable subsistence of the unemployed poor of our country," and it could provide "material relief" to the "labouring classes from the pressure of their own excessive competition."[29] But Mill was wary of unregulated flows of people; rational order was necessary to maximize utility. Emigration should be neither a piecemeal voluntaristic process nor a crude attempt to "shovel out paupers," but instead part of a coordinated state-sponsored scheme of colonization.[30] In pushing for the creation of further colonies in Australia, Mill waxed lyrical about the "the enlightened view of Colonization" and the "honesty and patriotism" that underpinned this ambition.[31] He emphasized two aspects. First, it would relieve socioeconomic pressure at home. And second, it would be financially self-supporting. The latter, Mill thought, was unprecedented: "[F]or the first time in the history of overpopulation, emigration will

---

[25] Riley, "Mill's Political Economy," in *The Cambridge Companion to Mill*, ed. John Skorupski (Cambridge, 1998), 294–95.

[26] Scholars disagree over whether Mill's support for Wakefield signaled a break from Ricardo and Say. Much turns on whether Wakefield's arguments on economic growth were—as he proclaimed—inconsistent with them, or whether he had misread Ricardo (as Mill claimed: *Principles*, 735–36). Donald Winch argues that Mill only supported Wakefield's policy proposals (Winch, *Classical Political Economy*, 139–40), while Samuel Hollander argues that Wakefield and Mill consistently extended Ricardian insights (*Economics of John Stuart Mill*, 1:166, 475–79). I here follow Hollander.

[27] For an example, see Mill, letter to Arthur Helps, March 28, 1870, *Collected Works*, 17:1710.

[28] For an early articulation, see Mill, "Wakefield's 'The New British Province of South Australia,'" 740–41. Mill argued that emigration, while vital, remained insufficient (*Principles*, 194).

[29] Mill, "The Emigration Bill," *Examiner*, February 27, 1831, *Collected Works*, 22:271–72.

[30] For the debates over the issue, see H.J.M. Johnson, *British Emigration Policy, 1815–1830* (Oxford, 1972).

[31] Mill, "The New Colony," [1], *Examiner*, June 29, 1834, *Collected Works*, 23:733–34.

now be made to pay its own expenses; and whatever relief it can allow to the pressure of population against subsistence in our own country, will be clear gain—pure, unalloyed good."[32] Indeed he suggested that colonization was the most important factor in the progressive development of the working classes. It would, he argued in 1837, "produce a more immediate and obvious benefit to the industrious classes generally, and to the labouring class above all, than even the great constitutional changes which we are contending for."[33] It was more far-reaching, that is, than the extension of the franchise. Systematic colonization, combined with the repeal of the Corn Laws, would unleash the productive promise of the British economy and help to emancipate the "labouring class."[34]

Mill's most thorough discussion of systematic colonization can be found in the *Principles of Political Economy*, first published in 1848.

> The system is grounded on the important principle, that the degree of productiveness of land and labour depends on their being in due proportion to one another; that if a few persons in a newly-settled country attempt to occupy and appropriate a large district, or if each labourer becomes too soon an occupier and cultivator of land, there is a loss of productive power, and a great retardation of the progress of the colony in wealth and civilization.[35]

Yet despite this obvious problem, the "instinct . . . of appropriation" meant that emigrant laborers typically tried to secure as much land as possible, aiming to "become at once a proprietor." Consequently there were too few laborers to support the investment of capital. Systematic colonization would disrupt this self-defeating process, so that "each labourer is induced to work a certain number of years on hire" before assuming a proprietary role. This was necessary to create a "perpetual stock" of laborers for the provision of public goods—roads, canals, irrigation projects—and the development of thriving towns.[36] He planned to "check the premature occupation of land" and the dangerous "dispersion of people" by instituting a strict regime of land pricing. The basic idea was to sell "all unappropriated lands at a rather high price, the proceeds of which were to be expended in conveying emigrant labourers from the mother country." The income could finance colonial emigration, creating

---

[32] Mill, "The New Colony" [2], *Examiner*, July 6, 1834, *Collected Works*, 23:737.

[33] Mill, "The Sale of Colonial Land," *Sun*, February 22, 1837, *Collected Works*, 24:792.

[34] Mill, *Principles*, 711. See also Mill, "Torrens's Letter to Sir Robert Peel," *Spectator*, January 28, 1843, *Collected Works*, 24:841; Mill, "On the Necessity of the Uniting of the Question of Corn Laws with That of the Tithes," *Examiner*, December 23, 1832, *Collected Works*, 23:539. On emigration as "palliative," see Mill, "The Claims of Labour," *Edinburgh Review* [1845], *Collected Works*, 4:387.

[35] Mill, *Principles*, 958.

[36] Ibid., 958.

a steady flow of wage-laborers fit to service an expanding capitalist economy. Wakefield and Mill added further refinements. They insisted on the importance of urbanization for creating "civilized" communities.

> It is a beneficial check upon the tendency of the population of colonists to adopt the tastes and inclinations of savage life, and to disperse so widely as to lose all the advantages of commerce, of markets, of separation of employments, and combination of labour.[37]

Metropolitan concentration, not the frontier virtues of agrarian republicanism, offered the greatest moral and political promise.[38] Bourgeois modernity was urban. Likewise, they argued that it was vital to prioritize the emigration of young families to normalize social relations and accelerate population growth.[39] In short, they conjoined three different types of argument: a diagnosis of the social question, a prescription for solving it, and the identification of specific institutional mechanisms to realize their plans.

It is unsurprising that Wakefield's analysis drew Marx's attention. For Marx, "virgin" colonies offered the potential to serve as free spaces for labor. While Wakefield had identified correctly the "anti-capitalist cancer of the colonies," he sought to excise it by privatizing property. Wakefield's "great merit," Marx proclaimed, was to have

> . . . discovered in the Colonies the truth as to the conditions of the capitalist production in them. As the system of protection at its origin attempted to manufacture capitalists artificially in the mother country, so Wakefield's colonisation theory . . . attempted to effect the manufacture of wage workers in the Colonies.[40]

Note, though, that for Marx the "evils" of British settler colonialism lay chiefly in the spread of capitalist social relations rather than in the injustice of occupation itself.[41] He seemed to think that an uncorrupted form of colonial emigration might allow people to escape the relentlessly dehumanizing logic of modern capitalism. This pointed to an alternative, noncapitalist form of colonial romance.

Mill's advocacy of systematic colonization was not insulated from his wider social and political theory. In the next section I discuss how it related to his

---

[37] Ibid., 958–59, 965–66. See also Mill, letter to Cairnes, December 12, 1864, *Collected Works*, 15:1046.

[38] For the republican view, see chapters 2, 4, and 12, in this volume.

[39] Wakefield, *England and America*, 2:215–17; Mill, "The Emigration Bill," 273. See also Mill, "Female Emigrants," *Examiner*, February 26, 1832, *Collected Works*, 23:419.

[40] Marx, *Capital*, 753, 758.

[41] On Marx's views on empire more broadly, see Gareth Stedman Jones, "Radicalism and the Extra-European World," in *Victorian Visions of Global Order*, ed. Duncan Bell (Cambridge, 2007), 186–215.

views on character and nationality. Here, however, it is worth stressing that in the *Principles* the argument was embedded in an account of the legitimate role of government, and especially of the justified exceptions to the policy of *laissez-faire*. In his analysis of the "functions of government in general" in Book 5, Mill divided "the province of government" into "necessary" and "optional" aspects. The former were those functions that were "either inseparable from the idea of government, or are exercised habitually and without objection by all governments," while the latter were those "which it has been considered questionable whether governments should exercise them or not." This did not render the optional aspects unimportant, it meant only that the "expediency" of the government exercising those functions did not amount to necessity.[42] Mill was concerned here, as elsewhere, with a dual task: defending a version of Ricardian economic science whilst identifying legitimate exceptions to a libertarian interpretation of the functions of government. He challenged the view that the state should only provide protection against "force and fraud."

Mill introduced systematic colonization in a discussion of "cases in which public intervention may be necessary to give effect to the wishes of the persons interested."[43] These cases identify a collective action problem in which the uncoordinated (instrumentally) rational actions of individual agents resulted in suboptimal outcomes for everyone involved. While individuals might benefit in the short term, the colony was damaged by existing emigration practices.

> However beneficial it might be to the colony in the aggregate, and to each individual composing it, that no one should occupy more land than he can properly cultivate, nor become a proprietor until there are other labourers ready to take his place in working for hire; it can never be the interest of an individual to exercise this forbearance, unless he is assured that others will not do so too ... It is the interest of each to do what is good for all, but only if others will do likewise.[44]

The lack of guaranteed reciprocity meant that there was an overriding case for government regulation. If colonization was to benefit everybody, the enterprise must "from its commencement" be undertaken "with the foresight and enlarged views of philosophical legislators."[45] Here we see an instance of Mill's long-standing belief in the role of disinterested expertise. Just as he thought that India was best governed by the bureaucracy of the East India Company,

---

[42] Mill, *Principles*, 800.

[43] Ibid., 965–67. He also discusses hours of labor. On Mill and collective action, see Richard Tuck, *Free Riding* (Cambridge, MA, 2008), 133–35.

[44] Mill, *Principles*, 959.

[45] Ibid., 963. See also Mill's letter to John Campbell, April 4, 1866, *Collected Works*, 26:1155.

and that representative democracy was best regulated by the expertise of the enlightened, so he also thought that colonial development needed to be directed by a class of "philosophical legislators" who understood the art and the science of political economy, and who recognized the duty to seek the improvement of humanity. The need for such legislators only increased as the century wore on, as the colonies grew in strength and size, and as their institutions increasingly diverged from those in Britain. In a letter written in 1870, for example, he argued that because colonial societies were "much more democratic than our own" it required imagination to support them. "[O]nly very exceptional persons in our higher and middle classes . . . could either reconcile themselves to it or have the foresight and mental adaptability required for guiding and organising the formation of such a community."[46] By then he had come to realize, much to his dismay, that such persons were very rare.

Whereas Mill's colonial advocacy in the 1830s and early 1840s had principally emphasized the domestic benefits of systematic colonization—its ability to address the "social problem" in Britain—this began to change in the late 1840s. The shift was apparent in the *Principles*, and became increasingly pronounced in the following years. In the *Principles* Mill stressed, in a way that he had not done previously, the global economic benefits of (British) systematic colonization.

> To appreciate the benefits of colonization, it should be considered in its relation, not to a single country, but to the collective economical interests of the human race. The question is in general treated too exclusively as one of distribution; of relieving one labour market and supplying another. It is this, but it is also a question of production, and of the most efficient employment of the productive resources of the world.[47]

Laborers in the colonies were more productive than those in Britain, and their migration would expand the colonial economies while easing the restrictions on domestic growth.[48] This in turn would catalyze further productivity. Everybody would benefit. While this line of argument had been implicit in the logic of Mill's earlier writings, he had placed little weight on it. From the late 1840s onwards it moved to center stage.

This shift in emphasis was the product of a series of changes in British, colonial, and global politics. This confluence of events reoriented Mill's normative account of the main purposes—the ultimate aims—of colonization. In 1846, the Corn Laws were repealed. In 1848, Britain avoided the revolutionary tumult that gripped the continent, in part because of the "safety valve"

---

[46] Mill, letter to Arthur Helps, March 28, 1870, *Collected Works*, 17:1710.

[47] Mill, *Principles*, 963.

[48] Ibid. Mill had long utilized the argument about differential labor productivity. "The Emigration Bill," 272.

provided by the empire.[49] The Chartist agitation ended in a damp squib. The economy prospered, while the "social question" receded from the forefront of political consciousness. The ghost of Malthus was temporarily exiled.[50] It was also a period during which the colonies were granted self-governing status (under the aegis of "responsible government"), and in which their populations and economies grew rapidly.[51] Mill saw confirmation of his optimistic predictions. Writing to an Australian correspondent in 1856, he was cheered by the fact that the colonies "seem to be the most prosperous and rapidly progressive communities." This "unexampled growth," was chiefly the result of the "Wakefield system."[52] A glorious new era was unfolding. Overcoming obdurate politicians and an indifferent public, outfoxing recalcitrant colonial officials and fighting the historical baggage of the pernicious "old colonial system," the once embattled colonial reformers had triumphed. This was the apotheosis of colonial romanticism.

As well as triggering a shift in the purposes of colonization, the change in empirical conditions also forced Mill to reassess the significance of specific elements of Wakefield's scheme. In the 1865 edition of the *Principles*, for example, he added a new passage to his discussion of the most effective ways to relieve pressure on the labor market. The onset of free trade, combined with a "new fact of modern history," had transformed the situation. While his argument for systematic colonization remained "true in principle," material advances had rendered it less urgent. "The extraordinary cheapening of the means of transport . . . and the knowledge which nearly all classes of the people have now acquired . . . of the condition of the labour market in remote parts of the world, have opened up a spontaneous emigration from these islands to the new countries."[53] The new dispensation, then, had both material and epistemic dimensions. The lowering of costs, combined with an increase in wages, meant that more people than ever had the economic *capacity* to emigrate without government support. As such, one of the key pillars of the

[49] Miles Taylor, "The 1848 Revolutions and the British Empire," *Past & Present*, 166 (2000), 146–80.

[50] Hilton, *A Mad, Bad, and Dangerous People?*; Anthony Howe, *Free Trade and Liberal England, 1846–1946* (Oxford, 1998)

[51] Increasing political independence was accompanied, however, by growing economic dependence. P. J. Cain and A. G. Hopkins, *British Imperialism, 1688–2000*, 2nd ed. (London, 2002), ch. 8.

[52] Letter to Hardy (1856), 511. This was despite the fact, Mill stated, that the plan had only ever been properly executed in New Zealand. He wanted to show that Australian growth could not be explained by the gold rush in the early 1850s. He also claimed that the "opinions" of the Australians were generally "ahead" of those in Britain. Letter to Henry Chapman, October 5, 1863, *Collected Works*, 15:888. Moreover, he wrote that he and Harriet "read every book we can get about the Australian colonies always with fresh interest" (Letter to Hardy [1856], 511).

[53] Mill, *Principles*, 378. Cf. Karl Marx and Friedrich Engels, *The Communist Manifesto* [1848], ed. Gareth Stedman Jones (Harmondsworth, 2002), 224.

Wakefield system—the self-financing provision—was less relevant than before.[54] But equally important was *knowledge*, and in particular a growing awareness of the opportunities available.[55] The novel communications technologies that were beginning to shrink the world in the imagination of Mill's contemporaries simultaneously aided in the diffusion of information, which made ocean-spanning travel seem appealing and feasible. This "new fact" offered further openings for civilizing the British, and perhaps most of all for educating the workers into responsible citizenship. The respite had, he argued, "granted to this overcrowded country a temporary breathing time, capable of being employed in accomplishing those moral and intellectual improvements in all classes of the people, the very poorest included, which would render improbable any relapse into the over-peopled state."[56] Moreover, the perceived change in conditions meant that political priorities had shifted: "[O]ur politicians," he wrote, "have grown more afraid of under than of over population."[57] As a result, any impetus to stimulate emigration would now have to come from the colonies.

Soon after Mill added this qualifier to the *Principles*, he was perturbed to discover that his arguments for the protection of infant industries were being utilized by advocates of protectionism in the United States and the colonies.[58] He engaged in an extensive correspondence on the issue—several of his letters were printed in the colonial press—rebutting the suggestion that his arguments applied there.[59] This led him to rethink aspects of his position. Indeed, he indicated in a couple of letters written in 1868 that he no longer supported protection, preferring instead the idea of an annual grant from the treasury.[60] Once again, we witness his prescriptions—aspects of his art—shifting in light of unforeseen developments.

From the start of his career, then, Mill advocated systematic colonization. During the 1830s, when the economic plight of Britain seemed desperate, he

[54] See also Hollander, *The Economics of John Stuart Mill*, 2:754–55, 756–57.

[55] See, in general, Robert Grant, *Representations of British Emigration, Colonisation and Settlement* (Basingstoke, 2005).

[56] The argument is found in Mill, *Principles*, vol. 5, ch. 10, sec. 1.

[57] Mill, letter to W. L. Johns, January 22, 1867, *Collected Works*, 16:1230. And conversely, "the colonies will not allow us to cast our paupers into them." Letter to Henry Chapman, January 14, 1870, *Collected Works*, 17:1685.

[58] See here Mill, *Principles*, vol. 5, ch. 10, sec. 1.

[59] See, for example, his letters to Frederick Miles Edge (of the *Chicago Tribune*), February 26, 1866, *Collected Works*, 16:1150–51; Henry Soden, May 2, 1865, *Collected Works*, 16:1043–44; George Kenyon Holden, July 5, 1868, *Collected Works*, 16:1419–20. He notes in a letter to the political economist J. E. Cairnes, on February 4, 1865 (*Collected Works*, 16:989–90), that he had modified various passages in the 6th edition (5:919–21) to "give a fuller expression of my meaning."

[60] Mill, letter to Archibald Michie, December 7, 1868, *Collected Works*, 16:1516; letter to Edward Stafford, December 11, 1868, *Collected Works*, 16:1520–21.

viewed it chiefly as a means to answer the "social question." Yet the situation was dynamic: the rapid development of the colonies and the stabilization of Britain rendered this narrow justification obsolete. His account of the utility of colonization therefore shifted along with his interpretation of empirical conditions. In particular, we witness two moves. First, his arguments from political economy increasingly emphasized the universal benefits of colonization. And second, as I explore in the rest of this chapter, the political economy arguments were increasingly reinforced, if not displaced, by a new range of geopolitical and ethical concerns.

Colonial Autonomy, Character, and Civilization

While both Mill and Wakefield agreed on the underlying economic causes of the crisis afflicting Britain, as well as the best remedy for it, they presented different visions of the future, although this was never made explicit. Wakefield was motivated by fear of revolution. In *England and America* (1833), the text that had drawn Marx's ire, he warned of the impending dangers:

> [F]or a country now situated like England, in which the ruling and the subject orders are no longer separated by a middle class, and in which the subject order, composing the bulk of the people, are in a state of gloomy discontent arising from excessive numbers; for such a country, one chief end of colonization is to prevent tumults, to keep the peace, to maintain order, to uphold confidence in the security of property, to hinder interruptions to the regular course of industry and trade, to avert the terrible evils which, in a country like England, could not but follow any serious political convulsion.[61]

His conception of colonization was ultimately more conservative than Mill's. He wanted to transpose hierarchical British social relations onto the colonies, recreating the new societies in the image of the old. Mill's vision was dynamic; he viewed the colonies as spaces for innovation and forms of progressive self-fashioning. They provided an escape from the parochialism and class-bound rigidities of British life, allowing—even demanding—experimentation in ways of living.

Experimentation was central to Mill's account of the development of "character," both individual and collective.[62] For Mill, character was not a biological given, but rather a product of the environment, and throughout his writings he stressed the "extraordinary susceptibility of human nature to external

---

[61] Wakefield, *England and America*, 2:105–6.

[62] Stefan Collini, *Public Moralists* (Oxford, 1991), ch. 3; Janice Carlisle, *John Stuart Mill and the Writing of Character* (Athens, 1991); Duncan Kelly, *The Propriety of Liberty* (Princeton, 2010); and, on India, Pitts, *A Turn to Empire*, ch. 5.

influences."[63] He saw the colonies, I would argue, as laboratories of character development, as vast case studies of his proposed science of "ethology."[64] Systematic colonization offered the opportunity to create new advanced political communities, populated by industrious, confident, democratic individuals. This points to a significant discrepancy between Mill's account of colonization and his views on India. Uday Singh Mehta suggests that liberalism "found the concrete place of its dreams" in empire.[65] For Mill, though, different elements of the empire spawned different dreams. India was a site for the reformist utilitarian project, for the mission to bring civilized enlightenment to a "backward" corner of the earth. Imperial governance, on this view, was a political technology that aimed to reshape the people who already lived there, bringing into being a different form of life, new modes of subjectivity, a fresh cultural-political constellation. Settler colonization, on the other hand, did not aim to transform the character of indigenous populations, or even to radically refashion the emigrants. It sought instead to provide an environment in which their existing civilizational potential could be realized. Such environments were conducive to the production of virtuous individuals and communities. The romance of colonialism was thus premised on the ethological opportunities opened up in distant "virgin" lands.

While Mill spent much of the early 1830s focusing on Australia, in the second half of the decade his attention was increasingly drawn across the Atlantic to Canada, which he had previously regarded as one of the decaying "colonies on the old system."[66] The rebellions in Canada in 1837–38 provided a rare chance to refound a corrupt polity. For Mill, the crisis was never simply about the status of Upper and Lower Canada. After all, he assumed that in the future Canada would achieve full political independence. It was important for two other reasons: the legitimacy of imperial rule *in general* and the fate of British political radicalism. The colonies and the metropole were once again figured as part of the same analytic field.

"[I]n an evil hour," Mill later reflected, the Canada question "crossed the path of radicalism."[67] The lightning rod here was the unlikely figure of Lord Durham. A vain, sickly, hugely wealthy scion of the Whig aristocracy, Durham had managed to alienate his colleagues in government while attaining

[63] Mill, *The Subjection of Women* [1869], *Collected Works*, 21:277; cf. Mill, *System of Logic, Collected Works*, vol. 8, bk. 6, pp. 904–5.

[64] On Mill's writings on women, democratic institutions, and himself, as ethological "case studies" see Terence Ball, "The Formation of Character," *Polity*, 33 (2000), 25–48.

[65] Mehta, *Liberalism and Empire*, 37. For a critical discussion of this argument, see chapter 2 in this volume.

[66] Mill, "New Australian Colony," *Morning Chronicle*, October 23, 1834, *Collected Works*, 23:750.

[67] Letter to Edward Lytton-Bulwer, March 5, 1838, *Collected Works*, 13:382. See William Thomas, *The Philosophic Radicals* (Oxford, 1979), ch. 8; Michael Turner, "Radical Agitation and the Canada Question in British Politics, 1837–1841," *Historical Research*, 79 (2006), 90–114.

great popularity among liberal and radical thinkers. Mill viewed Durham as a potential leader for the Radical party that he was attempting to create. In December 1837, news reached Britain that the French Canadians of Lower Canada had risen up against the colonial government. The rebellion was swiftly extinguished.[68] Durham, a man who had previously shown little interest in colonial affairs, was appointed Governor-General and instructed to resolve the situation. One product of his brief stay in Canada—he resigned in October 1838 following government censure of some of his activities—was his report on "the affairs of British North America," which came to be seen as one of the key documents in nineteenth-century British imperial history.[69]

The Canadian rebellions threatened an imperial legitimation crisis. For Mill the moral justification of the settler empire was different from that of the Raj. Empire in general could be justified if, and only if, it benefitted those subjected to it, but if those subjects lacked sufficient rationality—if they failed to pass a (fluid) threshold of civilization—then they could claim little control over their own form of government. Unless or until they passed that threshold, their destinies were best left to more enlightened peoples. This was, of course, how Mill saw India, and it generated a paternalist justification of despotism.[70] In settler communities, on the other hand, the purportedly civilized character of the populations meant that questions of recognition and reciprocity were paramount. The colonies were legitimate expressions of political power only insofar as this was accepted by those they ruled over. In this sense, the relationship was voluntaristic. Colonial rule depended on a stable normative order in which everyone knew their assigned place, and challenges to this order broke the compact between governments and subjects. Mill feared that an inappropriate response to the Canadian rebellion would threaten the legitimacy of the colonial empire. Britain, he argued, should treat its (settler) colonial populations fairly, on both intrinsic grounds (because justice demanded it) and for more instrumental reasons. It was vital that Britain maintained—and was *seen* to maintain—its reputation for "wisdom and foresight, for justice, clemency, and magnanimity" in the "eyes of all nations."[71] Legitimacy was as much a matter of perception as right action.

In line with many of his fellow radical liberals, Mill argued that the Canadians, while imprudent, had a "just cause" for revolting, for they had chal-

---

[68] A smaller uprising followed in Upper Canada in December 1837. See Peter Burroughs, *The Canadian Crisis and British Colonial Policy, 1828–1841* (London, 1972); P. A. Buckner, *The Transition to Responsible Government* (Westport, 1985).

[69] C. P. Lucas, ed., *Lord Durham's Report on the Affairs of British North America* [1839] (Oxford, 1912). Wakefield played a significant role in formulating the report. For a harsh indictment, see Ged Martin, *The Durham Report and British Policy* (Cambridge, 1972).

[70] Pitts, *A Turn to Empire*, ch. 5; and chapter 12 in this volume.

[71] Mill, "Lord Durham and His Assailants," *London and Westminster Review* (1838), *Collected Works*, 6: 448.

lenged a tyrannical system of government, an oppressive "foreign yoke": "They are styled rebels and traitors. The words are totally inapplicable to them."[72] The justice of the rebellion was a product of the illegal and immoral way in which the British government had overridden Canadian constitutional arrangements. "The people of Canada," argued Mill, "had against the people of England legitimate cause of war. They had the provocation which, on every received principle of public law, is a breach of the conditions of allegiance."[73] He insisted that it was important to "understand" and to address the legitimate grievances of the rebels. Refusal to do so undermined the legitimacy of British rule. He saw Durham's mission as an opportunity to transform Canada from an unjustly governed polity into a model colony. It was a "tabula rasa," open to Durham to "inscribe what character he pleases."[74]

Following what he assumed were the outlines of Durham's proposal, Mill argued for the creation of a broadly federal system uniting Lower and Upper Canada.[75] This would guarantee political justice to both sides. With skillful institutional design, minority protection could be assured. Moreover, in the long run it would also help to eliminate one of the residual problems encountered in Canada: the problem of nationalities. A positive side effect of federation, he claimed, was that it provided the "only legitimate means of destroying the so-much-talked-of nationality of the French Canadians," compelling them to see themselves not as a "separate body" but as "an integral portion of a larger whole." Combining the best characteristics of each "race" would create a "nationality of country," a sense of commitment to the state as opposed to the particularism of ethnic interests. It would forge them into "British Americans."[76] But it was not to be. Following Durham's humiliating resignation, Mill attempted to defend him, suggesting that he had demonstrated his fitness to lead the "great reform party of the empire."[77] This represented the triumph of hope over reality. By 1840 the plan was dead: Durham's activities

[72] Mill, "Radical Party and Canada," *London and Westminster Review* (1838), *Collected Works*, 6:414. See also Mill, "Penal Code for India," *London and Westminster Review* (1838), *Collected Works*, 30:30.

[73] Mill, "Radical Party and Canada," 417. "A constitution, once conferred, is sacred" (418). The point at issue was a series of punitive resolutions passed at Westminster in March 1837, which removed various powers from the Lower Canadian assembly, including the power of refusing to grant money for local administration, originally enshrined in the 1791 Constitution.

[74] Ibid.," 429.

[75] Ibid., 433–34. See also Mill's letter to John Robertson, December 28, 1838, *Collected Works*, 13:393–34. Mill's article on "Lord Durham and His Assailants" was heavily shaped by Charles Buller's inaccurate account of Durham's plans. Thomas, *The Philosophic Radicals*, 402–3.

[76] Mill, "Lord Durham and His Assailants," 458, 459. On Mill's "heterotic" view of national absorption, see Georgios Varouxakis, *Mill on Nationality* (London, 2002), esp. 15–19. Compare this with Will Kymlicka, *Multicultural Citizenship* (Oxford, 1995), 53, where Mill is accused of advocating "coercive assimilation."

[77] Mill, "Lord Durham and His Assailants," 461. See also Mill, *Autobiography* [1873], *Collected Works*, 1:164–66, 223.

had alienated many radicals, and he was not interested in the role that Mill envisaged for him.[78]

The intersection of race, nationality, and colonization can also be witnessed in Mill's analysis of the Irish famine a few years after the Canadian turmoil. As Pitts observes, he had a far more sympathetic understanding of the travails of the Irish peasantry than he did of the Indians, ascribing to the former "a moral dignity and rationality" he never accorded the latter.[79] Yet the Irish still remained subordinate in Mill's imperial topography; his sympathy did not translate into granting them civilizational equality. Once again, his comments on this issue emerged in relation to a set of ongoing arguments about how best to respond to crisis. Did state-sponsored colonization offer an apposite solution to the problems of Ireland? In a letter penned to Tocqueville's travelling companion, Gustave Beaumont, in October 1839, Mill argued that it did.[80] Yet by the mid-1840s, as the famine began to wreak its terrible havoc, he had changed his mind. While acknowledging the very serious problems in Ireland, he contended that they could be resolved by enacting a system of peasant proprietorship on reclaimed waste lands.[81]

He offered two reasons why systematic colonization was inappropriate in Ireland. First, it was prohibitively expensive: there were simply too many people who would need financial support to emigrate. The second reason goes to the heart of Mill's views on race, nationality, and ethology. He did not consider the Irish suitable apostles of civilization; their characters were too deformed by their blighted environment. This differentiated them from the settler populations in Australia, New Zealand, and Canada. In a newspaper article published in October 1846, he argued that "it is not well to select as missionaries of civilization a people who, in so great a degree, yet remain to be civilized." Encouraging Irish emigration would retard the progressive potential of colonization. "It is a serious question," he continued, "whether, in laying the foundation of new nations beyond the sea, it be right that the Irish branch of the human family should be the predominant ingredient." He thought it "desirable" that the Irish should "enter into the admixture," as the Saxon race needed "to be tempered by amalgamation with the more excitable and imaginative constitution and the more generous impulses of its Celtic kinsfolk," yet this process had to remain asymmetric, the Irish qualities tempering but not displacing the dominant Saxon racial configuration.[82] Mill's argument centered, once again, on the issue of character. The modern Irish character was deformed by economic exploitation and religious subservience. The Irish, he

[78] For Mill's recognition of this, see his letter to Robertson, April 6, 1839, *Collected Works*, 13:396–97.

[79] Pitts, *A Turn to Empire*, 148.

[80] Letter to Beaumont, October 18, 1839, *Collected Works*, 17:1990–92.

[81] See, in general, Bruce Kinzer, *England's Disgrace?* (Toronto, 2001), esp. chs. 2–3.

[82] Mill, "The Condition of Ireland," (11), *Morning Chronicle*, October, 26, 1846, *Collected Works*, 24:915.

continued, lack "individual hardihood, resource, and self-reliance"; they demanded instead "to be led and governed." And, moreover, they had been "made lawless and disorderly" by centuries of British misrule.[83] With this common liberal move, Mill simultaneously acknowledged an earlier British injustice while employing its results to undermine political claims in the present. Not only did the Irish fail to display the moral resources necessary for successful colonization, they now exhibited the potential to disrupt the colonial order through lack of discipline, even criminal excess. Their behavior would give colonization a bad name. Instead, he looked elsewhere: "The English and Scotch are the proper stuff for the pioneers of the wilderness."[84] Racial difference, figured as civilizational capacity, structured Mill's analytical field, identifying a hierarchy of peoples ranked according to their ability to fabricate civilization in wild and distant locations.

Melancholic Colonialism and the Pathos of Distance

During the last decade and a half of his life we witness a distinct shift in the *tone* of Mill's colonial writings. The romance faded, to be replaced by something more somber, even downcast. We also witness an increasing emphasis placed on noneconomic arguments. The most extensive analysis of colonization in Mill's later career is found in chapter 18 of the *Considerations on Representative Government* (1861). The direct economic benefits of colonization play only a subsidiary role in his analysis. His earlier concern with the urgency of emigration is also absent. Indeed Mill suggested that the material costs generated by the colonies offset the benefits. "England derives little advantage, except in prestige, from her dependencies; and the little she does derive is quite outweighed by the expense they cost her, and the dissemination they necessitate of her naval and military force."[85] Not only was it expensive to maintain a colonial empire, it was also potentially dangerous, leading to extensive global military commitments. Imperial overstretch beckoned. "Great Britain," Mill concluded, "could do perfectly well without her colonies." Despite this, he argued that the colonies were still valuable, for they produced a wide range of other benefits, both for Britain and (perhaps more importantly) the world.

Mill starts the chapter by noting that only in the "present generation" had the British realized the "true principle" of colonial government. Previously

---

[83] Ibid., 973.

[84] Mill, (25), *Morning Chronicle*, December 2, 1846, *Collected Works*, 24:973. Mill argued that the abject conditions meant that "Ireland was once more a tabula rasa, on which we might have inscribed what we pleased." Letter to the *Examiner*, May 1848, *Collected Works*, 25:1098.

[85] Mill, *Considerations*, 565. For his defense of the colonial system, see also his letter to Cairnes, November 8, 1864, 964–66.

they had meddled incessantly in colonial affairs. This was a "corollary" of the "vicious theory" of colonization that had long guided European policy, and which was premised on the view that colonies existed primarily for economic exploitation. The habit of meddling had outlasted the mercantile system, and it was the "persistence in domineering" that had caused the Canadian rebellion. However, out of this disaster had flowed enlightenment, for the foresight of Durham, Wakefield, Buller, and Roebuck—and of course Mill himself—had led to the abandonment of the "vicious theory." Durham's report had inaugurated a "new era" in which the colonies were granted "the fullest measure of internal self-government." This system bore little relation to previous modes of coercive colonial rule. Indeed if the colonies were to remain part of the British imperial system, it had to be on a voluntary basis. "[O]n every principle of morality and justice," he argued, "she [Great Britain] ought to consent to their separation, should the time come when, after full trial of the best form of union, they deliberately desire to be dissevered."[86] The lessons of the American Revolution were etched deeply into Mill's political consciousness.

Mill offered three separate reasons for maintaining the colonial empire. First, he sketched an argument about what international relations theorists refer to as the "security dilemma." The dilemma arises when two or more states coexisting in a condition of anarchy—lacking a global leviathan to regulate their interactions—are drawn into a conflictual posture despite their (potentially) nonaggressive intent.[87] In a condition of uncertainty, political leaders are compelled to engage in actions that can inadvertently generate further insecurity. The greater the number of sovereign units populating the international system, the greater the probability of conflict. Mill thought that the colonial empire helped to mitigate this problem. It was, he argued, a step "towards universal peace, and general friendly cooperation among nations." He offered two distinct arguments. In the first instance, it "renders war impossible among a large number of otherwise independent communities." It dampened the dilemma by reducing the number of units in the system. Second, it prevented any of the colonies "from being absorbed into a foreign state, and becoming a source of additional aggressive strength to some rival power, either more despotic or closer at hand, which might not always be so unambitious or so pacific as Great Britain."[88] It restrained the growth of potentially belligerent states while maintaining British predominance. A stable international system enhanced British security, as did the inability of other states to absorb the colonies. The rest of the world benefitted, moreover, for despite its faults Britain remained the most progressive of nations.

---

[86] Mill, *Considerations*, 562–63, 565.

[87] For a useful analysis of the idea, see Ken Booth and Nicholas Wheeler, *The Security Dilemma* (Basingstoke, 2007).

[88] Mill, *Considerations*, 565.

Mill's second reason for maintaining the colonial system concerned the moral and economic exemplarity of Britain's commitment to free trade. The existence of the colonies "keeps the markets of the different countries open to one another, and prevents that mutual exclusion by hostile tariffs, which none of the great communities of mankind, except England, have yet completely outgrown." Britain could offer an alternative, and superior, model of economic organization to the protectionism that was sweeping Europe and the United States. Mill's final argument focused on liberty. The colonial empire, he contended,

> ... has the advantage, specially valuable at the present time, of adding to the moral influence, and weight in the councils of the world, of the Power which, of all in existence, best understands liberty—and whatever may have been its errors in the past, has attained to more of conscience and moral principle in its dealings with foreigners, than any other great nation seems either to conceive as possible, or recognise as desirable.[89]

This conceited picture was a staple of British political thought. The British frequently saw themselves—and liked to think that they were seen by others—as the avatars of liberty. Consequently, the greater the reach of their institutions, the greater the benefits for all. Even Mill, a man deeply critical of many aspects of his society, held this as an article of political faith.

As I have suggested already, until the early 1860s Mill presented a remarkably optimistic picture of the potential of settler colonialization. This was colonization as romance: an uplifting story of progressive forces overcoming numerous obstacles, supplanting a "vicious" theory with an "enlightened" one, and consequently heralding a bright new dawn for the peoples of Britain and the world. Yet in the last decade of his life his optimism faded, to be replaced by a more disenchanted, anxious stance. In part this was because reality had caught up with the fantasy: as the colonies grew in population and power, and as they secured significant political autonomy, Mill realized that they were failing to play their allotted roles. There were three main problems. First, the colonies were becoming increasingly protectionist, thus adopting an economic system that he had spent decades inveighing against. Second, the new colonial authorities had failed to deal properly with the land question. Finally, and perhaps most devastatingly, the colonists themselves seemed to be resorting to barbarism in their treatment of indigenous peoples. Granting colonial autonomy had undercut the civilizing potential of colonization. When enacted, sound liberal principles came into destructive conflict.

An early hint of Mill's disquiet can be found in the *Considerations*. He observed that an example of "how liberal a construction has been given to the

---

[89] Ibid. On the debate over the morality of free trade, see Frank Trentmann, *Free Trade Nation* (Oxford, 2008).

distinction between imperial and colonial questions," was seen in the "uncontrolled disposal" of "unappropriated lands" in the colonies. "[W]ithout injustice," Mill lamented, the land could have been employed "for the greatest advantage of future emigrants from all parts of the empire."[90] In his correspondence he was adamant that in failing to fully implement systematic colonization the new colonies were undermining their own developmental potential. The "unoccupied" lands, he complained in 1871, should have been "reserved as the property of the empire at large until much greater progress had been made in peopling them."[91]

During the 1860s, Mill became increasingly critical of the violent behavior of the settlers.[92] While he had occasionally lamented brutality in the past, his earlier work was marked by a notable silence over colonial violence. During the 1830s and 1840s, the years of his most intense interest in Australia, some of the colonists were perpetrating the genocide of the Tasmanians, and engaging in widespread aggression against indigenous populations elsewhere.[93] Although this topic was discussed in Britain, Mill failed to address it. It would have disrupted his colonial romance. During the final decade of his life, however, he returned repeatedly to the topic, though never in print. The "common English abroad," he wrote, were "intensely contemptuous of what they consider inferior races" and sought to attain their ends by "bullying and blows."[94] This injustice threatened the normative justification of colonization. Mill appeared genuinely perturbed, yet he pulled back from arguing that colonization was *inherently* cruel, and thus from abandoning the colonial project. (His continued commitment to this project may explain why he refrained from publishing his concerns.) Instead, he implied that certain categories of people—oafish settlers and inexperienced officials among them—were more prone to violence than others. With the right policies and people the injustices could be corrected. This is an example of what Cheryl Welch calls "antiseptic containment," the attempt to confine colonial violence in a quarantined space.[95] By locating responsibility in this manner, Mill denied the possibility

[90] Mill, *Considerations*, 563–64, 92.

[91] Mill, letter to Arthur Patchett Martin, October 10, 1871, *Collected Works*, 32:232. But, he argued, "[t]he renunciation of them was by no means a necessary consequence of the introduction of responsible government" (232). See also letter to Chapman (1870), 1865–66.

[92] As detailed in Smits, "John Stuart Mill on the Antipodes." Cf. Pitts, *A Turn to Empire*, 159–60. For an argument that there is a general shift in justifications of British imperial rule during the closing decades of the century, see Karuna Mantena, *Alibis of Empire*.

[93] Benjamin Madley, "From Terror to Genocide," *Journal of British Studies*, 47 (2008), 77–106. The issue was raised, for example, in Herman Merivale's *Lectures on Colonisation and Colonies*, 2:150. Mill certainly read the second (1861) edition of these lectures. Letter to J. E. Cairnes, November 8, 1864, *Collected Works*, 15:647–48.

[94] Letter to A. M. Francis (1869), 1599. See also the following letters: to Robert Pharazyn, August 21, 1866, *Collected Works*, 16:1194–96; to Henry Chapman, August 7, 1866, *Collected Works*, 16: 1135–36; to Charlotte Manning, January 14, 1870, *Collected Works*, 17:1685–87.

[95] Welch, "Colonial Violence and the Rhetoric of Evasion," 251–52.

that violence and injustice were systemic. The main problem for Mill, and the source of his despondency, was that those best placed to control the colonists—the Crown government in London—no longer had the political power to do so. Rather than leading to progress, colonial autonomy facilitated injustice. This profound tension remained unresolved at the time of his death.

One final issue came to the fore in the 1860s, and it again goes to the heart of some core issues in Mill's political thinking. This concerned the most appropriate form of political organization suitable for coordinating a globe-spanning colonial empire. In the *Considerations*, Mill argued that it already constituted a weak quasi-federal political order. "Their union with Great Britain is the slightest kind of federal union; but not a strictly equal federation, the mother country retaining to itself the powers of a Federal Government, though reduced in practice to their very narrowest limits." This system was defensible, but it meant that the colonists had "no voice" in vital areas of foreign policy, above all in questions of war and peace.[96] In denying that the Irish should be accorded self-government, Mill explained that they were actually better off than the semi-autonomous Canadians, for through their incorporation in Westminster they "had something to say in the affairs of the empire," whereas Canada was but a dependency" and consequently voiceless. "A union such as this," he concluded, "can only exist as a temporary expedient, between countries which look forward to separation as soon as the weaker is able to stand alone, and which care not how soon it arrives."[97] Throughout the nineteenth century, various constitutional schemes had been proposed to give colonial governments an increased role in imperial decision-making, thus consolidating the colonial connection. Some advocated the representation of the colonies at Westminster, or, more radical still, the creation of a new supreme imperial legislature. The latter of these options was, Mill observed, a plan to constitute a "perfectly equal federation." But he dismissed further political integration. The idea was doomed to fail, he argued, for an equal federation of the colonies and Great Britain was so inconsistent with the "rational principles of government" that it is "doubtful if they have been seriously accepted as a possibility by any reasonable thinker." Quite simply, "[e]ven for strictly federative purposes, the conditions do not exist, which we have seen to be essential to a federation." The main obstacle was physical distance.

> Countries separated by half the globe do not present the natural conditions for being under one government, or even members of one federation. If they had sufficiently the same interests, they have not, and never can have, a sufficient habit of taking counsel together. They are not part

[96] Mill, *Considerations*, 564. A similar account of colonial "quasi-federalism" can be found in L. T. Hobhouse, *Democracy and Reaction* [1904], ed. P. F. Clarke (Brighton, 1972), 154. Cf. Bell, "The Victorian Idea of a Global State."

[97] Mill, "England and Ireland" [1868], 4th ed. 1869, *Collected Works*, 6:524–25.

of the same public; they do not discuss and deliberate in the same arena, but apart, and have only a most imperfect knowledge of what passes in the minds of one another. They neither know each other's objects, nor have confidence in each other's principles of conduct.

Representatives from Canada and Australia, he continued, "could not know, or feel any sufficient concern for, the interests, opinions, or wishes of the English, Irish or Scotch."[98] The size and spatial extent of the "public" was ultimately constrained by the immutability of physical space. Rational deliberation, the key to democratic development, was impossible across such vast expanses, as was the formation of a substantive political (national) identity.[99] It was cognitively impossible. Mill defended, then, a variant of Edmund Burke's influential argument from nature against colonial representation: "*Opposuit natura*—I cannot remove the barriers of the creation."[100] Similar arguments were adumbrated by Adam Smith, who once referred to British colonists living in North America as "strangers," and by Bentham, who asked incredulously of colonists whether it was to their "advantage to be governed by a people who never know, nor ever can know, either their inclinations or their wants."[101] On this view, which Mill reiterated until his death, geography circumscribed the spatial extent of political community. "I do not think," he wrote to a correspondent in 1871, "that the federal principle can be worked successfully when the different members of the confederacy are scattered all over the world," and he concluded that "the English people would prefer separation to an equal federation."[102]

The importance of physical space—and in particular of what we might call the pathos of distance—runs through Mill's colonial writings. We have already seen that Mill (following Wakefield) insisted that spatial dispersion undermined the potential of civilization.[103] Moreover, he argued that the role of distance was vital in shaping British attitudes toward various parts of the imperial system. This was one of the reasons why they were less prepared to tolerate dissent in Ireland than in Canada. "Canada is a great way off and British

---

[98] Mill, *Considerations*, 564, 565. Mill thought that a "loose federation" of the European states was a future possibility: letter to E. Cliffe Leslie, August 18, 1860, *Collected Works*, 15:703; letter to M. C. Halstead, January 19, 1871, *Collected Works*, 17:1800–1801.

[99] On the importance of deliberation in his political philosophy, see Nadia Urbinati, *Mill on Democracy* (Chicago, 2002).

[100] Edmund Burke, "Speech on Conciliation with America" (March 22, 1775), in *The Writings and Speeches of Edmund Burke*, ed. W. Elofson and John Woods (Oxford, 1996), 3:152.

[101] Smith, *Wealth of Nations*, 622; Jeremy Bentham, "Emancipate Your Colonies" [1830], in *Rights, Representation, and Reform*, ed. Philip Schofield, Catherine Pease-Watkin, and Cyprian Blamire (Oxford, 2002), 292.

[102] Mill, letter to Arthur Patchett Martin (1871), 233. See also, Mill, letter to Henry Chapman (1870), 1865.

[103] A point also made in Mill, "Civilization," *Collected Works*, 18:117–49.

rulers can tolerate much in a place from which they are not afraid that the contagion may spread to England."[104] Finally, the remoteness of the scattered elements of the empire—"at the distance of half the globe" from Britain[105]—had profound psychosocial consequences. One implication of Mill's "associationist" conception of character formation, albeit one that he never discussed, was that the colonies would never be suitable for full integration into a globe-spanning British colonial polity. While civilization could be transplanted, it would invariably assume different and increasingly divergent forms across the world, as it adapted to the local environment and developed its own constellation of institutions and *moeurs*. Over time, then, the underlying cultural unity necessary for maintaining a healthy political community would dissolve.

It was the argument from nature, above all, that marked the difference between Mill's promotion of the colonial empire and the proselytizers of the following generation. Mill himself had intimated change in an extraordinary letter in 1866:

> One of the many causes which make the age in which we are living so very important in the life of the human race—almost, indeed, the turning point of it—is that so many things combine to make it the era of a great change in the conceptions and feelings of mankind as to the world of which they form a part. There is now almost no place left on our planet which is mysterious to us, and we were brought within sight of practical questions which will have to be faced when the multiplied human race shall have taken full possession of the earth.[106]

Blending anxiety and awe, Mill recognized, without being able to put his finger on it, the profound transformation in political consciousness generated by the revolution in communications technology—the (purported) elimination of the "mystery." This revolution meant that the types of argument proffered by Burke, Bentham, Smith, and Mill were soon pushed aside, although they never disappeared completely. Whereas for Mill nature imposed definite limits on the spatial extension of community, many of his successors adopted a more ambitious line. From the early 1870s onwards, it was increasingly argued that the colonial empire formed part of a *single political field*, that it constituted a unified community stretching across the globe. As a result, it became a commonplace to argue that the federation of the British colonial world was feasible, even necessary.[107] This new generation of colonial advocates saw "the public," and with it the limits of political community itself, as open to reconfiguration by novel technologies. Deliberation across space was

---

[104] Mill, "England and Ireland," 525.
[105] Mill, "Lord Durham and His Assailants," 460.
[106] Mill, letter to Henry Chapman, August 7, 1866, *Collected Works*, 16:1137.
[107] See, for example, Seeley, *The Expansion of England*.

possible; the interests of Britain and the colonies could be harmonized. Likewise, Wakefield's ideas—the very backbone of Mill's colonial thought—fell
from favor. While emigration remained an abiding concern for colonial advocates, the specificities of Wakefield's scheme seemed redundant. As the author
of the 1878 entry on "emigration" in the *Encyclopaedia Britannica* wrote, the
"discussion thirty or forty years ago on organized methods of colonization
have mostly disappeared in these later times. We hear no more of Mr Wakefield's scheme."[108] Mill's insistence on the political limits imposed by geographical space and his adherence to Wakefield's theoretical ideas meant that his
arguments looked increasingly obsolete in the years following his death.

Conclusions

Recent scholarship on Mill has deepened our understanding of how his political thought was shaped by questions of empire, civilization, and progress. Yet
his evolving vision(s) of global order can only be grasped adequately by recognizing the importance that he accorded to settler colonization. This was an
issue he returned to repeatedly over the course of forty years, although as I
have argued we can discern various shifts in his thought over time. Above all,
we see an increased emphasis on the universal benefits of colonization, and on
geopolitical and moral, as opposed to political-economic, justificatory arguments. He always imagined the metropole and the colonies within the same
analytical field, a field structured but not exhausted by his political economy
and his utilitarianism, but he never regarded them as part of a single political
field, as part of the same community of interests, identity, and affect. The colonies were, as they had been for Bentham, nascent independent countries, distant spaces of hope. Because of their far-flung locations they would never constitute an integral element of the British polity. Ideally, and like their ancient
Greek exemplars, they would remain bound by ties of kinship, economic exchange, and the warm glow of a mythopoeic past.

---

[108] Robert Somers, "Emigration" [1878], *Encyclopaedia Britannica*, 9th ed. (London, 1875–
89), 8:176. For a brilliant analysis of the nature of the encyclopedia, see Alistair MacIntyre, *Three
Rival Versions of Moral Enquiry* (South Bend, IN, 1990), ch. 1.

CHAPTER 10

International Society in Victorian Political Thought

჻

T. H. Green, Herbert Spencer, and Henry Sidgwick

With Casper Sylvest

I grew up as an ardent believer in optimistic liberalism. I both hoped and
expected to see throughout the world a gradual spread of parliamentary
democracy, personal liberty, and freedom for the countries that were at that
time subject to European Powers, including Britain. I hoped that everyone
would in time see the wisdom of Cobden's arguments for Free Trade, and
that nationalism might gradually fade into a universal humanism.[1]

—BERTRAND RUSSELL

If . . . one were to press the theoretic issue, whether a state or nation is a
morally independent being, or whether it is in some sense or degree a
member of what maybe called an incipient society of states or nations,
nearly everyone would sustain the latter view.[2]

—J. A. HOBSON

Throughout the Victorian era, British liberal attitudes to international order
were shaped by a complex interplay between conceptions of universalism, sovereignty, progress, and civilization. This chapter explores a prominent idea
that permeated the thinking of the British liberal intelligentsia in the closing
decades of the century, at the very apogee of the imperial age: a vision of international society as both an empirical account of progressive trends identifiable
in global politics and as a normative project.[3]

[1] Bertrand Russell, "Hopes: Realized and Disappointed," in *Portraits from Memory and Other
Essays* (London, 1956), 46.

[2] J. A. Hobson, *The Morals of Economic Internationalism* (Boston, 1920), 3–4.

[3] In the late nineteenth century the terms "society" and "community" were often used interchangeably; in this chapter, for the sake of consistency, we stick to "society." In current interna-

This chapter analyzes the overlapping ideas about international society to be found in the political thought of three leading late Victorian liberal thinkers: T. H. Green (1836–82), Herbert Spencer (1820–1903), and Henry Sidgwick (1838–1900). In so doing it focuses on what Stefan Collini has labeled the world of the "public moralists"—the world, that is, of influential and well-connected British intellectuals who flourished in the universities, in Parliament, and in the press.[4] During the late nineteenth century it is possible to identify amongst the liberal sections of this elite a widely shared, if often only vaguely articulated, belief in the existence of a nascent and evolving international society. It was a belief that was to survive both world wars, albeit in a more disenchanted key. This was the vision that Bertrand Russell grew up believing in, only to have his hopes dashed by the horrors of the atom bomb and the Holocaust, and that Hobson claimed was "sustained" by "nearly everyone" in 1920.

Despite their manifold political and philosophical differences, Green, Spencer, and Sidgwick shared and articulated complementary visions of the past, present, and future of international society. This was not simply a happy coincidence of views—it was an understanding of international politics generated from within their distinctive intellectual systems. They simultaneously reflected and contributed to late Victorian liberal thinking about international affairs. Their significance in this respect lies, at least in part, in their attempt to theorize liberal internationalism in a sophisticated manner, thereby giving it both intellectual respectability and political force. Moreover, by approaching this theme from different philosophical viewpoints they managed to provide internationalism with an ideological flexibility that proved crucial for its survival and development in a period witnessing both major shifts in the intellectual current and considerable turbulence in global politics.[5]

---

tional relations theory "international society" is associated with the "English School"; see Hedley Bull, *The Anarchical Society* (London, 1977); Alex Bellamy, ed., *International Society and Its Critics* (Oxford, 2004). We are not using it in this latter sense.

[4] Collini, *Public Moralists* (Oxford, 1991).

[5] The degree to which their liberal internationalism permeated British society as a whole is, though, an open question. The dangers of over-generalization, often resulting from the frequent mismatch between authorial intention and audience reception, are manifest in many studies of Victorian political culture—on which see Peter Mandler, "The Problem of Cultural History," *Social and Cultural History*, 1 (2004), 94–118. However, it is not implausible to conjecture that this internationalist vision had a wide following outside the highbrow world of the public moralists, although in this chapter we limit our attention to this world. To take a few examples: the success of Gladstone's Midlothian campaign relied, at least in part, on the wide resonance of his views amongst significant elements of the electorate (H.C.G. Matthew, *Gladstone, 1809–1898* (Oxford, 1997), pt. 2, ch. 2); moreover, as Anthony Howe argues, from the 1860s onwards free trade was an essential element in popular political identity: Howe, *Free Trade and Liberal England, 1846–1946* (Oxford, 1997), 113, Furthermore, the relative prominence of the peace movement demonstrates the wide reception of broadly liberal internationalist ideas. Paul Laity, *The British Peace Movement, 1870–1914* (Oxford, 2001); N. W. Summerton, "Dissenting Attitudes to Foreign Relations, Peace

The structure of this chapter is as follows. Section 2 provides a sketch of the political context in which liberal internationalism flourished during the late Victorian era as well as a brief analysis of key arguments employed by its proponents. Section 3 examines the international thought of Green, Spencer, and Sidgwick, and the way in which they derived overlapping notions of international society from their divergent philosophical systems. Finally, section 4 highlights some of the ways in which their internationalism was circumscribed by ideas about the boundaries of civilization and the role of empire. It was the moral and practical standing of empire that brought to the surface the internal tensions, and the ethical limitations, of late nineteenth-century liberal conceptions of international society.

Progress, Justice, and Order: On Liberal Internationalism

During the late nineteenth century liberal internationalism was, like the liberalism that spawned it, a many-stranded phenomenon. Nevertheless, it had at its core a cluster of ideas about how best to organize and reform global politics, to which virtually all liberals subscribed, including, in their different ways, Green, Spencer, and Sidgwick. This liberal internationalism was founded on a belief that it was possible to build a just international order on the basis of existing patterns of cooperation between distinct political communities. Such thinking was neither strictly cosmopolitan (insofar as it did not attempt to transcend the state) nor was it crudely nationalist (insofar as it did not prioritize national self-interest over the interests of "humanity"). It drew on a combination of long-standing radical ideas about the dangers of militarism and aristocratic privilege and fused them with more mainstream liberal concerns about the value of commerce (and in particular free trade) in creating a morally acceptable international order. In short, liberal internationalists yoked a political project to the idea of sustained moral development.[6] In doing so, they projected, in what is often labeled the "domestic analogy," their conception of the nature and sources of domestic order onto the plane of international politics.[7] War was not a tragic inevitability. Internationalists insisted

---

and War, 1840–1890," *Journal of Ecclesiastical History*, 28 (1977), 151–78. Finally, much of the outlook of the labour movement, including the groups that later coalesced into the Labour Party, can also been seen as liberal in the sense that we employ the term. Henry Winkler, *British Labour Seeks a Foreign Policy, 1900–1940* (London, 2005), ch. 1. Popular liberalism could also be taken in a more militant (though not necessarily anti-internationalist) direction. See Eugenio Biagini, "Neo-Roman Liberalism," *History of European Ideas* 29 (2003), 55–72.

[6] On the continuity in radical attitudes, especially towards empire, see Miles Taylor, "Imperium et Libertas?," *Journal of Imperial and Commonwealth History*, 19 (1991), 1–23; Peter Cain, "Radicalism, Gladstone, and the Liberal Critique of Disraelian 'Imperialism,'" in *Victorian Visions*, ed. Bell, 215–39.

[7] Hidemi Suganami, *The Domestic Analogy and World Order Proposals* (Cambridge, 1989).

that the problem resulting from the lack of an overarching global leviathan—that determinate source of political authority identified by so many thinkers at the time (and today) as one of the primary causes of interstate conflict—was surmountable without recourse to the dreaded singularity of universal empire.

Nineteenth-century British liberalism was marked by two defining characteristics. The first was its political and ideological ascendancy, especially in the early and mid-Victorian eras. The second was its polyphonic variation, which was most marked in the closing decades of the century.[8] The two are not unrelated—liberalism was many things to many people. This was both a strength and a weakness. Its strength lay in the possibility of coopting and coordinating a variety of different political interests and philosophical outlooks and uniting them behind a broad vision of economic, political, social, and international reform. Its weakness resulted from the fragility of this compound. Liberalism's hold over both the popular political imagination and the intellectual elite was very pronounced, and for a few decades in the third quarter of the century it lay at the core of political discourse, the position against which others were forced to define (and often defend) themselves. Scholars often argue that the mid-Victorian era was comparatively harmonious, characterized by "stability, optimism, social solidarity, relative affluence, and liberality."[9] It was a moment of heightened confidence. Liberalism flourished in this comparatively sunny climate—although the "equipoise" was often qualified by the common dread of war. The "generation of William Whewell," noted Henry Maine in 1887, "may be said to have had a dream of peace," exemplified by the atmosphere in the years surrounding the Great Exhibition of 1851. But the "buildings of this Temple of Peace had hardly been removed when war broke out again, more terrible than ever," and Maine pointed to the Crimean War as having inaugurated a new period of conflict, which to believers in the possibility of peace had been "a bitter deception."[10] John Morley concurred: "Heavy banks of cloud hung with occasional breaks of brighter sky over Europe; and all the plot, intrigue, conspiracy, and subterranean scheming . . . was but the repulsive and dangerous symptom of a dire conflict in the depth of international politics."[11] Optimism about the future was tempered by fear about the potential derailment of progress, a fear that increased in intensity, as winter succeeded autumn, in the closing decades of the century.

[8] On parliamentary and popular politics, see J. P. Parry, *The Rise and Fall of Liberal Government in Victorian Britain* (London, 1993); John Vincent, *The Formation of the Liberal Party, 1857–1868* (London, 1966); Eugenio Biagini, *Liberty, Retrenchment, and Reform* (Cambridge, 1992).

[9] Lawrence Goldman, *Science, Reform, and Politics in Victorian Britain* (Cambridge, 2002), 59; Martin Hewitt, ed., *An Age of Equipoise?* (Aldershot, 2001).

[10] Maine, *International Law* (London, 1888), 3–5.

[11] Morley, *The Life of William Ewart Gladstone*, 3 vols. (London, 1903), 2:318–19.

From the late 1880s until their landslide electoral victory in 1906, liberals repeatedly found themselves cast in the party-political wilderness. Moreover, challenges to liberal ideology became evermore obvious to contemporaries, sympathetic and hostile alike. As L. T. Hobhouse wrote in 1911, "[w]hether at home or abroad those who represented Liberal ideas had suffered crushing defeats ... [i]ts faith in itself was waxing cold."[12] In the domestic sphere the furore over Irish Home Rule, increasing class antagonism, and the emergence of socialism as a serious political force, together with challenges to the shibboleth of free trade amid disappointment with the results of democratic expansion after 1867 and 1884, all combined to dampen the confidence of liberals. This trend was exacerbated by escalating European militarization, catalyzed in particular by the unification of Germany following the Franco-Prussian War (1870–71), the ensuing "scramble" for imperial territories in Africa, fear about a Russian challenge to British supremacy in India, and the perception that the British economy was rapidly weakening relative to other major states. But liberal optimism did not disappear altogether, and indeed the grim international environment led to a redoubling of efforts to find a way out of the political impasse. It was in this ideological milieu that *fin de siècle* liberal internationalism was forged, drawing on classical liberal (and radical) themes, Gladstone's global messianism, and the ideas of the "new liberals" and philosophical idealists.[13]

In general, liberal internationalists advocated the development of international law, arbitration, free trade, and multilateralism as the most appropriate strategies for states to pursue in search of a just international order. They also predicted the development of various supranational structures, including political federations, at the regional, inter-imperial or international level, although they rarely pushed for the immediate construction of such institutions. Two analytically distinct logics can be discerned in internationalist thought during this period, although they were usually interwoven in the writings of individual figures. Witness, for example, the Cambridge international lawyer T. J. Lawrence. One line of thought held that reform would come about mainly through a shift in moral norms ("international morality"); another held that the best route was through institutional engineering. The former, dominant, logic focused on transforming the values of domestic society and in particular it promoted democracy while lambasting aristocratic militarism and excessive capitalist accumulation. Writing in the 1880s Law-

---

[12] Hobhouse, *Liberalism and Other Writings* [1911], ed. J. Meadowcroft (Cambridge, 1994), 103. See also John Morley, *On Compromise* [1874], 2nd ed. (London, 1886), 29; A. V. Dicey, *Lectures on the Relation between Law and Public Opinion in England during the Nineteenth Century* [1905], 2nd ed. (London, 1914), 444.

[13] On new liberalism, see Peter Clarke, *Liberals and Social Democrats* (Cambridge, 1978); Michael Freeden, *The New Liberalism* (Oxford, 1978); Avital Simhony and David Weinstein, eds., *The New Liberalism* (Cambridge, 2001). On philosophical idealism see the references and discussion in section 3 below.

rence claimed that the three greatest forces of modern life, "Commerce, De-mocracy and Christianity," facilitated peace, and when he examined war "in light of the theory of Development" he "found reason for believing that a state of perpetual peace will be gradually evolved upon earth." The second logic foreshadowed and promoted the creation of a variety of institutional structures. These included regional and imperial federations and, rather less ambitiously, international arbitration bodies, or what Lawrence called "au-thoritative tribunals."[14] For most internationalists writing prior to the First World War, including Lawrence, the two logics were usually sequenced in a particular manner; moral transformation was seen as a necessary first step be-fore institutions could be created to harness and embed this internationalist vision.[15]

Commerce and law were generally seen as the two key engines of liberal internationalism. They were assigned distinctive and complementary roles in bringing about a new moral order. In the case of commerce it was held that free trade led to increasing levels of interdependence and cooperation be-tween states, and thus reduced the probability of violent conflict. In other words, political cooperation would follow from economic interaction. This view had found its most forceful advocate in Cobden, and was to reach its apotheosis in "Norman Angellism" during the late Edwardian era.[16] It can be seen today in the stultifying debates over the pacifying powers of neoliberal globalization. The legal vision focused mainly on constructing a regime based on international legal norms that would lock into place certain types of be-havior, including reciprocity and arbitration, with the expectation that over time states would become socialized into new modes of peaceable and coop-erative interaction. As the liberal historian Frederic Seebohm wrote in 1871, "we enter into commercial treaties, and become more and more dependent upon maintenance of international peace and justice," which in turn required "more adequate security for international justice which shall at the same time be less injurious to the interests of nations."[17] Law and commerce were not only symptomatic of the general progress of humanity but would also be the means of bringing about a more fundamental transformation: the necessary (if not inevitable) moral development of the species. For James Bryce, famed anatomist of democracy, this process could be identified in the unfolding of history, which, despite repeated frustrations, was moving ever "upwards." The best evidence for this was to be found in the fact that "evils which men once

[14] Lawrence, *Essays on Some Disputed Questions in Modern International Law* [1884], 2nd ed. (Cambridge, 1885), vii, 24, 240.

[15] See here Casper Sylvest, "Continuity and Change in British Liberal Internationalism, c.1900–1930," *Review of International Studies*, 31 (2005), 263–83; and, in general, Jens Bartelson, "The Trial of Judgement," *International Studies Quarterly*, 39 (1995), 255–79.

[16] See especially Norman Angell, *The Great Illusion* (London, 1910).

[17] Seebohm, *On International Reform* (London, 1871), 70, 91.

accepted as inevitable have now become intolerable."[18] The liberal jurist Sheldon Amos concurred:

> War, as modified by the laws and restrictions which the conscience of the civilised world, working in concurrence with the dictates of military and political convenience, imposes, marks an intermediate and, it may be hoped, transitory stage, between an absolute oblivion of moral obligations, and such an ascendancy of the sense of these obligations, as would render the cruel hardships and bitter passions, which are inevitable, even in the best conducted Wars, an anachronism.[19]

This fusion of moral and institutional technologies of reform characterized liberal internationalism from the mid-Victorian era through the early decades of the twentieth century.

International Society: Green, Spencer, Sidgwick

Green, Spencer, and Sidgwick occupied important positions in late Victorian intellectual life. Whereas Green, White's Professor of Moral Philosophy at Oxford, was the most important figure in translating philosophical idealism into a British creed, Herbert Spencer, a man who never held an academic post, has some claim to be described as the single most influential philosopher of the nineteenth-century Anglo-American world—and well beyond. The popularity of his social evolutionary ideas stemmed, at least in part, from their ability to crystallize the hopes and anxieties of educated Victorians, as well as quenching their thirst for knowledge of self and society.[20] Henry Sidgwick, the Knightbridge Professor of Moral Philosophy at Cambridge, provided the most sophisticated defense of utilitarianism in the closing decades of the century. Unlike Green, whose writings focused primarily on philosophical topics, Sidgwick's published output ranged widely across philosophy, history, political economy, and contemporary politics, although he never attained the level of popularity enjoyed by Spencer.

The three philosophers differed very considerably in temperament and style, and they were often found on opposite—and not always predictable—sides of major intellectual and political debates. Green and Sidgwick were both skeptical of Spencer's social evolutionism and his attempt (as they saw it)

---

[18] Bryce, "An Age of Discontent," *Contemporary Review*, 49 (1891), 14–29.

[19] Amos, *Political and Legal Remedies for War* (London, 1880), 340–41.

[20] Rom Harré, "Positivist Thought in the Nineteenth Century," in *The Cambridge History of Philosophy, 1870–1945*, ed. Thomas Baldwin (Cambridge, 2003), 11–26; C. A. Bayly, "European Political Thought and the Wider World during the Nineteenth Century," in *The Cambridge History of Nineteenth-Century Political Thought*, ed. Gregory Claeys and Gareth Stedman Jones (Cambridge, 2011), 835–62.

to reduce moral philosophy to a science. Green was also sharply critical of Spencer's metaphysical assumptions, and in particular how these translated into his writings on psychology.[21] Spencer and Sidgwick, meanwhile, remained unconvinced by the idealism that Green was so instrumental in elaborating. Spencer objected to what he saw as the speculative, "continental" nature of idealism, while Sidgwick was more concerned with Green's inability to address or resolve what he regarded as the fundamental conundrums of philosophy, such as the reconciliation of different modes of ethical reasoning.[22] While the two professional academics conducted their conversations in a technical philosophical language, Sidgwick's utilitarian ethical system was ultimately more compatible with that of Spencer, the academic outsider. They also diverged politically. Green and Spencer's views on the relationship between the individual and the state stood poles apart—indeed the idealist disciples of Green regarded Spencer's utilitarianism and radical individualism as one of their main targets, both theoretically (as an indefensible view of the self) and politically (as justifying damaging inequalities). And despite his support for an idiosyncratic form of socialism, Sidgwick was much more of a traditional individualist liberal, an exponent, as D. G. Ritchie put it, of utilitarianism grown "tame and sleek."[23]

Notwithstanding this plurality of ideas and ideals, when it came to international politics they shared a bifocal vision that implied, first, that an incipient international society was discernible, even if only faintly, in the existing configuration of global politics and, second, as a normative ideal, that it should be nourished, strengthened, and expanded in the future. In other words this society was immanent, if not imminent. While they differed on its potential structure as well as on the temporal dimensions of its full realization, their views coalesced behind a coherent (though vague) concern with the possibility of bringing a measure of order, justice, and tranquility to international politics. Moral transformation was central to this vision. But Green, Sidgwick, and Spencer thought that this transformation required some form of institutionalization, and they therefore advocated new legal mechanisms, including arbitration bodies; in the longer term it would mean working towards the creation of federal modes of government at the international level.

[21] Green, *Mr. Herbert Spencer and Mr. G. H. Lewes, Collected Works of T. H. Green*, ed., Peter Nicholson, 5 vols. (Bristol, 1997), 1:373–541. Hereafter *Collected Works*. The first three volumes of this new collection are reprints of *Works of Thomas Hill Green*, ed. R. L. Nettleship, 3 vols. (London, 1885–88).

[22] See, for example, Spencer to Alexander Bain, April 25, 1902, and Spencer to Professor Masson, April 26, 1902, in David Duncan, *The Life and Letters of Herbert Spencer* (London, 1908), 457–58. See also Henry Sidgwick, "Green's Ethics," *Mind*, 9 (1884), 169–87, and the discussion in Bart Schultz, *Henry Sidgwick* (Cambridge, 2004), 362.

[23] Ritchie, "Review of Henry Sidgwick, *The Elements of Politics*," *International Journal of Ethics*, 2 (1891–92), 256. See also Bernard Williams, "The Point of View of the Universe" [1982], in *Making Sense of Humanity* (Cambridge, 1994), 153–71.

Starting from very different philosophical premises, they ended up arguing for very similar political goals.

Thomas Hill Green

In approaching Green's international thought, it is crucial not to be swayed by the hostile interpretation of idealism orchestrated at the beginning of the twentieth century, largely but not exclusively by Hobson and Hobhouse. In a characteristic formulation, Hobhouse argued, with direct reference to idealism, that if "all that is real is rational, it is difficult to resist the view that what wins is right."[24] The prevailing view today is that idealism was not of itself anti-internationalist.[25] This is especially true of Green, who was, as Melvin Richter once remarked, "the last person in the world to be convinced of the moral virtue of a nation by its success in war."[26] There was always a radical tint to Green's liberalism, particularly in terms of foreign policy, as is illustrated by his great admiration for the anti-militarist internationalism of Bright and Cobden.[27] Moreover, his intellectual trademark—the focus on the ethical dimension and potential of "man"—was always carefully phrased in language that precluded militarism.

Green's liberalism can be seen as a halfway house between the classical liberalism of Mill and the new liberalism of the early twentieth century.[28] He valued individuality and freedom and defended a conception of persons as essentially communal and moral beings bearing social responsibilities and rights. The political implications of this philosophical vision were formulated most clearly in the posthumously published *Lectures on the Principles of Political Obligation* (1886), where Green argued that

[24] Hobhouse, "Introduction to the Second Edition" [1909], in *Democracy and Reaction* [1904], ed. P. F. Clarke (New York, 1973), 274. Hobhouse partly exonerated Green from this critique (276). See also Hobson, *International Government* (London, 1915), esp. 178; Hobhouse, *The Metaphysical Theory of the State* [1918] (London, 1960), 25. For an early, tentative suggestion along the same lines see Sidgwick, "Public Morality" [1897], in *Practical Ethics* (London, 1898), 66.

[25] Peter Nicholson, "Philosophical Idealism and International Politics," *British Journal of International Studies,* 2 (1976), 76–83; David Boucher, "British Idealism, the State, and International Relations," 671–94; Boucher, "Introduction," in *The British Idealists,* ed. Boucher (Cambridge, 1997), vii-xxxiii.

[26] Richter, *The Politics of Conscience* (London, 1964), 89.

[27] On Green's admiration for Bright and Cobden, and his corresponding hatred of Palmerston and Louis Napoleon, see R. L. Nettleship, "Memoir" [1888], in *Collected Works,* vol. 3, xx and xxiii-xxiv. Green was a staunch defender of the principle of non-intervention in international politics. See Green, "Can Interference with Foreign Nations in Any Case Be Justifiable?," *Collected Works,* 5:15–19; Christopher Harvie, *The Lights of Liberalism* (London, 1976), 102. On his domestic radicalism, see Colin Tyler, "T. H. Green, Advanced Liberalism and the Reform Question 1865–1876," *History of European Ideas,* 29 (2003), 437–58.

[28] Michael Freeden, *Ideologies and Political Theory* (Oxford, 1996), 179.

the claim or right of the individual to have certain powers secured to him by society, and the counter-claim of society to exercise certain powers over the individual, alike rest on the fact that these powers are necessary to the fulfilment of *man's vocation as a moral being, to an effectual self-devotion to the work of developing the perfect character in himself and others.*[29]

After setting out the objective of freedom as self-development and self-realization, Green argued that the true function of government was to make possible this ideal. Although this reformulation has often been seen as a precursor to "new liberal" arguments about the role of the state in achieving social equality, to Green the implications were not straightforwardly interventionist.[30] Although his view of state intervention was much more permissive than Spencer's, its task remained primarily ethical, being devoted to sustaining and harmonizing individual relations.[31] The state was a facilitating space for individual self-realization. On the other hand, Green also stressed that the citizen ideally should be an active participant in political life, not simply a passive recipient of its benefits, a view that fitted with his conception of "man" as inconceivable apart from community.[32] He was a persistent critic of dualisms—citizen-state, individual-society—and repeatedly insisted on their mutual interdependence. This philosophical notion of unity had a moral and political equivalent in Green's avowal of the social and individual dimensions of pursuing the common good, a common good that anchored collective life. With this guiding idea Green provided—or was seen to provide—an answer to materialistic hedonism in an age of increasing religious doubt.[33] This answer also embodied a progressive element in which institutions (including the state), and the individuals composing them, were seen as gradually fulfilling their true nature.[34]

Green's conception of the international was continuous with this vision of moral development. Green began his lecture "The Right of the State over the Individual in War," delivered in the academic year of 1879–80, with a discussion of the essential "wrongdoing" of war, arguing that even if it was undeniable that "many virtues are called into exercise by war, or that wars have been a means by which the movement of mankind ... has been carried on," this did

[29] Green, *Lectures on the Principles of Political Obligation* [1886], *Collected Works*, 2:347, sec. 21. Italics added.

[30] Mill, *Political Obligation*, 345–46, sec. 18.

[31] Mill, "Lecture on Liberal Legislation and Freedom of Contract" [1880], *Collected Works*, 3:365–86.

[32] Mill, *Political Obligation*, 454, 436, secs. 143, 122. See also Peter Nicholson, "Introduction," in *The Political Philosophy of the British Idealists,* ed. Nicholason (Cambridge, 1990), 1–6.

[33] For a discussion of Green's theology, see Colin Tyler, "T. H. Green," *Stanford Encyclopedia of Philosophy*, http://plato.stanford.edu.

[34] Richter, *The Politics of Conscience*, 105.

not diminish the wrong committed. Green then turned to the relationship between the right of (particular) states to act in their own interest and the rights that individuals acquired through membership in (a universal) human society. For Green, though, this implied a false dichotomy, because "the source of war between states lies in their incomplete fulfilment of their function; in the fact that there is some defect in the maintenance or reconciliation of rights among their subjects":

> There is no such thing as an inevitable conflict between states. There is nothing in the nature of the state that, given a multiplicity of states, should make the gain of the one the loss of the other. The more perfectly each one of them attains its proper object of giving free scope to the capacities of all persons living on a certain range of territory, the easier it is for others to do so; and in proportion as they all do so the danger of conflict disappears.[35]

This statement follows from Green's understanding of the relationship between state and citizen and was intended also as a challenge to the fatalistic view, which he associated with Spinoza and which he saw as resurgent in contemporary political life. In a previous lecture Green had discussed Spinoza's approach to war, and especially the view that "two commonwealths are enemies by nature." He complained that among "the enlightened . . . there has of late appeared a tendency to adopt a theory very like Spinoza's, without the higher elements which we noticed in Spinoza; to consider all right as a power attained in that 'struggle for existence' to which human 'progress' is reduced."[36] Green was to spend much time attempting to counter such crude notions of struggle, whether they were employed in debate about domestic or international politics.

The fulfillment of the real purpose of the state would remove the motives and opportunities for war, "while the bonds of unity become stronger." This development was linked directly to "Manchesterism." Despite some reservations about free trade, Green held that increasing levels of trade would strengthen "the sense of common interests" between citizens of different states, which war would otherwise violate. This logic can point in the direction of cosmopolitanism and a universal society of humankind, and there is indeed some evidence that this is what Green sought. Throughout his short life he argued against militarist patriotism, and he lamented that in international politics people were rarely influenced by "the idea of the universal brotherhood of men," and by the notion of "mankind as forming one society with a common good."[37] This suggests that Green was committed to a con-

---

[35] Green, *Political Obligation*, 473, 478, 476–77, secs. 163, 167, 166.
[36] Ibid., 357–59, 373, secs. 34–35, 50.
[37] Ibid., 483, 484, 464–65, secs. 174, 155. See also Richter, *Politics of Conscience*, 207, 216. For

ception of what might be labeled "transcendent" community, the belief that
ideally once individuals are members of one community they are members of
all communities.[38] Two factors, however, complicate a simple "cosmopolitan"
reading. First, Green was no straightforward individualist. Although he argued that in a nation, "however exalted its mission," there was nothing "which
is not in the persons composing the nation or the society" and that our "ultimate standard of worth is an ideal of *personal* worth," he also insisted that individuals could not possess "moral and spiritual qualities, independently of
their existence in a nation."[39] In thinking about morals, he suggested, we have
to start with a notion of moral community that does not encompass the whole
of humanity. Second, even if Green was a cosmopolitan, his attainable ideal,
his view, that is, of what it was at least plausible to aim for, was premised on
the existence of nation-states. This emerges from his discussion of the claim
that projects "of perpetual peace, to be logical, must be projects of all-
embracing empire." Although Green conceded that there was some merit in
this, he argued that a world of nations expressing particularistic sentiments
was more realistic and perhaps also more fulfilling. If these were properly constituted and directed towards the common good, not only would "the occa-
sions of conflict between nations disappear," those nations would also by virtue of the same development acquire a more altruistic "organ of expression
and action" for dealing with each other.[40]

Green's ideal was, then, of a society of rightly constituted nations coexisting in anti-egoistic ways and developing within a larger circle of humanity.
Even in *The Prolegomena to Ethics* (1883), wherein he discussed the possibility of communities widening continually so as to increase the range of persons
whose common good was sought, he did not dispense with (nation) states as
long as they fulfilled their potential. He employed, for example, the equivocal
phrase "the fraternity of men and nations." More importantly, Green acknowledged that the prime impediment to the maintenance and formation of
a fellowship was selfishness, a problem that was exacerbated as they expanded

---

examples of Green's criticisms of patriotism, see his undergraduate essay "Loyalty"; his speech
"Against Disraeli's Foreign Policy," January 26, 1878; and his speech on "National Loss and Gain
under a Conservative Government," December 5, 1879, *Collected Works,* 5:12–14, 313–17,
347–55.

[38] See Green, *Prolegomena to Ethics* [1883], in *Collected Works,* vol. 4, bk. 3, 160–314; Nettleship, "Memoir," cxxxviii-cxxxix.

[39] Green, *Prolegomena to Ethics,* 193, sec. 184. Original italics.

[40] Green, *Political Obligation,* 480–81, 484, secs. 170–71. This notion of "cosmopolitan nationalism," to use a slightly paradoxical formulation, was not uncommon. See Stuart Jones, "The
Idea of the National in Victorian Political Thought," *European Journal of Political Theory,* 5 (2006),
12–21; Duncan Bell, "Unity and Difference," *Review of International Studies,* 31 (2005), 559–79;
and Georgios Varouxakis, "'Patriotism,' 'Cosmopolitanism' and 'Humanity' in Victorian Political
Thought," *European Journal of Political Theory,* 5 (2006), 100–118. See also my discussion of J. R.
Seeley's political thought in chapter 11.

in scale and scope. Nevertheless he confidently asserted that "where selfishness of man has proposed, his better reason has disposed." Thus he saw the formation of independently law-governed nations and communities as an expression of reason because they facilitated both the subordination of the individual to the common good and underpinned the language of rights instrumental in realizing wider interpersonal commitments.[41] It was against this background that he could "dream of an international court with authority resting on the consent of independent states."[42] As with his conception of the relationship between individual and society the relationship between (nation) states and the "society" they form was potentially harmonious. But such a development depended on states becoming more fully realized and thereby recognizing their common interests.

Herbert Spencer

Unmistakably a child of the English provincial radicalism that flourished in his home town of Derby, Herbert Spencer was a self-made thinker who, from the 1850s onwards, worked out a "synthetic Philosophy" spanning biology, psychology, sociology, and ethics.[43] Following a brief career in the booming railway industry and as a journalist at the *Economist*, he published *Social Statics* in 1851. From an explicitly deist perspective, which he later abandoned, the book developed deductively a system of ethics for the perfect condition towards which mankind was progressing. In later life Spencer would move away from this exclusive focus on "absolute ethics" and begin to deal also with nonideal "relative ethics." At this stage, though, he had not yet identified the evolutionary mechanisms of progress even if its existence and direction was clear: "Progress . . . is not an accident, but a necessity. Instead of civilization being artificial, it is a part of nature." This conviction was so strong that Spencer could proclaim that evil and morality would disappear and that man would become "perfect."[44] In this projected future condition, a principle of equal freedom—"*Every man has freedom to do all that he wills, provided he infringes not the equal freedom of any other man*"[45]—would guide human action. Many essential elements of Spencer's utilitarianism and of his mature philosophical system were thus present in his early work.[46]

---

[41] Green, *Prolegomena to Ethics*, 218–19, 229–30, secs. 207, 216.

[42] Green, *Political Obligation*, 485, sec. 175.

[43] On his life and career see J.D.Y. Peel, *Herbert Spencer* (London, 1971); David Wiltshire, *The Social and Political Thought of Herbert Spencer* (Oxford, 1978). Since this chapter was first published, another important biographical study has appeared: Mark Francis, *Herbert Spencer and the Invention of Modern Life* (Ithaca, 2007).

[44] Spencer, *Social Statics* (London, 1851), 65.

[45] Ibid., 103. Italics in original.

[46] See David Weinstein, *Equal Freedom and Utility* (Cambridge, 1998); M. W. Taylor, *Men*

So too was his political liberalism. Spencer was a ruthless advocate of the ideal-typical "nightwatchman" state, as demonstrated both in *Social Statics* and in a series of letters to the *Nonconformist* entitled *The Proper Sphere of Government* (1842–43). Progress meant progressively less government.[47] The international consequences of this ideology corresponded with the arguments of the Anti-Corn Law League and its icons, Cobden and Bright, and as such Spencer can be located in a tradition of political radicalism highly critical of British foreign policy and imperialism.[48] This emerges clearly in *The Proper Sphere of Government*, where he argued that war was "the source of the greatest of England's burdens." War made nations aggressive and hindered industry and commerce, "the real sources of wealth." But it was the moral evils of war that exercised Spencer the most. It was, after all, "inconsistent with the spirit of Christianity," tending "greatly to retard the civilisation of the world," and it acted as "the grand bar to the extension of that feeling of universal brotherhood with all nations, so essential to the real prosperity of mankind."[49]

The same notion of an incipient and immanent society of nations is found in *Social Statics*, but at this stage he predicted that it would manifest itself in a global federal structure. It is vital to stress, however, that Spencer was not willing to actively advocate the establishment of such an institution. The logic was much more circumvented:

> A federation of peoples—a universal society, can exist only when man's adaptation to the social state has become tolerably complete. We have already seen ... that in the earliest state of civilization, when the repulsive force is strong, and the aggregative force weak, only small communities are possible; a modification of character causes these tribes and satrapies, and *gentes*, and feudal lordships, and clans, gradually to coalesce into nations; and a still further modification will allow for further union. That the time for this is now drawing nigh, seems probable ... The recognition of its desirableness foreshadows its realization. In peace societies, in proposals for simultaneous disarmament, in international visits and addresses, and in the frequency with which friendly interventions now occur, we may see that humanity is fast growing towards such a consummation. Though hitherto impracticable, and perhaps impracticable at the present moment, a brotherhood of nations is being made very practicable by the very efforts used to bring it about.[50]

versus the State (Oxford, 1992).

[47] Spencer, *The Proper Sphere of Government* [1842–43], in *Man versus the State* (Indianapolis, 1982), 187.

[48] For a valuable analysis (in which Spencer is not mentioned), see A.J.P. Taylor, *The Trouble Makers* (London, 1957); and also Taylor, "Imperium et Libertas?"; Cain, "Radicalism."

[49] Spencer, *The Proper Sphere of Government*, 211–13.

[50] Spencer, *Social Statics*, 272–73. Italics in original.

Impersonal forces governing human development would in time bring about a full manifestation of the international society that was then only discernable *in embryo*. Spencer indicated that this trajectory should be located in the larger timescales of history and that inter-societal conflict had acted as a crucial mechanism of development. In order to understand how this argument worked in any detail, it is important to briefly examine Spencer's understanding of social evolution.

A rudimentary notion of evolution was clearly present in Spencer's earlier writings, but it was not until he conceived of the "synthetic philosophy" that it was theorized more thoroughly, and arguably its full realization was parasitic on the development of the various branches of the entire philosophical system. In Spencer's philosophical groundwork, *First Principles*, published originally in 1860, evolution was defined as "an integration of matter and concomitant dissipation of motion; during which the matter passes from an indefinite, incoherent homogeneity to a definite, coherent heterogeneity; and during which the retained motion undergoes a parallel transformation."[51] At the core of this "total evolutionism" were two separate but interlinked concepts, individuation and differentiation.[52] At a general level Spencer held that organisms became distinct from other organisms—"individualised"—by a process of the differentiation of organs, but this process also implied another kind of individuation as the organism in question simultaneously became more integrated. The mechanism of these evolutionary developments was Lamarckian rather than Darwinian—that is, adaptation to the environment took place through the ability of organisms to inherit acquired characteristics from previous generations rather than through the more random Darwinian process of variation and selection. This allowed Spencer to conceive of progress in an orderly—and almost speculatively guidable—fashion.[53] It points to a crucial feature of the interlocking nature of Spencer's political ideology and theory of evolution: while the latter was presented as a disinterested scientific theory, in reality it was constantly fashioned and refashioned so as to confirm the main impetus of the former.[54]

Spencer's sociology, which encompassed what today we would term "political science," is important in understanding how he conceived of this process.[55] He contended that from the early stages of history the necessity for se-

---

[51] Spencer, *First Principles* (London, 1867), 396. The wording of this definition changed slightly as Spencer revised the work.

[52] The phrase is from Maurice Mandelbaum, *History, Man, & Reason* (London, 1971), 90.

[53] See especially John Burrow, "Historicism and Social Evolution," in *British and German Historiography, 1750–1950*, ed. Benedikt Stuchtey and Peter Wende (Oxford, 2000), 251–64.

[54] This had already been noted by Sidgwick, who castigated Spencer for his "irrepressible and unwarrantable optimism." Sidgwick, *Lectures on the Ethics of T. H. Green, Mr. Herbert Spencer and J. Martineau* (London, 1902), 228.

[55] Spencer, *Principles of Sociology*, 3 vols. (London, 1876–96), vol. 1, v.

curity and collective action caused humans to form groups, which in turn triggered a process of struggle that was followed by further "compounding" of groups and societies. In these early stages of history it was possible to discern an intercommunal struggle, where only the fittest survived and grew. These societies were mostly "militant" in an ideal-typical sense: hierarchical, oriented solely towards security and survival, and providing little space for individual freedom. As Spencer later described this turn in his thinking,

> It had to be reluctantly admitted that war, everywhere and always hateful, has nevertheless been a factor in civilization, by bringing about the consolidation of groups—simple into compound, doubly-compound, and trebly-compound—until great nations are formed. As, throughout the organic world, evolution has been achieved by the merciless discipline of Nature, "red in tooth and claw"; so, in the social world, a discipline scarcely less bloody has been the agency by which societies have been massed together and social structures developed.[56]

Yet the power of war was also limited because human societies could escape this logic. For example, the activity of war produced the skills needed for voluntary cooperation, and when a particular stage was reached the advantages of war were exceeded by its disadvantages.[57] According to Spencer, admitting the centrality of war in evolution was—viewed in the long term—not incompatible with "the belief that there is coming a stage in which survival of the fittest among societies, hitherto affected by sanguinary conflicts, will be affected by peaceful conflicts."[58] The outcome of the evolutionary process was the establishment of "industrial" societies characterized by, among other things, voluntary association, minimal government, individual freedom, and purely defensive military capabilities.[59] This development was paralleled in the domain of ethics, where egoism was gradually replaced by social altruism and rational/transfigured egoism until international conditions allowed for the emergence of internationalist altruism. Spencer could thus proclaim that there "needs but a continuance of absolute peace externally, and a rigorous insistence on nonaggression internally, to ensure the moulding of men into a form characterized by all the virtues."[60]

There are numerous problems with this explanatory logic, many of which are connected to the relationship between Spencer's ideology and his "sci-

---

[56] Spencer, "The Filiation of Ideas" [1899], in Duncan, *Life and Letters*, 569.

[57] Mike Hawkins, *Social Darwinism in European and American Thought, 1860–1945* (Cambridge, 1997), 92.

[58] Spencer, "Filiation of Ideas," 569.

[59] The importance of the distinction between militant and industrial societies to Spencer's sociology is hard to overestimate. It is developed in most detail in Spencer, *Political Institutions*, esp. chs. 17, 18; Spencer, *The Principles of Ethics* [1879–93], 2 vols. (Indianapolis, 1978), 2.

[60] Spencer, *Principles of Ethics*, 1, 504.

ence," but these can be left aside. It is more fruitful to focus on the consequences that followed for the way in which he viewed the future of international relations and, more specifically, the "brotherhood of nations," the burgeoning international society that figured in his early writings. First, the concept of social evolution and the distinction between militant and industrial societies possessed considerable rhetorical power for Spencer as a critic of foreign policy. Progress could be thrown into reverse by militaristic adventures and misconceived visions of empire as an agent of civilization. Consequently Spencer castigated the actions and ideas of politicians and aristocrats, the clergy, historians, generals, and imperialists of all stripes.[61] The lesson was obvious: accelerating social evolution was virtually impossible, but much could be done to obstruct the development of peace. Spencer's internationalism thus simultaneously embodied optimistic analysis and ferocious criticism. Second, it becomes clear that although he was not a nationalist (and certainly not a patriot), he was no straightforward cosmopolitan either. In line with many other liberals, Spencer seems to have "naturalized" the idea of the nation to the extent that a world without nations was unimaginable. However, the nation was not conceptualized in a sophisticated manner. Rather, Spencer's ideal demanded the development of complex industrial societies cooperating within a larger context of an evolving humanity. Indeed, the benign coexistence of nations amounted to an international society. This emerges again in the final pages of *The Principles of Sociology* (1896), although by this stage the ideal is much more heavily institutionalized. In speculating about the international order of the future, which Spencer thought (and hoped) would be federal, he argued that "future competitions" between nations would follow the general law of evolution, displaying not only increasing heterogeneity (in terms of structural and cultural differences) but also the trait of the "primary process of evolution," increasing integration. This development was necessary for completing human evolution; its potential benefits were obvious:

> As, when small tribes were welded together into great tribes, the head chief stopped inter-tribal warfare; as, when small feudal governments became subject to a king, feudal wars were prevented by him; so, in time to come, a federation of the highest nations, exercising supreme authority (already foreshadowed by occasional agreements among "the Powers"), may, by forbidding wars between any of its constituent nations, put an end to the re-barbarization which is continually undoing civilization. When this peace-maintaining federation has been formed, there may be effectual progress towards that equilibrium between constitution and conditions—between inner facilities and outer requirements—implied in the final stage of human evolution.[62]

[61] See the discussion below in section 4.
[62] Spencer, *Principles of Sociology*, 3:600, sec. 853.

Spencer, it should be stressed, did not advocate the construction of specific international institutions. In general, he held that the quality of political institutions was "relative to the natures of citizens," meaning that moral transformation had to precede successful institutional engineering. And of course, for Spencer, such transformation was slow and, to judge by its contemporary manifestations, sometimes regressive. Here lay the kernel of his increasing disenchantment with the conduct of international politics. Human evolution still had a long way to go before peace could break out. As with so many other aspects of his thought, the purported existence of a peaceful international society was more ideological assertion than scientific forecast.

Henry Sidgwick

Sidgwick appears at first markedly different from Spencer, and much more like his friend Green. Although he admired Spencer's ethical system, Sidgwick was unsympathetic to what he saw as its utopian implications. In particular he was critical of Spencer's (early) privileging of "absolute ethics," describing it as "an investigation not of what ought to be done here and now, but of what ought to be the rules of behaviour in a society of ideally perfect human beings." This was too far removed from political realities: "Thus the subject-matter of our study would be doubly ideal: as it would not only prescribe what ought to be done as distinct from what is, but what ought to be done if a society that itself is not, but only *ought* to be."[63] Although both Sidgwick and Spencer took the pursuit of truth—and perhaps especially moral truth—extremely seriously, this disagreement reflects a difference in confidence. Spencer relegated metaphysical uncertainty to his notion of the "Unknowable" on which it was intellectually fruitless (and, for Spencer, unhealthy) to dwell; instead, he focused on the remaining intellectual terrain where he felt confident that truths could be ascertained and then proselytized. Sidgwick, in contrast, was more skeptical and self-critical, often lambasting the emerging field of sociology, of which Spencer was the leading British light, for its predilection for utopian prophecy.[64] In a very un-Spencerian fashion, Sidgwick constantly agonized over the risk that ethical truths, like religious truths, were built on sand.[65] John Maynard Keynes's notorious remark that Sidgwick

---

[63] Sidgwick, *The Methods of Ethics* [1874], 7th ed. (London, 1907), 18, and the accompanying footnote. Italics in original. See also Sidgwick, "Mr. Spencer's Ethical System," *Mind*, 5 (1880), 216–26; Sidgwick, *Lectures*, 206. Already in 1873 Sidgwick felt moved to criticize Spencer "somewhat severely." H. S. to F.W.H. Myers [February 1873], Sidgwick papers, Wren Library, Trinity College, Cambridge, Add.ms.100/237.

[64] Sidgwick, "The Scope and Method of Economic Science" [1885] and "Political Prophecy and Sociology" [1894], in *Miscellaneous Essays and Addresses* (London, 1904), 170–99, 216–34; Sidgwick, "The Relation of Ethics to Sociology," *International Journal of Ethics*, 10 (1899), 1–21.

[65] Sidgwick acknowledged this gulf between him and Spencer: A. and E. M. Sidgwick, *Henry Sidgwick, A Memoir* (London, 1906), 421.

"never did anything but wonder whether Christianity was true and prove it wasn't and hope it was" should be read in this light.[66]

The readiness to engage the world as it really appeared is also testimony to Sidgwick's proximity to the British political elite; he had, after all, a future prime minister and a future Archbishop of Canterbury as brothers-in-law. His close links to the Tory establishment also raise a question about labeling Sidgwick a liberal. Like some other leading public moralists, including Henry Maine and A. V. Dicey, Sidgwick became increasingly conservative towards the end of his life. Although he displayed relatively little of the inflated fears about collectivism that beset Maine and Dicey, he was still skeptical about many contemporary political developments, most obviously the Gladstonian push for Irish Home Rule.[67] Sidgwick warmed to the Unionist perspective (sometimes even the Tory variant), and he was critical of party political liberalism. Nevertheless, the conservative elements in his thought should not be overestimated—the legacy of the academic liberalism of the 1860s and 1870s weighed heavily on him, shaping his views on various domestic issues, including female education.[68] Although he considered himself an independent, and although he has been described (with Maine) as a "terrible political hypochondriac," Sidgwick also remained decidedly liberal in his views about international politics.[69]

Despite these qualifications, Sidgwick and Spencer displayed close intellectual and political affinities. Unlike many later thinkers Sidgwick took Spencer's ideas very seriously, lecturing and writing widely on them. And as David Weinstein has argued, the philosophical differences between them should not be exaggerated.[70] In terms of international politics, moreover, they shared a number of fundamental assumptions and a normative vision. Sidgwick agreed with Spencer—reiterating an argument common at the time—that there existed an irreversible tendency towards ever-smaller numbers of large omnicompetent political units.[71] He shared (and often quoted) Spencer's dictum that "ideal conduct . . . is not possible for the ideal man in the

---

[66] John Maynard Keynes to Bernard Swithinbank, March 27, 1906 (Keynes Papers, King's College, Cambridge), quoted in Schultz, *Henry Sidgwick*, 4.

[67] Spencer also opposed Home Rule. See Spencer to Auberon Herbert, June 16, 1890, and Spencer to the Earl of Dysart, May 27, 1892, both in Duncan, *Life and Letters*, 300–301, 315.

[68] On "academic liberalism," see Harvie, *Lights of Liberalism*; on Sidgwick's reformist credentials, see Schultz, *Henry Sidgwick*.

[69] Collini, *Public Moralists*, 279; Collini, "My Roles and Their Duties," in *Henry Sidgwick*, ed. Ross Harrison (Oxford, 2001), 9–49, esp. 38.

[70] David Weinstein, "Deductive Hedonism and the Anxiety of Influence," *Utilitas,* 12 (2000), 329–46. See also Sidgwick, "Political Prophecy and Sociology," 222; Sidgwick, "The Relation of Ethics to Sociology," 2.

[71] Sidgwick, *The Elements of Politics* [1891], 3rd ed. (London, 1907), 218–19. Valorizing massive political units was common at the time, as for example in the writings of Sidgwick's colleague J. R. Seeley. For a liberal critique of the "megalophiles," see J. M. Robertson, *An Introduction to English Politics* (London, 1900), 251–58.

midst of men otherwise constituted."[72] One of the lessons that both men drew from this dictum was that it was impractical to work directly for the establishment of new political institutions. Nevertheless, Sidgwick also shared with Spencer the view that the future would (or at least should) be federal; the nations of the "civilized" world would be united under one government that ensured order on a global scale, although his optimism about this potential development increased during the 1890s. Following an exposition of the various factors generating the tendency towards larger unions—the dangers and economic burdens of war, increasing competition, the industrial character of modern societies, better facilities and habits of communication, and rising consciousness of a common civilization—Sidgwick warned that it would be vain to expect the development of a singular European nationality and of "an extensive federation of civilised states strong enough to put down wars among its members." In its pure form the ideal was not attainable, so Sidgwick opted for the second best:

> The practically dominant political ideal of the present age does not include an extension of government beyond the limits of the nation. As in Greek history the practically dominant ideal is a society of City-states, independent, though observing in their mutual relations some kind of common law, so, in the period to which we belong, it is a society of Nation-states under "International Law."[73]

Sidgwick's formulation of the internationalist ideal is interesting in several respects. First, his admiration of federalism grew stronger towards the end of his life.[74] As the 1890s unfolded, Sidgwick seems—despite his earlier criticisms of evolutionary optimism—to have become more open to the idea of evolutionary progress, and this in turn made him more inclined to speculate about the future.[75] In the final lecture of the course that was later published as *The Development of European Polity* (1903), he felt "disposed to predict a development of federality." As he argued, "When we turn our gaze from the past to the future, an extension of federalism seems to me the most probable of the political prophecies relative to the form of government."[76] Second, Sidgwick seems to have become steadily more internationalist during the 1890s. The tentative acceptance of evolutionary progress was indicative of his increasing

---

[72] See, e.g., Sidgwick, "Public Morality," 72. Sidgwick, *Elements of Politics*, 239–40nn. See also Spencer, *Principles of Ethics*, 1:307.

[73] Sidgwick, *Elements of Politics*, 219–20.

[74] Ibid., 267, 301–2, 310; Sidgwick, *Memoir*, 576.

[75] Weinstein, "Deductive Hedonism," 337.

[76] Henry Sidgwick, *The Development of European Polity*, ed. E. M. Sidgwick (London, 1903), 439. This book differed from the *Elements of Politics* in being inductive, historical, and avowedly "scientific," focusing on what *is* or *has been* (as opposed to his previous, deductive, and ethical concern with what *ought to be*).

optimism about international affairs—or perhaps "defiant optimism" considering the political developments at the time—which in turn might have catalyzed a more robust internationalist position. The most compelling evidence for such a development is to be found in some of the revisions Sidgwick made to writings published in the early 1890s.[77]

Finally, Sidgwick's internationalism contained a practical dimension. After setting out the ideal of a society of nations under International Law, he attempted to delineate the ethical principles that this idea involved and compared these to existing international practices. Behind this analysis lay the conviction that order and ethical progress in world politics were not only possible but also necessary. Although Sidgwick accepted the special anarchical character of international relations—the "absence of a common government which has hitherto rendered wars between nations inevitable"[78]—he nevertheless had a habit of distinguishing only in degree between domestic and international politics.[79] Despite the neo-Machiavellianism of "respectable," mainly German, "thinkers of our century," Sidgwick was adamant that statesmen and states were not exempt from the demands of public morality.[80] He conceded that if (when?) states could not expect reciprocity in their political dealings with other states, they were allowed a "corresponding extension of the right of self-protection, in the interest of humanity at large no less than in its own interest." But this did not mean that he drove a wedge between private and public morality, for a similar situation could also be imagined with regard to the dealings of individuals. Sidgwick pressed home the point that

> In both cases equally it must be insisted that the interest of the part is to be pursued only in such manner and degree as is *compatible with the interests of the larger community of which it is part*; and that any violation of the rules of mutual behaviour actually established in the common interests of this community, so far as it is merely justified by its conduciveness to the sectional interest of a particular group of human beings, must receive unhesitating and unsparing censure.[81]

Side-stepping the fundamental problem in this passage—the question of what censure can achieve in the face of the violation of rules—it is important to

[77] See, for example, "The Morality of Strife," in Sidgwick, *Practical Ethics*, 83–112 (first published in *International Journal of Ethics*, 1 (1890), 1–15); and compare ch. 15 of the first (1891) edition of *The Elements of Politics* to later editions (1896 onwards). See also Collini, "My Roles and Their Duties," 27–29.

[78] Sidgwick, "Public Morality," 77.

[79] See, for example, the simultaneous discussion of the ethical dimensions of domestic and international conflict in "Public Morality" and in the revised edition of "The Morality of Strife."

[80] Sidgwick, "Public Morality," 60. Sidgwick appears to have drawn this analysis from Lord Acton's introduction to Burd's edition of Machiavelli. Acton, "Introduction," in *Il Principe*, by Niccolò Machiavelli, ed. Burd (Oxford, 1891), xix–xl.

[81] Sidgwick, "Public Morality," 81–82. Italics added.

note how this insistence on viewing states as moral beings forming part of a "larger community" is as much a premise as it is a conclusion. If states are moral beings they form part of a community, and vice versa. The crucial point, however, is that insofar as moral progress is possible in international affairs (and Sidgwick clearly thought it was), such progress would manifest itself in strengthening that burgeoning international society that he had already identified.

Sidgwick was able to provide his readers with a more detailed discussion than Green and Spencer of what consequences for ethics followed from his internationalism, and in spelling this out he achieved a fuller balance between hardheaded analysis and ideological speculation. He was aware of the implausibility of internationalism ever gaining a complete victory, and in this sense he was a skeptic. But it was a skepticism that often translated into pragmatism rather than fatalism. It was this predilection for political pragmatism—which from another perspective simply means falling prey to power—and his criticism of Spencer's "unphilosophical" anti-imperialism, that with hindsight appear to compromise this brand of internationalism.

Civilization, Empire, and the Limits of International Morality

Green, Spencer, and Sidgwick adumbrated compatible understandings of "international society," and this vision formed part of their wider liberal internationalism, a generally optimistic picture of world order grounded on a progressive account of international development. However, they disagreed fundamentally over the role of empire, a topic that fiercely divided liberals in late Victorian Britain. Indeed many of the fault lines and silences in liberal thinking about empire that I explore throughout this book were reflected in their contrasting positions. In this section the limitations—conceptual, territorial, and political—of the liberal internationalist vision are explored.

Victorian internationalists sketched a highly circumscribed picture of the present and future, their implied universality constricted by a civilizational narrative of human moral and political development. Only those societies characterized as "civilized" were included within the scope of international society, at least in the present; most, though, were not accorded sovereign equality and were not considered bound by norms of legal and moral reciprocity. John Stuart Mill, famously, excluded from the remit of his "one very simple principle" of liberty "backward states of society in which the race itself may be considered as in its nonage."[82] The spatial limits of civilization—an elusive, always slippery concept—were not, however, etched naturally into the

---

[82] Mill, *On Liberty* [1859], *Collected Works*, 18:224.

fabric of the world. Liberal internationalism contained a dynamic conception of "international society," a picture in which civilization always emanated outwards, in concentric circles, from a European core. Progress was defined by a dual track of development, not only by the degree to which the already civilized powers were socialized into new and increasingly pacific modes of behavior, but also by the extent to which the sphere of civilization could be widened. The idea was that over time, and often with the explicit intervention of imperial powers, the uncivilized could reach the level of development necessary for reclassification. This notion of potentially expansive inclusion underpinned a progressive evolutionary conception of historical time, projecting the circumscribed "international society" from its embryonic present into an optimistic, but almost always deferred, global future.

Throughout the nineteenth century, liberal politicians and intellectuals contested the nature and boundaries of civilization. Debate tended to focus on "liminal" societies—those that, like China, Japan, and the Ottoman Empire, were thought to possess the potential for full inclusion.[83] Although opinions differed over the problems involved in bestowing the sacred moniker of civilization on these states, the overall trend was to argue that most societies were simply not prepared. Levels of civilization were calculated in relation to theological orientation, stage of technological development, ascribed racial characteristics, economic success, the form of political institutions that predominated, individual moral and intellectual competence, or (as was typically the case) some combination of these factors. It was, moreover, a common argumentative move to associate a civilized society with a particular form of political consciousness—nationality. A country that was civilized possessed a sense of nationhood, and as such displayed the political (and moral) capacity for self-determination. This was a necessary, but rarely sufficient, condition of entry into international society. India was, in the most common articulation of this argument, frequently seen as failing to meet the criteria. There was also a specific temporal dimension embedded in internationalist discourse. "Civilization" was a marker of the present, and a guide to the future; it was a classification independent of any historical greatness. Whilst the Indians could offer up their contributions to architecture, science, and philosophy as indicators of their civilizational status, this was not seen to reflect accurately the "barbarism" of the present. The Chinese, likewise, were frequently lambasted for their "stationariness," their failure to live up to the splendor of their own ancient history.[84] Different regions, and even different countries within a region, were labeled and judged (albeit often in conflicting ways) and placed on

---

[83] For debate amongst lawyers, see Jennifer Pitts, "The Boundaries of Victorian International Law," in *Victorian Visions*, ed. Bell, 67–89.

[84] On the trope of Chinese "stationariness," see Collini, *Public Moralists*, 108, 274.

a ladder, with the "white" countries, and especially Britain, perched at the top. But this account allowed for the possibility of movement up (and even down) the ladder, and thus for eventual inclusion in international society. This, at least, was the theory, although there were very few discussions of the actual timescale involved.

Questions of race, empire, and progress were woven through late Victorian political debate. Few internationalists followed Spencer in his almost complete opposition to empire (more on this below)—and most ended up defending at least some aspects of its existence. Many distinguished between varieties of "good" and "bad" imperialism. The aggressive, militaristic "jingo" imperialism associated with Disraeli and, later, Joseph Chamberlain, which reached its pinnacle in the "scramble for Africa" and the South African War, was widely condemned by liberal internationalists, including Morley, Hobson, and Hobhouse.[85] But empire itself was rarely considered unjustifiable. Two general lines of argument can be discerned; these were often but not always combined, although the weight afforded to each differed from individual to individual.[86] The first was a long-standing one, articulated most powerfully in the writings of John Stuart Mill, which stressed the benefits that enlightened imperial governance could bring to the "barbarous" regions of the world. This was often phrased, to use a pervasive metaphor, in terms of adults training children for induction into society.[87] Although faith in the "civilizing mission," which reached its peak in the 1830s and 1840s, had been slowly undermined by a series of imperial crises (most notably the 1857 Sepoy Rebellion and the Eyre controversy of the 1860s) and by a more general loss of confidence in the ability of the British to remake the world in their own image, belief in the civilizing role of empire still carried considerable weight (a topic I discuss further in chapter 2).[88] The empire, in this account, was seen as a giant engine for global social reform, the agent of civilization itself. The second line of argument focused more on the role of the settler empire, stressing the economic, cultural, political, and racial commonalities between the United Kingdom and Australia, New Zealand, and Canada—and often the United States. This union of the "Anglo-Saxon" peoples, whether cast in terms of a formal political alliance (most frequently in terms of "imperial federation") or a vague moral unity, was seen by a number of prominent internation-

[85] See also Bernard Porter, *Critics of Empire* (London, 1968).

[86] For debates among progressives, including Hobson, Herbert Samuel, J. M. Robertson, and C. P. Trevelyan, on the question of empire and civilization that bear out the following discussion, see Michael Freeden, ed., *Minutes of the Rainbow Circle, 1894–1924* (London, 1989), 45–46, 58–60, 69–79, 115–26.

[87] Ashis Nandy, "Reconstructing Childhood," in *Traditions, Tyranny, and Utopia* (Delhi, 1987), 56–76; Uday Singh Mehta, *Liberalism and Empire* (Chicago, 1999), 28–36.

[88] Mantena, *Alibis of Empire*.

alists, including Hobson and Hobhouse, as a step on the road to a more pacific global order.[89]

Green, Sidgwick, and Spencer embodied the ambiguities and ambivalences, as well as many of the prejudices, of liberal internationalism. Green had the least to say about civilization and empire, although this was largely a consequence of the level of abstraction at which his work was pitched. His undergraduate essays, written in the mid-1880s, had supported the conventional civilizing rationale of the British empire, arguing that "the progress of our dominion [in India] seems to have been the inevitable result of the action of civilization on barbarism."[90] He was never especially critical of the consequences of empire for Britain's imperial subjects.[91] However, in the *Lectures on the Principles of Political Obligation* he argued, albeit in an aside, that British rule in India was both internally and externally destabilizing, leading to the propagation of an unhealthy "military character" in England while simultaneously contributing to dangerous international rivalry.[92] Ironically, this muted critique was launched from Green's base in Balliol, an institution that, under the inspiring leadership of his former tutor, Benjamin Jowett (1817–93), primed young men for a life of service on the frontier: between 1874 and 1914, 27.1 percent of Balliol graduates worked in the imperial "outposts of progress" for at least two years.[93] Moreover, Green's teaching deeply influenced many of the men who left Balliol to become imperial administrators, and the impact of idealism on Edwardian conceptions of imperialism, ranging from ideas about the Anglo-Saxon "commonwealth" through to Tory visions of global grandeur, was pronounced.[94]

[89] Hobson, *Imperialism* [1902], ed. Philip Siegelman (Ann Arbor, 1997), 332; Hobhouse, *Democracy and Reaction*, 153–54. See also Bell, *The Idea of Greater Britain*. Hobson and Hobhouse later changed their positions on this issue, as I discuss in chapter 14.

[90] Green, "British Rule and Policy in India," *Collected Works*, 5:22. See also Green, "Interference with Foreign Nations," 15–19. In later writings the British empire, in India or elsewhere, is rarely mentioned.

[91] For example he argued that the only "lasting defence of the Indian Empire is in contentment of the Indian people." See Green's notes on his speech on "National Loss and Gain under a Conservative Government," delivered on December 5, 1879, in *Collected Works*, 5:352.

[92] Green, *Political Obligation*, 483, sec. 173.

[93] Richard Symonds, *Oxford and Empire* (Oxford, 1991), 28–29, 306. Since the 1850s, Jowett had been instrumental in directing Oxford and Cambridge graduates to the Indian Civil Service. See Phiroze Vasunia, "Greek, Latin, and the Indian Civil Service," *Proceedings of the Cambridge Philological Society*, 51 (2005), 35–71, esp. 44–47. In the years between 1888 and 1905, three successive viceroys of India came from Balliol. Vasunia, "Greater Rome and Greater Britain," in *Classics and Colonialism*, ed. Barbara Goff (London, 2005), 34–68, esp. 45. For the phrase "outposts of progress," see Joseph Conrad, "An Outpost of Progress" (1896–97), in *Heart of Darkness, and Other Tales*, ed. Cedric Watts (Oxford, 2002). See also the discussion in chapter 5.

[94] E.H.H. Green, *Ideologies of Conservatism* (Oxford, 2001), 42–72; Morefield, *Covenants without Swords*.

Sidgwick frequently wrote in a racialized idiom, and his work is studded with examples of crude (albeit standard) civilizational stereotyping.[95] It is the "business" of civilized nations to "educate and absorb" the savage nations, he wrote once when criticizing Spencer's ethics.[96] He was an ardent defender of the British empire; indeed he sought to replicate in Cambridge the success of Oxford in training young men for imperial service.[97] He argued that while the empire exhibited many potential downsides these were ultimately outweighed by its positive effects. The downsides included the loss of life involved (mainly but not only among the "civilized"), the geopolitical vulnerability to which it exposed Britain, the difficulty of defending such a globally extended frontier, and the temptation to drag other great powers into competition. These could in principle be offset, however, by a combination of material and moral benefits. Materially, imperialism could generate increased military power and national wealth, although this was by no means certain. Above all, though, it was ideas about Britain's civilizational task and "spiritual expansion," the "sentimental advantages, derived from justifiable conquests," that anchored Sidgwick's support for empire:

> Such are the justifiable pride which the cultivated members of a civilised community feel in the beneficent exercise of dominion, and in the performance by their nation of the noble task of spreading the highest kind of civilisation; and a more intense though less elevated satisfaction—inseparable from patriotic sentiment—in the spread of the special type of civilisation distinctive of their nation, communicated through its language and literature, and through the tendency to imitate its manners and customs which its prolonged rule, especially if on the whole beneficent, is likely to cause in a continually increasing degree.[98]

This was a vision of liberal civilizational imperialism, remaking the manners as well as the map of the world, and drawing on a long-standing argument about the occupation of "unoccupied" territory leavened with late Victorian moralism about the duty of imperialists to indigenous populations.[99]

However, as I have stressed throughout the chapters in this book, liberalism was far from monolithic when it came to justifying imperial ventures, and sweeping claims about the imperial logic inherent in liberalism, or of the es-

---

[95] See especially Sidgwick, *The Elements of Politics*, 311–28; Schultz, *Henry Sidgwick*, ch. 7.

[96] Sidgwick, *Lectures*, 236.

[97] Collini, Winch, and Burrow, *That Noble Science of Politics*, 354–55; Vasunia, "Greek, Latin, and the Indian Civil Service."

[98] Sidgwick, *The Elements of Politics*, 312, 313, 256.

[99] For a discussion of so-called *terra nullius* arguments, see Anthony Pagden, "Human Rights, Natural Rights, and Europe's Imperial Legacy," *Political Theory*, 31 (2003), 171–99. Since this chapter was originally published, a comprehensive study has appeared: Andrew Fitzmaurice, *Sovereignty, Property and Empire, 1500–2000* (Cambridge, 2014).

sential connection between liberal political thought and empire, need to be treated with caution. Spencer was a vitriolic critic of empire and imperialism. He was at his most acute in identifying the "re-barbarization" of England, the reversion to militarism and authoritarian practices, a process that he argued was inseparable from imperialism. At the turn of the century he wrote that the "coincidence in time between the South African war and the recent outburst of Imperialism, illustrates the general truth that militancy and Imperialism are closely allied—are, in fact, different manifestations of the same social condition. It could not, indeed, be otherwise."[100] As noted earlier, Spencer predicted the development of industrial societies and their peaceful coexistence. Although he had never specified a timeline, the closing years of the nineteenth century offered very little support for this prophecy. Spencer reacted by indicting the whole political culture of late Victorian Britain:

> From the people who daily read their Bibles, attend early services, and appoint weeks of prayer, there are sent out messengers of peace to inferior races, who are forthwith ousted from their lands by filibustering expeditions authorized in Downing Street; while those who resist are treated as "rebels," the deaths they inflict in retaliation are called "murders" and the process of subduing them is named "pacification."[101]

Most people took their "nominal creed" from the New Testament and their "real creed from Homer," and it was against this background that the by-now-agnostic Spencer claimed often to find himself trying to convert "Christians to Christianity."[102] This is not to suggest that he was free from the prejudices of his age; his writings are, after all, peppered with racialized turns of phrase (one only has to look closely at the passage just quoted).[103] The point is that Spencer's biting radicalism and his sense of betrayal gave him a critical distance from the establishment and the policies it pursued, especially in contrast to Sidgwick's "government house" internationalism. It was this distance that made it possible for him to refer to dark and white savages in the same breath, to identify the "diffusion of military ideas, military sentiments, military organization, military discipline . . . going on everywhere," and to lament the "general retrogression shown in the growing Imperialism and accompanying re-barbarization."[104]

---

[100] Spencer, "Imperialism and Slavery," in *Facts and Comments* (London, 1902), 112–21, esp. 113.

[101] Spencer, *Principles of Ethics*, 2:277.

[102] Spencer to E. Cazelles, December 6, 1896, in Duncan, *Life and Letters*, 399–400.

[103] Although see the discussion in Peel, *Herbert Spencer*, ch. 6. Note also that Spencer did offer heavily qualified support for privatized forms of settler colonialism, as I discuss in chapter 2.

[104] Spencer to Cazelles, and also Spencer to Moncure D. Conway, July 17, 1898, in Duncan, *Life and Letters*, 410; Spencer, "Re-Barbarization" and "Regimentation," in *Facts and Comments*, 236, 138.

Conclusions

Despite considerable political and philosophical differences, the views on international society articulated by Green, Spencer, and Sidgwick were overlapping. They emphasized the potential of a variety of trends discernible in international politics, in particular the importance of free trade and the evolution of international law, and they shared a broadly complementary normative vision of the future, of a pacific, stable, and expanding society of civilized states. Their conceptions of empire were, however, very different. The potential universalism of Sidgwick's vision was, like that of so many of his contemporaries, circumscribed by arrogance towards and ignorance about other societies. The sphere of civilization, whilst in principle capable of encompassing the whole planet, was still considered very small. This vision of international society was constrained, that is, by an account of racial difference. Green appears rather more ambivalent on this matter, whereas Spencer, while often prejudiced, was contemptuous of imperialism and feared the degrading effects of foreign dominion on British politics.

The intellectual life of the late Victorians was marked by often-vicious debate over a host of political issues. Despite the fissiparous nature of the period, it is nevertheless possible to identify a relatively coherent internationalist ideology promulgated by liberal public moralists. Green, Spencer, and Sidgwick were able to systematically theorize lines of thought which others held as articles of political faith. In the twentieth century the liberal ideal of international society was gradually, albeit incompletely, realized following two catastrophic world wars, reaching its formal legal recognition with the end of the drawn-out and bloody process of decolonization. Yet this new society embodied the Janus-faced approach to international order found in the tradition of British liberalism, one of its main intellectual progenitors. While finally achieving a form of universality through encompassing the entire globe, the new international society failed to completely escape the hierarchical differentiation associated with the always shifting standard of "civilization." This remains the case to this day.

CHAPTER 11

John Robert Seeley and the Political Theology of Empire

๛

When we have accustomed ourselves to contemplate the whole Empire together and call it England, we shall see that here too is a United States. Here too is a homogenous people, one in blood, language, religion, and laws, but dispersed over a boundless space.[1]

—J. R. SEELEY

John Robert Seeley (1834–95) was the most prominent imperial thinker in late nineteenth-century Britain. His writings about the past, present, and future of British expansion were hugely popular, and his name became a byword for the world-straddling ambition of the country. Lord Acton crowned him "the philosopher of national greatness."[2] Published in 1883, his most famous book, *The Expansion of England*, was an instant success, helping to set the terms of late Victorian debate about empire and remaining a standard reference point for decades to come. "I question," H.A.L. Fisher wrote in an obituary, "whether any historical work has exercised so great an influence over the general political thinking of a nation."[3] A quarter of a century later, G. P. Gooch marveled that it occupied "a place in political history as well as in a record of historiography," such was its impact.[4] It remained in print until 1956, the year of Suez.

Seeley set himself two main tasks in the book. First, he sought to rewrite the plotline of British historical development. Displacing the center of gravity

---

[1] Seeley, *The Expansion of England*, 158–59.

[2] Acton, review of Seeley, *A Short History of Napoleon*, *English Historical Review*, 2/7 (1887), 598. The most detailed discussions of Seeley are Deborah Wormell, *Sir John Seeley and the Uses of History* (Cambridge, 1980); David Worsley, "Sir John Robert Seeley and His Intellectual Legacy," unpublished PhD, University of Manchester, 2001.

[3] Fisher, "Sir John Seeley," *Fortnightly Review*, 60 (1896), 193.

[4] Gooch, *History and Historians in the Nineteenth Century* (London, 1920), 371. See also Gooch, "Imperialism," in *The Heart of Empire*, ed. C.F.G Masterman (London, 1901), 309. "Its influence can be traced in the pronouncements of three generations of political leaders (of all political parties)": John Darwin, "Empire and Ethnicity," *Nations and Nationalism*, 16/2 (2010), 394.

from domestic constitutional reform to imperial expansion, he contended that modern Britain was forged chiefly in conflicts over territory and sovereign control in North America and Asia, not in the corridors of Parliament or on the battlefields of Europe.[5] "History," he boomed, "is not constitutional law, nor parliamentary tongue-fence, nor biography of great men, nor even moral philosophy. It deals with states, it investigates their rise and development and mutual influence, the causes which promote their posterity or bring about their decay."[6] He thus rejected the Whiggish line that the epicenter of the national story was the evolution of constitutional government and individual liberty. Secondly, he emphasized the significance of what we might term the *second settler empire* in Australia, Canada, the Cape, and New Zealand, insisting that this transoceanic political association was both more durable and more important than India. "When we inquire into the Greater Britain of the future we ought to think much more about our colonial than our Indian empire."[7] Seeley presented these arguments as a case study of his historical method. Committed to the view that the main purpose of analyzing the past was to inculcate political knowledge in citizens and (especially) members of the political elite, he argued that history was a "school of statesmanship."[8] Through the rigorous inductive dissection of the historical record, and in particular through tracing the development of states, it was possible to cultivate political wisdom and foresight. If it was "worth anything," he argued, history must surely "anticipate the lessons of time. We shall all no doubt be wise after the event; we study history that we may be wise before the event." Studying the past necessarily involved a "practical object," insofar as it shaped perceptions of the world, and in doing so (hopefully) conditioned ethical judgment and political action.[9] "Though he did not coin the phrase 'History is past politics, and politics present history,'" G. W. Prothero once wrote, "it is perhaps more strictly applicable to his view of history than to that of its author."[10]

Despite its importance, and despite the apparent clarity of its argument, *The Expansion of England* remains poorly understood. This is partly a matter

[5] His claim about the primacy of Asia in eighteenth-century British history still sparks rebuttals. "It was not: the history of eighteenth-century Britain was in Europe." Brendan Simms, *Three Victories and a Defeat* (London, 2007), 1.

[6] Seeley, *Expansion*, 151.

[7] Ibid., 11.

[8] Seeley, "The Teaching of Politics," *Macmillan's Magazine*, 21 (1870), 433–44. On his methodological claims, see Collini, Winch, and Burrow, *That Noble Science of Politics*, ch. 7; Ian Hesketh, *The Science of History in Victorian Britain* (London, 2011); Wormell, *Seeley*, ch. 4.

[9] Seeley, *Expansion*, 169, 1.

[10] Prothero, "Preface," Edward Seeley, *The Growth of British Policy*, 2 vols. (Cambridge, 1895). The phrase was coined by Freeman (see chapter 13). Seeley had his own less pithy formulation: "Politics are vulgar when they are not liberalised by history, and history fades into mere literature when it lose sight of its relation to practical politics" (*Expansion*, 166).

of genre. Based on a course of undergraduate lectures, and rewritten for a general audience, it doesn't include any sustained discussion of the sources that Seeley drew from, the conceptual architecture underpinning his argument, or the political and intellectual positions he sought to overturn. In this chapter I argue that many of the ideas Seeley employed in his account of empire—nation, state, history, science, civilization—had specific theological connotations, and his political thought as a whole was underwritten by his eccentric interpretation of the sacred. Religion, he professed, was "the soul of all healthy political organization," and on it "depends the whole fabric of civilization, all the future of mankind."[11] This silence may also have been a matter of intention. Seeley wrote two major works of theological reflection, *Ecce Homo* (1866) and *Natural Religion* (1882), the former a literary sensation, the latter his most systematic treatment of the subject, but they were published anonymously, and even when their authorship was widely known Seeley refused to put his name to them.[12] Both *Ecce Homo* and *The Expansion of England*, "each in its own sphere," Fisher later reflected, "may be held to mark an epoch in the education of the Anglo-Saxon race."[13] Seeley did not regard those spheres as distinct or separable.

Seeley's brand of liberal political theology blended the impulse to transform aspects of society with a Burkean gradualism and respect for tradition. A willfully syncretic thinker, he drew on a variety of sources. Comtean positivism, Rankean historicism, German romanticism, the doctrines of Broad Churchmanship derived ultimately from Coleridge and transmitted through Thomas Arnold and F. D. Maurice, the "comparative method" so popular among late Victorian scholars: all found their allotted place in his capacious intellectual system. In the next section I dissect Seeley's understanding of theology and religion.[14] Section 3 probes his views on the sacred character of nationality, and shows how he attempted to reconcile particularism and universalism in what I will call a "cosmopolitan nationalist" vision. In section 4 I argue that *The Expansion of England* should be understood as an expression of his basic political-theological commitments, and I also make the case that he conceived of Greater Britain as a global federal nation-state, modeled on the United States. I conclude by discussing the role of India and Ireland in his polychronic, stratified conception of world order.

---

[11] [Seeley], *Natural Religion* (London, 1882), 259, 218.

[12] With *Ecce Homo* (London, 1866), he was keen to avoid upsetting his family; his reasons for keeping the authorship of *Natural Religion* secret are less clear. For a discussion of his anonymity, see Ian Hesketh, "Behold the (Anonymous) Man," *Victorian Review*, 38 (2012), 93–112.

[13] Fisher, "Sir John Seeley," 183.

[14] Good discussions of Seeley's theological views can be found in Richard Shannon, "John Robert Seeley and the Idea of a National Church," in *Ideas and Institutions of Victorian Britain*, ed. Robert Robson (London, 1967), 236–67; Wormell, *Seeley*, ch. 1. Neither, though, reads his conception of empire in theological terms (and nor does any other scholarship on Seeley).

Enthusiasm for Humanity

Seeley followed an intellectual trajectory typical of the son of "extreme" evan-
gelicals.[15] Bypassing the early crisis of faith so common amongst his contemporaries, he glided from a youthful immersion in evangelicalism to a less un-
forgiving incarnationalism, from a harsh and apocryphal vision of the cosmos
to a milder one in which the life of Jesus served as a noble example for human
behavior. In particular, Seeley drew inspiration from the "Broad Church"
theologians, A. P. Stanley, F. W. Robertson, and especially Thomas Arnold
and F. D. Maurice.[16] The term "Broad Church," happily embraced by Seeley,
had been introduced to encompass those sharing a more liberal theological
sensibility in the face of the radical supernaturalism and biblical literalism
that united the otherwise conflicting High (Anglo-Catholic, Tractarian-
influenced) and Low (Evangelical) Churches.[17] In the background hovered
Samuel Taylor Coleridge, whose ideas about the relationship between Church
and State influenced the Broad Church theologians, and whose notion of a
"clerisy" Seeley also embraced and updated.[18] Seeley's latitudinarianism seems
to have been reinforced by the time he spent in London, where he moved in
the overlapping circles of the emerging Comtean positivist movement and the
Christian Socialists.[19] Learning from both, he never fully joined either. Indeed
he can be seen as a fairly conventional Broad Church theologian, focusing on
the interrelationship between (the usually capitalized) Church and State, the
quest to reconcile modernity and tradition, and a concomitant desire to fashion national unity through the eradication of interdenominational and class

[15] Boyd Hilton, *The Age of Atonement* (Oxford, 1988), 334. His father was R. B. Seeley, a
prominent religious publisher and author of *Essays on the Church by a Layman* (London, 1834), a
fierce antiliberal, evangelical tract. For a comparison of father and son, see Reba Soffer, "History
and Religion," in *Religion and Irreligion in Victorian Society*, ed. R. W. Davis and R. J. Helmstadter
(London, 1992), 133–51. On the "familial" context of Victorian patterns of faith, see Frank
Turner, *Contesting Cultural Authority* (Cambridge, 1993), 73–101; David Hempton, *Evangelical
Disenchantment* (New Haven, 2008).

[16] By the late 1850s, in correspondence with his family, Seeley was expressing admiration for
the Broad Church. J. R. Seeley to R. B. Seeley, September 29, 185?, Seeley Papers, MS903/2A/2
and J. R. Seeley to Mary Seeley, April 3, 1855, Seeley Papers, MS903/2B/1. See also Seeley, "The
Church as a Teacher of Morality," in *Essays in Church Policy*, ed. W. L. Clay (London, 1868).

[17] See for example, W. J. Conybeare, "Church Parties," *Edinburgh Review*, 98 (1853), 273–342.
See also C. R. Sanders, *Coleridge and the Broad Church Movement* (London, 1972); Tod Jones, *The
Broad Church* (Lanham, MD, 2003).

[18] Coleridge, *On the Idea of the Constitution of the Church and State* (London, 1830). The most
explicit of Seeley's (published) references to Coleridge can be found in "Milton's Political Opinions," *Lectures and Essays*, 99. On the shifting meanings of clerisy, see Ben Knights, *The Idea of the
Clerisy in the Nineteenth Century* (Cambridge, 1978).

[19] Wormell, *Seeley*, ch. 1. His main contact with the positivists was through Edward Beesly. His
educational environment was also liberal. John Burrow, "The Age of Reform," in *Christ's* ed. David
Reynolds (London, 2004), 111–43.

strife. Extremely critical of the Church of England, Seeley believed that it was failing in its appointed task of educating the nation morally, of providing a sense of concord and purpose for society.[20] As the century unfolded, he began to shift the burden of this task away from traditional religious institutions and onto the shoulders of what he hoped would become a reconfigured historical discipline, a new clerisy. Historians were to act not simply as literary chroniclers of the past but as apostles of national destiny. It was their job to animate and inform public opinion and to guide wise statecraft.

In *Ecce Homo* he outlined a view of Christian morality appropriate for the modern world. Bracketing off the supernatural abilities attributed to Christ he focused on the life of Jesus, figuring him as a luminous moral exemplar.[21] Christians, Seeley averred, have a "divine inspiration" that should ideally allow them to identify the appropriate course of action in all circumstances, inspired by "the passion of humanity raised to high energy by the contemplation of Christ's character, and by the society of those in whom the same enthusiasm exists."[22] Jesus, according to Seeley, thus established a divine universal society dedicated to the "improvement of morality."

> His morality required that the welfare and happiness of others should not merely be remembered as a restraint upon action, but should be made the principal motive of action, and what he preached in words he preached still more impressively and zealously in deeds. He set the first and greatest example of a life wholly governed and guided by the passion of humanity.[23]

Central to Christ's revolutionary impact was a transformation of the idea of duty. "The Christian moral reformation may indeed be summed up in this— humanity changes from a restraint to a motive." By this, Seeley meant that an "active" dimension ("thou shalt") was added to the extant negative dictates of morality ("thou shalt not"), and as such the range of duties that human owed to one another was vastly expanded. "To the duty of not doing harm, which may be called justice, was added the duty of doing good, which may properly receive the distinctively Christian name of Charity."[24] This was both a historical assertion about the early development of Christianity, and a

---

[20] Seeley, *Natural Religion*, 43, 135–37. See also Seeley, "The Church as a Teacher of Morality."

[21] The degree to which Seeley "got rid" of the traditional deity and the supernatural paraphernalia accompanying it is far from clear: in *Ecce Homo* he gestured repeatedly to a belief in the transcendent realm, in *Natural Religion* his starting point was to disavow such a belief, and in the preface to the 3rd edition (1891) he restated his heterodox Christianity, therein describing supernaturalism as "accidental" to the religion.

[22] Seeley, *Ecce Homo*, 180.

[23] Ibid., 188.

[24] Ibid., 186, 189.

claim about the best way to understand morality in the present. Moral improvement was—or at least should be—the guiding task of Christianity, its continuing lesson and gift to the world. Much to the chagrin of his friend Henry Sidgwick, Seeley dismissed modern secular accounts of ethics as incapable of motivating right conduct, solely reliant as they were on rational argumentation. Only a system rooted in the passionate exemplarity of Christ was sufficient.[25]

Seeley's political theology developed in critical dialogue with Comtean positivism. Throughout his writings he attempted to combine elements of positivism, not least its respect for the wonders of modern science and its universalism, with a specifically Christian conception of moral life. He was far from alone in attempting this kind of synthesis. During the second half of the nineteenth century, numerous theologians grappled with Comte's elaborate system, which was widely understood to present a deep challenge to the main tenets of Christianity, principally through its corrosive skepticism about the ability to know the unobservable world. B. F. Westcott, J. B. Lightfoot, F.J.A. Hort, Charles Kingsley, and Maurice, among others, sought either to domesticate or tame its more radical epistemological claims.[26] Like many liberal theologians of the era, Seeley was both attracted to and repelled by positivism. We can catch a glimpse of his ambivalent attitude from a letter he wrote in 1869 to Kingsley, his predecessor at Cambridge:

> I certainly do not feel equal to the task of opposing Comte. But you are right in thinking that, if I could, I would oppose his atheism as strongly as yourself. But just at present Comtism seems so irresistibly triumphant, that I have contented myself lately with pointing out that it is in a sense a Christian movement and with trying to induce the Church to appropriate what is good in it.[27]

[25] Ibid., chs. 13–14. Unsurprisingly, Sidgwick rejected this argument: "Ecce Homo," *Westminster Review* (1866), reprinted in *Miscellaneous Essays and Addresses*, ed. Eleanor Sidgwick and Arthur Sidgwick (London: Macmillan, 1904). For analysis, see J. B. Schneewind, *Sidgwick's Ethics and Victorian Moral Philosophy* (Oxford, 1977), 28–35, 45–47.

[26] For Maurice's engagement with Comte, see, for example, Maurice, *Social Morality* (London, 1869), 18–19, Lecture 19. The positivists, as I discuss in chapter 2, were among the most ardent critics of imperialism. See Greg Claeys, *Imperial Sceptics*, ch. 1 (and p. 118) for Beesly's criticism of Seeley's *Expansion* as spreading the "poison of Imperialism." The positivist flavor of Seeley's writings did not go unnoticed, and it was a prominent theme in conservative criticisms of his views. Charles Cashdollar, *The Transformation of Theology, 1830–1890* (Princeton, 1989), 179, 198, 437. Rather surprisingly, Seeley plays no role in T. R. Wright's *The Religion of Humanity* (Cambridge, 1986).

[27] Seeley to Kinglsey, 1869, quoted in Cashdollar, *The Transformation of Theology*, 437. Kingsley had been tasked by Gladstone to sound out Seeley's views on Comte, before he recommended him for appointment to the Regius chair. See Sheldon Rothblatt, *The Revolution of the Dons* (London, 1968), 153, 160–61, 177; Wormell, *Seeley*, 41–42.

The influence of positivism was most pronounced in *Ecce Homo*, though it also inflected many of the concerns and categories of *Natural Religion*, including Seeley's advocacy of "enthusiasm" for humanity and his emphasis on love as the basis of morality. Throughout his writings, Seeley sought to undercut one of the main implications of Comte's teaching, the strict division, both epistemic and historical, between science and religion.[28] Rather than condemning the latter to a past rendered obsolete by the former, he (like Maurice) asserted that science itself could be seen as a form of divine revelation. Contra Comte and his legion of followers, then, science and religion were not only compatible, both were necessary to underpin a progressive vision of humanity.

Ecce Homo spawned impassioned debate about both the identity of its author and its religious teaching. Some theologians, including John Henry Newman, dismissed it as an amateurish essay.[29] The evangelical seventh Earl of Shaftesbury condemned it as the worst work "vomited from the jaws of hell."[30] Others, though, were far more receptive to its message. Among its greatest admirers was Gladstone, who published a sympathetic response and subsequently propelled Seeley into the Regius Professorship of Modern History at Cambridge.[31] Four decades after its publication, the liberal theologian and historian Hastings Rashdall described it as "the most striking expression of the appeal which Christ makes to the Conscience of the modern world," one that had "proved a veritable fifth Gospel to many seekers after light."[32] As the First World War engulfed the world Seeley had known, the American theologian Arthur McGiffert praised *Ecce Homo* as "epoch-making" due to its role in shifting attention to the personal example of Christ, while as late as 1927 Charles Gore, the Christian socialist Bishop, could write that there was "still no book about the teaching of our Lord which can rival *Ecce Homo*."[33]

Despite the success of *Ecce Homo*, or perhaps because of it, Seeley was determined to outline his basic theological commitments in a more comprehensive fashion. His friend Richard Jebb once asked him why he had not written

[28] Cashdollar, *The Transformation of Theology*, 426–30. Cashdollar claims that Seeley's theological thought was so heavily influenced by positivism that it "pushed the definition of Broad Church to its very limits, and some would have said beyond" (427). This is an exaggeration.

[29] Newman, "An Internal Argument for Christianity" [1866], in *Discussions and Arguments on Various Subjects*, 4th ed. (London, 1882), 363–98.

[30] Quoted in Wormell, *Seeley*, 23.

[31] Gladstone, *Ecce Homo* (London, 1868).

[32] Rashdall, *Philosophy and Religion* (London, 1909), 62. See also Rasgdall, "Professor Sidgwick on the Ethics of Religious Conformity," *International Journal of Ethics*, 7/2 (1897), where he described it as "the book from which in great measure I have learned all that I have been trying to convey" (166n).

[33] McGiffert, *The Rise of Modern Religious Ideas* (London, 1915), 271; Gore, *Christ and Society* (London, 1928), 59.

Ecce Deus, the sequel dedicated to the divine aspects of Christ promised in the preface to *Ecce Homo*. Much to Jebb's surprise, Seeley replied that he had done so in the *Life and Times of Stein*, his three-volume study of the reformist Prussian statesman.[34] This curious remark provides us with an insight into the profound relationship Seeley discerned between politics, history, and religion. His holistic vision was articulated in what he considered his two most important books, *Natural Religion* and *Stein*.[35] The former was an attempt to systematically explore the bases of belief and the purposes of faith in a world in which the naturalistic impulse, the will to science, was central. The latter was a detailed study of the career and ideas of a man whom Seeley regarded as a founding "father" of modern Germany, and as portending many of the crucial developments of the ensuing century. They were conceived and written during the same period and should be viewed as two elements of the same intellectual compound, one the articulation of his political theology, the other a case study of some of the most important aspects of this as put into political practice. They establish the conceptual architecture essential for understanding his argument in *The Expansion of England*.

Natural Religion never achieved the prominence of *Ecce Homo*. Anatomizing *The Varieties of Religious Experience*, William James observed that it was "too little read, I fear."[36] It was, nevertheless, a well-respected contribution to theological discussion. In 1911 W. W. Fenn, Unitarian theologian and Dean of the Harvard Divinity School, acknowledged that it was "almost forgotten" but went on to praise its "prophetic insight and power" and judged it "one of the most significant contributions ever made to the subject." He concluded that it should have "marked a turning-point in thought concerning natural religion."[37] Establishing the exact theological status of *Natural Religion* proved difficult, which may partly explain its muted reception. Praising it as "one of the most striking [books] in our theological literature," Alfred Caldecott argued that Seeley articulated a potent brand of "ethical theism," while a decade later the American theologian Durant Drake characterised it as the "clearest popular exposition of the pantheistic conception."[38] The philoso-

---

[34] Caroline Jebb, *The Life and Letters of Sir Richard Claverhouse Jebb* (Cambridge, 1907), 85–86. The nonconformist Joseph Parker did publish an *Ecce Deus* (Boston, 1868) in response to Seeley, arguing that the main problem with *Ecce Homo* was that it had failed to take the incarnation of Jesus seriously. Thanks to Michael Ledger-Lomas for this reference.

[35] *Natural Religion* was first published in serial form in *Macmillan's Magazine* between 1875–78, during the period in which Seeley was researching and writing *Stein*. It was published in 1882, the year during which the lectures on which the *Expansion of England* were being delivered.

[36] James, *The Varieties of Religious Experience* (London, 1902), 77n.

[37] Fenn, "Concerning Natural Religion," *Harvard Theological Review*, 4/4 (1911), 472.

[38] Caldecott, *The Philosophy of Religion in England and America* (London, 1901), 361, 191–92; Durant Drake, "Seekers after God," *Harvard Theological Review*, 12/1 (1919), 71–72. Formerly Dean of St. John's Cambridge, Caldecott was Professor of Logic and Mental Philosophy at King's College London. For his views on empire, see chapter 2.

pher A. W. Benn assigned Seeley a leading role in his influential history of rationalism, arguing that *Natural Religion,* more than any other book, marked the "retreat of religious belief before reason."[39] In contrast, the eminent church historian Francis Warre Cornish declared that Seeley, along with Arnold, had curbed the tide of the "forces which, since 1789, under the garb of liberation, were tending to irreligion."[40] Seeley would most likely have approved of the judgments of Caldecott and Cornish. He came not to bury existing religious practice, but to reanimate it. And in this he achieved some success. His writings, for example, exerted a powerful influence over the fledgling "ethical society" movement that flowered on both sides of the Atlantic from the 1890s onwards. One of its key texts listed the favored authors of the society as Matthew Arnold, Emerson, Milton, Burke, and Seeley.[41] Stanton Coit, a socialist and leading figure in the society, even dedicated his *National Idealism and a State Church* to Seeley, praising his visionary account of the moral mission of a national church.[42]

In *Natural Religion* Seeley attempted to move beyond both eighteenth-century natural theology and nineteenth-century Comtean positivism, whilst incorporating the most valuable aspects of both. He argued that there were two distinct but related forms of knowledge, the *theoretical* and the *practical.* In relation to the sacred—"in the realm of observing God"[43]—the two corresponded to theology (theoretical) and religion (practical). "By theology the nature of God is ascertained and false views of it eradicated from the understanding; by religion the truths thus obtained are turned over in the mind and assimilated by the imagination and the feelings." Theology was concerned with "the attitude of Nature towards human beings," where nature was defined as "the uniform laws of the Universe as known in our experience."[44] These included scientific laws of the kind revealed with ever-greater frequency during the nineteenth century, as well as social laws, such as those governing

---

[39] Benn, *The History of English Rationalism in the Nineteenth Century,* 2 vols. (London, 1906), 2:441. Benn defined rationalism as the use of reason for the (partial or total) destruction of religious belief ("Preface").

[40] Cornish, *The History of the English Church in the Nineteenth Century,* 2 vols. (London, 1910), 2:207. Cornish described Seeley as "less brilliant, but perhaps a more solid student of religion" than Thomas Arnold (206). Cf. Bridges, *Some Outlines,* 8, on Seeley as "liberator."

[41] Horace Bridges, Stanton Coit, G. E. O'Dell, and Harry Snell, *The Ethical Movement* (London, 1911), 12. On the movement, see I. MacKillop, *The British Ethical Societies* (Cambridge, 1986).

[42] Coit, *National Idealism and a State Church* (London, 1907). See also Horace Bridges, *Some Outlines of the Religion of Experience* (London, 1916), 8, 78–79, 232, 258. While Seeley admired the ambition of the Ethical Societies to incubate a broad ethical sensibility in a world that had lost its bearings, he cautioned against ignoring the role of the Christian churches. Seeley, "Ethics and Religion," *Fortnightly Review,* 45 (1889), 501–14

[43] Seeley, *Natural Religion,* 52.

[44] Ibid., 53, 66, 68.

the formation and growth of nations. It also examined meta-ethical questions including the character of virtue, the nature of temptation, and the role and limits of human conscience. "In one word," he inquired, "is life worth having, and the Universe a habitable place for one in whom the sense of duty has been awakened?"[45] Since for Seeley the scientific analysis of nature was an exploration of the laws of the universe, science was "in the strictest sense Theology," and since history was an exploration of the laws of social development, it was also, in the "proper sense," theological.[46] To read Seeley as a straightforward "scientific" historian or as a progenitor of a secular political science misses the point that his conceptions of history and science were themselves theological.

Religion, on the other hand, was grounded on admiration, on the impulse to (and act of) *worship*. Whereas theology engaged reason, religion was concerned chiefly with sensitivity, empathy, and imagination. It was as much about emotion as it was about rationality. This capacious understanding of religion attracted much commentary at the time.[47] Religion, for Seeley, was constituted by three elements: "that worship of visible things which leads to art, that worship of humanity which leads to all moral disciplines, and principally the Christian, and that worship of God which is the soul of all philosophy and science."[48] The third panel of this triptych focused on the worship of God-in-nature as clarified by the theological disciplines of history, natural science, and philosophy. *Natural Religion* was concerned primarily with this aspect. The aesthetic focus of the first panel pointed towards Seeley's intense love of literature and poetry, and in particular the works (and the sensibility) of the great romantic writers.[49] Like Maurice, Seeley admired Byron, Wordsworth, and above all Goethe, whom he regarded as the model of modern cultivation, the human embodiment of excellence in the simultaneous pursuit of art, science, and philosophy, and hence as a "religious" thinker of the highest rank.[50]

---

[45] Ibid., 66.

[46] Ibid., 56, 257.

[47] For positive accounts: Arthur McGiffert, *The Rise of Modern Religious Ideas* (London, 1915), 67–68; James, *Varieties*, 76–77. For rejection of his definition as "excessively broad," see J. H. Leuba, "The Definition of Religion," *American Journal of Theology*, 16/4 (1912), 644–45; Leuba, "The Psychological Nature of Religion," *American Journal of Theology*, 13/1 (1909), 84. A. C. Bradley engaged Seeley at length in his 1907 Gifford lectures, faulting him for failing to adopt the absolutist idealist metaphysics propounded by his brother, F. H. Bradley. Bradley, *Ideals of Religion* (London, 1940), ch. 5.

[48] Seeley, *Natural Religion*, 131–32.

[49] Seeley wrote widely on literature, including essays on Milton and a book on Goethe: *Goethe Reviewed after Sixty Years* (London, 1894). He also published some (bad) poetry of his own: [Seeley], *David and Samuel* (London, 1869).

[50] Seeley, *Natural Religion*, 96–111; Seeley, *Goethe Reviewed*. See also Frederick Denison Mau-

The middle panel of Seeley's triptych clarified his notion of morality: it was his understanding of religion as worship that underpinned his system of ethics. Again, when discussing Stein we can discern the lineaments of his own considered position: "As religion without morality would be to him a monstrosity, so he cannot understand any morality without religion."[51] In *Natural Religion* Seeley continued his campaign against the relevance of secular philosophy for ethics, arguing that it lacked the affective power to motivate action. Earlier, he had written to Sidgwick that utilitarian ethics were insufficient, for reason alone was incapable of identifying the "instinct for sympathy" that lay at the root of morality. Nor, he continued, could the "methodological" teachings of the philosophers help to inculcate the "one law which is to be obeyed for itself, viz., love."[52] It was this insight that he attempted to systematize in *Natural Religion*, and which remained the centerpiece of his moral vision. He was also deeply critical of a system of morality derived from supernaturalism, the belief that human behavior should be regulated by certainty in the eternal pleasures or punishments of the afterlife.[53] This "legal school of morals," as he termed it, was both theologically indefensible and the source of political inaction.[54] "To hope even with enthusiastic conviction for a future life is one thing; to be always brooding over it so as to despise the present life in comparison with it is another." Moreover, he continued, by "the side of such a vision everything historical, all the destiny of states and nations, fades away, and men become quietists if not monks."[55] Rather than subscribing to what he considered a fallacy of eighteenth-century deism, Seeley suggested that his view of natural religion as the worship of nature (broadly defined) could sustain a system of morality focused on the worship of humanity, of humans. People were to teach themselves, and be guided by the historical clerisy, to be generous and humane to one another. The religion "that leads to virtue," he intoned, "must be a religion that worships men."[56]

> It is worshipped under the form of a country, or of ancestors, or of heroes, or great men, or saints, or virgins, or in individual lives, under the form of a friend, or mother, or wife, or any object of admiration; who,

---

rice, *The Life of Frederick Denison Maurice*, vol. 2 (London, 1884), 59. On Seeley's "striking" account of the aesthetic dimension of religion, see Caldecott, *Philosophy of Religion*, 356–61.

[51] Seeley, *The Life and Times of Stein, or Germany and Prussia in the Napoleonic Age*, 2 vols. (Cambridge, 1878), 3:556.

[52] Seeley, letter to Sidgwick, July 2, 1867, Sidgwick Papers, Trinity College, Cambridge, Add Ms c95/64–73.

[53] Seeley, *Natural Religion*, 160.

[54] Ibid., 166.

[55] Ibid., 254.

[56] Ibid., 166.

once seizing the heart, made all humanity seem sacred, and turned all
dealings with men into a religious service.[57]

The ordering he gives to the objects of worship is indicative, for he places the
"country" at the top of his list. The state is the sphere within which the other
objects either live or lived, and as such it takes precedence over them. But as
we shall see, not all states were created equal.

On Nationalist Cosmopolitanism

Seeley was dismissive of the "modern" conception of the secular liberal state,
in which religion was pressed into a hermetically sealed private sphere.[58] It was
both ethically problematic and historically anomalous, for the vast panorama
of the human past was painted largely by the brush strokes of religious ferment. Religious institutions and patterns of belief had played a fundamental
role in social and political development, indeed in the origins and evolution of
the state system itself. The locus of religion in the modern world was the
nation-state. For Seeley, any human community could be labeled, almost interchangeably, "by the name State or Church."[59] Common among Broad Church
thinkers, this claim was derived from his view of the Church as an institution
constituting "the atmosphere of thought, feeling and belief that surrounds the
State; it is in fact its civilization made more or less tangible and visible."[60] An
ahistorical understanding of the interpenetration of politics and religion, one
that failed to grasp this point, was inadequate for the contemporary age. In
Arnoldian vein, he thought that a life without religion was mechanical and
largely meaningless.

For Seeley, the most important consequence of the "Anti-Napoleonic Revolution" was the increasing awareness and power of the "nationality doctrine."
In a quasi-Hegelian spirit, the nineteenth century witnessed the emergent
self-consciousness of the nation-state. This phenomenon was witnessed first
in Spain, where the armies of Napoleon had crushed the institutions of the
Spanish state but had then faced the onslaught of the Spanish nation, which
after surviving the initial destruction had sought to reclaim its political destiny. Seeley wrote admiringly that when "the state fell to pieces the nation
held together and proceeded to put forth out of its own vitality a new form of
state."[61] It was in this period that "a new idea took possession of the mind of

[57] Ibid., 168.
[58] Ibid., 183–85.
[59] Ibid., 185.
[60] Ibid., 200.
[61] Seeley, *Stein*, 2:20.

Europe. That idea was not democracy or liberty ... it was *nationality*."[62] This argument, and Seeley's vision of modern politics as a whole, presupposed a clear distinction between the "state" and the "nation." The former, Seeley wrote in *Stein*, "is merely a machinery by which a number of men protect their common interests." It was an administrative unit, a specified territory ruled over by government institutions. The latter was a distinct group of people whose bonds "are more instinctive, and as it were, more animal." Consequently, the "state which is also a nation is an organism far surpassing in vigour and vitality the state which is only a state."[63] In *The Expansion of England*, Seeley argued that there were three essential preconditions for (nation) state unity: the existence of a community of race, a community of religion, and a community of interest.[64] Of these, religion was the "strongest and most important"; it was the "great state-building principle."[65] Powerful nation-states would combine all three, and as both a presupposition and a consequence they would have to be socially and politically uniform to succeed. "States are composed of men who are in some sense homogeneous, and not only homogeneous in blood and descent, but also in ideas or views of the universe."[66] Modern history began with the completion of the state by the principle of nationality.

Seeley's vision of nationality drew on two main sources: the ideas of the German romantics, especially as instantiated by Stein, and the theology of the Broad Church, which was itself, through the work of Coleridge, influenced by the currents of Germanic organic romanticism. Seeley praised Fichte's *Addresses to the German Nation* (1807–8) for stressing the role of national education, promulgating a holistic ideal of national unity, and conceiving of the state as a moral entity.[67] "Here certainly is heard the tocsin of the anti-Napoleonic Revolution and of all the Nationality Wars that were to follow." Seeley discerned a foreshadowing of his distinction between the nation and the state. "Fichte proclaims the nation not only to be different from the state, but to be something far higher and greater."[68] Seeley's nationalism was ultimately a branch of his political religion, and the religiosity of his conception

---

[62] Ibid., 2:17. Italics added. See also Seeley, "Georgian and Victorian Expansion," 126.

[63] Seeley, *Stein*, 2:35, 17. See also Seeley, "History and Politics, II," *Macmillan's Magazine*, 40 (1879), 297; "Georgian and Victorian Expansion," *Fortnightly Review*, 48 (1887), 126.

[64] Seeley, *Expansion*, 11, 50, 220. He sometimes casually slipped between "state" and "nation-state."

[65] Ibid., 154.

[66] Seeley, *Political Science*, 137.

[67] See the extensive discussion in Seeley, *Stein*, 2:29–42. See also Fichte, *Addresses to the German Nation* [1807–8], ed. Isaac Nakhimovsky, Béla Kapossy, and Keith Tribe (Indianapolis, 2013). For the context of Fichte's argument, see Isaac Nakhimovsky, *The Closed Commercial State* (Princeton, 2011).

[68] Seeley, *Stein*, 2:34.

of nationality can be seen in his argument that, in Fichte's hands, the union of past and present in the doctrine of the nation "secures to the actions of man an earthly immortality."[69] It was the quest for the earthly immortality of the Anglo-Saxon race that ultimately shaped Seeley's vision of Greater Britain.

Seeley's thought was marked deeply by the ideas of Coleridge, and Coleridge's follower, F. D. Maurice. In a discussion of the prophetic seers of British politics, those who he labeled the "genius politicians," he focused on Milton, Carlyle, Ruskin, and Coleridge, arguing that the key to their powers as political thinkers was that they tended to have one simple idea that they reiterated tenaciously. For Coleridge, the "one conviction" that ran through his writings was "the hollowness of all hand-to-mouth statesmanship, and the necessity of grounding politics upon universal principles of philosophy and religion."[70] Seeley concurred wholeheartedly. Indeed, it is imperative to view Seeley's dogged intellectual exertion on behalf of Greater Britain in this light. Whilst he thought that Coleridge was the greatest philosopher, in formulating his conception of the state he drew more on Thomas Arnold and Maurice.[71] Coleridge had argued that the Church of England should be legally recognized as an integral component of the constitution, as a balance to the great landed and commercial interests of the country. It was an essential but quasi-autonomous element of the political nation.[72] Arnold went further, arguing that church and state were in a sense "perfectly identical" and, in his *Postscript to Principles of Church Reform* (1833), that the "state in its highest perfection becomes the Church."[73] Maurice, meanwhile, provided a forceful exposition of the ideal of a spiritual nation, in which church and state were coterminous and mutually constitutive.[74] Seeley's conception of nationality wove together the threads of Fichte's romantic nationalism and the reworking of liberal Anglican theology by Arnold and Maurice.

[69] Ibid., 2:41.

[70] Seeley, "Milton's Political Opinions," 99.

[71] The claim about Coleridge can be found in Seeley, "Milton's Political Opinions," 98. He once wrote in a letter to his father that he was "more of an Arnoldite than a Mauriceite." Seeley to R. B. Seeley, [n.d. 185?], Seeley Papers, MS903/2A/2. The respectful distance was reciprocated, as Maurice wrote of *Ecce Homo*, which he admired greatly (Maurice to A. Macmillan, January 2, 1886, Seeley Papers, MS903/3A/1). Despite these proclamations, I would argue that whilst Seeley might have shared more theological ground with Arnold (at least in the 1850s), his political thought appears to owe considerably more to Maurice, although this might simply be because Maurice lived longer and thus wrote on questions which were also pressing to Seeley.

[72] Coleridge, *Constitution of the Church and State*.

[73] Arnold, "The Church and the State" [1839] and "National Church Establishments" [1840], in *The Miscellaneous Works of Thomas Arnold*, ed. Arthur Stanley (London, 1845), 466–75, 486–92; Arnold, *Postscript to Principles of Church Reform* (London, 1833), 19. This was a vision supported by many Whig MPs.

[74] Maurice, *The Kingdom of Christ* (London, 1838); Maurice, *Social Morality*. On Maurice's social and political thought, see Jeremy Morris, *F. D. Maurice and the Crisis of Christian Authority* (Oxford, 2008), chs. 4–5.

Horace Bridges, leader of the Chicago Ethical Society, once called Seeley "the one great modern English philosopher of religious nationalism."[75] This underplays the universalism of Seeley's political theology. Indeed he is perhaps best characterized as a *cosmopolitan nationalist*. His conception of international politics and the empire was grounded in the idea of the ultimate (albeit only vaguely articulated) unity of humankind. And as we have seen, it was animated by an ethical system that centered on "enthusiasm for humanity." The future, he predicted, "will witness national religions flourishing inside a grand universal religion."[76] We see here echoes of Maurice's ideal of a "Universal Church" in which all of humanity was united in a nonsectarian spiritual society.[77] And it was the idea of love, expressed in the worship of humans, and grounded in a non-parochial attachment to national-political communities that underpinned this complex admixture. For Seeley, there were two churches: the universal church, accommodating all the species, believers and nonbelievers alike, and the national churches as institutionalized in the form of the modern state. The latter took priority, as the highest embodiment of human communal life, but it was embedded in the wider domain of the former. However, this neat binary was upset by Seeley's constant reference to a third (less clearly conceptualized) sphere; between the universal and the national he interposed an intermediary plane, namely Western Christendom, which he regarded as a form of transnational civilization.[78] He argued that the states of Europe—including their dynamic offspring in the United States—constituted a "society," bound to a certain extent by common values and a common culture.[79] The "European brotherhood of nation-states"were between them responsible for the glories of modern civilization.[80] Seeley thus adumbrated a multilayered and hierarchically arranged conception of global order, but one underwritten by a universal religious community.

Despite his constant avowal of the glories of the nation, Seeley was not an uncritical proponent of nationalism. In 1870 he warned that if left unchecked, the "more victories the nationality principle wins," the greater the likelihood that the world would be engulfed by a wave of violence, as "energetic popular states" waged war on each other with the "unrelieved fierceness of national

[75] Bridges, *Some Outlines of the Religion of Experience*, 228. Bridges was a British emigrant to the United States.

[76] Seeley, *Natural Religion*, 207. On the universalism of the church, see Seeley, letter to Sidgwick, May 15, 1866, Sidgwick Papers.

[77] *The Life of Frederick Denison Maurice*, 1:166.

[78] This was most apparent in Seeley, "United States."

[79] Seeley, "Our Insular Ignorance," *Nineteenth Century*, 18 (1885), 869. He continued: "In the main I hold that it is healthy for a nation to live in society. Like an individual a nation should study its behaviour to its fellows, and for this purpose it should listen respectfully and anxiously to their opinion" (869). See also Seeley, *Expansion*, 225.

[80] Seeley, *Political Science*, 88.

antipathy."[81] A decade later he complained that the pure ideal had often been corrupted, that in practice it was usually "too narrow and provincial."[82] He worried about the increasing militarization of Europe, of the great armies eyeing each other suspiciously from one end of the continent to the other.[83] Wary of the dangers of revolution, he was scathing of the Jacobite descent into terror. It was the association of the French Revolution with the thought of the *philosophes* that led Maurice to prefer the use of the term "humanity" to the otherwise equally appropriate "cosmopolitan" when outlining his own vision.[84] Given his admiration for Maurice, his hatred of Revolutionary France, and the theological vocabulary that he adopted, I think it plausible that Seeley's view was similar. In *Ecce Homo* he scorned "universal patriotism," which, without the instantiation of the state, was simply a form of "Jacobinism."[85] Critical of the abstract "universal man" of the Jacobins, he preferred to focus attention on individual persons and their communities. In *Stein* he had sided with his hero's critique of the purportedly disembodied cosmopolitanism of Goethe and Herder, whilst, drawing on Coleridge, he defended the virtues of national patriotism.[86] But as we can see from an earlier essay, his use of the term was qualified:

> The abuse of patriotism is not to be cured by destroying patriotism itself; but patriotism is to be strengthened by being purified, by being deprived of its exclusiveness, and ultimateness. The Christian unity of mankind is to be taught as a final lesson, which will be easiest learnt, or rather will only be learnt, by those who have already realized the unity of the state.[87]

The nation was not an insular political order, the antithesis of wide human sympathies. Rather, it was a necessary condition for their practical realization. Once again, Seeley was following in the wake of Maurice, who had argued that "Christ's Kingdom of Peace" was "a Kingdom for all *nations*. Unless there are Nations, distinct Nations, this Kingdom loses its character; it becomes a world Empire."[88] And world empires were associated with despotism and the

---

[81] Seeley, "United States," 447.

[82] Seeley, *Natural Religion*, 200.

[83] Seeley, "The Eighty-Eights," *Good Words* (1888), 380.

[84] Maurice, *Social Morality*, 19.

[85] Seeley, *Ecce Homo* [1866], ed. John Robinson (London, 1970), 121. See also the discussion in Shannon, "John Robert Seeley," 245–46; Maurice, *Social Morality*, 122–23.

[86] Seeley, *Stein*, 2:384–88. On patriotism (and its absence), see Seeley, "Our Insular Ignorance" and "Georgian and Victorian Expansion."

[87] Seeley, "The Church as a Teacher of Morality," 277. In *Constitution of the Church and State*, Coleridge had counterposed his conception of the national church with the universal church of Christ, which knew no legal or political borders. The two could coexist in the same space, but should not be confused.

[88] Maurice, *Social Morality*, 209. Italics in original. On the connection between nationalism

eradication of difference. "I have endeavored to shew [*sic*] you how much mischief has proceeded from every effort to constitute a Universal divine Society which shall swallow up . . . distinctions into itself."[89] It is little wonder that Seeley was so critical of Napoleon and his attempt to revive the ideal of a universal monarchy, or that he refused to label Greater Britain an empire, preferring instead to call it a "world-state." However, Seeley's cosmopolitanism was heavily attenuated. While his "purpose" was to seek an ideal of national coexistence within a wider framework of progressive humanity, it simultaneously helped to justify the existing power structures of international politics and the ethos of global racial hierarchy.

Expanding England: Democracy, Federalism, and the World-State

The early years of Seeley's career provided few hints about his later role as the leading ideologue of a united Greater Britain. Indeed during the late 1860s and early 1870s he appeared sanguine about the possible future independence of the colonies.[90] All of this was to change. During the 1880s the idea of strengthening the bonds between Britain and its settler colonies swept through the political elite, provoking numerous expressions of support and skepticism. The movement advocating unity coalesced under the rubric of "imperial federation."[91] *The Expansion of England* was its bible, Seeley one of its chief prophets. "I should like to be a working apostle of the doctrine which interests me so much."[92] He was so successful that W. T. Stead, the most famous journalist of the day, proposed that he be placed in charge of a college designed to spread the gospel of Greater Britain.[93] In 1894 Seeley was knighted at the instigation of Lord Rosebery, the prime minister and sometime president of the Imperial Federation League. The award, Rosebery wrote to him, was not merely a testimony to "my admiration for yourself and your

---

and internationalism, see Georgios Varouxakis, "'Patriotism,' 'Cosmopolitanism' and 'Humanity' in Victorian Political Thought," *European Journal of Political Theory*, 5 (2006), 100–118.

[89] Maurice, *Social Morality*, Lecture 13, 481.

[90] See, for example, Seeley, "The British Race" [1872], *Education*, vol. 1 (1881), 309–28; Seeley, "The British Empire," *Bradford Observer*, March 22, 1872.

[91] I explore this debate in Bell, *The Idea of Greater Britain*.

[92] "Sir John Seeley and National Unity," letter quoted by H. F. Wilson, *Cambridge Review*, 16 (1895), 197.

[93] Stead, *The Life of W. T. Stead*, ed. Frederick Whyte (London, 1925), 2:209–10. Influenced by Seeley, Stead was an ardent imperial federalist. See Stead, "The English beyond the Sea," *Pall Mall Gazette*, October 4, 1884, 1. He later wrote to his close confidant, Cecil Rhodes, that he was "drawing up . . . a course of reading" for Rhodes's assistant, "beginning with Seeley's The Expansion of England." Stead to Rhodes, May 21, 1891, Rhodes Papers, Rhodes House Library, Oxford, MSS Afr. s 228 C28, ff. 43–45.

work, but to my staunch adherence to the principles of empire that you have
so eloquently set forth."[94] While those principles could be read in secular
terms, as Seeley presumably intended, they were nevertheless grounded in his
political theology.

The central argument of *The Expansion of England*—and of much of Seeley's subsequent writings—was that the most important development of
modern history was the steady growth of the English state into a globe-
spanning empire. Furthermore, within the diffuse space of the empire, Greater
Britain had developed into a distinct political community, even a nascent
"world-state," and it constituted the most fundamental element of Britain's
enormous network of power. The most significant chapter in this story had
been victory over France in the second "hundred years' war" during the long
eighteenth century.[95] Both the public and the historians whose role it was to
shape the popular mind had missed the importance of these events due to the
prevailing "insular" comprehension of British history, a form of parochial
Whiggery that celebrated the history of parliamentary debate and the post-
1688 evolution of liberty.[96] Macaulay was the preeminent source of this erro-
neous view, with J. R. Green the latest popular exponent.[97] This was as much a
political as an intellectual failure, for in losing sight of the importance of
Greater Britain, Seeley warned that the people and the historians had forgotten the foundations as well as the purpose of colonial unity. The mid-Victorian
years had been pervaded by a dangerous "system of indifference" that nearly
led to a repeat of the American fiasco: "We began to provoke and suggest
secession."[98] Although things had improved since that dark time, Seeley
thought it was still essential to reconnect the people to their grand inheritance, to educate them about their sacred role.

Part of the background to this argument can be discerned in Seeley's outline of a theory of political development. For Seeley stagnation connoted political death.[99] "It is impossible that the history of any state can be interesting
unless it exhibits some sort of development. Political life that is uniform has

[94] Rosebery to Seeley, March 5, 1894, Seeley Papers, MS903/1B/14.

[95] Seeley, *Expansion*, 26, Lecture 2; Seeley, "Georgian and Victorian Expansion."

[96] In the most cogent critique of Seeley, John Morley argued that this claim to historiographical novelty was exaggerated. "The Expansion of England," *Macmillans's Magazine*, 49 (1884),
241–58.

[97] Seeley, *Political Science*, 236, 253, 385; Seeley, *The Growth of British Policy*, 1–2. Seeley later
upset the young G. M. Trevelyan by dismissing his great uncle as a "charlatan." David Cannadine,
G. M. Trevelyan (London, 1992), 27. Seeley cited Green's *Short History of the English People* in the
original manuscript of the *Expansion*, but was persuaded to drop it by Alexander Macmillan, the
publisher of both men. Leslie Howsam, "Imperial Publishers and the Idea of Colonial History,
1870–1916," *History of Intellectual Culture*, 5/1 (2005), 5.

[98] Seeley, "Introduction," to *Her Majesty's Colonies* (London, 1886), xv. On the trope of indifference, see also chapter 7, section 2.

[99] Seeley, *Natural Religion*, 61. See also Seeley, "Roman Imperialism" [1869], vol. 2, in *Lectures
and Essays*, 45.

no history, however prosperous it might be." Associated habitually with "Asiatic" modes of political order, reverting to a "stationary" condition was a characteristic liberal fear during this period.[100] Averse to violent revolution, and drawing on fashionable biological metaphors, Seeley suggested that political "organisms" demonstrated their health in perpetual change, in their active response to internal and external pressures. "Surely we moderns do not believe much in cataclysms. Development is our word. The present grows out of the past."[101] In a revealing passage analyzing the development of the Church, he argued that an "institution is healthy in proportion to its independence of its own past, to the confident freedom with which it alters itself to meet new conditions." Elsewhere he wrote of the state that the "development of its institutions [was] the result of the effort which organisms make to adapt themselves to their environment."[102] To remain healthy, therefore, institutions needed to be adaptable, fitting comfortably into the evolving political environment in which they were embedded. Failure in this delicate process of adjustment and calibration would result in inexorable degeneration. Grasping what we might term this "environmentalist" conception of politics sheds light on the reason why Seeley considered imperial federation a necessity and also on his belief that it could be realized. The shifting—and increasingly threatening—geopolitical situation, combined with the febrile condition of British domestic politics, sparked both the internal and external stimuli for change. This in turn necessitated constitutional revision and the strengthening of Greater Britain. To stand still, frozen, was to court disaster. *The Expansion of England* at once sought to alert people to the dangers and present them with the best solution.

Seeley warned that the people of Greater Britain faced a stark choice: separation or federal unification. "Such a separation would leave England on the same level as the states nearest to us on the continent, populous, but less so than Germany and scarcely equal to France."[103] Shorn of its dominions, England would be dwarfed. "The other alternative," he suggested, was that "England may prove able to do what the United States has done so easily, that is, hold together in a federal union countries very remote from each other." If it achieved this goal, Greater Britain would become, "in time far greater than any political union the world has known."[104] As if to prove his disinterested "scientific" curiosity about the subject, he cautioned that, "[w]e ought by no

---

[100] Seeley, *Expansion*, 117. For Seeley's views on Asia, see "Roman Imperialism," 3:66–68; *Natural Religion*, 61. See, for other examples, Matthew Arnold, "Democracy," in *Culture and Anarchy, and Other Writings*, ed. Stefan Collini (Cambridge, 1993), 10, 21; John Stuart Mill, *On Liberty* [1859], *Collected Works*, 18:273.

[101] Seeley, "Ethics and Religion," 514.

[102] Seeley, *Natural Religion*, 217; Seeley, *Political Science*, 340.

[103] Seeley, *Expansion*, 15–16.

[104] Seeley, "Introduction," xi, xii. Intriguingly, he also referred to America as a "world state" (*Expansion*, 293).

means to take for granted that this is desirable."[105] His lectures sought, he stated, to explore the two options in order to divine which was best for the country. The answer, though, was predetermined by the very language, structure, and tone of his analysis, and it was underpinned by his suggestion that the aim of British policy should be to secure "the foundation of a solid and permanent union."[106]

In *The Idea of Greater Britain* I argued that debate over Greater Britain was motivated by two intersecting fears, of international geopolitical competition and of the dangers posed by mass democracy to British greatness. Many saw a united colonial empire as an answer to both challenges, a means to buttress British preeminence and to diffuse the worst excesses of democracy, the latter chiefly through the agency of large-scale emigration, which could neutralize the rise of socialism and the insurrectionary dangers fostered by intensive urbanization.[107] Seeley was no exception. During the 1880s he too became increasingly nervous about democracy. In 1881, for example, he wrote to his sister that "[w]e are nearer to a Revolution than we have been since before I was born." "Radicalism," he fretted, "is triumphant everywhere." By the end of the decade, he had become, he admitted, "a great skeptic about the current political system."[108] This skepticism was less about franchise extension and the institutional paraphernalia of representative democracy, than it was about the underlying social conditions, and in particular the pronounced deficit in the English "character." "We have everything except decided views and steadfast purpose—everything in short except character! We have emotions, sentiment, thought, knowledge in abundance, only not character! And so to foreigners this nation seems degenerate—a nation in decay."[109]

The British educational system (and the Church) was to blame for the debasement of culture, the rise of crass materialism, and the divorce of the majority of the population from their glorious national heritage. An appreciation of the "higher" aspects of life was conspicuously absent from society. "That bareness in ideas, that contempt for principles, that Philistinism which we hardly deny to be an English characteristic, was not always so," he lamented.[110] This was not simply the complaint of a cultural elitist (although it was that also), for as we have seen Seeley's conception of culture was ultimately

---

[105] Seeley, *Expansion*, 16.

[106] Seeley, "Georgian and Victorian Expansion," 139.

[107] Bell, *The Idea of Greater Britain*, ch. 2.

[108] Seeley to Bessie Seeley, April 9, 1881, Seeley papers, MS903/2B/1; Seeley, "The Impartial Study of Politics," *Contemporary Review*, 54 (1888), 59. On the important role of Irish Home Rule in this switch, see Seeley, letter to Oscar Browning, April 6, 188[?], Browning Papers, Modern Archive Centre, King's College, Cambridge, OB/1/1455A.

[109] Seeley, "Ethics and Religion," 503, 508.

[110] Seeley, "Liberal Education in Universities" [1867], *Lectures and Essays* (London, 1870), 215.

theological, and it underlay his notion of the "higher" life of the nation. To be uneducated was to lack the refinement and knowledge necessary to imagine oneself as part of a community; it was to be deficient in the prerequisites of full citizenship. The "man" lacking a decent awareness of national literatures, suggested Seeley, "can have no link whatever with the past, he can have no citizenship, no country."[111] For Seeley, then, the lack of a proper education, including a wide schooling in English literature and history, as well as in the centrality of empire, was an important *political* problem. Although it beset all classes, it affected the workers in particular for the majority of them were "childishly ignorant of larger political questions."[112] Their ignorance endangered the country: as well as being unaware of their heritage and lacking adequate national consciousness, they were still beholden to superstitions, including the belief in the possibility of a political "utopia," such as that promised by socialists. This was a potential harbinger of revolution. "In England the ideas of the multitude are perilously divergent from those of the thinking class."[113] Now, more than ever, it was essential for the historian to fulfill his destiny as shaper of the national mind and as spiritual healer of the body politic. For Seeley, the ideal nation-state needed to strike a fine balance between democracy and aristocracy (understood in its classical sense as rule by the most suitably qualified).[114] Progress was fragile and in need of constant sustenance and supervision. The lack of national bonds of unity led to alienation between the individual and the state, and also between the different classes. This portended the possibility of increasing unrest, even revolt. It is little surprise, then, that Seeley emphasized the importance of mobilizing the support of the working classes to create a viable Greater Britain.[115]

Seeley fretted that the collective "imagination" and "ways of thinking" about the empire acted as a brake on necessary reforms. Most people continued to view the colonies as entirely separate from the homeland, fragments of foreign land scattered over the distant reaches of the planet. It was thus imperative for the historical clerisy to bring "home to our imaginations" the true nature of the situation, for until that task was achieved "[w]e have not really then as yet a Greater Britain."[116] Political consciousness preceded legislative action; shifts in imagination initiated parliamentary change. The "true mo-

---

[111] Seeley, "English in Schools," *Lectures and Essays*, 238.

[112] Seeley, "Political Somnambulism," *Macmillan's Magazine*, 43 (1880), 42.

[113] Seeley, "The Political Education of the Working Classes," *Macmillan's Magazine*, 36, (1877), 145; Seeley, *Natural Religion*, 208.

[114] Seeley, *Introduction to Political Science*, 357. For his extended discussion on the nature of aristocracy, see 321–31. He is here echoing a Coleridgian argument about the necessity of aristocracies of talent.

[115] Seeley, "Sir John Seeley and National Unity," *Cambridge Review*, 197; Seeley, "Political Education of the Working Classes," 143–45.

[116] Seeley, "Introduction," vii; Seeley, *Expansion*, 8, 61.

ment of revolution," he had written in a different context, "is not so much that in which the new legislation takes place as that in which the conviction becomes universal that a change must come."[117] National education and political mobilization were thus interwoven, and in particular Seeley emphasized the increasing influence of public opinion in shaping British politics.[118] But public opinion needed to be organized and directed. The conditions were ripe, he argued, for the previous decades had witnessed the power of public opinion and the role of pressure groups in catalyzing momentous political change. One of the most important forces guiding the "English Revolution of the Nineteenth Century," and one of the main reasons for the corrosion of the pervasive monopolies of the *ancien régime*, was the influence of the assorted "Leagues" that had demanded the repeal of the Corn Laws, and extensive parliamentary and religious reform. "These Leagues may be considered as a kind of occasional system of government set up for a particular purpose beside the permanent government of the country." It is in the context of his views on the efficacy of the "occasional systems of government" that Seeley's involvement with the Imperial Federation League should be understood.[119]

The year 1887 was, declared Seeley, a time of "of depression, confusion, and anxiety."[120] Despite this, and many similar proclamations, he was not an abject pessimist, and his views about the future were somewhat ambiguous. While at times he wrote in the vein of a doom-laden prophet, a latter-day Carlyle, he also preserved a large measure of optimism. Apprehensive about the political life of the "mother country," he was also keen to stress that things had improved markedly since the first few decades of the century, and as he became increasingly concerned about the international situation—warning of the "international danger, the gigantic discords, the gigantic armies!"—so he was also keen to stress the increasing strength and unity of the colonial empire. The continued expansion of England, and its consolidation since the troubled midcentury years, represented the "brightest side" of the Victorian age, and it gave him great hope for the future.[121] In Greater Britain lay a potential resolution to his fears about both the "mother country" and the wider world.

[117] Seeley, "The English Revolution in the Nineteenth Century," *Macmillan's Magazine*, 22 (1870), 1:241, 2:353. See also the comments on public opinion (in regard to India) in *Expansion*, 190.

[118] For context, see James Thompson, *British Political Culture and the Idea of "Public Opinion," 1867–1914* (Cambridge, 2013), 85–86, 93.

[119] Seeley, "English Revolution," 2:353. On his support for the IFL, see Seeley, "The Journal of the League," *Imperial Federation*, 1/1 (1886), 4; Seeley, "The Object to Be Gained by Imperial Federation," *Imperial Federation*, 1/6 (1886), 206; Seeley, Speech to the Imperial Federation League in Cambridge, May 29, 1891, reprinted in "Professor Seeley at Cambridge," *Imperial Federation*, 6/6 (1891), 176.

[120] Seeley, "Georgian and Victorian Expansion," 124.

[121] Seeley, "The Eighty-Eights," 380; Seeley, "Georgian and Victorian Expansion," 127.

But what kind of polity did Seeley envisage when he wrote that "England has left Europe altogether behind it and become a world-state," or when he argued that it was essential to create a "great and solid World-State" that would supplant the existing fragile one?[122] I would argue that he had in mind a supra-parliamentary federal polity, a United States of Greater Britain. In the *Introduction to Political Science*, based on lectures delivered in the mid-1880s, Seeley traced the various forms that states had assumed across time and space. Seeley initially defined the state so broadly that it encompassed nearly all forms of human community, and as such it might be argued that there was nothing unusual in his assertion that Greater Britain was a state.[123] But in evaluating the status of Greater Britain, he was actually drawing on a much narrower conception of the "nation-state." Recall his three essential preconditions for (nation) state unity: the existence of a "community of race," a "community of religion," and a "community of interest."[124] All existed in the colonial empire. Colonists were not simply deracinated migrants lost to distant, alien lands, but (echoing Robert Browning) citizens of a "world-Venice, with the sea for the streets."[125] While in the past there had been a Greater France, a Greater Spain, and a Greater Holland, the experience of the late Victorian British was unique, and the expansion of England, he maintained, "can be paralleled by nothing in the history of any other state."[126] Previous empires had neither the geographical extension nor the degree of cultural and political unity exhibited by Greater Britain. In an age that had witnessed the power of the "nationality doctrine," a new form of global British political consciousness was beginning to emerge, fusing together the scattered components of a global state. Greater Britain, wrote Seeley,

> . . . is a vast English nation, only a nation so widely dispersed that before the age of steam and electricity its strong natural bonds of race and religion seemed practically dissolved by distance. As soon as it is proved by the example of the United States and Russia that political union over

---

[122] Seeley, *Expansion*, 293, 169, 75.

[123] Seeley, *Political Science*, 16–18. On this broad account, "human beings almost everywhere belong to states." This point is noted in Meadowcroft, *Conceptualizing the State* (Oxford, 1995), 45–47; Jens Bartelson, *The Critique of the State* (Cambridge, 2001), 52. The volume was, wrote philosopher D. G. Ritchie, "a valuable addition to political science and, it might be added, to English literature." Ritchie, review of *Political Science*, *International Journal of Ethics*, 7/1 (1896), 114. For further discussion of Seeley's conception of the state, see Henry Ford Jones, *The Natural History of the State* (Princeton, 1916), 4–5, 150–52. Jones was Professor of Politics at Princeton.

[124] Seeley, *Expansion*, 11, 50, 220; also Seeley, *Political Science*, 68–70.

[125] Seeley, *Expansion*, 288. In "A Toccata of Galuppi's" [1855], Browning wrote of Venice: "Ay, because the sea's the street there; and 't'is arched by . . . what you call / . . . Shylock's bridge with houses on it, where they kept the carnival: / I was never out of England . . . it's as if I saw it all." Browning, *Poetical Works*, ed. Ian Jack (Oxford, 1970), 579.

[126] Seeley, "Introduction," xv.

vast areas has begun to be possible, so soon Greater Britain starts up, not only a reality, but a robust reality.[127]

Seeley acknowledged that it was hardest to make the case for a "community of interest." Indeed one of the main criticisms leveled at the imperial federalists was that Greater Britain was little more than a sentimental dream, based on an inability to recognize the divergent interests of the far-flung colonies.[128] In the *Considerations on Representative Government*, Mill had argued that spatial dispersion of the colonial empire meant that it was incapable of "rational government."[129] Seeley rejected this line of reasoning, arguing that new conditions meant that the "old Utopia" of Greater Britain was now realizable—indeed it was necessary.[130] The construction of a "great and solid" political association was predicated on a cognitive and affective revolution. Spread so widely, the empire had until recently been "practically dissolved by distance." Separated by great distances, and working under a warped mercantile economic system, the fragments of the first British empire did not share the same vital interests. But new communications and transport technologies had fundamentally reshaped the world and its political potential.[131] "Science has given the political organism a new circulation, which is steam, and a new nervous system, which is electricity." A world of glorious possibility was opening up. In the eighteenth century Burke "thought a federation quite impossible across the Atlantic Ocean," but since then the Atlantic had "shrunk till it seems scarcely broader than the sea between Greece and Sicily."[132] This was an age, he hymned, "when inventions have drawn the whole globe close together, and a new form of state on a larger scale than was known in former ages has appeared in Russia and the United States."[133] Greater Britain was such a state—or at least it could be.

Although Seeley never discussed the institutional form that he thought Greater Britain would or should assume, I believe that he had in mind a fully-fledged federal state, encompassing the assorted settler colonies and Britain. During the closing decades of the ninetieth century, federation was a topic of

---

[127] Seeley, *Expansion*, 72–73, 75; Seeley, "Georgian and Victorian Expansion," 138–39.

[128] See, for example, Robert Lowe, "The Value to the United Kingdom of the Foreign Dominions of the Crown," *Fortnightly Review*, 22 (1877), 618–30.

[129] Mill, *Considerations on Representative Government*, *Collected Works*, 19, 564–65.

[130] Seeley, *The Expansion of England*, 74. On utopianism and Greater Britain, see Duncan Bell, "Dreaming the Future: Anglo-America as Utopia, 1880–1914," in *The American Experiment and the Idea of Democracy in British Culture, 1776–1914*, ed. Ella Dzelzainis and Ruth Livesey (Aldershot, 2013), 197–210.

[131] For further discussion, see Bell, *Greater Britain*, ch. 3, and chapters 6 and 8 in this volume.

[132] Seeley, *Expansion*, 74–75. Cf. Burke, "Speech on Conciliation with America" (March 22, 1775) and "Address to the Colonists" (January 1777), in *The Writings and Speeches of Edmund Burke*, ed. W. M. Elofson (Oxford, 1996), 3:285, 152.

[133] Seeley, *Expansion*, 257, 288; Seeley, "Georgian and Victorian Expansion," 137.

intense interest among liberal political thinkers, chiefly due to the dynamic success of the United States. Sidgwick was far from alone in predicting that "an extension of federalism seems to me the most probable of the political prophecies relative to the form of government."[134] In "The United States of Europe" Seeley had argued that a "close" federation, modeled on the United States, was the only way to halt the internecine violence that plagued Europe. What was required was "Europe constituted into a single State, with a Federal executive and legislature," wherein its "authority must be brought to bear directly upon individuals."[135] In the long term it might come about, following a social revolution, but there were many obstacles in the way. In particular, the divergent national identities of the European states generated a clash of interests, meaning that if aggregated they could not satisfy his three conditions for proper statehood. Without such unity, Seeley argued elsewhere, a successful federation was impossible—it was, after all, "an arrangement so extremely difficult" to construct.[136] Such problems did not afflict Greater Britain, which was, he argued in the *Expansion of England*, "on the whole free from that weakness which brought down most empires, the weakness of being a mere mechanical forced union of alien nationalities."[137] The social and technological conditions for crafting a successful federation were in place.

Seeley's most thorough examination of federalism is found in the *Introduction to Political Science*.[138] He argued that the strict distinction drawn between "federal" and "unitary" states was misleading, as it was "too purely formal and verbal." Since all large countries were ultimately composite states, insofar as they comprised a number of semi-autonomous administrative units, it made little sense to sharply differentiate them from federations. "I deny, then, that between the unitary state and the federation or federal state there is any fundamental difference in kind; I deny that the one is composite in any sense in which the other is simple." As such, there was "no fundamental difference in the kind of union" between French Departments, American States, and British Counties. The key to assessing states was to determine the extent of authority vested in local government. "Where locality prevails, we can call this federal, where centralization prevails, we can call this unitary."[139] Indeed, he proclaimed that every "political union which has not sufficient central power

[134] Sidgwick, *The Development of European Polity*, ed. Eleanor Sidgwick (London, 1903), 439.

[135] Seeley, "United States," 445, 443.

[136] Seeley, *Stein*, 3:238.

[137] Seeley, *Expansion*, 46.

[138] Like many other federalists, Seeley used the terms "federation" and "confederation" interchangeably (e.g., *Political Science*, 63, 85, 205). As his later discussion made clear, however, he was well aware of the differences pertaining between different forms of federation. See Seeley, "United States," 440–44.

[139] Seeley, *Political Science*, 94–95. Rather confusingly, Seeley then proceeds to identify two kinds of unitary state, the centralised and decentralised, before moving on to discuss different types of federation (97).

to deserve the name of a unitary state must in our system be called federal,"
and he surmised that "almost all very large empires" are federations, "because
in them the central power cannot act vigorously at such a great distance." Just
as all polities could be called states, so all empires could be called federations.
But once again Seeley had something much more specific in mind for Greater
Britain. It was essential to distinguish between two different types of federal
entity: the "federal state" and the "system of confederate states." Seeley was
very critical of confederations, arguing that they were intrinsically weak. The
vast majority of empires fitted that category. Federal states, on the other
hand, could prosper, but they required "a complete apparatus of powers, legislative, executive and judicial . . . raised above all dependence on the State
governments."[140] He pointed to the United States as a "vigorous, strongly and
sufficiently organized" example.[141] And like the United States, successful federations were predicated on a unified nation. Once again, Greater Britain fitted
the bill. Already an immanent polity, it had the potential to become a fully-
fledged federal nation-state, if only the imagination of the people and their
leaders could be reoriented.

Empire as Polychronicon: India and Ireland

One of the most striking things about Seeley's imperial political thought was
the absence of Africa. In his 1887 Rede Lecture on "Georgian and Victorian
Expansion," published at the pinnacle of the European frenzy to carve up the
world, he declared that the greatest achievement of the Victorian age was the
expansion and consolidation of the British empire. Africa did not warrant a
single mention. India and Ireland, on the other hand, were frequent points of
reference in his writings.

Part 2 of *The Expansion of England* was dedicated to an analysis of the past,
present, and future of British rule in India. Far more ambiguous about the
benefits of the imperial mission in South Asia than he was about Greater Britain, Seeley maintained that the two zones were simply not comparable. While
Greater Britain was populated by transplanted British citizens bound loyally
to the mother country, India comprised a separate and degraded political
order, its countless inhabitants falling outside the scope of the English state
and nation. Drawing on the findings of contemporary philology he argued
that the Indians were an Aryan race, but that this was where the similarity
with Europe ended. Once great, they had fallen by the wayside of history.
"The country has achieved nothing in modern times."[142] Now moribund,

---

[140] Seeley, "United States," 440.

[141] Seeley, *Political Science*, 97–99. See also the discussion in Seeley, "United States," 440–43.

[142] Seeley, *Expansion*, 242, 243. He (242n) cites Max Müller's, *India, What Can It Teach Us?*

India displayed the unmistakable symptoms of a diseased body politic, denuded of the "vigour" that Seeley considered essential for a healthy political "organism."

> The colonies and India are in opposite extremes. Whatever political maxims are most applicable to one, are most inapplicable to the other. In the colonies everything is brand-new. There you have the most progressive race put in the circumstances most favourable to progress. There you have no past and an unbounded future. Government and institutions are all ultra-English. All is liberty, industry, invention, innovation, and as yet tranquility.

In contrast, India "is all past and, I may almost say, has no future."[143] This was a vision of empire as a polychronic space, carved into zones characterized by diverse temporal stages of development within an imagined universal history. The ancient, medieval, and modern were juxtaposed in Seeley's fertile imagination, the various constellations of territory and time forming stratified levels of civilization. Arrayed hierarchically, each was subject to different modes of assessment and political prescription.

In the *Introduction to Political Science* Seeley divided states into two broad classes, the *organic* and the *inorganic*, and while the book was mainly dedicated to classifying the varieties of organic states, he occasionally drew comparisons between the two types. Organic states were typically vibrant and capable of progress, whereas inorganic states were inert, thus failing to meet the criteria of proper statehood. They owed any substantive unity that they displayed to interference from outside powers. Products of conquest, they manifested a "similar appearance to the organic state" only because they adopted and imitated "the organisation of it." They were more accurately termed "quasi-states," the two defining features of which were low vitality and massive size. Again with Seeley we find ambiguity on a key point. Given both his conceptual analysis and his reading of Asian history, India could be classified as an example—perhaps the prime example—of an inorganic state. It was composed of multiple nationalities, immense, lacking in political consciousness—and it had been subjected to invasions for centuries. Never a "conscious political whole," the "homogeneous community does not exist there, out of which the State properly so called arises."[144] Yet Seeley rejected the obvious inference. This is probably because he regarded such states as the victims of aggressive conquest, where "everything is founded on violence and conquest" and a

---

(Oxford, 1883). On the discourse of Aryanism, see Tony Ballantyne, *Orientalism and Race* (Basingstoke, 2001).

[143] Seeley, *Expansion*, 51, 244, 176. For discussion of this passage, see also chapter 5.

[144] Seeley, *Expansion*, 185–86, 202, 204. This is why only a localized "village-patriotism" could be found (206).

grim despotism was the norm, and he didn't want to associate the British with this pattern of behavior.[145] This is also the most likely explanation for his determination to prove that the English had never actually "conquered" India in the first place. To conquer a country, he argued, is to presuppose that it was a unified entity in the first place, and since India had "no sense whatever of nationality" there had been "no India" to defeat. Rather, the spread of the early British traders and later the East India Company was due to the fortuitous circumstance of an "internal revolution."[146] It was as if they were sucked into a political vacuum, and both for their own good and that of the Indians, took control and brought stability and order.

For Seeley, then, India was an artificial country populated by a mix of races and religious creeds. Indeed any unity it possessed was created, not extinguished, by the British. A condition of "anarchy seems almost to have been chronic in India since Mahmoud," and "it may be said that India has never really been united so as to form one state except under the British," at least during the Governorship of Lord Dalhousie. Self-determination meant nothing there, for the "love of independence presupposes political consciousness," and the name India, he argued, "ought not to be classed with such names as England or France, which correspond to nationalities, but rather with such as Europe, marking a group of nationalities which have chanced to obtain a common name owing to some physical separation."[147] Since it did not constitute a nation, the "fundamental postulate cannot be granted, upon which the whole political ethics of the West depend."[148] The liberal maxims that Seeley applied to the states of Europe and North America were irrelevant. This was not to suggest that India would remain permanently locked in a servile position, for "Brahmanism" presented the "germ" of a potential nationality movement, but independence was not on the horizon, and for the moment the British should accede to such demands. "It is impossible for the present to think of abandoning the task we have undertaken there."[149] A man with no direct experience of or knowledge about Indian culture or political life, Seeley could discern no signs of it at the time.[150] Two years after *The Expansion of England* was published, the Indian National Congress was formed.

---

[145] Seeley, *Political Science*, 73–74, 76, 367–68, 168.

[146] Seeley, *Expansion*, 203, 207–8, 228. For a similar argument, drawing on Seeley, see Alfred Caldecott, *English Colonization and Empire*, 69–70.

[147] Seeley, *Expansion*, 228, 221.

[148] Ibid., 205. According to Charles Dilke, Seeley wrote "more suggestively and more profoundly upon the history of British government in all parts of the world than any other writer," and yet when it came to India his analysis was contradictory. Dilke, *Problems of Greater Britain* (London, 1898), 2:98. Dilke also disagreed with Seeley over the priority of the settler colonies, insisting that India was more important: Dilke, *The British Empire* (London, 1899), 17.

[149] Seeley, *Expansion*, 194.

[150] Ibid., 198, 224, 226–27.

Seeley's views on Ireland exhibit a family resemblance to his account of India. Underpinning his assessment of the Irish question was a fiercely critical portrayal of Catholicism. In this, he shared the prejudices of his fellow Broad Church thinkers, who saw Catholicism as embodying all that they rejected in religious life, most notably dogmatic and exclusive adherence to doctrine. Viewing it as the least developed of the Christian denominations, Seeley argued that Catholicism was bound by rigidity and prone to undermine the possibility of good government.[151] The mysticism of the Indians and the feudal superstitions of the priests both obscured the horizon of progress. Ireland, like India, fell outside the boundaries of the British nation. Or so he argued in 1870.[152] However, by the time he published *The Expansion of England* his position had changed, and he claimed that all of Greater Britain (including Ireland, but still excluding India) was bound together as one consolidated nation. In order to argue against home rule he modified his understanding of the boundaries of nationality; theoretical consistency gave way to the convenience of political maneuver. In a letter to his wife written in 1887 he noted that the "public struggle goes pretty well. The *Times* is really tackling Parnell with some vigour."[153] He would have regarded it as energy well spent. He also sought to improve relations between the English and the Irish, believing that the ideal solution lay in the trends that had fermented the nineteenth-century "English Revolution," chiefly the destruction of monopolies, including the closed labor market in the industrialized North.[154] In 1870 at least, he thought that such a course of action would create a more just relationship. But his optimism faded, and by 1885 he was writing that the Irish were "more hopelessly alienated than ever."[155] No solution appeared to be forthcoming. This was all the more reason to focus on a perceived British success story, to find in Greater Britain a distraction from the fraught situation in Ireland.

Like numerous other Victorian liberals, Seeley was critical of many facets of the history of British expansion. He lamented British behavior in Ireland.[156] He also regretted the "unjustifiable means" by which the early imperial pioneers in India acquired power. The greatest crime of all was slavery. In the seventeenth century, he reminded his audience, Great Britain had pioneered the abominable practice: "From this date I am afraid we took the leading share, and stained ourselves beyond other nations in the monstrous and enormous atrocities of the slave trade." Even in the Victorian age, there was "noth-

---

[151] Seeley, *Natural Religion*, 168–69; see also Seeley, "English Revolution," 2:450.

[152] Seeley, "English Revolution," 2:446.

[153] Seeley, letter to Mary Seeley, April 22, 1887, Seeley Papers, MS903/2A/1. See also Christopher Harvie, *The Lights of Liberalism* (London, 1976), 225–26.

[154] Seeley, "English Revolution," 2:446–48.

[155] Seeley, "Our Insular Ignorance," 862. On his darkening view of British politics in the 1870s and 1880s, see Bell, *Greater Britain*, 164–68.

[156] Seeley, "English Revolution," 2:446.

ing to boast of" in the treatment of indigenous populations under British control. But he always qualified his critique by arguing that that the behavior of the British was "not as bad as many others," and he stressed that such "crimes" as had been committed "have been almost universal in colonisation."[157] He thus employed what Cheryl Welch calls a "rhetoric of evasion."[158] In particular, Seeley utilized the argumentative strategy of "comparison as vindication," at once admitting that the British had acted reprehensibly at times but also that their record was morally superior to their competitors. Past injustice, on this account, was no bar continued British involvement in India.

But why? Given the polychronic variation between Greater Britain and the Indian empire, why not simply advocate the abandonment of the latter, perhaps (even especially) in order to strengthen the former? After all, Seeley was skeptical of the material advantages accrued by holding India: "[I]t is not at once evident that we reap any benefit from it."[159] While acknowledging the economic importance, he also stressed the substantial noneconomic costs that occupation imposed, notably the dangers of war with other great powers, and especially Russia.[160] Despite these worries, and the priority he assigned to Greater Britain, he recoiled from separation. The debates over Greater Britain were infused by a marked dissonance between skepticism about the benefits of the Indian empire and a fervent but often poorly explained desire to hold onto it anyway.

Seeley argued that in the distant future it might be necessary to leave India, but that in the meantime it was "obligatory to govern her as if we were to govern her forever." This was nothing to do with honoring the past, for such groundless romanticism belonged to a "primitive and utterly obsolete class of ideas." Rather, Seeley presented two arguments. The first was that the British had a duty to remain. Because they had incapacitated Indian governing institutions, the British could not simply depart, leaving chaos in their wake. If political judgments were to be made purely on the grounds of national interests, the British would probably be better off withdrawing; however, it was imperative to place the interests of the Indians first. A "very moderately good Government," argued Seeley, "is incomparably better than none. The sudden withdrawal even of an oppressive government is a dangerous experiment." This echoed the argument made by Henry Maine.[161] The British, Seeley professed, had a duty to finish the mission, with "vast and almost intolerable re-

---

[157] Seeley, "Our Insular Ignorance," 135–36; Seeley, "Introduction," xiii.

[158] Cheryl Welch, "Colonial Violence and the Rhetoric of Evasion," *Political Theory*, 31 (2003), 235–64.

[159] Seeley, *Expansion*, 183.

[160] Ibid., 187, 191–92, 289–90. On the importance of Indian trade, see Seeley, *Expansion*, 191, 258–59, 263–64, 304.

[161] On which, see Mantena, *Alibis of Empire*.

sponsibilities" to uphold.[162] This was owed as much to themselves as to the Indians, for self-denying conceptions of duty were a central tenet in the moral and political discourse of the Victorians, a core component in the formation of an admirable character.

The second argument centered on what we might call a sacred conception of the "civilizing mission."[163] Seeley argued that the ancients taught a valuable lesson about the nature of good governance and the priorities of virtuous politics. Liberty was not the only admirable quality in politics, nor was it necessarily the most suitable at any given time. Bewitched by vague and illusory notions about the irreducibility of freedom, this was an important truth that many of his countrymen failed to grasp.[164] Other great qualities included civilization and nationality. What distinguished, and also in a sense justified, the Roman and Greek Empires was that they were of a vastly superior level of civilization in comparison with those they were ruling.[165] So too the British in India. His compatriots had huge reservoirs of knowledge to impart to a people stranded in time. A "grand object of the modern Church," he proclaimed in *Natural Religion*, "would be to teach and organise the outlying world, which for the first time in history now lies prostrate at the feet of Christian civilisation." For Seeley, then, civilization had an explicitly sacred connotation: it was the "public aspect" of the religious impulse.[166] His conception of the civilizing mission was religious not in the sense that its principal aim was to proselytize Christianity (though it might include that goal), but that the very practice of spreading civilization was itself a religious act, an expression of admiration and worship motivated by "enthusiasm for humanity."

Western civilization was defined by three main features. Firstly, it facilitated and encouraged science and the set of attitudes towards truth and verification that accompanied it. Secondly, it presumed a cosmopolitan view of humanity, defined as the ability to think beyond the confines of the tribe or nation, and including such features as respect for women and the principle of liberty. And finally, it generated "delight and confidence" in nature, as opposed to the besetting superstition and mysticism of other, less sophisticated ways of life. Seeley thought it important to export this complex of values and

---

[162] Seeley, *Expansion*, 194–96, 183, 195.

[163] Rather surprisingly, Deborah Wormell asserts that Seeley disdained the civilizing mission and criticized the moralizing vision of "helping" other races. Wormell, *Seeley*, 159.

[164] Liberty, he argued, "in all cases will be but comparative," and moreover it "will appear to be a good, or a bad thing according to circumstances." Seeley, *Political Science*, 26–27. To the American political philosopher W. W. Willoughby, Seeley analyzed the concept of liberty "in a thoroughly philosophical manner, and the idea in its correct meaning is applied to concrete conditions in a way that cannot but afford sound practical information." Willoughby, review of *IPS*, *Political Science Quarterly*, 11/3 (1896), 548.

[165] Seeley, *Expansion*, 238–39.

[166] Seeley, *Natural Religion*, 221, 201.

beliefs to "backward" regions, both at home and abroad. It was necessary, he argued, to teach "the races outside it or the classes that have sunk below it."[167] India was one such target, a vast tissue of superstitious beliefs and torpid social and political institutions. It had been civilized once, and the British were not therefore dealing with a properly "backward" people, but rather with one stuck in time. England's sacred mission was "to raise India out of the medieval and into the modern phase." It was ripe for education. We "stand out boldly," he proclaimed, "as teachers and civilizers," imparting the "superior enlightenment we know we ourselves possess."[168] This education required the erasure of indigenous traditions and knowledges, the wiping clean of the slate. "The true view of the universe must be opened to the population of India, even though it should seem to blot out and cancel all the conceptions in which they have lived for three thousand years."[169] Such was the nature of progress.

[167] Ibid., 201–2.
[168] Seeley, *Expansion*, 244–45, 248, 252, 260.
[169] Seeley, *Natural Religion*, 243.

CHAPTER 12

Republican Imperialism

૱

J. A. Froude and the Virtue of Empire

So far as I can judge, the characteristics of modern mankind, French,
English, or American, are levity and selfishness, and out of these
qualities you cannot build up republics.[1]

—J. A. FROUDE

In recent years, much scholarly attention has been lavished on the ideology
of "liberal imperialism." Against a backdrop of the omnipresent debates
over the dynamics and consequences of globalization and the aggressive foreign policy of the United States and its allies, historians and political theorists
have revisited the history of Western political thinking in order to identify the
conceptual structure and to track the diffusion of liberal visions of imperial
rule. This has propelled some scholars back to early modern Europe, and in
particular to the colonial writings of John Locke. The other most popular des-
tination is the nineteenth century, the crucible of liberalism and a period during which the power, geographical extent, and sheer ambition of the Western
empires reached an unprecedented level.

Focusing on liberal imperialism in this manner, whilst an important exercise, often generates more heat than light. First, the term itself is problematic:
"liberal imperialism" implies commonalities and coherence, where the political thought of the nineteenth century was marked by dissonance and diversity. As I argued in chapter 2, not all liberals were imperialists, and those who
were diverged very significantly in the intensity of their support, the types of
empires that they envisaged, and the justifications that they offered. For example, alongside the standard "liberal imperial" position there existed a parallel and frequently overlapping mode of justification that I term republican (or

---

[1] J. A. Froude, letter to Theodor Stanton, 1888, reprinted in Waldo Hilary Dunn, *James Anthony Froude*, 2 vols. (Oxford, 1961–63), 2:560. Stanton was a professor at Cornell.

civic) imperialism.[2] The main purpose of this chapter is to elaborate on this claim. I proceed as follows. Utilizing John Stuart Mill's writings for illustrative purposes, section 2 sketches the basic features of the "liberal civilizational" position. The following section outlines, in broad terms, the republican alternative. The complex relationship between empire and liberty has been a prominent theme in European political thought for over two millennia. For many writers, the two were intimately linked: liberty at home was compatible with (or even required) empire abroad—although empire itself, if understood and enacted improperly, could pose a threat to that very liberty.[3] Such concerns also permeated Victorian public debate. Sections 4 and 5 interpret the political thought of the eminent Victorian historian and public moralist J. A. Froude (1818–94) in republican terms.

In ideal-typical form, the two types of imperial justification differed in both motivational structure and geographical orientation. The Millian variant of liberal imperialism contended that in the modern world empire was legitimate if (and only if) it was primarily intended to benefit the populations subjected to it. Any other benefits that it generated were derivative and incidental. It sought to "civilize" the "barbarian," and it focused consequently on specific spaces in the imperial archipelago (most commonly India). It is this line of argument that has been at the center of recent scholarship. Republican imperialism, on the other hand, was primarily motivated by a concern with the character of the imperial power, defending empire in terms of the benefits that it generated for the state. Its proponents sought to foster individual and collective virtue in their compatriots, while striving to defend or enhance national honor and glory. Any other benefits that it generated—including the gift of "civilization"—were derivative and incidental. Given these concerns, republican imperialism tended to focus more on the settlement colonies, most notably (in the British case) in North America and the South Pacific. Yet republican and liberal civilizational modes of imperial justification were not antithetical, either in theory or practice. Republican defenses of empire were offered by self-professed liberals, as well as by non-liberals, while advocates of the "civilizing" potential of empire could be found across the political spectrum. Like those today, Victorian languages of imperial justification were complex, contested, and frequently inconsistent.

---

[2] I am not arguing that this distinction captures all of the variety of nineteenth-century imperial thought, only that it helps us to understand some significant aspects of it. For other modulations of imperial ideology, see the discussion in Chapter 3.

[3] David Armitage, "Empire and Liberty," in *Republicanism*, ed. Quentin Skinner and Martin van Gelderen (Cambridge, 2003), 2:29–47; Andrew Fitzmaurice, *Humanism and America* (Cambridge, 2003); Mikael Hörnqvist, *Machiavelli and Empire* (Cambridge, 2004); Mikael Hörnqvist, "The Two Myths of Civic Humanism," in *Renaissance Civic Humanism*, ed. James Hankins (Cambridge, 2000), 105–43.

John Stuart Mill and Liberal Civilizing Imperialism

Liberal imperialism is usually understood to center on the "civilizing mission," the idea that liberal states have a right—and, in a strong version of the argument, a duty—to spread "civilization" to the purportedly non-civilized peoples of the world. It is thus structured by a bifocal vision, dividing peoples into two separate categories: "civilized" and "barbarian/savage."[4] Societies are arrayed along (and judged according to their position on) a single developmental trajectory, where both the logic and pace of change, as well as the status to be realized, are characterized in terms of "progress." Although this vision allows for considerable variation within each category, crossing the threshold from "barbarity" to "civilization" is conceived of as a monumental step, one which (depending on the version of the argument employed) will either take an inordinate amount of time given prevailing social and political conditions, or would be impossible without exogenous assistance.[5] Both versions justify imperial rule, and both were common in the nineteenth century, above all in Britain, France, and Germany.

Most articulations of this generic liberal imperial argument link civilization to sovereignty. Civilization is seen as a necessary if not sufficient condition for the emergence of a sense of national self-consciousness, which in turn is regarded as essential to trigger liberal claims about the rights of national self-determination. Since most political communities were not thought to exhibit a sense of nationality, imperialism was legitimate if (and only if) it was intended to help bring about a significant progressive change in the social, political, and moral status of the subject people. Once a society had developed to the point where it could be classified as civilized, and once it exhibited authentic national self-consciousness, it could justifiably claim independence, and the job of the liberal imperial power was complete. Froude, who as we shall see was a critic of this argument, summarized the narrative of liberal transformation as follows:

[4] It is important to note, however, that during the nineteenth century "civilization" remained a highly fluid concept, lacking specificity and open to various ideological uses. See here: Gerritt Gong, *The Standard of "Civilization" in International Society* (Oxford, 1984); Bruce Mazlish, *Civilization and Its Contents* (Stanford, 2005); Jennifer Pitts, "Boundaries of Victorian International Law," in *Victorian Visions of Global Order*, ed. Duncan Bell (Cambridge, 2007), 67–89.

[5] Most nineteenth-century European thinkers ranked the "civilized" powers according to a variety of criteria, usually placing their own society at the peak. See Georgios Varouxakis, "'Great' versus 'Small' Nations," in *Victorian Visions*, ed. Bell, 136–59. Non-Western peoples were also coded in hierarchical terms, often with indigenous Australians placed at the bottom, and the more "warlike" of the Indian peoples, as well as the Maoris of New Zealand, accorded a higher position. Some of these peoples were thought to be heading for inevitable extinction. Patrick Brantlinger, *Dark Vanishings*; Mark Hickford, "'Decidedly the Most Interesting Savages on the Globe,'" *History of Political Thought*, 27 (2006), 122–67.

At present in our enthusiasm for self-government we imagine that our Eastern subjects are by-and-by to learn to govern themselves as we do. We are their trustees while they are in their political infancy. Our duty is to train them in our own image, that when they are fit to receive their inheritance, we may pass it into their own hands. The Asiatic, we are persistently told, is the inferior of the European only in the disadvantages with which he has been surrounded. If he be educated, as we are educated, lifted gradually into freedom, with his rights and powers enlarged as he shows himself capable of their exercise, we shall elevate him into an equality with ourselves, and our mission will be ended.[6]

The projected *telos* of this liberal project, was a world of "civilized" nation-states coexisting on a formally equal basis under an expanding regime of international law and commerce. Imperialism was thus part of a wider international reformist vision.[7] But the temporal coordinates of this process were very rarely specified; freedom remained deferred to some indefinite point in the future. In the meantime, attention was focused on refining the modes and modulations of imperial rule.

John Stuart Mill was the archetypal nineteenth-century proponent of liberal civilizing imperialism. He was certainly not the first to preach the creed, and nor were his imperial arguments especially novel, but he was nevertheless one of its most systematic and forceful advocates. He stands at the heart of contemporary scholarship on the subject—indeed at times he almost seems to exhaust it.[8] This is partly a result of his prominence during the Victorian era, his reputation as a philosopher, political economist, social reformer, and public moralist.[9] But it is also a function of his place in the canon of modern political thought, a canon that retrospectively classifies individuals as worthy of scholarly attention, and which often identifies them (sometimes explicitly, often implicitly) as representatives either of their age or of the politico-

---

[6] Froude, "England's War," *Fraser's Magazine*, 1871, reprinted in *Short Studies on Great Subjects*, 5 vols. (London, 1907) (hereafter *Short Studies*), 3:272–73.

[7] Some variations of this argument also envisaged the eventual creation of regional (and even global) federations. On liberal internationalism, see Jens Bartelson, "The Trial of Judgement," *International Studies Quarterly*, 39 (1995), 255–79; Casper Sylvest, *British Liberal Internationalism, 1880–1930* (Manchester, 2009); and chapter 10.

[8] For examples, see the discussion in chapter 2. Notably absent from the recent wave of scholarship on Mill is recognition of the value he placed on (and the arguments he offered for) settler colonization. For correctives, see Katherine Smits, "John Stuart Mill on the Antipodes," *Australian Journal of Politics and History*, 51 (2008), 1–15; and the discussion in chapter 9.

[9] Yet it is important to note that while Mill was widely admired, he also had numerous detractors, including self-proclaimed liberals, and his political writings in particular were subjected to sustained attack, both during his lifetime and afterwards. He was not, in other words, a straightforward representative figure of any position. See, for example, Stefan Collini, *Public Moralists* (Oxford, 1991), esp. chs. 4, 8; Bruce Kinzer, *A Moralist In and Out of Parliament* (Toronto, 1992).

theoretical positions they articulated. Mill is thus often seen as a symbol of nineteenth-century liberalism, and through this, of liberal imperialism. Yet as I argue in chapter 2, and as I further elaborate on below, this type of identification can lead to misinterpretations of the wider ideological context. The reasons for Mill's identification with liberal imperialism, though, are not hard to fathom. Following in the footsteps of his father, he went to work at the East India Company at the age of seventeen, and there he remained, rising to senior rank, until the charter of the Company was revoked in 1858. Having left the services of the Company, he continued to ruminate on the nature and value of the British empire until his death in 1873.

For Mill, civilization was a rare and fragile achievement; it was a status attained by only a very few communities.[10] India was not one of them. He had very decided views on "barbarians."[11] Like many of his contemporaries Mill argued that India had once been an advanced society, but that this was no longer the case. It was moribund, mired in superstition, and beholden to primitive traditions. The scope of his putatively universal ambitions was circumscribed—spatially not temporally—by the limits of civilization. His famed definition of liberty, the "one very simple principle" that governed his ideal conception of society, did not apply to those who had failed to reach the "maturity of their faculties." Children, the mentally disabled, and those "backward states of society in which the race itself may be considered as in its nonage" were not included within its embrace. "Liberty, as a principle, has no application to any state of things anterior to the time when mankind have become capable of being improved by free and equal discussion."[12] This was the spatial limitation—for Mill, this argument excluded the vast majority of the world's population. Only a select few states had reached the prescribed level of maturity. The link to national self-consciousness is clear. "[B]arbarians," Mill stated in an essay published in 1859, "have no rights as a *nation*, except a right to such treatment as may, at the earliest possible period, fit them for becoming one."[13] This was because they were incapable of reciprocity and of following rules. The "minds" of those lacking civilization, he wrote, "are not capable of so great an effort."[14] The universality was reinscribed in temporal terms: in the future the "barbarians" will reach civilization, and when they do they will be welcomed into a society of states regulated by binding laws and

[10] Mill, "Civilization" [1836], in *Collected Works,* 18:117–49.

[11] From a very early age Mill was exposed to his father's highly influential writings on India, which he seems to have absorbed. For Mill's shifting ideas about race in India, see Zastoupil, *John Stuart Mill and India.*

[12] Mill, *On Liberty* [1859], *Collected Works,* 18:224.

[13] Mill, "A Few Words on Non-Intervention" [1859], *Collected Works,* 21:119. Italics in original. See also Mill, *Considerations on Representative Government* [1861], *Collected Works,* 19:566–67.

[14] Mill, "A Few Words on Non-Intervention," 118.

enforceable rights. The job of the liberal state was to help them in this process, to act as the midwife of modernity.

For Mill, ever the utilitarian, the British empire, and in particular the empire in India, was an engine of improvement. It provided a vast laboratory for his "ethology," the science of individual and collective "character" that he sketched (although never fully developed) in the *System of Logic* (1843).[15] Since human character—both individual and collective—was relatively plastic, and could be (re)shaped by environmental conditioning, it was possible to transform barbarous societies into progressive ones, given time, patience, and skill.[16] This was the only legitimate type of imperial rule in the modern world. As he wrote in *On Liberty* (1859), "[d]espotism is a legitimate mode of government in dealing with barbarians, provided the end be their improvement, and the means justified by actually effecting that end."[17] He reiterated the point in the *Considerations on Representative Government*, published two years later, arguing that imperialism as a

> ... mode of government is as legitimate as any other, if it is the one which in the existing state of civilization of the subject people, most facilitates their transition to a higher stage of improvement. There are ... conditions of society in which a vigorous despotism is in itself the best mode of government for training the people in what is specifically wanting to render them capable of a higher civilisation.[18]

Traditional motives for conquest, whether financial gain, geopolitical rivalry, or national glory, were obsolete.

Mill argued, then, that the primary duty of an imperial power was, through a combination of coercion and example-setting, to help educate subject populations until they were "capable" of attaining responsible self-government. The key point for the present discussion is that for Mill—and for many other liberals—this was the *only* way in which despotism could be justified. Empire may generate other benefits (and Mill certainly argued that it did so), but these were necessarily incidental to the transformative project.

Republican Themes in Victorian Political Thought

The term "republican" has played an important role in historical writing over the last few decades, although it has assumed a number of different and some-

---

[15] Mill, *A System of Logic* [1843], *Collected Works*, 7:861–75.

[16] This view of development was grounded in an "associationist" account of psychology, a view that Mill had inherited from his father. For the most illuminating account of how this was to work in practice, see Mill's account of his own education in his *Autobiography* (1873).

[17] Mill, *On Liberty*, 224.

[18] Mill, *Considerations on Representative Government*, 416.

times conflicting meanings.[19] In applying it to British imperial discourse, it is essential to be clear about the nature of the claims being advanced. (For example, I am not employing republican in the sense it is often used to describe French imperialism, especially in the years of the Third Republic, a vision in which *la mission civilatrice* played a constitutive role.)[20] It is therefore necessary to explore briefly both the generic structures of republican argumentation and the ways in which scholars have discussed republican legacies in the Victorian era.

Historians have traced republican themes in various nineteenth-century contexts. Two stand out. Firstly, they have identified a powerful republican inheritance among radicals, a line of argument that was transmitted from Thomas Paine and through to the Chartists, and which lingered until the 1880s when it was supplanted by socialist theories of political economy (especially those inspired by Karl Marx).[21] Radical republicans stressed the close connection between the ownership of property and liberty, they criticized the Crown and the aristocracy for holding arbitrary power over them, and they regarded the state as corrupt. The solution to these problems lay, they argued, in political (as opposed to economic or social) transformation. A second stream of research has charted how republican themes shaped various aspects of an emergent liberalism, focusing in particular on the transmission belts of Whiggism. These themes were expressed in a variety of commonplace Victorian tropes. Stefan Collini, for example, argues that eighteenth-century conceptions of "virtue" and Victorian notions of "character" shared a number of key features, most notably their asceticism and demanding political ethic. Victorian thought, he concludes, was marked by "survivals and mutations" of the earlier language of civic humanism.[22]

[19] For examples, see Skinner and van Gelderen, eds., *Republicanism*; Eric Nelson, "Republican Visions," in *The Oxford Handbook of Political Theory*, ed. John Dryzek, Bonnie Honig, and Anne Phillips (Oxford, 2005), 193–211; Iseult Honohan, *Civic Republicanism* (London, 2002). This section extends my discussion of civic imperialism in Bell, *The Idea of Greater Britain*, ch. 5.

[20] Alice Conklin, *A Mission to Civilize* (Stanford, 1998), esp. ch. 1. Nor am I employing it to map the history of "republican" arguments about freedom and security, as in Daniel Deudney's fascinating, *Bounding Power* (Princeton, 2007).

[21] Mark Bevir, "Republicanism, Socialism, and Democracy in Britain," *Journal of Social History*, 34 (2000), 351–68. For examples, see Eugenio Biagini, "Neo-Roman Liberalism," *History of European Ideas*, 29 (2003), 55–72; Biagini, "Radicalism and Liberty," in Peter Mandler, ed., *Liberty and Authority in Victorian Britain* (Oxford, 2006), 101–25; Duncan Kelly, "Reforming Republicanism in Nineteenth-Century Britain," in *Republicanism in Theory and Practice*, ed. Iseult Honohan and Jeremy Jennings (London, 2006), 41–52; Gregory Claeys, "The Origins of the Rights of Labor," *Journal of Modern History*, 66 (1994), 249–90; and, most influentially, Gareth Stedman Jones, "Rethinking Chartism," in *Languages of Class* (Cambridge, 1983).

[22] Collini, *Public Moralists*, 108–10. See also John Burrow, *Whigs and Liberals* (Oxford, 1988). Some scholars have pointed to the continuities between Mill's language and that of the civic humanists of the eighteenth century (for example, Burrow, *Whigs and Liberals*, 85), but this does not refer to his vision of empire.

What unites these streams of scholarship is that they bypass empire. Yet it is in the domain of empire that we hear some of the clearest and most consistent echoes of republicanism in the Victorian age. The key point of imaginative anchorage lay in the prevalence and cultural authority of narratives of imperial decline and fall (a topic I explore in chapter 5). The dangers and the dynamics of imperial corruption, heralded by Sallust and Polybius and rearticulated most famously by Edward Gibbon, infused Victorian political consciousness.[23] Collini maintains that the Victorians and their civic humanist predecessors differed in at least one important respect: their "sense of nemesis."[24] This difference resulted from divergent conceptions of historical time, for the eighteenth-century humanists, he argues, feared corruption, grounded in a cyclical account of rise and decline, while the Victorians feared stagnation as a threat to their open-ended notion of a progressive future. For many of those with their eyes fixed on the fortunes of the British empire, however, the sense of nemesis remained exactly the same: the seemingly inexorable logic of imperial declension. The imperial imagination was partially structured by interpretations of the political dynamics of the ancient world.

The most significant context for republican imperialism was the late nineteenth-century debate over the future of the settler colonies. Because India has been the focus of so much recent research, the pivotal importance of Canada, New Zealand, Australia, and the Cape in the Victorian political imagination has often been overlooked. The three best-selling books on imperial questions published during the second half of the century—Charles Dilke's, *Greater Britain* (1868), J. A. Froude's, *Oceana* (1886), and J. R. Seeley's, *The Expansion of England* (1883)—all stressed the primary importance of the settler colonies. And all exhibited, to varying degrees, the complex and diffuse legacy of republican thinking. Republican imperialism was opposed to radical individualism, emphasizing instead public duty, self-denying altruism, and the promotion of a virtuous patriotism; its proponents worried, to varying degrees, about the corrupting powers of materialism, capitalism, and "luxury"; they stressed duty above rights, politics above economics, and the enchanted national above the unencumbered cosmopolitan. They contrasted the passive subject with the active imperial patriot. They also repeatedly invoked the benefits bestowed by propertied independence, and especially the ownership and active usage of productive agricultural land (at home and especially in the

---

[23] In his highly critical overview of eighteenth-century political thought, Leslie Stephen scoffed that the discourse of the time was comprised of "generalities about liberty, corruption, and luxury." Leslie Stephen, *English Thought in the Eighteenth Century* (London, 1876), 2:111. Mill made a similar point about Gibbon: "Carlyle's French Revolution" (1837), *Collected Works*, 20:134, 136. On the pervasiveness of the classics in the Victorian era, see Frank Turner, *The Greek Heritage in Victorian Britain* (New Haven, 1981); and Norman Vance, *The Victorians and Ancient Rome* (Oxford, 1997).

[24] Collini, *Public Moralists*, 108–10.

colonies). This helps to explain the suspicion expressed by many Victorian imperialists about urbanization.[25] This anxiety is not surprising given the deep
historical roots, stretching back to Rome, of the connection between farming
and the planting of people. After all, the Latin term *colonia*, derived from the
verb *colere*, means to cultivate, or to farm.[26] This imaginative link has been a
central theme in the history of Western imperial expansion.

The late Victorian colonial debates were not an unmediated replay of the
eighteenth-century clash over the respective merits of the ancients and moderns. Rather, republican imperialism was a language adapted to and shaped by
the late nineteenth-century imperial context.[27] Born of an industrial capitalist
society, its advocates were simultaneously proud of the achievements of modern commerce and wary of the dangers of the commercial spirit extending too
far. Republican imperialism was defined as much by what it was opposed to as
by what it stood for. Among the main targets were liberals infected with the
"virus of Manchesterism."[28] This strand of liberalism was characterized, it was
claimed, by utilitarian reasoning, a debilitating individualism, and a narrow
obsession with profit and the doctrines of *laissez-faire* political economy.
Above all else, it was seen to underpin an attitude critical of empire: during
the 1860s in particular liberalism came to be associated, albeit inaccurately,
with "indifference, if not hostility, towards the Colonies."[29] It was against
these forms of liberalism (or at least a crude caricature of them) that the republican imperial position was articulated most forcefully. Materialism, it was
thought, was destructive in three distinct ways, although they frequently overlapped. First, it could corrupt individuals. The perfidious sensuality and vice
of the East rebounding to undermine the polity from within was a long-
standing (orientalist) concern, rising to prominence in the eighteenth century
where it was exemplified in Burke's dogged pursuit of Warren Hastings. It re-
verberated throughout the nineteenth century.[30] Modern luxury could even
damage those not directly involved in the empire, either by entrenching social
and economic conditions that debilitated the working classes, emasculating

---

[25] In classical republican thought, the city was often viewed as the most appropriate site of political life. During the nineteenth century the idea of the city was transformed, in the wake of industrialism and the vast growth of urban populations. Cities were reimagined as vast spaces of vice
and danger rather than the seedbed of virtue.

[26] Moses Finley, "Colonies—An Attempt at a Typology," *Transactions of the Royal Historical
Society*, 5th series, 6 (1976), 173.

[27] For an analysis of the wide-ranging eighteenth-century debates over luxury, see Istvan Hont,
"Luxury and Commerce," in *The Cambridge History of Eighteenth-Century Political Thought*, ed.
Mark Goldie and Robert Wokler (Cambridge, 2006), 379–419.

[28] Edward Salmon, "The Colonial Empire of 1837," *Fortnightly Review*, 61 (1897), 863.

[29] The quotation is from Hugh Egerton, *A Short History of British Colonial Policy* (London,
1897), 455. Froude concurred: *The Earl of Beaconsfield* (London, 1890), 238–39.

[30] Miles Taylor, "Imperium et Libertas?," *Journal of Imperial and Commonwealth History*, 19
(1991), 1–23.

their virile energies, or through the creation of a rich but effete ruling class. Combined, this fashioned a society unable to, and uninterested in, expanding its strength and glory. The second dimension reinforced this polarization. Commercial society generated increasing economic inequality, triggering potentially destabilizing political consequences as well as fueling fear of the working classes rising to challenge their oppressors. Finally, there was a further indirect effect: the commercial spirit, it was often argued, corroded patriotism and the belief in a transcendent common good. Individuals became increasingly egotistical, placing self-interest above public duty.[31] The "materialists" were perfectly happy to see the empire either fall into a state of disrepair or, in some cases—most notably that of the self-proclaimed "last of the Manchester school," Goldwin Smith—to demand the "emancipation" of the colonies.[32] Julius Vogel, a former premier of New Zealand, warned in 1877 of the dangers of Britain, stripped of its colonies, "sinking into a small money-loving State—a second Holland."[33]

These lines of thought came together in a powerful defense of the virtues of settler colonialism. Much of the debate over "Greater Britain"—as the unity of Britain and the settler colonies was frequently labeled—centered on the type of character necessary for and produced by successful colonization. Emigration lay at the heart of this process.[34] For much of the nineteenth century, emigration was looked upon either as a "safety valve" for social problems or as a means of escape for greedy young men and the less talented sons of the aristocracy. While political economists had repeatedly insisted on the financial benefits of colonies, the colonists themselves were frequently scorned. The "colonial reformer" and political economist E. G. Wakefield wrote in *A View on the Art of Colonization* (1849), that "speaking generally, colonies and colonists are in fact, as well as in the estimation of the British gentry, inferior, low, unworthy of much respect, properly disliked and despised by people of honour here, who happen to be acquainted with the state of society in the colonies."[35] Throughout the century settlers were also routinely criticized for their brutality to indigenous populations, often by Britons (including John Stuart Mill) who supported the empire but were worried about how some of

---

[31] Seeley's defense of classical notions of (merit-based) aristocracies, above party intrigue, noble, and acting in the name of the common good, can be seen as a response to this. Seeley, *Stein*, 3:564; Seeley, *Introduction to Political Science*, ed. Henry Sidgwick (Cambridge, 1896), 328–30.

[32] Goldwin Smith, *The Empire* (London, 1863); Smith, "The Expansion of England," *Contemporary Review*, 45 (1884), 524–40; Smith, "The Empire," in *Essays on Questions of the Day* [1893], 2nd ed. (New York, 1894), 141–95.

[33] Vogel, "Greater or Lesser Britain," *Nineteenth Century*, 1 (1877), 831.

[34] On the importance of emigration, see Bell, *The Idea of Greater Britain*, ch. 2.

[35] Wakefield, *A View on the Art of Colonization* [1849], in *The Collected Works of Edmond Gibbon Wakefield*, ed. M. F. Lloyd-Prichard (Glasgow, 1968), 837. See also Arthur Mills, *Systematic Colonization* (London, 1847), 33–34.

its constituent elements were governed.[36] The debates over Greater Britain witnessed a sustained attempt to transform this negative image, both to help encourage further emigration and to shift the general perception of the value of the colonies. As I discuss in Chapter 2, the colonies were reimagined as integral elements of the "mother country"; the existing colonists as loyal, hardy, and rugged patriots.[37] Republican imperialism was not exclusively found in Britain. It can be seen, for example, in Alexis de Tocqueville's writings on Algeria. Unlike many other French nineteenth-century thinkers, Tocqueville was not especially interested in "civilizing" imperial subjects. He was concerned primarily with the benefits that colonialism would bring to mainland France, and he sought to reinvigorate the *patria* through foreign conquest. With "time, perseverance, ability, and justice," he prophesized, "I have no doubt that we will be able to raise a great monument to our country's glory on the African coast."[38] This monument would restore French greatness and transform the citizenry. American political thought at the turn of the twentieth century expressed many of the same concerns. It was in nineteenth-century Britain, however, that we find some of the most powerful echoes of republican imperialism.

J. A. Froude and the Pathologies of the Moderns

An anatomist of religious crisis, an influential historian, and a fierce social critic, Froude was one of the leading "public moralists" of the second half of the nineteenth century.[39] His monumental twelve-volume study of the En-

---

[36] Mill, *Considerations on Representative Government*, 771–72. This was one of the central concerns of the prosecutors of Governor Eyre. See here Rande Kostal, *A Jurisprudence of Power* (Oxford, 2006); Smits, "John Stuart Mill on the Antipodes."

[37] The representation of the colonies in publicity material often drew on classical images of the virtue (and purity) of femininity. Dominic David Alessio, "Domesticating 'The Heart of the Wild,'" *Women's History Review*, 6 (1997), 239–69. On the gendering of colonialism, see also Robert Grant, *Representations of British Emigration, Colonisation, and Settlement* (Basingstoke, 2005), ch. 8.

[38] Tocqueville, "Second Letter on Algeria" [1837], in *Writings on Empire and Slavery*, ed. J. Pitts (Baltimore, 2001), 24. Though for a switch in tone and emphasis, see also his "First Report on Algeria" [1847], *Writings*, 146. For a valuable discussion of Tocqueville's thought, which identifies its republican dimensions, see Pitts, *A Turn to Empire*, chs. 6–7.

[39] Froude's writings on his brutalized youth (*Shadows of the Clouds*, 1847) and the spiritual turmoil of his early adulthood (*The Nemesis of Faith*, 1849) provide two of the most psychologically rich explorations of the Victorian crisis of faith. Julia Markus contends that he was the author of the most important pre-Freudian biography (on Jane and Thomas Carlyle) in the English language: Markus, *J. Anthony Froude* (New York, 2005), 76. Other studies of Froude, none of which make the argument I am pursuing, include Dunn, *James Anthony Froude*; A. L. Rowse, *Froude as Historian* (Gloucester, 1987); and Walter Thompson, *James Anthony Froude on Nation and Empire* (London, 1998). Since this chapter was originally published, a major new intellectual biography

glish reformation, the *History of England from the Fall of Wolsey to the Defeat of the Spanish Armada* (1856–70), sold tens of thousands of copies. His writings on empire reached a similarly large audience.[40] In these writings we see the articulation of a distinctive republican argument.

Froude is often characterized as a straightforward disciple of Thomas Carlyle. However, although he admired Carlyle enormously, and although he followed him in various ways, Froude was nevertheless an independent thinker, fully capable of carving out his own path. The complexion of his political thought has proven notoriously elusive—something of which he would be proud. Michael Bentley characterizes him as a "great liberal," Peter Mandler a "liberal Carlylean," while for John Burrow he was a "radical Tory."[41] By the 1850s he had shed his youthful radicalism and he increasingly identified with conservative policies and politicians. His writings grew increasingly reactionary in tone and content. He hated Gladstone and was an enthusiastic admirer of Disraeli. He was no "great liberal." But nor was he a great Tory. He liked to project himself as a man above and beyond trivial partisan struggles, his energies focused on the good of the "commonwealth." Indeed his writings, like those of Seeley, abound with harsh criticisms of the factionalism and myopia of "party." He once wrote:

> [I]t is the very nature of "party" that party leaders shall never see things as they really are, but only as they affect for the moment the interests of one section of the community. They are as men who, having two eyes

---

has appeared: Ciaran Brady, *James Anthony Froude* (Oxford, 2013). In relation to the empire, it is especially good on Ireland and the Caribbean.

[40] For his conception of history, see John Burrow, *A Liberal Descent* (Cambridge, 1981); Jane Garnett, "Protestant Histories," in *Politics and Culture in Victorian Britain*, ed. Peter Ghosh and Lawrence Goldman (Oxford, 2006), 171–92; Rosemary Jann, *The Art and Science of Victorian History* (Columbus, OH, 1985), 105–40; Jeffrey von Arx, *Progress and Pessimism* (Cambridge, MA, 1985), 173–200. Burrow also notes Froude's reliance on the "language of Bolingbroke and the eighteenth-century Country Party" (*Liberal Descent*, 282), though he does not make enough of the civic elements of his imperialism. On Froude's largely negative reception among professionalizing historians at the time, see Ian Hesketh, "Diagnosing Froude's Disease," *History and Theory*, 47 (2008), 373–95.

[41] Bentley, *Lord Salisbury's World* (Cambridge, 2001), 225; Burrow, *Liberal Descent*, Part III; Mandler, *The English National Character* (London, 2006), ch. 3. Elsewhere, Mandler writes that Froude and Carlyle were "as close to organic conservatives as British intellectual life gets," but that they were ultimately paternalists who believed in the ability of leaders to shape the people "at will." Mandler, "The Consciousness of Modernity?," in *Meanings of Modernity*, ed. Bernhard Rieger and Martin Daunton (Oxford, 2001), 123. The letter to Stanton cited in note 1 above also indicated Froude's ambivalent attitude towards radicalism and political change during the 1880s: "The future of Radicalism these days I conceive to be the burning up of rubbish. The grass will spring up again by and by out of the ashes. But the burning process is disagreeable to me however I may see it to be inevitable." He also referred to radical reformers as "indispensable persons" because they were at the forefront of criticizing corruption and excess luxury in government. Froude, "Party Politics," *Short Studies*, 4:351 (*Fraser's Magazine*, 1874).

given them by nature, deliberately extinguish one. There is the point of view from the "right" and the point of view from the "left," and from each, from the nature and necessity of the case, only half the truth can be seen. A wise man keeps both his eyes, belongs to no party, and can see things as they are.[42]

Froude's eyes were fixed on the multifarious failings of his contemporaries, on the lessons that could be drawn from both the character and the fate of the Roman Republic and, ultimately, on how to secure the future glory of the British "race" in the wide expanses of the colonies.

Froude had nearly become a colonist. In the 1840s he was on the verge of emigrating to Hobart, in Van Diemen's Land, to take up a teaching position, before the offer was rescinded in the wake of the controversy generated by the publication of his autobiographical novel *The Nemesis of Faith* (1849). Burned publicly in his Oxford college, the book cost him his cherished fellowship as well as a potential new career. Yet it was only in the 1870s that he turned to writing at length about the empire. In a series of essays and books published between 1870 and his death in 1894 (two years after being appointed Regius Professor of History at Oxford), Froude elaborated a distinctive republican vision of the empire. It was republican in two specific senses. First, his imperial thought was shaped by an interpretation of the corruption of the Roman republic. From this narrative, Froude drew lessons that he applied directly to the contemporary world, identifying the same (or analogous) mechanisms at work in Britain. This was a fairly common argumentative strategy amongst his contemporaries, although (as I show in Chapter 5) it could be used to defend a wide variety of positions. Second, in a more innovative move, he argued that the answer to this impending catastrophe lay in creating a global polity populated by individuals exhibiting many of the same virtuous characteristics that he discerned amongst the inhabitants of the Roman Republic. Both his diagnosis and his prescriptions were drawn from the Greco-Roman world. Froude mixed these arguments with an idealized view of the "ancient" feudal system in Britain. Although he often talked in vague terms about the greatness of the "English Empire," he placed little emphasis on the providential rights and duties of the British to "civilize" the rest of the world, and he prioritized the settler colonies above all.[43] They were, he argued, "infinitely more important to

---

[42] Froude, *Oceana*, cited in Dunn, *James Anthony Froude*, 523–24. He uses a similar formulation in "Party Politics," 326–27. Froude's *Oceana* is of course named after James Harrington, *The Commonwealth of Oceana* (London, 1656).

[43] Aside from *Oceana*, which focused mainly on Australia, the Cape, and New Zealand (as well as the United States), Froude also wrote *The English in the West Indies, or the Bow of Ulysses* (London, 1888). Pessimistic and deeply racist, this is his most Carlylean book. It focuses more on the degraded state of the British settlers than on "civilizing" the nonwhite population. He very briefly mentions that Russia and Britain were both engaged in bringing "civilization" to the "Eastern nations" in *The Earl of Beaconsfield* (244), but he did not expand on this issue.

us than even India." The reason for this was simple: "[I]t is because the entire future of the English Empire depends on our availing ourselves of the opportunities which those dependencies offer to us."[44] Indeed he barely touched on India, and when he did it was in terms that would have horrified Mill. He suggested that, due to its role in promoting national greatness, the British should stay in India in perpetuity. "Our Indian Empire was won by the sword, and by the sword it must be held; and to suppose that we can ever abandon it except in defeat and disgrace is to surrender ourselves wilfully to the wildest illusion."[45]

Froude saw corruption wherever he looked in the modern world. "[W]e are passing," he warned, "through a crisis in our national existence."[46] Obsessed with the "genius of English freedom," a genius he saw as largely consigned to the past, he believed that the only hope for the future lay in the unity of the settler empire. But it was important, he argued, to recognize that the colonies were not simple imperial possessions, and that "[o]ne free people cannot govern another free people."[47] With the necessary checks and balances they could govern a non-free people—this is presumably how he saw India—but to impose their will on a "free" people was both to commit an injustice (made worse in this case because they were "English" and therefore part of the same "nation") and also to potentially corrupt the polity.

Froude's views on the specific content of "freedom" were rather elusive. He was not a systematic theorist, and his comments on the issue are scattered and frequently opaque. It is nevertheless clear what he was opposed to. The modern state, he argued, "disclaims abstract considerations of justice, and knows nothing but expediency." It existed only "to secure the greatest liberty to the greatest number—liberty meaning the absence of constraint," and it was driven by a simple philosophy: "Let every man prove his private advantage with all the faculties that belong to him, and nature and competition will take care of the rest."[48] His own conception of freedom was much less clearly articulated. He repeatedly harked after an "old" England—the dates of which remained unspecified—where the people were free in a different sense; it was this historical phantasm that he often linked to (or conflated with) the early Roman Republic. In this feudal ideal, freedom was an attribute of citizenship granted for the performance of valuable social roles. In such a society everybody knew their place, recognizing that they were enmeshed in a complex web of obligations and duties. "In the old days a 'freeman' was a master of his craft, and not till he had learnt to do, and do well, some work which was use-

[44] Froude, "England's War," 276.

[45] Ibid., 274–75.

[46] Froude, *Oceana*, 395.

[47] Ibid., 2.

[48] Froude, "Reciprocal Duties of State and Subject," *Short Studies*, 3:118–20 (*Fraser's Magazine*, 1870).

ful for society did he enter upon his privileges as a citizen."[49] In such a world, "[l]iberty in the modern sense, liberty where the rights of man take the place of the duties of man," was neither "sought nor desired."[50] He summarized this view in "On Progress," arguing that:

> As a member of society man parts with his natural rights, and society in turn incurs a debt to him which it is bound to discharge. Where the debt is adequately rendered, where on both sides there is a conscious-ness of obligation, where the rulers and ruled alike understand that more is required of them than attention to their separate interests, and where they discern with clearness in what the "more" consists, there is at once good government, there is supremacy of law . . . and there, and only there, is freedom.[51]

As long as they were enacted for the betterment of the commonwealth, laws were not (as liberals purportedly argued) impediments to liberty. "Just laws are no restraint upon the freedom of the good, for the good man desires noth-ing which a just law will interfere with. He is as free under the law as without the law, and he is grateful for its guidance when want of knowledge might lead him wrong."[52] But freedom was increasingly undermined by the logic of capitalism, for under the iron rule of the political economists, Froude argued, English workers were overly dependent on their masters. The worker existed in "an enchanted circle of necessity—that he must stay passive under the bar-est of wages which will keep life in him and his, under penalty of starvation if he resist to make an effort to escape." We "mock him with the name of free-dom," he declared.[53] Independence, which he routinely (although inconsis-tently) tied to property, was the anchor of freedom; and the freedom of the individual and the freedom of the polity were intimately connected, for the "units composing it [the state] are free in the freedom of the body. If they seek a separate freedom of their own, they can obtain it only by degradation."[54]

Dreaming of Rome: The Uses of History and the Future of "Oceana"

In order to understand the nature of and the inspiration for Froude's views on Britain and the empire it is necessary to turn to his interpretation of ancient history, and in particular the history of Rome. This was a constant point of

[49] Froude, *The Earl of Beaconsfield*, 189.
[50] Ibid., 75–76.
[51] Froude, "On Progress," *Short Studies*, 3:173 (*Fraser's Magazine*, 1870).
[52] Froude, "Reciprocal Duties of State and Subject," 138.
[53] Froude, "England's War," 287; Froude, *The Earl of Beaconsfield*, 189.
[54] Froude, "Party Politics," 341.

reference in his writings, and it played a fundamental role in shaping his political thought. It is this imaginative engagement with the ancients, as much as
anything else, that marks his distance from Carlyle. The early republic offered
Froude a partial template for his global British polity; and the causes of its
decline presented a stark warning about both the mechanisms and the consequences of corruption. "To the student of political history, and to the English
student above all others," he wrote in the opening passage of his biography of
Julius Caesar, "the conversion of the Roman Republic into a military empire
commands peculiar interest. Notwithstanding many differences, the English
and the Romans essentially resemble one another."[55] The twilight of the republic was, he continued, a period "in so many ways the counterpart of our
own," and the "[t]endencies now in operation may a few generations hence
land modern society in similar conclusions." If this came to pass, "free institutions" would be destroyed.[56]

The reason that Rome seemed such an apposite exemplar derived, at least
in part, from Froude's conception of historical time. He believed that all living
things, including "commonwealths," followed the same trajectory: "recurring
stages of growth and transformation and decay."[57] This was one of the reasons
why he was generally suspicious of the cult of progress that he discerned
amongst his contemporaries. But the pattern of history was not fully predetermined. The speed at which decay metastasized through the body politic
remained within the domain of human agency, and as such, Froude thought
that the Commonwealth could be ruled in such a manner as to extend its existence—and conversely, that certain courses of action would accelerate decline. Fate could not be defeated, but it could be held at bay. "The life of a nation, like the life of a man, may be prolonged in honour into the fullness of its
time, or it may perish prematurely, for want of guidance, by violence or internal disorders." The study of history offered one way in which to inculcate wisdom, for the causes of decline could be identified and acted upon.[58] This was
yet another reason why he insisted that the fall of Rome was of such "peculiar" interest to the "English student." Although Froude dissented from Harrington's specific proposals for overcoming the tension between expansion
and liberty, he nevertheless thought that through reordering the moral and
political constitution of the British people, and through incorporating vast
expanses of the colonies within an enlarged polity, the inevitability of decline
could be resisted, perhaps even indefinitely.

[55] Froude, *Caesar* (London, 1879), 1. See also Froude, "Society in Italy in the Last Days of the
Roman Republic," *Short Studies*, 5:205.

[56] Froude, *Caesar*, 4, 8.

[57] Ibid., 2 (and also 536). Carlyle also held to a cyclical conception of historical time, though
his was more violent and destructive than Froude's. See the discussion in Burrow, *Liberal Descent*,
253. Compare this with Mill's ambiguous view: Mill, *Considerations*, 388.

[58] Froude, *Caesar*, 3–4. "[T]here are courses of action which have uniformly produced the
same results" (4).

Froude's vision of "Oceana" demanded the translation of the virtues of the early Roman republicans into the contemporary world. This was partly a matter of recovering their personal virtues. The inhabitants of the "early commonwealth of Rome," he wrote, were "distinguished by remarkable purity of manners." The "marriage tie was singularly respected" and the "Latin yeomen, who were the back-bone of the community, were industrious and laborious," living their lives "with frugality and simplicity," and raising their children "in a humble fear of God or the gods as rulers to whom they would one day have to give an account." This was a society where "[t]he whole duty of man lay in *virtus*— virtue, manliness." Then corruption set in, and the last years of the republic were marked by the "incredible depravity of manners, the corruption of justice, the oppression of the provinces [and] the collapse of the political fabric in a succession of civil wars."[59] The result was catastrophic: the "free institutions which had been the admiration of mankind were buried under the throne of the Caesars."[60]

Froude argued that a sense of religion had regulated the life of the republicans, motivating and giving shape to the other virtues.[61] Under the wise rule of Augustus, order and justice were reinstated, but following his death it soon became apparent that the moral fabric of the republic had disintegrated.

The administration of Augustus was the most perfect system of secular government ever known, and the attributes assigned to Augustus were the apotheosis of it. The principle of Augustus was the establishment of law and order, of justice and decency of conduct. Of the heroic virtues, or even the modest virtues of purity and sense of moral responsibility, such a system knew nothing, and offered no motive for moral enthusiasm. Order and law and decency are the body of society, but are a body without a soul; and, without a soul, the body, however vigorous its sinews, must die and go to corruption.[62]

And so it came to pass. The reign of justice could not last, and the decline and fall of Rome ensued as corruption and vice spread widely and decisively. The moral orientation provided by an overarching religiosity disappeared, and the

[59] Ibid., 257.

[60] Froude, "Divus Caesar" [1867?], *Short Studies*, 5:258, 257; Froude, "Society in Italy," 215.

[61] Froude, "Divus Caesar," 250, 290. In "Party Politics," Froude wrote that religion leads people "into a recognition of their higher destiny and of the obligations attaching to it" (342). In *Caesar*, he refers to the religion of the Romans as "the foundation of the laws and rule of personal conduct" (7). He also writes that: "The 'virtues' which the Romans made into gods [valor, truth, good faith, modesty, charity and concord] contain in them the essence of real religion, that in them and in nothing else has the characteristic which distinguished human beings from the rest of animated things" (14).

[62] Froude, "Divus Caesar," 283. Froude's most famous discussion of the "heroic" virtues amongst his (Elizabethan) countrymen came in his early essay, "England's Forgotten Worthies," *Short Studies*, vol. 3 [1852].

collapse of virtue invariably followed. Such was the story that Froude recounted. The focus on religion was unusual—and drew directly from Froude's own fragile spiritual sensibility—but the general narrative of rise and decline was firmly etched in the consciousness of educated late Victorians. The ancient republic provided Froude with a model for the future, and a way to judge—and judge scathingly—the world around him. The character traits that he most admired in the ancients—a sense of public duty, hardiness and frugality, "manliness," an intimate connection with the land, and so forth— were those that he considered necessary to escape the debasement of the moderns.[63] The mechanisms of corruption that had destroyed the republic were those that he feared were hollowing out his beloved England from within. Froude also employed the fate of Rome to inculcate a number of specific lessons. One concerned the depredations of urbanization. England, he warned, was in danger of becoming a "country of cities."[64] This had two main consequences. First, it was leading to the moral and physical degeneration of the population. He drew on a passage from Horace to illustrate the point. As people flocked from the fields to the cities they were exposed to ever increasing levels of vice. "Decay is busy at the heart of them, and all the fate of Rome seemed to me likely to be the fate of England if she became what the political economists desired to see her."[65] Second, it meant that the number of "free holders"—those owning their own plots of land or with secure tenure—went into rapid decline. The ownership of property, the very anchor of freedom, was being eliminated. The likely consequences could again be traced in the fate of Rome.

> The armies which made the strength of the Roman republic were composed of the small holders of Latium and afterwards of Italy. When Rome became an empire, the freeholder disappeared; the great families bought up the soil and cultivated it with slaves, and the decline and fall followed by inevitable consequence.[66]

A similar process was happening around him, for as the people left the countryside to work in the factories large landowners increasingly swallowed up

---

[63] Froude's portrait of the early Romans mirrors his admiring description of Dutch colonists— the "true colonists"—in southern Africa. See his speech at Bloemfontein, December 1874, reprinted in Dunn, *Froude*, 2:414. See also his positive assessment in "Leaves from a South African Journal," 378, 397. Froude was keen to see the Boers and the English settlers confederate. He was sent on a mission by the Colonial Secretary, the Earl of Carnarvon, during 1874–75 to investigate this possibility. On this episode, see Dunn, *Froude*, vol. 2, ch. 26.

[64] Froude, "England and Her Colonies," *Short Studies*, 3:19 (*Fraser's Magazine*, 1870).

[65] Froude, *Oceana*, 10. Elsewhere he lamented "the poisoned atmosphere of our huge and hideous towns." Froude, "England's War," 278.

[66] Froude, "England and Her Colonies," 21. The same was true, he argued, of the famous commercial cities—Venice, Genoa, Florence: "Their greatness was founded upon sand." See also Froude, "On Progress," 153.

the lands they had vacated.[67] Many of these men sat in Parliament, which partly explained the shameful state of British politics, for their main interest lay not in defending the common good but in the pursuit of personal gain. "Their grandfathers cared for the English commonwealth. It is hard to say what some of these high persons care for except luxury."[68] Froude also looked to puncture what he saw as facile complacency about progress. Gibbon, he noted, had identified the period between the accession of Trajan and the death of Marcus Aurelius as the "time in which the human race had enjoyed more general happiness than they had ever known before." But this was a fatal mistake, for "during that very epoch, and in the midst of all that prosperity, the heart of the empire was dying out of it. The austere virtues of the ancient Roman were perishing with their faults. The principles, the habits, the convictions, which held society together were giving way, one after the other, before luxury and selfishness."[69] As with the Romans, warned Froude, so with his compatriots.

Froude argued that the problems of the modern world could be laid squarely at the feet of liberalism, or at least a species of it. Liberalism promoted three crippling vices: materialism, individualism, and a minimalist ("nightwatchman") conception of the state. Materialism was the popular religion of the country; and luxury, understood as the excessive accumulation of personal wealth and its ostentatious display, was its progeny. "Luxury," he lamented, was "no longer deprecated as an evil," as it was by the ancient writers, but was instead "encouraged as a stimulus to labour." Again: the "modern creed [of liberalism] looks complacently on luxury as a stimulus to trade. Fact says that luxury has disorganized society, severed the bonds of goodwill which unite man to man, and class to class, and generated distrust and hatred."[70] Luxury was allowed to polarize society because the modern liberal conception of the state failed to provide the necessary resources to deal with the threat— indeed it encouraged it. In this rendering, the state was no more than the uncoordinated aggregation of egoistic individuals, a hollow shell lacking common purpose. This vision itself was premised on a rampant individualism that, according to Froude, corroded the affective bonds necessary to unite communities, reconcile classes, and ensure greatness. "In these modern times men govern themselves, and therefore their loyalty is to themselves."[71] He

---

[67] There was one difference, however. While the "Roman capitalists" filled their lands with slaves, the same was not true of the moderns. While this meant that the specific mechanisms of decline were somewhat different, it did not alter the general picture of freedom being eradicated, and of a dangerous migration to the overcrowded cities. See Froude, *Caesar*, 7, 8–9; and Froude, "On the Uses of a Landed Gentry," *Short Studies*, 4:310 [1876].

[68] Froude, "The Colonies Once More," *Short Studies*, 3:207 (*Fraser's Magazine*, 1870).

[69] Froude, "On Progress," 151.

[70] Froude, "Reciprocal Duties," 123; Froude, "On Progress," 181.

[71] Froude, "Reciprocal Duties," 118.

hankered after an older understanding of self, society, and state, praising the "ancient notion of a community," one which fostered virtues "which Englishmen used most to desire," the virtues of "Patriotism, loyalty, fidelity, self-forgetfulness, a sense of duty." In such a society the "sense of what is due to a man's self—his rights, as he calls them—is conspicuously absent."[72] Individuals should be bound by duty, not seen as possessing inalienable rights; society was a cooperative hierarchical arrangement united by common purpose and interests; and the state was a moral entity, the priorities of which were clear: "To repress needless luxury, to prevent capitalists from making fortunes at the cost of the poor, and to distribute in equitable proportions the profits of industry."[73] A "sound nation," he declared,

> . . . is a nation composed of sound human beings, healthy in body, strong of limb, true in word and deed—brave, sober, temperate, chaste, to whom morals are more important than wealth or knowledge—where duty is first and the rights of man are second—where, in short, men grow up and live and work hard, having in them what our ancestors called the "fear of God."

This was, of course, exactly the way he had described the virtues of the inhabitants of the "early republic." Unlike the radical republicans, Froude believed that democracy fostered rather than eliminated these dangers. In democracies, he warned, the "pursuit of wealth becomes the predominant passion, degrades the national character, raises to eminence the least worthy of elevation, corrupts those who obtain it by luxury."[74] The main counter to these tendencies was strong government and, ideally, a patriotic aristocracy ruling in the best interests of the commonwealth. "The natural leaders in a healthy country are the gentry; public-spirited and patriotic because their own fortunes are bound up with the fortunes of their country."[75] They would act as a bulwark against the vagaries of "commercial speculation." Here lay the roots of his (qualified) admiration for Disraeli. Whereas Carlyle "despised" Jews and had regarded Disraeli as a "fantastic ape," Froude described himself as a "*quasi* follower" of the Tory politician, although this is unsurprising as he attributed to him a vision of politics that almost exactly mirrored his own.[76] After all, he claimed,

---

[72] Froude, "Party Politics," 342–43.

[73] Froude, "Reciprocal Duties," 122.

[74] Froude, "Party Politics," 329–30.

[75] Froude, "Landed Gentry," 312. He frequently criticized aristocracies, past and present, for failing in their duties. In his Rector's address at St. Andrews in 1869, he praised John Knox for challenging an "unworthy aristocracy." "Education," *Short Studies*, 3:227. He scalded the existing British aristocracy for falling into the grip of luxury and for diverting its attention from the common good. Froude, "England's War," 278; "Party Politics," 356–57. *Caesar* was a harsh indictment of the corruption of the Roman aristocracy.

[76] Froude, *Beaconsfield*, 84, 92, 93. Italics in original. For Froude's assessment of Disraeli's po-

Disraeli venerated the "old conception of the commonwealth," where a just and beneficent aristocracy ruled in the name of the people, and he hoped that some version of this might be restored if only the aristocrats could relearn "the habits of their forefathers."[77] Once again we witness Froude's admixture of classical ideals and a mythopoeic vision of the feudal past. Aristocratic rule provided the backbone for republican life.

> Republics have held together as long as they have been strong with patrician sinews; when the sinews crack the republic becomes a democracy, and the unity of the commonwealth is shivered into a heap of disconnected atoms, each following its own laws of gravitation towards its imagined interests. Athens and Rome, the Italian Republics, the great kingdoms which rose out of the wreck of the Roman Empire, tell the same story.[78]

And this story was repeating itself before his very eyes. In language strikingly similar to that he employed to chart the decline of Rome, he argued that the Reform Acts of 1832 and 1867 had created an environment in which individuals focused solely on their own interests, "a process under which the English people are becoming a congregation of contending atoms, scrambling every one of them to snatch a larger portion of good things than its fellow."[79] Froude's vision was a paternalistic one in which a beneficent elite governed a contented free people, bound together in loyalty to the nation and by the interdependence and mutual reliance of all classes.

Froude argued that the cure for the assorted evils that he identified lay in the wide-open spaces of Greater Britain. His dream, which was never specified with any precision, was of a "united Oceana," a polity "united as closely as the American states are united."[80] The colonies were important for two different, though related, reasons. The first concerned scale and power. "These are not the days for small states: the natural boundaries are broken down which once divided kingdom from kingdom; and with the interests of nations so much intertwined as they are now becoming, every one feels the benefit of

---

litical thought, see 107, 216–18. He ultimately remained ambivalent about Disraeli, regarding his years in office as a wasted opportunity (ch. 16).

[77] Ibid., 82, 107. The connections between this and the civic humanist vision are not, however, that distant. The key link—at least for Disraeli—was Viscount Bolingbroke, whose *Idea of a Patriot King* (1838) was a key "country party" text (Disraeli, though, stripped much of the radicalism from Bolingbroke's prescriptions). See Richard Faber, *Beaconsfield and Bolingbroke* (London, 1961); David Armitage, "A Patriot for Whom?," *Journal of British Studies*, 36 (1997), 397–418. See also the discussion of Victoria as a patriot queen in chapter 6.

[78] Froude, "Cheneys and the House of Russell," *Short Studies*, 5:347–48.

[79] Ibid., 375. Elsewhere he wrote that in a democracy the state was in danger of being "reduced finally to the congregation of self-seeking atoms" ("Party Politics," 356).

[80] Froude, *Oceana*, 91, 354–56.

belonging to a first-rate Power."[81] Only a united Oceana could secure the freedoms of the (global) English nation. Secondly, the colonies offered vast tracts
of land that could absorb millions of emigrants from the "mother country."
Froude was obsessed with emigration—both the dangers of the continuing
flow of people to the United States, and also the need for the British government to finance a system of systematic emigration to the colonies. The former
was a problem because it simultaneously weakened Britain whilst strengthening a formidable competitor. The latter was vital because of the increasing urbanization and consequent degradation of Britain. In the colonies emigrants
would be transfigured into freemen and patriots—rugged, hardy, and industrious. "You who are impatient with what you call a dependent position at
home, go to Australia, go to Canada, go to New Zealand, or South Africa."[82]
The vile cities could be halved in size, the colonies restocked. Fearful of the
"plagues which are consuming us," Froude argued that emigrants would be
able to lead "a happier and purer life" in the colonies.[83] "If," he argued,

> ... the millions of English and Scotch men and women who are wasting
> their constitutions and wearing out their souls in factories and coal
> mines were growing corn and rearing cattle in Canada and New Zea-
> land, the red colour would come back to their cheeks, their shrunken
> sinews would fill out again, their children, now a drag upon their hands,
> would be elements of wealth and strength while here at home the sun
> would shine again, and wages would rise to the colonial level, and land
> would divide itself, and we should have room to move and breathe.[84]

The aim of British government policy should be to create a polity strong and
"healthy" enough to postpone the inevitable, to "defy the storms of fate."[85]

Was Froude simply reiterating Carlyle's views on empire? Their positions
overlapped on many points. Both contended that the settler colonies were
more important than India.[86] Both expressed horror at the state of British
cities, demanded more support for emigration, and waxed lyrical about the
revivifying open spaces of the colonies. Both called for an end to the reign of
the political economists and a more interventionist role for the state. But

---

[81] Froude, "England and Her Colonies," 29. On the geopolitical necessity of Oceana, see also
Froude, "Party Politics," 333–34; "England's War," 276.

[82] Froude, "Landed Gentry," 319.

[83] Froude, "England's War," 282–83.

[84] Ibid., 283–84. The "wealth of a nation," he argued in *Oceana*, "depends in the long run upon
the conditions mental and bodily of the people of whom it consists, and the experience of all mankind declares that a race of men sound in soul and limb can be bred and reared only in the exercise
of plough and spade, in the free air and sunshine, with country enjoyments and amusements, never
amidst foul drains and smoke blacks and the eternal clank of machinery" (8, 246).

[85] Froude, *Oceana*, 15.

[86] For Carlyle's views on India, see John Morrow, *Thomas Carlyle* (London, 2006), chs. 2–3.

their thinking was marked by numerous differences, and when they did concur it did not necessarily mean that they had arrived at their conclusions in the same manner.[87] We should not be surprised by this: their writings on empire were produced in different political contexts. Carlyle's scattered remarks on colonization were published during the 1840s and 1850s (primarily in *Chartism* and *Past and Present*), while Froude's date mainly from the 1870s and 1880s. Carlyle's conception of the spiritual value of labor shaped his views on colonization, whereas Froude, who did not share Carlyle's account, articulated a more instrumental position—it was beneficial for everybody to have a trade so that they could be independent, and thus capable of securing their freedom.[88] Whereas Carlyle looked benignly on British emigration to America, Froude was horrified by it, regarding the United States as a challenger to British preeminence.[89] "We have raised up against us a mighty empire to be the rival, it may be the successful rival, of our power."[90] For Carlyle, the colonies were important mainly as an answer to the "social question," and he placed little emphasis on geopolitics; for Froude, on the other hand, the domestic and the international were combined in an intricate dialectic. Due to a combination of geopolitical competition and internal decay British greatness was under threat, and the colonies offered the only solution. Finally, while Carlyle expostulated on the benefits of emigration and colonial life, he never conceived of the empire, or the settlement empire within it, as a distinctive and integrated social and political unit. Froude, meanwhile, dreamed of a united Oceanic commonwealth.

Conclusions

Recent interest in tracing the history of "liberal imperialism" has illuminated important dimensions of nineteenth-century political thought and action. The relevance of this exercise for contemporary political theory and social criticism is palpable. Yet focusing exhaustively on ideas about the liberal desire

[87] Even on these points, however, tracing a direct line of influence is far from straightforward, for many of them were commonplaces of imperial political discourse.

[88] For example: "I accept without qualification the first principle of our forefathers, that every boy born into the world should be put in the way of maintaining himself in honest independence." Froude, "Education," 240, and also, 250–51; see also, Froude, "On Progress," 164–69, and for his admiring views of the multi-dimensional education (and the "universal practical accomplishments") of the Romans, *Caesar*, 231. On Carlyle's metaphysical view of labor, see Morrow, *Thomas Carlyle*, chs. 4–5.

[89] For Carlyle's views, see Carlyle, *Collected Works*, 6:378; and, in general, K. J. Fielding, "Carlyle and the Americans,'" *Carlyle Studies Annual*, 15 (1995), 55–64.

[90] Froude, "Education," 249. Indeed he feared that unless they were united with Britain the colonies might seek to join the United States. Froude, "England and Her Colonies," 29–30.

to "civilize" the "barbarian," and to transmit British manners, values, and institutions throughout the world, has also meant that the variety and complexity of Victorian imperial thought is often obscured. Many liberals, and indeed many non-liberals, looked on the map of the world as an open invitation for projects of transformation—social, political, and moral. But not all did so. Other parallel, intersecting, and sometimes contradictory forms of argument were also common, offering different accounts of justification for overseas expansion, coercion, and rule. In this chapter I have highlighted one such position, which I have termed republican. Yet it is important to stress that republican imperialism was not a discrete autonomous "tradition" completely separate from other imperial ideologies—it was instead a bundle of arguments, even a sensibility, concerning the sources, nature, and value of overseas conquest and government. It was possible, for example, to offer a republican defense of settler colonization and insist on the imperatives of the civilizing mission elsewhere. Republican themes were threaded through the tapestry of Victorian political thought, cutting across liberalism, conservatism, even socialism. The clearest and most consistent articulation of republican imperial argument can be found in Froude's writings. Much as Froude was indebted to Carlyle, his hero and often his inspiration, those interested in tracing the sources and character of his political thought need to pay more attention to the imaginative debt he owed to the ancient world, and in particular to his appropriation of Roman republicanism, than is usually the case. His understanding of the pathologies and potential of the British (global) polity was shaped by, and anchored in, his understanding of the practices and intellectual worlds of the early Romans. Only by drawing vital lessons from the precapitalist past, he insisted, would it be possible to map a glorious future for "Oceana." Otherwise the fate of Rome would befall the corrupted British.

CHAPTER 13

Alter Orbis

⁂

E. A. Freeman on Empire and Racial Destiny

Where there is Empire, there is no brotherhood;
where there is brotherhood, there is no Empire.[1]

—E. A. FREEMAN

Freeman was a celebrated historian in a culture that venerated the historical arts as a privileged source of truth about the human condition. His historical writing was always political; his political thinking always historical. Indeed he once defined history in Aristotelian terms as "the science of man in his character as a political being."[2] A scholar of prodigious energy, he pioneered the application of the "comparative method" to the study of politics and contributed to a wide range of contemporary debates. He was, that is, an archetypal public moralist. Freeman gave the role two distinctive twists. The first, inspired by Thomas Arnold, stressed the "unity of history," denying any radical break between the ancient and the modern—"that wretched distinction"—and emphasizing continuities and "survivals" more than rupture and innovation. The "great truth" to be discerned from studying the past was that "history is one," that "every part has a bearing on every other part."[3] This led him to see events in a deep (and often distorting) historical perspective and to express suspicion of novelty. Freeman's second characteristic move was to underscore the spatial dimensions of political life, contrasting the unity of historical time with the disunity of geographical space, the manner in which different constellations of geology, climate, and territory shaped political institutions, racial

---

[1] Freeman, "George Washington, the Expander of England," in *Greater Greece and Greater Britain* (London, 1886), 102.

[2] Freeman, "A Review of My Opinions," *The Forum* (1892), 152; Freeman, *The Methods of Historical Study* (London, 1886), 117.

[3] Freeman, *Comparative Politics* (London, 1873), 293–94.

character, and individual subjectivities. Indeed he can be seen as an early exponent of geopolitics.[4] In combination, these intellectual commitments produced a body of work at once expansive in ambition and attenuated in
execution.

Oscillating between Burkean gradualism and sentimental radicalism, Freeman was a self-declared searcher after truth and justice, his political activity
marked, he claimed, by "zeal for right against wrong." Proud of his devotion
to individual and collective freedom, he boasted that he was "for the oppressed everywhere, whoever may be the oppressor."[5] While his myopic vision of justice rarely extended beyond the limits of Western Christendom, it
nevertheless underpinned his skepticism about imperial order. Unconvinced
by the purported benefits of British rule in India and Africa, he was hostile to
plans for further imperial expansion and advocated immediate independence
for the settler colonies. Yet Freeman was no straightforward "Little Eng-
lander," for he defended an alternative model of global racial imperium in
which the "Teutonic" peoples, and above all "the English folk," would order
the world. The English nation, on this account, was an immanent community
distributed across North America, Britain, southern Africa, and the South Pacific. Its potential as an agent of progress was undermined by the misguided
pursuit of empire. The bonds of "race" were more fundamental than those of
formal political institutions. "Surely the burthen of barbaric Empire is at most
something that we may school ourselves to endure; the tie of English brotherhood is something that we may rejoice to strive after."[6]

I start by dissecting some of Freeman's arguments about time, space, and
politics. The rest of the chapter analyzes his views on racial kinship and empire, focusing initially on his critique of the idea of imperial federation, one of
the most prominent political debates of the 1880s and 1890s, before moving
to his alternative conceptualization of global order. He argued that dismantling the British settler empire was both a matter of justice and a precondition
for establishing the proper sense of racial "brotherhood" necessary to realize
the higher purpose of the English-speaking peoples. The manifest destiny of
the race was thus premised on recognition of the deep unity of Britain and the
United States.

---

[4] This novelty was acknowledged. C.R.M., "The Late Professor E. A. Freeman and His Services to Geography," *Proceedings of the Royal Geographical Society*, 14 (1892), 401. Halford Mackinder critiqued Freeman in "The Geographical Pivot of History," *Geographical Journal*, 23 (1904),
423–24.

[5] Freeman, "A Review of My Opinions," 150, 157. On this uneasy oscillation, as well as shifts
in the emphasis of his thought between the 1860s and 1880s, see Collini, Winch, and Burrow,
That Noble Science of Politics, 219–26; Burrow, *A Liberal Descent* (Cambridge, 1981), pt. 3.

[6] Freeman, "George Washington," 84.

Palimpsest: A World of Worlds

On us a new light has come.[7]

—E. A. FREEMAN

Freeman once claimed that reading Aristotle taught him the "power of discerning likenesses and unlikeness, of distinguishing between real and false analogies," and that this lesson informed both his historical and political thought.[8] Supremely confident in his ability to decipher the palimpsest of human experience, Freeman carved multiple worlds from the historical record, each defined by a specific configuration of territory and social organization, each subject to the perennial forces of expansion, contraction, dispersal, and even annihilation. Populated by civilizations, races, empires, cities, and states, his imaginative geography ranged across different scales, from the local to the planetary, but the practice of worlding—of classifying communities and assigning them meaning in a universal story of human endeavor—was a recurrent theme in his writings. It enabled him to trace patterns of continuity and change across continents and centuries. The privileged role of the historian was to map the fate of worlds and divine salutary lessons from the perpetual cycle of creativity and destruction.

The most fundamental division was expressed in the "eternal Eastern Question," the millennia-long struggle between East and West. Stretching from "the opening chapters of Herodotus" to "this morning's telegrams," it was an epic battle between "light and darkness, between freedom and bondage," an enduring topography of fear and loathing. Originally centered on the Greek conflict against the barbarians, its most recent incarnation was the clash between Christianity and Islam.[9] His hatred of the "Turk" motivated Freeman's political interventions during the 1850s and 1870s, when he took a lead in campaigning against the depredations of the Ottoman Empire.[10] The Ottomans—with the insidious support of the "Jew" Disraeli—presented a fundamental threat to the progressive Western world, centered on Teutonic Europe. Blending anti-Semitism with a vitriolic hatred of Islam and the barbarism of "the Orient," Freeman's racism infected his political vision and his historical writing in equal measure.[11]

[7] Freeman, "Unity of History," *Comparative Politics*, 301.

[8] Freeman, "Review," 152.

[9] Freeman, "A Review," 155, 156. See Vicky Morrisroe, " 'Eastern History with Western Eyes,' " *Journal of Victorian Culture*, 16 (2011), 25–45; William Kelley, "Past History and Present Politics," in *Making History*, ed. G. A. Bremner and Jonathan Conlin (Oxford, 2015), 119–39.

[10] Richard Shannon, *Gladstone and the Bulgarian Agitation, 1876* (London, 1963), 81, 223–30.

[11] On Freeman's racism, see the contrasting accounts in Vicky Morrisroe " 'Sanguinary Amuse-

Freeman was drawn above all to the ancient Greeks. The rediscovery of classical learning in the fifteenth and sixteenth centuries, he marveled, must have "been like the discovery of a new sense," indeed like the "discovery of a new world of being, as it opened up the vistas of human knowledge and experience, granting access to the manifold treasures that had been lost from view."[12] The Hellenic world provided Freeman with a uniquely rich inventory of ideas and institutions to measure all other worlds against, and as we shall see this classicizing gaze undergirded his account of the pathologies of empire and the potentiality of racial kinship. It also shaped his understanding of historical pedagogy. He once wrote that the "great lesson of history is that the nature of man, or at any rate of civilized European man, is the same in all times and places, and that there is no time or place whose experience may not supply us with some teaching."[13] Yet some times and places taught the true philosophical historian more than others. By focusing on a great but comprehensible civilization, students and scholars could uncover universal truths about history, politics, and the human condition.[14] A microcosm of human experience, the Greek world was a laboratory of enlightenment and political virtue. While Freeman's views can be read as an expression of bathetic nostalgia, he never yearned for a mimetic recreation of the past; rather, the ancient Greek order was a yardstick and a navigation aid, both map and compass, for helping to comprehend his own world.

Freeman regarded the "comparative method" as the intellectual polestar of the nineteenth century, a "new light" arguably more significant that the Renaissance encounter with the ancients—the illuminator of worlds.[15] Scholars such as Max Müller and Henry Maine provided tools to analyze the Aryan race and its Teutonic heirs through the study of symbols, myths, and above all language. They had demonstrated that unity could be found in difference and that human progress was essentially the story of the Aryans and their offspring. "Civilization," as Maine once declared, "is nothing more than a name

---

ment,'" *Modern Intellectual History*, 10 (2013), 27–56; Theodore Koditschek, *Liberalism, Imperialism and the Historical Imagination* (Cambridge, 2011), 240–50; Christopher Parker, "The Failure of Liberal Racialism," *Historical Journal*, 24/4 (1981), 825–46.

[12] Freeman, "Unity of History," 297. The downside, he continued, was that it led people to venerate the Greeks and the Romans at the expense of the rest of history.

[13] Freeman, "Greater Greece and Greater Britain," *Greater Greece*, 59.

[14] This was a thought that he tried to translate into pedagogical reform: R. N. Berard, "Edward Augustus Freeman and University Reform in Victorian Oxford," *History of Education*, 9 (1980), 287–301. It is little surprise that one of his main political preoccupations was the fate of modern Greece: "A Review of My Opinions," 148.

[15] Freeman, "Unity of History," 301–2; Freeman, *Comparative Politics*, 1, 18. On the "comparative method," see Collini, Winch, and Burrow, *That Noble Science of Politics*, ch. 7; Sandra den Otter, "The Origins of a Historical Political Science in Late Victorian and Edwardian Britain," in *Modern Political Science*, ed. Robert Adcock, Mark Bevir, and Shannon Stimson (Princeton, 2007), 66–96.

for the old order of the Aryan world, dissolved but perpetually reconstituting itself."[16] But Freeman thought that more still could be achieved, that enacting the "true philosophy of history" required knowledge of the important *institutional* similarities connecting descendants of the ur-race, and he thus sought to track distinctive "forms of government" across time and space—this was the overarching aim of the field he named "comparative politics."[17] Chains of racial descent could now be ascertained beneath ephemeral surface phenomena.

> Like the revival of learning, it has opened to its votaries a new world, and that one not an isolated world, a world shut up within itself, but a world in which times and tongues and nations which before seemed parted poles asunder, now find each one its own place, its own relation to every other, as members of one common primeval brotherhood.[18]

Harnessing this dazzling intellectual power necessitated the cultivation of a new scholarly identity. The creation and maintenance of scholarly personae express a form of spirituality, characterized as they are by "an array of acts of inner self-transformation, of work on the self by the self," with the intention of fostering "an open ended variety of ethical aspirations, psychological deportments, cognitive dispositions, public duties, and private desires."[19] Freeman's historico-political project is a telling example. To become a true comparative scholar required arduous training in various scholarly arts and the mastery of a vast body of historical knowledge—"[o]f some branches he must know everything, but of every branch he must know something."[20] Moreover, it fostered a cognitive disposition to view the sensory output of the everyday with suspicion, allowing the scholar to delineate the fundamental patterns of history and politics. This was a kind of second sight, a trained capacity to identify "analogies which are to be seen between the political institutions of times and countries most remote from one another" and in particular where the "most profitable analogies, the most striking cases of direct derivation, are not those which are most obvious at first sight."[21] He was exceed-

---

[16] Maine, "The Effects of the Observation of Modern European Thought," in *Village Communities in the East and West*, 3rd ed. (London, 1876), 230.

[17] Freeman, *Comparative Politics*, 33, 19. Maine said that Freeman's lectures on the topic were the most interesting he had ever heard. Maine to Freeman, December 22, 1873, Freeman papers, John Rylands Library, University of Manchester, EAF/1/7.

[18] Freeman, "Unity of History," 302.

[19] Ian Hunter, "The Persona of the Philosopher and the History of Early Modern Philosophy," *Modern Intellectual History*, 4 (2007), 574. See also the discussion in Duncan Bell, "Writing the World," *International Affairs*, 85/1 (2009), 3–22, and Joel Isaac, "Tangled Loops," *Modern Intellectual History*, 6 (2009), 397–424. For the sources of this argument, see especially Pierre Hadot, *Philosophy as a Way of Life*, trans. M. Chase (Oxford, 1995).

[20] Freeman, "Unity of History," 308.

[21] Freeman, *Comparative Politics*, 18, 20. On his understanding of historical "method," see

ingly proud of his mastery of the method, his self-proclaimed ability to perceive the importance of the unfamiliar and the counterintuitive.

The project of comparativism was predicated on an account of racial descent, the original Aryan ur-people spawning assorted lineal descendants, the
most important of which were the Greeks, Romans, and Teutons. These three
races—of which the Teutons were the greatest—either had been or were the
"rulers and the teachers of the world."[22] This was at once their burden and
their sacred mission. While Müller and Maine had focused on the philological, mythical, and cultural connections between them, Freeman traced the
descent of "forms of government," including state, monarchy, and representative assembly.[23] Whereas the splendor of the Greeks and the Romans lay in
the past, the Teutons now stood as the foremost race in the world, with the
English their dominant branch. The itinerant English had three homes: their
primeval base on the European mainland, their main dwelling in Britain, populated by those who travelled with Hengst in the fifth century, and their new-
est offshoot in the United States.[24] Whether they realized it or not, they were
united by the indestructible bonds of kinship.

The intercalating of geography and politics shaped Freeman's conception
of both the possibilities and limitations of British power. He presented Britain as an "alter orbis," another world, due to its island status. This spatial accident was freighted with historical meaning. "It is the insular character of Britain which has, beyond anything else, made the inhabitants of Britain what
they are and the history of Britain what it has been."[25] Geographical other-
ness was the most important fact about British history, more significant even
than the Norman Conquest. It explained crucial variations between the "insular" and the "continental" branches of the Teutons, and in particular why the
Romans (and romance languages) never fully colonized Britain.[26] "We grew
up as a Teutonic people, in some things more purely Teutonic than our kinsfolk of the mainland. For we never accepted the law of Rome, we never saw a
roman empire of the English Nation."[27] Shaped by a fortuitous concatena-

---

Herman Paul " 'Habits of Thought and Judgment,' " in *Making History*, ed. Bremner and Conlin,
273–93.

[22] Freeman, *Comparative Politics*, 38.

[23] Freeman, *Lectures* 3–5. On Freeman and "democratic Teutonism," see Peter Mandler, *The
English National Character* (London, 2006), 86–105. On Freeman as a "universal historian," see
Arnaldo Momigliano, "Two Types of Universal History," *Journal of Modern History*, 58/1 (1986),
235–46.

[24] Freeman, "The English People in Its Three Homes," in *Lectures to American Audiences* (Philadelphia, 1882), 7–204.

[25] Freeman, "Alter Orbis," *Historical Essays*, 4th series (London, 1892), 221. See also Freeman,
Comparative Politics, 47–50; Freeman, *The History of the Norman Conquest of England, Its Causes
and Its Results* (London, 1870),1:556.

[26] Freeman, "Alter Orbis," 223, 229.

[27] Ibid., 234.

tion of history and physical geography, the liberty-loving character of the English was present wherever they settled, including the United States, that "newer and vaster England beyond the Oceans."[28]

Space could be recoded—at least in part—by human agency. Like so many of his contemporaries, Freeman was fascinated by the power of machines to master nature, though rather unusually he thought that this induced a welcome sense of temporal dislocation. Technological prosthetics, above all the electrical telegraph, furnished the recovery of the greatest of Greek political gifts: active citizenship. Freeman followed convention by arguing that small city-states (and their analogues) provided the ideal ground for the creation of political "character." In such communities—with Athens the template—men "are raised to the highest level and sharpened to the finest point," as all citizens had a stake in the life of the society.[29] Such social intimacy was impossible to recreate in large communities, but the wondrous products of Victorian technoscience finally allowed people separated by vast distances "direct personal knowledge" of political affairs, creating a bond of solidarity between individuals and groups who might never meet face-to-face. For Freeman, always the time-traveler, this meant that it was now possible to replicate the political ethos of the Greeks.

> Very few Englishmen ever saw or heard Walpole or Pulteney, Pitt or Fox. Now the whole land has well-nigh become a single city; we see and hear our leading men almost daily; they walk before us as the leaders of the Athenian democracy walked before their fellow-citizens; they take us into their counsels; they appeal to us as their judges; we have in short a share in political life only less direct than the share of the Athenian freeman, a share which our forefathers, even two or three generations back, never dreamed of.[30]

Those inventions meant that the world of Freeman's fellow subjects was closer to that of Periclean Athens than to their Georgian predecessors. The same technological developments also made it both possible and necessary to harness the power of race and the links of kinship uniting the English-speaking peoples.

The "Dark Abyss": Freeman on Imperial Federation

"I am no lover of 'empire,'" Freeman once declared. "I am not anxious for my country to exercise lordship over other lands, English-speaking or otherwise."

---

[28] Ibid., 221–22.

[29] Freeman, "Greater Greece," 13; Freeman, *History of Federal Government in Greece and Italy*, ed. J. B. Bury (London, 1893), 29–32; Freeman, *Comparative Politics*, 93–97.

[30] Freeman, "Greater Greece," 14–15.

While such lordship was sometimes a necessary evil—"a solemn and fearful duty"—it was never a "matter for rejoicing or boasting."[31] His main intervention in imperial debates came during the 1880s and early 1890s, at a time when arguments raged about the possible unification of Britain and its settler colonies. Plans for "imperial federation" tended to fall into three categories. Some advocated parliamentary representation for the colonists, others called for the creation of an extra-parliamentary council (or some equivalent institution) to offer nonbinding advice to Parliament on imperial affairs, while the most radical plans envisaged a globe-spanning federal polity. Railing against the "dark abyss" of imperial federation, Freeman established himself as one of the most trenchant critics of the project.[32]

A great admirer of federalism, Freeman was widely regarded as the leading British authority on the subject. He was prone to wax lyrical about its possibilities. *The Federalist*, he once wrote to Bryce, "[is] one of the wisest books ever written. I used to call Polybius and it the Old and New Testament on the subject."[33] He was skeptical, though, that many of his compatriots understood the complexities of the system—"so few know," he complained.[34] For a government to be classified as federal, Freeman had argued in his *History of Federal Government*, it had to meet two conditions: "On the one hand, each of the members of the Union must be wholly independent in those matters that concern each member only. On the other hand, all must be subject to a common power in those matters which concern the whole body of members collectively." An ideal federation, then, "in its perfect form, is one which forms a single state in its relations to other nations, but which consists of many states with regard to its internal government."[35] As such, an authentic "federal commonwealth" could be seen simultaneously as a state and a collection of states, as singular and plural. It all seemed to depend on the angle of vision. Yet he had been clear that colonies could not be parts of a federal commonwealth, for despite their high degree of internal independence their "relations

---

[31] Freeman, "The Physical and Political Bases of National Unity," in *Britannic Confederation*, ed. Arthur Silva White (London, 1892), 56; Freeman, "George Washington," 90.

[32] Freeman, "The Physical and Political Bases of National Unity," 45. On the debates over imperial federation, see Bell, *The Idea of Greater Britain*, and the chapters in part II of this volume. Freeman's nemesis, J. A. Froude—the subject of chapter 12—was among the most prominent imperial federalists, which may well have stoked Freeman's animosity to the idea.

[33] Letter to Bryce, July 10, 1884, *The Life and Letters of Edward A. Freeman*, 2 vols, ed. W.R.W. Stephens (London, 1895), 2:324.

[34] Letter to Bryce, May 22, 1887, *Life and Letters*, 2:367.

[35] Freeman, *History of Federal Government* (London, 1863), 3, 9. "It is enough," he wrote, "for a commonwealth to rank . . . as a true Federation, that the Union is one which preserves to the several members their full internal independence, while it denies to them all separate action in relation to foreign powers" (15). Criticizing Freeman's definition, Murray Forsyth argues that once a polity is federal it takes on its own state-like properties and cannot be seen in this bifocal manner. Forsyth, *Unions of States* (Leicester, 1981), 7.

towards other nations are determined for [them] by a power over which the Colony nor its citizens have any sort of control."[36]

To Freeman's fastidious mind "imperial federation" could only be interpreted coherently in two senses: the federation of either the whole British empire or the totality of the English-speaking peoples.[37] Both were fatally flawed. In the former, the nonwhite population of the Empire would have a huge numerical advantage, which denoted, he wrote to James Bryce, "a Federation in which we shall be outvoted by Hindoos and Mahometans." This entailed the ludicrous conclusion that "barbarians" would rule over their racial superiors.[38] Encompassing the English-speaking peoples, on the other hand, meant incorporating the independent United States while excluding most of the extant British empire.[39] Although this would solve one problem—getting "rid of the barbarians"—it was predicated on the fantasy that the US would willingly rejoin the very colonial power against which it had rebelled.[40] However, he at least acknowledged the possibility. "I believe that no-one proposes that the Federation of the English-speaking people shall take in the United States of America; if any one does so propose, I honour him as being more logical than his brethren."[41] In both cases, Freeman was being disingenuous. Most imperial federalists were explicit about the racial exclusivity of their plans and some did argue for the absorption of the United States.[42]

He lambasted imperialists for misunderstanding the true meaning of both federalism and empire. "On the principle that language was given to man to conceal his thoughts, 'Imperial Federation' is surely the wisest name ever thought of. On any other principle it is surely the most foolish."[43] Freeman found it hard to believe that any sentient being might support it, and he was astonished when Bryce accepted the Presidency of the Oxford branch of the Imperial Federation League. "For to me," he wrote to his friend, "Imperial Federation seems to be, not an intelligible proposal which one deems unjust or inexpedient, and therefore argues against, but a mere heap of vague, meaningless, and contradictory phrases." The reasoning was simple: "[W]hat is Imperial cannot be Federal, and what is Federal cannot be Imperial."[44] Derived from Roman usage, empire had a distinct meaning, "the rule of some person

---

[36] Freeman, *History of Federal Government*, 3, 9, 26.

[37] Freeman, "Imperial Federation," 140–41.

[38] Letter to Bryce, February 7, 1887, *Life and Letters*, 2:359.

[39] Freeman, "Greater Greece," 38

[40] Letter to Bryce, February 7, 1887, 359; Freeman, "Greater Greece," 39, 87.

[41] Freeman, "Imperial Federation," 141.

[42] S. R. Mehrota, "Imperial Federation and India, 1868–1917," *Journal of Commonwealth Political Studies*, 1 (1961), 29–40. For American incorporation, see, for example, John Redpath Dougall, "An Anglo-Saxon Alliance," *Contemporary Review*, 48 (1885), 693–707.

[43] Freeman, "The Physical and Political Bases of National Unity," 45.

[44] Letter to Bryce, December 16, 1886, 356; Freeman, "The Physical and Political Bases of National Unity," 45. He also dismissed the idea of "Greater Britain." Freeman, "Greater Greece," 1.

or power over some other," whereas Federation was a system of government that implied "the unity of certain powers or communities, presumably on equal terms."[45] The former was premised on political hierarchy, the latter on parity. They were antithetical.

Freeman contrasted the superior Greek model of colonization with the ruinous behavior of post-Renaissance Europeans. In the Hellenic world, political obligation and patriotic loyalty were directed to a fixed space: the city. "The Greek was before all things a citizen." The modern European notion of personal allegiance, a type of feudal fealty that bound individuals to the sovereign, was alien to them: "The Greek would have regarded himself degraded by the name of 'subject.' "[46] The difference between subjecthood and citizenship determined the modality of colonization, for "while the active duties of the citizen of a commonwealth can hardly be discharged beyond the territories of that commonwealth, the duties of the subject of . . . a personal master, are as binding on one part of the earth's surface as on another." The Greeks planted free cities populated by free citizens, as Corinth seeded Syracuse.

> Parent and child were on the political side necessarily parted; the colonist could exercise no political rights in the mother-city, nor did the mother city put forward any claim to be lady and mistress of her distant daughter. Still the love, the reverence, due to a parent was never lacking. The tie of memory, the tie of kindred, the tie of religion, were of themselves so strong that no tie of political allegiance was needed to make them stronger.[47]

In contrast, the modern European colonists, including the British, remained bound to their "mother land" by formal and subordinate ties of political allegiance.[48] Freeman's sympathies were clear: the connections between metropole and colony were the "brightest facts of Greek or Phoenician political life," while those of the modern colonial system were "among the darkest."[49] This history of subjection bestowed a dangerous legacy, for when the modern colony sought independence, as it invariably would, the relations between it and the "mother country" were often poisoned, as demonstrated by lingering Anglophobia in the United States.[50]

Freeman suggested that imperial federation would be more theoretically intelligible if it drew on the Roman precedent: absorbing colonies within an expanded state. "By this process the ruling state gives up nothing; it simply admits others, not so much to its own level as into its own substance."[51] How-

---

[45] Freeman, "The Physical and Political Bases of National Unity," 45.
[46] Freeman, "Greater Greece," 18, 23; Freeman, "Imperial Federation," 142.
[47] Freeman, "Greater Greece," 29.
[48] Ibid., 23, 30, 27.
[49] Freeman, "Imperial Federation," 121.
[50] Freeman, "Greater Greece," 36.
[51] Ibid., 55.

ever, this act of constitutional transubstantiation would mean extending full parliamentary representation to the British settler colonies, an idea that Freeman thought open to a battery of objections. Perhaps the most important "moral" taught by Roman history, he argued, was that the quest for empire resulted in the extinction of freedom at home and abroad, with citizens demoted from citizenship to subjecthood.[52] But there were also practical difficulties to overcome. Despite the wonders of modern science, the colonial empire was still too geographically dispersed for political unification.[53] Moreover, the colonies would be unwilling to cede their *de facto* autonomy to a federal government dominated by England. "[S]ubjection, in short, formally abolished, would practically be made more complete."[54] Many colonial subjects concurred.

Sir John Colomb's idea of "Britannic Confederation" struck Freeman as the most intellectually credible plan for colonial unity. Its name was not self-contradictory and its scope was clearly specified: a federation of Britain, Australia, Canada, and South Africa.[55] Yet it was neither feasible nor desirable. Establishing a durable connection was impossible between geographically fragmented territories bound only by sentimental attachment, especially when that sentiment was directed at the metropole but not each other. Colonial affect was bidirectional not multilateral, and Freeman predicted that this augured badly for the longevity of the empire. He regarded competition between constituent units as a weakness of all federations, but he thought it would be exacerbated in a distended noncontiguous one. Finally, he pointed to the lack of historical precedent for creating such a political association.[56] Neither space nor time were on Colomb's side.

Many advocates of imperial federation had failed to grasp the implications of their plans for the fate of Britain itself. Federation, he complained to Bryce, meant "the degradation, if not the destruction, of England and its institutions," chiefly because Parliament would either be abolished or transformed "into the Legislature of a Canton."[57] Elsewhere he compared the status of a federated England to that of "the State of New York or the State of Delaware."[58] Again, history offered no precedent. Federations were typically instituted when a number of small states banded together against an external threat, but

[52] Freeman, *Comparative Politics*, 99. On ancient models in imperial thought, see chapter 5.

[53] Freeman, "Greater Greece," 56–57.

[54] Freeman, "Imperial Federation," 125; Freeman, "The Physical and Political Bases of National Unity," 53–55.

[55] Freeman, "Political and Physical," 49; Colomb, "A Survey of Existing Conditions," in *Britannic Confederation*, ed. White, 1–31. Colomb was a Tory MP and prominent writer on naval affairs.

[56] Freeman, "The Physical and Political Bases of National Unity," 52, 53–54.

[57] Freeman to Bryce, February 7, 1887, 360. See also his letter to Bryce (February 7, 1887), 360, where he picks out Rhode Island. Freeman had consulted A. V. Dicey on the constitutional status of the British colonies. Dicey to Freeman, February 21, 1885, Freeman papers, EAF/1/7.

[58] Freeman, "Greater Greece," 52; Freeman, "The Physical and Political Bases of National Unity," 55.

the imperialists proposed to conjoin a dominant state with several weaker entities, and as such "a great power, an ancient power, a ruling power, is asked to come down from its place, to rank for the future simply as one member alongside its own dependencies, even though most of those dependencies are its own children."[59] This upset the natural order of things. The lack of precedent carried great epistemological and moral authority. The historian G. W. Prothero once observed that "if a proposal threatened to change the fundamental character of a thing or an institution, then, for Mr Freeman, it stood condemned."[60] Such was the case with empire. Absence of a precedent "does not of itself prove the proposed scheme is either impossible or undesirable," he admitted, but it was "a fact worth bearing in mind," and it was always "dangerous to imagine a precedent where there is none."[61] Bryce too acknowledged the role of past experience in shaping the political views of his friend. Freeman's reading of the Greeks prompted him to think "that the relation between the 'metropolis' and her colonies to be one not of political interdependence, but of cordial friendliness and a disposition to render help, nothing more."[62] The historical record taught colonial independence, not union.

Freeman played a Janus-faced role in the debates over imperial federation, cited as an authority by advocates and opponents alike. Both Sir Frederick Young, enthusiastic unionist and Honorary Secretary of the Royal Colonial Institute, and Francis De Labilliere, one of the most radical federalists, drew inspiration from Freeman's earlier influential work on federalism.[63] So too did liberal politician W. E. Forster, the co-President of the Imperial Federation League, who utilized Freeman's account in outlining his own vision of a federal Greater Britain.[64] Freeman retorted that Forster was confusing the *Bundesstadt*, the "perfect" type of federation, with the *Staatenbund*, a much weaker form that was bound to fail, and he attacked those who claimed the colonial empire already constituted a nascent federation.

> All the elements of federation are wanting. There is no voluntary union of independent states, keeping some powers to themselves and granting other powers to a central authority of their own creation. There is instead a number of dependent bodies, to which a central authority older

[59] Freeman, "Greater Greece," 54–55; Freeman, "Imperial Federation," 120; Freeman, *Federal Government*, ch. 2.

[60] Prothero, *English Historical Review*, 8 (1893), 385. Casper Sylvest, *British Liberal Internationalism, 1880–1930* (Manchester, 2009), emphasizes Freeman's influence on Bryce. See also H.A.L. Fisher, *James Bryce* (London, 1927), 1:113–14, 2:308–9.

[61] Freeman, "Imperial Federation," 122.

[62] Bryce, "Edward Augustus Freeman," *English Historical Review*, 7 (1892), 502.

[63] Young, *On the Political Relations of Mother Countries and Colonies* (London, 1883), 22; de Labilliere, *Federal Britain* (London, 1894), 94–95.

[64] Forster, *Our Colonial Empire* (Edinburgh, 1875), 31; Forster, *Imperial Federation* (London, 1885), 1. See also James Stanley Little, *The United States of Britain* (Guilford, 1887), 17.

than themselves has been graciously pleased to grant certain powers. This state of things is not federation, but subjection.

The colonies, indeed, were not "states" in the relevant sense, but rather subordinate "municipalities on a great scale."[65]

While he complained that his objections fell on deaf ears, numerous critics deployed Freeman's arguments to bolster their attacks on imperial federation.[66] Imperial federalists, meanwhile, often felt the need to respond to him. George Parkin, an energetic Canadian proselytizer, sought to rebut Freeman's argument about the absence of intra-colonial sentiment.[67] He also suggested that Freeman's failure to understand imperial federation could be traced to his admission that he knew little about commerce, manufacturing, or agriculture. Praising Freeman for keeping "faith" in federalism during the American Civil War, Labilliere "regretted" that the great historian had "written decadently against Imperial Federation" and questioned the significance of historical precedent. He also denied that imperial federation would damage relations with the United States.[68] Others acknowledged the force of Freeman's objections while stressing their limited scope. The journalist W. T. Stead conceded that Freeman was "quite right in pointing out . . . [that] Imperial Federation is an absurdity when used by those who are really aiming at the federation of all the English-speaking peoples," but insisted that "this criticism advances the matter very little," presumably because such a union wasn't the main object of the debate. "Against those who have plans and are ready with paper constitutions for an Imperial England," wrote Sir Robert Stout, a senior colonial politician, "Mr Freeman's criticism may hold good," but it failed to challenge those "who strive to prevent separation and who are as yet unable to formulate the new form of government."[69] Indeed it was a common federalist trope that preaching the general *idea* of unity was more important than specifying constitutional details. Vagueness, on this account, was a political virtue, albeit not one that Freeman would have acknowledged. Archly characterizing Freeman

---

[65] Freeman, "Imperial Federation," 114, 117, 118–19.

[66] Letter to Bryce, February 7, 1887, 360. For examples, see: P. Glynn, *Great Britain and Its Colonies* (Adelaide, 1892), 3; Anon., "Greater Greece and Greater Britain," *Spectator*, September 18, 1886, 15; E. Burton, "Federation and Pseudo-Federation," *Law Quarterly Review*, 5 (1889), 176; Alpheus Henry Snow, "Neutralization versus Imperialism," *American Journal of International Law*, 2:3 (1908), 569–70; G. W. Wilton, "Solidarity without Federation," pts. 1 and 2, *Juridical Review*, 4 (1892), 317–34; 5 (1893), 248–62.

[67] Parkin, *Imperial Federation* (London, 1892), 40–43, 44n. See also, E. T. Stuart-Linton, *The Problem of Empire Governance* (London, 1912), 60–61. For other responses, see H. Mortimer-Franklyn, *The Unit of Imperial Federation* (London, 1887), 20, 24, 32, 41, 60; *Imperial Federation League in Canada* (Montreal, 1885), 28; [Urquart Forbes], "Imperial Federation," *London Quarterly Review*, 4 (1885), 325–26.

[68] Labilliere, *Federal Britain*, 89n1, 206–7, 213.

[69] Stead, *Review of Reviews*, 4/20 (1891), 164; Stout, "A Colonial View of Imperial Federation," *Nineteenth Century*, 21 (1887), 356.

as a man "with a keen sense for the political antiquities of political terms," the idealist philosopher D. G. Ritchie accepted that imperial federation was an "absurd" idea if projected onto historical empires, but he argued that modern political experience demonstrated its feasibility.

> [J]ust as representative government was the great political invention of the middle ages, so federation (as distinct from mere leagues or confederacies) is the greatest political invention of modern times. To the Greek philosopher a republican *nation* would have seemed an impossibility. A federal Empire (like Germany), a federal republic, a federation of self-governing communities with dependencies more or less autocratically governed according to their degree of civilization—all these forms now seem possible to us.[70]

Ultimately, though, Freeman's skepticism was more realistic and support for imperial federation drained away after the turn of the century. But it did not disappear. The leading post-Victorian theorist of imperial union, Lionel Curtis, drew mixed messages from Freeman's work. Writing during the First World War, Curtis embraced Freeman's Teutonism, and borrowed heavily from his account of ancient federalism, to construct a celebratory narrative about "English" racial destiny, but he dismissed his criticisms of imperial federation.[71] Like Freeman, though, Curtis sought legitimacy in historical precedent, claiming that the principle of "commonwealth," which he regarded as the chief intellectual justification for imperial federation, was itself a product of Teutonic political experience.

On Racial Solidarity

> To me most certainly the United States did not seem like a foreign country;
> it was simply England with a difference.[72]
>
> —E. A. FREEMAN

Although skeptical of constitutional models of union, Freeman nevertheless propounded a form of racial "brotherhood," declaiming that true greatness was to be found in the diffusion of the English people(s) across the world. His was one voice among many. While debates between imperial federalists and their critics were heated, the participants often shared more than they were

[70] Ritchie, "War and Peace," *International Journal of Ethics*, 11 (1901), 152.

[71] Curtis, *The Commonwealth of Nations* (London, 1916), ch. 2 (on Teutonism) and pp. 227–30, 594–95 (for criticism of Freeman). Curtis was the chief ideologue of the Round Table movement.

[72] Freeman, *Some Impressions of the United States* (London, 1883), 10.

willing to concede, including a commitment to the basic unity and superiority of the "English-speaking peoples" (or "Anglo-Saxons").[73] Their disagreements centered on the best means of realizing this racialized form of global dominion. Thus Goldwin Smith, widely reviled as an anti-imperialist, insisted that he had the "greatest respect for the aspirations of the Imperial Federationists, and myself most earnestly desire the moral unity of our race and its partnership in achievement and grandeur."[74] Freeman promoted a similar vision. Racial unity was, he argued, "a thought higher and dearer than any thought of a British Empire."[75] Above all, he vested his hopes in the United States, "brethren in a higher brotherhood, born of one ancient stock, speaking one ancient tongue, sharer under different forms of one ancient freedom."[76] Race was the basic ontological category of global politics, far more significant than the state, let alone the artificial shell of empire.

Primed by the "comparative method" to recognize "survivals" of the Teutonic order, Freeman unsurprisingly found them wherever he looked during his 1882 visit to the United States. He regarded his public lectures as an act of filial persuasion, an attempt to remind Americans that they were part of one great racial family. "The feeling of unity between the two severed branches is really present in the American breast, but it needs something special to wake it up."[77] He was happy to serve as an alarm clock. Like many keen on strengthening cooperation with the United States, Freeman sought to defuse lingering Anglophobia, which he interpreted optimistically as a sign of familial intimacy, although he admitted that memory of the War of Independence and of 1812 remained "a formidable historic barrier" to reconciliation.[78] As it was, the very existence of the British empire circumvented the transformation of sentiment necessary to unlock racial destiny. Not only did the existence of a large "dependent colony" (Canada) on the borders of the "independent colony" (the United States) stand as a permanent reminder of the historical injustice of British rule, "inconsistent with the full acknowledgement of the general brotherhood of the English folk," but the mixture of dependent and independent polities in the English world meant that suspicion would remain the norm. This quandary could only be resolved by granting independence to the colonies.[79] Intra-racial equality was a perquisite for justifying global inequality between races.

[73] Freeman rejected the designation "Anglo-Saxon," largely on etymological grounds (*Lectures*, 38–67).

[74] Smith, "Straining the Silken Thread," *Macmillan's Magazine*, 58 (1888), 242.

[75] Freeman, *Some Impressions of the United States*, 16.

[76] Freeman, *Lectures to American Audiences*, 10.

[77] Freeman, *Some Impressions of the United States*, 19. For an account of his trip, see Conlin, "The Consolations of Amero-Teutonism," in *Making History*, ed. Bremner and Conlin, 101–19.

[78] Freeman, *Some Impressions of the United States*, 7–9, 21.

[79] Ibid., 23, 24.

In a lecture delivered in Oxford in 1886 to commemorate the birth of George Washington, he criticized the imperial unionists and outlined an alternative vision. Entitled "George Washington, the Expander of England," the lecture was a provocative riposte to J. R. Seeley's *The Expansion of England*, the bible of the imperial federation movement. As I discuss in chapter 11, Seeley argued that the true greatness of British history lay in its imperial expansion during the eighteenth and nineteenth centuries rather that in a Whiggish unfolding of liberty, and he promoted the creation of a "great and solid world-state."[80] Freeman turned the historical argument on its head, arguing that Washington—rebel and founder—was the real "Expander of England," not the men who had pilfered swathes of South Asia. True expansion meant establishing permanent independent communities, a feat that Washington had achieved through dismembering the British empire.[81] The act of rebellion was thus a paradoxical but productive moment in the history of racial "brotherhood."

In a world thrown into close communion by modern technoscience, it was possible to deepen those racial bonds through replicating the political ideas and ethos of the ancients. "Geographical distance, political separation, fierce rivalry, cruel warfare, never snapped the enduring tie which bound every Greek to every other Greek. So the Englishman of Britain, of America, of Africa, of Australia, should be each to his distant brother as were the Greek of Massalia, the Greek of Kyrênê, and the Greek of Chersôn."[82] Misunderstanding the power of affect, the imperial federalists failed to grasp that the "tie of national brotherhood, the abiding feeling of the oneness of the folk, lives on through physical distance, through political separation, through political rivalry and wasting war."[83] A heterogeneous assemblage of territories, peoples, and forms of government, "patched up out of men of every race and speech under the sun," the empire failed even to approximate the necessary conditions for successful union. In prioritizing empire over the race-nation they endangered racial unity. He concluded his peroration on Washington by sketching a glorious future:

> I shall hardly see the day; but some of you may see it, when the work of Washington and Hamilton may be wrought again without slash or blow, when, alongside the Kingdom of Great Britain and the United States of America, the United States of Australia, the United States of

[80] Freeman, "George Washington," 66; Seeley, *The Expansion of England*, 169, 75.

[81] Freeman, "George Washington," 89, 69–70. A quarter of a century later, an American scholar was still praising the lecture: "[T]he English historian was right, and the title was correct." Edwin Mead, "The United States as a World Power," *Advocate of Peace*, 75 (1913), 58.

[82] Freeman, *Some Impressions of the United States*, 24.

[83] Freeman, "George Washington," 72. See also Freeman, *Comparative Politics*, 82–85.

South Africa, the United States of New Zealand, may stand forth as independent homes of Englishmen, bound together by the common tie of
brotherhood, and bound by loyal reverence, and by no meaner bond, to
the common parent of all.[84]

Here, then, was a suitable application of federalism to the English-speaking
world. Just as communications technologies had transformed the potential
scope of citizenship, so they had reanimated federalism, allowing its extension
across vast political spaces. "It is by the help of modern discoveries that the
federal systems of old Greece can be reproduced on a gigantic scale, that a
single Union of States can embrace a continent stretching from Ocean to
Ocean instead of a peninsula stretching from sea to sea." The United States
exemplified the wonderful possibilities. It demonstrated that federal government was appropriate for uniting territorially contiguous colonial polities,
thus fashioning powerful independent states like Australia that would constitute the elements of an immense racial brotherhood.[85] But empire itself was of
little value. "The sentiment is possibly unpatriotic," Freeman wrote, "but I
cannot help looking on such a friendly union of the English and English-
speaking folk as an immeasurably higher object than the maintenance of any
so-called British Empire."[86]

Although wary of formal political institutions, Freeman hinted at a political technology that could help to fuse the brotherhood: *common citizenship*.
"I have often dreamed," he wrote, "that something like the Greek συμπολιτεία,
a power in the citizens in each country of taking up the citizenship of the
other at pleasure, might not be beyond hope; but I have never ventured to
dream of more than that."[87] Although he didn't live to see it, the idea of common citizenship attracted considerable support during the 1890s and beyond,
its advocates including Bryce and A. V. Dicey.[88] In the early 1890s the industrialist Andrew Carnegie demanded the "reunion" of Britain and America.
His call resonated widely, feeding the intellectual currents helping to drive the
"rapprochement" between the two powers. Carnegie commended Freeman's
"wider and nobler patriotism"—the elevation of race over empire—and he
likewise advocated "a common British-American citizenship" while calling for

---

[84] Freeman, "George Washington," 102–3.

[85] Freeman, "Greater Greece," 16. See also Freeman, *Federal Government*, 4, 86–87.

[86] Freeman, "Imperial Federation," 143.

[87] Ibid., 142. In a letter to Goldwin Smith, August 19, 1888, *Life and Letters*, 2:384, he summarized the idea as the "taking up of citizenship at pleasure—between Great Britain, United States
of America, United States of Australia, and so on."

[88] Bryce, "The Essential Unity of England and America," *Atlantic Monthly*, 82 (1898), 29;
Dicey, "A Common Citizenship for the English Race," *Contemporary Review*, 71 (1897), 457–76.
For an analysis of the idea, see Duncan Bell, "Beyond the Sovereign State," *Political Studies*, 62
(2014), 418–34.

the independence of the British settler colonies as a precondition for racial union.[89]

Freeman's greatest intellectual influence, though, was exercised in the "western home" of his beloved English folk. His Teutonist account of the racial foundations of the English-speaking peoples, and his outline of the field of "comparative politics," played a formative role in the development of the human sciences in North America.[90] His main disciple was the historian Herbert Baxter Adams, who established a famous "seminary" at Johns Hopkins University to train American scholars in the arts of "historical and political science"—a veritable laboratory for constructing "comparativists." Alongside Bluntschli and Maine, Freeman was one of its guiding lights, his pithy motto "history is past politics and politics are present history" adorning both the wall of the library, where it "stares every man in the face who enters," and the front page of the influential *Johns Hopkins University Studies in Historical and Political Science*.[91] During his visit to the United States, Freeman spent time with Adams and his students, lecturing on the "eternal Eastern question."[92] Adams hailed the sage: "He had come to the Western Empire of the English people, which, expanding with the great Teutonic race from local centres, is repeating in the continental island of Atlantis and in the continent of Asia, with Egypt and Ocean between, the experiment of the Roman People upon a grander and nobler scale." He also endorsed Freeman's mission to inculcate "national belief in the civic kinship and religious unity of Britain and America."[93] Adams considered Freeman "the founder of our new walls," the "godfather" of his project. Freeman reciprocated, contributing an article to the first edition of Adams's journal, arguing that local institutions in the United States were expressions of the Teutonic branch of the "Aryan family."[94]

[89] Carnegie, *The Reunion of Britain and America* (Edinburgh, 1893), 22, 10. On Carnegie, see Duncan Bell, "Race, Utopia, Perpetual Peace," in *Intellectual Histories of American Foreign Policy,* ed. Jean-Francis Drolet and James Dunkerley (forthcoming).

[90] Anthony Brundage and Richard Cosgrove, *The Great Tradition* (Stanford, 2007), 34–42; Dorothy Ross, *The Origins of American Social Science* (Cambridge, 1991), 68–73; James Farr, "The Historical Science(s) of Politics," in *Modern Political Science*, ed. Adcock, Bevir, and Stimson, 66–96. On the role of the seminary at Johns Hopkins, see Robert Adcock, *Liberalism and the Emergence of American Political Science* (Oxford, 2014), ch. 5. Freeman's Saxonism was also influential in Australia. Marilyn Lake and Henry Reynolds, *Drawing the Global Colour Line* (Cambridge, 2008), 50–52.

[91] Adams to Freeman, July 10, 1883, Freeman papers, EAF/1/7. Freeman called the motto a "chance proverb." "A Review of My Opinions," 157. See also Adams, "Is History Past Politics?," *Johns Hopkins University Studies*, 13 (1895), 67–70. Following Adams's death in 1901 the motto was removed, symbolizing the shifting fortunes of the Teutonic thesis.

[92] Adams, "Mr. Freeman's Visit to Baltimore," *Johns Hopkins University Studies*, 1/1 (1882), 10. On why Freeman's work—and his historical method—should play a central role in American education, see Adams, *The Study of History in American Colleges and Universities* (Washington, 1887).

[93] Adams, "Mr. Freeman's Visit to Baltimore," 11.

[94] Adams to Freeman, January 12, 1885, June 9, 1882, and December 25, 1882, Freeman pa-

Contra Freeman, Adams praised the ambition to federate the Teutons, although he also recognized that the solidarity of race was stronger and more enduring than institutions. "England and the United States will probably never be federated together in that magnificent imperial system which some people in your country are now advocating; but they will always remain one in blood and thought and speech, which are better ties than politics."[95]

Freeman also exerted a powerful spell over the philosopher and historian John Fiske, who was arguably the most widely read Teutonist in the United States.[96] "No student of political development in our time," Fiske declared, "has made more effective use of the comparative method," and none had done as much to establish the continuities in transatlantic Teutonic history.[97] Fiske even shared Freeman's prejudices, congratulating him for expressing "very sound and wholesome views of the unspeakable Turk and the Everlasting Eastern Question."[98] Like many of its adherents, he translated Teutonism into a conservative and racist vision of the present, and it is no coincidence that he served as Honorary President of the Immigration Restriction League, for he believed that the Teutonic greatness of the people was threatened by an influx of racial inferiors. The admiration was returned. Praising Fiske's attempt to trace the Teutonic origins of American history, Freeman lamented that it "is so strangely hard to get people on either side of the Ocean to take in the simple fact that Englishmen on both sides of the Atlantic are one people."[99] "Truly," Freeman wrote after reading Fiske's popular *American Political Ideas Viewed from the Standpoint of Universal History*, "you preach exactly the same doctrine as I do."[100] Fiske later dedicated *The Discovery of America* to Freeman, a "scholar who inherits the gift of Midas, and turns into gold whatever subject he touches."[101]

Not all American intellectuals were so impressed. Henry Adams, for one, derided Freeman's "parade of knowledge" and asserted that he had never written anything "really solid."[102] Unsurprisingly, the Teutonic interpretation of American institutions generated fierce criticism. Describing Freeman, Goldwin Smith, Froude, and Matthew Arnold as the most distinguished "British

pers, EAF/1/7; Freeman, "An Introduction to American Institutional History," *Johns Hopkins University Studies*, 1/1 (1882), 13.

[95] Adams to Freeman, September 5, 1884, Freeman papers, EAF/1/7.

[96] Fiske, *American Political Ideas Viewed from the Standpoint of Universal History* (Boston, 1885).

[97] Fiske, "Edward Augustus Freeman," in *A Century of Science and Other Essays* (Boston, 1899), 268.

[98] Ibid., 275.

[99] Freeman to Fiske, August 9, 1889, in John Spencer Clark, *The Life and Letters of John Fiske* (Boston, 1917), 414.

[100] Freeman to Fiske, November 10, 1889, in *Life and Letters*, 415.

[101] Fiske, *The Discovery of America*, 2 vols. (Boston, 1892).

[102] W. C. Ford, *The Letters of Henry Adams* (New York, 1930), 1:236.

chauvinists," one commentator talked of "an idea received with enthusiasm by some here in America, with indifference by others, but by a large section of our people by dislike, because it is false and because it is offensive."[103] The archaeologist Charles Waldstein called it a "modern version of the old story of national lust for power," and dismissed the Saxonist account for its "pedantic pretensions of its inaccurate ethnological theories," while historian H. Morse Stephens labeled it a "perverted and inaccurate view of the past as a source for political arguments in the present."[104] While popular during the 1880s and early 1890s, by the turn of the century Teutonism had largely been displaced as the central interpretive framework to understand American political development, though it claimed a dwindling band of enthusiasts deep into the twentieth century. As it sank, so too did Freeman's reputation in the most recent "home" of the English.

[103] John Fleming, "Are We Anglo-Saxon?," *North American Review*, 153 (1891), 253.
[104] Waldstein, "The English-Speaking Brotherhood," *North American Review*, 167 (1898), 227; Stephens, "Nationality and History," *American Historical Review*, 21/2 (1916), 227.

CHAPTER 14

Democracy and Empire

꙰

J. A. Hobson, L. T. Hobhouse, and the Crisis of Liberalism

What would the new century bring?" At the close of the nineteenth century, according to Jay Winter, most European and American writers, politicians, and artists were sanguine about the coming era: "[I]maginings of the twentieth century celebrated progress on a global scale and projected it optimistically into the foreseeable future." Although dark prognostications were penned by H. G. Wells and Joseph Conrad, among others, it was confidence that triumphed.[1] Winter may be correct about the general tenor of literary and artistic life, but many of those in Britain concerned with the future of geopolitics were deeply anxious. Threats appeared to emanate from multiple directions, at home and abroad. British global power was being challenged: foreboding abounded.[2] Thinkers across the political spectrum grappled incessantly with questions about the past, present, and future of world order.

In this chapter, I explore how two of the leading social and political thinkers in *fin de siècle* Britain—J. A. Hobson (1858–1940) and L. T. Hobhouse (1864–1929)—viewed the prospects for international affairs in the decade and a half before the outbreak of the First World War. A self-described "economic heretic," Hobson was and is best known as the author of *Imperialism: A Study* (1902), arguably one of the most influential political tracts of the twentieth century.[3] Hobhouse, meanwhile, was trained as a philosopher, held the first chair in sociology in Britain, and quickly made a name for himself as

---

[1] Winter, *Dreams of Peace and Freedom* (London, 2006), 11.

[2] This sense of foreboding found literary expression in a genre of fiction imaging future wars: I. F. Clarke, *Voices Prophesying War*, 2nd ed. (Oxford, 1992); Charles Gannon, *Rumors of War and Infernal Machines* (Liverpool, 2005), chs. 1–4. Some of the stories are reprinted in I. F. Clarke, ed., *The Tale of the Next Great War, 1871–1914* (Liverpool, 1995).

[3] Hobson, *Imperialism* (London, 1902). His autobiography was entitled *Confessions of an Economic Heretic* (London, 1938).

an innovative political theorist. Both men were political radicals, pivotal in the emergence of the "new liberalism."[4] Both were public moralists, combining scholarship with abundant political campaigning and popular writing. And both wrote widely on international and imperial affairs. Their work provides a revealing insight into how reflective liberals thought about the future of world order as a new century dawned.

Hobson and Hobhouse have drawn considerable scholarly interest, and in what follows I do not attempt an exhaustive analysis of their political thought.[5] Rather, I outline some of the key issues shaping political thought at the time, and then explore how Hobhouse and Hobson conceived of the relationship between democracy, empire, and international politics. I focus on two main themes, neither of which has received sufficient attention. First, I highlight how they figured themselves within narratives charting the evolution of liberal thought and practice, allowing them simultaneously to pay homage to their predecessors while carving out a space for the new liberal project. Second, I discuss their writings about the settler colonies in Australia, Canada, and New Zealand. Their accounts of colonialism undermine neat distinctions between "domestic," "international," and "imperial" politics and political theory. For Hobson and Hobhouse, as well as for many of their contemporaries, the colonies exhibited characteristics of all three: constitutive elements of the empire, they were nevertheless semi-autonomous states purportedly composed of people of the same nationality and race as the inhabitants of the United Kingdom. According to this perspective, the British colonial empire could be viewed as an embryonic intermediary institution occupying the space between the territorially delimited modern state and an all-encompassing world state. Grounded in and bound by the cultural singularity of the "British race," it promised, if understood properly, to unite colonial communities scattered across the planet, creating a vast polity that would maintain or expand British geopolitical strength while acting simultaneously as an agent of global progress. This was the apotheosis of British imperial ambition.

Confronting Modernity

British international thought at the turn of the twentieth century was structured by a wide variety of assumptions and preoccupations, some old, others

[4] See, for example, Peter Clarke, *Liberals and Social Democrats* (Cambridge, 1978); Michael Freeden, *The New Liberalism* (Oxford, 1978); Aviral Simhony and David Weinstein, eds., *The New Liberalism* (Cambridge, 2001).

[5] Stefan Collini, *Liberalism and Sociology* (Cambridge, 1979); Peter Cain, *Hobson and Imperialism* (Oxford, 2002); Michael Freeden, ed., *Reappraising J. A. Hobson* (London, 1990); Jules Townshend, *J. A. Hobson* (Manchester, 1990); David Long, *Towards a New Liberal Internationalism* (Cambridge, 1995); David Weinstein, "Consequentialist Cosmopolitanism," in *Victorian Visions of Global Order*, ed. Duncan Bell (Cambridge, 2007), 267–91.

new. It is productive to interpret many of the thinkers in this period as wrestling with the politics of modernity—as confronting, that is, a world that seemed to be undergoing a period of intense and rapid transition in which many of the existing categories and concerns of politics were being transformed, even revolutionized.[6]

First, as I have stressed throughout this book, technology was radically altering the way in which individuals perceived the physical world. New sociopolitical possibilities—new horizons of expectation—were opened up as a result.[7] From the 1860s onward, the electrical telegraph, which promised instantaneous global communication, spawned fantasies about the elimination of geographical distance, the "annihilation of time and space," that prefigure late twentieth-century accounts of globalization.[8] Vast ocean liners, the motorcar, and the airplane all reinforced this belief during the two decades straddling 1900.[9] Yet the political conclusions drawn from these changes were indeterminate. Many saw technological developments as facilitating, even necessitating, the construction of institutions and modes of politics that in the past would have seemed the stuff of dreams. But to others, they were potentially threatening, intensifying the dangers of competition and conflict.[10]

This cognitive shift reinforced the sense that Britain's global position was under threat. The dominance of the mid-Victorian years, when the country was thought of as the "workshop of the world," was superseded by a period of anxiety and tension, especially from the 1880s onward. The "age of equipoise," of stability, prosperity, and untrammelled optimism, had come to an end.[11] An economic depression bit deeply. The post-Civil War dynamism of the United States, the rise of Germany at the heart of Europe and of Russia at the periphery, and, in the early Edwardian years, the emergence of Japan as a formidable force in Asia, seemed to augur the end of British hegemony. A new

---

[6] I pursue this line of argument in more detail in Bell, "Dreaming the Future," in *The American Experiment and the Idea of Democracy in British Culture, 1776–1914*, ed. Ella Dzelzainis and Ruth Livesey (Aldershot, 2013), 197–210. For the connotations of modernity in Britain, see Martin Daunton and Bernhard Rieger, eds., *Meanings of Modernity* (Oxford, 2001).

[7] On "horizons of expectation," see Reinhard Koselleck, *Futures Past*, trans. Keith Tribe (Cambridge, MA, 1985).

[8] In general, see Stephen Kern, *The Culture of Time and Space, 1880–1914* (Cambridge, MA, 1983); on how this affected views of global order, see Bell, *The Idea of Greater Britain*, ch. 3; Jo-Ann Pemberton, *Global Metaphors* (London, 2001).

[9] Bernhard Rieger, *Technology and the Culture of Modernity in Britain and Germany, 1890–1945* (Cambridge, 2005).

[10] The language of competition was also fueled by the popularity of evolutionary arguments, although they too were politically indeterminate. Mike Hawkins, *Social Darwinism in European and American Thought, 1860–1945* (Cambridge, 1997); Paul Crook, *Darwinism, War and History* (Cambridge, 1994).

[11] W. L. Burn, *The Age of Equipoise* (London, 1964); Martin Hewitt, ed., *An Age of Equipoise?* (Aldershot, 2000).

geopolitical constellation was materializing. This was felt keenly throughout the British intellectual and political elite.

Political thought in Britain, meanwhile, was in a state of transitional flux. As I discuss in chapter 3, liberalism was being revised and reformulated by a new generation of thinkers, Hobson and Hobhouse prominent among them. The emergence of the "new liberalism" pointed many liberals in a social democratic direction, eschewing the perceived atomism of an older generation of reformers and focusing instead on the value of an interventionist state and on questions of social justice. In this their arguments overlapped, and sometimes fused, with those made by socialists, who since the 1880s had become an increasingly significant force in British political culture, terrifying many conservatives while expanding the space of political debate. British international thought was dominated, though far from exhausted, by forms of liberal internationalism. Liberal internationalists insisted on both the possibility and the moral necessity of progressive change in the structures and norms of world order. They sought to tame, even to eliminate, conflict while intensifying cooperation between "civilized" states, chiefly through the powers of international commerce and international law.[12] The question of empire, however, divided the new liberals as it had the old. It was also a point of contention among socialist writers.[13] Although some thinkers argued that empire was inimical to progress, for others it was, if enacted properly, a virtuous agent of it. The contest for the souls of liberalism and socialism was mirrored in a diverse array of visions of global order.

During the closing decades of the century, democracy came to play a central role in debates over domestic and global politics. For much of the nineteenth century, mass democracy in Britain was a liberal aspiration and a conservative nightmare, its possible impact predicted but not yet felt. America acted as a model—often mediated through the writings of Alexis de Tocqueville—for this new form of politics, but it was far from clear how it would function in a European context. The Reform Bills of 1867 and, above all, 1886 were seen by many, despite their manifold limitations—not least the failure to enfranchise women—to initiate a democratic age. Yet a general sense of disillusionment with the realization of democracy and its failure to live up to expectations soon set in. The relationship between democracy and empire, which came to a head during the South African War (1899–1902), became a touchstone for debates over the future of liberalism and world politics.

In light of these various challenges, many commentators came to regard federalism as an answer to the political perplexities of the modern age. In a world undergoing profound changes, institutional technologies that could reconcile unity with difference were eminently desirable. Federalism seemed

---

[12] For further discussion of liberal internationalism, see chapter 10.
[13] Gregory Claeys, *Imperial Sceptics*, ch. 3.

to fit the bill. It was prescribed for local, regional, imperial, and global politics. Although federalism had often been floated as a possible answer to the internecine warfare of European politics, it had rarely been considered a realistic option for governing on a global scale. At the end of the nineteenth century, as the world itself seemed to shrink, this skepticism receded. In Britain, debate raged about the potential unification of the settler colonies into an "imperial federation," a vast polity stretching across the face of the earth. The possibilities for international organization were reshaped. Federalism joined democracy as an object of desire, confusion, and endless debate. All of this helped to fuel an ever-increasing fascination with the past, present, and future of the United States.

Finally, this was a period marked by a growing tension between specialist and expert knowledge.[14] Intellectuals increasingly had to negotiate between appealing to an ever-expanding public hungry for information (and entertainment) and the imperatives of a rapidly professionalizing academic world. At the same time, universities were being transformed by the development of new disciplinary fields constituted by professional norms that derided, and institutional structures that hampered, existing models of knowledge production.[15] Such pressures were reinforced by the emergence of a global news service that helped to expand the geographical scope of the "public."[16] These shifts complicated the role of the "public moralist," for it became progressively more difficult to satisfy the conflicting demands of multiple audiences. Some managed to navigate the terrain, including Hobhouse and Hobson, but it was treacherously difficult.

Hobson and Hobhouse were both contributors to, and shaped by, these various political and intellectual trends. They addressed questions that many of their contemporaries were puzzling over and in doing so they drew on a wide range of existing intellectual resources. But they were also important agents in structuring the terms of those debates, outlining arguments that were to play a significant role in fashioning the political thinking of their age.

Hobhouse and the Ironies of Liberal History

In 1901–1902, Hobhouse published a series of hard-hitting essays in the liberal weekly the *Speaker*. These were republished, in amended form, as *Democracy and Reaction* (1904). His central message was clear: in recent years, Brit-

---

[14] See, in general, Martin Daunton, ed., *The Organisation of Knowledge in Victorian Britain* (Oxford, 2005); Amanda Anderson and Joseph Valente, eds., *Disciplinarity at the Fin de Siècle* (Princeton, 2002).

[15] Collini, Winch, and Burrow, *That Noble Science of Politics*; Robert Adcock, Mark Bevir, and Shannon Stimson, eds., *Modern Political Science* (Princeton, 2007), chs. 1–6.

[16] See, for example, Simon Potter, *News and the British World* (Oxford, 2003). On the perceived shift in the scope of the public, see chapter 7.

ain had entered a period of "reaction" that infected most aspects of public life and threatened to undermine the progress that had characterized the previous century. "The nineteenth century," Hobhouse wrote later, "might be called the age of Liberalism, yet its close saw the fortunes of that great movement brought to their lowest ebb."[17] This reaction, which manifested itself most obviously in the war in South Africa, demanded a reconsideration of the limits of and opportunities for progressive politics. In his writings between the turn of the century and the First World War, Hobhouse meditated on the ironies of history, the unintended effects of success, and the failures of judgment that had befallen him and his colleagues.

He identified two main problems infecting British political life. First, the victorious march of liberalism had helped to seed its nemesis, its triumph paving the way for its supersession. In this dialectical movement, progress was potentially, although not necessarily, self-undermining. The key to this historical tragedy could be found in the recent history of the empire, and in particular the settlement colonies. Second, the historical self-understanding of the new liberals had contributed to the growth of reaction by failing to grasp the similarities between the old and the new liberalism.

Liberals, Hobhouse observed, were only very rarely opposed to all aspects of empire. Historically, they had denigrated the "old colonial system," but this was often conjoined with support for the establishment of settler colonies, which were seen as pioneer outposts of civilization. Indeed, the phenomenal growth of the settler colonies during the nineteenth century, from minor appendages of the imperial order to large self-governing political communities, was attributable chiefly to the ideas and energy of the Benthamite radicals. "Paradoxical as it may seem," Hobhouse argued, "the new conception of empire had its roots, politically speaking, in the older Liberalism." Cloaked in the language of progress and freedom, the new imperialism was thus powerfully "seductive" to the "modern liberal."[18] Looking to the settler colonies, they thought that "the problem of reconciling Empire with liberty had been solved."

Under this mild sway each component State of the Empire enjoyed full internal self-government, and yet the whole had advantages which small free States cannot claim. Over a great area of the world there was, it seemed, peace; there was the machinery for adjusting disputes between different parts, should such disputes arise; and there was the consciousness of a wider fraternity, of a vaster common heritage, than the citizens

[17] Hobhouse, *Liberalism* [1911], ed. J. Meadowcroft (Cambridge, 1994), 103.

[18] Hobhouse, *Democracy and Reaction* [1904], ed. Peter Clarke (Brighton, 1972), 18. On Bentham's views, see Philip Schofield, *Utility and Democracy* (Oxford, 2006), ch. 7; Jennifer Pitts, *A Turn to Empire* (Princeton, 2005), ch. 4. On utilitarianism, see Bart Schultz and Georgios Varouxakis, eds., *Utilitarianism and Empire* (Oxford, 2005).

of any small community, however proud, could enjoy. In all of this taken in full sincerity, there was much to appeal to Liberals, little to repel them.[19]

Yet the seduction was dangerous. Some liberals, he observed later, were becoming "imperialists in their sleep." Falling for the rhetoric, they ignored the squalid reality—a form of dissonance that could be applied to numerous liberal advocates of empire, then and now. This was an acute failure of moral and political judgment, for a political theory "must be judged not only by its profession but by its fruits."[20] And the fruits of the new imperialism were strange indeed. "Under the reign of Imperialism the temple of Janus is never closed. Blood never ceases to run. The voice of the mourner is never hushed."[21] Imperialism, for Hobhouse, was antithetical to liberalism properly understood. The "central principle" of the former was self-government; that of the latter, the "subordination of self-government to Empire." They were impossible to reconcile. Those liberals who had supported imperialism, above all in South Africa, had fallen into a trap, and were now committed to an incoherent set of beliefs. "The trap laid for Liberals in particular consisted in this—that they were asked to give in their adhesion to Imperialism as representing admiration for an Empire which more and more has been shaped upon Liberal lines. Having given their assent, they were insensibly led on to the other meaning of Imperialism—a meaning which, for all practical purposes, these principles set aside."[22] Liberal success in reshaping the colonial empire in the second half of the century, then, had dulled the senses of many liberals, anesthetizing them against the profoundly antiliberal character of modern imperialism.

The second problem was a function of the historical understanding and intellectual self-fashioning of the new liberals. Hobhouse argued that they had erred badly in traducing their immediate predecessors, ignoring their strengths while exaggerating their weaknesses. To mark their distance from the *laissez-faire* liberals of the mid-Victorian years, the new generation had glossed over the points of similarity, the connections in "spirit and intention" that linked them. "The old individualism was standing in our way and we were for cutting it down."[23] The consequences of this act of youthful rebellion were deeply regrettable, for in their rush to fell the old liberalism, the new liberals had inadvertently aided their reactionary adversaries. "The socialist development of Liberalism paved the way for Imperialism by diminishing the

---

[19] Hobhouse, *Democracy and Reaction*, 24–25.

[20] Ibid., 107, 28.

[21] Ibid., 28.

[22] Ibid., 48. One definition of imperialism that he offered was "the doctrine of racial ascendency and territorial aggression." Hobhouse, "The Growth of Imperialism," *Speaker*, January 25, 1902, 474. This conception of the empire spawned the view, upheld by "Lord Milner and Mr. Rhodes," that it comprised a "great gold-producing machine."

[23] Hobhouse, *Democracy and Reaction*, 11, 210.

credit of the school which had stood most for the doctrines of liberty, fair dealing, and forbearance in international affairs."[24] In *Democracy and Reaction*, Hobhouse lavished praise on Cobden for his assiduous defense of freedom and his sustained anti-imperialism. In his classic volume *Liberalism* (1911), he went much further, sketching a historical narrative that charted, albeit briefly and in rather vague terms, the origins and trajectory of liberalism. This account identified the "old liberalism" as a necessary step in the evolution of liberal political thought and practice.[25] On this view, liberal history had largely comprised a "negative" account in which liberals fought against the excessive and unjust powers of state and church.

> Thus Liberalism appears first as a criticism, sometimes even as a destructive and revolutionary criticism. Its negative aspect is for centuries foremost. Its business seems not to be so much to build up as to tear down, to remove obstacles which block human progress, rather than to point out the positive goal of endeavour or fashion the fabric of civilization. It finds humanity oppressed, and would set it free. It finds a people groaning under arbitrary rule, a nation in bondage to a conquering race, industrial enterprise obstructed by social privileges or crippled by taxation, and it offers relief.[26]

The closing years of the century had witnessed the emergence of a more constructive form of liberalism, marked by greater attention to questions of economic inequality, social justice, and the positive role of state intervention. It is arguable that Hobhouse's narration of liberal history was, at least in part, a belated response to his perception of the failures of liberals to recognize the continuities in their own tradition. And as I suggested in Chapter 3, it played an important role in the reimaging of the liberal tradition that took place during the Edwardian years.

Hobhouse viewed the relationship between old and new liberal views on international affairs through the same prism. Whereas the old liberalism had prescribed strict adherence to the doctrine of nonintervention and skepticism about international entanglements, the "positive" dimension of the new liberalism, adapted for a democratic age, necessitated instead the creation of powerful international institutions.[27] Although the means differed, the ends re-

[24] Ibid., 12. For a spirited defense of classical liberalism against the charges leveled by the new liberals (among others), see Goldwin Smith, "The Manchester School," *Contemporary Review*, 67 (1895), 377–90.

[25] *Liberalism* was once described by C. Wright Mills as the "best twentieth-century statement of Liberal ideals." Mills, *The Marxists* (Harmondsworth, 1963), 25n. On Cobden, see Peter Cain, "Capitalism, War, and Internationalism in the Thought of Richard Cobden," *British Journal of International Studies*, 5 (1979), 229–45; Claeys, *Imperial Sceptics*, ch. 2.

[26] Hobhouse, *Liberalism*, 8.

[27] See Casper Sylvest, *British Liberal Internationalism* (Manchester, 2009), on the difference between "moral" and "institutional" conceptions of progress in international politics.

mained the same: peace and cooperation in world politics. And the enemies of this vision remained the same also: the imperialists. The tragedy of the situation was palpable. Although Hobhouse deplored the avarice and violence found throughout the British empire—he focused repeatedly on the issue of racial injustice, without wholly escaping many of the racialized assumptions of his age—he was primarily concerned with the destruction wrought on British society and politics. In this, he followed in a long line of radical critics of empire, from Bentham and Constant through to Cobden, Spencer, and beyond. Above all, he feared that the imperialist reaction "paralysed democratic effort at home."[28] Imperialism, that is, threatened to undermine Britain from within, infecting both political institutions and public morality. Like Constant, writing nearly a century beforehand, Hobhouse worried that the corruption of political discourse—triggered above all by the disingenuous recourse to justifying imperial aggression in terms of honor, glory, and national defense—was as dangerous as imperial policy itself. It was, Hobhouse averred, perhaps more corrupting than "the unblushing denial of right."[29] The spirit of conquest was malevolently intoxicating.

Democracy had failed to live up to its promise. The period of reaction had confounded the commonplaces of political prophecy. "Both the friends and enemies of democracy," he noted, had previously "inclined to the belief that when the people came into power there would be a time of rapid and radical domestic change combined in all probability with peace abroad." Democracy was supposed to usher in a new world order, yet the democratic state had been slow to reform, and its people had been enthusiastic supporters of the unjust war in South Africa. Moreover, the "humanitarian sentiment" that had shaped much of nineteenth-century British politics was being eroded. Humanitarianism was concerned "not merely with the direct alleviation of suffering and prevention of cruelty, but with the removal of fetters, the opening of opportunity to individual and national self-development, the utilisation of vastly increased material resources for the common benefit, the bringing in of the humblest to the banquet of civilisation."[30] It was a constituent element of the emergent liberalism. The corrosion of humanitarianism was caused by a number of factors, but above all Hobhouse emphasized the role played by mistaken understandings of evolutionary biology and the rise of philosophical idealism, both of which he thought legitimated a potentially authoritarian account of the state. This latter worry became an increasing fixation, reaching its peak in his polemical attack on *The Metaphysical Theory of the State* (1918). The combination of German metaphysics and notions of the "survival of the

[28] Hobhouse, *Democracy and Reaction*, 49.
[29] Ibid., 29. Constant, "The Spirit of Conquest and Usurpation and Their Relation to European Civilization" [1814], in *Political Writings*, ed. B. Fontana (Cambridge, 1988), 51–81.
[30] Hobhouse, *Democracy and Reaction*, 49–50, 58–59.

fittest" meant the naturalization of might over right, the validation of selfishness and aggression in politics.

Yet rather than dismiss evolution and democracy as fatally flawed, Hobhouse defended specific articulations of each of them. His general philosophy was grounded in an account of "orthogenic" evolution.[31] As an essentially ethical process, he affirmed, evolution was capable of rational human control; its end result and index was cooperation, not conflict. It served as an antidote to brute competition, not its justification. The political implications of this vision were obvious. Progress was defined by increasing cooperation between individuals in society and between different societies. The logical conclusion was a form of global institution that simultaneously entrenched political and economic interdependence while fostering particularity, and especially nationality, which Hobhouse, in common with many liberals, regarded as a progressive force in world politics.[32] Imperial federation, as we shall see, offered him a microcosmic variant of this ambitious project.

Democracy, properly understood, was both an agent and a *telos* of progress. Democracy and imperialism, he argued, were opposed in principle: "Democracy is government of the people by itself. Imperialism is government of one people by another." But although the theory of democracy was clear on the matter, Hobhouse wondered whether modern political and economic developments had rendered it obsolete. He focused in particular on the issue of scale. Was democracy impossible in a world of vast states? To answer this question, he delineated two conceptions of democracy: *direct participation* and *popular sovereignty*. On the former view, democracy implied "a direct participation of the masses of ordinary citizens in the public life of the commonwealth." This was an ideal that had nearly been realized in "the great assemblies and large popular juries" of ancient Athens. It meant that ordinary citizens were entrusted with complex public functions, despite having little appropriate training or expertise. The modern way to neutralize this tendency was the creation of a bureaucracy, a disinterested technocratic civil service. Popular sovereignty, on the other hand, implied that the people constituted the only legitimate source of authority, which was achieved in practice through the institutions of representative government and through free and full public discussion.[33] "Given these conditions, on the one hand the recognised supremacy of the law which it makes, on the other hand perfect free-

---

[31] See especially, Hobhouse, *Mind in Evolution* (London, 1901); *Morals in Evolution*, 2 vols. (London, 1906); *Social Evolution and Political Theory* (New York, 1911); *Development and Purpose* (London, 1913).

[32] On liberal conceptions of nationality, see H. S. Jones, "The Idea of the National in Victorian Political Thought," *European Journal of Political Theory*, 5 (2006), 12–21.

[33] Hobhouse, *Democracy and Reaction*, 147, 148–49, 151. Without providing details, Hobhouse also argued that the idea of "direct participation" was "held by observers to have materially influenced American public life, and not to have influenced it for the good," 149.

dom to inform itself and make itself heard, democracy in the sense of ultimate popular sovereignty, is not necessarily incompatible with vastness of territory or complexity of interests." But this alone did not eliminate the conjoined problems of scale and complexity, for local differences threatened to undermine the unity, and thus the viability, of modern political communities. Centrifugal forces challenged their "democratic character."[34]

Federalism presented the best answer to the conundrum. Although the United States offered the world the main example of "strict federalism," there were other forms available. For example, the British colonial empire was linked by what Hobhouse characterized as a "loose, informal quasi-Federalism," in which the "development of internal autonomy for each separate part is the means of reconciling democracy with empire." Although he recognized the potential friction that might arise between the claims of a united colonial empire and the nationalist aspirations of the individual colonies, he nevertheless argued that democracy, federalism, and empire (not imperialism) were theoretically compatible, and that this compound was partly, if precariously, realized in the British colonial system. "Democracy," he argued, "may be compatible with Empire in the sense of a great aggregation of territories enjoying internal independence while united by some common bond, but it is necessarily hostile to Empire in the sense of a system wherein one community imposes its will on others no less entitled by race, education, and capacity to govern themselves." This was to distinguish between progressive and reactionary forms of imperial government, those that were on the right side of history from those that held it back. He concluded by arguing that whatever its fate in the British colonial context, federalism, "as the natural means whereby over large areas unity can be reconciled with the conditions of popular government," had a bright future.[35] This argument aligned Hobhouse with the numerous proponents of imperial federation, who had been campaigning actively on behalf of the ideal since the late 1870s. Imperial federation was a vague term, identifying plans that ranged from the moderate—simply reinforcing existing ties between Britain and its colonies—to the truly audacious—including the creation of a globe-spanning racial-national state ruled by directly elected representatives sitting in a new imperial senate in London. However, the very vagueness of the project, or at least its elasticity, was also part of its strength, for it allowed individuals and groups, often with different agendas, to form a broad coalition to pressure the government over the direction of British foreign and imperial policy.

In an earlier article reviewing *Imperialism*, Hobhouse praised the imperial federal project outlined by Hobson—to which I will return later—although his endorsement was qualified. "It is true," he wrote, "that a democratic Em-

---

[34] Ibid., 152–53.
[35] Ibid., 154, 156–57, 155.

pire, or let us say a democratic world State, might be conceived as a possibility," but, he continued, such a "state could only be built up by Federation, probably by a complex system of Federation within Federation, and it would rest not on the annihilation, but in the peaceful development of nationality."[36] Once again, and more forcefully than Hobson, Hobhouse insisted on the need to reconcile nationality and imperial federation. If the correct balance could be struck between demands for national autonomy and the centralizing tendencies of an overarching political structure, imperial federation would be a normatively desirable objective. Returning to the issue in *Liberalism*, Hobhouse sketched a powerful, albeit highly abstract, argument for the viability, even necessity, of imperial federation. A united British colonial empire could act as both a model for the future and a possible agent of global transformation. Modes of international organization had to adapt to a changing world. "Physically the world is rapidly becoming one," he argued, "and its unity must ultimately be reflected in political institutions." In this quasi-determinist account, new technologies were modifying the conditions of both political possibility and of necessity. These developments were generated by, and further helped to generate, the orthogenic evolution of mind. The result was the simultaneous growth of support for the principle of nationality and a challenge to traditional conceptions of state sovereignty. The "old doctrine" of "absolute sovereignty" was "absolutely dead." The largest modern states, continued Hobhouse, "exhibit a complex system of government within government, authority limited by authority, and the world-state of the not-impossible future must be based on a free national self-direction as full and satisfying as that enjoyed by Canada and Australia within the British Empire at this moment."[37] Here the British colonies acted as the vanguard of a democratic future, harbingers of a global polity to come. The fate of the indigenous populations of these "free" states was not considered worthy of attention.

Although liberalism was antithetical to the "imperial idea," it was fully alive to the forces that bound the colonies together, that is, "to the sentiment of unity pervading its white population, to all the possibilities involved in the bare fact that a fourth part of the human race recognizes one flag and one supreme authority."[38] This raised an important challenge for the new liberals. Because the colonial communities were the most democratic in the world, their union with Britain was often viewed as a force for progress, and as such

[36] Hobhouse, "Democracy and Empire," *Speaker*, October 18, 1902, 75. He concluded that "Mr. Hobson's book will become one of the text-books of reviving Liberalism—the Liberalism which is finding itself again in opposition to Imperialism, and is recognising that a choice must be made between Democracy and Empire." Hobhouse was far from alone in thinking that the end result of imperial federation was better characterized as a "world state" not an empire. Bell, *The Idea of Greater Britain*, ch. 4.

[37] Hobhouse, *Liberalism*, 105, 115.

[38] Ibid., 115–16. Note the conflation here between the "white" settler colonies and the remainder of the empire.

it was considered imperative that the empire was not left to the reactionary imperialists. It was therefore vital "to devise means for the more concrete and living expression of this sentiment without impairing the rights of self-government on which it depends."[39] This was a difficult balancing act. As a first step, he proposed the creation of an Imperial Council to coordinate relationships between the colonial states, although he failed to offer any details about how it might work. This move would constitute, he implied, an initial step toward a deeper union, a union that would help to bind together, and give institutional expression to, the "sentiments" of the English-speaking peoples. "Such a union is no menace to the world's peace or to the cause of freedom. On the contrary, as a natural outgrowth of a common sentiment, it is one of the steps towards a wider unity which involves no backstroke against the ideal of self-government. It is a model, and that on no mean scale, of the International State."[40] Like many thinkers of his generation, Hobhouse saw a dual challenge. Not only was it vital to calibrate relationships with the colonies, it was simultaneously important to deepen the connection with "the other great commonwealth of the English-speaking people," namely, the United States. If the democratic peoples of the Anglo-Saxon race could be aligned, then progress could be secured.

For Hobhouse, then, *imperialism*, understood as the aggressive foreign expansion of the state, offered a dangerous challenge to the progressive development of humanity. It was the ultimate manifestation of reaction, antithetical to democratic theory and practice. But *empire*, if regarded as a political vehicle uniting the colonial communities, was not only compatible with democracy, it could help to bring about the democratization of the international system through strengthening the bonds, moral and political, that linked the various Anglo-Saxon communities scattered across the earth. History had come full circle. Although the success of liberalism had helped to spawn the period of reaction, the rise of imperialism in turn triggered the revival of liberalism, waking many—though not all—liberals from their slumber. In the preface to the second edition of *Democracy and Reaction*, published in 1909, Hobhouse identified the span of the period of reaction as 1880 to 1902, although it had antecedents and "some currents" were "still flowing."[41] In *Liberalism*, published two years later, he identified the key turning point as Campbell-Bannerman's famous speech delivered in 1901 on the "methods of barbarism" employed by the British in South Africa.[42] "Liberalism," he concluded, "has passed through its Slough of Despond, and in the give and take of ideas with

---

[39] Ibid, 116.

[40] Ibid.

[41] Hobhouse, *Democracy and Reaction*, 247, 250. 1886 saw the rejection of Gladstone's Home Rule Bill while 1902 was marked by the Peace of Vereeniging, bringing hostilities in South Africa to a close.

[42] See here C. C. Eldridge, *Victorian Imperialism* (London, 1978), 13; John Ellis, "'The Methods of Barbarism' and the 'Rights of Small Nations,'" *Albion*, 30 (1998), 49–75.

Socialism, has learnt, and taught, more than one lesson."[43] It seemed that Minerva's owl had flown: the period of reaction could only be comprehended at the moment it drew to a close.

Hobson and the Crisis of Liberalism

When Hobson came to reflect on *The Crisis of Liberalism* in 1909, his analysis dovetailed neatly with that of Hobhouse.[44] He sketched, albeit in less detail and with less finesse, a grim account of recent political and intellectual developments. Liberals, he argued, had "shown defects of vision and of purpose," with the result that for "over a quarter of a century Liberalism has wandered in this valley of indecision, halting, weak, vacillating, divided, and concessive." Hobson sought to anatomize and correct this drift.

Like Hobhouse, Hobson thought that liberals were engaged in a bitter conflict with the forces of reaction. He maintained that the Tories controlled the press, the political machinery, the city, the church, the armed services, and even the sporting establishment.[45] Yet he remained optimistic, interpreting the intensity of the conservative reaction as a sign of the popularity and power of new liberal ideas. In characteristic radical style, he distinguished the people from the elites who ruled (and manipulated) them, placing his hope in the progressive potential of the former. The vitality of the new liberalism was demonstrated above all by the fact that the "vested interests" defended their class privileges by appeals to reason and justice; they were forced, that is, to use the terms of their opponents. This appeal took two main forms. First, they denied the existence of (structural) social and economic problems, focusing instead on "individual moralization" as the engine of progress. This was an attempt to neutralize demands for systemic social reform. Second, they tried to "foster the combative competitive instincts of the lower nature of man by urging the necessity and utility of industrial competition with other States." They legitimated brutal competition through a combination of misapplied biological arguments, which led to politics being conceived of as a "struggle for life," and the "authoritative conservatism of Hegelian dogmas."[46] The overlap with Hobhouse is clear.

The Crisis of Liberalism was Hobson's call to arms, an attempt to inject fighting spirit into the liberals by reorienting their priorities. The new liberalism, he argued, stood for an assault on monopolies and "unearned property."

---

[43] Hobhouse, *Liberalism*, 107, 109.

[44] Hobson, *The Crisis of Liberalism* (London, 1909). This volume, like *Democracy and Reaction*, was composed of a series of previously published articles.

[45] Ibid., x. All of this was "thrown together by the class instinct of self-preservation," 188.

[46] Ibid., 183–84, 185, 187. Like Hobhouse, Hobson thought that evolution, properly understood, generated "mutual aid or conscious co-operation," 185.

To achieve this, it demanded a "new conception of the functions of the State," and a reinterpretation of the meaning of, and the conditions necessary for securing, individual liberty.[47] Like Hobhouse, Hobson also sought to embed the new liberalism in a developmental history of liberal thought and practice. This historical emplotment allowed him to argue that although the older individualist liberalism was in many respects obsolete, it nevertheless contained important truths that should not be jettisoned. Principles always needed to be adapted to contemporary conditions. "Each new generation of liberals will be required to translate a new set of needs and aspirations into facts." It also meant that time was of the essence; reaction had to be defeated before it was too late. "This is the last chance for English Liberalism."[48] Hobson stressed two points. First, that the older liberalism had never been as etiolated as both its critics and its heirs proclaimed. "The negative conception of liberalism, as a definite mission for the removal of certain political and economic shackles upon personal liberty, is not merely philosophically defective," he contended, "but historically false." Liberals had never been committed to a radically atomistic individualism. Although he aimed to save the older liberals from the condescension of posterity, he nevertheless criticized their arguments, maintaining that the "old Radicalism" had been "crippled" by "positive hostility to public methods of cooperation," and had placed "an excessive emphasis upon the aspect of liberty which consists in the absence of restraint, as compared with the other aspect which consists in presence of opportunity."[49] Second, he identified the continuities between the old and the new, which centered on the value assigned to individual liberty. In seeking the "fuller realization of individual liberty contained in the provision of equal opportunities for self-development," [50] the new liberals could be seen as completing the historical mission inaugurated by their predecessors.

Again like Hobhouse, he argued that liberal weakness and indecision had encouraged the enemies of liberalism, facilitating their assaults on its core achievements in politics and social policy. Above all, he lamented that imperialism, the "great arch-enemy of the age," had "found a too facile entrance among the ranks of her dejected followers." Its popularity, then, was partly a function of liberal vacillation and loss of confidence. Imperialism, he contin-

---

[47] Ibid., xi. The American Progressive scholar Charles Beard observed that "At Albany or Harrisburg, Mr. Hobson's philosophy would be instantly branded as 'rank socialism' and dangerous utopianism, but at Westminster things are different." Beard, *Political Science Quarterly*, 25 (1910), 530.

[48] Hobson, *The Crisis of Liberalism*, 135.

[49] Ibid., 92–94. Yet he painted liberalism with a very broad brush, for, as Michael Freeden notes, he expended little effort in engaging with past thinkers, even Mill, and preferred to discuss his contemporaries. Freeden, *Liberal Languages* (Princeton, 2005), 94.

[50] Hobson, *The Crisis of Liberalism*, xii. This was a "more constructive and evolutionary idea of liberty," 93.

ued, had been exploited by the conservatives to derail projects for reform, and it served as a natural ally for economic protectionism.[51] In a perverse turn of events, liberals were thus colluding in the destruction of their own creed and the overturning of their historical achievements. Few of Hobson's readers were likely to be surprised by this diagnosis. He was, after all, well known as the author of *Imperialism: A Study* (1902), a coruscating attack on the "new imperialism" being practiced by the United States, Germany, France, and, above all, the United Kingdom. This volume had followed in quick succession from two earlier books, both based on his experiences as a correspondent for the *Manchester Guardian* during the South African War.[52]

During the first few years of his career, Hobson had been a fairly conventional supporter of the liberal imperial mission to civilize, only transmuting into a new liberal thinker, and avowed enemy of imperialism, in the early 1890s. Yet this transition was never complete, and pronounced traces of his earlier views remained. His political thinking selectively combined elements of Fabian thought, Spencer's political sociology of industrial modernization, utilitarianism, positivism ultimately derived from the writings of Auguste Comte, and Ruskin's conception of organic economic society.[53] By the late 1890s, he became convinced that the "new" imperialism, unfolding mainly in Africa and Asia, represented an overriding danger to British democracy. It threatened "peace, economy, reform, and popular self-government," catalyzing instead militarism, reaction, and jingoism.[54] *Imperialism* presented a multicausal explanation for the emergence of the "earth hunger" that had gripped the imperial powers since roughly 1870. Its "leading characteristic" was competition between great capitalist empires.[55]

The main stimulus was investment. Oversaving among capitalists and underconsumption by the masses meant that the rich could not invest their money profitably in the domestic market. In search of a high rate of return, they pushed for the opening of foreign markets, which in turn required territorial acquisitions. This system benefitted the few—chiefly financiers and their allies in the political establishment—at the expense of the many. The "business interests of the nation as a whole are subordinated to those of certain sectional interests that usurp control of the national resources and use them for their private gain."[56] Employing a common radical trope, he argued

---

[51] Ibid., viii.

[52] Hobhouse, *The War in South Africa* (London, 1901); Hobhouse, *The Psychology of Jingoism* (London, 1901).

[53] On Ruskin and Spencer, see Cain, *Hobson and Imperialism*; on the links to positivism, see Claeys, *Imperial Sceptics*, ch. 4; and on utilitarian themes, see David Weinstein, *Utilitarianism and the New Liberalism* (Cambridge, 2007), ch. 6.

[54] Hobson, *Imperialism*, 126.

[55] Ibid., 13, 19.

[56] Ibid., 46. Like many contemporary critiques of finance capitalism, Hobson's views were

that imperialism was "irrational from the standpoint of the whole nation," although "it is rational enough from the standpoint of certain classes in the nation." Using various forms of manipulation and misleading propaganda, this profit-driven imperialism was disguised as necessary government policy; it was a "calculating, greedy type of Machiavellianism" wrapped in the evocative language of "national destiny" and the spread of "civilization."[57] Like Hobhouse, he warned against the corrupting effects of disingenuous language.

Empire was not the problem, only its malignant forms. Hobson never gave up on the idea that higher civilization bestowed rights on some states or peoples to override the claims to self-determination of others. He also offered a strong defense of the value of settler colonization, insisting on the "radical distinction between genuine colonialism and Imperialism."[58] An advocate of imperial federation, he once sketched out an ambitious outline of the future of international organization in which vast federations, each rooted in "common blood, language, and institutions," dominated, and helped to pacify, world politics.

> Holding, as we must, that any reasonable security for good order and civilization in the world implies the growing application of the federation principle in international politics, it will appear only natural that the earlier steps in such a process should take the form of unions of States most closely related by ties of common blood, language, and institutions, and that a phase of federated Britain or Anglo-Saxondom, Pan-Teutonism, Pan-Slavism, and Pan-Latinism might supervene upon the phase already reached . . . Christendom thus laid out in a few great federal empires, each with a retinue of uncivilized dependencies, seems to me the most legitimate development of present tendencies and one which would offer the best hope of permanent peace on an assured basis of inter-Imperialism.[59]

Imperial federation would also derail the aggressive ambitions of the rapidly expanding colonies. Hobson worried that the colonies were in danger of turning into semi-autonomous imperial powers, seeking to dominate the "lower races" in their regions and dragging Britain into hazardous entanglements

---

tainted with anti-Semitism (Cain, *Hobson and Imperialism*, 84, 92–93). On earlier socialist and radical theories of finance imperialism, see Claeys, *Imperial Sceptics*. His account highlights that Hobson's argument about finance capital was not especially original.

[57] Hobson, *Imperialism*, 47, 12–13. Claeys (*Imperial Sceptics*, ch. 4) shows that this was grounded in, among other things, a Vattelian argument about the rights of occupation of underutilized land. See also Andrew Fitzmaurice, "The Resilience of Natural Law in the Writings of Sir Travers Twiss," in *British International Thinkers from Hobbes to Namier*, ed. Ian Hall and Lisa Hill (New York, 2009), ch. 8.

[58] Hobson, *Imperialism*, 36.

[59] Ibid., 332.

with other powerful states. The threat was the same as in the "mother coun-try": the influence of local cohorts of financiers pushing for market expansion and plotting the "subversion of honest, self-developing democracy."[60] On this account, empires bred other empires, as the will to dominate and exploit spread from the "mother country" to its imperial outposts like a virus.

In a book long remembered as a model of anti-imperialism, Hobson unam-biguously defended the benefits of imperial federation and the civilizing po-tential of global Anglo-Saxon power. However, over the course of the next few years, his views on imperial federation shifted, and by the time he came to publish *The Crisis of Liberalism*, he had lost his earlier enthusiasm for the proj-ect. Indeed, he poured scorn on those who professed support for it —while conveniently failing to mention his earlier advocacy. "Those British imperial-ists who with the events of the last few years before their eyes, still imagine a closer Imperial federation in any shape or form practicable, are merely the dupes of a Kiplingesque sentimentalism."[61]

What spurred his change of heart? Part of the answer lies in Hobson's changing views on the practical effects of federalism and the dynamics of co-lonial development. When he turned to discussing the postwar situation in South Africa, he noted that much support for the union of South Africa, which was to be achieved in 1910, emanated from those (notably Carnarvon and Chamberlain) who had long sought a "larger federation, or other recon-stitution of the self-governing sections of the British Empire." They had as-sumed that the federation of South Africa would be a step on the road to im-perial federation, a vanguard that heralded wider transformation of the imperial system. Hobson doubted this logic, arguing that federation and state consolidation in Australia, Canada, and South Africa made imperial federa-tion *less* feasible, for as the colonies have "grown in size and strength, they have increasingly asserted their larger rights of independent government." Na-tional federation acted as a centrifugal force, reducing the likelihood of the wider imperial federal project acquiring sufficient support among the newly emboldened colonists. The leaders of the colonies would not think it in their national interest to federate with the "mother country." Contrary to popular belief, moreover, the links between the colonies and Britain were growing weaker despite the "greater physical accessibility" facilitated by new commu-nications and transport technologies and that space-eliminating instrument of modern capitalism, the "great machinery of modern investment."[62] These were outweighed by countervailing tendencies demanding increased national autonomy. Such skepticism about the transformative powers of technology highlights the political indeterminacy of technological change.

[60] Ibid., 345.
[61] Hobhouse, *The Crisis of Liberalism*, 238.
[62] Ibid., 236, 237, 239.

In the movement of Joseph Chamberlain's ideas, Hobson divined the direction of imperial federalist discourse, and above all the shift from arguments propounding political federation to those focusing on economic unity. "Mr Chamberlain," he wrote, "soon saw that the front-door of political federation was shut, bolted and barred. He thereupon sought the tradesman's entrance, claiming to knit the colonies and the mother country into an indissoluble union by means of a set of preferences which he hoped might eventually give free trade within the Empire." But, Hobson continued, this new project was also doomed to fail—it was "futile"—and for the same reasons: the perceived national interests of the colonial states.[63] As such, the only possible mechanism for drawing the empire together was imperial defense. Here too he was skeptical. In particular, he turned his attention to the hollowness of imperial rhetoric:

> It might well appear a profitable and glorious task to co-operate in the protection of a "free, tolerant, unaggressive Empire." But it is not equally glorious or profitable to enter a confederation under which a necessarily dominant partner can claim his blood and money to help hold down India, to quell some struggles for liberty in Egypt, or to procure some further step in the tropical aggrandisement at the bidding of some mining or rubber syndicate.[64]

Although this was a powerful critique from the perspective of a metropolitan new liberal, it was not convincing in its own terms. As Hobson lamented in *Imperialism*, the colonies themselves claimed a right to engage in their own imperial activities. Indeed, one of the reasons that he had originally defended imperial federation was that he thought it would limit their expansionist ambitions. He concluded his dissection of imperial federation with the summary claim that "no abiding unity can be found for an Empire half autocratic and half self-governing."[65]

A further reason for the unacknowledged switch lies in Hobson's interpretation of the nefarious role of Chamberlain. Although in the 1890s Hobson had been a cautious admirer of Chamberlain, he soon came to associate him with the forces of imperialist reaction, above all in South Africa.[66] This was made all the worse by Chamberlain's early political radicalism; his subsequent trajectory was a gross act of betrayal. The tariff reform campaign, launched by Chamberlain in 1903, was the final nail in the coffin for Hobson.[67] He was

---

[63] Ibid., 239. On Chamberlain's own change of heart, see Bell, *The Idea of Greater Britain*, 56–58.

[64] Hobson, *The Crisis of Liberalism*, 241.

[65] Ibid., 242.

[66] On his early support for and respect of Chamberlain, see Cain, *Hobson and Imperialism*, 53, 61.

[67] On the debates around tariff reform, see, inter alia, Anthony Howe, *Free Trade and Liberal England, 1846–1946* (Oxford, 1998); Frank Trentmann, *Free Trade Nation* (Oxford, 2008).

also confronted with empirical evidence that challenged the feasibility of any constitutional scheme for imperial federation. During 1905, Hobson traveled around Canada, writing reports for the *Daily Chronicle*, which he soon turned into a short book. Two main themes ran through it: the increasing "Americanization" of Canada and the failings of protectionism as an economic policy. Canada, he argued, was undergoing a profound transformation. Following the lead of its southern neighbor, its people were displaying boundless optimism; the country was "conscious, vocally, uproariously conscious, that her day has come." Despite the professed anti-Americanism he discerned among many of its elite, Canada was also becoming more American. The food, the architecture, the economic infrastructure, even the accents and physical dispositions of the people: all were more American than British. Average Canadians, he proclaimed, "are American through and through," although they retained a substantial residue of Britishness. "In fact," Hobson concluded, "Canada presents as yet a sub-American variety of civilization, though in some ways rapidly assimilating to the States."[68] He maintained that Canada's destiny was bound up with increasing economic interaction with the United States. Imperial federation, which was based on an assumption about the cultural unity of the global British diaspora, would find it extremely difficult to flower in this environment.

Canada was also gaining a sense of national unity, drawing the distinct interests and peoples of the country together. "Every visitor to Canada is powerfully impressed by a growing conscious spirit of nationality," a spirit that was bound to "find expression in demands for even larger liberty than is enjoyed now." This further undermined schemes for imperial federation. Despite widespread sentimental attachment to the British empire—Hobson discerned little enthusiasm for complete independence—he contended that "it would not be possible to devise, even in general terms, any scheme of Imperial federation to which the most pro-British group of Canadians would assent when they understood what it implied." This was a consequence of both national consciousness and democratic development. Canadians were not prepared to lose "one jot of the power of self-government" or shut themselves off from "any further degree of independence to which they may aspire in the future." Yet this is exactly what any serious federal scheme would involve. "For, either an Imperial Council would be an amiable farce, or it would be a real political body, capable of committing the peoples of the Colonies to some course of action, involving pecuniary and military obligations, and directing, at any rate, their foreign policy." The idea that a "democratic country" like Canada would "hand powers over to some Privy Council committee" was, he thought,

---

[68] Hobson, *Canada To-Day* (London, 1906), 3, 50–51. Although it had long been in use, the term "Americanization" was popularized by W. T. Stead, *The Americanization of the World* (London, 1902).

"preposterous." Democratic sentiment heralded the death knell for federalist dreams—a diagnosis that was largely accurate. The future for Canada lay elsewhere: "Canada is not staying as she was: both in sentiment and in practical policy she is moving along the road towards national independence, either within or outside the Empire."[69] Whereas imperial federation had once seemed an appealing prospect—and there is no reason to think that he changed his mind on the abstract arguments in its favor—it had now been rendered obsolete by a combination of political developments. Not only was it less feasible than before, it had also been hijacked by the forces of reaction. Hobson clearly agreed with Hobhouse's injunction to take the "fruits" as well as the intentions of political theories seriously.

Yet despite his disavowal of formal schemes for imperial federation, Hobson did not give up on the civilizing potential of empire. The problem with contemporary imperialism, he argued, was its lack of accountability and the fact that it was often pursued for self-interested motives. The "radical moral defect of Imperialism," he contended, "is due to lack of any true sanction from a society of nations to the interference of an imperialist nation with the life of a lower people." This implied that if such sanctions could be enacted, then it would be possible to distinguish morally corrupt from just forms of imperial governance. Indeed, he looked forward to a paternalist form of multilateral imperialism, the legitimacy of which could be secured through the collaboration of a variety of "civilized" states.

> If there existed a fairly developed form of international society, in which all peoples, great and small, were in some sense represented, and such a society delegated England or France in the interests of civilisation to take under her tutelage some backward or degraded people which lay on their borders, maintaining order, developing the natural resources of the country, and helping to teach the arts of civilisation, this would afford some moral basis for Imperialism. Actual imperialism differs widely from this condition.[70]

In a move that prefigures the arguments of many late twentieth-century liberal imperialists, and arguably some of the most powerful norms of the post-1945 international order, Hobson defended a vision of a benevolent multinational civilizing imperialism.

Conclusions

In the wake of the war in South Africa, a war that divided British liberals like no other, Hobson and Hobhouse set out a penetrating autocritique of the re-

---

[69] Hobson, *Canada To-Day*, 99–101, 103.
[70] Hobhouse, *The Crisis of Liberalism*, 259.

cent failings of liberalism and offered an alternative vision for the future. They focused their critical energies on the purported enemies of liberalism: neo-Hegelian philosophy, misapplied notions of evolution, and vested class interests. But they also addressed the failings of liberalism in general, and the new liberals in particular. These failings were both practical and cognitive. Liberalism had been a successful force during the nineteenth century, but it had grown weak and divided, hamstrung by the moral and political limits of the older liberalism and by the failure of the new liberals to recognize the powerful intellectual resources bequeathed by their predecessors. Liberalism, that is, had been partially undermined by the careless way in which its history had been narrated and absorbed by the new liberals. Hobson and Hobhouse sought to rectify this failure of historical judgment by offering an alternative account of development, one that simultaneously allowed them to praise the virtues and the foresight of the earlier liberals while insisting that new conditions meant that it was essential to adopt new arguments—to at once acknowledge and redirect the legacy of their forebears. In doing so, they provide an early example of what would become common practice as the twentieth century wore on: the writing and rewriting of the "liberal tradition," with a canon of great thinkers at its core. This had been largely absent in prominent nineteenth-century constructions of liberalism.

Empire played a central, although ambivalent, role in their political projects. Initially both Hobson and Hobhouse supported the federation of the British colonies, arguing that it could harness unity and diversity within a single political organization and provide an institutional foundation for further progress in international politics. It had the potential to become a democratic new liberal polity stretched across the globe. During the Edwardian years, however, Hobson changed his mind. He came to regard imperial federation as both impractical and reactionary. Hobhouse, meanwhile, appeared to strengthen his support for the idea, although he rarely engaged with concrete details. Their shifting arguments about empire exemplified the deep ambiguity of liberal visions of global order at the turn of the twentieth century.

Coda

๕

(De)Colonizing Liberalism

In 2004, with American and British troops fighting in Iraq and Afghanistan, and a ferocious global "war on terror" in full swing, empire was once again high on the agenda. In a now infamous outburst an anonymous official in Washington boasted that "[w]e're an empire now, and when we act, we create our own reality . . . We're history's actors . . . and you, all of you, will be left to just study what we do."[1] Most of the protagonists I have (just) studied in this book would likewise have seen themselves as belonging to an exclusive group of history's actors, the handful of states that had fundamentally remade the world, shaping their own reality, and whose political and intellectual leaders often believed that they were entitled, even destined, to continue doing so deep into the future. Like empire, hubris is a transhistorical phenomenon.

The preceding chapters have addressed a variety of themes and thinkers in the history of modern British imperial ideology (and beyond). Although I have concentrated on the "age of empire," the half century prior to the out-break of the First World War, I have also pushed back into the early Victorian era to trace the development of assorted doctrines, and moved through the twentieth century and into the present, across decades in which the British empire dissolved and the United States achieved a long foretold position of global supremacy. Whether wittingly or not, the anonymous official hymning the power and virtue of contemporary American empire was a lineal heir of those earlier ideologists, imaginatively beholden to a mythopoeic vision of the British empire and its role in the long nineteenth century. My analysis has been motivated by curiosity about the ways in which historical actors made

---

[1] Ron Suskind, "Faith, Certainty and the Presidency of George W. Bush," *New York Times Magazine*, October 17, 2004. The phrase is often attributed to Karl Rove. On the debate over American empire, see Paul Macdonald, "Those Who Forget Historiography Are Doomed to Republish It," *Review of International Studies*, 35/1 (2006), 45–67; Craig Calhoun, Frederick Cooper, and Kevin Moore, eds., *Lessons of Empire* (New York, 2006).

sense of their world, and a conviction that studying their ideas can shed light on key moments and movements in the past, while also helping to inform contemporary political thinking. I have probed the meanings of liberalism, forms of imperial argumentation, conceptions of time and history, and accounts of global racial order. In doing so, I have investigated the writings of various individuals, some still famous, venerated even, but the majority of whom have been lost to the condescension of posterity. Only by recovering the political concerns, languages, anxieties, and fantasies of such a motley cast of characters can we begin to apprehend the content and complexity of imperial political thought at the apogee of the largest empire in history.

Throughout *Reordering the World* I have emphasized the importance of both "historical-mindedness" and of settler colonialism in nineteenth-century imperial discourse. Emigration and settlement had long been a conspicuous theme in English (and later British) political discourse. The colonization of North America provoked vociferous debate, drawing in many of the leading minds of the age.[2] The subsequent loss of the thirteen colonies haunted later imperial thinkers, prompting anguish about the future, and melancholy ruminations about what might have been if only the British empire had remained intact. Although I am skeptical that we can learn much about modern imperial ideology from studying the writings of John Locke, it is nevertheless clear that in order to understand the character of much early modern political thought it is necessary to grapple with attitudes to settlement and occupation.[3] I have traversed less well-trodden ground, analyzing intellectual debates over what I call the second settler empire. Whereas the first settler empire was geographically concentrated in North America, and was fatally wrenched apart by what Seeley termed the "Schism in Greater Britain," the second was spread across oceans and continents, encompassing vast territories (and more modest populations) in Canada, the South Pacific, and southern Africa.[4]

This new empire—or imperial subsystem—was slow to form and slower still to ignite the political imagination. It coalesced piecemeal from the scattered remnants of the late eighteenth-century colonial order and the steady accumulation of new territories. Initially maligned, frequently ignored, its inhabitants routinely derided, it was only during the second half of the nine-

---

[2] For two important accounts of early modern colonization, see David Armitage, *The Ideological Origins of the British Empire* (Cambridge, 2000); Andrew Fitzmaurice, *Humanism and America* (Cambridge, 2007).

[3] For wide-ranging analyses of imperial justification and contestation, see Lauren Benton, *A Search for Sovereignty* (Cambridge, 2010); Andrew Fitzmaurice, *Sovereignty, Property, and Empire, 1500–2000* (Cambridge, 2014); Anthony Pagden, *The Burdens of Empire* (Cambridge, 2015). For a brilliant meditation on the construction of political space in European political thought, see Annabel Brett, *Changes of State* (Princeton, 2011).

[4] This is the title of chapter 8 in Seeley, *The Expansion of England*.

teenth century that it came to be seen as part of a single integrated system.[5] During the same period it was transvalued: colonization was recoded as a laudable ideal, the colonies reimagined as spaces of virtue and desire. This fundamental switch in fortunes had several sources, some deep-rooted, others proximate. The early nineteenth century was marked by what James Belich terms a "Settler Revolution," the "explosive" development of two interconnected geo-economic regions, the "American West" and the "British West" (Canada, Australia, New Zealand, and South Africa). Although the seeds of the revolution could be located earlier, a phase of "hyper-colonialism" erupted with the "settler transition" of 1815–20, as emigration reached a critical mass and became a significant historical force. It was the joint product of novel transport technologies and a shift in collective psychology, such that embarking on life in the colonies came to seem both practicable and attractive to millions of people. It was sustained by a new ideology of "settlerism," praising the manifold benefits, material and spiritual, of colonization.[6] In a wave of creative destruction—characterized by an economic cycle that saw frenetic booms followed by sudden collapse and then sustained periods of "regrowth"—the settler world became a powerful engine of economic development and a space for the reproduction of Anglo-societies. The nineteenth-century "great divergence," then, was powered by the astonishing rise of an Angloworld formed by the "organic unity" of the British settler empire and the United States.[7]

Economic vitality alone was insufficient to captivate and enthuse generations of liberal thinkers. It was the specific political status—or at least self-image—of the colonies that provided the key. The period of the "great transition" was also, as Lisa Ford argues, the moment when settler sovereignty was consolidated.[8] Exclusive spaces of jurisdiction were established, such that (for example) indigenous resistance was no longer treated as a matter for diplomatic resolution between distinct communities but as an instance of domestic criminality to be dealt with by the settler legal system. Regulated by violence, this new regime of territorial sovereignty established the juridical and symbolic foundations of the settler state. Above all, though, it was the grant of "responsible government" in the 1840s and 1850s that elevated the colonies

---

[5] For a near-contemporary account of the gestalt switch, see J. E. Cairnes, "Colonization and Colonial Government" (1863), in *Political Essays* (London, 1873), 158. On some of the key midcentury protagonists, see Edward Beasley, *Empire as the Triumph of Theory* (London, 2004); Beasley, *Mid-Victorian Imperialists* (London, 2005).

[6] Belich, *Replenishing the Earth*, 153–56. For a comprehensive account of emigration around the British empire, see Marjory Harper and Stephen Constantine, eds., *Migration and Empire* (Oxford, 2010).

[7] Belich, *Replenishing the Earth* (Oxford, 2009), 51.

[8] Lisa Ford, *Settler Sovereignty* (Cambridge, MA, 2010). Her book is based on a comparative analysis of Georgia and New South Wales. See also the discussion in Russell Smandych, "Colonialism, Settler Colonialism, and Law," *Settler Colonial Studies*, 3/1 (2013), 82–101.

in the eyes of so many liberal thinkers, rendering them worthy subjects of sustained attention and affirmation. Imagining colonies as semi-autonomous, collectively self-governing communities, free of the feudal vestiges of British society, and populated overwhelmingly by energetic "civilized" white people, aligned them with liberal visions of political progress. Indeed it was this political transformation that many liberals later boasted was the major liberal contribution to the British empire during the nineteenth century. This was *their* empire, something of which they could be proud and in which they could invest their hopes. While most were happy to claim the title of preeminent civilizing agent for Britain, many also felt that the occupied territories in India, the Caribbean, and Africa were ultimately fated for independence and that the despotism required to govern them, while in principle compatible with liberal ideology, was not something that they could endorse with the same confidence as the project of settler colonization. This is why I have suggested, contra Uday Singh Mehta, that it was in the colonies, not India, that many liberals found the concrete place of their dreams.[9] Liberal support for settler colonialism was premised on the belief that the colonies had performed a remarkable act of political synthesis, reconciling liberty and empire in a manner unprecedented in the annals of Western history. It was usually based on a willful downplaying of the violence necessary to construct and govern settler communities. The colonies were polities based on the *herrenvolk* principle of white racial supremacy.

While liberals frequently celebrated the progressive dimensions of colonization, they disagreed fiercely about how best to institutionalize the settler world. At midcentury, one of the most common positions—maybe even the dominant one—was a modern variation on the ancient Greek template, which envisaged the colonies securing formal independence and thereafter remaining tightly bound to Britain through a dense web of economic interactions, migrant flows, and the power of racial affect. Encompassing a cluster of geographically dispersed states—including the United States—joined symbolically by shared culture, history, and political institutions, the Angloworld would comprise a microcosmic international order. Despite the mosaic of independent polities, however, its underlying racial unity meant that it would remain one of history's actors. Others, including John Stuart Mill, were keen to maintain the sovereign connection between the "mother-country" and the colonies, but only on a voluntary basis, anchored in common interests and mutual recognition.[10] During the 1880s and 1890s plans for consolidating the settler empire shaped the terms of debate, often under the elastic rubric of "imperial federation." Whether formal or informal, visions of colonial unity

---

[9] The quote is from Mehta, *Liberalism and Empire*, 37.
[10] Mill, *Considerations on Representative Government* (1861), *Collected Works,* vol. 18, ch. 18. For the details of his argument, see chapter 9.

were predicated on a cognitive revolution, a transformation in perceptions of time and space, and thus of the parameters of political feasibility, that allowed the scattered fragments of the settler world to be imagined as a single united domain. For all the intellectual energy exerted on the subject, little came of plans to create a Greater British polity, though the idea of closer Angloworld collaboration advocated by more judicious imperialists sowed a far more enduring legacy.[11]

Antoinette Burton has recently called on historians to study phenomena that cannot be enclosed within the imaginative or juridical boundaries of nation or empire.[12] One such transversal was the ideology of whiteness, "at once global in its power and personal in its meaning, the basis of geo-political alliances and a subjective sense of self."[13] Claims about the nature and value of whiteness were central to debate over settler colonialism and imperial federation. During the 1880s and beyond, moreover, conceptions of whiteness (and in particular Anglo-Saxonism) underlay numerous calls to reconcile Greater Britain and the United States. Once again, liberals assumed a leading role. Ambitious demands emanated from such apparently incongruent figures as H. G. Wells, Andrew Carnegie, Cecil Rhodes, and W. T. Stead, who fired some of the opening salvos in the campaign to politically unify the Angloworld.[14] This represented an attempt to wrestle with the problem of *translatio imperii*, of calibrating the transition from one imperial order to another, only this time it was construed as both an interstate and an intra-racial predicament, a shift in the balance of power between polities that were composed of the same people. In chapter 13 I discussed one of the main intellectual sources for the ideology of transatlantic whiteness, namely E. A. Freeman's argument for the shared Teutonic foundations of Britain and the United States. For Freeman, race was the most basic ontological element of the sociopolitical world, and as such political institutions should be arrayed to reflect this primacy. The British empire failed this test, incorporating as it did copious "alien" elements while excluding the most significant political expression of the race. Some prophets of Angloworld unity, such as Rhodes and Wells, called for the foundation of a vast transatlantic Anglo-American polity.[15] Less

---

[11] On the legacies of the Angloworld in twentieth-century global politics, see Srdjan Vucetic, *The Anglosphere* (Stanford, 2011); Peter Katzenstein, ed., *Anglo-America and its Discontents* (London, 2012). On the weaknesses of the imperial federal movement, see Duncan Bell, *The Idea of Greater Britain*, ch. 10.

[12] Burton, "Getting Outside of the Global," in *Empire in Question* (Durham, NC, 2011), 279–80.

[13] Marilyn Lake and Henry Reynolds, *Drawing the Global Colour Line* (Cambridge, 2008), 3. See also Bill Schwarz, *The White Man's World* (Oxford, 2011).

[14] I analyze fantasies of Anglo-America in Bell, *Dreamworlds of Empire* (forthcoming).

[15] Rhodes, *The Last Will and Testament of Cecil J. Rhodes*, ed. W. T. Stead (London, 1902); *Anticipations of the Reaction of Mechanical and Scientific Progress upon Human Life and Thought* [1902] (Mineola, 1999). For more detailed proposals for formal union, see W. T. Stead, *The Amer-*

ambitious proponents, including Freeman and James Bryce, recommended the creation of an "isopolity," based on shared (racial) citizenship.[16] More cautious devotees of the Angloworld simply emphasized the importance of closer cooperation between its two main powers, destined to reorder the world between them. As I discussed in chapter 8, the overlapping discourses of Greater Britain and Anglo-America spawned a variety of other models of global governance during the twentieth century, including leagues of democracies and world federalism. They continue to inform debates about global order today.

Reordering the World makes no claims to comprehensiveness. A broader study of the thought-worlds of the settler empire would incorporate a greater range of material, as well as shifting between different modalities of historical investigation. It would need to scrutinize conceptions of the world produced in the colonies, identifying how they helped to mold local politics and how they circulated around the imperial commons. It would need to address the gendered character of colonial discourse, as well as its theological dimensions. It would need to engage with the complex legal arguments utilized to claim land and establish sovereign jurisdiction.[17] It would need to move beyond elite discourses to excavate the political languages of a larger cast of individuals, organizations, and movements. It would need to recover, where possible, the intellectual production of the assorted indigenous communities that were the main victims of the "settler revolution." It would need to address the interstitial status of Ireland, at once a zone of colonial settlement and an integral part of the British state. There is also much work to be done in analyzing the intellectual history of the metropolitan elite. In this book, and especially in part III, I have dedicated a considerable amount of space to the work of historians and philosophers. This choice is not accidental, insofar as they produced some of the most interesting and influential accounts of colonialism, but nor is it exhaustive. Poets and novelists were amongst the most searching colonial fabulists, and appraising their output offers rich rewards for students of political thought.[18] Political economists, in particular, are due greater attention. Al-

---

icanization of the World (London, 1902); John Dos Passos, *The Anglo-Saxon Century and the Unification of the English-Speaking Peoples*, 2nd ed. (New York, 1903). See further discussion in chapter 8.

[16] Bryce, "The Essential Unity of England and America," *Atlantic Monthly*, 82 (1898), 22–29. For Freeman's account, see chapter 13. On isopolity, see Duncan Bell, "Beyond the Sovereign State," *Political Studies*, 62 (2014), 418–34.

[17] See, for examples, Benton, *A Search for Sovereignty*; P. G. McHugh, *Aboriginal Societies and the Common Law* (Oxford, 2004); Fitzmaurice, *Sovereignty, Property and Empire*; Mark Hickford, *Lords of the Land* (Oxford, 2011).

[18] For recent examples of work on this topic, see Helen Lucy Blyth, *The Victorian Colonial Romance with the Antipodes* (Basingstoke, 2014); Terra Walston Joseph, "Bulwer-Lytton's *The Coming Race* and an Anglo-Saxon Greater Britain," *Nineteenth-Century Contexts*, 37 (2015), 233–48; Philip Steer, "Greater Britain and the Imperial Outpost," *Victorian Review*, 35 (2009), 79–95;

though I have touched on aspects of the political economy of settler colonialism—for example, in my discussion of Mill's work—I have not engaged it in depth. Metropolitan political economists were especially significant in shaping debate during the first half of the century, chiefly through the theoretical work and activism of the colonial reform movement, but they also played a significant role in arguments over imperial federation, and later returned to center stage in the Edwardian clashes over Chamberlain's plans for imperial tariff reform.[19] A new comprehensive study of the economic thought of empire across the nineteenth century is long overdue.

Elucidating the impact of alien rule in the history of modern European political thought produces a relatively clear dividing line between supporters and critics of empire, facilitating the creation of canons of "anti-imperial" and "imperialist" thinkers, liberal or otherwise. Injecting settler colonialism back into the narrative blurs this distinction. Most so-called "anti-imperialists" from the late eighteenth century to the late nineteenth, from Bentham through Spencer to Hobson and Hobhouse, promoted settler colonialism of one kind or another. Although there is no necessary conceptual or theoretical connection between liberalism and settler colonialism, such that authentic liberals must sanction the practice, the historical record demonstrates that (British) liberals overwhelmingly endorsed it. This support was frequently conjoined with the rejection, even fierce denunciation, of empire-as-alien-rule. The crucial task of decolonizing liberalism thus needs to start with an acknowledgment that many (liberal) critics of imperialism were simultaneously proponents of settler colonialism. This Janus-faced attitude was at once simple and complex. It was simple insofar as it was based on a claim that colonization belonged to a completely different category of political order—that "[w]hatever political maxims are most applicable to one, are most inapplicable to the other," as Seeley put it in one of the pithier renditions of the mantra.[20] They shouldn't be confused or conflated. The complexity resided in disentangling them, specifying exactly how and why settler colonies were different, when all forms of empire involved conquest and repressive governance. Here there was considerable disagreement, though most supporters concurred on a few basic points, above all the importance of racial similarity and self-government. The settler colonies were imagined as *white*, as populated by civilized peoples capable of governing themselves (preferably within

---

Lyman Tower Sargent, "Colonial and Postcolonial Utopias," in *The Cambridge Companion to Utopian Literature*, ed. Gregory Claeys (Cambridge, 2010), 200–223.

[19] See, for example, the discussion in A. C. Howe, *Free Trade and Liberal England, 1846–1946* (Oxford, 1998); E.H.H. Green, *The Crisis of Conservatism* (London, 1996), chs. 2, 7; Gregory Claeys, *Imperial Sceptics*; P. J. Cain, *Hobson and Imperialism* (Oxford, 2002). As far as I am aware, there are no recent histories of political economy that focus on colonial thought from the early Victorian era to the First World War.

[20] Seeley, *The Expansion of England*, 244. Seeley was comparing the settler colonies to India.

an overarching imperial framework) and of instituting sovereign control over territory that could be appropriated legitimately from its unworthy original inhabitants. The liberal case for exceptionalism, for transcending or escaping the despotic logic of traditional modes of imperial rule, was premised on a racialized picture of global hierarchy.

Thinking through the political and theoretical implications of settler colonialism, past and present, involves formidable challenges.[21] Such states are usually founded on acts of systematic violence against indigenous peoples. (The same could of course be said of many other states as well). The United States is but the largest example. Throughout the eighteenth and nineteenth centuries a succession of presidents, including Jefferson, Jackson, Grant, and Roosevelt, were quite open about the genocidal character of the frontier wars waged against the "Indian."[22] Civilization or extermination: such was the choice. In a discussion of Michael Walzer's account of American citizenship, Mahmood Mamdani writes that the "American [national] biography is written as the autobiography of the settler. The native has no place in it."[23] As such, pluralism and multiculturalism "flowered on a bed prepared by the conquest and decimation of tribes in America," and "[t]he uncritical embrace of the settler experience explains the blind spot in the American imagination: an inability to coexist with difference, indeed a preoccupation with civilizing natives." "American cosmopolitanism," he concludes, "has been crafted through settler lenses."[24] Facing up to this situation is not only a matter of recognizing an obligation to address past injustice, but admitting that the current political order is founded on, and continues to be shaped by, an ideology of settlerism. "Engaging with the native question would require questioning the ethics and politics of the very constitution of the United States of America. It would require rethinking and reconsidering the very political project called the USA."[25] Efforts to rethink and reconsider have been attempted with varying degrees of

---

[21] The journal *Settler Colonial Studies* is an excellent source of analysis. Now a vibrant, multi-disciplinary enterprise, the field of settler colonial studies was in its infancy when I embarked on my research into discourses of Greater Britain. I have learned much from it since then. For a valuable overview, see Lorenzo Veracini, *The Settler Colonial Present* (Basingstoke, 2015).

[22] Benjamin Madley, "Reexamining the American Genocide Debate," *American Historical Review*, 120 (2015), 109–110.

[23] Mamdani, "Settler Colonialism," *Critical Inquiry*, 41 (2015), 596. For an excellent discussion that takes this settler dimension into account, see Aziz Rana, *The Two Faces of American Freedom* (Cambridge, MA, 2010). See also Alyosha Goldstein, ed., *Formations of United States Colonialism* (Durham, NC, 2014); Kevin Bruyneel, "The American Liberal Colonial Tradition," *Settler Colonial Studies*, 3 (2013), 311–21.

[24] Mamdani, "Settler Colonialism," 598–99. He is critiquing a line of argument that runs through Michael Walzer, *What It Means to Be an American* (New York, 1996). On the peculiar form of sovereignty enacted by indigenous populations in the US, see Kevin Bruyneel, *The Third Space of Sovereignty* (Minneapolis, MN, 2007).

[25] Mamdani, "Settler Colonialism," 602–3.

enthusiasm across the other elements of the British settler world in recent years, spawning controversial campaigns for restitution, apology, and new forms of political participation, though with mixed results.[26]

I offer no solutions to this quandary. But if the legacy of empire in general, and settler colonialism in particular, is to be confronted properly it will require a fundamental reconsideration of the political institutions and norms of settler states, including the ideologies that they created and profess. Liberalism is one such ideology. This rethinking need not entail a wholesale rejection of liberalism—if such a thing is even possible now. Even at the height of British imperial arrogance, liberalism contained resources to both justify empire (of various kinds) and to launch stinging critiques of it. If those criticisms were often muted, their very possibility at least offers some hope. Today liberalism has expanded so broadly that it virtually monopolizes political theory and practice in the Angloworld, and as such it is vital to establish whether there are liberal forms of anti-imperialism suitable for the contemporary world, and what they might look like. It is essential to creatively engage with liberalism, joining the conflict between its tessellated factions.[27]

In *Liberalism and Empire*, Mehta argued that the "liberal involvement ←
with the British empire was largely coeval with liberalism itself."[28] I have challenged this historical narrative, suggesting that it both misdates the origins of liberalism and oversimplifies the character of liberal attitudes to empire in the nineteenth century. The British empire was forged long before the emergence of liberal political ideology: liberalism supervened on, while adapting and supplementing, existing ideas and practices. A relentless focus on the assumptions, theoretical architecture, and political entailments of liberalism carries the risk of overlooking the deeper intellectual and political currents on which it drew and to which it was a response—perhaps above all the coevolving relationship between the modern state and global capitalism.[29] In particular, I would contend that British liberalism was broadly coeval with the second settler empire. It was, in large part, a product of the violent dissolution of the thirteen colonies in North America, the revolutionary upheavals in France, and the tidal wave of economic, social, and political change that they unleashed. Perhaps more importantly, the development of liberal political the-

[26] On official policies of reconciliation and apology, see Miranda Johnson, "Reconciliation, Indigeneity, and Postcolonial Nationhood in Settler States," *Postcolonial Studies*, 14/2 (2011), 187–201; Dirk Moses, "Official Apologies, Reconciliation, and Settler Colonialism," *Citizenship Studies*, 15/2 (2011), 145–59.

[27] For valuable attempts to rethink liberalism, see Duncan Ivison, *Postcolonial Liberalism* (Cambridge, 2002); Tully, *Strange Multiplicity* (Cambridge, 1995). See also the discussion in Charles Mills, "Occupy Liberalism!," *Radical Philosophy Review*, 15/2 (2012), 305–23.

[28] Mehta, *Liberalism and Empire*, 4.

[29] For a magisterial account of the political thought of these developments, to which I am much indebted, see Istvan Hont, *Jealousy of Trade*.

ory and the second settler empire was interconnected. The repercussions of this historical imbrication have yet to be fully explored. In order to decolonize liberalism, it is first necessary to (re)colonize it, acknowledging the vital role that the project and ideology of settler colonialism played in its emergence and historical evolution.

BIBLIOGRAPHY

৯১

Manuscript Sources

Oscar Browning papers, Modern Archive Centre, King's College, Cambridge
Andrew Carnegie papers, Library of Congress, Washington
E. A. Freeman papers, John Rylands Library, University of Manchester
Imperial Federation League papers, British Library, London
John Robert Seeley papers, University of London Library
Henry Sidgwick papers, Trinity College, Cambridge
W. T. Stead papers, Churchill Archives Centre, Churchill College, Cambridge
Cecil Rhodes papers, Rhodes House Library, University of Oxford
Royal Commonwealth Society papers, University of Cambridge Library
Clarence Streit papers, Library of Congress, Washington
H. G. Wells papers, Rare Book and Manuscript Library, University of Illinois at Urbana-Champaign
Frederick Young papers, University of Cambridge Library

Primary Printed Sources

Anon., "A Colony and Parliament," in *Imperial Federation of Great Britain and Her Colonies*, ed. Frederick Young (London: Silver, 1876), 151–56.

Anon., "The Federation of the British Empire: Thoughts for the Queen's Jubilee on Imperial Federation," *Westminster Review*, 128 (1887), 484–94.

Anon., "Greater Greece and Greater Britain," *Spectator*, September, 18, 1886, 15–16.

Anon., "Imperium et Libertas," *Westminster Review*, 57 (1880), 91–111.

Anon., "Our Australian Possessions," *London Quarterly Review*, 1 (1853), 517–57.

Anon., "A Proposed Reform of the English Constitution," *Fraser's Magazine*, 8 (1873), 600–607.

Abbott, Lyman, "The Basis of an Anglo-American Understanding," *North American Review*, 166 (1898), 513–21.

Acton, John Emerich Edward Dalberg, "Nationality," in *Selected Writings of Lord Acton, Vol. 1: Essays on the History of Liberty*, ed. J. Rufus Fears (Indianapolis: Liberty, 1985), 409–39.

———, review of Seeley, *A Short History of Napoleon*, *English Historical Review*, 2/7 (1887), 593–603.

———, "Introduction," in *Il Principe*, by Niccolò Machiavelli, ed. L. Arthur Burd (Oxford: Clarendon Press, 1891), xix–xl.

Acton, John Emerich Edward Dalberg, *Lectures on Modern History*, ed. J. N. Figgis and R. V. Laurence (London: Macmillan, 1906).

Adams, Brooks, *The Law of Civilization and Decay: An Essay on History* (London: Macmillan, 1895).

Adams, Herbert, "Mr. Freeman's Visit to Baltimore," *Johns Hopkins University Studies in Historical and Political Science*, 1 (1882), 5–12.

———, *The Study of History in American Colleges and Universities* (Washington: Government Printing Office, 1887).

———, "Is History Past Politics?," *Johns Hopkins University Studies in Historical and Political Science*, 13 (1895), 67–81.

Alexander, Samuel, *Locke* (London: Constable, 1908).

Amery, Leopold Stennett, "Imperial Defence and National Policy," *The Empire and the Century*, ed. Goldman, 174–97.

———, "Imperial Unity," in *Union and Strength: A Series of Papers on Imperial Questions*, ed. Leopold Stennett Amery (London: Edward Arnold, 1912), 1–21.

Amos, Sheldon, *Political and Legal Remedies for War* (London: Cassell, 1880).

———, *The Science of Politics* (London: Kegan Paul, 1890).

Angell, Norman, *The Great Illusion: A Study of the Relation of Military Power in Nations to Their Economic and Social Advantage* (London: Heinemann, 1910).

———, *The Political Conditions of Allied Success: A Plea for the Protective Union of the Democracies* (New York: Putnam, 1918).

———, "The English-Speaking World and the Next Peace," *World Affairs*, 105 (1942), 7–12.

———, "The British Commonwealth in the Next World Order," *Annals of the American Academy of Political and Social Science*, 228 (1943), 65–70.

———, "Angell Sums Up at 85—Urges Union of the West," *Freedom & Union*, 13/12 (December 1958), 7–11.

Arendt, Hannah, *The Origins of Totalitarianism* (New York: Harcourt, Brace, 1985 [1951]).

———, *The Origins of Totalitarianism* (New York: Schocken, 2000 [1954]).

———, *On Violence* (New York: Mariner, 1970).

Arnold, Edwin, "The Duty and Destiny of England in India," *North American Review*, 154/423 (1892), 168–88.

Arnold, Thomas, *Postscript to Principles of Church Reform* (London: Fellowes, 1833).

———, "The Church and the State" [1839], in *The Miscellaneous Works of Thomas Arnold . . . Collected and Republished*, ed. Arthur Stanley (London: Fellowes, 1845), 466–75.

———, "National Church Establishments" [1840], in *Miscellaneous Works of Thomas Arnold*, ed. Stanley, 486–92.

———, "Democracy" [1861], *Culture and Anarchy and Other Writings*, ed. Stefan Collini (Cambridge: Cambridge University Press, 1993), 1–25.

Austin, John, *The Province of Jurisprudence Determined* (London: John Murray, 1832).

Bagehot, Walter, "Sir George Cornewall Lewis" [1863], in *Biographical Studies*, 2nd ed., ed. Richard Holt (London: Longmans, 1889).

———, "The Meaning and the Value of the Limits of the Principle of Nationalities"

[1864], in *The Collected Works of Walter Bagehot*, ed. Norman St. John-Stevas (London: Routledge, 1965–86), 8:149–53.

———, *The English Constitution* [1867], ed. Paul Smith (Cambridge: Cambridge University Press, 2001).

———, "An Anglo-Saxon Alliance" [1875], *Collected Works*, 8:335–39.

Balfour, Arthur, *Decadence* (Cambridge: Cambridge University Press, 1908).

Baring, Evelyn, *Ancient and Modern Imperialism* (London: John Murray, 1910).

Barker, Ernest, *Political Thought in England from Herbert Spencer to the Present Day* (London: Williams, 1915).

———, "Democracy since the War and Its Prospects for the Future," *International Affairs*, 13 (1934), 751–71.

Beard, Charles, "Review of *The Crisis of Liberalism*, by J. A. Hobson; *Liberalism and the Social Problem*, by Winston Spencer Churchill," *Political Science Quarterly*, 25 (1910), 529–31.

Benn, A. W., *The History of English Rationalism in the Nineteenth Century*, 2 vols. (London: Longmans, 1906).

Bentham, Jeremy, "Emancipate Your Colonies!" [1793/1830], in *Rights, Representation, and Reform: Nonsense upon Stilts and Other Writings on the French Revolution*, ed. Philip Schofield, Catherine Pease-Watkin, and Cyprian Blamires (Oxford: Oxford University Press, 2002), 289–90.

Beresford, Charles, "The Future of the Anglo-Saxon Race," *North American Review*, 171 (1900), 802–10.

Berlin, Isaiah, "Political Ideas in the Twentieth Century," *Foreign Affairs*, 28 (1950), 351–85.

———, "Two Concepts of Liberty" [1958], in *Liberty*, ed. David Miller (Oxford: Oxford University Press, 1991), 33–57.

Besant, Walter, "The Future of the Anglo-Saxon Race," *American Review*, 163 (1896), 129–43.

———, *The Future of the Empire* (London: Marshall, 1897).

Blease, W. Lyon, *A Short History of English Liberalism* (London: Unwin, 1913).

Bluntschli, Johann, *The Theory of the State*, trans. D. G. Ritchie, P. E. Matheson, and R. Lodge (Oxford: Clarendon, 1885).

Bolingbroke, Viscount Henry St. John, *The Idea of a Patriot King* [1738], in *Bolingbroke's Political Writings*, ed. Bernard Cottret (London: Houndmills, 1997), 329–421.

Borgese, G. A., *Foundations of a World Republic* (Chicago: University of Chicago Press, 1953).

Brabazon, Reginald, "State-Directed Colonization," *National Review*, 9 (1887), 525–37.

Bradley, F. H., *Ideals of Religion* (London: Macmillan, 1940).

Bradshaw, W. J., "Imperial Federation," in London Chamber of Commerce, *England and Her Colonies* (London: Swan Sonnenschein, 1887), 73–89.

Brassey, Lord, "On Work and Wages in Australia," in *Papers and Addresses of Lord Brassey*, ed. Arthur H. Loring and R. J. Beardon (London, 1895), 235–47.

Bridges, Horace, *Some Outlines of the Religion of Experience* (London: Macmillan Books, 1916).

Bridges, Horace, Stanton Coit, G. E. O'Dell, and Harry Snell, *The Ethical Movement: Its Principles and Aims* (London: Union of Ethical Societies, 1911).

Brown, Ivor, *English Political Theory* (London: Methuen, 1920).

Browning, Robert, *Poetical Works*, ed. Ian Jack (Oxford: Oxford University Press, 1970).

Bryce, James "An Age of Discontent," *Contemporary Review*, 49 (1891), 14–29.

——, "Edward Augustus Freeman," *English Historical Review*, 7 (1892), 497–509.

——, "The Essential Unity of England and America," *Atlantic Monthly*, 82 (1898), 22–29.

——, "The Ancient Roman Empire and the British Empire in India," in *Studies in History and Jurisprudence* (Oxford: Clarendon, 1901), 1:1–84.

Buckle, George, ed., *The Letters of Queen Victoria, 1879–1885*, 2nd series, vol. 3 (London: John Murray, 1926).

Bull, Hedley, "What Is the Commonwealth," *World Politics*, 11 (1959), 577–87.

Burke, Edmund, "Opening of Impeachment" [February 16, 1788], in *The Writings and Speeches of Edmund Burke: Vol. VI, India: The Launching of the Hastings Impeachment 1786–1788*, ed. P.J. Marshall (Oxford: Oxford University Press, 1991), 312–73.

——, "Speech on Conciliation with America," in *The Writings and Speeches of Edmund Burke*, ed. Warren Elofson and John A. Woods (Oxford: Oxford University Press, 1996), 3:102–69.

Burrows, Montague, "Imperial Federation," *National Review*, 4 (1884–85), 365–80.

Burton, E., "Federation and Pseudo-Federation," *Law Quarterly Review*, 5 (1889), 170–78.

Burton-Adams, George, *The British Empire and a League of Peace; Suggesting the Purpose and Form of an Alliance of the English-Speaking Peoples* (New York: Putnam, 1919).

Bury, John Bagnell, "Inaugural Speech" [March 15, 1869], *Proceedings of the Royal Colonial Institute*, vol. 1 (1869–70), 51–62.

——, "The British Empire and the Roman Empire," *Saturday Review*, June 27, 1896.

——, *The Idea of Progress: An Inquiry into Its Origin and Growth* (London: Macmillan, 1920).

——, *Selected Essays of J. B. Bury*, ed. Howard Temperley (Cambridge: Cambridge University Press, 1930).

C.R.M., "The Late Professor E. A. Freeman and His Services to Geography," *Proceedings of the Royal Geographical Society*, 14 (1892), 401–4.

Cairnes, J. E., "Colonization and Colonial Government," *Political Essays* (London: Macmillan, 1873), 1–58.

Caldecott, Alfred, *English Colonization and Empire* (London: J. Murray, 1891).

——, *The Philosophy of Religion in England and America* (London: Methuen, 1901).

Campbell Fraser, A., *Locke* (Edinburgh: Blackwood, 1890).

Carnegie, Andrew, "Imperial Federation: An American View," *Nineteenth Century*, 30 (1891), 490–508.

——, *The Reunion of Britain and America: A Look Ahead* (Edinburgh: Andrew Elliott, 1893).

————, "The Venezuelan Question," *North American Review*, 162 (1896), 129–44.

————, "Distant Possessions: The Parting of the Ways," *North American Review*, 167/501 (1898), 239–48.

————, "Americanism versus Imperialism," *North American Review*, 162 (1899), 129–44.

Carr, Edward Hallett, *The Twenty Years' Crisis, 1919–1939: An Introduction to the Study of International Relations* (London: Macmillan, 1939).

Catlin, George, *The Anglo-Saxon Tradition* (London: Kegan, 1939).

————, *The Story of the Political Philosophers* (New York: McGraw-Hill, 1939).

Chamberlain, Joseph, "The True Conception of the Empire," in *Mr Chamberlain's Speeches*, vol. 2, ed. Charles W. Boyd (London: Constable, 1896), 1–6.

————, *The Life of Joseph Chamberlain* [1902], ed. Garvin and Amery (London: Macmillan, 1968).

Cheng, Seymour, *Schemes for the Federation of the British Empire* (New York: Columbia University Press, 1931).

Churchill, Winston, *A History of the English-Speaking Peoples*, vols. 1–4 (London: Cassell, 1956–58).

Clarke, G. S., "Imperial Responsibilities a National Gain," *North American Review*, 168 (1899), 129–41.

Cobden, Richard, "How Wars Are Got Up in India: The Origin of the Burmese War," in *Writings of Richard Cobden* (London: Unwin, 1886), 397–460.

Coit, Stanton, *National Idealism and a State Church: A Constructive Essay on Religion* (London: Williams and Norgate, 1907).

Coker, Francis, "Some Present-Day Critics of Liberalism," *American Political Science Review*, 47 (1953), 1–27.

Cole, Robert, *The Struggle for Empire: A Story of the Year 2236* [1900], in *Political Future Fiction, Vol. 1: The Empire of the Future*, ed. Kate MacDonald (London: Pickering and Chatto, 2013).

Coleridge, Samuel Taylor, *On the Idea of the Constitution of the Church and State* (London: Hurst, Chance, 1830).

Collingwood, Robin George, "Translator's Preface," in *The History of European Liberalism* [1927], by Guido De Ruggiero, trans. R. G. Collingwood (Boston: Beacon, 1959), vii-viii.

————, "Review," *English Historical Review*, 43/186 (1931), 461–65.

Colomb, John, "A Survey of Existing Conditions," in *Britannic Confederation*, ed. White, (London: Council of the Royal Scottish Geographical Society, 1892), 1–31.

Comte, Auguste, *System of Positive Polity*, ed. and trans. Richard Congreve, 4 vols. (London: Longmans, 1877 [1854]).

Congreve, Richard, et al., *International Policy* (London: Chapman and Hall, 1866).

Conrad, Joseph, "An Outpost of Progress" [1896–97], in *Heart of Darkness, and Other Tales*, ed. Cedric Watts (Oxford: Oxford University Press, 2002), 1–26.

————, *Heart of Darkness*, ed. Ross Murfin, 2nd ed. (London: St. Martins, 1996).

Constant, Benjamin, "The Spirit of Conquest and Usurpation and Their Relation to European Civilization" [1814], in *Political Writings*, ed. Biancamaria Fontana (Cambridge: Cambridge University Press, 1988), 51–165.

Conybeare, William John, "Church Parties," *Edinburgh Review*, 98 (1853), 273–342.

Cook, Thomas, *History of Political Philosophy from Plato to Burke* (New York: Prentice-Hall, 1936).

Cornewall Lewis, George, *An Essay on the Government of Dependencies* (London: John Murray, 1841).

Cornish, F. W., *The History of the English Church in the Nineteenth Century*, 2 vols. (London: Macmillan, 1910).

Cotton, Henry, "The Political Future of India," *North American Review*, 181/584 (1905), 110–16.

Craik, Henry, "John Locke," *Quarterly Review*, 169 (1889), 460–91.

Cramb, J. A., *Reflections on the Origins and Destiny of Imperial Britain* (London: Macmillan, 1900).

Cromer, Lord, "History and Politics," *Classical Review*, 24 (1910), 114–16.

Crossman, Richard, *Government and the Governed* (London: Christopher, 1939).

Cunningham, Granville, *A Scheme for Imperial Federation* (London: Longmans, 1895).

Curtis, Lionel, *The Commonwealth of Nations* (London: Macmillan, 1916).

——, *The Problem of Commonwealth* (London: Macmillan, 1916).

——, *Civitas Dei: The Commonwealth of God*, 3 vols. (London: Macmillan, 1937).

——, "World Order," *International Affairs*, 18 (1939), 301–20.

——, "The Fifties as Seen Fifty Years Hence," *International Affairs*, 27 (1951), 273–84.

Curzon, George, *Frontiers* (Oxford: Clarendon, 1907).

Dalton, J. N., "The Federal States of the World," *Nineteenth Century*, 16 (1884), 96–118.

Davidson, William L., *Political Thought in England from Bentham to J. S. Mill* (London: Williams, 1915).

de Labillière, Francis, "Present Aspects of Imperial Federation," *Imperial Federation*, 1 (1886), 5–6.

——, "British Federalism: Its Rise and Progress," *Proceedings of the Royal Colonial Institute*, 24 (1893), 95–120.

——, *Federal Britain, or, Unity and Federation of the Empire* (London: S. Low, 1894).

De Ruggiero, Guido, *The History of European Liberalism* [1927], trans. R. G. Collingwood (Boston: Beacon, 1959).

——, "Liberalism," in *Encyclopaedia of the Social Sciences*, ed. E. R. Seligman, vol. 11 (London: Macmillan, 1933), 276–82.

de Vitoria, Francisco, "On the American Indians (*De Indis*)," in *Francisco de Vitoria: Political Writings*, ed. Anthony Pagden and Jeremy Lawrence (Cambridge: Cambridge University Press, 1991), 231–92.

Deutsch, Karl W., et al., *Political Community and the North Atlantic Area: International Organization in the Light of Historical Experience* (Princeton: Princeton University Press, 1957).

Dewey, John, *Liberalism and Social Action* (New York: Putnam, 1935).

Dicey, Albert Venn, *Lectures Introductory to the Study of the Law of the Constitution* (London: Macmillan, 1885).

——, "A Common Citizenship for the English Race," *Contemporary Review*, 71 (1897), 457–76.

——, *Lectures on the Relation between Law and Public Opinion in England during the Nineteenth Century* [1914], 2nd ed., ed. Richard VandeWetering (Indianapolis: Liberty, 2008).

——, *Introduction to the Study of the Law of the Constitution*, 8th ed. (London: Macmillan, 1915), lxxxiv.

Dilke, Charles, *Greater Britain: A Record of Travel in English-Speaking Countries during 1866 and 1867* (London: Macmillan, 1868).

——, *Problems of Greater Britain* (London: Macmillan, 1890).

——, *The British Empire* (London: Chatto and Windus, 1899).

Doane, William Crosswell, "Patriotism: Its Defects, Its Dangers and Its Duties," *North American Review*, 166 (1898), 310–23.

Doré, Gustave, and Blanchard Jerrold, *London: A Pilgrimage* (London: Grant, 1872).

Dos Passos, John Randolph, *The Anglo-Saxon Century and the Unification of the English-Speaking People*, 2nd ed. (New York: Putnam, 1903).

Douglas, James, *Canadian Independence, Annexation and British Imperial Federation* (New York: G. P. Putnam, 1894).

Doyle, Arthur Conan, *The White Company* (London: Smith, 1891).

——, "The Adventures of the Noble Bachelor," in *The Adventures of Sherlock Holmes* (London: Newnes, 1892), 235–60.

Doyle, J. A., *The English in America*, 5 vols. (London: Longmans, 1882–1907).

——, "Freeman, Froude, Seeley," *Quarterly Review*, 182/364 (1895), 281–305.

Drake, Durant, "Seekers after God," *Harvard Theological Review*, 12/1 (1919), 67–83.

DuBois, W.E.B., *The Souls of Black Folk* (New York: Dover, 1903).

Dulles, John Foster, *War, Peace, and Change* (New York: Harper, 1939).

Dunning, William Archibald, "A Century of Politics," *North American Review*, 179/577 (1904), 801–14.

——, *A History of Political Theories from Luther to Montesquieu* (London: Macmillan, 1905).

Egerton, H. E., *A Short History of British Colonial Policy* (London: Methuen, 1897).

Fanon, Frantz, *The Wretched of the Earth* (London: Penguin, 2001).

Fenn, W. W., "Concerning Natural Religion," *Harvard Theological Review*, 4/4 (1911), 460–76.

Ferguson-Bowen, George, "The Federation of the British Empire," *Proceedings of the Royal Colonial Institute*, 17 (1885–86), 282–315.

Fichte, Johann Gottlieb, *Addresses to the German Nation* [1807–8], ed. Isaac Nakhimovsky, Béla Kapossy, and Keith Tribe (Indianapolis: Hackett, 2013).

Field, G. C., "*The Rise of European Liberalism* by H. J. Laski," *Mind*, 45 (1936), 525–29.

Fisher, H.A.L., "Sir John Seeley," *Fortnightly Review*, 60 (1896), 183–98.

——, *James Bryce*, 2 vols. (London: Macmillan, 1927).

Fiske, John, *American Political Ideas Viewed from the Standpoint of Universal History* (Boston: Houghton Mifflin, 1885).

——, *The Discovery of America*, 2 vols. (Boston: Houghton Mifflin, 1892).

——, "Edward Augustus Freeman," in *A Century of Science and Other Essays* (Boston: Houghton Mifflin, 1899), 265–85.

Fleming, John, "Are We Anglo-Saxons?," *North American Review*, 153 (1891), 253–56.

Forbes, Duncan, *The Liberal Anglican Idea of History* (Cambridge: Cambridge University Press, 1952).

Forbes, Urquhart, "Imperial Federation," *London Quarterly Review*, 4 (1885), 320–35.

Ford, W. C., *The Letters of Henry Adams* (New York: Constable, 1930).

Forster Boulton, A. C., "Liberalism and Empire," *Westminster Review*, 151 (1899), 486–91.

Forster, William Edward, *Our Colonial Empire* (Edinburgh: Edmonston and Douglas, 1875).

———, *Imperial Federation: Report of the Conference Held July 29, 1884, at the Westminster Palace Hotel* (London: Cassell, 1884).

———, "A Few More Words on Imperial Federation," *Nineteenth Century*, 17 (1885), 552–56.

———, "Imperial Federation," *Nineteenth Century*, 17 (1885), 201–18.

Fowler, Thomas, *Locke* (London: Macmillan, 1880).

Fox-Bourne, H. R., *The Life of John Locke* (London: King, 1876).

Freeman, Edward A., "Grote's History of Greece," *North British Review*, 25 (1856), 141–72.

———, *History of Federal Government, from the Foundation of the Achaian League to the Disruption of the United States* (London: Macmillan, 1863).

———, *The History of the Norman Conquest of England, Its Causes and Its Results* (London: Macmillan, 1870).

———, *Comparative Politics: Six Lectures Read before the Royal Institution in January and February 1873* (London: Macmillan, 1873).

———, "An Introduction to American Institutional History," *Johns Hopkins University Studies in Historical and Political Science*, 1/1 (1882), 13–39.

———, *Lectures to American Audiences* (Philadelphia: Porter, 1882).

———, *Some Impressions of the United States* (London: Longmans, Green, 1883).

———, "Imperial Federation," *Macmillan's Magazine*, 51 (1885), 430–35.

———, "George Washington, the Expander of England," in *Greater Greece and Greater Britain* (London: Macmillan, 1886), 62–103.

———, *The Methods of Historical Study* (London: Macmillan, 1886).

———, "Alter Orbis," *Historical Essays*, 4th series (London: Macmillan, 1892), 219–48.

———, "Historical Cycles," in *Historical Essays*, 4th series (London: Macmillan, 1892), 249–58.

———, "The Physical and Political Bases of National Unity," in *Britannic Confederation*, ed. Arthur Silva White (London: Council of the Royal Scottish Geographical Society, 1892), 33–56.

———, "A Review of My Opinions," *The Forum* (1892), 145–57.

———, *History of Federal Government in Greece and Italy*, ed. J. B. Bury (London: Macmillan, 1893).

———, *The Life and Letters of Edward A. Freeman*, 2 vols., ed. W.R.W. Stephens (London: Macmillan, 1895).

Friedrich, Carl, "The Political Thought of Neo-Liberalism," *American Political Science Review*, 49 (1955), 509–25.

Froude, James Anthony, *Shadows of the Clouds* (Farnborough: Gregg, 1847).

————, *Nemesis of Faith* (London: John Chapman, 1849).

————, "England's Forgotten Worthies," *Westminster Review*, 2 (1852), 42–67.

————, "Divus Caesar" [1867], in *Short Studies on Great Subjects* (London: Longmans, 1907), 4:252–91.

————, "The Colonies Once More" [1870], in *Short Studies on Great Subjects* (London: Longmans, 1907), 3:188–223.

————, "England and Her Colonies," *Fraser's Magazine*, 1 (1870), 1–16.

————, "On Progress" [1870], in *Short Studies on Great Subjects* (London: Longmans, Green, 1907), 3:149–87.

————, "Reciprocal Duties of State and Subject," *Fraser's Magazine*, 81 (1870), 285–392.

————, "Calvinism" [1871], in *Short Studies on Great Subjects* (London: Macmillan, 1907), 2:1–51.

————, "England's War," *Fraser's Magazine*, 3 (1871), 135–50.

————, "Leaves from a South African Journal" [1874], in *Short Studies on Great Subjects* (London: Longmans, 1907), 4:358–415.

————, "Party Politics" [1874], in *Short Studies on Great Subjects* (London: Longmans, Green, 1907), 4:322–57.

————, "On the Uses of a Landed Gentry" [1876], in *Short Studies on Great Subjects*, (London: Longmans, Green, 1907), 4:292–321.

————, *Caesar: A Sketch* (London: Longmans, 1879).

————, *Oceana, or England and Her Colonies* (London: Longmans, 1886).

————, *The English in the West Indies, or the Bow of Ulysses* (London: Longmans, 1888).

————, *The Earl of Beaconsfield* (London: S. Low, 1890).

————, "Cheneys and the House of Russell," in *Short Studies on Great Subjects* (London: Longmans, 1907), 5:346–90.

————, "Education," in *Short Studies on Great Subjects* (London: Longmans, Green, 1907), 3:224–57.

————, "Society in Italy in the Last Days of the Roman Republic," in *Short Studies on Great Subjects* (London: Longmans, Green, 1907), 4:191–215.

Gandhi, Mahatma, *Hind Swaraj and Other Writings* [1909], ed. Anthony Parel (Cambridge: Cambridge University Press, 1997).

Gardiner, A. G., *Life of Sir William Harcourt* (London: Constable, 1923).

Gladstone, William, "England's Mission," *Nineteenth Century*, 4 (1878), 560–84.

Glynn, P., *Great Britain and Its Colonies* (Adelaide: W. K. Thomas, 1892).

Goldman, C. S., ed., *The Empire and the Century, A Series of Essays on Imperial Problems and Possibilities* (London: John Murray, 1905).

Gooch, George P., *The History of English Democratic Ideas in the Seventeenth Century* (Cambridge: Cambridge University Press, 1898).

————, "Imperialism," in *The Heart of Empire*, ed. C.F.G Masterman (London: Unwin, 1901), 309–63.

————, *History and Historians in the Nineteenth Century* (London: Longmans, Green, 1920).

Gore, Charles, *Christ and Society: The Halley Stewart Lectures* (London: Allen and Unwin, 1928).

Graham, William, *English Political Philosophy from Hobbes to Maine* (London: Arnold, 1899).

Green, John Richard, *A Short History of the English People* [1874] (London: Harper, 1878).

Green, Thomas Hill, "Introduction to Hume's Treatise of Human Nature" [1874], *Collected Works*, 1:1–13.

———, "Against Disraeli's Foreign Policy" [1878], *Collected Works*, 5:313–17.

———, "National Loss and Gain under a Conservative Government" [1879], *Collected Works*, 5:347–55.

———, "Lecture on Liberal Legislation and Freedom of Contract" [1880], *Collected Works*, 3:365–86.

———, *Prolegomena to Ethics* [1883], *Collected Works*, 3:160–314.

———, *Lectures on the Principles of Political Obligation* [1886] (Bristol: Thoemmes, 1997).

———, *Lectures on the Principles of Political Obligation, and Other Writings*, ed. Paul Harris and John Morrow (Cambridge: Cambridge University Press, 1986).

———, "Can Interference with Foreign Nations in Any Case Be Justifiable?," *Collected Works* (Bristol: Thoemmes, 1997), 5:15–19.

———, *Collected Works of T. H. Green*, ed. Peter Nicholson (Bristol: Thoemmes, 1997).

———, "Loyalty," *Collected Works* (Bristol: Thoemmes, 1997), 5:12–14.

———, "Mr Herbert Spencer and Mr G. H. Lewes: Their Application of the Doctrine of Evolution to Thought," *Collected Works* (Bristol: Thoemmes, 1997) 1:373–541.

Greswell, William, "Imperial Federation: Prize Essay," in London Chamber of Commerce, *England and Her Colonies* (London: Swan Sonnenschein, 1887), 1–42.

Grey, Earl, "How Shall We Retain the Colonies?," *Nineteenth Century*, 5 (1879), 935–54.

Grote, George, "Institutions of Ancient Greece," *Westminster Review*, 5 (1826), 269–331.

Guizot, François, *General History of Civilization in Europe* [1828], ed. G. Knight (New York: Appleton, 1896).

Hallowell, John, *The Decline of Liberalism as an Ideology* (Berkeley: University of California Press, 1943).

———, *Main Currents in Modern Political Thought* (New York: Holt, 1950).

Hammond, J. L., "Colonial and Foreign Policy," in *Liberalism and the Empire*, by F. W. Hirst, Gilbert Murray, and J. L. Hammond, (London: R. B. Johnson, 1899), 158–211.

Harrington, James, *The Commonwealth of Oceana, and, A System of Politics* [1656], ed. J.G.A. Pocock (Cambridge: Cambridge University Press, 1992).

Harrison, Benjamin, "Musings upon Current Topics II," *North American Review*, 172 (1901), 352–66.

Harrison, Frederic, "Our Venetian Constitution" *Fortnightly Review*, 7 (1867), 261–83.

———, "Empire and Humanity," *Fortnightly Review*, 27/158 (1880), 288–308.

———, *Studies in Early Victorian Literature* (London: Edward Arnold, 1895).

———, "The Modern Machiavelli," *Nineteenth Century*, 42/247 (1897), 462–71.

Hartz, Louis, *The Liberal Tradition in America* (New York: Harcourt, 1955).

———, ed., *The Founding of New Societies* (New York: Harcourt, 1964).

Haultain, Arnold, ed., *A Selection from Goldwin Smith's Correspondence* (London: Werner Laurie, 1910).

Hayek, Friedrich A., "Liberalism" [1973], in *New Studies in Philosophy, Politics, Economics and the History of Ideas* (London: Routledge, 1978), 119–51.

Hazeltine, Mayo, "The United States and Great Britain: A Reply to Mr. David A. Wells," *North American Review*, 162 (1896), 594–606.

Henley, William Ernest, "Epilogue" [1897], in *Poems* (London: Macmillan, 1926), 241.

Herkless, John L., "Introduction" to *Sir John Robert Seeley* [1912], by Gustav Adolf Rein, trans. Herkless (Wolfeboro, NH Longwood Academic, 1987), i-xxiv.

Hirst, F. W., Gilbert Murray, and J. L. Hammond, *Liberalism and the Empire* (London: R. B. Johnson, 1900).

Hobhouse, Leonard T., *Mind in Evolution* (London: Macmillan, 1901).

———, "Democracy and Empire," *Speaker*, October 18, 1902.

———, "The Growth of Imperialism," *Speaker*, January 25, 1902.

———, *Democracy and Reaction* [1904], ed. Peter Clarke (Brighton: Harvester, 1972).

———, *Morals in Evolution: A Study in Comparative Ethics*, 2 vols. (London: Chapman and Hall, 1906).

———, *Liberalism and Other Writings* [1911], ed. James Meadowcroft (Cambridge: Cambridge University Press, 1994).

———, *Social Evolution and Political Theory* (New York: Columbia University Press, 1911).

———, *Development and Purpose: An Essay Towards a Philosophy of Evolution* (London: Macmillan, 1913).

———, *The Metaphysical Theory of the State* [1918] (London: Allen and Unwin, 1960).

Hobsbawm, Eric, *The Age of Empire, 1875–1914* (London: Abacus, 1987).

Hobson, John A., *The Psychology of Jingoism* (London: Richards, 1901).

———, *The War in South Africa: Its Causes and Effects* (London: Nisbet, 1901).

———, *Imperialism: A Study* (London: Allen and Unwin, 1902).

———, *Imperialism: A Study* [1902], ed. Philip Siegelman (Ann Arbor: University of Michigan Press, 1997).

———, *Canada To-Day* (London: T. Fisher Unwin, 1906).

———, *The Crisis of Liberalism* (London: King, 1909).

———, *International Government* (London: George Allen and Unwin, 1915).

———, *The Morals of Economic Internationalism* (Boston: Houghton Mifflin, 1920).

———, *Confessions of an Economic Heretic* (London: Allen and Unwin, 1938).

———, "Thoughts on Our Present Discontents," *Political Quarterly*, 9 (1938), 47–57.

Holland, Bernard, *Imperium et Libertas: A Study in History and Politics* (London: Edward Arnold, 1901).

Hume, David, "Hume's Early Memoranda, 1729–1740: The Complete Text," ed. E. C. Mossner, *Journal of the History of Ideas*, 9 (1948), 492–518.

Hutchins, Robert M., Mortimer J. Adler, Erich Kahler, and Robert Redfield, *Preliminary Draft of a World Constitution* (Chicago: University of Chicago Press, 1948).

Ireland, W. Alleyne, "The Growth of the British Colonial Conception," *Atlantic Monthly* (April 1899), 488–98.

———, "The Victorian Era of British Expansion," *North American Review*, 172/533 (1901), 560–72.

James, Henry, *The Letters of Henry James*, ed. Percy Lubbock, 2 vols. (New York: Charles Scribner's, 1920).

James, William, *The Varieties of Religious Experience* (London: Longmans, 1902).

Jebb, Caroline, *The Life and Letters of Sir Richard Claverhouse Jebb* (Cambridge: Cambridge University Press, 1907).

Jebb, Richard, "Imperial Organization," in *The Empire and the Century*, ed. Goldman, 332–48.

Jenkins, Edward, "An Imperial Confederation," *Contemporary Review*, 17 (1871), 60–79.

———, "Imperial Federalism," *Contemporary Review*, 16 (1871), 165–88.

Jenkyns, Henry, *British Rule and Jurisdiction beyond the Seas* (Oxford: Clarendon Press, 1902).

Jones, Henry Ford, *The Natural History of the State: An Introduction to Political Science* (Princeton: Princeton University Press, 1916).

Kant, Immanuel, "Idea for a Universal History with a Cosmopolitan Purpose" [1784], in *Kant, Political Writings*, ed. Hans Reiss (Cambridge: Cambridge University Press, 1990), 41–54.

King, Lord, *The Life of John Locke* (London: Colburn, 1830).

Kipling, Rudyard, "Deep-Sea Cables" [1896], in *Rudyard Kipling's Verse, 1885–1932* (London: Hodder and Stoughton, 1932), 173.

———, "Recessional," *Times*, July 17, 1897.

———, *Something of Myself for My Friends Known and Unknown* (London: Macmillan, 1937).

Lamprecht, Sterling, *The Moral and Political Philosophy of John Locke* (New York: Columbia University Press, 1918).

Laski, Harold J., *Political Thought in England from Locke to Bentham* (London: Williams, 1920).

———, *A Grammar of Politics* [1925] (London: Allen and Unwin, 1926).

———, *The Rise of European Liberalism* (London: Allen and Unwin, 1936).

Lawrence, Thomas Joseph, *Essays on Some Disputed Questions in Modern International Law* [1884], 2nd ed. (Cambridge: Deighton, Bell, 1885).

Lecky, William E. H., *The Empire: Its Value and Growth* (London: Longmans, 1893).

Leighton, Joseph Alexander, *Social Philosophies in Conflict* (New York: Appleton, 1937).

Lenin, Vladimir Illich, *Imperialism, The Highest Stage of Capitalism* [1917], in *Selected Works* (Moscow: Progress, 1963), 1:667–766.

Leuba, J. H., "The Psychological Nature of Religion," *American Journal of Theology*, 13/1 (1909), 77–85.

Lippmann, Walter, *US Foreign Policy: Shield of the Republic* (Boston: Little Brown, 1943).

Little, James Stanley, *The United States of Britain* (Guilford: Billing, 1887).

————, *Progress of British Empire in the Century* (London, 1903).

Lodge, Henry Cabot, "England, Venezuela, and the Monroe Doctrine," *North American Review*, 160 (1895), 651–58.

Lowe, Robert, "The Value to the United Kingdom of the Foreign Dominions of the Crown," *Fortnightly Review*, 22 (1877), 618–30.

————, "Imperialism," *Fortnightly Review*, 24 (1878), reprinted in *Empire and Imperialism: The Debate of the 1870s*, ed. P. J. Cain (Bristol: Thoemmes, 1999).

Lucas, C. P., ed., *Lord Durham's Report on the Affairs of British North America* [1839] (Oxford: Clarendon Press, 1912).

————, "Introduction" to *An Essay on the Government of Dependencies* by George Cornewall Lewis (Oxford: Clarendon, 1891), vii–lxvii.

————, *Greater Rome and Greater Britain* (Oxford: Clarendon, 1912).

Macaulay, Thomas Babington, "Speech on the Renewal of the East India Company Charter" [July 10, 1833], reprinted in *The Complete Works* (London: Longmans, Green, 1898–1906), 111–42.

————, "Minute of 2 February 1835 on Indian Education" [1835], in *Macaulay, Prose and Poetry*, ed. G. M. Young (Cambridge, MA: Harvard University Press, 1957), 721–24.

————, "Sir James Mackintosh" [1835], in *Critical and Historical Essays* (London: Longman, 1848) 200–279.

————, "Ranke's History of the Popes" [1840], in *Critical and Historical Essays*, ed. A. J. Grieve (London: Everyman, 1907), 2:38–72.

MacDonald, Ramsay, *Labour and the Empire* (London: George Allen, 1907).

Macdonell, Philip J., "Historic Bases of Liberalism," in *Essays in Liberalism* (London: Cassell, 1897), 219–76.

Macfie, Andrew Robert, "On the Crisis of the Empire: Imperial Federation," *Proceedings of the Royal Colonial Institute*, 3 (1871–72), 2–12.

Machiavelli, Niccolo, *Discourses on Livy*, ed. Julia Conaway Bondanella and Peter Bondanella (Oxford: Oxford University Press, 1997).

Mackinder, Halford, "The Geographical Pivot of History," *Geographical Journal*, 23 (1904), 421–37.

Macpherson, Crawford Brough, "The History of Political Ideas," *Canadian Journal of Economics and Political Science*, 7 (1941), 564–77.

————, "*Main Currents in Modern Political Thought* by John H. Hallowell," *Western Political Quarterly*, 4 (1951), 145–46.

————, *The Political Theory of Possessive Individualism* (Oxford: Clarendon, 1962).

Mahan, Alfred T., and Charles Beresford, "Possibilities of an Anglo-American Reunion," *North American Review*, 159 (1894), 551–73.

Maine, Henry S., *Village Communities in the East and West*, 3rd ed. (London: Murray, 1876).

————, *International Law: A Series of Lectures Delivered before the University of Cambridge, 1887* (London: John Murray, 1888).

————, *Ancient Law* [1861] (London: Murray, 1908).

Maitland, Frederick William, *The Constitutional History of England* (Cambridge: Cambridge University Press, 1908).

————, *A Historical Sketch of Liberty and Equality* [1875] (Indianapolis: Liberty, 2000).

Martin, Boyd, "Liberalism," *Western Political Quarterly*, 1 (1948), 295–97.

Martineau, John, "New Zealand and Our Colonial Empire," *Quarterly Review*, (1870), 134–62.

Marx, Karl, *Capital*, vol. 1, in *Collected Works*, by Marx and Engels (London: Lawrence and Wishart, 1975).

Marx, Karl, and Friedrich Engels, *The Communist Manifesto* [1848], ed. Stedman Jones (Harmondsworth: Penguin, 2002).

Maurice, Frederick Denison, *The Kingdom of Christ* (London: Darnton and Clark, 1838).

———, *Social Morality* (London: Macmillan, 1869).

———, *The Life of Frederick Denison Maurice* (London: Macmillan, 1884).

Mayer, J. P., *Political Thought: The European Tradition* (London: Dent, 1939).

Mazzini, Guiseppe, "Principles of International Politics" [1871], in *Cosmopolitanism and Nations: Giuseppe Mazzini's Writings on Democracy, Nation Building and International Relations*, ed. Stefano Recchia and Nadia Urbinati (Princeton: Princeton University Press, 2009), 224–41.

McGiffert, Arthur, *The Rise of Modern Religious Ideas* (London: Macmillan, 1915).

McLachlan, Jean, "The Origin and Early Development of the Cambridge Historical Tripos," *American Historical Review*, 9 (1947), 78–105.

Mead, Edwin, "The United States as a World Power," *The Advocate of Peace*, 75 (1913), 57–62.

Merivale, Herman, *Lectures on Colonisation and Colonies*, 2 vols. (London: Longmans, 1841).

Merriam, Charles, "*Liberalism in America* by Harold Stearns," *American Political Science Review*, 14/3 (1920), 511–12.

Mill, James, "Review of Voyage aux Indes Orientales," by Le P. Paulin De S. Barthélemy, *Edinburgh Review*, 15 (1810), 363–84.

———, "Colony" [1818], in *Essays from the Supplement to the Encyclopaedia Britannica, Collected Works* (London: Thoemmes, 1995), 3–33.

Mill, John Stuart, "The Emigration Bill," *Examiner*, February 27, 1831, *Collected Works*, 22:270–72.

———, "Female Emigrants," *Examiner*, February 26, 1832, *Collected Works*, 23:419–20.

———, "On the Necessity of the Uniting of the Question of Corn Laws with That of the Tithes," *Examiner*, December 23, 1832, *Collected Works*, 23:534–39.

———, "New Australian Colony," *Morning Chronicle*, October 23, 1834, *Collected Works*, 23:749–51.

———, "The New Colony" [2], *Examiner*, July 6, 1834, *Collected Works*, 23:735–36.

———, "De Tocqueville on Democracy in America [I]" [1835], *Collected Works*, 28:47–91.

———, "Civilization" [1836], *Collected Works*, 28:117–49.

———, "Carlyle's French Revolution" (1837), *Collected Works*, 20:131–67.

———, "The Sale of Colonial Land," *Sun*, February 22, 1837, *Collected Works*, 24:791–92.

———, "Lord Durham and His Assailants," *London and Westminster Review* (1838), *Collected Works*, 6:437–44.

————, "Penal Code for India," *London and Westminster Review* (1838), *Collected Works*, 30:17–30.

————, "Radical Party and Canada: Lord Durham and the Canadians," *London and Westminster Review* (1838), *Collected Works*, 6:405–36.

————, "Coleridge" [1840], *Collected Works*, 10:117–64.

————, *A System of Logic, Ratiocinative and Deductive, Being a Connected View of the Principles of Evidence and the Methods of Scientific Investigation* [1843], *Collected Works*, 7:861–75.

————, "Torrens's Letter to Sir Robert Peel," *Spectator*, January 28, 1843, *Collected Works*, 24:836–40.

————, "Wakefield's 'The New British Province of South Australia,'" *Examiner*, July 20, 1843, *Collected Works*, 23:738–42.

————, "The Claims of Labour," *Edinburgh Review* [1845], *Collected Works*, 4:363–90.

————, "The Condition of Ireland [25]," *Morning Chronicle*, December 2, 1846, *Collected Works*, 24:972–75.

————, *Principles of Political Economy* [1848], *Collected Works*, vol. 3.

————, "Grote's *History of Greece*," vol. 2 [1853], *Collected Works*, 11:271–306.

————, "A Few Words on Non-Intervention" [1859], *Collected Works*, 21:111–24.

————, "Grote's History of Greece [IV]," *Spectator*, March 10, 1859, *Collected Works*, 25:1128–35.

————, *On Liberty* [1859], *Collected Works*, 18:213–310.

————, *Considerations on Representative Government* [1861], *Collected Works*, 18:371–72.

————, *The Subjection of Women* [1869], *Collected Works*, 21:259–340.

————, *Autobiography* [1873], *Collected Works*, 1:4–290.

————, *The Collected Works of John Stuart Mill*, ed. John Robson (Toronto: University of Toronto Press, 1963–91).

————, "Use and Abuse of Political Terms," *Collected Works*, 18:1–14.

Miller, J.D.B., "The Utopia of Imperial Federation," *Political Studies*, 4 (1956), 195–97.

Mills, Arthur, *Systematic Colonization* (London: John Murray, 1847).

————, *Colonial Constitutions* (London: John Murray, 1856).

Mills, Charles Wright, *The Marxists* (Harmondsworth: Penguin, 1963).

Mills, Richard, *The Colonization of Australia (1829–1842)* [1915] (London: Dawsons, 1968).

Milner, Alfred, "Credo," *Times*, July 25, 1925.

Minogue, Kenneth R., *The Liberal Mind* (London: Methuen, 1962).

Mises, Ludwig von, *Liberalism* (Indianapolis: Liberty Fund, 2005).

Monypenny, W. F., "The Imperial Ideal," in *The Empire and the Century*, ed. Charles Sydney Goldman (London: John Murray, 1905), 5–28.

Monypenny, W. F., and G. E. Buckle, *The Life of Benjamin Disraeli*, 6 vols. (London: John Murray, 1910–20).

Morley, John, *The Life of Richard Cobden*, 2 vols. (London: Macmillan, 1881).

————, "The Expansion of England," *Macmillan's Magazine*, 49 (1884), 241–58.

————, *On Compromise* [1874], 2nd ed. (London: Macmillan, 1886).

————, *The Life of William Ewart Gladstone* (London: Macmillan, 1903).

————, "Democracy and Reaction" [1904], *Critical Miscellanies* (London: Macmillan, 1908), 4:267–328.

Morley, John, *Recollections*, 2 vols. (London: Macmillan, 1917).

Mortimer-Franklyn, H., *Imperial Federation League in Canada* (Montreal, 1885).

————, *The Unit of Imperial Federation* (London: Swan Sonnerchein, 1887).

Muirhead, J. H., "What Imperialism Means," *Fortnightly Review*, 68 (1900), reprinted in *The British Idealists*, ed. David Boucher (Cambridge: Cambridge University Press, 1997), 237–52.

Müller, Max, *India, What Can It Teach Us?* (London: Longmans, 1883).

Murphy, Arthur, "Ideals and Ideologies, 1917–1947," *Philosophical Review*, 56 (1947), 374–89.

Murray, Gilbert, "The Exploitation of Inferior Races in Ancient and Modern Times," in *Liberalism and the Empire*, by F. W. Hirst, Gilbert Murray, and J. L. Hammond (London: R. B. Johnson, 1899), 118–57.

Murray, Robert, *The History of Political Science from Plato to the Present* (Cambridge: Heffer, 1926).

Nettleship, R. L., "Memoir" [1888], in *Works of Thomas Hill Green*, vol. 3, ed. Richard Lewis Nettleship, (London, 1885–88), xi-clxi.

Newman, John Henry, "An Internal Argument for Christianity" [1866], in *Discussions and Arguments on Various Subjects*, 4th ed. (London: Pickering, 1882), 363–98.

Niebuhr, Reinhold, "Liberalism," *New Republic*, July 4, 1955, 11–13.

Oakeshott, Michael, ed., *The Social and Political Doctrines of Contemporary Europe* (Cambridge: Cambridge University Press, 1939).

Oliver, Frederick Scott, *Alexander Hamilton: An Essay on American Union* (London: Constable, 1906).

Oman, Charles William, *England in the Nineteenth-Century* (London: Edward Arnold, 1899).

Parker, Joseph, *Ecce Deus: Essays on the Life and Doctrine of Jesus Christ* (Boston: Roberts, 1868).

Parkin, George, *Imperial Federation: The Problem of National Unity* (London: Macmillan, 1892).

————, *The Rhodes Scholarship* (London: Constable, 1912).

Parmlees, M., "Liberal Democracy, Fascism, and Bolshevism," *Annals of the American Academy of Political and Social Science*, 180 (1935), 47–54.

Parrington, Vernon, *Main Currents in American Thought*, 3 vols. (New York: Harcourt-Brace, 1927–30).

Pattison, Mark, "Philosophy at Oxford," *Mind*, 1 (1876), 82–97.

Pearson, Charles H., *National Life and Character: A Forecast* (London: Macmillan, 1894).

Peterson, W., "The Future of Canada," in *The Empire and the Century*, ed. Charles Sydney Goldman (London: John Murray, 1905), 363–84.

Plamenatz, John, *On Alien Rule and Self-Government* (London: Longmans, 1960).

Platt, Charles Malcolm, "A Triad of Political Conceptions: State, Sovereign, Government," *Political Science Quarterly*, 10 (1895), 292–323.

Polanyi, Karl, *The Great Transformation: The Political and Economic Origins of Our Time* (Boston: Beacon, 1944).

Pollock, Frederick, *An Introduction to the History of the Science of Politics* (London: Macmillan, 1890).

———, "Locke's Theory of the State," *Proceedings of the British Academy*, (1903–4), 80–102.

———, "The Social Contract in Hobbes and Locke," *Journal of the Society of Comparative Legislation* (1907), reprinted in *Essays in the Law*, by Frederick Pollock (London: Macmillan, 1922), 80–109.

Rashdall, H., "Professor Sidgwick on the Ethics of Religious Conformity," *International Journal of Ethics*, 7/2 (1897), 137–68.

———, *Philosophy and Religion* (London: Duckworth, 1909).

Redpath Dougall, John, "An Anglo-Saxon Alliance," *Contemporary Review*, 48 (1885), 693–706.

Rhodes, Cecil, *The Last Will and Testament of Cecil J. Rhodes*, ed. W. T. Stead (London: Review of Reviews, 1902).

Ritchie, D. G., *Principles of State Interference* (London: Swan, 1891).

———, "Review of Henry Sidgwick, *The Elements of Politics*," *International Journal of Ethics*, 2 (1891–92), 254–57.

———, "The Teaching of Political Science at Oxford," *Annals of the American Academy of Political and Social Science*, 2 (1891), 85–95.

———, *Natural Rights: A Criticism of Some Political and Ethical Conceptions* (London: Swan, 1895).

———, review of *Political Science*, *International Journal of Ethics*, 7/1 (1896), 114–16.

———, "War and Peace," *International Journal of Ethics*, 11 (1901), 137–58.

Robertson, J. M., *An Introduction to English Politics* (London: G. Richards, 1900).

———, *Patriotism and Empire*, 3rd ed. (London: Grant Richards, 1900).

———, "The Moral Problems of War," *International Journal of Ethics*, 11/3 (1901), 273–90.

Robinson, John, "The Future of the British Empire," *Westminster Review*, 38 (1870), 47–74.

Rockow, Lewis, *Contemporary Political Thought in England* (London: Parsons, 1925).

Roebuck, John Arthur, *The Colonies of England: A Plan for the Government of Portion of Our Colonial Possessions* [*sic*] (London: Parker, 1849).

Ruskin, John, *The Works of John Ruskin*, 39 vols., ed. E. T. Cook and A. Wedderburn (London: George Allen, 1903–12).

Russell, Bertrand, *History of Western Philosophy* (London: Unwin, 1945/1948).

———, "Hopes: Realized and Disappointed," in *Portraits from Memory and Other Essays* (London: Simon and Schuster, 1956), 45–50.

Russett, Bruce, *Community and Contention: Britain and America in the Twentieth Century* (Cambridge, MA: MIT Press, 1963).

Sabine, George H., *A History of Political Theory* (London: Harrap, 1937).

———, "The Historical Position of Liberalism," *American Scholar*, 10 (1940–41), 49–58.

———, "*The Political Tradition of the West: A Study in the Development of Modern Liberalism* by Frederick Watkins," *Political Science Quarterly*, 64 (1949), 147–49.

Salmon, Edward, "The Crown and the Colonies," *National Review*, 14 (1889–90), 200–207.

————, "The Colonial Empire of 1837," *Fortnightly Review*, 61 (1897), 862–70.

————, "Imperial Federation: The Condition of Progress," *Fortnightly Review*, 58 (1900), 1009–19.

Samuel, Herbert, *Liberalism: An Attempt to State the Principles of Contemporary Liberalism in England* (London: Grant Richards, 1902).

Schumpeter, Joseph, *Imperialism: Social Classes: Two Essays* [1919] (New York: Meridian, 1955).

Seebohm, Frederic, *On International Reform* (London: Longmans, 1871).

————, "Imperialism and Socialism," *Nineteenth Century* (1880), 726–36.

Seeley, John Robert, *Ecce Homo: A Survey of the Life and Work of Jesus Christ* (London: Macmillan, 1866).

————, "English in Schools" [1867], *Lectures and Essays* (London: Macmillan, 1870), 217–44.

————, "Liberal Education in Universities" [1867], *Lectures and Essays* (London: Macmillan, 1870), 182–216.

————, "The Church as a Teacher of Morality," in *Essays in Church Policy*, ed. Walther Clay (London: Macmillan, 1868), 247–91.

————, *David and Samuel; With Other Poems, Original and Translated* (London: Seeley, 1869).

————, "Roman Imperialism" [1869], *Lectures and Essays* (London: Macmillan, 1870), 1–58.

————, "The English Revolution of the Nineteenth Century," pts. 1–3, *Macmillan's Magazine*, 22 (1870), 241–51, 347–58, 441–51.

————, *Lectures and Essays* (London: Macmillan, 1870).

————, "The Teaching of Politics," *Macmillan's Magazine*, 21 (1870), 433–44.

————, "The United States of Europe," *Macmillan's Magazine*, 23 (1871), 436–48.

————, "The Political Education of the Working Classes," *Macmillan's Magazine*, 36, (1877), 143–45.

————, *The Life and Times of Stein, or Germany and Prussia in the Napoleonic Age*, 2 vols. (Cambridge: Cambridge University Press, 1878).

————, "History and Politics," pts. 1–3, *Macmillan's Magazine*, 40 (1879), 289–99, 369–78, 449–58.

————, "Political Somnambulism," *Macmillan's Magazine*, 43 (1880), 28–44.

————, "The British Race" [1872], *Education I*, 4, (1881), 309–28.

————, *Natural Religion* (London: Macmillan, 1882).

————, *The Expansion of England; Two Courses of Lectures* (London: Macmillan, 1883).

————, "Our Insular Ignorance," *Nineteenth Century*, 18 (1885), 861–73.

————, "Introduction," in *Her Majesty's Colonies* (London: William Clowes and Son, 1886), viii–xxvi.

————, "The Journal of the League," *Imperial Federation*, 1/1 (1886), 4–5.

————, "The Object to Be Gained by Imperial Federation," *Imperial Federation*, 1/6 (1886), 205–6.

————, *A Short History of Napoleon the First* (London: Seeley, 1886).

————, "Georgian and Victorian Expansion," *Fortnightly Review*, 48 (1887), 123–39.

————, "A Midlands University," *Fortnightly Review*, 42 (1887), 703–16.

————, "The Eighty-Eights," *Good Words* (1888), 272–360.

————, "The Impartial Study of Politics: Inaugural Address to the Cardiff Society for the Impartial Discussion of Politics and Other Questions, October 18th 1886," *Contemporary Review*, 54 (1888), 52–65.

————, "Ethics and Religion," *Fortnightly Review*, 45 (1889), 501–14.

————, *Introduction to Political Science* [1891], ed. Henry Sidgwick (London: Macmillan, 1919).

————, "Professor Seeley at Cambridge," *Imperial Federation*, 6/6 (1891), 176.

————, *Goethe Reviewed after Sixty Years* (London: Seeley, 1894).

————, *The Growth of British Policy: An Historical Essay* (Cambridge: Cambridge University Press, 1895).

————, "Sir John Seeley and National Unity," letter quoted by H. F. Wilson, *Cambridge Review*, 16 (1895), 197.

————, *Introduction to Political Science: Two Series of Lectures* [1896], ed. Henry Sidgwick (London: Macmillan, 1923).

Seeley, Robert Benton, *Essays on the Church by a Layman* (London: R. B. Seeley and W. Burnside, 1834).

Senior, Nassau, *Remarks on Emigration* (London: R. Clay, 1831).

————, *An Outline of a Science of Political Economy* (London: W. Clowes, 1836).

Shaw, Albert, "An American View of Home Rule and Federation," *Contemporary Review*, 62 (1892), 305–18.

Sibley, N. W., "Edmund Burke," *Westminster Review*, (1897), 496–509.

Sidgwick, Arthur, and Eleanor Mildred Sidgwick, *Henry Sidgwick, A Memoir* (London: Macmillan, 1906).

Sidgwick, Henry, *Principles of Political Economy* (London: Macmillan, 1873).

————, *The Methods of Ethics* [1874], 7th ed. (London: Macmillan, 1907).

————, "Philosophy at Cambridge," *Mind*, 1 (1876), 235–46.

————, "Mr. Spencer's Ethical System," *Mind*, 5 (1880), 216–26.

————, "Green's Ethics," *Mind*, 9 (1884), 169–87.

————, "The Scope and Method of Economic Science" [1885], in *Miscellaneous Essays and Addresses* (London: Macmillan, 1904), 170–99.

————, "The Historical Method," *Mind*, 11/42 (1886), 203–19.

————, *The Elements of Politics* [1891], 2nd ed. (London: Macmillan, 1897).

————, *The Elements of Politics* [1891], 3rd ed. (London: Macmillan, 1907).

————, "Political Prophecy and Sociology" [1894], in *Miscellaneous Essays*, 216–34.

————, "Editor's Preface" to *Introduction to Political Science: Two Series of Lectures* [1896], by J. R. Seeley, ed. Henry Sidgwick (Cambridge: Cambridge University Press, 1923), v-xi.

————, "Public Morality" [1897], in *Practical Ethics: A Collection of Addresses and Essays* (London: Swan Sonnenschein, 1898), 52–82.

————, "The Morality of Strife," in *Practical Ethics A Collection of Addresses and Essays* (London: Swan Sonnenschein, 1898), 83–112.

————, "The Relation of Ethics to Sociology," *International Journal of Ethics*, 10 (1899), 1–21.

————, *Lectures on the Ethics of T. H. Green, Mr. Herbert Spencer and J. Martineau* (London: Macmillan, 1902).

————, *The Development of European Polity*, ed. Eleanor Sidgwick (London: Macmillan, 1903).

Smith, Adam, *An Inquiry into the Nature and Causes of the Wealth of Nations* [1776], ed. R. H. Campbell, Andrew S. Skinner, and W. B. Todd (Oxford: Oxford University Press, 1976).

Smith, Arthur Lionel, "English Political Philosophy in the Seventeenth and Eighteenth Centuries," in *The Cambridge Modern History*, vol. 6, ed. Adolphus W. Ward, George W. Prothero, and Stanley Leathes (Cambridge: Cambridge University Press, 1909), 785–821.

Smith, Goldwin, *The Empire, A Series of Letters Published in "The Daily News," 1862, 1863* (Oxford: J. Henry and J. Parker, 1863).

———, "The Policy of Aggrandizement," *Fortnightly Review*, 22 (1877), 303–24.

———, "The Expansion of England," *Contemporary Review*, 45 (1884), 524–40.

———, "Straining the Silken Thread," *Macmillan's Magazine*, 58 (1888), 241–46.

———, "The Hatred of England," *North American Review*, 150/402 (1890), 547–62.

———, "The Empire," in *Essays on Questions of the Day* [1893], 2nd ed. (New York: Macmillan, 1894), 141–95.

———, "The Manchester School," *Contemporary Review*, 67 (1895), 377–90.

Smith, William Roy, "British Imperial Federation," *Political Science Quarterly*, 36 (1921), 274–97.

Snow, Alpheus Henry, "Neutralization versus Imperialism," *American Journal of International Law*, 2/3 (1908), 569–70.

Sohn, Louis, and Grenville Clark, *World Peace through World Law* (Cambridge, MA: Harvard University Press, 1958).

Somers, Robert, "Emigration" [1878], *Encyclopaedia Britannica*, 9th ed. (London: A. C. and Black, 1875–89), 8:174–76.

Sonenscher, Michael, "Barbarism and Civilisation" in *A Companion to Intellectual History,* ed. Richard Whatmore and Brian Young (Oxford: Blackwell, 2016), 288–302.

Sorel, Georges, *Reflections on Violence* [1908], ed. Jeremy Jennings (Cambridge: Cambridge University Press, 1999).

Sorley, William Ritchie, "John Locke," in *The Cambridge History of English Literature*, ed. Adolphus W. Ward and Alfred Rayney Waller (Cambridge: Cambridge University Press, 1912), 8:328–48.

Spencer, Herbert, *The Proper Sphere of Government* [1842–43], in *Man versus the State: With Six Essays on Government, Society and Freedom* (Indianapolis: Liberty Classics, 1982), 181–264.

———, *Social Statics: Or, the Conditions Essential to Human Happiness Specified, and the First of Them Developed* (London: John Chapman, 1851).

———, *First Principles* (London: Williams and Norgate, 1867).

———, *Principles of Sociology*, 3 vols. (London: Williams and Norgate, 1876–96).

———, *The Man versus the State* [1884] (Indianapolis: Liberty, 1969).

———, *The Principles of Ethics* [1879–93], 2 vols. (Indianapolis: Liberty, 1978).

———, "The Filiation of Ideas" [1899], in *The Life and Letters of Herbert Spencer*, ed. David Duncan (London: Methuen, 1908), 533–76.

———, "Imperialism and Slavery," in *Facts and Comments* (London: Williams and Norgate, 1902), 112–21.

———, "Re-barbarization" and "Regimentation," in *Facts and Comments* (London: Williams and Norgate, 1902), 172–200.

Stead, William Thomas, "The English beyond the Sea," *Pall Mall Gazette*, October 4, 1884, 1.

———, "To All English-Speaking Folks," *Review of Reviews*, 1/1 (1890), 15–20.

———, *The Americanization of the World; Or, the Trend of the Twentieth Century* (London: Horace Markley, 1902).

Stearns, Harold, *Liberalism in America: Its Origins, Its Temporary Collapse, Its Future* (New York: Boni, 1919).

Stephen, James Fitzjames, "Liberalism," *Cornhill Magazine*, 5/25 (1862), 70–83.

———, "Deus Ultionum," *Saturday Review*, October 15, 1867.

———, "Locke on Government" [1867], *Horae Sabbaticae*, vol. 2 (London: Macmillan, 1892), 206–8.

———, *Liberty, Equality, Fraternity* (London: Smith, 1873).

———, "Manchester on India," *Times*, January 4, 1878.

———, "Foundations of the Government of India," *Nineteenth Century*, 14/80 (1883), 541–68.

———, *The Story of Nuncomar and the Impeachment of Sir Elijah Impey* (London: Macmillan, 1885).

Stephen, Leslie, *History of English Thought in the Eighteenth Century* (London: Smith, 1876).

———, "Locke, John (1632–1704)," *The Dictionary of National Biography* (London: Smith, 1893), 34:27–36.

———, *The Life of Sir James Fitzjames Stephen* (London: Smith, Elder, 1895).

Stephens, H. Morse, "Nationality and History," *American Historical Review*, 21/2 (1916), 225–36.

Stokes, Eric, *The English Utilitarians and India* (Oxford: Clarendon Press, 1959).

Strauss, Leo, *Liberalism Ancient and Modern* (Chicago: University of Chicago Press, 1968).

Strauz-Hupe, Robert, James Dougherty, and William Kintner, *Building the Atlantic World* (New York: Harper, 1963).

Streit, Clarence, *Union Now: A Proposal for a Federal Union of Democracies of the North Atlantic* (New York: Harper, 1938).

———, *Union Now with Britain* (New York: Harper, 1941).

———, "Atlantic Union—Freedom's Answer to Malenkov," *Annals of the American Academy of Political and Social Science*, 288 (1953), 2–12.

———, "Lionel Curtis—Prophet of Federal Freedom," *Freedom & Union*, 10 (January 1956), 10.

———, *Freedom's Frontier: Atlantic Union Now* (New York: Harper, 1961).

Stout, Robert, "A Colonial View of Imperial Federation," *Nineteenth Century*, 21 (1887), 351–62.

Stuart-Linton, E. T., *The Problem of Empire Governance* (London: Macmillan, 1912).

Sutherland, John Douglas, Marquis of Lorne, *Imperial Federation* (London: Sonnenschein, 1885).

———, "The Annual Address on the Progress of Geography, 1885–1886," *Proceedings of the Royal Geographical Society*, 8 (1886), 417–36.

Taylor, A.J.P., *The Trouble Makers: Dissent over Foreign Policy 1792–1939* (London: Hamilton, 1957).

Tennyson, Alfred, *Poetical Works, Including the Plays* (Oxford: Oxford University Press, 1953).

Thonton, A. P., *The Imperial Idea and Its Enemies* (London: Macmillan, 1959).

Tocqueville, Alexis de, *Democracy in America* [1835–40], trans. Henry Reeve, 2 vols. (London: Longmans, 1862).

——, "Second Letter on Algeria" [1837], *Writings*, 14–26.

——, "Essay on Algeria (October 1841)," *Writings*, 59–116.

——, "First Report on Algeria" [1847], *Writings*, 129–73.

——, *Writings on Empire and Slavery*, ed. J. Pitts (Baltimore: Johns Hopkins University Press, 2001).

Todd, Alpheus, *On Parliamentary Government in England* [1867] (London: S. Low, 1887).

——, *Parliamentary Government in England: Its Origin, Development and Practical Operation* (London: Longmans, 1867).

——, *Parliamentary Government in the British Colonies* (London: Longmans, 1880).

Torrens, Robert, *Colonisation of South Australia* (London: Longmans, 1835).

——, *Self-Supporting Colonization* (London: J. Ridgeway, 1847).

Tourgée, Albion, "The Twentieth Century Peacemakers," *Contemporary Review*, 75 (1899), 886–908.

Trollope, Anthony, *The New Zealander*, ed. N. J. Hall (Oxford: Clarendon, 1972).

Trotter, L. J., "British India under the Crown," *Contemporary Review*, vol. 15 (1870), 113–32.

Tupper, Sir Charles, "Federating the Empire, A Colonial Plan," *Nineteenth Century*, 30 (1891), 509–20.

Turner, Frederick Jackson, "The Significance of the Frontier in American History" [1893], in *Rereading Frederick Jackson Turner*, ed. J. M. Faragher (London: Yale University Press, 1998), 31–60.

Vaughan, Charles E., *Studies in the History of Political Philosophy*, 2 vols. (Manchester: Manchester University Press, 1925).

Vincent, C. E. Howard, "Inter-British Trade and Its Influence on the Unity of the Empire," *Proceedings of the Royal Colonial Institute*, 22 (1891–92), 265–88.

Voegelin, Eric, "Liberalism and Its History," *Review of Politics*, 36 (1974), 504–20.

Vogel, Julius, "Greater or Lesser Britain," *Nineteenth-Century*, 1 (1877), 809–31.

——, "The British Empire: Mr. Lowe and Lord Blachford," *Nineteenth Century*, 3 (1878), 617–36.

Wakefield, Edward Gibbon, *A Letter from Sydney, the Principal Town in Australasia, Together with the Outline of a System of Colonization*, ed. Robert Gouger (London: Joseph Cross, 1830).

——, *England and America*, 2 vols. (London: R. Bentley, 1833).

——, *A View on the Art of Colonization* [1849], in *The Collected Works of Edward Gibbon Wakefield*, ed. Muriel Florence Lloyd Prichard (Glasgow: Collins, 1968), 758–1040.

Waldstein, Charles, "The English-Speaking Brotherhood," *North American Review*, 167 (1898), 223–38.

Wallace, Edwin, "John Locke," *Westminster Review*, 107 (1877), 163–95.

Wallas, Graham, *Human Nature in Politics*, 3rd ed. (London: Constable, 1909).

Watkins, Frederick M., *The Political Tradition of the West: A Study in the Development of Modern Liberalism* (Cambridge: Harvard University Press, 1948).

Wells, H. G., *The War of the Worlds* (London: William Heinemann, 1898).

———, *Anticipations of the Reaction of Mechanical and Scientific Progress upon Human Life and Thought* [1902] (Mineola, NY: Dover, 1999).

———, *The Outline of History: Being a Plain History of Life and Mankind* (London: Cassell, 1925).

———, *The New America: The New World* (London: Cressett, 1935).

Westgarth, William, "The Unity of the Empire: Federation, Intercolonial and Imperial," *National Review*, 4 (1884), 504–11.

Whatley, Richard, *Letters on the Church, by an Episcopalian* (London: Longmans, 1826).

White, Arthur Silva, "An Anglo-American Alliance," *North American Review*, 158 (1894), 484–93.

———, ed., *Britannic Confederation: A Series of Papers* (London: George Philip, 1892).

Whyte, Frederick, *The Life of W. T. Stead*, 2 vols. (London: Jonathan Cape, 1925).

Willkie, Wendell, *One World* (New York: Cassell, 1943).

Willoughby, W. W., review of *Introduction to Political Science*, *Political Science Quarterly*, 11/3 (1896), 548–51.

Wilson, Samuel, "Imperial Federation," *National Review*, 4 (1884), 380–86.

———, "A Scheme for Imperial Federation," *Nineteenth-Century*, 17 (1885), 590–98.

Wilton, G. W., "Solidarity without Federation," pts. 1 and 2, *Juridical Review*, 4 (1892), 317–34; *Juridical Review*, 5 (1893), 248–62.

Wright, Quincy, "International Law and Ideologies," *American Journal of International Law*, 48 (1954), 616–26.

Young, Frederick, *Imperial Federation of Great Britain and Her Colonies; in Letters Edited by Frederick Young* (London: S. W. Silver, 1876).

———, *An Address on Imperial Federation, at Cambridge* (London: E. Stanford, 1885).

———, *On the Political Relations of Mother Countries and Colonies* (London: Chapman and Hall, 1885).

———, *Exit Party: An Essay on the Rise and Fall of "Party" as the Ruling Factor of the Governments of Great Britain* (London: George Allen, 1900).

———, *A Pioneer of Imperial Federation in Canada* (London: G. Allen, 1902).

Zimmern, Alfred, *The Greek Commonwealth: Politics and Economics in Fifth Century Athens* (Oxford: Clarendon, 1911).

———ed., *Modern Political Doctrines* (Oxford: Oxford University Press, 1939).

Secondary Sources

Aarsleff, Hans, "Locke's Influence," in *The Cambridge Companion to Locke*, ed. Vere Chappell (Cambridge: Cambridge University Press, 1997), 252–89.

Abernethy, David, *The Dynamics of Global Dominance: European Overseas Empires, 1415–1980* (New Haven: Yale University Press, 2000).

Abizadeh, Arash, "Citizenship, Immigration, and Boundaries," in *Ethics and World Politics*, ed. Bell, 358–77.

Adas, Michael, "Contested Hegemony: The Great War and the Afro-Asian Assault on the Civilizing Mission Ideology," *Journal of World History*, 15/1 (2004), 31–63.

Adcock, Robert, *Liberalism and the Emergence of American Political Science: A Transatlantic Tale* (Oxford: Oxford University Press, 2014).

Adcock, Robert, Mark Bevir, and Shannon Stimson, eds., *Modern Political Science: Anglo-American Exchanges since 1880* (Princeton: Princeton University Press, 2007).

Alessio, Dominic David, "Domesticating 'The Heart of the Wild': Female Personifications of the Colonies, 1886–1940," *Women's History Review*, 6 (1997), 239–69.

Allard, James, "Idealism in Britain and the United States," in *The Cambridge History of Philosophy, 1870–1945*, ed. Thomas Baldwin (Cambridge: Cambridge University Press, 2003), 43–59.

Allardyce, Gilbert, "The Rise and Fall of the Western Civilization Course," *American Historical Review*, 87 (1982), 695–725.

Allen, H. C., *Great Britain and the United States: A History of Anglo-American Relations* (New York: St. Martin's, 1954).

Anderson, Amanda, and Joseph Valente, eds., *Disciplinarity at the Fin de Siècle* (Princeton: Princeton University Press, 2002).

Anderson, Perry, "Renewals," *New Left Review*, 1 (2000), 5–24.

Anievas, Alexander, ed., *Marxism and World Politics: Contesting Global Capitalism* (London: Routledge, 2010).

Appadurai, Arjun, *Modernity at Large: Cultural Dimensions of Globalization* (Minneapolis: University of Minnesota Press, 1996).

———, "Sovereignty without Territoriality: Notes for a Postnational Geography," in *The Geography of Identity*, ed. Patricia Yaeger (Ann Arbor: University of Michigan Press, 1996), 40–58.

Armitage, David, "A Patriot for Whom? The Afterlives of Bolingbroke's Patriot King," *Journal of British Studies*, 36 (1997), 397–418.

———, ed., *Theories of Empire, 1450–1800* (Aldershot: Ashgate, 1998).

———, *The Ideological Origins of the British Empire* (Cambridge: Cambridge University Press, 2000).

———, "Empire and Liberty," in *Republicanism: A Shared European Heritage*, 2 vols., ed. van Gelderen and Skinner (Cambridge: Cambridge University Press, 2002), 2:29–47.

———, "The Fifty Years' Rift: Intellectual History and International Relations," *Modern Intellectual History*, 1 (2004), 97–109.

———, *Foundations of Modern International Thought* (Cambridge: Cambridge University Press, 2013).

Arneil, Barbara, *John Locke and America* (Oxford: Oxford University Press, 1996).

———, "Citizens, Wives, Latent Citizens and Non-Citizens in the *Two Treatises*: A Legacy of Inclusion, Exclusion and Assimilation," *Eighteenth-Century Thought*, 3 (2007), 209–22.

———, *Domestic Colonies: The Colonial Turn Inward* (Oxford: Oxford University Press, forthcoming).

Arnstein, Walter, "Queen Victoria," *Victorian Studies*, 36 (1993), 377–80.

———, *Queen Victoria* (Basingstoke: Palgrave, 2003).

Bain, William, *Between Anarchy and Society: Trusteeship and the Obligations of Power* (Oxford: Oxford University Press, 2003).

Baji, Tomohito, "Commonwealth: Alfred Zimmern and World Citizenship," PhD thesis, University of Cambridge (2016).

Baldwin, Thomas, "The Territorial State," in *Jurisprudence: Cambridge Essays*, ed. Gross and Harrison (Oxford: Clarendon Press, 1992), 207–30.

Ball, Terence, "The Formation of Character: Mill's Ethology Reconsidered," *Polity*, 33 (2000), 25–48.

Ballantyne, Tony, *Orientalism and Race* (Basingstoke: Palgrave Macmillan, 2002).

———, "Remaking the Empire from Newgate," in *Ten Books That Shaped the British Empire*, ed. Antoinette Burton and Isabel Hofmeyr (Durham, NC: Duke University Press, 2014), 29–50.

Baratta, Joseph Preston, "The International Federalist Movement: Toward Global Governance," *Peace & Change*, 24 (1999), 340–72.

———, *The Politics of World Federation*, 2 vols. (Westport, CT: Praeger, 2004).

Barkawi, Tarak, "Empire and Order in International Relations and Security Studies," in *The International Studies Encyclopaedia*, ed. Robert Denemark (Oxford: Blackwell, 2010), 3:1360–79.

Barry, Brian, "On Self-Government," in *The Nature of Political Theory*, ed. David Miller and Larry Siedentop (London: Clarendon Press, 1983), 121–54.

Bartelson, Jens, "The Trial of Judgement: A Note on Kant and the Paradoxes of Internationalism," *International Studies Quarterly*, 39 (1995), 255–79.

———, *The Critique of the State* (Cambridge: Cambridge University Press, 2001).

———, "Making Sense of Global Civil Society," *European Journal of International Relations*, 12 (2006), 371–95.

———, *Visions of World Community* (Cambridge: Cambridge University Press, 2009).

Bateman, Fiona, and Lionel Pilkington (eds.), *Studies in Settler Colonialism: Politics, Identity and Culture* (New York: Palgrave, 2011).

Bayly, Christopher Alan, *The Birth of the Modern World: Global Connections and Comparisons 1780–1914* (Oxford: Blackwell, 2004).

———, "European Political Thought and the Wider World during the Nineteenth Century," in *The Cambridge History of Nineteenth-Century Political Thought*, ed. Claeys and Stedman Jones (Cambridge: Cambridge University Press, 2011), 835–63.

———, *Recovering Liberties: Indian Thought in the Age of Liberalism and Empire* (Cambridge: Cambridge University Press, 2012).

———, "Michael Mann and Modern World History," *Historical Journal*, 58/1 (2015), 331–41.

Bayly, Susan, *Caste, Society and Politics in India from the Eighteenth Century to the Modern Age* (Cambridge: Cambridge University Press, 1999).

Beasley, Edward, *Empire as the Triumph of Theory: Imperialism, Information, and the Colonial Society of 1868* (London: Routledge, 2005).

———, *Mid-Victorian Imperialists: British Gentlemen and the Empire of the Mind* (London: Routledge, 2005).

Behm, Amanda, "The Bisected Roots of Imperial History: Settler World Projects and the Making of a Field in Modern Britain, 1883–1912," *Recherches Britanniques*, 1/1 (2011), 54–77.

Belich, James, *Replenishing the Earth: The Settler Revolution and the Rise of the Anglo-World, 1783–1939* (New York: Oxford University Press, 2009).

Bell, Duncan, "Mythscapes: Memory, Mythology and National Identity," *British Journal of Sociology*, 54/1 (2003), 63–81.

———, "Dissolving Distance: Technology, Space, and Empire in British Political Thought, 1770–1900," *Journal of Modern History*, 77/3 (2005), 523–63.

———, "Unity and Difference: John Robert Seeley and the Political Theology of International Relations," *Review of International Studies*, 31/3 (2005), 559–79.

———, "Empire and International Relations in Victorian Political Thought," *Historical Journal*, 49 (2006), 281–98.

———, "From Ancient to Modern in Victorian Imperial Thought," *Historical Journal*, 49 (2006), 1–25.

———, "The Idea of a Patriot Queen? The Monarchy, the Constitution, and the Iconographic Order of Greater Britain, 1860–1900," *Journal of Imperial and Commonwealth History*, 34 (2006), 3–22.

———, "The Victorian Idea of a Global State," in *Victorian Visions*, ed. Bell, 159–86.

———, *The Idea of Greater Britain: Empire and the Future of World Order, 1860–1900* (Princeton: Princeton University Press, 2007).

———, "Agonistic Democracy and the Politics of Memory," *Constellations*, 15/1 (2008), 148–66.

———, "Democracy and Empire: J. A. Hobson, Leonard Hobhouse, and the Crisis of Liberalism," in *British International Thinkers*, ed. Hall and Hill (New York: Palgrave Macmillan, 2009), 181–207.

———, "Republican Imperialism: J. A. Froude and the Virtue of Empire," *History of Political Thought*, 30 (2009), 166–91.

———, "Imagined Spaces: Nation, State, and Territory in the British Colonial Empire, 1860–1914," in *The Primacy of Foreign Policy in British History*, ed. William Mulligan and Brendan Simms (Basingstoke: Palgrave, 2010), 197–214.

———, "John Stuart Mill on Colonies," *Political Theory*, 38 (2010), 34–64.

———, "Empire and Imperialism," in *The Cambridge History of Nineteenth-Century Political Thought*, ed. Gregory Claeys and Gareth Stedman Jones (Cambridge: Cambridge University Press, 2011), 864–92.

———, "Dreaming the Future: Anglo-America as Utopia, 1880–1914," in *The American Experiment and the Idea of Democracy in British Culture, 1776–1914*, ed. Ella Dzelzainis and Ruth Livesey (Aldershot: Ashgate, 2012), 197–210.

———, "The Project for a New Anglo Century: Race, Space, and Global Order," in *Anglo-America and Its Discontents*, ed. Peter Katzenstein (New York: Routledge 2012), 33–56.

———, "Making and Taking Worlds," in *Global Intellectual History*, ed. Samuel Moyn and Andrew Sartori (New York: Colombia University Press, 2013), 254–82.

———, "On J. A. Hobson's 'The Ethics of Internationalism,'" *Ethics*, 125 (2014), 220–22.

———, "To Act Otherwise: Agonistic Republicanism and Global Citizenship," in

On Global Citizenship: James Tully in Dialogue, ed. David Owen (London: Bloomsbury, 2014), 181–207.

———, "Before the Democratic Peace: Racial Utopianism, Empire and the Abolition of War," *European Journal of International Relations*, 20/3 (2014), 647–70.

———, "Beyond the Sovereign State: Isopolitan Citizenship, Race, and Anglo-American Union," *Political Studies*, 62 (2014), 418–34.

———, "Alter Orbis: E. A. Freeman on Empire and Racial Destiny," in *Making History*, ed. Bremner and Conlin, 217–35.

———, "Desolation Goes before Us," *Journal of British Studies*, 54/4 (2015), 987-93.

———, *Dreamworlds of Empire* (forthcoming).

———, "Race, Utopia, Perpetual Peace: Andrew Carnegie's Dreamworld," in *Intellectual Histories of American Foreign Policy,* ed. Jean-Francis Drolet and James Dunkerley (forthcoming).

———, ed., *Victorian Visions of Global Order: Empire and International Relations in Nineteenth-Century Political Thought* (Cambridge: Cambridge University Press, 2007).

Bell, Duncan, and Joel Isaac, eds., *Uncertain Empire* (Oxford: Oxford University Press, 2012).

Bell, Duncan, and Casper Sylvest, "International Society in Victorian Political Thought: T. H. Green, Herbert Spencer, and Henry Sidgwick," *Modern Intellectual History*, 3 (2006), 1–32.

Bellamy, Alex, *Responsibility to Protect: A Defense* (Oxford: Oxford University Press, 2014).

———, ed., *International Society and Its Critics* (Oxford: Oxford University Press, 2004).

Bellamy, Richard, *Liberalism and Modern Society: An Historical Argument* (Cambridge: Polity, 1992).

———, ed., *Victorian Liberalism: Nineteenth Century Political Thought and Practice* (Abingdon: Routledge, 1990).

Bennett, Bruce, *New Zealand's Moral Foreign Policy 1935–39* (Wellington: New Zealand Institute of International Affairs, 1962).

Bennett, George, *The Concept of Empire*, 2nd ed. (London: Adam and Charles Black, 1962).

Bennett, James C., *The Anglosphere Challenge: Why the English-Speaking Nations Will Lead the Way in the Twenty-First Century* (Lanham, MD: Rowman and Littlefield, 2007).

———, *The Third Anglosphere Century: The English-Speaking World in an Era of Transition* (Washington: Heritage Foundation, 2007).

Bentley, Michael, *Politics without Democracy: England, 1815–1918*, 2nd ed. (Oxford: Blackwell, 1999).

———, *Lord Salisbury's World: Conservative Environments in Late Victorian Britain* (Cambridge: Cambridge University Press, 2001).

———, "Review of Uday Singh Mehta, *Liberalism and Emapire*," *Victorian Studies*, 43/4 (2001), 620.

Benton, Lauren, *A Search for Sovereignty: Law and Geography in European Empires, 1400–1900* (Cambridge: Cambridge University Press, 2010).

Berard, R. N., "Edward Augustus Freeman and University Reform in Victorian Oxford," *History of Education*, 9 (1980), 287–301.

Berman, Sherri, *The Primacy of Politics: Social Democracy and the Making of Europe's Twentieth Century* (Cambridge: Cambridge University Press, 2006).

Bevir, Mark, "Republicanism, Socialism, and Democracy in Britain: The Origins of the Radical Left," *Journal of Social History*, 34 (2000), 351–68.

———, "The Long Nineteenth Century in Intellectual History," *Journal of Victorian Culture*, 6 (2001), 313–36.

Bevir, Mark, "Political Studies as Narrative and Science, 1880–2000," *Political Studies*, 54 (2006), 583–606.

Bhabha, Homi, *The Location of Culture* (London: Routledge, 1994).

Biagini, Eugenio, *Liberty, Retrenchment, and Reform: Popular Liberalism in the Age of Gladstone, 1860–1880* (Cambridge: Cambridge University Press, 1992).

———, "Neo-Roman Liberalism: 'Republican' Values and British Liberalism, ca. 1860–1875," *History of European Ideas*, 29 (2003), 55–72.

———, "Radicalism and Liberty," in *Liberty and Authority in Victorian Britain*, ed. Peter Mandler (Oxford: Oxford University Press, 2006), 101–25.

Bodelson, Carl Adolf, *Studies in Mid-Victorian Imperialism* [1924] (London: Heinemann, 1960).

Booth, Ken, and Nicholas Wheeler, *The Security Dilemma: Fear, Cooperation and Trust in World Politics* (Basingstoke: Palgrave, 2007).

Bosco, Andrea, "Lothian, Curtis, Kimber and the Federal Union Movement (1938–1940)," *Journal of Contemporary History*, 23 (1988), 465–502.

Boucher, David, "British Idealism, the State, and International Relations," *Journal of the History of Ideas*, 55 (1994), 671–94.

———, "Introduction," in *The British Idealists*, ed. Boucher (Cambridge: Cambridge University Press, 1997), vii–xxxiii.

Boucher, David, and Andrew Vincent, *British Idealism and Political Theory* (Edinburgh: Edinburgh University Press, 2001).

Bourke, Richard, "Pocock and the Presuppositions of the New British History," *Historical Journal*, 53/3 (2010), 747–70.

Bowden, Brett, *The Empire of Civilization: The Evolution of an Imperial Idea* (Chicago: University of Chicago Press, 2009).

Bradley, Mark, "Introduction," in *Classics and Imperialism in the British Empire*, ed. Bradley (Oxford: Oxford University Press, 2010), 1–29.

Brady, Ciaran, *James Anthony Froude: An Intellectual Biography of a Victorian Prophet* (Oxford: Oxford University Press, 2013).

Brake, Laurel, et al., eds., *W. T. Stead: Newspaper Revolutionary* (Chicago: University of Chicago Press, 2012).

Brantlinger, Patrick, *Dark Vanishings: Discourse on the Extinction of Primitive Races, 1800–1930* (Ithaca: Cornell University Press, 2003).

Bremner, Alex, and Jonathan Conlin, eds., *Making History: Edward Augustus Freeman and Victorian Cultural Politics* (Oxford: Oxford University Press, 2015).

Brendon, Piers, *The Decline and Fall of the British Empire: 1781–1997* (London: Jonathan Cape, 2007).

Brett, Annabel, *Changes of State: Nature and the Limits of the City in Early Modern International Law* (Princeton: Princeton University Press, 2011).

Brewer, Anthony, *Marxist Theories of Imperialism: A Critical Survey*, 2nd ed. (London: Routledge, 1990).

Brown, Gordon, "Enlarging the Anglosphere," *Wall Street Journal*, April 16, 2008.

Brundage, Anthony, Richard Cosgrove, *The Great Tradition: Constitutional History and National Identity in Britain and the United States, 1870–1960* (Stanford: Stanford University Press, 2007).

Bruyneel, Kevin, *The Third Space of Sovereignty: The Postcolonial Politics of U. S.–Indigenous Relations* (Minneapolis: University of Minnesota Press, 2007).

———, "The American Liberal Colonial Tradition," *Settler Colonial Studies*, 3 (2013), 311–21.

Buchan, Bruce, *Empire of Political Thought: Indigenous Australians and the Language of Colonial Government* (London: Pickering and Chatto, 2008).

Buckner, P. A., *The Transition to Responsible Government* (Westport, CT: Greenwood Press, 1985).

Burbank, James, and Frederick Cooper, *Empires in World History: Power and the Politics of Difference* (Princeton: Princeton University Press, 2010).

Burgess, Michael, *The British Tradition of Federalism* (London: Leicester University Press, 1995).

Burgin, Angus, *The Great Persuasion: Reinventing Free Markets since the Depression* (Cambridge: Harvard University Press, 2012).

Burn, W. L., *The Age of Equipoise: A Study of the Mid-Victorian Generation* (London: Allen and Unwin, 1964).

Burroughs, Peter, *Colonial Reformers and Canada, 1830–1849* (London: McClelland, 1969).

———, *The Canadian Crisis and British Colonial Policy, 1828–1841* (London: Macmillan, 1972).

———, "John Robert Seeley and British Imperial History," *Journal of Imperial and Commonwealth History*, 1 (1973), 191–213.

———, "Imperial Institutions and the Government of Empire," in *The Oxford History of the British Empire*, ed. Andrew Porter (Oxford: Oxford University Press, 1999), 4:170–97.

Burrow, John, *Evolution and Society: A Study in Victorian Social Theory* (Cambridge: Cambridge University Press, 1966).

———, *A Liberal Descent: Victorian Historians and the English Past* (Cambridge: Cambridge University Press, 1981).

———, *Whigs and Liberals: Continuity and Change in English Political Thought* (Oxford: Oxford University Press, 1988).

———, *The Crisis of Reason: European Thought, 1848–1914* (London: Yale University Press, 2000).

———, "Historicism and Social Evolution," in *British and German Historiography, 1750–1950: Traditions, Perceptions, and Transfers*, ed. Benedikt Stuchtey and Peter Wende (Oxford: Oxford University Press, 2000), 251–64.

———, "The Age of Reform," in *Christ's: A Cambridge College over Five Centuries*, ed. David Reynolds (London: Palgrave, 2004), 111–43.

Burrow, John, Stefan Collini, and Donald Winch, *That Noble Science of Politics: A Study in Nineteenth-Century Intellectual History* (Cambridge: Cambridge University Press, 1983).

Burton, Antoinette, *Empire in Question: Reading, Writing, and Teaching British Imperialism* (Durham, NC: Duke University Press, 2011).

Burton, Antoinette, and Isabel Hofmeyr, "The Spine of Empire? Books and the Making of an Imperial Commons," in *Ten Books That Shaped the British Empire: Creating an Imperial Commons*, ed. Burton and Hofmeyr (Durham, NC: Duke University Press, 2014), 1–28.

Butler, Sarah J., *Britain and Its Empire in the Shadow of Rome* (London: Bloomsbury, 2012).

Buzan, Barry, and George Lawson, *The Global Transformation: History, Modernity and the Making of International Relations* (Cambridge: Cambridge University Press, 2015).

Cabrera, Luis, "World Government: Renewed Debate, Persistent Challenges," *European Journal of International Relations*, 16 (2010), 511–30.

Cain, Peter, "Capitalism, War, and Internationalism in the Thought of Richard Cobden," *British Journal of International Studies*, 5/3 (1979), 229–47.

———, "The Economic Philosophy of Constructive Imperialism," in *British Politics and the Spirit of the Age: Political Concepts in Action*, ed. Cornelia Navari (Keele: Keele University Press, 1996), 42–65.

———, "Empire and the Languages of Character and Virtue in Later Victorian and Edwardian Britain," *Modern Intellectual History*, 4/2 (2007).

———, "Radicalism, Gladstone, and the Liberal Critique of Disraelian 'Imperialism,'" in *Victorian Visions*, ed. Bell, 215–319.

———, *Hobson and Imperialism: Radicalism, New Liberalism, and Finance, 1887–1938* (Oxford: Oxford University Press, 2002).

———, "Capitalism, Aristocracy and Empire: Some Classical Theories of Imperialism Revisited," *Journal of Imperial and Commonwealth History*, 35/1 (2007), 25–47.

———, "Character, 'Ordered Liberty,' and the Mission to Civilise: British Moral Justification for Empire, 1870–1914," *Journal of Imperial and Commonwealth History*, 40/4 (2012), 557–78.

Cain, Peter, and Antony G. Hopkins, *British Imperialism, 1688–2000* (London: Pearson, 2002).

Calhoun, Craig, Frederick Cooper, and Kevin Moore, eds., *Lessons of Empire: Imperial Histories and American Power* (New York: New Press, 2006).

Callinicos, Alex, *Imperialism and the Global Political Economy* (Cambridge: Polity, 2009).

Cannadine, David, *G. M. Trevelyan: A Life in History* (London: Harper Collins, 1992).

———, "The Context, Performance, and Meaning of Ritual: The British Monarchy and the 'Invention of Tradition' c. 1820–1977," in *The Invention of Tradition*, ed Hobsbawm and Ranger (Cambridge: Cambridge University Press, 1993), 101–65.

Canovan, Margaret, *The People* (Cambridge: Polity, 2005).

Capaldi, Nicholas, *John Stuart Mill: A Biography* (Cambridge: Cambridge University Press, 2004).

Carlisle, Janice, *John Stuart Mill and the Writing of Character* (Athens: University of Georgia Press, 1991).

Cashdollar, Charles, *The Transformation of Theology, 1830–1890: Positivism and*

Protestant Thought in Britain and America (Princeton: Princeton University Press, 1989).

Ceadel, Martin, *Semi-Detached Idealists: The British Peace Movement and International Relations, 1854–1945* (Oxford: Oxford University Press, 2000).

Chakrabarty, Dipesh, *Provincializing Europe: Postcolonial Thought and Historical Difference* (Princeton: Princeton University Press, 2000).

Chatterjee, Partha, *Nationalist Thought and the Colonial World* (London: Zed Books, 1986).

———, *The Nation and Its Fragments: Colonial and Postcolonial Histories* (Princeton: Princeton University Press, 1993).

Claeys, Gregory, "The Origins of the Rights of Labor: Republicanism, Commerce, and the Construction of Modern Social Theory in Britain, 1796–1805," *Journal of Modern History*, 66 (1994), 249–90.

———, *Imperial Sceptics: British Critics of Empire, 1850–1920* (Cambridge: Cambridge University Press, 2010).

Clarke, Ignatius Frederick, *Voices Prophesying War: Future Wars, 1763–3749*, 2nd ed. (Oxford: Oxford University Press, 1992).

———, ed., *The Tale of the Next Great War, 1871–1914: Fictions of Future Warfare and of Battles Still-to-Come* (Liverpool: Liverpool University Press, 1995).

Clarke, Peter, *Liberals and Social Democrats* (Cambridge: Cambridge University Press, 1978).

———, "The English-Speaking Peoples before Churchill," *British Scholar*, 4 (2011), 199–231.

Cocks, Raymond, *Sir Henry Maine: A Study in Victorian Jurisprudence* (Cambridge: Cambridge University Press, 1988).

Cohn, Bernard, *Colonialism and Its Forms of Knowledge* (Princeton: Princeton University Press, 1996).

Colaiaco, James, *James Fitzjames Stephen and the Crisis of Victorian Thought* (London: Macmillan, 1983).

Colás, Alejandro, *Empire* (Cambridge: Polity, 2007).

Cole, Douglas, "The Problem of 'Nationalism' and 'Imperialism' in British Settlement Colonies," *Journal of British Studies*, 10 (1971), 160–82.

Colley, Linda, "What Is Imperial History Now?," in *What Is History Now?*, ed. David Cannadine (Basingstoke: Palgrave, 2002), 132–48.

Collini, Stefan, *Liberalism and Sociology: L. T Hobhouse and Political Argument in England, 1880–1914* (Cambridge: Cambridge University Press, 1979).

———, *Public Moralists: Political Thought and Intellectual Life in Britain, 1850–1930* (Oxford: Clarendon Press, 1991).

Conklin, Alice, *A Mission to Civilize: The Republican Idea of Empire in France and West Africa, 1895–1930* (Stanford: Stanford University Press, 1998).

Conlin, Jonathan, "The Consolations of Amero-Teutonism: E. A. Freeman's Tour of the United States, 1881–1882," in *Making History*, ed. Bremner and Conlin, 101–19.

Conquest, Robert, *Reflections on a Ravaged Century* (London: Norton, 2000).

Cooley, Alexander, *Logics of Hierarchy: The Organization of Empires, States, and Military Occupations* (Ithaca: Cornell University Press, 2005).

Coombes, Annie, ed., *Rethinking Settler Colonialism: History and Memory in Austra-*

lia, Canada, New Zealand and South Africa (Manchester: Manchester University Press, 2006).

Cooper, Frederick, *Colonialism in Question: Theory, Knowledge, History* (Berkeley: University of California Press, 2005).

Cooper, Frederick, and Ann Laura Stoler, "Between Metropole and Colony: Rethinking a Research Agenda," in *Tensions of Empire: Colonial Cultures in a Bourgeois World*, ed. Cooper and Stoler (Berkeley: University of California Press, 1997), 1–59.

Coupland, Philip, "H. G. Wells' 'Liberal Fascism,'" *Journal of Contemporary History*, 35 (2000), 541–58.

Craig, Campbell, *Glimmer of a New Leviathan: Total War in the Realism of Niebuhr, Morgenthau, and Waltz* (New York: Columbia University Press, 2003).

Craig, David M., "The Crowned Republic? Monarchy and Anti-Monarchy in Britain, 1760–1901," *Historical Journal*, 46 (2003), 167–85.

———, "The Origins of 'Liberalism' in Britain," *Historical Research*, 85 (2012), 469–87.

Crook, Paul, *Darwinism, War and History: The Debate over the Biology of War from the 'Origin of Species' to the First World War* (Cambridge: Cambridge University Press, 1994).

Cull, Nicholas J., "Selling Peace: The Origins, Promotion and Fate of the Anglo-American New Order during the Second World War," *Diplomacy and Statecraft*, 7 (1996), 1–28.

Cunliffe, Philip, ed., *Critical Perspectives on the Responsibility to Protect: Interrogating Theory and Practice* (London: Routledge, 2011).

Curthoys, Ann, "Genocide in Tasmania: The History of an Idea," in *Empire, Colony, Genocide*, ed. Moses, 229–53.

Daalder, Ivo, and James Lindsay, "Democracies of the World, Unite," *American Interest*, 2 (2007), 5–15.

Daly, Nicholas, *Literature, Technology, and Modernity, 1860–2000* (Cambridge: Cambridge University Press, 2004).

Darwin, John, "The Fear of Falling: British Political and Imperial Decline since 1900," *Transactions of the Royal Historical Society*, 36, 5th series, (1986), 27–45.

———, *After Tamerlane: The Rise and Fall of Global Empires, 1400–2000* (London: Penguin, 2007).

———, "Empire and Ethnicity," *Nations and Nationalism*, 16/2 (2010), 383–401.

———, *The Empire Project: The Rise and Fall of the British World-System, 1830–1970* (Cambridge: Cambridge University Press, 2011).

Daunton, Martin, ed., *The Organisation of Knowledge in Victorian Britain* (Oxford: Oxford University Press, 2005).

Daunton, Martin, and Bernhard Rieger, eds., *Meanings of Modernity: Britain in the Age of Imperialism and World Wars* (Oxford: Berg, 2001).

Davis, Mike, *Late Victorian Holocausts: El Nino Famines and the Making of the Third World* (London: Verso, 2003).

den Otter, Sandra, *British Idealism and Social Explanation: A Study in Late Victorian Thought* (Oxford: Clarendon, 1996).

———, "The Origins of a Historical Political Science in Late Victorian and Edwardian Britain," in *Modern Political Science*, ed. Adcock, Bevir, and Stimson, 37–65.

Deudney, Daniel, "Greater Britain or Greater Synthesis? Seeley, Mackinder, and Wells on Britain in the Global Industrial Era," *Review of International Studies*, 27/2 (2001), 187–208.

——, *Bounding Power: Republican Security Theory from the Polis to the Global Village* (Princeton: Princeton University Press, 2007).

Diamond, Alan, ed., *The Victorian Achievement of Sir Henry Maine* (Cambridge: Cambridge University Press, 2006).

Dillon, Brian, *Ruin Lust: Artists' Fascination with Ruins, from Turner to the Present Day* (London: Tate, 2014).

Dingley, Robert, "The Ruins of the Future: Macaulay's New Zealander and the Spirit of the Age," in *Histories of the Future: Studies in Fact, Fantasy and Science Fiction*, ed. Dingley and Alan Sandison (Basingstoke: Palgrave, 2000), 15–33.

Dirks, Nicholas, *Castes of Mind: Colonialism and the Making of Modern India* (Princeton: Princeton University Press, 2001).

Dorsett, Shaunnagh, "Sovereignty as Governance in the Early New Zealand Crown Colony Period," in *Law and Politics in British Colonial Thought: Transpositions of Empire*, ed. Dorsett and Hunter (Basingstoke: Palgrave, 2010), 209–28.

Doyle, Michael, *Empires* (Ithaca: Cornell University Press, 1986).

——, "Liberalism and World Politics," *American Political Science Review*, 80 (1986), 1151–69.

——, *The Question of Intervention: John Stuart Mill and the Responsibility to Protect* (New Haven: Yale University Press, 2015).

Driver, Felix, *Geography Militant: Cultures of Exploration and Empire* (Oxford: Blackwell, 2001).

Dunn, John, *The Political Thought of John Locke* (Cambridge: Cambridge University Press, 1969).

——, *Western Political Theory in the Face of the Future* [1979] (Cambridge: Cambridge University Press, 1991).

Dunn, Waldo Hilary, *James Anthony Froude* (Oxford: Clarendon Press, 1961).

Dunne, Tim, and Trine Flockhart, eds., *Liberal World Orders* (Oxford: Oxford University Press, 2013).

Durrans, Peter J., "The House of Commons and the British Empire, 1868–1880," *Canadian Journal of History*, 9 (1974), 19–45.

Dworkin, Ronald, *A Matter of Principle* (Oxford: Clarendon, 1985).

Eldridge, C. C., *Victorian Imperialism* (London: Hodder and Stoughton, 1978).

Elkins, Caroline, and Susan Pedersen, "Settler Colonialism: A Concept and Its Uses," in *Settler Colonialism in the Twentieth Century*, ed. Elkins and Pedersen (London: Palgrave, 2005), 1–20.

Elliott, J. H., *Empires of the Atlantic World: Britain and Spain in America, 1492–1830* (London: Yale University Press, 2006).

Ellis, John S., "'The Methods of Barbarism' and the 'Rights of Small Nations': War Propaganda and British Pluralism," *Albion*, 30 (1998), 49–75.

Evans, Julie, et al., *Unequal Rights: Indigenous People in British Settler Colonies, 1830–1910* (Manchester: Manchester University Press, 2003).

Faber, Richard, *Beaconsfield and Bolingbroke* (London: Faber and Faber, 1961).

Falk, Richard, *A Study of Future Worlds* (New York: Free Press, 1975).

Farr, James, "The Historical Science(s) of Politics: The Principles, Association, and Fate of an American Discipline," in *Modern Political Science*, ed. Adcock, Bevir, and Stimson, 66–96.

———, "Locke, Natural Law, and New World Slavery," *Political Theory*, 36 (2008), 495–522.

Ferguson, Niall, *Empire: How Britain Made the Modern World* (London: Allen Lane, 2003).

———, "Hegemony or Empire?," *Foreign Affairs*, 82/5 (2003), 154–61.

———, *Colossus: The Price of America's Empire* (London: Penguin, 2004).

Fielding, Kenneth Joshua, "Carlyle and the Americans: 'Eighteen Million Bores,'" *Carlyle Studies Annual*, 15 (1995), 55–64.

Fine, Sarah, "Democracy, Citizenship, and the Bits in Between," *Critical Review of International Social and Political Philosophy*, 14/5 (2011), 623–40.

Finley, Moses, "Colonies—An Attempt at a Typology," *Transactions of the Royal Historical Society*, 26, 5th series (1976), 167–88.

Finnemore, Martha, and Kathryn Sikkink, "International Norm Dynamics and Political Change," *International Organization*, 52 (1998), 887–917.

Fitzmaurice, Andrew, *Humanism and America: An Intellectual History of English Colonization, 1500–1625* (Cambridge: Cambridge University Press, 2003).

———, "The Genealogy of *Terra Nullius*," *Australian Historical Studies*, 129 (2007), 1–15.

———, "Neither Neo-Roman nor Liberal Empire," *Renaissance Studies*, 26/4 (2012), 479–91.

———, "The Resilience of Natural Law in the Writings of Sir Travers Twiss," in *British International Thinkers*, ed. Hall and Hill (New York: Palgrave Macmillan, 2009), 137–61.

———, *Sovereignty, Property, and Empire, 1500–2000* (Cambridge: Cambridge University Press, 2014).

Fitzpatrick, Matthew P., ed., *Liberal Imperialism in Europe: Expansionism and Nationalism, 1848–1884* (Basingstoke: Palgrave, 2012).

Foley, Tadhg, "'An Unknown and Feeble Body': How Settler Colonialism Was Theorized in the Nineteenth Century," in *Studies in Settler Colonialism*, ed. Bateman and Pilkington, 10–28.

Ford, Lisa, *Settler Sovereignty: Jurisdiction and Indigenous People in America and Australia, 1788–1836* (Cambridge, MA: Harvard University Press, 2010).

Foucault, Michel, "Afterword: The Subject and Power," *Michel Foucault: Beyond Structuralism and Hermeneutics*, by Hubert Dreyfus and Paul Rabinow, 2nd ed. (Chicago, Illinois: University of Chicago Press, 1983), 216–26.

Freeden, Michael, *The New Liberalism: An Ideology of Social Reform* (Oxford: Clarendon Press, 1978).

———, *Liberalism Divided: A Study in British Political Thought 1914–1939* (Oxford: Oxford University Press, 1986).

———, ed., *Minutes of the Rainbow Circle, 1894–1924* (London: RHS, 1989).

———, ed., *Reappraising J. A. Hobson: Humanism and Welfare* (London: Unwin, 1990).

———, *Ideologies and Political Theory: A Conceptual Approach* (Oxford: Oxford University Press, 1998).

———, "Ideology, Political Theory and Political Philosophy," in *Handbook of Political Theory*, ed. Gerald Gaus and Chandran Kukathas (London: Sage, 2004), 3–17.

———, *Liberal Languages: Ideological Imaginations and Twentieth-Century Progressive Thought* (Princeton: Princeton University Press, 2005).

———, "What Should the 'Political' in Political Philosophy Explore?," *Journal of Political Philosophy*, 13 (2005), 113–34.

———, "The Coming of the Welfare State," in *The Cambridge History of Twentieth-Century Political Thought*, ed. Terence Ball and Richard Bellamy (Cambridge: Cambridge University Press, 2006), 7–45.

———, *The Political Theory of Political Thinking* (Oxford: Oxford University Press, 2013).

Freeden, Michael, and Marc Stears, "Liberalism," in *The Oxford Handbook of Political Ideologies*, ed. Michael Freeden, Lyman Tower Sargent, and Marc Stears (Oxford: Oxford University Press, 2013), 329–48.

Fukuyama, Francis, *America at the Crossroads: Democracy, Power and the Neoconservative Legacy* (London: Yale University Press, 2006).

Gannon, Charles, *Rumors of War and Infernal Machines: Technomilitary Agenda-Setting in American and British Speculative Fiction* (Liverpool: Liverpool University Press, 2005).

Garnett, Jane, "Protestant Histories: James Anthony Froude, Partisanship and National Identity," in *Politics and Culture in Victorian Britain: Essays in Memory of Colin Matthew*, ed. Peter Ghosh and Lawrence Goldman (Oxford and New York: Oxford University Press, 2006), 171–92.

Gaus, Gerald, and Shane Courtland, "Liberalism," *The Stanford Encyclopaedia of Philosophy*, ed. Edward Zalta, http://plato.stanford.edu/entries/liberalism/.

Gerlach, Murney, *British Liberalism and the United States: Political and Social Thought in the Late Victorian Age* (Basingstoke: Palgrave, 2001).

Gerstle, Gary, "The Protean Character of American Liberalism," *American Historical Review*, 99 (1994), 1043–73.

Geuss, Raymond, *History and Illusion in Politics* (Cambridge: Cambridge University Press, 2001).

———, *Private Goods, Public Goods* (Princeton: Princeton University Press, 2001).

———, "Liberalism and Its Discontents," *Political Theory*, 30 (2002), 320–38.

Gibson, Nigel, *Fanon: The Postcolonial Imagination* (Cambridge: Polity, 2003).

Gieryn, Thomas, "Boundary-Work and the Demarcation of Science from Non-Science," *American Sociological Review*, 48 (1983), 785–95.

Gilman, Nils, *Mandarins of the Future: Modernization Theory in Cold War America* (Baltimore: Johns Hopkins University Press, 2004).

Gilroy, Paul, *The Black Atlantic: Modernity and Double Consciousness* (Cambridge, MA: Harvard University Press, 1993).

Glanville, Luke, *Sovereignty and the Responsibility to Protect* (Chicago: University of Chicago Press, 2014).

Gleason, Abbott, *Totalitarianism: The Inner History of the Cold War* (Oxford: Oxford University Press, 1997).

Goldberg, Jonah, *Liberal Fascism: The Secret History of the American Left, from Mussolini to the Politics of Change* (London: Doubleday, 2007).

Goldhill, Simon, *Victorian Culture and Classical Antiquity: Art, Opera, Fiction and the Proclamation of Modernity* (Princeton: Princeton University Press, 2012).

Goldie, Mark, "Introduction," in *The Reception of Locke's Politics*, ed. Goldie (London: Pickering, 1999), vol. 1, xvii–lxxiii.

Goldman, Lawrence, *Science, Reform, and Politics in Victorian Britain: The Social Science Association, 1857–1886* (Cambridge: Cambridge University Press, 2002).

Goldstein, Alyosha, ed., *Formations of United States Colonialism* (Durham, NC: Duke University Press, 2014).

Goldstein, Alyosha, and Alex Lubin, eds., "Settler Colonialism," *South Atlantic Quarterly*, 107/4 (2008).

Goldstein, Lawrence, *Ruins and Empire: The Evolution of a Theme in Augustan and Romantic Literature* (Pittsburgh: University of Pittsburgh Press, 1977).

Gong, Gerritt, *The Standard of "Civilization" in International Society* (Oxford: Clarendon, 1984).

Gorman, Daniel, *Imperial Citizenship: Empire and the Question of Belonging* (Manchester: Manchester University Press, 2006).

Gould, Eliga, "A Virtual Nation? Greater Britain and the Imperial Legacy of the American Revolution," *American Historical Review*, 104 (1999), 476–89.

Grafton, Anthony, "The History of Ideas: Precept and Practice, 1950–2000 and Beyond," *Journal of the History of Ideas*, 67 (2006), 1–32.

Grant, Robert, *Representations of British Emigration, Colonisation and Settlement: Imagining Empire, 1800–1860* (Basingstoke: Palgrave, 2005).

Green, E.H.H., *Ideologies of Conservatism: Conservative Political Ideas in the Twentieth Century* (Oxford: Oxford University Press, 2001).

Gregory, Derek, *The Colonial Present: Afghanistan, Palestine, and Iraq* (Oxford: Blackwell, 2004).

Guilhot, Nicolas, "Imperial Realism: Postwar IR Theory and Decolonisation," *International History Review*, 36/4 (2014), 698–720.

Guillory, John, *Cultural Capital: The Problem of Literary Canon Formation* (Chicago: University of Chicago Press, 1993).

Gunn, Simon, and James Vernon, eds., *The Peculiarities of Liberal Modernity in Imperial Britain* (Berkeley: University of California Press, 2011).

Gunnell, John, *The Descent of Political Theory: The Genealogy of an American Vocation* (Chicago: University of Chicago Press, 1993).

——, "The Archaeology of American Liberalism," *Journal of Political Ideologies*, 6 (2001), 125–45.

——, *Imagining the American Polity: Political Science and the Discourse of Democracy* (Philadelphia: Penn State University Press, 2004), 183–219.

Hadley, Elaine, *Living Liberalism: Practical Citizenship in Mid-Victorian Britain* (Chicago: University of Chicago Press, 2010).

Hadot, Pierre, *Philosophy as a Way of Life: Spiritual Exercises from Socrates to Foucault*, trans. M. Chase (Oxford: Blackwell, 1995).

Hagerman, Christopher, *Britain's Imperial Muse: The Classics, Imperialism, and the Indian Empire, 1784–1914* (Basingstoke: Palgrave, 2013).

Hall, Catherine, *Civilising Subjects: Metropole and Colony in the English Imagination, 1830–1867* (Cambridge: Polity, 2002).

———, *Macaulay and Son: Architects of Imperial Britain* (London: Yale University Press, 2012).

Hall, Ian, "History, Christianity, and Diplomacy: Sir Herbert Butterfield and International Relations," *Review of International Studies*, 28/4 (2002), 719–36.

Hall, Ian, and Lisa Hill, eds., *British International Thinkers from Hobbes to Namier* (Basingstoke: Palgrave, 2009).

Hardt, Michael, and Antonio Negri, *Empire* (Cambridge, MA: Harvard University Press, 2000).

———, *Multitude: War and Democracy in the Age of Empire* (Cambridge, MA: Harvard University Press, 2004).

Harper, Marjory, and Stephen Constantine, eds., *Migration and Empire* (Oxford: Oxford University Press, 2010).

Harré, Rom, "Positivist Thought in the Nineteenth Century," in *The Cambridge History of Philosophy, 1870–1945*, ed. Thomas Baldwin (Cambridge: Cambridge University Press, 2003), 11–26.

Harris, Jose, "Political Thought and the Welfare State, 1870–1914: An Intellectual Framework for British Social Policy," *Past & Present*, 135 (1992), 116–41.

Harrison, Ross, ed., *Henry Sidgwick* (Oxford: Oxford University Press, 2001).

Hartley, Livingston, *Atlantic Challenge* (New York: Dobbs Ferry, 1965).

Harvey, David, *The New Imperialism* (Oxford: Oxford University Press, 2003).

———, *A Brief History of Neoliberalism* (Oxford: Oxford University Press, 2005).

Harvie, Christopher, *The Lights of Liberalism: University Liberals and the Challenge of Democracy 1860–86* (London: Allen Lane, 1976).

Hawkins, Mike, *Social Darwinism in European and American Thought, 1860–1945* (Cambridge: Cambridge University Press, 1997).

Hay, Daisy, "Liberals, *Liberales* and *The Liberal*," *European Romantic Review*, 19 (2008), 307–20.

Heater, Derek, *World Citizenship and Government: Cosmopolitan Ideas in Western Political Thought* (Basingstoke: Macmillan, 1996).

Hechter, Michael, *Alien Rule* (Cambridge: Cambridge University Press, 2013).

Hell, Julia, "*Katechon*: Carl Schmitt's Imperial Theology and the Ruins of the Future," *Germanic Review*, 84 (2009), 283–326.

———, "The Twin Towers of Anselm Kiefer and the Trope of Imperial Decline," *Germanic Review*, 84/1 (2009), 84–93.

Hell, Julia, and Andreas Schonle, eds., *Ruins of Modernity* (Durham, NC: Duke University Press, 2010).

Hempton, David, *Evangelical Disenchantment: Nine Portraits of Faith and Doubt* (New Haven: Yale University Press, 2008).

Herbert, Christopher, *War of No Pity: The Indian Mutiny and Victorian Trauma* (Princeton: Princeton University Press, 2007).

Hesketh, Ian, "Diagnosing Froude's Disease: Boundary Work and the Discipline of History in Late-Victorian Britain," *History and Theory*, 47/3 (2008), 373–95.

———, "Behold the (Anonymous) Man," *Victorian Review*, 38 (2012), 93–112.

Hewitt, Martin, ed., *An Age of Equipoise? Reassessing Mid-Victorian Britain* (Aldershot: Ashgate, 2000).

Hickford, M., "'Decidedly the Most Interesting Savages on the Globe': An Approach to the History of Maori Property Rights, 1837–1853," *History of Political Thought*, 27 (2006), 122–67.

———, *Lords of the Land: Indigenous Property Rights and the Jurisprudence of Empire* (Oxford: Oxford University Press, 2011).

Hilton, Boyd, *The Age of Atonement: The Influence of Evangelicalism on Social and Economic Thought, 1795–1865* (Oxford: Clarendon, 1988).

———, *A Mad, Bad, and Dangerous People?* (Oxford: Oxford University Press, 2006).

Hind, Robert "'We Have No Colonies': Similarities within the British Imperial Experience," *Comparative Studies in Society and History*, 26 (1984), 3–35.

Hingley, Richard, *Roman Officers and English Gentlemen: The Imperial Origins of Roman Archaeology* (London: Routledge, 2000).

Hobson, John M., *The Eurocentric Conception of World Politics: Western International Theory, 1760–2010* (Cambridge: Cambridge University Press, 2012).

Hollander, Samuel, *The Economics of John Stuart Mill*, 2 vols. (Oxford: Blackwell, 1985).

Holmes, Stephen, "The Permanent Structure of Anti-Liberal Thought," in *Liberalism and the Moral Life*, ed. Nancy Rosenblum (Cambridge: Harvard University Press, 1989), 227–53.

———, *Passions and Constraint: On the Theory of Liberal Democracy* (Chicago: University of Chicago Press, 1995).

———, "Making Sense of Liberal Imperialism," in *J. S. Mill's Political Thought: A Bicentennial Reassessment*, ed. Urbinati and Zakaras, 319–47.

Homans, Margaret, and Adrienne Munich, "Introduction," in *Remaking Queen Victoria*, ed. Homans and Munich (Cambridge: Cambridge University Press, 1997), 1–13.

Honohan, Iseult, *Civic Republicanism* (London: Routledge, 2002).

Hont, Istvan, *Jealousy of Trade: International Competition and the Nation-State in Historical Perspective* (Cambridge, MA: Harvard University Press, 2005).

———, "Luxury and Commerce," in *The Cambridge History of Eighteenth-Century Political Thought*, ed. Mark Goldie and Robert Wokler (Cambridge: Cambridge University Press, 2006), 379–419.

———, *Politics in Commercial Society: Jean-Jacques Rousseau and Adam Smith*, ed. Béla Kapossy and Michael Sonenscher (Cambridge, MA: Harvard University Press, 2015).

Hopkins, A. G., ed., *Globalization in World History* (London: Pimlico, 2002).

Hoppen, Theodore K., *The Mid-Victorian Generation, 1846–1886* (Oxford: Oxford University Press, 1998).

Hörnqvist, Mikael, "The Two Myths of Civic Humanism," in *Renaissance Civic Humanism: Reappraisals and Reflections*, ed. James Hankins (Cambridge: Cambridge University Press, 2000), 105–43.

———, *Machiavelli and Empire* (Cambridge: Cambridge University Press, 2004).

———, "Machiavelli's Three Desires: Florentine Republicans on Liberty, Empire, and Justice," in *Empire and Modern Political Thought*, ed. Muthu, 7–30.

Howe, Anthony, *Free Trade and Liberal England, 1846–1946* (Oxford: Oxford University Press, 1998).

——, "Free Trade and Global Order: The Rise and Fall of a Victorian Vision," in *Victorian Visions of Global Order*, ed. Bell, 26–46.

Howe, Anthony, and Simon Morgan, eds., *Rethinking Nineteenth-Century Liberalism: Richard Cobden Bicentenary Essays* (London: Ashgate, 2006).

Howsam, Leslie, "Imperial Publishers and the Idea of Colonial History, 1870–1916," *History of Intellectual Culture*, 5/1 (2005), 1–15.

Hunter, Ian, "The Persona of the Philosopher and the History of Early Modern Philosophy," *Modern Intellectual History*, 4 (2007), 571–600.

Huntley, James, *Pax Democratica: A Strategy for the 21st Century* (London: St. Martin's, 1998).

Hurd, Elizabeth Shakman, "The Political Authority of Secularism in International Relations," *European Journal of International Relations*, 10 (2004), 235–62.

Ignatieff, Michael, *Empire Lite: Nation-Building in Bosnia, Kosovo and Afghanistan* (London: Vintage, 2003).

Ikenberry, G. John, *After Victory: Institutions, Strategic Restraint, and the Rebuilding of Order after Major Wars* (Princeton: Princeton University Press, 2001).

——, "Liberalism and Empire: Logics of Order in the American Unipolar Age," *Review of International Studies*, 30 (2004), 609–30.

——, *Liberal Order and Imperial Ambition: Essays on American Power* (London: Polity, 2006).

——, "Liberal Internationalism 3.0: America and the Dilemmas of Liberal World Order," *Perspectives on Politics*, 7/1 (2009), 71–87.

Ikenberry, G. John, and Anne-Marie Slaughter, *Forging a World of Liberty under Law: U. S. National Security in the 21st Century* (Princeton Project on National Security, 2006), accessed July 22, 2011, http://www.princeton.edu/~ppns/report/Final Report.pdf.

Immerman, Richard H., *Empire for Liberty: A History of American Imperialism from Benjamin Franklin to Paul Wolfowitz* (Princeton: Princeton University Press, 2010).

Inayatullah, Naeem, and David Blaney, *International Relations and the Problem of Difference* (New York: Routledge, 2004).

Isaac, Joel, "Tangled Loops: Theory, History and the Human Sciences in Modern America," *Modern Intellectual History*, 6 (2009), 397–424.

Isabella, Maurizio, *Risorgimento in Exile: Italian Émigrés and the Liberal International in the Post-Napoleonic Era* (Oxford: Oxford University Press, 2009).

Ivison, Duncan, *Postcolonial Liberalism* (Cambridge: Cambridge University Press, 2002).

——, "Locke, Liberalism and Empire," in *The Philosophy of John Locke*, ed. Peter R. Anstey (London: Routledge, 2003), 86–105.

Ivison, Duncan, Paul Patton, and Will Sanders, eds., *Political Theory and the Rights of Indigenous Peoples* (Cambridge: Cambridge University, 2001).

Jackson, Ben, "At the Origins of Neo-Liberalism: The Free Economy and the Strong State, 1930–1947," *Historical Journal*, 53 (2010), 129–51.

Jahn, Beate, "Barbarian Thoughts: Imperialism in the Philosophy of John Stuart Mill," *Review of International Studies*, 31 (2005), 599–618.

——, *Liberal Internationalism: Theory, History, Practice* (London: Palgrave, 2013).

James, Robert Rhodes, ed., *Winston S. Churchill: His Complete Speeches, 1897–1963* (New York: Chelsea House, 1974).

Jann, Rosemary, *The Art and Science of Victorian History* (Columbus: Ohio State University Press, 1985).

Jenkyns, Richard, *The Victorians and Ancient Greece* (Oxford: Blackwell, 1980).

Johnson, Chalmers, *Nemesis: The Last Days of the American Republic* (New York: Metropolitan Books, 2007).

Johnson, Miranda, "Reconciliation, Indigeneity, and Postcolonial Nationhood in Settler States," *Postcolonial Studies*, 14/2 (2011), 187–201.

Johnston, H.J.M., *British Emigration Policy, 1815–1830: "Shovelling Out Paupers"* (Oxford: Clarendon, 1972).

Jones, Emily, "Conservatism, Edmund Burke, and the Invention of a Political Tradition, c. 1885–1914," *Historical Journal*, 58 (2015), 1115–39.

Jones, H. S., "The Idea of the National in Victorian Political Thought," *European Journal of Political Theory*, 5 (2006), 12–21.

———, *Victorian Political Thought* (Basingstoke: Macmillan, 2000).

———, "The Victorian Lexicon of Evil: Frederic Harrison, the Positivists and the Language of International Politics," in *Evil, Barbarism and Empire: Britain and Abroad, c. 1830–2000*, ed. Tom Cook, Rebecca Gill, and Bertrand Taithe (Basingstoke: Palgrave, 2011), 126–43.

Jones, Tod, *The Broad Church: A Biography of a Movement* (Lanham, MD: Lexington Books, 2003).

Joseph, Terra Walston, "Bulwer-Lytton's *The Coming Race* and an Anglo-Saxon Greater Britain," *Nineteenth-Century Contexts*, 37 (2015), 233–48.

Katzenstein, Peter, ed., *Anglo-America and Its Discontents: Civilizational Identities beyond West and East* (London: Routledge, 2012).

Katznelson, Ira, *Desolation and Enlightenment: Political Knowledge after Total War, Totalitarianism, and the Holocaust* (New York: Columbia University Press, 2003).

———, *Fear Itself: The New Deal and the Origins of Our Time* (New York: Norton, 2013).

Kearns, Gerry, *Geopolitics and Empire: The Legacy of Halford Mackinder* (Oxford: Oxford University Press, 2009).

Kelley, William, "Past History and Present Politics: E. A. Freeman and the Eastern Question," in *Making History*, ed. Bremner and Conlin, 119–39.

Kelly, Duncan, "Reforming Republicanism in Nineteenth-Century Britain: James Lorymer's *The Republican* in Context," in *Republicanism in Theory and Practice*, ed. Iseult Honohan and Jeremy Jennings (London: Routledge, 2006), 41–52.

———, *The Propriety of Liberty: Persons, Passions and Judgment in Modern Political Thought* (Princeton: Princeton University Press, 2010).

Kelly, John D., ed., *Anthropology and Global Counterinsurgency* (Chicago: University of Chicago Press, 2010).

Kendle, John, *The Round Table Movement and Imperial Union* (Toronto: University of Toronto Press, 1975).

———, *Federal Britain: A History* (London: Routledge, 1997).

Kennedy, Dane, "The Imperial History Wars," *Journal of British Studies*, 54/1 (2015), 1–22.

Kern, Stephen, *The Culture of Time and Space, 1880–1914* (Cambridge, MA: Harvard University Press, 1983).

Kilgore, DeWitt Clinton, *Astrofuturism: Science, Race and Visions of Utopia in Space* (Philadelphia: University of Pennsylvania Press, 2003).

King, Richard, and Dan Stone, eds., *Hannah Arendt and the Uses of History: Imperialism, Racism, Nationalism and Genocide* (Oxford: Berghahn, 2007).

Kinzer, Bruce, *A Moralist In and Out of Parliament: John Stuart Mill at Westminster, 1865–68* (Toronto: University of Toronto Press, 1992).

———, *England's Disgrace? J. S Mill and the Irish Question* (Toronto: University of Toronto Press, 2001).

Kirkby, Coel, "The Politics and Practice of 'Native' Enfranchisement in Canada and the Cape Colony, c.1880–1900," PhD thesis, University of Cambridge, 2013.

Klausen, Jimmy Casas, "Room Enough: America, Natural Liberty, and Consent in Locke's *Second Treatise*," *Journal of Politics*, 69/3 (2007), 760–69.

Kloppenberg, James, *Uncertain Victory: Social Democracy and Progressivism in European and American Thought, 1870–1920* (Oxford: Oxford University Press, 1986).

Knights, Ben, *The Idea of the Clerisy in the Nineteenth Century* (Cambridge: Cambridge University Press, 1978).

Koditschek, Theodore, *Liberalism, Imperialism, and the Historical Imagination: Nineteenth Century Visions of a Greater Britain* (Cambridge: Cambridge University Press, 2011).

———, "Past Politics and Present History: E. A. Freeman's Invention of Racial Tradition," in *Making History*, ed. Bremner and Conlin, 199–217.

Kohn, Margaret, and Keally McBride, *Political Theories of Decolonization: Postcolonialism and the Problem of Foundations* (Oxford: Oxford University Press, 2011).

Kohn, Margaret, and Daniel O'Neill, "A Tale of Two Indias: Burke and Mill on Empire and Slavery in the West Indies and America," *Political Theory*, 34 (2006), 198–228.

Koselleck, Reinhart, *Futures Past: On the Semantics of Historical Time*, trans. Keith Tribe (Cambridge, MA: MIT Press, 1985).

———, "Crisis," *Journal of the History of Ideas*, 67 (2006), 357–400.

Koskenniemi, Martti, *The Gentle Civilizer of Nations: The Rise and Fall of International Law, 1870–1960* (Cambridge: Cambridge University Press, 2001).

Kostal, Rande, *A Jurisprudence of Power: Victorian Empire and the Rule of Law* (Oxford: Oxford University Press, 2005).

Kratochwil, F., "Of Systems, Boundaries and Territoriality: An Inquiry into the Formation of the State System," *World Politics*, 39 (1986), 27–52.

Kristol, Irving, *Reflections of a Neoconservative* (New York: Basic Books, 1983).

Kuhn, William, *Democratic Royalism: The Transformation of the British Monarchy, 1861–1914* (London: Macmillan, 1997).

Kumar, Krishan, *The Making of English National Identity* (Cambridge: Cambridge University Press, 2003).

Kymlicka, Will, *Multicultural Citizenship* (Oxford: Oxford University Press, 1995).

Laborde, Cécile, "The Concept of the State in British and French Political Thought," *Political Studies*, 48 (2000), 540–57.

———, *Pluralist Thought and the State in Britain and France, 1900–1925* (Basingstoke: Palgrave, 2000).

Laity, Paul, *The British Peace Movement, 1870–1914* (Oxford: Clarendon, 2001).

Lake, Marilyn, and Henry Reynolds, *Drawing the Global Colour Line: White Men's*

Countries and the International Challenge of Racial Equality (Cambridge: Cambridge University Press, 2008).

Larson, Victoria Tietze, "Classics and the Acquisition and Validation of Power in Britain's 'Imperial Century' (1815–1914)," *International Journal of the Classical Tradition*, 6/2 (1999), 185–225.

Lavin, Deborah, *From Empire to International Commonwealth: A Biography of Lionel Curtis* (Oxford: Clarendon Press, 1995).

Le May, G.H.L., *The Victorian Constitution: Conventions, Usages and Contingencies* (London: Duckworth, 1979).

Lear, Jonathan, *Radical Hope: Ethics in the Face of Cultural Devastation* (Cambridge, MA: Harvard University Press, 2006).

Lebovics, Herman, *Imperialism and the Corruption of Democracies* (Durham, NC: Duke University Press, 2006).

Leonhard, Jörn, "From European Liberalism to the Languages of Liberalisms: The Semantics of Liberalism in European Comparison," *Redescriptions*, 8 (2004), 17–51.

Lester, Alan, and Fae Dussart, *Colonization and the Origins of Humanitarian Governance: Protecting Aborigines across the Nineteenth-Century British Empire* (Cambridge: Cambridge University Press, 2014).

Levin, Michael, *J. S. Mill on Civilization and Barbarism* (London: Routledge, 2004).

Levine, Philippa, *The Amateur and the Professional Antiquarians, Historians and Archaeologists in Victorian England 1838–1886* (Cambridge: Cambridge University Press, 1986).

Lieven, Dominic, *Empire: The Russian Empire and Its Rivals* (New Haven: Yale University Press, 2002).

Linstrum, Erik, "The Politics of Psychology in the British Empire, 1898–1960," *Past & Present*, 215 (2012), 214–33.

Long, David, *Towards a New Liberal Internationalism: The International Theory of J. A. Hobson* (Cambridge: Cambridge University Press, 1995).

Long, David, and Brian Schmidt, eds., *Imperialism and Internationalism in the Discipline of International Relations* (Albany: SUNY Press, 2005).

Long, David, and Peter Wilson, eds., *Thinkers of the Twenty Years' Crisis: Interwar Idealism Re-Assessed* (Oxford: Clarendon, 1995).

Lootens, Tricia, "Victorian Poetry and Patriotism," in *The Cambridge Companion to Victorian Poetry*, ed. Joseph Bristow (Cambridge: Cambridge University Press, 2000), 255–80.

Losurdo, Domenico, *Liberalism*, trans. Gregory Elliott (London: Verso, 2011).

MacDonald, Paul, "Those Who Forget Historiography Are Doomed to Republish It," *Review of International Studies*, 35/1 (2006), 45–67.

Mackenzie, John, ed., *Imperialism and Popular Culture* (Manchester: Manchester University Press, 1986).

———, "The British Empire," *Journal of Imperial and Commonwealth History*, 43/1 (2015), 99–124.

MacKillop, I., *The British Ethical Societies* (Cambridge: Cambridge University Press, 1986).

MacIntyre, Alistair, *Three Rival Versions of Moral Enquiry: Encyclopedia, Genealogy, and Tradition* (South Bend, IN: University of Notre Dame Press, 1990).

MacMillan, Margaret, "Isosceles Triangle: Britain, the United States, and the Dominions, 1900–1926," in *Twentieth-Century Anglo-American Relations*, ed. Jonathan Hollowell (Basingstoke: Palgrave, 2001), 1–25.

Madley, Benjamin, "From Terror to Genocide: Britain's Tasmanian Penal Colony and Australia's History Wars," *Journal of British Studies*, 47 (2008), 77–106.

———, "Tactics of Nineteenth Century Colonial Massacre: Tasmania, California and Beyond," in *Theatres of Violence*, ed. Philips Dwyer and Lyndall Ryan (New York: Bergham, 2012), 110–25.

———, "Reexamining the American Genocide Debate: Meaning, Historiography, and New Methods," *American Historical Review*, 120/1 (2015) 98–139.

Magee, Gary, and Andrew Thompson, *Empire and Globalisation: Networks of People, Goods and Capital in the British World, c. 1850–1914* (Cambridge: Cambridge University Press, 2010).

Maier, Charles, *Among Empires: American Ascendancy and Its Predecessors* (Cambridge, MA: Harvard University Press, 2006).

Majeed, Javeed, *Ungoverned Imaginings: James Mill's "The History of British India" and Orientalism* (Oxford: Clarendon, 1992).

Malamud, Margaret, *Ancient Rome and Modern America: Classical Receptions* (Oxford: Blackwell, 2008).

Mamdani, Mahmood, "Settler Colonialism: Then and Now," *Critical Inquiry*, 41 (2015), 1–19.

Mandelbaum, Maurice, *History, Man, & Reason: A Study in Nineteenth-Century Thought* (Baltimore: Johns Hopkins University Press, 1971).

Mander, W. J., *British Idealism: A History* (Oxford: Oxford University Press, 2011).

Mandeville, Peter, "Territory and Translocality: Discrepant Idioms of Political Identity," *Millennium*, 28 (1999), 653–67.

Mandler, Peter, "'Race' and 'Nation' in Mid-Victorian Thought," in *History, Religion and Culture: British Intellectual History, 1750–1950*, ed. Stefan Collini, Richard Whatmore, and Brian Young (Cambridge: Cambridge University Press, 2000), 224–45.

———, "The Consciousness of Modernity? Liberalism and the English 'National Character,' 1870–1940," in *Meanings of Modernity: Britain from the Late-Victorian Era to World War II*, ed. Bernhard Rieger and Martin Daunton (Oxford: Berg, 2001), 119–45.

———, "The Problem of Cultural History," *Social and Cultural History*, 1 (2004), 94–118.

———, *The English National Character: The History of an Idea from Edmund Burke to Tony Blair* (London: Yale University Press, 2006).

———, "Looking around the World," in *Time Travelers*, ed. Adelene Buckland and Sadiah Qureshi (Chicago: University of Chicago Press, forthcoming, 2016).

———, ed., *Liberty and Authority in Victorian Britain* (Oxford: Oxford University Press, 2006).

Manent, Pierre, *An Intellectual History of Liberalism*, trans. R. Balinski (Princeton: Princeton University Press, 1996).

Mantena, Karuna, "The Crisis of Liberal Imperialism," in *Victorian Visions*, ed. Duncan Bell, 113–36.

———, *Alibis of Empire: Henry Maine and the Ends of Liberal Imperialism* (Princeton: Princeton University Press, 2010).

———, "Another Realism: The Politics of Gandhian Nonviolence," *American Political Science Review*, 106 (2012), 455–70.

Markus, Julia J., *Anthony Froude: The Last Undiscovered Great Victorian* (New York: Scribner, 2005).

Martin, Ged, *The Durham Report and British Policy: A Critical Essay* (Cambridge: Cambridge University, 1972).

———, "Empire, Federalism and Imperial Parliamentary Union, 1820–70," *Historical Journal*, 16 (1973), 65–92.

Matthew, Colin, *The Liberal Imperialists: The Ideas and Politics of a Post-Gladstonian Elite* (Oxford: Oxford University Press, 1973).

Mayall, James, and Ricardo Soares de Oliveira, eds., *The New Protectorates: International Tutelage and the Making of Liberal States* (London: Hurst, 2011).

Mayers, David, *Dissenting Voices in America's Rise to Power* (Cambridge: Cambridge University Press, 2007).

Mazlish, Bruce, *Civilization and Its Contents* (Stanford: Stanford University Press, 2005).

Mazower, Mark, *No Enchanted Palace: The End of Empire and the Ideological Origins of the United Nations* (Princeton: Princeton University Press, 2009).

———, *Governing the World: The History of an Idea* (London: Penguin, 2012).

McCain, John, "An Enduring Peace Built on Freedom," *Foreign Affairs*, 86 (2007), 19–34.

McHugh, P. G., *Aboriginal Societies and the Common Law: A History of Sovereignty, Status, and Self-Determination* (Oxford: Oxford University Press, 2004).

Meadowcroft, James, *Conceptualizing the State: Innovation and Dispute in British Political Thought, 1880–1914* (Oxford: Clarendon, 1995).

Mehrota, S. R., "Imperial Federation and India, 1868–1917," *Journal of Commonwealth Political Studies*, 1 (1961), 29–40.

Mehta, Pratap Bhanu, "Cosmopolitanism and the Circle of Reason," *Political Theory*, 28/5 (2000), 619–39.

Mehta, Uday Singh, *Liberalism and Empire: A Study in Nineteenth Century British Liberal Thought* (Chicago: University of Chicago Press, 1999).

Metcalf, Thomas, *Ideologies of the Raj* (Cambridge: Cambridge University Press, 1995).

Middleton, Alexander, "French Algeria in British Imperial Thought, 1830–70," *Journal of Colonialism and Colonial History*, 16/1 (2015), 1–15.

Mills, Charles, *The Racial Contract* (Ithaca: Cornell University Press, 1997).

———, "White Right: The Idea of a Herrenvolk Ethics," in *Blackness Visible: Essays on Philosophy and Race* (Ithaca: Cornell University Press, 1998), 139–67.

———, "Occupy Liberalism!," *Radical Philosophy Review*, 15/2 (2012), 305–23.

———, "Decolonizing Western Political Philosophy," *New Political Science*, 37/1 (2015), 1–24.

Mitchell, Leslie, "Britain's Reaction to the Revolutions," in *The Revolutions in Europe, 1848–1849: From Reform to Reaction,* ed. Robert Evans and Hartmut Pogge von Strandmann (Oxford: Oxford University Press, 2000), 83–99.

Mitchell, Timothy, *Colonising Egypt* (Berkeley: University of California Press, 1991).

————, *Rule of Experts: Egypt, Techno-Politics, Modernity* (Berkeley: University of California Press, 2002).

Moir, Martin I., Douglas Peers, and Lynn Zastoupil, eds., *J. S. Mill's Encounter with India* (Toronto: University of Toronto Press, 1999).

Momigliano, Arnaldo, "Two Types of Universal History: The Cases of E. A. Freeman and Max Weber," *Journal of Modern History*, 58/1 (1986), 235–46.

Morefield, Jeanne, "Hegelian Organicism, British New Liberalism, and the Return of the Family State," *History of Political Thought*, 23 (2002), 141–70.

————, *Covenants without Swords: Idealist Liberalism and the Spirit of Empire* (Princeton: Princeton University Press, 2004).

————, " 'An Education To Greece': The Round Table, Political Theory, and the Uses of History," *History of Political Thought*, 28 (2007), 328–61.

————, *Empires without Imperialism: Anglo-American Decline and the Politics of Deflection* (Oxford: Oxford University Press, 2014).

Morris, Jeremy, *F. D. Maurice and the Crisis of Christian Authority* (Oxford: Oxford University Press, 2008).

Morrisroe, Vicky, " 'Eastern History with Western Eyes': E. A. Freeman, Islam, and Orientalism," *Journal of Victorian Culture*, 16 (2011), 25–45.

————, " 'Sanguinary Amusement': E. A. Freeman, the Comparative Method and Victorian Theories of Race," *Modern Intellectual History*, 10 (2013), 27–56.

Morrow, John, *Thomas Carlyle* (London: Hambledon, 2006).

Moses, Dirk A., ed., *Genocide and Settler Society: Frontier Violence and Stolen Indigenous Children in Australian History* (New York: Berghahn, 2004).

————, ed., *Empire, Colony, Genocide: Conquest, Occupation, and Subaltern Resistance in World History* (New York: Berghahn, 2008).

————, "Official Apologies, Reconciliation, and Settler Colonialism: Australian Indigenous Alterity and Political Agency," *Citizenship Studies*, 15/2 (2011), 145–59.

————, "Das römische Gespräch in a New Key: Hannah Arendt, Genocide, and the Defense of Imperial Civilization," *Journal of Modern History*, 85/4 (2013), 867–913.

Motyl, Alexander, *Imperial Ends: The Decay, Collapse, and Revival of Empires* (New York: Columbia University Press, 2001).

Muldoon, James, *Empire and Order: the Concept of Empire, 800–1800* (Basingstoke: Palgrave, 1999).

Muthu, Sankar, *Enlightenment against Empire* (Princeton: Princeton University Press, 2003).

————, ed., *Empire and Modern Political Thought* (Cambridge: Cambridge University Press, 2012).

Nabulsi, Karma, *Traditions of War: Occupation, Resistance, and the Law* (Oxford: Oxford University Press, 1999).

Nagel, Thomas, "Rawls and Liberalism," in *The Cambridge Companion to Rawls*, ed. Samuel Freeman (Cambridge: Cambridge University Press, 2003), 62–86.

Nakhimovsky, Isaac, *The Closed Commercial State: Perpetual Peace and Commercial Society from Rousseau to Fichte* (Princeton: Princeton University Press, 2011).

Nandy, Ashis, "Reconstructing Childhood: A Critique of the Ideology of Adulthood," in *Traditions, Tyranny, and Utopia: Essays in the Politics of Awareness* (Delhi; Oxford: Oxford University Press, 1987), 56–76.

Nash, David, and Antony Taylor, eds., *Republicanism in Victorian Society* (Stroud: Sutton, 2003).

Nelson, Eric, "Republican Visions," in *The Oxford Handbook of Political Theory*, ed. John Dryzek, Bonnie Honig, and Anne Phillips (Oxford: Oxford University Press, 2005), 193–211.

Nexon, Daniel, *The Struggle for Power in Early Modern Europe: Religious Conflict, Dynastic Empires, and International Change* (Princeton: Princeton University Press, 2009).

Nicholls, David, *The Lost Prime Minister: A Life of Sir Charles Dilke* (London: Hambledon, 1995).

Nicholson, Peter, "Philosophical Idealism and International Politics: A Reply to Dr. Savigear," *British Journal of International Studies*, 2 (1976), 76–83.

———, *The Political Philosophy of the British Idealists: Selected Studies* (Cambridge: Cambridge University Press, 1990).

Novik, Peter, *That Noble Dream: The "Objectivity Question" and the American Historical Profession* (Cambridge: Cambridge University Press, 1988).

O'Brien, Patrick, "Historiographical Traditions and Modern Imperatives for the Restoration of Global History," *Journal of Global History*, 1 (2006), 3–39.

O'Neill, Daniel, "Rethinking Burke and India," *History of Political Thought*, 30/3 (2009), 492–523.

———, *Edmund Burke and the Conservative Logic of Empire* (Berkeley, forthcoming).

Osterhammel, Jürgen, *Colonialism: A Theoretical Overview*, 2nd ed. (Princeton: Princeton University Press, 2005).

———, *The Transformation of the World: A Global History of the Nineteenth Century*, trans. Patrick Camiller (Princeton: Princeton University Press, 2014).

Owen, Nicholas, *The British Left and India: Metropolitan Anti-Imperialism, 1885–1947* (Oxford: Oxford University Press, 2007).

Pagden, Anthony, *Lords of All the World: Ideologies of Empire in Spain, Britain and France, 1500–1850* (London: Yale University Press, 1995).

———, *Peoples and Empires: Europeans and the Rest of the World, from Antiquity to the Present* (London: Phoenix, 2001).

———, "Human Rights, Natural Rights, and Europe's Imperial Legacy," *Political Theory*, 31 (2003), 171–99.

———, "The Empire's New Clothes: From Empire to Federation, Yesterday and Today," *Common Knowledge*, 12/1 (2006), 36–46.

———, *The Burdens of Empire: 1539 to the Present* (Cambridge: Cambridge University Press, 2015).

Palen, Marc-William, "Protection, Federation and Union: The Global Impact of the McKinley Tariff upon the British Empire, 1890–94," *Journal of Imperial and Commonwealth History*, 38 (2010), 395–418.

———, "Adam Smith as Advocate of Empire," *Historical Journal*, 57/1 (2014), 179–98.

Parekh, Bhikhu, *Gandhi's Political Philosophy: A Critical Examination* (London: Macmillan, 1989).

———, "Decolonizing Liberalism," in *The End of "Isms?": Reflections on the Fate of Ideological Politics after Communism's Collapse*, ed. Alexander Shtromas (Oxford: Blackwell, 1994), 85–105.

————, "Liberalism and Colonialism: A Critique of Locke and Mill," in *The Decolonization of Imagination*, ed. J. N. Pieterse and Parekh (London: Zed Books, 1995), 81–98.

Parel, Anthony, *Gandhi's Philosophy and the Quest for Harmony* (Cambridge: Cambridge University Press, 2006).

Parker, Christopher, "The Failure of Liberal Racialism: The Racial Ideas of E. A. Freeman," *Historical Journal*, 24/4 (1981), 825–46.

Parmar, Inderjeet, "Anglo-American Elites in the Interwar Years: Idealism and Power in the Intellectual Roots of Chatham House and the Council on Foreign Relations," *International Relations*, 16 (2002), 53–75.

Parry, Jonathan Philip, *The Rise and Fall of Liberal Government in Victorian Britain* (New Haven; London: Yale University Press, 1993).

————, *The Political of Patriotism: English Liberalism, National Identity, and Europe, 1830–86* (Cambridge: Cambridge University Press, 2009).

Parsons, Jotham, "Defining the History of Ideas," *Journal of the History of Ideas*, 68 (2007), 682–89.

Pateman, Carole, and Charles Mills, *Contract and Domination* (Cambridge: Polity, 2007).

Paul, Herman, "'Habits of Thought and Judgement: E. A. Freeman on Historical Methods," in *Making History*, ed. Bremner and Conlin, 273–93.

Pedersen, Susan, *The Guardians: The League of Nations and the Crisis of Empire* (Oxford: Oxford University Press, 2015).

Peel, J.D.Y., *Herbert Spencer: The Evolution of a Sociologist* (London: Heinemann, 1971).

Pemberton, Jo-Ann, *Global Metaphors: Modernity and the Quest for One World* (London: Pluto, 2001).

Pettit, Philip, "A Republican Law of Peoples," *European Journal of Political Theory*, 9 (2010), 70–94.

Pick, Daniel, *Faces of Degeneration: A European Disorder, 1848–1918* (Cambridge: Cambridge University Press, 1989).

Pietsche, Tamsin, *Empire of Scholars: Universities, Networks and the British Academic World, 1850–1939* (Manchester: Manchester University Press, 2013).

Pitts, Jennifer, *A Turn to Empire: The Rise of Imperial Liberalism in Britain and France* (Princeton: Princeton University Press, 2005).

————, "The Boundaries of Victorian International Law," in *Victorian Visions*, ed. Bell, 67–89.

————, "Political Theory of Empire and Imperialism," *Annual Review of Political Science*, 13 (2010), 211–35.

Plunkett, John, *Queen Victoria: First Media Monarch* (Oxford: Oxford University Press, 2003).

Pocock, J.G.A., "The Myth of John Locke and the Obsession with Liberalism," in *John Locke: Papers Read at a Clark Library Seminar, 10 December 1977*, ed. Richard Ashcraft and J.G.A. Pocock (Los Angeles: Clark Library, 1980), 1–24.

————, "Between Gog and Magog: The Republican Thesis and the *Ideologia Americana*," *Journal of the History of Ideas*, 48 (1987), 325–46.

————, *The Machiavellian Moment: Florentine Political Thought and the Atlantic Republican Tradition* (Princeton, 2003).

———, *Barbarism and Religion: Vol. 4: Barbarians, Savages and Empires* (Cambridge: Cambridge University Press, 2005).

———, *The Discovery of Islands* (Cambridge: Cambridge University Press, 2005).

Pombeni, Paolo, "Starting in Reason, Ending in Passion: Bryce, Lowell, Ostrogorski and the Problem of Democracy," *Historical Journal*, 37 (1994), 319–41.

Porter, Bernard, *Critics of Empire: British Radical Attitudes to Colonialism in Africa, 1895–1914* (London: Macmillan, 1968).

———, *The Absent-Minded Imperialists: Empire, Society, and Culture in Britain* (Oxford: Oxford University Press, 2004).

———, *Empire and Superempire: Britain, America, and the World* (London: Yale University Press, 2006).

Potter, Simon, *News and the British World: The Emergence of an Imperial Press System, 1876–1922* (Oxford: Oxford University Press, 2003).

Prager, Carol A., "Intervention and Empire: John Stuart Mill and International Relations," *Political Studies*, 53 (2005), 621–41.

Prochaska, Frank, *Royal Bounty: The Making of a Welfare Monarchy* (London: Allen Lane, 1995).

———, *The Republic of Britain, 1760–2000* (London: Yale University Press, 2000).

Purdy, Jedediah, "Liberal Empire: Assessing the Arguments," *Ethics & International Affairs*, 17/2 (2003), 35–47.

Rajan, Balachandra, "Excess of India," *Modern Philology*, 95/4 (1998).

Rana, Aziz, *The Two Faces of American Freedom* (Cambridge, MA: Harvard University Press, 2010).

Rawls, John, *A Theory of Justice* (Oxford: Oxford University Press, 1971).

———, *Lectures on the History of Political Philosophy*, ed. Samuel Freeman (Cambridge: Harvard University Press, 2007).

Read, Donald, *Cobden and Bright: A Victorian Political Partnership* (London: Edward Arnold, 1967).

Reeves, Richard, *John Stuart Mill: Victorian Firebrand* (London: Overlook Press, 2007).

Reus-Smit, Chris, "Struggles for Individual Rights and the Expansion of the International System," *International Organization*, 65 (2011), 207–42.

Reynolds, David, *The Creation of the Anglo-American Alliance, 1937–41: A Study in Competitive Cooperation* (London: Europa, 1981).

———, "Roosevelt, Churchill, and the Wartime Anglo-American Alliance, 1939–45," in *The Special Relationship: Anglo-American Relations Since 1945*, ed. Roger Louis and Hedley Bull (Oxford: Clarendon Press, 1986), 17–41.

Reynolds, Matthew, *The Realms of Verse, 1830–1870: English Poetry in a Time of Nation-Building* (Oxford: Oxford University Press, 2001).

Richter, Melvin, *The Politics of Conscience: T. H. Green and His Age* (London: Weidenfeld and Nicolson, 1964).

Rieger, Bernhard, *Technology and the Culture of Modernity in Britain and Germany, 1890–1945* (Cambridge: Cambridge University Press, 2005).

Riley, Jonathan, "Mill's Political Economy: Ricardian Science and Liberal Utilitarian Art," in *The Cambridge Companion to Mill*, ed. John Skorupski (Cambridge: Cambridge University Press, 1998), 293–338.

Roberts, Andrew, *A History of the English-Speaking Peoples since 1900* (New York: Harper Collins, 1997).

Roberts, Priscilla, "The Transatlantic American Foreign Policy Elite: Its Evolution in Generational Perspective," *Journal of Transatlantic Studies*, 7/2 (2009), 163–83.

Robertson, John, "Gibbon's Roman Empire as a Universal Monarchy," in *Edward Gibbon and Empire*, ed. Rosamond McKitterick and Roland Quinault (Cambridge: Cambridge University Press, 1997), 247–71.

Robinson, Ronald, and John Gallagher, "The Imperialism of Free Trade," *Economic History Review*, 6 (1953), 1–15.

Robinson, Ronald, and John Gallagher, with Alice Denny, *Africa and the Victorians: The Official Mind of Imperialism* (London: Macmillan, 1961).

Rodgers, Daniel, *Atlantic Crossings: Social Politics in a Progressive Age* (Cambridge, MA: Harvard University Press, 2000).

———, "The Traditions of Liberalism," in *Questions of Tradition*, ed. Mark Salber Phillips and Gordon Schochet (Toronto: University of Toronto Press, 2004), 203–33.

Rorty, Richard, "The Historiography of Philosophy," in *Philosophy in History: Essays in the Historiography of Philosophy*, ed. Richard Rorty, Jerome Schneewind, and Quentin Skinner (Cambridge: Cambridge University Press, 1984), 49–76.

Rosen, Frederick, "Eric Stokes, British Utilitarianism, and India," in *J. S. Mill's Encounter with India*, ed. Moir, Peers, and Zastoupil (Toronto: University of Toronto Press, 1999) 18–33.

Ross, Dorothy *The Origins of American Social Science* (Cambridge: Cambridge University Press, 1991).

Rothblatt, Shedon, *The Revolution of the Dons: Cambridge and Society in Victorian England* (London: Faber and Faber, 1968).

Rowse, A. L., *Froude as Historian: Victorian Man of Letters* (Gloucester: Sutton, 1987).

Ruggie, John Gerard, "Territoriality and Beyond: Problematizing Modernity in International Relations," *International Organization*, 47 (1993), 139–74.

Runciman, David, *Pluralism and the Personality of the State* (Cambridge, 1997).

———, "The Concept of the State: The Sovereignty of a Fiction," in *States and Citizens: History, Theory, Prospects*, ed. Quentin Skinner and Bo Stråth (Cambridge: Cambridge University Press, 2003), 28–39.

Russell, Lynette, ed., *Colonial Frontiers: Indigenous—European Encounters in Settler Societies* (Manchester: Manchester University Press, 2001).

Ryan, Alan, "Liberal Imperialism" [2004], in *The Making of Modern Liberalism*, 107–23.

———, "Bureaucracy, Democracy, Liberty: Some Unanswered Questions in Mill's Politics," in *J. S. Mill's Political Thought*, ed. Urbinati and Zakaras, 147–66.

———, *The Making of Modern Liberalism* (Princeton: Princeton University Press, 2012).

Ryan, Henry Butterfield, *The Vision of Anglo-America: The US-UK Alliance and the Emerging Cold War, 1943–1946* (Cambridge: Cambridge University Press, 1987).

Sahlins, Marshall, *How "Natives" Think: About Captain Cook, for Example* (Chicago: University of Chicago Press, 1995).

Said, Edward, *Orientalism* (London: Routledge, 1978).

———, *Culture and Imperialism* (London: Chatto and Windus, 1993).

Sanders, C. R., *Coleridge and the Broad Church Movement* (London: Weidenfeld and Nicolson, 1972).

Sargent, Lyman Tower, "Utopianism and the Creation of New Zealand National Identity," *Utopian Studies*, 12/1 (2001), 1–18.

———, "Colonial and Postcolonial Utopias," in *The Cambridge Companion to Utopian Literature*, ed. Gregory Claeys (Cambridge, 2010), 200–223.

Sartori, Andrew, "The British Empire and Its Liberal Mission," *Journal of Modern History*, 78 (2006), 623–42.

———, *Liberalism in Empire: An Alternative History* (Berkeley: University of California Press, 2014).

Saunders, Francis Stonor, *Who Paid the Piper? The CIA and the Cultural Cold War* (London: Granta, 1999).

Schivelbusch, Wolfgang, *The Railway Journey: The Industrialization and Perception of Time and Space* (Oxford: Oxford University Press, 1986).

Schneewind, J. B., *Sidgwick's Ethics and Victorian Moral Philosophy* (Oxford: Clarendon, 1977).

Schofield, Philip, *Utility and Democracy: The Political Thought of Jeremy Bentham* (Oxford: Oxford University Press, 2006).

Schultz, Bart, *Henry Sidgwick: Eye of the Universe* (Cambridge: Cambridge University Press, 2004).

Schultz, Bart, and Georgios Varouxakis, eds., *Utilitarianism and Empire* (Lanham, MD: Lexington, 2005).

Scott, David, *Conscripts of Modernity: The Tragedy of Colonial Enlightenment* (Durham, NC: Duke University Press, 2004).

Scott, James, *Weapons of the Weak: Everyday Forms of Peasant Resistance* (New Haven: Yale University Press, 1985).

———, *Domination and the Arts of Resistance: Hidden Transcripts* (New Haven: Yale University Press, 1990).

———, *Seeing like a State: How Certain Schemes to Improve the Human Condition Have Failed* (London: Yale University Press, 1998).

———, *The Art of Not Being Governed: An Anarchist History of Upland Southeast Asia* (New Haven: Yale University Press, 2009).

Searle, Geoffrey Russell, *A New England? Peace and War, 1886–1914* (Oxford: Oxford University Press, 2004).

Semmel, Bernard, *Imperialism and Social Reform: English Social-Imperial Thought, 1895–1914* (Cambridge, MA: Harvard University Press, 1960).

———, *The Governor Eyre Controversy: Jamaican Blood and Victorian Conscience* (London: MacGibbon and Kee, 1962).

———, *The Rise of Free Trade Imperialism: Classical Political Economy the Empire of Free Trade and Imperialism 1750–1850* (Cambridge: Cambridge University Press, 1970).

———, *The Liberal Ideal and the Demons of Empire: Theories of Imperialism from Adam Smith to Lenin* (Baltimore: Johns Hopkins University Press, 1993).

Shannon, Richard, *Gladstone and the Bulgarian Agitation 1876* (London: Harvester, 1963).

———, "John Robert Seeley and the Idea of a National Church: A Study in Churchmanship, Historiography, and Politics," in *Ideas and Institutions of Victorian Brit-*

ain: Essays in Honour of George Kitson Clark, ed. Robert Robson (London: Bell, 1967), 236–67.

Shaw, Timothy, *Commonwealth: Inter- and Non-State Contributions to Global Governance* (London: Routledge, 2008).

Shklar, Judith N., "The Liberalism of Fear" [1989], in *Political Thought and Political Thinkers* (Chicago: University of Chicago Press, 1998), 3–20.

Simhony, Aviral, and David Weinstein, eds., *The New Liberalism: Reconciling Liberty and Community* (Cambridge: Cambridge University Press, 2001).

Simms, Brendan, *Three Victories and a Defeat. The Rise and Fall of the First British Empire, 1714–1783* (London: Penguin, 2007).

Skilton, David, "Tourists at the Ruins of London: The Metropolis and the Struggle for Empire," *Cercles*, 17 (2007), 93–119.

Skinner, Quentin, "From the State of Princes to the Person of the State," in *Visions of Politics, Volume II: Renaissance Virtues* (Cambridge: Cambridge University Press, 2002), 368–414.

———, *Visions of Politics, Volume I: Regarding Method* (Cambridge: Cambridge University Press, 2002).

———, *Hobbes and Republican Liberty* (Cambridge: Cambridge University Press, 2008).

———, "On the Slogans of Republican Political Theory," *European Journal of Political Theory*, 9 (2010), 95–102.

Slee, Peter, *Learning and a Liberal Education: The Study of Modern History in the Universities of Oxford, Cambridge and Manchester, 1800–1914* (Manchester: Manchester University Press, 1986).

Smandych, Russell, "Colonialism, Settler Colonialism, and Law: Settler Revolutions and the Dispossession of Indigenous Peoples through Law in the Long Nineteenth Century," *Settler Colonial Studies*, 3/1 (2013), 82–101.

Smith, K.J.M., *James Fitzjames Stephen: Portrait of a Victorian Rationalist* (Cambridge: Cambridge University Press, 1988).

Smith, Rogers, *Civic Ideals: Conflicting Visions of Citizenship in U. S. History* (London: Yale University Press, 2007).

Smith, Tony, *A Pact with the Devil: Washington's Bid for World Supremacy and the Betrayal of America's Promise* (London: Routledge, 2007).

Smits, Katherine, "John Stuart Mill on the Antipodes: Settler Violence against Indigenous Peoples and the Legitimacy of Colonial Rule," *Australian Journal of Politics and History*, 51 (2008), 1–15.

Soffer, Reba N., "History and Religion: J. R. Seeley and the Burden of the Past," in *Religion and Irreligion in Victorian Society: Essays in Honor of R. K. Webb*, ed. R. W. Davis and R. J. Helmstadter (London: Routledge, 1992), 133–51.

———, *Discipline and Power: The University, History, and the Making of an English Elite, 1870–1930* (Stanford, CA: Stanford University Press, 1994).

Spivak, Gayatri, "Can the Subaltern Speak?," in *Marxism and the Interpretation of Culture*, ed. Cary Nelson and Lawrence Grossberg (Urbana: University of Illinois Press, 1988), 271–313.

Stanton, Tim, "John Locke and the Fable of Liberalism," *Historical Journal* (forthcoming).

Stapleton, Julia, "James Fitzjames Stephen: Liberalism, Patriotism, and English Liberty," *Victorian Studies*, 41/2 (1998), 243–63.

Stears, Marc, *Progressive, Pluralists, and the Problems of the State: Ideologies of Reform in the United States and Britain, 1909–1926* (Oxford: Oxford University Press, 2002).

Stedman Jones, Gareth, "Rethinking Chartism," in *Languages of Class: Studies in English Working Class History, 1832–1982* (Cambridge: Cambridge University Press, 1983), 90–179.

———, "Radicalism and the Extra-European World: The Case of Marx," in *Victorian Visions*, ed. Bell, 186–225.

Steer, Philip, "Greater Britain and the Imperial Outpost: The Australasian Origins of *The Riddle of the Sands* (1903)," *Victorian Review*, 35 (2009), 79–95.

Steger, Manfred, *Gandhi's Dilemma: Nonviolent Principles and Nationalist Power* (Basingstoke: Macmillan, 2000).

———, *The Rise of the Global Imaginary: Political Ideologies from the French Revolution the War on Terror* (Oxford: Oxford University Press, 2008).

Steger, Manfred, "The Changing Face of Political Ideologies in the Global Age," *New Political Science*, 31 (2009) 423–30.

Stoler, Ann Laura, *Race and the Education of Desire: Foucault's History of Sexuality and the Colonial Order of Things* (Durham, NC: Duke University Press, 1995).

———, "On Degrees of Imperial Sovereignty," *Public Culture*, 18/1 (2006), 125–46.

———, *Along the Archival Grain: Epistemic Anxieties and Colonial Common Sense* (Princeton: Princeton University Press, 2010).

Stray, Christopher, *Classics Transformed: Schools, Universities, and Society in England, 1830–1960* (Oxford: Clarendon, 1998).

———, ed., *Gilbert Murray Reassessed: Hellenism, Theatre and International Politics* (Oxford: Oxford University Press, 2007).

Studdert-Kennedy, Gerald, "Christianity, Statecraft and Chatham House: Lionel Curtis and World Order," *Diplomacy & Statecraft*, 6 (1995), 470–89.

Suganami, Hidemi, *The Domestic Analogy and World Order Proposals* (Cambridge: Cambridge University Press, 1989).

Sullivan, Eileen P., "Liberalism and Imperialism: J. S. Mill's Defense of the British Empire," *Journal of the History of Ideas*, 44 (1983), 599–617.

Summerton, N. W., "Dissenting Attitudes to Foreign Relations, Peace and War, 1840–1890," *Journal of Ecclesiastical History*, 28 (1977), 151–78.

Suskind, Ron, "Faith, Certainty and the Presidency of George W. Bush," *New York Times Magazine*, October 17, 2004.

Sylvest, Casper, "Interwar Internationalism, the British Labour Party and the Historiography of International Relations," *International Studies Quarterly*, 48 (2004), 409–32.

———, "Continuity and Change in British Liberal Internationalism, c. 1900–1930," *Review of International Studies*, 31 (2005), 263–83.

———, "International Law in Nineteenth-Century Britain," *British Yearbook of International Law 2004* (Oxford: Oxford University Press, 2005), 9–70.

———, *British Liberal Internationalism, 1880–1930: Making Progress?* (Manchester: Manchester University Press, 2009).

———, "James Bryce and the Two Faces of Nationalism," in *British International*

Thinkers, ed. Ian Hall and Lisa Hill (New York: Palgrave Macmillan, 2009), 161–81.

Symonds, Richard, *Oxford and Empire: The Last Lost Cause?*, rev. ed. (Oxford: Clarendon, 1991).

Taylor, Antony, *"Down with the Crown": British Anti-Monarchism and Debates about Royalty since 1790* (London: Reaktion, 1999).

Taylor, Charles, *Modern Social Imaginaries* (Durham, NC: Duke University Press, 2004).

Taylor, M. W., *Men versus the State: Herbert Spencer and Late Victorian Individualism* (Oxford: Oxford University Press, 1992).

Taylor, Miles, "Imperium et Libertas? Rethinking the Radical Critique of Imperialism during the Nineteenth Century," *Journal of Imperial and Commonwealth History*, 19 (1991), 1–23.

——, "The 1848 Revolutions and the British Empire," *Past & Present*, 166 (2000), 146–80.

——, "Republics versus Empires: Charles Dilke's Republicanism Reconsidered," in *Republicanism in Victorian Society*, ed. David Nash and Antony Taylor (Stroud: Sutton, 2003), 25–34.

——, "Queen Victoria and India, 1837–61," *Victorian Studies*, 46 (2004), 264–74.

Thomas, William, *The Philosophic Radicals: Nine Studies in Theory and Practice, 1817–1841* (Oxford: Oxford University Press, 1979).

Thompson, Andrew, *Imperial Britain: The Empire in British Politics, 1880–1932* (London: Longman, 2000).

——, *The Empire Strikes Back: The Impact of Imperialism on Britain since the Mid-Nineteenth Century* (London: Longmans, 2005).

——, ed., *Writing Imperial Histories* (Manchester: Manchester University Press, 2014).

Thompson, Dorothy, *Queen Victoria: Gender and Power* (London: Virago, 1990).

Thompson, J. Lee, *A Wider Patriotism: Alfred Milner and the British Empire* (London: Pickering and Chatto, 2007).

Thompson, James, *British Political Culture and the Idea of "Public Opinion," 1867–1914* (Cambridge: Cambridge University Press, 2013).

Thompson, Walter, *James Anthony Froude on Nation and Empire: A Study in Victorian Racialism* (London: Garland, 1998).

Todorov, Tzvetan, *The Conquest of America: The Question of the Other*, trans. Richard Howard (New York: Harper Perennial, 1992).

Tomes, Jason, *Balfour and Foreign Policy: The International Thought of a Conservative Statesman* (Cambridge: Cambridge University Press, 1997).

Townshend, Jules, *J. A. Hobson* (Manchester: Manchester University Press, 1990).

Toye, Richard, *Churchill's Empire: The World That Made Him and the World He Made* (London: Macmillan, 2010).

Trentmann, Frank, "The Strange Death of Free Trade: The Erosion of the 'Liberal Consensus' in Great Britain, c. 1903–1932," in *Citizenship and Community: Liberals, Radicals and Collective Identities in the British Isles, 1865–1931*, ed. Euginio Biagini (Cambridge: Cambridge University Press, 1996), 219–51.

——, *Free Trade Nation: Commerce, Consumption and Civil Society in Modern Britain* (Oxford: Oxford University Press, 2008).

Tuck, Richard, *The Rights of War and Peace: Political Thought and International Order from Grotius to Kant* (Oxford: Oxford University Press, 1999).

———, *Free Riding* (Cambridge, MA: Harvard University Press, 2008).

Tully, James, *An Approach to Political Philosophy: Locke in Contexts* (Cambridge: Cambridge University Press, 1993).

———, *Strange Multiplicity: Constitutionalism in an Age of Diversity* (Cambridge: Oxford University Press, 1995).

———, "The Kantian Idea of Europe: Critical and Cosmopolitan Perspectives," in *The Idea of Europe*, ed. Anthony Pagden (Cambridge: Cambridge University Press, 2002), 331–58.

Tully, James, *Public Philosophy in a New Key*, 2 vols. (Cambridge: Cambridge University Press, 2008).

———, "Lineages of Contemporary Imperialism," in *Lineages of Empire: The Historical Roots of British Imperial Thought*, ed. Duncan Kelly (Oxford: Oxford University Press, 2009), 3–30.

———, " 'Two Concepts of Liberty' in Context," in *Isaiah Berlin and the Politics of Freedom: "Two Concepts of Liberty" 50 Years Later*, ed. Bruce Baum and Robert Nichols (Abingdon: Routledge, 2013), 23–52.

Tunick, Mark, "Tolerant Imperialism: John Stuart Mill's Defense of British Rule in India," *The Review of Politics*, 68 (2006), 586–611.

Turner, Frank M., *Between Science and Religion: The Reaction to Scientific Naturalism in Late Victorian England* (New Haven: Yale University Press, 1974).

———, *The Greek Heritage in Victorian Britain* (New Haven: Yale University Press, 1981).

———, *Contesting Cultural Authority: Essays in Victorian Intellectual Life* (Cambridge: Cambridge University Press, 1993).

Turner, Jack, "John Locke, Christian Mission, and Colonial America," *Modern Intellectual History*, 8 (2011), 267–97.

Turner, John, ed., *The Larger Idea: Lord Lothian and the Problem of National Sovereignty* (London: Lothian Foundation, 1988).

Turner, Michael, "Radical Agitation and the Canada Question in British Politics, 1837–1841," *Historical Research*, 79 (2006), 90–114.

Tyler, Colin, "T. H. Green," *Stanford Encyclopaedia of Philosophy*, http://plato.stanford.edu.

———, "T. H. Green, Advanced Liberalism and the Reform Question 1865–1876," *History of European Ideas*, 29 (2003), 437–58.

———, *Idealist Political Philosophy: Pluralism and Conflict in the Absolute Idealist Tradition* (London: Continuum, 2006).

Urbinati, Nadia, *Mill on Democracy: From the Athenian Polis to Representative Government* (Chicago: University of Chicago Press, 2002).

Urbinati, Nadia, and Alex Zakaras, eds., *J. S. Mill's Political Thought: A Bicentennial Reassessment* (Cambridge: Cambridge University Press, 2007).

van Gelderen, Martin, and Quentin Skinner, eds., *Republicanism: A Shared European Heritage*, 2 vols. (Cambridge: Cambridge University Press, 2002).

Vance, Norman, *The Victorians and Ancient Rome* (Oxford: Blackwell, 1997).

———, "Anxieties of Empire and the Moral Tradition: Rome and Britain," *International Journal of the Classical Tradition*, 18/2 (2011), 246–61.

Varouxakis, Georgios, *Mill on Nationality* (London: Routledge, 2002).

———, "Empire, Race, Euro-Centrism: John Stuart Mill and His Critics," in *Utilitarianism and Empire*, ed. Bart Schultz and Georgios Varouxakis (Lanham, MD: Lexington, 2005), 137–54.

———, "'Patriotism,' 'Cosmopolitanism' and 'Humanity' in Victorian Political Thought," *European Journal of Political Theory*, 5 (2006), 100–118.

———, "'Great' versus 'Small' Nations: Size and National Greatness in Victorian Political Thought," in *Victorian Visions of Global Order*, ed. Bell, 136–59.

———, *Liberty Abroad: J. S. Mill on International Relations* (Cambridge: Cambridge University Press, 2013).

Vasunia, Phiroze, "Greater Rome and Greater Britain," in *Classics and Colonialism*, ed. Barbara Goff (London: Duckworth, 2005), 34–68.

———, "Greek, Latin, and the Indian Civil Service," *Proceedings of the Cambridge Philological Society*, 51 (2005), 35–71.

———, *The Classics and Colonial India* (Oxford: Oxford University Press, 2013).

Veracini, Lorenzo, *Settler Colonialism: A Theoretical Overview* (Basingstoke: Palgrave, 2010).

———, "Introducing Settler Colonial Studies," *Settler Colonial Studies*, 1/1 (2011), 1–12.

———, "Settler Colonialism: Career of a Concept," *Journal of Imperial and Commonwealth History*, 41/2 (2013), 313–33.

———, *The Settler Colonial Present* (Basingstoke: Palgrave, 2015).

Vernon, James, ed., *Re-Reading the Constitution: New Narratives in the Political History of England's Long Nineteenth Century* (Cambridge: Cambridge University Press, 1996).

Vincent, John, *The Formation of the Liberal Party, 1857–1868* (London: Constable, 1966).

Vitalis, Robert, "The Noble American Science of Imperial Relations and Its Laws of Race Development," *Comparative Studies in Society and History*, 52 (2010), 909–38.

———, *White World Order, Black Power Politics: The Birth of American International Relations* (Ithaca: Cornell University Press, 2015).

von Arx, Jeffrey, *Progress and Pessimism: Religion, Politics and History in Late Nineteenth Century Britain* (Cambridge, MA: Harvard University, 1985).

Vucetic, Srdjan, "Anglobal Governance?," *Cambridge Review of International Affairs*, 23 (2011), 455–74.

———, *The Anglosphere: A Genealogy of a Racialized Identity in International Relations* (Stanford: Stanford University Press, 2011).

Waldron, Jeremy, "Theoretical Foundations of Liberalism," *Philosophical Quarterly*, 37 (1987), 127–50.

Walker, Robert B. J., *Inside/Outside: International Relations as Political Theory* (Cambridge: Cambridge University Press, 1993).

Walzer, Michael, *Just and Unjust Wars: A Moral Argument with Historical Illustrations* (London: Allen Lane, 1978).

Watson, Nicola J., "Gloriana Victoriana: Victoria and the Cultural Memory and Elizabeth I," in *Remaking Queen Victoria*, ed. Homans and Munich, 79–105.

Weinstein, David, *Equal Freedom and Utility: Herbert Spencer's Liberal Utilitarianism* (Cambridge: Cambridge University Press, 1998).

————, "Deductive Hedonism and the Anxiety of Influence," *Utilitas*, 12 (2000), 329–46.

————, "Imagining Darwinism," in *Utilitarianism and Empire*, ed. Schultz and Varouxakis, 189–209.

————, *Utilitarianism and the New Liberalism* (Cambridge: Cambridge University Press, 2007).

————, "Consequentialist Cosmopolitanism," in *Victorian Visions*, ed. Bell, 267–91.

Weisberg, Jacob, "George Bush's Favourite Historian: The Strange Views of Andrew Roberts," *Slate*, March 28, 2007, accessed July 26, 2011, http://www.slate.com/id/2162837/.

Weiss, Thomas, "What Happened to the Idea of World Government?," *International Studies Quarterly*, 53 (2009), 253–71.

Welch, Cheryl, "Colonial Violence and the Rhetoric of Evasion: Tocqueville on Algeria," *Political Theory*, 31 (2003), 235–64.

Wendt, Alexander, "Why a World State Is Inevitable," *European Journal of International Relations*, 9 (2003), 491–542.

Whelan, Frederick, *Edmund Burke and India* (Pittsburgh: University of Pittsburgh Press, 1996).

————, *Enlightenment Political Thought and Non-Western Societies* (London: Routledge, 2009).

Williams, Bernard, "The Point of View of the Universe: Sidgwick and the Ambitions of Ethics" [1982], in *Making Sense of Humanity, and Other Philosophical Papers, 1982–1993* (Cambridge: Cambridge University Press, 1994), 153–71.

Williams, Michael, *The Realist Tradition and the Limits of International Relations* (Cambridge: Cambridge University Press, 2005).

Williams, Paul, "A Commonwealth of Knowledge: Empire, Intellectuals and the Chatham House Project, 1919–1939," *International Relations*, 17 (2003), 35–58.

Williams, Richard, *The Contentious Crown: Public Discussion of the British Monarchy in the Reign of Queen Victoria* (Aldershot: Ashgate, 1997).

Wilson, Jon, "Taking Europe for Granted," *History Workshop Journal,* 52 (2001), 287–95.

Wiltshire, David, *The Social and Political Thought of Herbert Spencer* (Oxford: Oxford University Press, 1978).

Winch, Donald, *Classical Political Economy and Colonies* (Cambridge, MA: Harvard University Press, 1965).

Winkler, Henry, *British Labour Seeks a Foreign Policy, 1900–1940* (London: Transaction Publishers, 2005).

Winter, *Dreams of Peace and Freedom: Utopian Moments in the Twentieth Century* (London: Yale University Press, 2006).

Wolf, Eric, *Europe and the People without History* (Berkeley: University of California Press, 1982).

Wolfe, Patrick, "History and Imperialism: A Century of Theory, from Marx to Postcolonialism," *American Historical Review*, 102 (1997), 388–420.

————, *Settler Colonialism and the Transformation of Anthropology* (London: Cassell, 1999).

————, "Settler Colonialism and the Elimination of the Native," *Journal of Genocide Research*, 8/4 (2006), 387–409.

————, "Recuperating Binarism: A Heretical Introduction," *Settler Colonial Studies*, 3/4 (2013), 257–79.

Wolin, Sheldon, *Politics and Vision: Continuity and Innovation in Western Political Thought*, rev. ed. (Princeton: Princeton University Press, 2004).

Wood, J. C., *British Economists and the Empire* (London: Croom Helm, 1983).

Wooley, Wesley T., *Alternatives to Anarchy: American Supranationalism since World War II* (Bloomington: Indiana University Press, 1988).

Wormell, Deborah, *Sir John Seeley and the Uses of History* (Cambridge: Cambridge University Press, 1980).

Worsley, David, "Sir John Robert Seeley and His Intellectual Legacy: Religion, Imperialism, and Nationalism in Victorian and Post-Victorian Britain," unpublished PhD thesis, University of Manchester, 2001.

Wright, T. R., *The Religion of Humanity: The Impact of Comtean Positivism on Victorian Britain* (Cambridge: Cambridge University Press, 1986).

Zastoupil, Lynn, *John Stuart Mill and India* (Stanford, CA: Stanford University Press, 1994).

Zastoupil, Lynn, and Martin I. Moir, eds., *The Great Indian Education Debate: Documents Relating to the Orientalist-Anglicist Controversy, 1781–1843* (London: Curzon, 1999).

Ziegler, Philip, *Legacy: Cecil Rhodes, the Rhodes Trust and Rhodes Scholarships* (London: Yale University Press, 2008).

INDEX

50 years pre- WWI

settler colonialism